THE
CODEX
MENDOZA

The Codex Mendoza

by
Frances F. Berdan
and
Patricia Rieff Anawalt

UNIVERSITY OF CALIFORNIA PRESS
Berkeley   Los Angeles   Oxford

University of California Press
Berkeley and Los Angeles, California

University of California Press
Oxford, England

Copyright © 1992 by The Regents of the University of California

Library of Congress Cataloging-in-Publication Data

The Codex Mendoza / [edited] by Frances F. Berdan and Patricia Rieff Anawalt.
     p.   cm.
   Vol. 1 contains revised versions of six papers originally presented at a symposium
organized at the International Congress of Americanists held in Manchester, England.
   Includes bibiographical references (p.   ) and index.
   ISBN 0-520-06234-5 (cloth)
   1. Codex Mendoza.   2. Aztecs.   3. Manuscripts, Aztec—Facsimiles.   I. Berdan,
Frances. 1944–   . II. Anawalt, Patricia Rieff. 1924–   .   III. International
Congress of Americanists (44th : 1982 : University of Manchester)
F1219.56.C625C64   1992
972′.018—dc20   91-15397
                                                            CIP

Printed in the United States of America

1   2   3   4   5   6   7   8   9

Contents

VOLUME 1

Preface   xiii

Acknowledgments   xvii

About the Authors   xix

PART I: The *Codex Mendoza* in Perspective

CHAPTER 1
The History of the *Codex Mendoza*,
by H. B. Nicholson   1

CHAPTER 2
A Physical Description of the *Codex Mendoza*,
by Wayne Ruwet   13

Addendum
by Bruce Barker-Benfield   20

CHAPTER 3
The Relationship of Indigenous and European Styles
in the *Codex Mendoza:* An Analysis of Pictorial Style,
by Kathleen Stewart Howe   25

CHAPTER 4
The Aztec Pictorial History of the *Codex Mendoza*,
by Elizabeth Hill Boone   35

CHAPTER 5
The Imperial Tribute Roll of the *Codex Mendoza*,
by Frances F. Berdan   55

CHAPTER 6
The Ethnographic Content of
the Third Part of the *Codex Mendoza*,
by Edward E. Calnek   81

CHAPTER 7
Glyphic Conventions of the *Codex Mendoza*,
by Frances F. Berdan   93

CHAPTER 8
A Comparative Analysis of the Costumes
and Accoutrements of the *Codex Mendoza*,
by Patricia Rieff Anawalt   103

PART II: Appendices

APPENDIX A.
The Founding of Tenochtitlan and the Reign Dates
of the Mexica Rulers According to
Thirty-nine Central Mexican Sources,
by Elizabeth Hill Boone   152

APPENDIX B.
Annual Tribute in *Codex Mendoza* Part 2,
by Frances F. Berdan   154

APPENDIX C.
Tribute Totals in the *Codex Mendoza*,
Matrícula de Tributos, and *Información of 1554*,
by Frances F. Berdan   158

APPENDIX D.
Reconstructed *Tira* of the *Codex Mendoza* Part 3,
by Edward E. Calnek   160

APPENDIX E.
The Place-Name, Personal Name, and Title Glyphs
of the *Codex Mendoza:* Translations and Comments,
by Frances F. Berdan   163

APPENDIX F.
Warrior Costumes: The *Codex Mendoza*
and Other Aztec Pictorials,
by Patricia Rieff Anawalt   240

APPENDIX G.
Shields: The *Codex Mendoza* and Other Aztec Pictorials,
by Patricia Rieff Anawalt   242

APPENDIX H.
Ehuatl Styles: The *Codex Mendoza* and Other Aztec Pictorials,
by Patricia Rieff Anawalt   244

APPENDIX I.
Codex Mendoza Tribute Textile Design Motifs,
by Patricia Rieff Anawalt   247

APPENDIX J.
Codex Mendoza Tribute Textile Design Motifs
Names and Citations,
by Patricia Rieff Anawalt   248

APPENDIX K.
Descriptions of the Warrior Insignia in
Primeros Memoriales (1926) *estampas* XXII–XXVII
Based on Thelma D. Sullivan Translations
(*Primeros Memoriales* n.d.: chap. 4, par. 8)   249

VOLUME 2

Description of *Codex Mendoza*

A Guide to the Page Descriptions   vii

PART 1.
The History Year to Year   1

PART 2.
The Tribute Year to Year   27

PART 3.
The Daily Life Year to Year   143

Bibliography   239
Place Names Index   257
Subject Index   263

VOLUME 3

A Facsimile Reproduction of *Codex Mendoza*

VOLUME 4

Parallel Images, Transcriptions, and Translations of
Codex Mendoza

Tracings by Jean Cuker Sells

Paleographic and Translation Conventions   1

Parallel Images, Transcriptions, and Translations   5

For past, present, and future Mesoamerican scholars:
*ce qualli ohtli.**

*"May you find a good road."

VOLUME I
Interpretation of *Codex Mendoza*

Preface

The *Codex Mendoza*, currently residing in the Bodleian Library at Oxford University, England, is a vivid rendering of many aspects of pre-Contact Aztec life. It is the only Mesoamerican manuscript that pictorially combines Aztec conquests, tribute demands, and an ethnographic account of life from cradle to grave. As such, it is the most comprehensive of the Mesoamerican codices, serving as a major source for studies of Aztec history, geography, economy, social and political organization, glyphic writing, costumes, textiles, military attire, and indigenous art styles. In addition, this rich repository of information on pre-Hispanic central Mexican life has a further significance. Because the Aztecs were the most fully documented of all the newly discovered peoples in the Age of Exploration, they provide a gateway through which scholars can work back in time to even more ancient pre-Hispanic peoples. And of all the Aztec chronicles, none offers a fuller range of pictorial content than *Codex Mendoza*. At many levels this manuscript is truly extraordinary.

There has long been a recognized need for an accessible facsimile edition as well as a scholarly update of the information contained in the *Codex Mendoza*, particularly in light of recent breakthroughs in ethnohistorical and archaeological research. The goal of the present edition is to fill these desiderata.

THE STRUCTURE OF CODEX MENDOZA

The *Codex Mendoza* contains seventy-two annotated pictorial leaves and sixty-three pages of commentary in Spanish. These folios are divided into three discrete parts. Part 1 (nineteen pictorial pages) documents the founding of Tenochtitlan and the history of Mexica conquests, chronologically by individual ruler. Part 2 (thirty-nine pictorial pages) is a detailed tally of the tribute demanded (or received) from thirty-eight provinces subject to the Triple Alliance in the early sixteenth century. It begins with two folios showing imperial garrison towns. Part 3 (fifteen pictorial pages) is an ethnographic account of Mexica daily existence, including colorful details on life cycle and education, warfare, political life, priestly training, crime and punishment, preparations for various livelihoods, and avenues to high social esteem.

The codex was compiled some twenty years after the Conquest. It was drawn on European paper by native scribes under the supervision of missionary priests, who added annotations and commentaries in Spanish. While it appears that the document as a whole was prepared for the Spanish crown, there is little doubt that parts 1 and 2 were copied from earlier pictorials dating from pre-Hispanic times. Part 3 has no known indigenous analogue, and probably was composed specifically for inclusion in this document. After a long and eventful history, *Codex Mendoza* has come safely to rest in the Bodleian Library.

THE STRUCTURE OF THIS FOUR-VOLUME EDITION

This edition of *Codex Mendoza* is divided into four separate but related volumes. The first, volume 1, is devoted to a thorough examination of the content of *Codex Mendoza*. The initial section is composed of eight interpretive essays written by Aztec scholars, each of whom analyzes a specific aspect of the document. Part 2 contains eleven appendices—some textual, others pictorial—to aid further in understanding the wealth of information contained in the complex manuscript. Volume 2 provides a descriptive, page-by-page discussion of *Mendoza*, concluding with an extensive bibliography and index. Volume 3 provides a color facsimile of *Codex Mendoza*, and volume 4 contains its parallel image, complete with transcriptions and translations of the sixteenth-century Spanish commentaries and glosses.

Volume 1

PART 1: INTERPRETATION OF CODEX MENDOZA

Each of the eight analytical commentaries included in volume 1 deals with a separate aspect of the document. The first article, "The History of the *Codex Mendoza*" by H. B. Nicholson, provides the backdrop for better understanding the manuscript, recounting its colorful history and important place among the Mesoamerican pictorials. Nicholson considers the many difficult questions involving the time and circumstances of the codex's composition; solution of these problems, he stresses, could lead to a far more accurate interpretation of the information contained within the *Mendoza*.

The following two chapters, by Wayne Ruwet—with an addendum by B. C. Barker-Benfield—and Kathleen Howe, provide important information on the physical properties of the manuscript and the art style used in composing the pictorial. Ruwet (chapter 2), in "A Physical Description of the *Codex Mendoza*," focuses on origins and methods of European paper manufacture, types of watermarks and their significance, and the method of binding used in producing the document. Barker-Benfield provides additional new information on *Mendoza* watermarks. Howe, in "The Relationship of Indigenous and European Styles in the *Codex Mendoza:* An Analysis of Pictorial Style" (chapter 3), discusses indigenous and European stylistic conventions of the time, analyzing each section of the *Mendoza* in turn. She reaches conclusions also supported in chapter 8 by Anawalt.

The next three chapters, by Elizabeth Hill Boone, Frances F. Berdan, and Edward E. Calnek, focus on the three major sections of the codex: part 1, the history of Aztec conquests; part 2, tribute; and part 3, social and political life. Each of these chapters discusses the format and content of the section, compares and contrasts the data with analogous information from other contemporary sources (be they ethnohistorical, archaeological, or ethnographic), and highlights persistent problems of interpretation.

Boone, in "The Aztec Pictorial History of the *Codex Mendoza*" (chapter 4), addresses the especially baffling problems of chronology through a comparison of the history of conquests contained in the *Codex Mendoza* with similar histories in other contemporary ethnohistorical sources. She discusses several typologies of historical codices, concluding that the *Codex Mendoza* part 1 is a victory chronicle. Berdan, in "The Imperial Tribute Roll of the *Codex Mendoza*" (chapter 5), deals with part 2 of the document. She systematizes the large amount of tribute portrayed, unraveling its repetitive presentations into an understandable system, and placing the depicted tribute into the context of the spectrum of goods utilized by the growing population of Tenochtitlan. Calnek, in "The Ethnographic Content of the Third Part of the *Codex Mendoza*" (chapter 6), suggests the possible social background of the native authors of this unique section as well as diagrams the convoluted progression of the narrative throughout the fifteen folios.

The two remaining chapters, by Frances F. Berdan and Patricia Rieff Anawalt, each address a major theme exemplified by the codex: the glyphic writing system and the costumes and acccoutrements. Berdan, in "Glyphic Conventions of the *Codex Mendoza*" (chapter 7), elucidates specific stylistic patterns used in the rendering of the glyphs and focuses on the problems of the extent of flexibility and scribal preference exhibited in the document. Anawalt, in "A Comparative Analysis of the Costumes and Accoutrements of the *Codex Mendoza*" (chapter 8), compares the dress modes and warrior costumes portrayed in the document with similar items depicted in contemporary Aztec pictorials, using these data to shed light on the composition of *Codex Mendoza*.

PART 2: THE APPENDICES

Much of the content of *Codex Mendoza* is more easily understood when tabulated or charted, as is done in the eleven appendices in this volume. Appendix A provides a ready reference to the dates of the Mexica reigns, drawing on extensive comparative data. Appendices B and C pertain to the massive quantities of tribute demanded by the Mexica of their imperial provinces, adding up the amounts and comparing these totals with similar documentary sources. Appendix D provides a fold-out, *tira*-style reconstruction of the narrative of part 3 of *Codex Mendoza*. Appendix E is a compilation of all the name glyphs found in the codex, including translations, varying interpretations, and discussions of curious details about these indigenous terms. Appendices F–H compare the war-

rior costumes, shields, and *ehuatl* styles that appear in *Codex Mendoza* with similar apparel from other Aztec pictorials. Appendix I displays all the textile motifs that appear in *Mendoza*; these images are correlated with their Nahuatl names in appendix J. Appendix K provides the reader with translations of the Nahuatl terms for the warrior insignia in the referenced *estampas* of Sahagún's early work, the difficult-to-obtain *Primeros Memoriales*.

Volume 2:

THE PAGE DESCRIPTIONS OF CODEX MENDOZA

This descriptive material provides the reader with a page-by-page explanation of the specific content of each folio, including discussion of perplexing pictorial details. In the history and tribute sections, a series of maps are provided which pinpoint a large number of the pre-Hispanic centers represented by *Mendoza's* 612 place glyphs. It is thus possible to locate the whereabouts of many of the communities conquered by the expanding Aztec empire as well as the general boundaries of the thirty-eight imperial tribute provinces.

For the ethnographic section, the content of each page has been described with the aid of sixteenth-century indigenous data. An "Image Description" section is also included for these fifteen folios. Here every pictorial depiction on each page is discussed in detail, often with reference to analogous material contained in other Aztec pictorials.

Volumes 3 & 4

Volume 3 of this edition provides the reader with a facsimile of the *Codex Mendoza*. Thanks to the generosity of the Bodleian Library, the color transparencies were photographed directly from the original manuscript. As a result, these folios display an exceptional degree of clarity and color accuracy. The accessibility of such a reliable facsimile is particularly fortuitous given the scarcity of copies of the 1938 James Cooper Clark edition.

Volume 4 is a parallel image replica of the facsimile. Here the depictions on each pictorial folio have been faithfully duplicated in outline, and the accompanying Spanish glosses have all been translated into English and placed in their original positions on each page. In the case of the sixteenth-century Spanish commentaries, all the paleography has been transcribed into printed form and then translated into English. The reader is thus more easily able to study all aspects of the original text.

CONTRIBUTIONS OF CODEX MENDOZA

With volume 3's facsimile, volume 4's direct transcription and translation of the sixteenth-century paleography, and volume 1's interpretive and volume 2's descriptive material, the information contained within *Codex Mendoza* is now available at a number of levels.

The totality of this work converges on several common themes. There is agreement among the scholars involved that the document illustrates only a portion of the complex and bustling metropolis that was pre-Hispanic Tenochtitlan. For example, the all-pervasive indigenous religion is almost totally ignored. This, of course, is not surprising, given that the pictorial was compiled under the watchful eyes of a Spanish priest.

An additional point of agreement is the recurring evidence that Aztec social structure was neither so regimented nor so controlled as prior scholars have believed. The embellishing of clothing for the entire spectrum of the social order, the constant recombining of many elements of military insignia, the flexibility in the glyphic writing system, and the range of occupation options open to many young men all attest to more fluidity in Aztec culture and society than previously presumed.

Although *Codex Mendoza* was compiled some twenty years after the Conquest, evidence of the resultant acculturation is not consistent throughout. The first two parts probably were copied from pre-Hispanic cognates, and hence retain their indigenous style with very few European intrusions. This is not the case in part 3.

The manner of depicting the images on the ethnographic folios reflects the influence of two decades of Spanish rule. However, the content of these life-cycle scenes, as well as the native scribes' pictorial response to the questions asked of them, attest to the perseverance of indigenous thought patterns from a vanquished world. A reflection of that bygone age still abides in the magnificent *Codex Mendoza*.

Frances F. Berdan
Patricia Rieff Anawalt
June 27, 1989

Published with the assistance of
the Getty Grant Program

Acknowledgments

It is the nature of complex undertakings to involve large commitments of time and patience. Certainly this four-volume edition of *Codex Mendoza* has demanded a great deal of both.

Preliminary to this publication, a symposium on *Codex Mendoza* was organized at the 1982 International Congress of Americanists held in Manchester, England. The six papers presented at that well-attended gathering were highly abbreviated versions of six of the commentaries contained here, in volume 1. We wish to thank our collaborators for their forbearance with the time needed for the subsequent completion of this complex manuscript.

The intellectual and moral support given by Dr. H. B. Nicholson during these years must be acknowledged early on. He has sustained us from the inception of the project through its completion. The encyclopedic knowledge of this foremost of Aztec specialists was always available to us; however, if there are errors on these pages they are ours, not his. Dr. Mary Elizabeth Smith was also a source of early encouragement, for which we are most grateful.

Dr. Nicholson, Dr. Hasso von Winning, and Dr. Alan Grinnell each carefully read early drafts of the descriptive pages of the ethnographic section. Their suggestions consistently improved the work. Dr. Stanley Robe was also most generous with time and expertise; his careful review of the volume 4 transcriptions and translations of the Spanish commentaries are most appreciated. In the same "parallel image" volume, it is the painstaking work of Jean C. Sells to which we owe those carefully detailed tracings, as well as volume I's excellent renderings of warrior paraphernalia in appendices F–H.

Luther Wilson is to be thanked for his early encouragement of the project as well as for obtaining a National Endowment for the Humanities grant. We are most grateful for that generous support from NEH. It was Dr. Ludwig Lauerhass, Jr., who subsequently put us in touch with the University of California Press, whose Stanley Holwitz, Assistant Director, and Scott Mahler, Sponsoring Editor, brought this long-term project to fruition. They also obtained a J. Paul Getty Foundation grant. We are most appreciative to the Foundation for having made this beautiful, *de luxe* edition possible.

We are also most beholden to Dr. David Vaisey, Director of the Bodleian Library, for his generous cooperation. He was very supportive of the undertaking from its beginning and has remained so. His enthusiasm has been contagious. Dr. B. C. Barker-Benfield, Assistant Librarian, Department of Western Manuscripts, also has given generously of his time and expertise; both have been very much appreciated.

This work has also received three grants from California State University, San Bernardino, to whom we are grateful. In addition, that campus's Audio-Visual Department has been exceptionally supportive. Both Trina Whiteside and Victoria Willis have pleasantly and proficiently produced all the maps for volume 2, part 1, the history section, as well as two sets of maps for each of the thirty-eight Aztec provinces discussed in the tribute section, part 2 of volume 2. We are also indebted to the Fowler Museum of Cultural History at the University of California, Los Angeles, for their generous support. The seemingly endless typing required to produce a manuscript of this proportion was cheerfully shared by Linda Stockham of California State University, San Bernardino and Lisa Chisholm. Margaret Ambler Nicholson kindly provided early research assistance.

Bridget Hodder Stuart was a valued aide in the initial stages of preparing the ethnographic folios in part 3 of volume 2. She was followed by the equally multifaceted Lisa Chisholm, whose linguistic skills, meticulous organization, and high standards guaranteed that this potentially overwhelming enterprise stayed on a well-ordered track.

Finally, our deepest appreciation for the patience of our families. They—like *Codex Mendoza*—continue to inspire. We are indeed fortunate.

Our profound thanks to all.

Frances F. Berdan
Patricia Rieff Anawalt

About the Authors

AUTHORS

FRANCES F. BERDAN (Ph.D. University of Texas at Austin, 1975) is Professor of Anthropology and Chair of the Anthropology Department at California State University, San Bernardino. Her research areas include Aztec economics and Mexican Colonial Nahuatl documentation. She has published *The Aztecs of Central Mexico: An Imperial Society* (Holt, Rinehart and Winston, 1982), as well as five other books and numerous articles.

PATRICIA RIEFF ANAWALT (Ph.D. UCLA, 1975) is Director of the Center for the Study of Regional Dress, Fowler Museum of Cultural History, University of California, Los Angeles, and a 1988–1989 Guggenheim Fellow. Her research centers on pre-Hispanic and modern Middle American costumes and textiles. In addition to numerous articles, she has published *Indian Clothing Before Cortés: Mesoamerican Costumes from the Codices* (University of Oklahoma Press, 1981; paperback edition 1990).

CONTRIBUTORS

B. C. BARKER-BENFIELD (D. Phil. Oxford, 1976) is an Assistant Librarian in the Department of Western Manuscripts at the Bodleian Library and part-time University Lecturer in Latin Palaeography at Oxford University.

ELIZABETH HILL BOONE (Ph.D. University of Texas at Austin, 1977) is Director of Studies, Pre-Columbian Studies, at Dumbarton Oaks, Washington, D.C. Her research contributions focus on Aztec art history and ethnohistory. Among her numerous publications is *The Codex Magliabechiano* (University of California Press, 1983).

EDWARD E. CALNEK (Ph.D. University of Chicago, 1962) is Associate Professor of Anthropology at the University of Rochester. His research concentrates on the social organization of Aztec Mexico, especially urban Tenochtitlan, and he has published numerous articles on the subject.

KATHLEEN STEWART HOWE is completing her Ph.D. degree in art history at the University of New Mexico. She has worked intensively with the *Codex Mendoza* at the Bodleian Library, Oxford University, England.

H. B. NICHOLSON (Ph.D. Harvard, 1958) is Professor of Anthropology at the University of California, Los Angeles. His research focuses on Mesoamerican religion and ethnohistory. He has published numerous articles, authored an Aztec exhibition catalog, and edited *Origins of Religious Art and Iconography in Preclassic Mesoamerica* (UCLA Latin American Studies Series, 1976).

WAYNE RUWET is a dedicated student of pre-Hispanic Mexican documentation, focusing particularly on the enormous Sahagún corpus. He has studied the physical properties of the *Codex Mendoza* in depth.

PART I

The *Codex Mendoza* in Perspective

CHAPTER I

The History
of the *Codex Mendoza*

H. B. Nicholson

Undoubtedly the best known Colonial native tradition pictorial from central Mexico is the *Codex Mendoza* (Bodleian Library, Oxford University, Arch. F.c. 14, Ms. Arch. Seld. A.1). In spite of its renown and the existence of a substantial literature concerning it, this priceless illustrated document, which also includes an extensive Spanish text, deserves considerable further study. Remarkably, although the *Codex Mendoza* was the first important Mesoamerican pictorial to be published nearly in its entirety, it did not appear in an adequate color photoreproduction until 1938—and most of this edition (Clark 1938) was destroyed two years later during the London Blitz of World War II. This chapter is devoted to a general discussion of the problems surrounding the origin of the *Codex Mendoza* and a summary of its publication history prior to the present edition.

First, a few notes on the manuscript itself.[1] No thorough physical description of the *Codex Mendoza* has hitherto been published, nor did any earlier edition reproduce all of its leaves. The Paso y Troncoso/Galindo y Villa edition of 1925 contained excellent black-and-white photographs, at the same scale as the original, of the seventy-one leaves of what can be considered the "*Codex Mendoza* proper." The Clark edition of 1938 reproduced in color photographs, also at the same scale, all of these plus a third of the preliminary leaves. A reasonably accurate notion of the original manuscript can be formed by careful study of these editions, particularly the latter.

What has not been made clear is that the first of the three preliminary leaves, not hitherto published, is pasted on the inside cover of the present vanilla-colored vellum binding. Written on it is the name of its first recorded possessor, "A. Thevet." The second preliminary leaf, which also to my knowledge has hitherto not been published, contains various annotations on its reverse, most of them apparently added after the manuscript reached the Bodleian Library. The third preliminary leaf, reproduced in the Clark edition, features on its obverse a Latin title in the handwriting of the last private owner of the document, John Selden: *Historia mexicana cum figuris quasi hieroglyphicis* (Selden's motto, "Above all—freedom," is also written in Greek on folio 1r). On the reverse of this third preliminary leaf, in the lower left corner, is a brief notation in English, whose correct interpretation has posed a considerable problem.[2] In any case, the facts that it is in English and that it contains the date September 7, 1587, and the word "londen" appear to indicate that the document was on its way to or had reached England by that time. The second and third preliminary leaves are now numbered, in pencil, "i" and "ii" in their upper right corners.

None of the watermarks of the *Codex Mendoza* manuscript has hitherto been illustrated. Clark (1938 1:1) identified them, with their foliation, apparently in terms of their principal use as given in Briquet's (1907) classic compendium. He did not mention that the watermark he designated "Clermont Ferrand" on the third preliminary leaf is also found on the second. Because the first is pasted to the binding, it is impossible to determine whether it also displays a watermark. Nor did Clark point out that the so-called "pelligrino" watermark is also present on the last leaf, 71. The possible relevance of the watermarks of the manuscript for the dating of *Codex Mendoza* will be discussed below.

Because of the present binding, the gatherings of the manuscript are difficult to discern with precision, but numerical annotations on certain leaves provide indications of groupings. Apart from the preliminary leaves, there appear to be at least seven gatherings in the manuscript, all but the sixth in sets of five folio leaves, with half leaves possibly constituting the final six folios. The beginning of the seventh gathering, when a different type of paper also commences, coincides with the start of part 3 (ethnography), thus lending support to the view of Barlow (1949a:5) that parts 1 (conquests) and 2 (tributes) were copied from the *Matrícula de Tributos* (or a cognate, HBN), while the third section was probably prepared independently, "the only one painted especially for it."

The circumstances surrounding the preparation of the *Codex Mendoza* are obscure. A breakthrough appeared to have been achieved in 1938 when Silvio Zavala published the text of a *parecer* concerning the distribution of *encomiendas*. Prepared at the request of Viceroy Antonio de Mendoza by the ex-conquistador Jerónimo López, it probably can be dated to 1547. To illustrate his point that something similar to the *encomienda* system existed prior to the coming of the Spaniards, López described how

> it must have been about six years ago more or less that entering one day into the home of an Indian who was called Francisco Gualpuyogualcal, master of the painters, I saw in his possession a book with covers of parchment and asking him what it was, in secret he showed it to me and told me that he had made it by the command of Your Lordship, in which he had to set down all the land since the founding of the city of Mexico and the lords that had governed and

ruled until the coming of the Spaniards and the battles and clashes that they had and the taking of this great city and all the provinces that it ruled and had made subject and the assignment of these towns and provinces that was made by Motezuma to the principal lords of this city and of the fee that each one of the knights gave him from the tributes of the towns that he had and the plan that he employed in the aforesaid assignment and how he sketched [?] the towns and provinces for it.[3]

Zavala (1938:61) suggested that this passage "explains the history of the preparation of the famous *Codex Mendoza.*"[4] The following year this view was strongly reiterated by Federico Gómez de Orozco in a paper presented to the Sociedad Mexicana de Antropología, published in 1941. The Zavala/Gómez de Orozco hypothesis has been widely accepted, but it must be recognized that the manuscript shown to López by its Indian preparator appears to have included some coverage of the Spanish Conquest. Aside from a brief reference accompanying the last of the three years (3 Calli: 1521) crudely added on folio 15v and a one-paragraph summary at the end of the textual account of the career of Motecuhzoma II (folio 15r), this event receives no coverage in the *Codex Mendoza,* which is clearly complete in its present state. Also, López made no mention of the third, ethnographic part—although, as Gómez de Orozco (1941:47) suggested, this last section might have been prepared and added later.

Gómez de Orozco also identified the person who interpreted into Spanish the information provided by the Indian informants for the *Codex Mendoza* as "a modest and virtuous canon of Mexico called Juan González."[5] This cleric is mentioned in a Spanish annotation, in the trembling hand of Fray Bernardino de Sahagún, to a Nahuatl passage in the *Códice Matritense de la Academia de la Historia* (Sahagún 1905–1907 8: folio 3r). It corresponds to folio 1v, libro octavo, capítulo 1, of the *Florentine Codex* (Sahagún 1979 2) version of the *Historia general (universal) de las cosas de Nueva España* and describes the reign of Axayacatl, sixth official ruler of Mexico Tenochtitlan. Diverging from the fourteen years assigned to this reign in the Nahuatl, Sahagún adds, "The Tenochca say that he reigned twelve years. These additions were taken from the relation that the Tenochca gave to the canon Juan Gonçalez in pictures and in writing."[6] Noting that the regnal durations (for Chimalpopoca, Itzcoatl, Axayacatl, and Ahuitzotl) specified in Sahagún's Spanish additions "correspond approximately with those of the *Codex Mendoza,*"[7] Jiménez Moreno (1938:xxxix, note 88) had already suggested that this relation "perhaps was none other than the *Codex Mendoza,*"[8] and Gómez de Orozco endorsed this view.[9]

In further support of his opinion that the author of the Spanish annotations of the *Codex Mendoza* was Juan González, Gómez de Orozco (1941:48–50) proposed that the final passage of the manuscript (fol. 71v), in which the scribe apologized for the crude style of the Spanish explanatory annotations because of the imperative haste of their preparation, is signed by the initial *G.* Clark (1938 1:1) had previously identified it as a *J,* speculating that it might have been the signature of Martín Jacobita, one of Sahagún's principal Indian informants and the rector of the Imperial Colegio de Santa Cruz de Tlatelolco. Woodrow Borah and Sherburne F. Cook (1963:31) expressed a third opinion. To them it looked "far more like a standard Q of the sixteenth century," leaving to "some more energetic scholar" the task of "locating an interpreter of the middle sixteenth century whose name began with Q."[10]

Acceptance of the Zavala/Gómez de Orozco view concerning the origin of the *Codex Mendoza* would justify the name by which it

has become generally known—although, as will be seen, the employment of Mendoza's name to designate this document dates only from 1780/1781. There are also other indications that might provide additional evidence for Mendoza's role in its genesis. In book 33, chapter 50, of Gonzalo Fernández de Oviedo y Valdés's *Historia general y natural de las Indias* (1944–1945 10:103–110), the official *cronista de Indias* paraphrased a "breve relación" sent by the viceroy of New Spain, Antonio de Mendoza, to Emperor Charles V, with a copy to Mendoza's brother, Diego de Mendoza, Spanish ambassador to Venice. The latter's secretary, Fernández de Oviedo's "especial amigo," Giovanni Battista Ramusio, had sent a version of this copy to the chronicler, resident in Santo Domingo. Following a very garbled summary of the history of Mexico Tenochtitlan, the account refers to

> all this and other histories they have in their books of sacrifices illustrated by figures, which the viceroy arranged to have interpreted in order to send to His Majesty with a book that he is arranging to have made which includes the particular description of the provinces, towns, and fruits of the land, and the laws, and the customs, and origins of the people.[11]

Oviedo y Valdés then wrote to the viceroy, questioning him concerning some of the statements contained in this account; Mendoza replied in a letter dated October 6, 1541. He confirmed that he was preparing "the relation of the things of this land,"[12] remarking that he was being very diligent in ascertaining the facts in the face of considerable diversity of opinion caused by the presence of "many lords in each province."[13] He promised to send a copy to the *cronista* when it was completed, "because it appears to me that it would be very embarrassing that you would send on this relation and that you allege me to be the author thereof, not being very truthful" (Oviedo y Valdés 1944–1945 10:118).[14]

Could this "libro" or "relación" being prepared by the viceroy be the *Codex Mendoza?* In my doctoral dissertation (Nicholson 1957:131) I suggested that apparently it was. The date neatly coincides with that of ca. 1541 that can be calculated from the López reference, lending credence to the view that the document seen by him and the account of native history and culture that, according to his own statements, was being compiled at that time by Viceroy Mendoza were one and the same. However, the apparent inclusion in the illustrated manuscript seen by López of some coverage of the Conquest contrasts with the virtual omission of this topic in the *Codex Mendoza,* raising doubts concerning this identification.

Certainly Viceroy Mendoza must have commissioned, if not the Bodleian document itself, something very similar to it, intending to send it to the mother country. If other than the *Codex Mendoza,* did this manuscript reach its destination? There is one bit of evidence that a pictorial source containing a historical section similar to that of the *Codex Mendoza* must have been in Spain in the sixteenth century and was available to a later *cronista de Indias,* Antonio de Herrera. One of the title-page vignettes of the *Descripción de las Indias Occidentales* of Juan López de Velasco (fig. 1), included with the first four decades of Herrera's *Historia general de los hechos de los castellanos en las islas y tierra firme de Mar Océano* (1601–1615), is labeled "Acamapich first king of Mexico."[15] It portrays that enthroned ruler surrounded by the same four place signs (Quauhnahuac, Mizquic, Cuitlahuac, Xochimilco) that are positioned, on *Codex Mendoza* folio 2v, in front of Acamapichtli (here seated on a simple mat rather than a backed mat throne), to indicate conquests undertaken during his reign (1376–1396). Sty-

Fig. 1. Title page of *Descripción de la Indias Occidentales*, Herrera 1601–1615.

listically and iconographically the place signs are very similar to those in the *Codex Mendoza*, which by this time was already in England.[16]

Another vignette on this title page pictures a native temple, while four vignettes on the title page of the *Década Segunda* of the *Historia general* (fig. 2) depict, inter alia, warriors in full regalia; Motecuhzoma in his litter, surrounded by his retinue, going to the temple; probably at least one (greatly enlarged) place sign (apparently Coyucac, on the Costa Grande of Guerrero, also present in differing versions in the *Codex Mendoza*); Mexican landscape features, etc. All or some of these might also derive from the same (lost) pictorial source as the Acamapichtli vignette.[17] Significantly,

one vignette includes a Spanish crossbowman shown aiming at an Indian warrior brandishing an obsidian-edged club, *macuahuitl*, seemingly a Conquest scene.

In a document replying to a charge by the nephew of Pedrarias Dávila (governor of Panama, 1519–1526) that he had besmirched the reputation of his uncle, Herrera provided an extensive list of his principal sources (Herrera 1882:143; Medina 1913–1920 2: 530–531), which includes this entry: "A colored book of figures of Indians and deeds of Spaniards with . . ."[18]

Both Boone (1977, 1983) and Riese (1986) have suggested that this "Libro de Figuras," as they prefer to abbreviate it, was a key (lost) member of the sixteenth-century Magliabechiano Group of

Fig. 2. Title page of *Década Segunda*, Herrera 1601–1615.

annotated native tradition pictorial manuscripts. Space limitations preclude even a summary of their intricate arguments for their somewhat differing reconstructions of the complex interrelationships of the members of this group—nor can we explore here the possibility that the original prototype(s) for the group could conceivably have had a *Mendoza* connection. For our purposes it is sufficient to note that Herrera's somewhat generalized title for one source he listed as having used, "un libro de figuras de colores de indios e fechos despañoles con . . . ," would seem to fit rather well the type of source utilized for those vignettes, described above, which are not cognate, as are others on these two title pages, with illustrations in extant members of the Magliabechiano Group. All

the Herreran title-page vignettes were apparently completed by 1597–1598 by Juan Peyrou (León Pinelo 1923–1926 16:165; Medina 1962 2:11).

As indicated, some close relationship between—if not outright identification with—the pictorial manuscript inspected ca. 1541 in Mexico City by Jerónimo López in the house of a native "maestro de los pintores" and the "libro" or "relación de las cosas desta tierra" reported by Viceroy Mendoza himself to be in preparation about this same time does seem likely. If it was completed and sent to the Spanish monarch, there might be a possibility that it could be connected with Herrera's "libro de figuras." And, if so, the *Codex Mendoza* must have had a different origin. However, with the limited data at hand, one must be wary of piling conjecture on conjecture. Nevertheless, the recognition of this possibility suggests that the wide acceptance of the Zavala/Gómez de Orozco hypothesis regarding the time and circumstances of the preparation of the *Codex Mendoza* was perhaps somewhat premature.[19]

Unfortunately, there appears to be no internal evidence that dates our document with any real precision. All folios of the codex proper that have discernible watermarks display the "Heart-Cross" and "Pilgrim" or "Caballero with Staff" watermarks, except one (folio 69: five-pointed star adjoining circle containing an inner linear motif; cf. Briquet 1907: nos. 13995–14072). These are known to have been typical of locally produced or imported (probably North Italian and/or French) paper in use in Spain in the sixteenth century (e.g., Briquet 1907: nos. 5677–5704, 7563–7607; Mena 1926; Valls i Subirà 1980:128–132, 163–165, 197–202, 232–235, 396; Dibble 1982). A *terminus post quem* is provided by the designation (folio 15r) of Cortés as Marqués del Valle, a title granted him in Toledo, July 6, 1529. A *terminus ante quem* is seemingly provided by the date 1553 written twice (folios 1r, 71v) below the name of its first recorded European possessor (see below).

Possibly the reference on folio 71v to the "flota" would support a post-1543 date, since apparently not until that year was the system of annual sailings of the convoyed treasure fleet to Spain formally instituted (e.g., Haring 1963:304; Hoffman 1980:33). However, it is also possible that the reference is to a more informal fleet of an earlier period. Although the evidence, as we have seen, is not conclusive, a date within the span of the viceregal administration of Antonio de Mendoza (1535–1550) would not be unlikely. Certainly New Spain's first viceroy was genuinely interested in his Indian subjects and gathered pertinent information concerning their culture. It is known that he also instigated, during the period 1539–1542, the preparation, probably by a pioneer Franciscan missionary to Michoacán, Fray Jerónimo de Alcalá, of a somewhat similar historical/ethnographic account of a major West Mexican Indian group (Tarascan), the *Relación de Michoacán* (Warren 1971).

Mendoza's predecessor as chief crown authority in the new colony, Sebastián Ramírez de Fuenleal, was also quite interested in collecting information on indigenous cultural patterns (León-Portilla 1969), so it perhaps would not be inconceivable that the *Codex Mendoza* was prepared as early as the period of his administration (1531–1536). None of the major students of our document, however, has suggested such an early date for it. At the other end, a very late dating, 1550–1553, the initial years of Mendoza's successor as viceroy, Luis de Velasco, should also probably not be ruled out altogether. Manuel Orozco y Berra, in his truncated 1877–1882 commentary on the *Codex Mendoza*, suggested a date around 1549 for its composition, but he did not present the reasons for the "simples conjeturas" that led him to this opinion (Orozco y Berra 1877–1882:182).

In any case, it is virtually certain that a remarkable and controversial French cleric, André Thevet (1502/1504? 1516/1517?–1592; see Schlesinger and Stabler 1986:xix–xxvi; Lestringant in Thevet 1985:XIII–XC), possessed our document by 1553. He wrote his name (Latinized) on folios 1r and 71v, adding this date under both signatures. On the latter page, below Thevet's name and the date 1553, are five crossed-out lines, apparently in Latin and in mirror writing, possibly in Thevet's hand. The first line seems to read "Anno Domini 1571"; the remainder is virtually illegible.

Thevet's name, in its French form and without the date, also appears, as mentioned, on the reverse of the preliminary leaf pasted to the front cover of the binding and, additionally, on folios 2r and 70v. After his signature on folio 2r appears an annotation, "cosmographe du Roy." This must have been added sometime after 1553, for Thevet does not seem to have enjoyed the position of royal cosmographer until late in the reign of Henri II (1547–1559), at the earliest (Cardozo 1944:21). Perhaps all three of his signatures in the French form were added at this time. Thevet might also have added the three preliminary leaves after obtaining the manuscript, for the watermarks are of the type that Briquet (1907: nos. 7223–7258) identified as being found mainly on French-manufactured paper.

Whether Thevet acquired the *Codex Mendoza* precisely in 1553 is uncertain. Apparently others of his surviving manuscripts also bear this date. Adhemar (1947:29) suggested that at this time, following his famous trip to the Levant, he was adding significantly to his manuscript and book collection. Compounding the question of when Thevet came into possession of our document is the larger problem of how and from whom. In his *Cosmographie universelle* (1575 2:996v), in connection with his discussion of the pre-Hispanic Mexican writing system, Thevet wrote

> of such writing that I have in my cabinet, engraved on two disks of ivory, or of other wild beasts, that I have recovered from the taking of a ship that came from those countries; in the middle of the said disks can be seen certain letters made like frogs, or toads, and some other animals, both terrestrial as well as aquatic, around the said letters.[20]

Keen (1971:152), followed by Joppien (1978:130) and Schlesinger and Stabler (1986:204), assumes that this passage refers to Thevet's acquisition of the *Codex Mendoza*, but "two disks of ivory" would hardly seem to fit our document. However, it is possible that the royal cosmographer did obtain these pieces, if they really were Mexican, as a result of the capture of the same Spanish ship that was conveying the *Codex Mendoza* (see below).

Nine years after the appearance of his *Cosmographie universelle* Thevet published his *Vrais pourtraits et vies des hommes illustres* (Thevet 1584). In his section on Johannes Gutenberg, Thevet, discussing the origin of printing, mentions that some had ascribed its invention to the indigenous Mexicans. He goes on to say:

> But this is entirely contrary to the truth, for the Mexicans have never used printing. However, I will confess that the Mexicans, in order to express their ideas, use characters resembling divers terrestrial and aquatic animals and the head, feet, arms, and other limbs of a man, just as the Egyptians and Ethiopians did formerly in their hieroglyphic letters—a subject which I have treated amply in my Cosmography. Two such books I have by me, written by hand in the city of Themistitan, and filled with their characters and figures and the interpretations of them.[21]

In his *Grand insulaire*, another major cosmography written by Thevet, ca. 1586/1588, which exists only in manuscript and of which only certain portions have been published, while discussing the native Mexican deities he states:

> I have in my possession two books about the idols writ by hand containing the genealogy and history of the kings and great lords of that country, and the pictures of the idols they adored, painted and pictured in two books, written by hand by a monk who lived there around thirty-four years, exercising the charge of a bishop in that country. [These] books came into my hands after having been presented to the late Queen of Spain, daughter of King Henry II of France. . . .

The reader who might be curious and wants to go thoroughly into the matter will have patience, if it please him, to wait until I have published these books, which will be soon with God's help. Still, if he were too famished [to wait], I would advise him to come see me and I will show him something that will be able to satisfy him.[22]

Later, in describing the city of "Themistitan" (Tenochtitlan), Thevet describes it as built on an island, "as I show on the map which I had from him who provided me with these two books, which I told you about before."[23]

Some serious problems are posed by these statements. Schlesinger and Stabler (1986:219), who first published the excerpt just quoted from the *Grand insulaire* in English translation, held that "Thevet is here referring to his possession of the *Codex Mendoza* and possibly of the *Histoyre du Mechique*." As they also recognized, Thevet's "late Queen of Spain" was Elizabeth of Valois, third wife of Philip II. The eldest daughter of Henri II and his queen, Caterina de' Medici, she was born in 1545—which would have made her only eight years old in 1553, by which time Thevet almost certainly had acquired the *Codex Mendoza*. As part of the arrangements in 1559 in connection with the Treaty of Cateau-Cambrésis ending the long, intermittent war between Spain and France, Elizabeth, then only fourteen, married Philip II following the death of his second wife, Mary Tudor, Queen of England. She resided with her husband, as Queen of Spain, until her death, in childbirth, in 1568. It does not seem likely that the *Codex Mendoza* would have been "presented" to Elizabeth when such a young child or that Thevet would have referred to her as the "Queen of Spain" if he had obtained it from her at least six years before she had assumed that title.

Thevet states that both books were "about the idols" but also contained "the genealogy and history of the kings and great lords." Only this latter topic would fit the *Codex Mendoza*, which contains no material on the native deities. Another problem concerns the date of the writing of this passage. The *Grand insulaire* is often dated 1588 (e.g., Schlesinger and Stabler 1986:272; but cf. xxiv: 1586), but on internal evidence some of it, at least, was being composed in 1587. If, as will be seen, the *Codex Mendoza* had come into the hands of its next documented possessor, Richard Hakluyt, by September, 1587, Thevet could hardly have written after that date that he intended, "with God's help," to publish it. Quinn (1974 1:292) suggested that possibly Hakluyt acquired it from Thevet on the occasion of his visit to him in 1587, accompanied by the young French mathematician Martin Basanier, to present him with a copy of René de Laudonniére's *L'histoire notable de la Floride*, published by them, "the manuscript of which Hakluyt had earlier borrowed from Thevet and now returned." Thevet bitterly condemned this publication of his manuscript of Laudonniére as plagiarism and "a villainy against me," but, as Quinn noted, "Hakluyt and Basanier could scarcely have presented themselves in a friendly way to Thevet if the situation had been precisely as he indicated."

Compounding the problems surrounding these two illustrated books that Thevet claimed to have owned is his attribution of their authorship to a "monk" who allegedly lived in Mexico for about thirty-four years and who also held the office of bishop. It was mentioned above that Schlesinger and Stabler suggested that one was the *Codex Mendoza* and the other was possibly the *Histoyre du Mechique*. The latter, which will be discussed in more detail below, is a French copy by Thevet of portions of an original Spanish manuscript that had come into his hands; it may have been the extensive ethnography of the native peoples of central Mexico compiled, possibly between 1533 and 1539, by the Franciscan missionary Fray Andrés de Olmos. If Schlesinger and Stabler's suggested identification was correct, Thevet was obviously describing not his French copy (which contains no illustrations) but the original illustrated Spanish manuscript.

But who was this alleged author of his two "books" who had, according to Thevet, spent around thirty-four years in Mexico and who had also served as a bishop? Olmos's missionary career in New Spain spanned some forty years (1528–1568; Baudot 1977: 119–157), but he never became a bishop. Olmos accompanied Fray Juan de Zumárraga, who did come to New Spain in 1528 as the first Bishop of Mexico and continued his missionary career there for twenty years until his death in 1548. But Zumárraga is not known to have ever written an illustrated account of the native religion. Another missionary who wrote extensively on the native culture and who also served as a bishop (of Chiapa) was the Dominican "Apostle of the Indies," Fray Bartolomé de las Casas, but he derived his material mainly from that of others (including Olmos), and his surviving manuscripts are not illustrated. Las Casas also spent only about seven years (1535–1540, 1545–1547) in Middle America (Wagner and Parish 1967).

And who was the unnamed "him" who supposedly supplied Thevet with his two books, together with a map of the Mexica capital?[24] Just how reliable are the statements of Thevet concerning the authorship of these works and the circumstances of his acquisition of them? Schlesinger and Stabler (1986:219), assuming that one at least was the *Codex Mendoza*, regarded Thevet's assertions as "almost certainly a fabrication, as the document never reached Spain." Thevet's frequent unreliability is well established, yet these statements should probably not be completely dismissed out of hand. In passages both before and after them Thevet provides material that clearly derives from both the *Histoyre du Mechique* and the *Codex Mendoza*, particularly the former. There are, however, a few items, especially concerning the deities Huitzilopochtli, Citlalicue, and Citlalatonac and the specification of the date May 10 for a native ceremony, which cannot be clearly linked to these or to others of the sources Thevet is known to have used for his accounts of native Mexican culture. Although typically somewhat garbled and containing some dubious material, these tidbits of information might be derived from the original Spanish source from which he extracted the *Histoyre du Mechique*. However, it is also possible, if the two illustrated books he supposedly obtained from the French queen of Spain were other than the *Histoyre* and the *Codex Mendoza*, that they came from one or both of them.

In any case, there is no doubt that Thevet acquired the *Codex Mendoza* no later than 1553, as well as, at some undetermined date, the Spanish manuscript from which he extracted the *Histoyre du Mechique*. What is difficult to resolve—considering Thevet's well-known penchant for vagueness and inaccuracy—is whether these two documents can positively be identified with the two illustrated books he alluded to in his 1584 and 1586/1588 works cited above. If so, his statement that he obtained them from an unnamed person after they had been presented to the Queen of Spain is puzzling in the extreme. If they were not the *Mendoza* or the *Histoyre*, it is perhaps even more puzzling why he didn't make greater use of them in his writings—apart from the question of what happened to them.[25]

Thevet did utilize a few data in the *Codex Mendoza* in the four chapters he devoted to Mexico in his *Cosmographie universelle* (1575, bk. 22, chaps. 14–17, 2:984v–1000r)—and, as we have seen, to some extent also in his *Grand insulaire*. His engraving of Motecuhzoma II, especially the shield, in his *Vrais pourtraits et vies des hommes illustres* (Thevet 1584: folio 644r; fig. 3) was clearly influenced by certain representations in the *Codex Mendoza* (discussion in Joppien 1978:129–137).

As indicated, Thevet apparently kept possession of our document until 1587. What happened next, to account for its conveyance to another country, was told in 1625 by Samuel Purchas (3:1065–1066):

> Reader, I here present unto thee the choicest of my Jewels. . . . Such an one we here present, a present thought fit for him whom the senders esteemed the greatest of Princes, and yet now presented to thy hands before it could arrive in his presence. For the Spanish Governour having with some difficultie (as the Spanish Preface imports) obtained the Booke of the Indians with Mexican interpretations of the Pictures (but ten daies before the departure of the Ships) committed the same to one skillful in the Mexican language to be interpreted; who in a very plaine stile and verbatim performed the same, using also some Morisco words, as Alfaqui and Mezquitas (for Priest and Temples) import. This Historie thus written, sent to Charles the fifth Emperour, was together with the Shippe that carried it taken by Frenchmen of war, from whom Andrew Thevet, the French Kings Geographer, obtained the same: after whose death Master Hakluyt (then Chaplaine to the English Embassadour in France) bought the same for 20. French crownes, and procured Master Michael Locke in Sir Walter Raleighs name to translate it. It seems that none were willing to be at the cost of cutting the Pictures, and so it remained amongst his papers till his death, whereby (according to his last will in that kinde) I became the possessor thereof, and have obtained with much earnestnesse the cutting thereof for the Presse.

In 1613 Purchas had published *Purchas His Pilgrimage*, which, although focusing on religious customs, was very geographically oriented and included many travel accounts. It was well received and popular, and the following year a much expanded edition appeared. Purchas in the meantime had gained access to the important collection of manuscripts of the preeminent English editor of collections of voyages and travels, Richard Hakluyt, including one of his prime documents, the *Codex Mendoza*. Purchas referred to it, among his manuscript sources, as the "Mexican Historie" and the "Mexican picture history." He made some use of it in his coverage of the history of Mexico Tenochtitlan, the educational system, the calendar, and, especially, tributes (Purchas 1614:790, 793–794, 803, 806–812). On page 793, in the passage describing the reign of Ahuitzotl, derived from José de Acosta's 1590 *Historia natural y moral de las Indias*, mention is made of "the Annales of Mexico; which booke is now in the Vatican Librarie at Rome." His marginal note reads: "And Master Hakluit hath a copie of it translated into English. It was in the Mexican language, sent to Charles 5. intercepted by *Florinus*." Various confusions are evident here. Acosta's reference to the pictorial annals in the Vatican Library (which have their own problems that cannot be discussed here) has nothing to do, of course, with the *Codex Mendoza*, nor is the latter in the "Mexican language." Whoever the French corsair was who seized the ship conveying it to Spain, it was certainly not Florin, or Fleury, of La Rochelle (who did capture in 1523 many of the treasures Cortés had sent to Spain after the Conquest), for Fleury was

Fig. 3. Portrait of Motecuhzoma II. Thevet 1584: fol. 644r.

captured by the Spanish in 1527 and hanged as a pirate (Gaffarel 1902).[26]

Purchas acquired the *Codex Mendoza* some time after 1616, the year of Hakluyt's death. By 1625 he appears to have obtained fuller and more accurate information concerning its history. As the passage quoted above from the 1625 edition indicates, "Florinus" has disappeared, replaced by "Frenchmen of war." However, Purchas was still in error concerning the date of Hakluyt's acquisition of our document, since it is known that the latter, after having served since 1583 as chaplain to the English ambassador to the French court, Sir Edward Stafford, left Paris, never to return, in the fall or winter of 1588 (Parks 1961:274–250; Quinn 1974 1:300). As mentioned, according to the English annotation on the verso of the third preliminary leaf—but apparently not in Hakluyt's hand, as Clark (1938 1:2 [cf. Quinn 1974 1:294]) recognized—the document had apparently reached or was on its way to England by September 7, 1587, five full years before Thevet's demise.

In 1625 Purchas published his magnum opus, *Hakluytus Posthumus: Or, Purchas His Pilgrimages*, in four volumes. Included in volume 3 (pp. 1065–1117) was Michael Lok's English translation of the Spanish text of our document, now Purchas's property, along with woodcuts of much of the pictorial material. However quaint, these illustrations (fig. 4) constituted a much larger portion of a Mesoamerican native tradition pictorial than had ever been published before.[27]

What is not made clear by the early history of the *Codex Mendoza* summarized by Purchas is precisely when it was captured by the French on the high seas. If 1553 was the actual year of its acquisition by Thevet, could it also have been the year of its abortive shipment from Mexico? Certainly French privateering was especially active at this time, when France and Spain were formally at

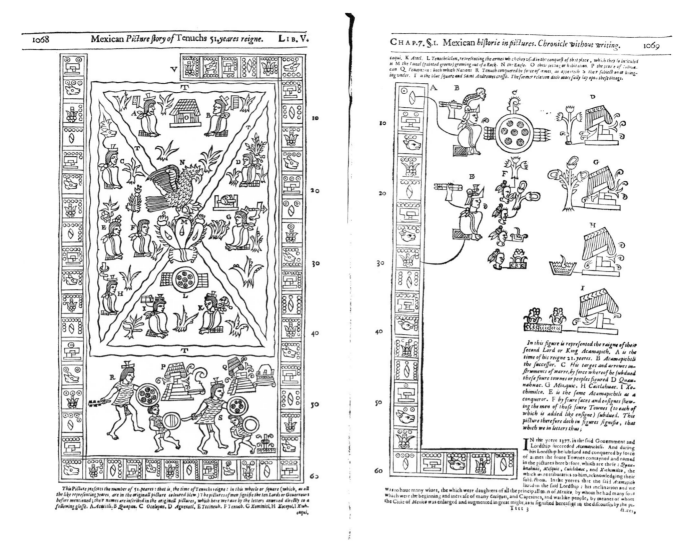

Fig. 4. Pages 1068–1069, Purchas 1625 vol. 3, with woodcuts
of *Codex Mendoza* fols. 2r and 2v.

war (1552–1556). On the other hand, open conflict between the two nations had also prevailed a decade before (1542–1544). The earlier date would actually be more conformable with the chronological implications of the López document and Viceroy Mendoza's statements quoted by Fernández de Oviedo y Valdés.

It may be significant that Thevet also acquired, as was indicated above, another Spanish manuscript concerned with indigenous Mexican Indian culture. His French translation of this, the *Histoyre du Mechique*, is still extant (Bibliothèque Nationale de Paris, Fonds Française 19031) and was published in 1905 by de Jonghe. Thevet made extensive use of this document in chapters 14–17 of book 22 of his *Cosmographie universelle* and, to a somewhat lesser extent, in his *Grand insulaire*. The circumstances of Thevet's acquisition of the Spanish manuscript from which the *Histoyre du Mechique* was derived are unknown, but it is conceivable that it might have been captured together with the *Codex Mendoza*, and the French savant may have obtained both at the same time from the same source. If so, its date, if it could be ascertained, might be relevant to that of the *Codex Mendoza*.

Unfortunately, the *Histoyre du Mechique* is undated, although a reference to Mexico as an "archévesché" provides a *terminus post quem* of 1547 for the manuscript in its present form, for the archbishopric was not established until that year. It has been long agreed that at least part of the *Histoyre* stems from the writings, surviving only in fragments, of the important pioneer missionary/ethnographer in New Spain Fray Andrés de Olmos. The em-

broiled issues surrounding the "Olmos problem" cannot be entered into here. Baudot (1977:119–240) has published the most thorough recent discussion. He believes that the original, comprehensive account of Olmos, which he calls *Traité des antiquites mexicaines* and which was commissioned by the president of the Segunda Real Audiencia de México, Sebastián Ramírez de Fuenleal, and the *custodio* of the Franciscan order, Fray Martín de Valencia, was compiled between 1533 and 1539. After all copies had been sent to Spain, Olmos, apparently at the insistence of Fray Bartolomé de las Casas, prepared a concise summary of his work, a *Suma*, probably in 1546, which some later writers, especially the Franciscan chronicler Fray Gerónimo de Mendieta, utilized in part. Baudot, with others, believes that certain later accounts of aspects of indigenous Central Mexican culture were copies of portions of Olmos's earlier, longer work, including the invaluable *Historia de los mexicanos por sus pinturas* and, in French, the *Histoyre du Mechique*. Baudot also suggested that, while copying the latter, Thevet heavily edited it and interpolated many observations of his own. These would include one chronological statement that has been used, he believes erroneously, to date the original Spanish document at 1543 and the characterization of Mexico as an archbishopric.

The problems surrounding the *Histoyre du Mechique* are obviously too complicated for it to be utilized very effectively to help solve the kinds of problems connected with the *Codex Mendoza*. However, if Thevet did acquire the *Codex Mendoza* and the *Histoyre de Mechique* together and if Baudot's dates for Olmos's two treatises are accepted along with his view that the earlier, more extensive one was the principal source for the *Histoyre du Mechique*, it would suggest a relatively early date (ca. 1539–1542?) for the *Codex Mendoza* as well. This is all quite conjectural, but it is noteworthy that this possible dating for our document about this time keeps recurring as various lines of evidence are considered.

Fray Andrés de Olmos was also possibly directly connected with the *Codex Mendoza* in a tantalizing but still obscure fashion. Chapters 34–36 of Libro Segundo of Gerónimo de Mendieta's 1596 *Historia eclesiástica indiana* contain an account of the royal dynasty of Mexico Tenochtitlan that is textually almost identical to that of the *Codex Mendoza*. It immediately follows a passage that almost certainly derived from the lost Olmos *Suma*. According to his own statement, Mendieta (1980:75–76) based all of his material on the Indian cultures on the earlier chronicles of either Olmos (the *Suma*) or Fray Toribio de Benavente (Motolinía). Was the Spanish text of the *Codex Mendoza* also included in the Olmos *Suma*? If so, it has some interesting implications. Not the least of these is the possibility that the fluent *Nahuatlato* Fray Andrés de Olmos, rather than the canon Juan González, could have been the interpreter who interrogated the Indian informants, conveying their replies to the obviously rather harassed scribe of the *Codex Mendoza*.[28] Olmos, then, might have incorporated this historical resumé of the Tenochca dynasty in his *Suma*, possibly, if Baudot's arguments have cogency, in 1546. It should also be kept in mind that Thevet attributed the authorship of both of the illustrated books that he owned to the same person, a "monk" who had spent many years in Mexico—a characterization that, in spite of various anomalies, probably best fits Fray Andrés de Olmos.

The later history of the *Codex Mendoza* can be summarized rather briefly. After the death of Purchas in 1626 it was apparently inherited by his son. Sometime before 1654 it was acquired by Samuel Purchas's good friend John Selden, the prominent English jurist and antiquary, who also obtained, from an unknown source or sources, two other Mexican native tradition pictorials, *Codex Selden* and the *Selden Roll*, both originally from western Oaxaca.[29] In 1659, five years after Selden's death, all three entered the collection of the Bodleian Library, Oxford University, where their existence passed almost unnoticed for many years.

In the same year that Purchas published his major work, 1625, the Flemish geographer, naturalist, and philologist connected with the West India Company of Leiden, Holland, Joannes de Laet, published in Leiden his *Nieuwe Wereldt ofte Beschrijvinghe van West-Indien* (Laet 1625). It included a concise resumé of the geography and ethnography of New Spain, largely drawn from various published Spanish sources. In 1630 appeared a second and considerably augmented edition, which now included woodcuts taken from the 1625 Purchas publication of the *Codex Mendoza*: the first thirteen years (1 Tecpatl–13 Tecpatl) of Acamapichtli's reign; the New Fire symbol (fire-making implements and smoke puffs); five banners indicating the numerical value $5 \times 20 = 100$; the copal incense pouch, *xiquipilli*, indicating 8,000; and the hair, *tzontli*, symbol for 400 attached to a gourd vessel. These illustrations were repeated in the Latin (1633), French (1640), and third Dutch (1644) editions.

The renowned pioneer student of Egyptian hieroglyphics, the erudite German Jesuit Athanasius Kircher, in his *Oedipus Aegyptiacus* (1652–1654 3:28–36), copied the Purchas woodcuts that correspond to the first two illustrated pages of the *Codex Mendoza* part 1 (folios 2r, 2v) and the initial page of part 3 (folio 57r). He also reproduced the column of thirteen years (1 Tecpatl–13 Tecpatl) which corresponds to the reign of Itzcoatl, fourth official

HISTOIRE
DE L'EMPIRE MEXICAIN·
repreſentée par figures·
RELATION
DV MEXIQUE, OV DE LA NOUVELLE ESPAGNE,
Par Thomas Gages.

A PARIS,
Chez ANDRE' CRAMOISY, ruë de la vieille Bouclerie, au Sacrifice d'Abraham.

Fig. 5. Title page of Thevenot 1596, with copy of woodcut published by Purchas (1625 3: 1115) of *Codex Mendoza* fol. 69r.

ruler of Mexico Tenochtitlan (folio 5v). His text featured a Latin version of Lok's English translation of the Spanish explanations of the relevant plates. A virtually literal copy of the Purchas woodcuts was published in 1672 in Paris by Melchisedec Thevenot, with a French translation of nearly all of Lok's English version of the Spanish text. Republished in 1696 (transposing the reigns of Ahuitzotl and Motecuhzoma II [XI, XII] and omitting two tribute figures [XXI, XXII]), Thevenot's French editions made the *Codex Mendoza* more widely known on the Continent (fig. 5). In a work first published in 1738–1741, *The Divine Legation of Moses Demonstrated*, William Warburton also copied Purchas's first plate. A partial French translation of Warburton's work in 1744 added the rumor that the original manuscript of the *Codex Mendoza* was in the library of the French monarch. This error—apparently the result of confusion with the *Codex Telleriano-Remensis*—was later repeated by various others (see Quiñones Keber 1984:12–13).

This period of relative ignorance concerning the location of the *Codex Mendoza* was accentuated by the unawareness of its existence in the Bodleian Library on the part of the Scottish historian William Robertson, author of the influential *The History of America* (1777), who was particularly interested in the Mexican native tradition pictorials. Francisco Clavigero (1780–1781), Lino Fábrega (1792–1797 [1899]), and Alexander von Humboldt (1813), other leading pioneer students and publishers of Mesoamerican pictorials, were also ignorant of the location of the *Codex Mendoza* and the four other important examples in the Bodleian Library.

In his widely read *Storia antica del Messico* (1780–1781), Clavigero, who apparently knew it only through Thevenot's 1696 publication, christened our document for the first time *Raccolta di Mendoza* (Spanish: *Colección de Mendoza* [Clavigero 1958–1959 1:31]). He obviously assumed that Thevenot's "gouverneur du Mexique" best fitted this personage—and the name stuck, particularly after its acceptance by Humboldt and Kingsborough.

Although certain brief, sometimes vague reports of the Bodleian Library group of Mesoamerican pictorials appeared earlier, it was not until the publication of the first version of Lord Kingsborough's *Antiquities of Mexico* (1831–1848) that the curtain was really lifted on the Bodleian corpus. The *Codex Mendoza* occupied the place of honor as the first item reproduced in the first volume of Kingsborough's mammoth nine-volume set. Based on tracings by the Italian artist Agostino Aglio, these color lithographs constituted the first complete reproduction of the *Codex Mendoza* (Spanish text, vol. 5; English translation, plus some indices, vol. 6). It completely superseded Purchas's quaint woodcuts and became the standard reproduction for nearly a century.

In 1925 the Mexican government published an excellent set of black-and-white photographs of all the illustrated and textual leaves of the *Codex Mendoza* that had been printed in Madrid for Francisco del Paso y Troncoso. This edition was accompanied by a brief introduction by Paso y Troncoso's protégé and ex-assistant, Jesús Galindo y Villa. This was followed thirteen years later, in 1938, by the ill-fated James Cooper Clark three-volume edition, published by Waterlow and Sons Limited, London. It included an English translation of the Spanish text and an extensive commentary. Although the latter is somewhat uneven in quality, the color photographic reproduction was superb, one of the best ever issued of a native tradition Mesoamerican pictorial. The unfortunate destruction of most of this edition in a warehouse during the 1940 London bombings has been mentioned.

In 1964 the Secretaría de Hacienda y Crédito Público, Mexico, in the first volume of its four-volume re-edition of Kingsborough's *Antiquities of Mexico*, published color photographs of the illustrated pages of the *Codex Mendoza*. They were accompanied by transcriptions of the Spanish text and a page-by-page commentary by José Corona Núñez. In 1978 a popular edition appeared, published by Productions Liber S.A., Fribourg, Switzerland, with reduced color photographs of all illustrated pages, plus numerous larger photos of details, with a general commentary in English by Kurt Ross. The following year the Mexican government, through San Angel Ediciones S.A., published an excellent color photographic reproduction of the *Codex Mendoza*, derived from the 1938 Clark edition, edited by José Ignacio Echeagaray, with a preface by Ernesto de la Torre Villar. It constituted a limited edition of only 2,000 copies, which were not generally made available to persons outside of Mexican government circles. The same year, Editorial Cosmos, Mexico, republished, in offset, the Paso y Troncoso/Galindo y Villa black-and-white photographic edition of 1925.

To summarize, the entire question of the precise time and exact circumstances surrounding the preparation of the *Codex Mendoza* should still be considered open. The evidence is often ambiguous and conflicting. More technical analysis of the document itself (watermarks, chain lines, laid lines, inks, etc.) might result in a more accurate dating than now seems possible, but the limitations of this type of investigation are familar to all students of historical manuscripts. Additional exploration in the archives might uncover new information that could lead to more definitive solutions to the problems discussed above. Clearly, the Zavala/Gómez de Orozco hypothesis, identifying the *Codex Mendoza* with the manuscript volume observed by Jerónimo López while it was being prepared by an Indian artist for Viceroy Mendoza in Mexico City ca. 1541, still must be seriously considered. However, the difficulties with it must also be recognized. It should not be regarded as having conclusively solved the question of the time of its composition and identity of its native preparer. Regarding the identity of the interpreter, both Canon Juan González and Fray Andrés de Olmos were certainly competent and probably available. I suggest that the case for the latter should be more seriously considered than it has been in previous discussions of the problems surrounding the *Codex Mendoza*. As for the dating, most indications do appear to converge on the decade of the 1540s, favoring the earlier end. Finally, it should be emphasized that, in spite of the many versions of *Codex Mendoza* that have been published over a long time span, the need for a more accessible, accurate color reproduction of this fundamental source of information concerning late pre-Hispanic central Mexican culture has been obvious for some time. It is to be hoped that the present edition more than adequately fills this major desideratum in Mesoamerican studies.

NOTES

1. I would like to express my appreciation to the staff of the Bodleian Library, Oxford University, for permitting me to examine the original of the *Codex Mendoza*. I would also like to thank Dr. Nancy P. Troike and Wayne Ruwet for expressing to me their views concerning the manuscript, based on their personal inspections of it, and Dr. Eloise Quiñones Keber for her constructive criticism of this article in manuscript. See Ruwet, this volume, for a more detailed physical description of the manuscript.

2. Clark (1938 1:2) transcribed it as "O. yourself in gold rydinge to londen ỹ 7th of september 1587/vⁱ." Clark assumed this notation recorded the purchase by Hakluyt of the document from Thevet for five pounds, the equivalent of twenty French crowns, commenting that "the date shows that the manuscript changed hands before the death of Thevet." Recent correspondence with a number of scholars (David Vaisey and Bruce Barker-Benfield, Bodleian Library, and Malcolm Blyn, Keble College, Oxford; David Quinn, University of Liverpool; A. I. Doyle, University Library, Durham; and Laetitia Yeandle, Folger Shakespeare Library, Washington, D.C.) familiar with manuscripts and the handwriting of this period indicates that there is now a consensus that the first letter is actually "D.," probably standing for "deliver"

or "debitur." It is also generally agreed that the notation probably constituted a memorandum written by the sender or the courier who carried it to London to collect five pounds as compensation for the delivery service. Quinn (in litt., 7/20/85), who had earlier (1974 1:294) opted for the "O." and now agrees that it is a "D.," states his view: "I am convinced that it has nothing to do with the price Hakluyt paid for it to Thevet, whatever Purchas (not noted for accuracy) might say 38 years later. 20 crowns would be about £5 but I cannot see Thevet parting with the MS for such a small sum and I should not pay any attention seriously to Purchas's figure." I would like to thank all these experts for their helpful comments concerning this still somewhat enigmatic notation.

3. The Spanish reads: "Puede haber seis años poco más o menos que en entrando un dia en casa de un yndio que se decía Francisco Gualpuyogualcal maestro de los pintores vide en su poder un libro con cubiertas de pergamino, e preguntádole qué era, en secreto me lo mostró e me dijo que lo hacía por mandado de Vuestría Señoría, en el cual había de poner toda la tierra desde la fundación desta cibdad de México y los señores que la oviesen gobernado e señoreado hasta la venida de los españoles y las batallas y reencuentros que ovieron y la toma desta gran cibdad y todas las provincias que señoreó y lo a

ellas sujeto y el repartymiento que destos pueblos e provincias se hizo por Motezuma en los señores principales desta cibdad y del feudo que le daban cada uno de los encomendatarios de los tributos de los pueblos que tenía y la traza que llevó en el dicho repartimiento e cómo trazó los pueblos e provincias para ello."

4. In Spanish: "Ilustra la historia de la redacción del famoso códice mendocino."

5. In Spanish: "Un modesto y virtuoso canónigo de México llamado Juan González."

6. In Spanish: "Dizen los tenuchcas q reyno doze años. Estas additiones se tomarō de la relatiō que dierō los tenuchcas al canonigo Juã gonçalez en pintura y ē escripto."

7. In Spanish: "corresponde aproximadamente con el *Códice Mendocino*."

8. In Spanish: "quizá no era otra cosa que el *Códice Mendocino*."

9. Gibson and Glass (1975:365) expressed skepticism concerning the views of Jiménez Moreno and Gómez de Orozco that these Sahaguntine additions closely resembled chronologically those of the *Codex Mendoza*, stating that "their differences indicate that this is unlikely." However, only one reign length differs, that of Chimalpopoca: ten (*Codex Mendoza*) versus eleven (Sahagún annotation) years.

10. Even if this really is a letter and constituted a kind of sign-off, it must have been written by the *scribe*, who appears, from the final statements in the document commenting on crudities in the translation due to the haste with which it had to be done, to be a different person from the translator.

11. In Spanish: "E todo este é otras historias tienen ellos en sus libros de sacrificios escriptos por figuras, los quales hace el visorey interpretar para enviar á Su Magestad con un libro, que hace hacer de la descripcion particular de las provincias, pueblos é fructos de la tierra, é leyes, é costumbres é origenes de la gente."

12. In Spanish: "la relacion de las cosas desta tierra."

13. In Spanish: "muchos señores en cada provincia."

14. In Spanish: "porque me paresce que seria cosa muy vergoncosa que os enviasse yo relacion y que me alegásedes por auctor dello, no siendo muy verdadera."

15. In Spanish: "Acamapich primero rey de Mexico."

16. There could also be a relationship between the Herreran Acamapichtli vignette and a one-leaf document currently in the manuscript collection of the Escorial library (X-II-7, no. 59, fols. 343–344), *Relación de los señores que fueron de Méjico* (Miguelez 1917–1925 1:237; Tudela de la Orden 1954:388). This brief prose account lists the nine official rulers of Mexico Tenochtitlan, with the number of years of their reigns and the number of towns conquered. Acamapichtli is credited with having conquered four communities. The regnal years and numbers of towns conquered in some cases conform to those of the *Codex Mendoza*, but in others vary to some extent. If this textual summary derived from a pictorial chronicle (a section of the "Libro de Figuras"?), it could possibly have been that which served as the source for the Herreran Acamapichtli vignette.

17. Glass and Robertson (1975:132) listed this "unknown source" for those Herreran vignettes not cognate with depictions in extant members of the Codex Magliabechiano Group as number 133 of their census of Mesoamerican pictorials in the native tradition; they also recognized that this putative source might have consisted of "one or more unknown manuscripts." Riese (1986:16–25, 150–154) has undertaken the most detailed scrutiny of the entire corpus of Herreran vignettes derived from Mesoamerican sources.

18. In the 1882 published Spanish version of this list, the entry reads: "Un libro de figuras de colores de yndios e fechos despañoles con . . ." What appears to be the next entry reads: "Hystoria. En la Cámara de Su Maxestad." Medina's 1913–1920 version is the same except for some modernized spellings. Boone (1983:51), who cites only Medina's version, obviously believed that the "Hystoria" that seems to follow "Un libro de figuras . . ." was a separate item. Riese (1986:46–47), however, citing only the 1882 version, obvi-

ously believed that they constituted a single item, which he gives as "un libro de colores de yndios e fechos despáoles con hystoria," and, as a corollary, believes that it was assigned to the "Cámara de Su Magestad." However, the word "con," which terminates the second line of the "libro de figuras" entry in both the 1882 and 1907–1920 versions, seems, on the face of it, to imply some damage to the manuscript at this point which prevented a clear reading of the following word or words. Perhaps only an examination of the original document, in the Archivo General de las Indias, Seville, could conclusively resolve this difference of opinion.

19. The Marquis Spineto (1829:240) claimed that he had seen, many years before 1829, the original of the *Codex Mendoza* in the library of the Escorial. Glass (1975:706), probably correctly, dismisses this statement as simply a mistake on the part of the marquis. The remote possibility remains, however, that he saw something similar to the *Codex Mendoza* and which has since been lost (the *Codex Borbonicus* and the *Relación de Michoacán*, which were in this repository at this time, seem too distinct to qualify).

20. In French: "Et de telle escriture i'en ay á mon cabinet, engrauee sur deux rondeaux d'yuire, ou d'autres bestes farouches, que i'ay recouuerts á la prinse d'vn Nauire qui venoit de ces pais lá: au mitan desdits rondeaux l'on y voit certaines lettres faites comme crapaux, ou grenouilles, & quelques autres bestes, tant terrestres que aquatiques, autour les dittes lettres."

21. The English translation is taken from McMurtrie 1926:4. In French: "Mais cela est du tout contraire á la verité, car ils n'ont iamais vse d'Imprimerie. Toutesfois ie confesseray bien que les Mexicains vsent de characteres, ressemblans á diuers animaux terrestres & aquatiques, & de testes, pieds, bras, & autres membres de l'homme, par lesquels ils donnent à entendre leur conception, comme faisoient iadis les Aegptiens & Aethiopiens par leurs lettres Hyeroglyphiques, donti'ay assés amplement traitté en ma Cosmogra(p)hie: & de tels liures l'en ay deux par deuers moy, escripts à la main en la ville de Themistitan & remplis de leurs characteres & figures auec l'interpretation d'iceux."

22. The only published version (Schlesinger and Stabler 1986:218–219) of this passage is available just in English.

23. Schlesinger and Stabler 1986:224.

24. Lestringant (1984:489), in his catalog of maps in the *Grand insulaire*, lists one of "Themistitan" as number 74 (fol. 180v). To my knowledge, it has never been published.

25. Is it conceivable that one of these "books," assuming that they were other than the *Codex Mendoza* and the *Histoyre du Mechique*, might have been the *Codex Telleriano-Remensis*? Thevet's description would fit it quite well, and if he obtained it through the agency of the Queen of Spain, its date, ca. 1562–1563, would also be appropriate. The history of the *Codex Telleriano-Remensis* in France cannot be traced any earlier than 1700, when it was donated to the Bibliothèque du Roi by Charles-Maurice Le Tellier, Archbishop of Reims. However, I have noted no information in any of Thevet's available writings that might have derived from this source, nor did its putative major compiler, Fray Pedro de los Ríos, a Dominican lay brother who served in New Spain at least from ca. 1541 to 1565, ever serve as a bishop. See Quiñones Keber 1984:11–12, 42–45.

26. The two later editions of *Purchas His Pilgrimage* (1617, 1626) repeat these statements—even that of 1626, which was published long after Purchas had acquired the original of the *Codex Mendoza*.

27. See Glass 1975, table 5, for a useful tabulation of the pre-1810 publication of illustrations from Mesoamerican pictorials in the native tradition.

28. Another possibility, of course, is that Juan González did serve as the interpreter for the *Codex Mendoza* and that Fray Andrés de Almos obtained a copy of that portion of the text concerned with the dynastic history of Mexico Tenochtitlan, which he incorporated into his *Suma*—to be copied, in turn, by Gerónimo de Mendieta in his *Historia eclesiástica indiana*.

29. Selden apparently bound the manuscript with its present vellum covers, including with it another, wholly unrelated item (cf. Clark 1938 1:2, note 6). See Ruwet, chapter 2, this volume.

A Physical Description
of the *Codex Mendoza*

Wayne Ruwet

The *Codex Mendoza* is one of the most famous and glorious post-Hispanic Mexican manuscripts known, yet to date no adequate description of its contents, let alone its physical attributes, has been published. True, the contents are outlined in the *Summary Catalogue of Western Manuscripts in the Bodleian Library* (Madan and Craster 1922 2, 1:595–596), but the binding, watermarks, and other physical features of this remarkable volume are not mentioned. Such detail is not to be expected in a general catalog. James Cooper Clark did address some aspects of the technical makeup of the volume when they pertained to the history of the manuscript. However, he did not include a full physical description of the *Codex Mendoza* in his superb facsimile edition (1938 1:ix). Such description would help to clarify numerous problems concerning the history and composition of the manuscript.

The manuscript volume known as *Codex Mendoza* is kept in the Bodleian Library, with the shelfmark MS. Arch. Seld. A.1. Its eighty-five folios contain two works: the first is the annotated sixteenth-century Mexican pictorial manuscript of seventy-one folios known as *Codex Mendoza*; the second manuscript of fourteen folios is a series of tables comparing the values of Greek and Roman monetary units with their English and French equivalents (fig. 1) of the late sixteenth century (English silver of 1563 is mentioned on folio 74r). This item was probably written in England, since the headings are in English. Folios 83–84 comprise a smaller folding bifolio pasted onto folio 82v and contain an opinion of John Greaves (d. 1652) about the inaccuracy of the tables. There are a number of blank leaves that complete the count of eighty-five folios.

The *Codex Mendoza* manuscript has suffered in its travels through the years. For example, folio 1 has a major tear starting at the bottom of the page and terminating at a point midway up the page toward the fore-edge. This tear was repaired in the distant past with crude patches in a blank area of text and at the bottom of folio 1r. Many other folios of *Codex Mendoza* have been reinforced at the inner margin with later repairing of the paper, especially at the beginning of the manuscript. Also, a parchment strengthener has been glued around the outside of the monetary manuscript, as in the gutter of folios 73r and 82v.

THE PAPER:
ITS HISTORY, DATING, AND ORIGIN

Each page measures 210–215 millimeters wide by 300–315 millimeters high. In the sixteenth-century papermaking process, a pulp prepared from rags or other fibrous material was mixed with water. By the use of sievelike screens—or molds, as the screens are called—the fibers were lifted from the water in a thin sheet. The water was then drained through the small holes of the screen, leaving a sheet of matted fiber, which when pressed and dried became paper (Hunter 1967:5).

We can establish that the pictorial was compiled on paper of European manufacture, specifically Spanish. It is possible to rule out the two other sixteenth-century candidates of paper manufacture, Asia and Mexico, by comparing briefly the contemporary papermaking technologies of Asia and Mexico with that of Spain.

The types of watermarks found in the *Codex Mendoza* paper will at once rule out an Asian origin. While Chinese paper production indeed predates all European papermaking, watermarks were not used in early Oriental papers (Hunter 1967:260). Asian watermarks usually portray Oriental design motifs. The watermarks in the *Codex Mendoza* are typical European designs.

Paper production spread from China to Europe via the Muslims, who started producing paper in Spain in the tenth century (Valls i Subirà 1978:87). Watermarks were introduced by the Italians in 1281. Similar versions of such watermarks found in the *Codex Mendoza* are probably of Spanish origin. Further, during the sixteenth century, the New World was denied access to non-Spanish paper by imperial prohibition.

Papermaking was well established in pre-Hispanic Mexico. The indigenous population of Mexico made a form of paper by beating the well-soaked bark of specific types of trees. This produced a heavy brown paper completely unlike that of the *Codex Mendoza*. The earliest paper mill in New Spain was not authorized until 1575 (Hunter 1967:479), which dates long after the completion of this pictorial.

The Watermarks

There are three types of watermarks present in the pages of the *Codex Mendoza*. Watermarks are made by applying a design onto the mold on which the paper is cast. Normally, there is only one watermark per sheet; however, on some occasions two different watermarks appear on a single sheet. The larger design is then known as the watermark; the second, smaller design is called the countermark. Countermarks were introduced in the seventeenth century.

Watermarks can often help date a document with some precision. This is accomplished by comparing the watermarks from

FIG. I TABLE OF CONTENTS AND INSCRIPTIONS IN THE *CODEX MENDOZA* VOLUME

Location	Inscriptions
Cover (spine)	I X
Front pastedown	s.c. 3134 A. Thevet
Folio ir	blank

Folio iv	77 (3134)
	    8 6 MS Arch. A.1. Seld
	  13 28
	
	Arch. Seld. A.1
	[Kept as Arch. F.c.14]
	"The Mendoza collection"

Folio iir	m.s. fo.
	Historia mexicana Hispanica cum figures
	    quasi hieroglyphicis./
	
	See Purchas' Pilgrims Lib. v. Cap. vii.
	    p. 1066 (1625) I.1. 3. Art. Seld.

Folio iiv	[vertical inscription in lower left corner] d. youreselfe in gold rydinge to londen ye 7th of september 1587/v^t
Folio 1r	A. Thevetus 1553 Περὶ παντὸς τὴν ἐλευθερίαν
	[start of history section]
Folio 2r	A. Thevet cosmographe du Roy
Folio 7r	Blank
Folio 9r	Blank
Folio 11r	Blank
Folio 14r	Blank
Folio 17r	Blank
Folio 18r	fin de la partida primera de esta ystoria
Folio 18v	La segunda parte de la historia./
Folio 54v	fin de la parte segunda./
Folio 55r	[illustration showing the tribute for Oxitipan province]
Folio 55v	Blank
Folio 56r	Blank
Folio 56v	La partida tercera de esta historia./
Folio 70v	A. Thevet
Folio 71v	A. Thevetus 1553 [five lines of mirror writing—all lines crossed out] Anno domini 1571 [remaining four lines illegible] (see fig. 10) [end of third part]
Folio 72	Blank
Folio 73r	Blank
Folio 73v	Start of monetary tables
Folio 82r	End of monetary tables
Folio 82v	Blank
Folio 83r	Note by J. Greaves
Folio 83v	Blank
Folio 84	Blank
Folio 85	Blank
Back pastedown—Blank	

dated documents, such as legal papers, with those found in the undated document. Unfortunately, the watermarks in *Codex Mendoza* were widely used for a long period; hence the paper can be dated only generally, to the middle of the sixteenth century.

Codex Mendoza's preliminary leaves, folios i and ii, both are marked with a fleur-de-lis surmounted by a crown and flanked by the letters *A* and *B* (see fig. 2). While this particular design cannot be precisely identified in the monumental compendium of watermarks by Briquet (1923) or in the recent and highly specialized work by Piccard (1983), the items most similar in Briquet are numbers 9234 and 9239. Briquet identifies these particular watermarks as dating to 1571 and states that they are of French manufacture.

The Pilgrim watermark (fig. 3), common to Spain in that period, is found on the paper in the first and second parts of the *Codex Mendoza*. This watermark shows a pilgrim within a circle with the letters *AMF* below. Briquet (1923:415) argues that this watermark originated in Italy and was most prominent there. However, Valls i Subirà (1970:396) has demonstrated that the Pilgrim watermark was used much earlier in Spain and frequently appeared on a commonly used standard grade of sixteenth-century Spanish paper.

Part 3 of *Codex Mendoza* carries a watermark that shows a Latin cross flanked by the letters *F* and *A* within a teardrop-shaped circle (fig. 4). This common type of watermark is identified by Briquet (1923:334–335, nos. 5677–5688) as dating between 1565 and 1596 and coming from Spain or France. Again, Valls i Subirà (1980:128–131) demonstrated that it is much older in Spain and appears on a widely used type of paper.

A distinctive watermark is located on folio 69: a sphere surmounted by a star and bisected by a pole (fig. 5). Versions of this watermark are described in Briquet (1923:712, nos. 13995–14026). These date from 1501 to 1589 and most frequently appear in paper from either France or Spain. I have been unable to locate a more precise match that might better date this singular watermark in *Codex Mendoza*. On folio 71, the Pilgrim watermark reappears.

The non-Mexican document bound with the *Codex Mendoza*, the tables of Greek and Roman monetary standards, is written on heavy paper that has no visible watermarks. However, a preliminary leaf, folio 72, which is positioned between *Codex Mendoza* and the later document, does have an unusual watermark showing three hats over an *M* (fig. 6). Heawood (1950: nos. 2596–2600) describes similar watermarks that have three hats, but none positioned above the letter *M*. He attributes these similar watermarks to English or Italian manufacture.

Still another watermark occurs on the final sheet of the volume, folio 85, which is clearly conjoined with the back pastedown. This watermark bears the letters "A. GOVTON" and has a countermark of grapes (fig. 7). The grape countermark should appear on the back pastedown, but since the sheet is pasted down it is impossible to view the countermark. Heawood (1950: no. 2252) dates this design to 1607, originating in England.

The Binding

The volume is currently bound with plain, vellum-covered boards. On the fore-edge there is evidence that there once were two sets of ties. These ties are now entirely lost, and it is difficult even to make out what their material or color may have been. There is a graininess to the tie remnants as one feels through the thickness of the pastedowns, which suggests they were of fabric. However, leather cannot be ruled out.

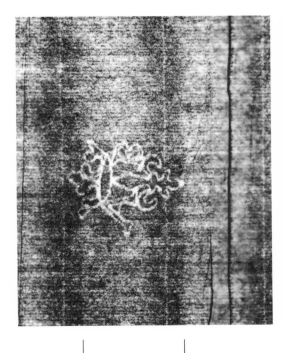

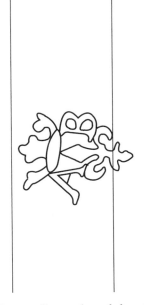

Fig. 2. Beta-radiograph and drawing of the fleur-de-lis watermark on folio ii.

Fig. 3. Beta-radiograph and drawing of the Pilgrim watermark on folio 36.

Fig. 4. Beta-radiograph and drawing of the teardrop and cross watermark on folio 64.

The binding probably dates to the seventeenth century when this manuscript was owned by John Selden (1584–1654), as evidenced by his customary insertion of a Greek motto at the bottom of folio 1r (see fig. 1). Dating the binding to John Selden's time was assumed by H. H. E. Craster of the Bodleian Library when James Cooper Clark (1938 1:ix) wrote his commentary on *Codex Mendoza*. Clark gives no further evidence to support this idea.

Christopher Clarkson, currently conservation officer of the Bodleian Library, also believes that the binding dates to the seventeenth century. He and B. C. Barker-Benfield, librarian at the Bodleian Library, base their opinions on the following argument. The signature of André Thevet (1502–1590), the cosmographer to the king of France in whose hands *Codex Mendoza* rested in the sixteenth century prior to Selden's acquisition (see Nicholson's article in this volume), appears on the verso of the front pastedown of the volume. This fact might be taken to show that the binding was already in existence during Thevet's ownership. However, the inclusion of the second document on Greco-Roman monetary values indicates that the binding must have been done after *Codex Mendoza* had reached England. As Barker-Benfield notes:

In the *Summary Catalogue* entry of 1922, F. Madan and H. H. E. Craster describe fols. 73–82 as "insititious," and indeed this chunky section does not lie particularly happily

with its famous companion; nevertheless, the vellum of the binding seems to allow space for it and shows no sign of the stretching at the spine which would have resulted if the monetary section had been forced into an already existing binding. The conclusion is that the present binding was designed from the first to accommodate both sections, and must therefore have been done after the *Codex Mendoza* had reached England.

Barker-Benfield concludes:

The apparent conflict between these two pieces of evidence may be resolved by a re-examination of the front pastedown. This has a marked vertical pleat running down the center, which is exactly mirrored in the two front flyleaves, fols. i–ii. The conclusion is that the pastedown must originally have been a loose fly-leaf with fols. i–ii, and therefore Thevet could well have written his name on it *before* it had been transformed into an integral part of the present binding.

Our conclusion, then, is that this is an English binding of John Selden's time or shortly before. The monetary table as well as the exotic Aztec material would certainly have interested Selden.[1]

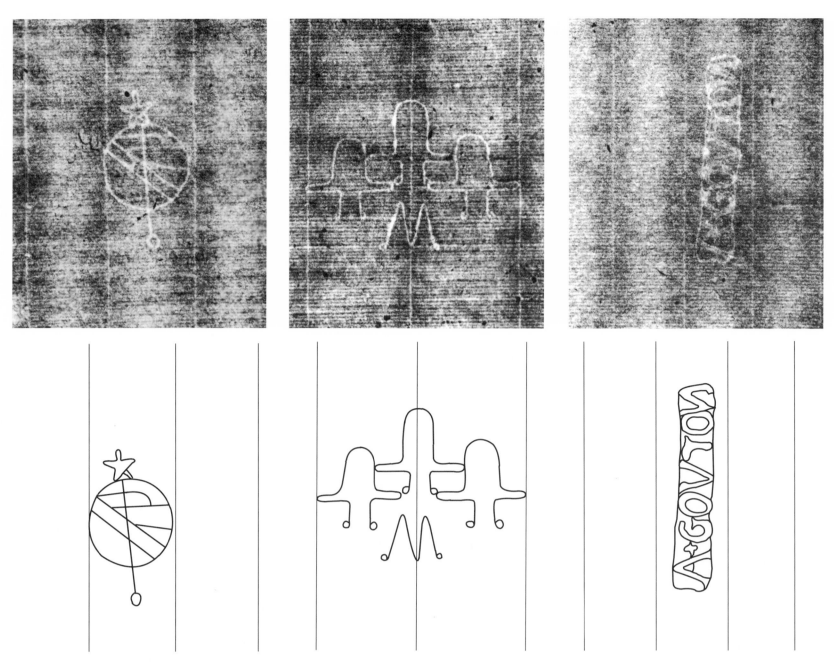

Fig. 5. Beta-radiograph and drawing of the sphere and star watermark on folio 69.

Fig. 6. Beta-radiograph and drawing of the three hats watermark on folio 72.

Fig. 7. Beta-radiograph and drawing of the "A. GOVTON" watermark on folio 85.

It seems, then, that the English binder who bound the volume in the seventeenth century cannibalized one of the flyleaves already present (added by A. Thevet) as his front endpaper. The binder also added new endpapers at the back. This conclusion is supported by the provenance of the watermarks and the physical layout of the volume (see fig. 8).

At this point it is useful to review the method of binding a large-sized sixteenth-century manuscript. A large paper sheet was folded to make two folios or four pages. Folios are numbered on the recto sides only, while pages are numbered on both the recto and verso sides. Several of these bifolios would be gathered together, one inside the other, into a group called a quire or signature. Four sheets per quire was the norm in sixteenth-century Mexico. Quires normally have between three and eight sheets. The quires would be lettered or, as in *Codex Mendoza*, numbered so that the binder could keep them in correct order. This marking is known as a signature, and, by extension, the whole gathering is also called a signature. In *Codex Mendoza*, the signature marks are on the first folio of each of the first seven gatherings next to the folio number, separated from it by a slash (e.g., 11/2, 21/3, 31/4). The mark of the first signature, however, is at the bottom of folio 1. The reconstruction of the gatherings (fig. 8) is based on these signature marks and the location of the various watermarks, since the bind-

ing is still too tight to enable one to follow the connection from folio to folio.

As mentioned above, there is evidence of at least two sewings of the *Codex Mendoza* gatherings. In numerous folios of the manuscript, traces of old stitching holes of an earlier sewing can be seen in the gutters (inner margins of the facing pages). Because no trace of this earlier sewing can be seen in the monetary tables, it seems clear that the *Codex Mendoza* had a previous sewing, if not a previous binding, prior to its being joined with the monetary tables, in the seventeenth century.

Codex Mendoza offers other indicators of an earlier binding. A vertical fold runs about one hundred millimeters from the fore-edge of many of the folios in the initial part of the manuscript. There are also horizontal folds about halfway down the pages. The double folds are most pronounced in the first part of the manuscript. They gradually fade in part 2, and there are only faint traces in part 3. The folds probably represent marks of the handling of the manuscript prior to its being bound, because it could not be folded once the covers were added. However, the manuscript could have been sewn, but not bound. Because similar folds are not found in the monetary tables at the end of the volume, *Codex Mendoza*'s folds must predate the joining of these two manuscripts. As these folds are found in the preliminary leaves, which appear to be

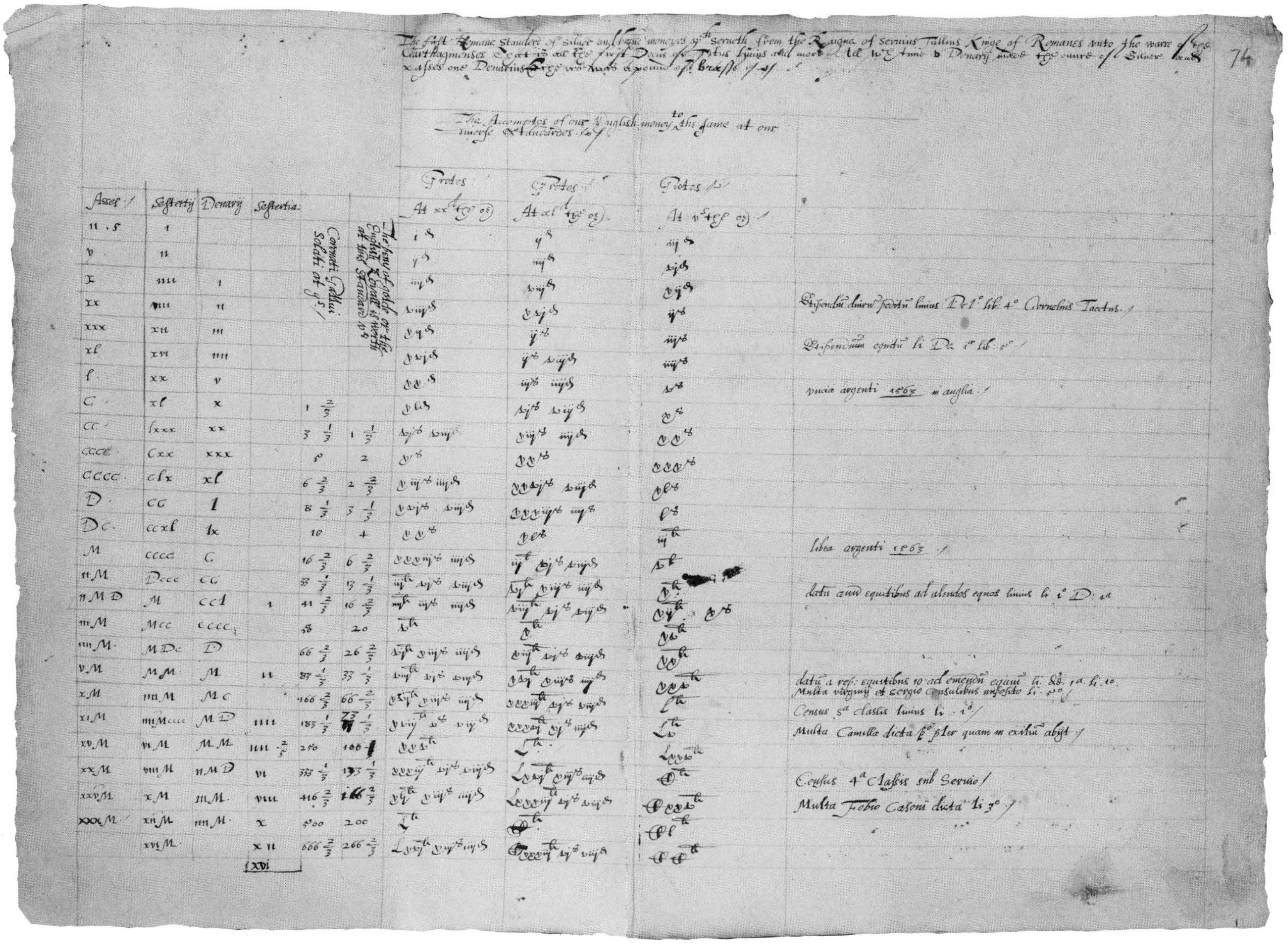

Fig. 9. Photograph of folios 73v–74r
showing the first of the monetary tables.

of French manufacture, it would seem that the earlier sewing dates to the time of the manuscript's residence in France.

SPECIFIC PROBLEMS WITH THE ASSEMBLY OF THE MANUSCRIPT

Close examination reveals several interesting discrepancies in the way the *Codex Mendoza* manuscript was assembled. There are two obvious problems with the reconstruction, as can be seen when studying figure 8. First, folios 2 and 9 are joined, and they both have watermarks of the same design; however, an examination of folio 9 shows that it is pasted to a stub connecting it with folio 2. This could be evidence of a correction made by the scribe when preparing the manuscript. The scribe probably copied text on the recto side of folio 8 and left the reverse side, the verso, blank. In that way, the text did not face its accompanying illustration. The incorrect folio, therefore, was probably removed and a new one pasted in, with the recto now blank and the verso properly containing the text.

There is a similar error correction problem with folio 69. Because folios 65 through 71 are on halfsheets, there is no stub to indicate the page replacement as was the case with folio 2. How-

ever, folio 69 has a distinctive watermark that is out of place in this part of *Codex Mendoza*, indicating that the folio was most likely added later. Perhaps the content of folio 69 has the answer to the problem. On the recto of folio 69, the rather complex illustration attempts to show European perspective, unfamiliar to native pictorialists of the period. This style may have created such problems for the artist that his first work, proving unsuccessful, had to be removed and a new sheet added (see Howe's essay in this volume).

A further problem has to do with the reappearance of the Pilgrim watermark—used previously only in parts 1 and 2—on folio 71 of part 3. Folio 71 may have been added as an afterthought when the section turned out to be longer than expected. Thus, the paper for this new folio probably was obtained from a lot different from the rest of part 3.

Although the folios are numbered in the upper-right-hand corner of the recto of each folio and there are no missing folios or misnumberings, folio 55 is misbound between 52 and 53. The folio is correctly numbered, but the binder inserted it into the wrong place. No doubt the binder felt that the illustration on folio 55 really belonged before 54v, which states that it is the end of the second part. All modern editions of the *Codex Mendoza* correct this error.

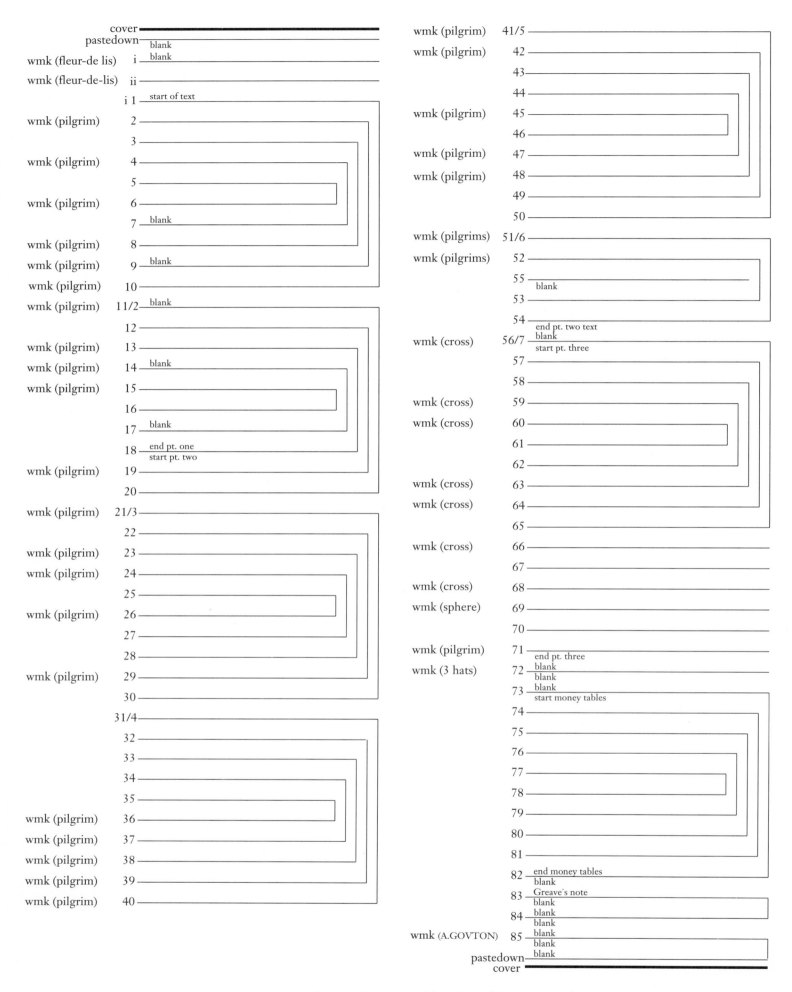

Fig. 8. Diagram of the gatherings and location of the watermarks along with the contents of the volume.

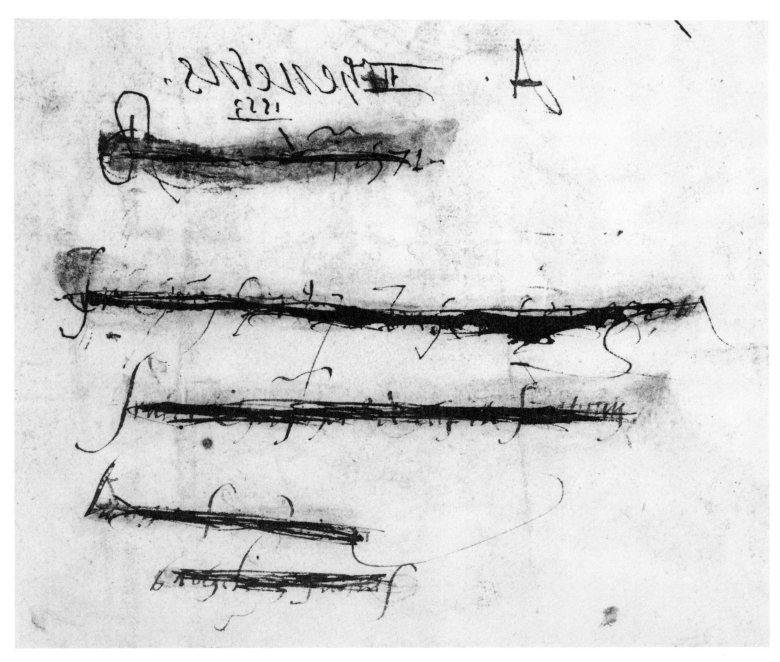

Fig. 10. Photograph of the effaced writing at the end of folio 71v. The picture has been printed in reverse so that the mirror writing can be read.

GUIDELINES AND SKETCHINGS

Another problem for the scribe(s) preparing *Codex Mendoza* was the lack of any lines ruled on the textual pages of the document. Guidelines used by the artists for illustrations can be seen on several folios of *Codex Mendoza*—for example, on folio 2 recto and folio 5 verso. However, on the textual folios, neither the margins nor the lines of text are straight, as would be expected if they had been ruled. Also, the number of lines differs from folio to folio, which is inconsistent with preruled pages. By comparing *Codex Mendoza* with the monetary tables manuscript, one can see the problem the scribes of the former manuscript faced. The monetary tables clearly show that the pages were ruled and laid out prior to the copying of the text (see fig. 9).

PHYSICAL EVIDENCE AND PROBLEMS OF PROVENANCE

Codex Mendoza's physical composition bears evidence of its adventures before reaching a safe haven in the Bodleian Library. The third part of *Codex Mendoza*, which is not based on native accounts, was composed separately from the first two parts, which form a unified whole. This is borne out by both the gatherings and the change in watermarks in the third part. Folds and tears indicate careless handling during its travels. Its various owners have also left their marks on the manuscript. The signatures of André Thevet bear witness to its residence for a time in France, and the Greek motto of John Selden on folio 1r and the addition of the Greco-Roman monetary tables speak of the eclectic tastes of its English owners. The scratched-out mirror writing that appears at the bottom of folio 71v (fig. 10) is mostly indecipherable, except for one portion that reads "Anno domini 1571." Who wrote the inscription, and for what purpose, is not known.

An investigation of the inks and colors used in the *Codex Mendoza* might answer many questions. Unfortunately, the inks and colors used in the manuscript have never been analyzed. In the past such a study required direct chemical analysis, which meant that small scrapings had to be taken from the document for the tests. Librarians and conservation officers have always shown considerable reluctance to take such samples from their greatest treasures. Now a nondestructive method of trace element analysis may be made through external beam Proton-induced X-ray Emission (PIXE) techniques (Cahill, Kusko, and Schwab 1981). This method involves bombarding a minuscule area with protons from a cyclotron. This exposes the item to very low levels of energy of no more than a one-hundred-watt light bulb shining on it at a distance of fifty centimeters. This method has been used recently in the analysis of the Gutenberg 42-line Bible (Schwab et al. 1983). It is to be hoped that the inks and colors of the *Codex Mendoza* may someday be analyzed by this technique, which might give us more precise information on the origins and types of colors used. The variations in the ink formulas might allow us to identify exactly which sections were written by each of the scribes or artists.

The above analysis of the physical properties of *Codex Mendoza* suggests some tentative conclusions. For example, the scribe's corrections seem to have resulted in the cancellation of folio 9 and the additional cancellation of folio 69, which may reflect a lack of familiarity with European perspective on the scribe's part. Also, regarding the baffling location of folio 55, it could be argued that last-minute haste in compiling *Codex Mendoza* caused the page misplacement. It is just as likely, however, that the folio was misbound into the center of the gathering closest to the end of part 2, in order to make the binder's job easier.

The number of halfsheets used at the end of part 3 presents a further enigma. It appears that the scribe who laid out this section may have been less experienced than the artist who copied parts 1 and 2 and arranged those folios into gatherings in such a manner that no halfsheets occurred (except for the replacement of folio 9).

In conclusion, it is through close analyses of the physical aspects of the *Codex Mendoza* that we can gain additional insight into the history and composition of this unique and invaluable manuscript.

ACKNOWLEDGMENTS

I would like to express my gratitude to William Hunt, Bruce Barker-Benfield, H. B. Nicholson, Patricia Rieff Anawalt, Margaret A. Nicholson, Wendy Soderburg, and Victoria Haselton for their help in preparing this essay. Dr. Hunt graciously arranged for me to examine the document at the Bodleian Library; Dr. Barker-Benfield, also of the Bodleian, was extremely generous with his time and his expertise; Dr. Nicholson visited the Bodleian and examined the document to provide answers to some of my specific questions; Dr. Anawalt, with the help of Mrs. Nicholson, consulted with me regarding technical problems in presenting the article; Ms. Soderburg and Ms. Haselton gave their editorial help in preparing the article.

NOTE

1. Letter from B. C. Barker-Benfield, Bodleian Library, to Wayne Ruwet, dated March 12, 1985.

ADDENDUM: FURTHER DATA AND ANALYSES OF *CODEX MENDOZA* WATERMARKS

B. C. Barker-Benfield
Assistant Librarian
Department of Western Manuscripts, Bodleian Library

NOTE: The following beta-radiographs and accompanying analyses were received as Codex Mendoza *was at the typesetter. We include them here as additional new information on the* Codex Mendoza *watermarks, complementing the research completed earlier by Wayne Ruwet. We are grateful for the work Dr. Barker-Benfield has done to assemble this special contribution.*

F.F.B.
P.R.A.

PART I (FOLS I−7I): *CODEX MENDOZA*

The original text-block of *Codex Mendoza* is made up of paper containing six watermark patterns, some of which can be subdivided further into their twin moulds.

Four of the six patterns (A–D) are of the same general design which Briquet[1] classifies under the general heading "Homme", sub-heading "Pélerin" (nos. 7567–7603). Apart from the differences in the letters beneath, the pilgrims themselves are close in design, each with his wide-brimmed hat, pointed chin, and crutched staff. Briquet's examples are mostly Italian, but Valls i Subirà[2] provides a number of Spanish examples from 1500 to 1597 (pp. 163–165, 232–235, nos. 212–227). As it happens, the non-Spanish examples of "pilgrim" papers reproduced by Briquet provide the closer parallels to the watermarks of *Codex Mendoza*, but none are identical and the papers are no doubt of Spanish origin.

Pattern A: "Pilgrim"

Pattern B: "Pilgrim"

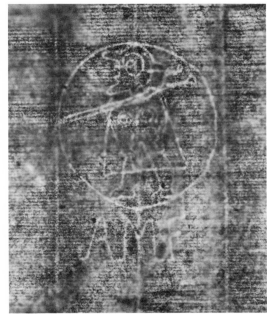

Pattern C(i): "Pilgrim"

Pattern C(ii)

Pattern D: "Pilgrim"

Pattern A: "Pilgrim"

"Pilgrim" facing left (as seen from the wire side), in a circle; beneath, two(?) capital letters of which the first is "B" (second illegible). The closest parallel in the two repertories is Briquet 7586 (Provence, 1568), where the letters are "B F", but it is not very similar.

Folio 2 only.

Pattern B: "Pilgrim"

"Pilgrim" facing left (as seen from the wire side), in a circle, with no letters or other additional designs outside the circle. No match in Valls i Subirà; fairly similar but by no means identical to Briquet 7570 (Milan, 1567).

Folios 4, 8, 19 (no clear division into twin moulds).

Pattern C: "Pilgrim"

"Pilgrim" facing left (as seen from the wire side), in a circle; beneath, three letters, "A M F". The only comparable example in the two repertories is Briquet 7582 (Milan, 1570), with "A M F": quite a good match, but not identical.

Folios 6, 9, 10, 11, 13, 14, 15, 21, 23, 24, 26, 29, 36, 37, 38, 39, 40, 41, 42, 45, 47, 48, 51, 52.

Amongst these, the clearer specimens provide examples of at least two moulds, e.g.:
  (i) Folios 6, 29, 36, 37, 42, 48. Lower legs shapelier.
  (ii) Folios 9, 41, 52. Lower legs straighter.

Pattern D: "Pilgrim"

"Pilgrim" facing left (as seen from the wire side), in a circle: beneath, two letters, perhaps "I P". No match for a pilgrim with these letters appears in the two repertories.

Folio 71 only.

Pattern E(i): Cross (Latin), in pointed shield

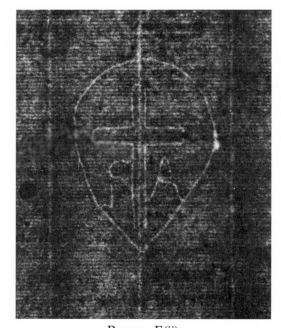

Pattern E(ii)

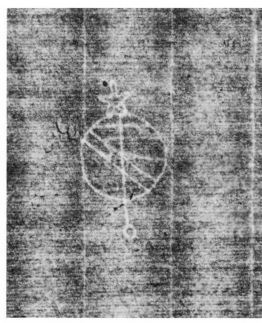

Pattern F: Sphere, with five-pointed star above

Pattern G(i): Fleur-de-lis, crowned

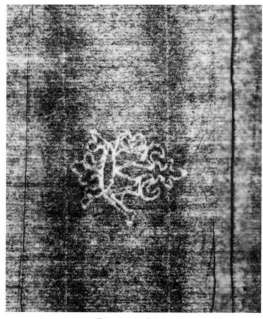

Pattern G(ii)

Pattern E: Cross (Latin), in pointed shield

On each side of the cross, within the shield, is a capital letter. The design makes sense from either direction, but as seen from the wire side the letters read "F"(?) on the left and "A" on the right. Valls i Subirà describes the shield pattern as "abundant throughout Spain", and provides examples from 1495 to 1600 (pp. 129–132, 197–202, nos. 79–101). Briquet reproduces examples from Spain, Italy and France (nos. 5677–5704, "très nombreux"). If the design were reversed (i.e., read from the "felt" side), the closest parallel, by no means identical, would be Briquet 5678, with the letters "A R" (Spain, 1576. *Var. simil.:* Rodez, 1579; Madrid, 1586). Two moulds are readily distinguishable:

(i) Folios 56, 63, 64.
(ii) Folios 59, 60, 66, 68.

Pattern F: Sphere, with five-pointed star above

Similar but not identical to Briquet 14013 (Angoulême, 1570). No examples of this pattern are reproduced by Valls i Subirà.

Folio 69 only.

EARLY ENDPAPERS ASSOCIATED WITH PART I
(FRONT PASTEDOWN, FOLS. i–ii, 72)

Evidence such as pleats and sewing-holes suggests that these leaves pre-date the present seventeenth-century English binding. Thevet's signature on the former flyleaf which is now the front pastedown confirms the sixteenth-century date.

Pattern G: Fleur-de-lis, crowned

The fleur-de-lis and its crown are of equal size; at the point where they join, the letter "A" appears on the left and "B" on the right. No Spanish examples of the crowned fleur-de-lis are reproduced by Valls i Subirà or amongst Briquet's specimens (nos. 7223–7258); the closest parallels, with different initials, are Briquet 7249 (Poitiers, 1574, with "G L") and Piccard, *Lilie*,[3] no. 786 (Florence 1579, with "B G").

The two examples here are not quite identical and presumably represent different moulds:

(i) Folio i.
(ii) Folio ii.

The front pastedown with Thevet's signature is probably of the same paper. No watermark can be discerned, but the chain-lines are approximately the same distance apart (c. 27–28 mm).

Pattern H: "W" over three swords or daggers   Pattern K: Bunch of grapes, with
                                                  Countermark "A. GOUTON"

Pattern H: "W" over three swords or daggers

The interpretation of the letter as "W" rather than "M" depends on the watermark being read from the wire side (i.e., present verso) and with the swords or daggers hilts upward (i.e., with the leaf reversed). I have been unable to match this pattern in the published repertories.

Folio 72 only.

PART 2 (FOLS. 73–84): MONETARY TABLES

Two patterns may be discerned; but since the leaves of the monetary tables each consist of two sheets pasted together, it is difficult to observe the fine detail or to distinguish between moulds. No beta-radiographs have been made.

*Pattern I: Fleur-de-lis in crowned shield,
over "WR" monogram*

This pattern was common throughout the seventeenth century (cf. Heawood[4] nos. 1660, 1721, 1721A, 1724, 1761–1762, 1768–1769, 1781).

*Pattern J: Crozier in crowned shield, over the initials
"NCH/M"*

This pattern, less common, seems very similar to Heawood no. 1199 ("Schieland Records", 1616).

LOWER ENDPAPERS OF THE
SEVENTEENTH-CENTURY BINDING

Unlike those at the front, the lower endpapers clearly belong to the period of the present parchment-covered boards (seventeenth-century English work).

*Pattern K: Bunch of grapes, with Countermark
"A. GOUTON"*

The countermark on the flyleaf (fol. 85), running vertically between chain-lines with the name "A. GOUTON" in a narrow cartouche, is close to Heawood no. 2252 (London, 1607). The position of the Grapes watermark in the pastedown makes the pattern less clear and a beta-radiograph impossible, but the tip of the bunch seems to terminate with a small cross, as in Heawood 2252.

Lower pastedown (Grapes) plus folio 85 ("A. GOUTON"), conjoint.

NOTES

1. C. M. Briquet, *Les filigranes: Dictionnaire historique des marques du papier dès leur apparition vers 1282 jusqu'en 1600*, facsimile of 1907 ed., Allan Stevenson, ed., 4 vols. (Amsterdam: Paper Publications Society, 1968).

2. Oriol Valls i Subirà, *XV–XVI Centuries*, vol. 2 of *The History of Paper in Spain*, Sarah Nicholson, trans. (Madrid: Empresa Nacional de Celulosas, 1980).

3. Gerhard Piccard, ed., *Wasserzeichen Lilie*, vol. 13 of *Die Wasserzeichenkartei Piccard im Hauptstaatsarchiv Stuttgart* (Stuttgart: Verlag W. Kohlhammer, 1983).

4. Edward Heawood, *Watermarks, Mainly of the 17th and 18th Centuries*, vol. 1 of *Monumenta Chartae Papyraceae* . . . (Hilversum, the Netherlands: Paper Publications Society, 1950).

CHAPTER 3

The Relationship of Indigenous and European Styles in the *Codex Mendoza*: An Analysis of Pictorial Style

Kathleen Stewart Howe

Style is the means of communication, a language not only as a system of devices for conveying a precise message by representing or symbolizing objects and actions but also as a qualitative whole which is capable of suggesting diffuse connotations as well. . . . By an effort of imagination based on experience of his medium, the artist discovers the elements and formal relationships which will express the values of the content and look right artistically.

Meyer Shapiro (1962:295)

Information is presented in the *Codex Mendoza* in a pictorial form. The picture elements, the objective vehicle for the subject matter, may be studied in terms of the formal elements in which they are composed: their line, color, organization, and representational quality.[1] These elements make up the style of the work. The creation of the physical forms that make up the *Codex Mendoza* involved choices on the part of the artist. The choices made by an artist at the center of the cultural maelstrom created by the collapse of indigenous structures under the intrusion of the Spanish offer an excellent opportunity to view the response of a strong indigenous tradition to the new cultural realities. The amalgam of European and indigenous elements produced by the Mendoza artist speaks eloquently of both the speed of acculturation and the resilience of the pictorial manuscript tradition.[2] An examination of the formal elements of style in this manuscript also provides some interesting clues to the manner in which it was produced.

The artist of the *Codex Mendoza* faced a complex commission; the pictorial writing system had to be used within defined limits. The content was undoubtedly selected by the patron. It had to be adapted to the European book format, and the painter had to adjust the spatial organization to leave space for a Spanish translation. Aside from the stated limitations of his commission, the artist also had to deal with the internal stresses generated by his familiarity with the new dominant pictorial system and his training as a pictorial writer in the indigenous tradition.

The *Codex Mendoza* was a hybrid, a European commission grafted onto an indigenous tradition. An analysis of the pictorial style of this manuscript can be carried out only after a short discussion of the two stylistic traditions that were its parent stock. The basis of the differences between the two stylistic traditions may be elucidated by a discussion of the purpose of manuscript illustration in Mesoamerican pictorial documents versus the European pictorial tradition.

MESOAMERICAN AND EUROPEAN PICTORIAL STYLES

In pre-Conquest Mesoamerican manuscripts, the images are the text. Edward Calnek (1978:239–262) described the Valley of Mexico pictorial writing system as an "episodic information storage system." In such a system, the image must either carry the complete information and thus function as a sign or function as a mnemonic device and elicit a particular oral text.[3] The system was composed of signs that represented both general concepts (ideograms) and analogues to specific Nahuatl words (logograms). The victory chronicle of part 1 contains an example of the use of a sign representing a concept: the burning temple platform represents the subjugation of a town. The concept is anchored to a specific location by the addition of a place sign in which the pictorial elements phonetically spell out the name of the location. The burden placed on the pictorial writing system of carrying both general concepts and specifying detail required that all elements of the image be equally readable. Conventions of depiction which might obscure the identity of a pictorial element were not used. Elements were drawn in their most significant aspect and were carefully positioned with regard to other elements so that no part of the message was obscured.

By the sixteenth century, the European pictorial tradition had long been divorced from the responsibility of being the primary vehicle for verbal information. While no one would deny the use of images to convey meaning, an alphabetic writing system was the principal means of preserving and conveying the types of information stored in Mesoamerican documents. The image system was not necessary to information retrieval and had become a system for recreating a sensuous reality, inextricably bound up in the naturalistic representation of optical experience. In the European manuscript tradition, pictures carried complex cultural messages that were best presented by naturalistic conventions.

PRE-CONQUEST MANUSCRIPT STYLE

The complex and populous society in the Valley of Mexico at the time of the Spanish Conquest was a literate society that maintained records in a pictorial idiom. Bernal Díaz del Castillo (1956: 211) reported hundreds of volumes in Motecuhzoma's library. Unfortunately, this wealth of material was destroyed in the aftermath of the Spanish occupation, and a specific reconstruction of the Valley of Mexico manuscript style awaited Donald Robertson's synthesis (1959:9–11). The Robertson reconstruction was based on three sources: post-Conquest manuscripts from the Valley of Mexico; the style of Aztec art in other media, especially that of relief sculpture; and the style of known pre-Conquest manuscripts from the Mixtec-speaking region of southern Mexico. Using the sources listed above, but primarily that of Mixtec manuscripts, and, in particular, the *Codex Nuttall*, Robertson proposed a set of stylistic traits that would define pre-Conquest Valley of Mexico manuscripts.[4]

The indigenous Valley of Mexico manuscript style proposed by Robertson was characterized by conventions of composition, line, color, figural representation, and architectural representation. Conventions of composition determine the manner in which forms are placed in relationship to one another and to the surface on which they appear. In the pre-Conquest tradition the forms were "sifted" evenly over the page, with attention paid to the clarity of each element of the image. Thus, the conventions developed to indicate spatial recession in the European tradition, foreshortening and overlap, were not used. The characteristic composition of pre-Columbian manuscripts appeared to Robertson to reflect the *horror vacui* associated with some types of "primitive" art (Robertson 1959:16). There was no attempt to represent three-dimensional illusionistic space on the pages of Mesoamerican manuscripts.

The line, referring simply to the artists' marks creating the pictorial forms, was defined as a frame line of unvarying width, used to enclose areas of color applied in flat, unshaded washes. Neither the line, by variations in width, nor the application of color, by the use of highlight and shadow, was used to suggest modeling or contour.

The human form was squatly proportioned, with proportions of less than 1:4 head to body ratio, and was presented as if made up of distinct, nonintegrated body parts with no differentiation of right and left extremities. Costume elements were affixed to the figures as additive elements designed to specify the actor and the role. A limited range of hand and body positions was used to indicate the actions of the figures.[5] Architecture was iconically represented, with a limited number of schematized forms indicating building types and standing for what we assume to be a specific building at a site defined by the place sign associated with it. The relative scale of figures, accessories, and architecture was variable; the primary consideration was not realistic depiction of scale but the necessity of showing all elements in the pictorial message with maximum legibility.

This reconstruction of the stylistic attributes of pre-Conquest Valley of Mexico manuscripts was the accepted benchmark against which all Colonial manuscripts from the Valley of Mexico were compared. This reconstruction has been amended in light of recent work defining an Aztec painting style based on the murals at Malinalco and the *Codex Borbonicus*. Elizabeth Boone (1982) has proposed that a consideration of the Aztec painting style must take cognizance of the penchant for naturalistic representation that is a hallmark of some Aztec sculpture and the Malinalco murals. The murals demonstrate more elongated figural proportions, generally about 1:5, and a naturalistic differentiation of right and left extremities (Boone 1982:158–163). The line used in Aztec painting was also more cursive than that found in the Mixtec *Codex Nuttall*, as evidenced in both the mural paintings and the first part of the *Codex Borbonicus*. However, this more cursive line was still not used to suggest volume.

For the purposes of this analysis, we shall follow Robertson's proposed characteristics of indigenous manuscript style for the late pre-Conquest period in the Valley of Mexico (composition, line, color, and figural and architectural representation). These characteristics will be amended along the lines Boone proposed, in that the line will be more cursive, the figural proportions more elongated, and overall there will be a greater tendency to naturalistic detail and representation within the confines of a system whose main aim was still to produce images comprising clear signs with specific meanings.

EUROPEAN PICTORIAL STYLE

Compared to Mesoamerica, the European pictorial style at the time of the conquest of the New World placed greater premium on naturalistic representation. As such, the depiction of a coherent, readable, three-dimensional space through the devices of linear perspective, aerial perspective, overlap, and foreshortening was a priority. The human figure was presented with proportions of approximately 1:7 head to body ratio and was shown in a variety of naturalistic postures with clear differentiation of right and left extremities. Line was used to further the illusion of optical reality by suggesting contour and volume through variations in width or by use as shading. Paint was applied with gradations of value to approximate the optical presentation of light striking three-dimensional bodies in a defined space. Postures and activities conveyed the narrative sense of the image in such a way as to emphasize the illusion of actors moving in a defined space. These pictorial conventions can be seen in a sixteenth-century European print reproduced as figure 1.

THE CODEX MENDOZA

The three sections of the *Codex Mendoza* are distinguished by the different types of information presented in each. Part 1 is a historical document chronicling the Aztec rulers and the years of their reign, and listing the victories achieved under their rule. Part 2 is a tribute list organized by region. Part 3 sets forth the life and customs of the Mexica-Aztec. The types of information presented in the first two parts had conventions of format and idiom in the pre-existing manuscript tradition. The detail of everyday life presented in part 3 is assumed to be unique to the pre-Conquest tradition and to represent a response to Spanish questions.

Because of the distinctive nature of each of the three parts that make up the *Codex Mendoza*, the manuscript is frequently discussed almost as if it were three separate documents sharing the same binding.[6] However, the *Codex Mendoza* is a single work, conceived and executed as such. The content was undoubtedly determined by the patron and is unified by its attention to the secular matters that might have been most interesting to the Spanish king. And, most importantly, it can be seen from internal evidence that the manuscript is the work of one primary artist, working within a workshop tradition.

The attribution of the *Codex Mendoza* to a single hand was advanced in a detailed analysis of Colonial manuscripts by Donald Robertson (1959:102–103). Robertson based his attribution on the characteristic "S" curve of the artist's line. My personal inspection of the manuscript supports that attribution.[7] Details such as toes, the inferior surface of the nose, and the curve of feathers in headdresses are drawn with the same curving strokes throughout the manuscript.[8] The line drawings are the work of one hand. Variation in application of color supports the hypothesis that other artisans worked on the manuscript. The arguments supporting this view can be most logically presented in the discussion of color.

Fig. 1. Early sixteenth-century woodcut illustration of the Nativity for Missale Traiectense showing European pictorial conventions (*Missale ad venu cathedralis ecclesie Traiectensis . . .*) Utrecht Missal, f. 10r, by Lucas van Leyden. (From Jacobowitz and Stepanek 1983:139.)

In this essay, the style of the *Codex Mendoza* will be analyzed by reference to the characteristic uses of line, color, composition, and figural and architectural representation as previously defined. The separate sections of the manuscript will be discussed under each topic, and a statement regarding style that applies to the entire manuscript will be made.

Line

Qualities of line are excellent stylistic markers in any discussion of differences between pre- and post-Conquest manuscripts. Pre-Conquest linear technique did not use the swell and taper of line to indicate contour and modeling. Rather, line was used as a frame line, although the Aztec use of line might be assumed to be more cursive than that used in Mixtec manuscripts.

Line in the *Codex Mendoza* is certainly cursive, tending to vary in width on every stroke. The start of each stroke is of uniform width, becoming thicker toward the middle and then thinning at the end as the writing instrument, a split reed pen, was brought off the paper. But within part 1, the quality of line seems to change with its use in different pictorial elements. Examples of variations in line which occur throughout the section can be seen on folio 12r. The line is a cursive frame line (i.e., one varying in width but not indicating volume) seen in the representations of temple platforms, year signs, and the shield and arrow war emblem. Line begins to be used to indicate volume in the place signs that have figural elements (see especially the signs for the towns of Tonalimoquetzayan and Miquetlan). The line delineating the nude corpse in the name of Miquetlan in the lower right corner swells over the shoulders and buttocks and tapers as it delineates the axilla.[9] A subtle sense of volumetric modeling is conveyed. Likewise, the lower leg that forms the name sign of the ruler Tiçoçicatzin in the

center of the folio is rendered with a line that swells over the bulge of the calf and tapers at the ankle, again rendering a sense of volume and substance different from the unvarying frame line of pre-Conquest documents. It would seem that in depicting conventionalized signs—for example, the war emblems and the temple platforms—the artist had no sense of rendering objects that possessed a reality other than that of glyphic signifiers. However, in depicting portions of place signs that draw on a vocabulary of naturally occurring objects to form the phonetic or logographic equivalent of a place name, the artist slipped into the characteristic contour line that was the new and dominant style in the Valley of Mexico and one that permitted a more naturalistic rendering of the object.

The line in part 2 is also cursive, variable in width, and shows a characteristic ending sweep. It occasionally defines volume as it does in part 1 and under the same circumstances. The banners affixed to tribute items, which indicate units of twenty, and the hill portions of place signs are drawn with a cursive frame line that does not convey any sense of volume. However, tribute goods that must have been known to the artist from everyday experience are drawn to suggest volume. The warriors' costumes are excellent markers for this European style of contour line; the line is tapered at the junction of the sleeve and torso of the garments to suggest overlap and modeling, creating the illusion of a plastic form rather than a flat symbol. The variation in the use of line may be seen, for example, on folio 28r.

The increased naturalism as a result of the use of a modeling line is a distinct change from pre-Conquest style. This can be seen by comparing the place signs in part 2 of the *Codex Mendoza* with corresponding signs from its cognate, the *Matrícula de Tributos*.[10] A comparison of the third place sign on folio 32r to the corresponding place sign from the *Matrícula* (fig. 2) demonstrates the difference in style. The place sign for Chapolmoloyan consists of an arm and a grasshopper. In the *Codex Mendoza*, the arm is rendered as a swelling plastic form by the use of line that broadens and tapers as the contours of an arm would. The grasshopper is drawn with a complex series of lines that use both changes in width and techniques of overlap to represent the three-dimensionality of the insect form. In the *Matrícula*, the same structures are drawn with a line of unvarying width. They are easily recognized symbols that do not seem to have any reference to naturalism. Robertson (1959: 105) described the difference between the pictorial signs in the two manuscripts as that between an image (*Codex Mendoza*) and a sign (*Matrícula de Tributos*).

The line in part 3 shows the same cursive sweep as that in parts 1 and 2. In the previous two sections, the line had occasionally been a contour line; however, in part 3, the use of line to suggest contour is the rule rather than the exception. The first folio of pictorial text sets the tone for the rest of the section. On folio 57r, the figures are drawn with a contour line, and their robes are shaded with color and line to indicate the volumetric folds of drapery. This convention persists throughout part 3. The images in this section seem to occupy a curious position between pictorial language and textual illustration. There is a mix of schematized pre-Conquest signs with a depiction of narrative, almost European, action, best seen on folio 60r. This folio apparently answered inquiries about the teaching and disciplining of children. Their ages and food consumption are shown by pre-Conquest signs, while their activities are presented in genre scenes. A small but telling difference can be seen in the famous scene of Aztec discipline in which a disobedient child is held in the smoke from burning chiles.

Fig. 2. Comparison of the place signs for Chapolmoloyan from (a) *Codex Mendoza*, f. 32r, detail and (b) Matrícula de Tributos 1980: f. 6v, detail.

In part 1, where defeat was shown as a burning temple roof, smoke and flames were drawn as stylized volutes and then colored. Here the smoke and flames are rendered naturalistically by unbounded and blended colors, although a sense of the curved volute shape is maintained so that the depiction is not quite identical to the European convention.

Throughout the manuscript the characteristics of line vary with use. We might broadly categorize the use of line as either delineating standard pictorial signs that are abstracted from immediate natural referents or presenting naturally occurring objects known to the painter. Where the painter is reproducing pictorial signs such as indicators of quantity, generic temple platforms, or the standard hill portion of a place sign, the line follows the characteristics of pre-Conquest linear tradition. It is a slightly cursive frame line, which does not indicate volume. However, where the line represents naturally occurring objects known to the painter, such as the mundane articles of the tribute tally and portions of place signs which incorporate parts of the human body or animals and insects, the use of line reflects the European convention of volumetric depiction. In the third portion of the manuscript, where conventionalized symbols for much of the information simply did not exist, the characteristic line is furthest from the pre-Conquest model.

Color

Color in pre-Conquest manuscript painting is laid on in flat washes enclosed by the artist's line. There is no attempt to indicate modeling by changes in value. The application of color in part 1 gener-

ally follows the indigenous model. However, colors vary in the manner in which they have been applied. For example, the application of red seems to have been done with less care or less skill than that of blue, green, and yellow. The red textile headdress worn by Atonal on folio 7v is rather carelessly painted, with the red pigment overflowing the frame line. An even more obvious example occurs on the facing folio (folio 8r), where there is a qualitative difference between the coloring of the red hill in the place sign for Tlatlauhquitepec and the coloring of the green hills making up the other place signs on the same folio. This qualitative difference in the application of specific colors is maintained throughout the manuscript.

There is a rather anomalous use of color in depicting the thatched roof of the temple platforms in part 1. On folios 2r and 2v, the thatch is represented by lines, and the entire roof is painted a solid shade. From folio 3v on, the lines indicating thatch disappear, only to reappear randomly and infrequently throughout the rest of part 1. The thatch on folio 6r is no longer a wash of solid color but is represented by distinct banding of brown and yellow; on folios 3v, 4v, and 5v the lines indicating thatching are combined with banding of brown and yellow. The thatch on folio 8r appears as subtle gradations of brown and yellow. In fact, the different representations of thatch may all be seen on the same page, folio 8r, making it likely that all the techniques were used by a single colorist. This variance in a key pictorial element in the victory chronicle is problematic and does not, to my mind, represent the acquisition of intrusive stylistic characteristics but, rather, may represent the flexibility allowed in a pictorial writing system.

While the color in part 2 is usually applied as a flat wash, there are interesting exceptions to the pre-Columbian standard. A close examination of the color in this section has yielded some observations that may shed some light on the production techniques used. There is, as in part 1, a difference in the ways specific colors are applied. Yellow and blue are always applied in flat washes; the reds and yellows are blended to give a naturalistic depiction of the color of feathers, shells, and amber; and green is shaded to indicate modeling.[11] The only place in this section of the manuscript where highlighting and shading are used to create modeling is in the application of green pigment for warrior costumes (folios 22r, 23r, 29r, and 32r, for example). The costumes are consistently painted in graduated values of green pigment to indicate a rounded shape, as if they were being worn. This use of value to suggest the way in which light falls on a rounded form is a European stylistic trait. The use of a European convention on a pictorial sign is illustrative of the tension between sign and image found throughout the manuscript. The dramatic differences in the use of color, including both degrees of care in application and the difference between flat washes and shaded and highlighted areas, would seem to indicate that there were different painters involved in applying color to the manuscript.

The black design elements within the warrior costumes were either added after the color wash or painted before the primary color was applied, in which case they were evenly covered with the wash.[12] This varies with the color of the costumes, so that black elements were added last on the yellow and red costumes and first on the blue and orange costumes. Such variations occur throughout part 2 and may be seen by comparing the jaguar costume on folio 20r, where the black was added after the yellow wash, to the jaguar costume on folio 23v, where the orange color wash covers the black. Again, the implication would be that a group of people, working in a particular order, painted the manuscript.

Under a workshop method of production, the artist who drew the pictorial elements would probably not apply the color. Evidence in support of this statement is found on a later folio in the tribute section. On folio 47r, the third line of tribute items includes two representations of birds. When the second bird from the left was drawn, the artist neglected to draw the feet as he had on the first bird. A colorist rectified the mistake by drawing in the feet with brown pigment. There is an obvious difference in hand between the feet drawn with ink on the first bird and the feet on the second bird. The feet on the first bird are very economically drawn as two concentric curves, with the talons suggested but not individually drawn. The feet on the second bird are painted with each talon separately indicated. The result is a rather awkward splaying of the feet. The difference in style is too great to be explained by the difference in media but must represent the work of two different artists.

In light of these observations, a definition of color as a formal element of style in part 2 has to reflect the fact that the color was applied by more than one person. The artist who painted with green pigment was following European conventions of changes in value to indicate rounded forms. The persons applying the other pigments, especially yellow and blue, were following the indigenous convention of flat color washes. This would suggest that, in this workshop setting, a primary artist drew the outline of the forms and his assistants applied the colors in some sort of order. We might further conjecture that the painter assigned to apply the green pigment may have been a younger apprentice whose association with the older pre-Conquest style was more tenuous than that of older assistants, who painted the other colors.

The variations in the application of colors noted in the previous sections, and especially in part 2, are present in part 3. The costumed warriors on folios 64r, 65r, and 67r show the same type of difference in color application that we saw in the tribute costumes. However, the emphasis in part 3 on the volumetric rendering of the human figure adds another dimension to the use of pigment in this section. It would appear that the primary artist participated in the coloring of part 3. The white cloaks worn by the figures in this section are shaded with a gray wash to indicate volumetric folds of drapery. These folds are also indicated by lines drawn on the cloaks. There is a constantly changing relationship between the lines and the gray wash; sometimes the lines are drawn over the wash, sometimes the wash covers the line. An examination of the original manuscript shows that this relationship changes within the same figure. The obvious conclusion is that a single person did both the wash and the line and worked back and forth between them to achieve the sense of volume which the figures show. This concern with the volumetric rendering of figures is alien to the pre-Conquest manuscript tradition and was acquired from the Spanish. It should be noted that, on folio 68r, the use of line and shade in cloaks to indicate volume occurs much more frequently in the plaintiff figures, which have a narrative quality to their postures and attitudes, than in the figures that stand as signs for magistrate or judge in the Aztec legal system.

The use of color in the *Codex Mendoza* reflects both indigenous conventions and European conventions. The consistent use of a particular system of color application for individual pigments indicates a workshop system. The choice of the system of pigment application made by individuals within the workshop would seem to reflect the strength of their tie to the indigenous manuscript tradition rather than the newly introduced European system.

Composition

Within the constraints of the customary ordering of historical information in part 1, there are stylistic characteristics of page composition. Pages are composed in registers with an even sifting of pictorial elements over the surface of the page, a trait that Donald Robertson (1959:10) defines as pre-Conquest. There are some exceptions to this standard method of composition. The artist composed folio 2v leaving a large space at the bottom of the folio empty; in fact, the pictorial elements are reduced in size compared to similar elements on the following folios. The scribe added a rather lengthy annotation in this empty space, and one might conclude that the patron asked for space on the first register of conquests so that the scribe would have room to explain the pictorial conventions separately from the translating Spanish text opposite the folio. Another disruption in the usual pattern of composition occurs on folio 16v, where two horizontal registers of falling temples finish the record of Motecuhzoma's conquests. The rigid maintenance of horizontal registers and the resultant empty space reflects the adoption of the European reading order.

There is never an attempt to create the illusion of three-dimensional space on the page in part 1. The figures and architectural forms are placed on the page as flat signs in horizontal registers; they are not placed within the context of a landscape or a perspectival scheme. It might be argued that a register of conquests would not require a reference to landscape. However, where there is a depiction of an event other than the tally of victories there is still no depiction of landscape space. On folio 4v, the destruction of Aztec canoes and the murder of Aztec citizens are recorded as justification for the subjugation of Chalco. This scene is presented without reference to a landscape space. The canoes float on the page, and the protagonist is painted next to the canoes unrelated to any ground line that would define the space in which the action took place.

The composition of folio space in part 1 shows elements of European style in the adherence to European bibliographic conventions of reading order and recto/verso organization, while simultaneously maintaining the indigenous composition style of "sifting" pictorial elements evenly over the page and presenting them as discrete elements. There is no attempt to render a landscape space.

The composition of the folio space in part 2 follows, to some extent, those criteria that we earlier defined as pre-Conquest. The placement of forms reflects a compromise between the pre-Conquest scattering of elements in loose registers over the surface of the page and the rigid horizontal registers required by European reading conventions. The dual approach to composition may be seen by comparing folio 34r, in which the horizontal registers are maintained and, consequently, a large space at the bottom of the folio is left empty, to folios 50r and 51r, in which the few forms on the folio are scattered over the page, although a sense of registers is maintained. It seems evident that the artist had a conflict between compositional devices and that he used both in this section of the codex.

Information in part 3 is generally presented in horizontal registers, except for folio 69r, which is a full-page depiction of Motecuhzoma in his palace. The horizontal registers are translated in such a way that a left-to-right reading order is presumed. This system of horizontal registers of information still allows the artist to compose the folio in a way that reflects the pre-Conquest *horror vacuii*. However, the folio space is now, for the first time in this manuscript, used to depict illusionistic space.

The artist made an extremely ambitious attempt at creating the illusion of three-dimensional space on folio 69r. The painting shows Motecuhzoma and his councillors dispensing justice in the royal palace. Here the artist has attempted to use the system of one-point perspective to render human figures accurately in an interior space. Perspective is a European artistic convention, employed here by an artist from the indigenous native tradition who almost certainly would not have had any formal instruction in the theory or technique. His knowledge of the system must have been derived from the European prints circulating in the New World at the time. We can conclude that the execution of this systematic perspectival painting gave the artist a great deal of difficulty; as it appears in the manuscript it is far from accurate. If one were to continue the orthogonal lines of the rooms in which the magistrates sit, the lines would not meet at a common vanishing point, a requisite for accurate one-point perspective. The degree of difficulty that this painting presented to the artist is also indicated by the fact that the drawing is on a different type of paper from that used for the rest of this section. The obvious conclusion to be drawn is that the first attempt to master this difficult and little-understood technique was a failure and that the folio was cut from the section and another more satisfactory painting bound in its place.

On the folio that follows this bravura attempt at a perspectival drawing, the pre-Conquest sign for a majordomo and his storehouse occurs (folio 70r). The storehouse (*petlacalco*) is shown in the standard T-elevation with the person seated in front of it. The scale of building to person is not intended to be realistic, and the image is intended to be read as a sign. However, the artist had not discarded the use of perspective after his difficulties with folio 69r, for he attempted a perspectival drawing of the basket element in the sign for public works (associated with two boys), which is immediately contiguous with the sign for "personage in a building." The artist had a choice between the schematic sign for a personage in his building and the illusion of placing figures in an interior. The artist's choice must reflect a conviction that the information about Motecuhzoma's legal system could best be conveyed by the depiction of the setting and, conversely, that general information about work levies would be more economically presented with the pre-Conquest sign.

Perspective had been tried by the artist in less ambitious contexts before folio 69r. In the first pictorial text of this section (folio 57r), the birth and naming ceremony of an infant are shown. The infant is shown in a cradle that appears to be drawn in perspective. However, our ability to perceive it as a perspectival image is confounded because the infant in the cradle is not shown foreshortened, as the angle of vision would demand. Although the artist had a choice of image conventions, he did not have a complete understanding of the nuances of European spatial conventions.

Landscape in pre-Conquest manuscripts is depicted by conventionalized signs standing for a type of geographic feature. Hills are signified by the standard sign already familiar to us by its use in place signs in this manuscript. Bodies of water are depicted in cross section, as in the example from the *Codex Nuttall* (fig. 3). The presentation of landscape as a space rendered as the eye would see it is a European concept. There are rudimentary depictions of landscape in part 3 of the *Codex Mendoza*. On folios 60r and 63r, men are shown in canoes that float on the surface of an undefined body of water, creating a primitive sense of optical reality. This attempt at depicting conventions of space as the Europeans did is followed on folio 67r by a schematized representation of a river that probably reflects European cartographic traditions.[13] The river is shown

Fig. 3. Body of water represented in cross section from the *Codex Nuttall*, detail. (From Nuttall 1975:9.)

as a band of blue as if seen from above; footprints, a pre-Conquest sign for travel, are shown crossing the river. The information here is written in a combination of pre-Conquest signs and European mapping conventions. It is clear that the *Mendoza* artist could draw on many ways of presenting information and selected the convention that suited his purposes best. The paintings of men in canoes were intended to convey information about the genre activities of fishing and transport, and it seems likely that merely placing the figures in a landscape context conveyed a good deal of that information. On folio 67r, the informational burden of the image was more complex. A scouting mission into a specific territory is indicated, and so cartographic conventions derived from both the European and the indigenous traditions were used in order to present the information economically.

The Human Figure

A section-by-section comparison of the representation of the human figure in the *Codex Mendoza* is hampered by the relative paucity of figural representation in the first two sections of the manuscript. With few exceptions, the representation of the human figure in the first section is confined to the sign for ruler, a figure seated on the *icpalli* and wearing a diadem. These figures are nothing more than draped, rounded forms with attached heads and feet. There is no sense of the anatomy beneath the cloak. The feet are differentiated into right and left, but that is the only concession to naturalism.[14]

In one of the few instances in the victory chronicle in which the rather laconic information about rulers and their conquests has been expanded, the reason for the conflict with Chalco which resulted in its defeat is depicted on folio 4v. A figure, identified as being from Chalco by the line that connects it to the Chalco place sign, is shown dropping a rock into a canoe. This rather lean figure displays a 1:6 head to body ratio. The extremities are clearly differentiated into right and left limbs. The figure's posture conveys the narrative sense of his action; he leans forward over the canoe as he prepares to drop the rock through the bottom of the craft.

The reconquest of Tlatelolco is recorded on folio 10r by the spectacular suicidal leap of its ruler, Moquihuiztli. The figure is disproportionately large in comparison to the temple platform from which he falls. The relative scale of figures, accessories, and architecture was variable in pre-Hispanic manuscripts. It was more important to show elements with maximum legibility than to depict realistic values of scale. Part of the falling figure is obscured by the architectural representation of the twin temple platform of Tlatelolco. This obscuration of parts of the figure would be appropriate in a European narrative scene but flies in the face of indigenous manuscript conventions, which dictated that all parts of the figure must be shown in their most significant aspect. The costume elements that identify this figure as the ruler are carefully shown. While the back standard and shield are placed on the figure in a naturalistic manner, the diadem that identifies the figure as the ruler of Tlatelolco is painted on the head as an additive element. The diadem does not fit the shape of the head, nor does it seem likely that it would have remained on the ruler's head given his head-first plunge from the heights of the temple platform. Although the entire figure is not shown, it also has the long, lean proportions of the Chalcoan figure on folio 4v. The disparity among the additive costume elements, the figural proportions, the partial view of the figure, and the scale disparity between the figure and the architectural setting mark the representation of Moquihuiztli as an amalgam of European and pre-Hispanic traditions of representing the human figure. The compromise achieved by the painter of the *Codex Mendoza* sought to maintain those indigenous devices that would define the character in the drama while adopting the European conventions that contribute to the narrative impact of this recorded event. It would seem that in the first section the combination of European and indigenous pictorial conventions associated with the human figure was reserved for two situations that had a richer narrative content. The native artist, after twenty years of exposure to European pictorial conventions, could use selected elements of European style to heighten the drama of the epic he was painting.

Part 2 of the *Codex Mendoza* is a list of goods and the regions from which they came. As might be expected of an accounting document, human actors are not recorded.

The figural proportions in part 3 are European in their elongation. The standard proportion is 1:6.2, which is somewhat more elongated than Elizabeth Boone's (1982) redefinition of Aztec style, which noted that the standard proportion was 1:5. These long, lean figures are depicted in a variety of postures that reflect the activities being performed. On folio 62r, the figures carrying burdens lean into the tumplines, their postures graphically representing the work involved. The more naturalistic posture in these tall figures represents the acquisition of European stylistic traits.

The painted figures in the vignettes of daily life in part 3 are not anatomically correct as demanded by the European figural tradition. They have a rather boneless quality as they sit in improbable positions (see, for example, folio 59r). Although anatomically incorrect, these seated figures may be contrasted with the seated rulers on the *icpalli* depicted in part 1. Rather than a rounded bundle with attached head and feet, the seated human figure in this section (on folio 70r) is depicted with upper and lower extremities. The robes worn by these figures are drawn with line and shade to indicate the volume of the body beneath the garment. The postures are animated as these figures interact with the children they instruct. Clearly, these figures are images of activities as opposed to the stereotyped representations of rulers.

In this section of the manuscript, the artist used the sign of the seated personage when the information to be conveyed dealt with a class of officials. On folio 68r, the artist delineated the steps in the Aztec judicial system. The seated human figures on the left-hand side of the lower half of the folio represent different officials within the judicial system. The figures are represented as rounded bundles with attached head and feet. They clearly derive from the pre-Conquest pictorial sign tradition. The plaintiffs before the court are presented as animated figures who sit and gesticulate in attitudes associated with the European naturalistic style of figural representation.

The same dichotomy between codified sign for a personage and animated figural drawings is demonstrated on folio 70r. The personage defined as the majordomo or director of public works is shown in the same manner as the seated rulers in part 1. The rank of this figure is indicated by the decoration on his *manta* and the symbol for public works placed in front of him. The other figures are defined by their activities; they are images that convey information about vice and virtue. A complex of pre-Conquest pictorial signs defines the majordomo, but the other figures represent elements of information that have no codified sign. The European tradition of naturalistic depiction of figures in a genre scene was deemed most suitable for pictorially writing the information.

The use of both pre-Conquest conventions for human figures and a more naturalistic and European depiction of human figures occurs because part 3 is neither a copy nor a restatement of any known pre-Conquest document. It represents the attempt by an artist, trained to transmit information through pictorial conventions, to answer the questions of his Spanish patron in a pictorial form. It should not be considered to be, in any sense, a loose rendering of daily scenes. It was constructed as carefully and as tightly as the pre-Conquest historical, economic, or religious documents were. The artist in this case had to adapt pictorial conventions to the information requested. His principal aim was to communicate information, and his use of pre-Conquest convention, European convention, and an amalgam of the two was determined by that aim. The use of either pre-Conquest pictorial elements or European narrative elements in part 3 was determined by the artist's decision as to which would best carry the information. The change from copying a preexisting manuscript to the production of a new manuscript released the artist from stylistic restrictions but did not release him from the principal obligation of a native manuscript painter, the clear conveyance of information.

Architectural Representations

Architecture throughout the *Codex Mendoza* is shown by a limited number of schematized forms. The standard form is the T-elevation, a term first applied by Robertson (1959:19) to indicate the schematized profile view with cutaway lateral wall. Representations of buildings in this manuscript might be considered logograms standing for specific types of structure. The only exception to the use of indigenous pictorial signs for buildings is the large painting of Motecuhzoma's palace on folio 69r. This folio was discussed earlier in this essay, in the section dealing with composition.

CONCLUSIONS

An analysis of the pictorial style of the *Codex Mendoza* demonstrates the elements of European pictorial style which had been incorporated in native manuscript painting since the Conquest of Mexico.

The conventions governing line had changed from the pre-Conquest use of a frame line to a more cursive and volumetric use of line.[15] The use of the newer European style of line is seen to a different degree in each section of the *Codex Mendoza*. As might be expected, line depicts volumetric form most often when it is used on naturally occurring figural elements and is most similar to a frame line when it is presenting a direct copy of a pre-Conquest sign. Parts 1 and 2, which are composed in pre-Conquest pictorial signs, show less evidence of European linear style than does part 3, which records information for which indigenous pictorial signs did not always exist.

Color in the *Codex Mendoza* seems to deviate from the pre-Conquest style least of all the formal elements, with the single exception of the application of green pigment. If color was applied in the workshop manner as I have postulated, it would follow that color application would be delegated to a specific group of artisans trained in color application. Their training probably would have been in the preparation of pigments and the traditional application of color in flat washes. Another artist, the *maestro de los pintores*, was responsible for composing the pages and drawing the figures. The colorists would probably continue to apply color as they had been trained to do, and it would take the addition of a younger and more acculturated artist to the workshop to show style changes in the application of the color for which he was responsible.

The change in figural proportions from the squat pre-Conquest depictions of personages or ritual activities to elongated, naturally posed figures moving in a space is a primary difference between indigenous manuscript style and European pictorial style. The artist chose between pre-Hispanic pictorial conventions and images of figures based on his perception of the most economical and legible way in which information could be "written" in a pictorial system. In part 3, where pre-Conquest pictorial texts did not, for the most part, exist for the range of information solicited by the European patron, the artist used a European style of figural representation. The artist had evidently learned that there were other ways of relaying information than the pre-Conquest convention of figures with attached attributes. Obviously, the depiction of narrative scenes in European prints would have been seen as an option in communicating via pictures; and, as visually sophisticated as an artist in this medium would have had to have been, it would have been possible for him to integrate the new system with the old, as he so effectively did in this section.[16]

The artist of the *Codex Mendoza* used the pre-Conquest pictorial conventions almost exclusively for the depiction of architecture. The one exception to this is the attempt at a perspectival drawing of the emperor's palace on folio 69r. Architectural signs, as opposed to the rendering of single-view perspectives of buildings, must have seemed more legible to the artist.

The adoption of European linear conventions and the single instance of European conventions of color may be viewed as an almost unconscious process of acculturation. The preference for composing pages without regard for illusionistic space speaks to the artist's judgment that, for the most part, spatial representation would blur the message. The few instances where spatial illusionism is attempted seem to be very self-conscious efforts that may have been an exhibition of skill for an important patron. The tension between stereotyped convention and representational image in the presentation of the human figure reflects careful judgments about economy and legibility of pictorial information. Where signs for actions and personages did not exist, the artist developed a pictorial system based on European models that could depict genre activities. The almost total retention of indigenous pictorial conventions for architecture clearly indicates the artist's perception that these were more legible than scale perspectival drawings. This may be attributable to the difficulty that someone from outside the European tradition has in reading Western artistic conventions for presenting architecture.

The analysis of the mixture of pre-Conquest and European pictorial elements in the *Codex Mendoza* may help us to understand more clearly the way in which a pictorial language carries information. The artist who drew the Mendoza sections was exercising his ability to choose between the two traditions and yet still convey the necessary information. The choices he made, particularly in part 3, indicate his flexibility in applying European pictorial conventions when appropriate and, perhaps, his perception that the pre-Conquest pictorial system was not flexible enough to transcribe information that did not fit into already established and well-defined categories.

ACKNOWLEDGMENTS

This essay is a portion of an M.A. thesis completed under the direction of Mary Elizabeth Smith at the University of New Mexico, 1987. I would like to express my deep appreciation for Professor Smith's encouragement and assistance in the completion of this manuscript.

·

NOTES

1. Kubler (1981) and Shapiro (1962) provide valuable discussions of the significance of style in discussions of cultural artifacts.

2. See Kubler (1961) for an overview of the relative preservation of indigenous remnants in the Colonial period.

3. It is not within the scope of this paper to consider the connections between pictorial manuscripts and the oral tradition. The loss of most of the indigenous oral tradition has precluded investigation in this area. We do know that the religious manuscripts from the region required a reader trained in the indigenous priesthood (Dibble 1971:330).

4. Robertson returned to the problem of defining the Mixtec manuscript style, and by inference the Valley of Mexico manuscript style, in "The Mixtec Religious Manuscripts" in *Ancient Oaxaca*, edited by John Paddock (1966). James Ramsey, in a 1975 doctoral dissertation, *An Analysis of Mixtec Minor Art, with a Catalogue*, also discussed stylistic characteristics of Mixtec manuscript painting. Both of these works amplify but do not differ from the broad outlines presented by Robertson in his earlier work.

5. Nancy Troike (1982:175–206) advances the theory that stereotyped poses were used in the Mixtec manuscripts to convey attitudes and emotions.

6. The study that presents the *Codex Mendoza* as a unified work is Donald Robertson's discussion of Colonial manuscript style in the Valley of Mexico (1959:94–107). It is not coincidental that the study that deals with the manuscript as a whole is one focusing on style. A close study of the style of the manuscript reveals that it is the work of one workshop under the direction of a single master.

7. This discussion is based on my personal inspection of the manuscript in June of 1984. I am indebted to the staff of the Bodleian Library, Oxford University, for their assistance.

8. These telling details can be appreciated when the original manuscript is examined with a good magnifying lens. They may not be as apparent in details of photographic facsimiles.

9. The use of a nude corpse as the sign for a dead man has no precedent in pre-Conquest manuscripts. The usual convention is to show a mummy bundle. The artist was clearly drawing from a knowledge of the European convention for depicting a dead figure, and it is not inconsistent that European linear style would be used rather than the indigenous style. The proportions of this figure also agree with European conventions.

10. Nicholson (1973), in a discussion of the phonetic elements in central Mexican writing systems, states that iconographically and stylistically the *Matrícula* shows no evidence of Hispanic influence, and that the style and composition of place signs in the manuscript may be considered a faithful reflection of pre-Conquest signs.

11. Green feathers shown in the list of tribute items are also painted with gradations in color. This process appears to be the same as that used on the bundles of red and yellow feathers. The use of gradations of color was necessary to increase the specificity of the tribute record. The more accurate naturalistic depiction of color in the feathers would fix the precise type of feather required as tribute. Color was not used as a vehicle for suggesting volume in those cases.

12. This variance in the application of color cannot be clearly seen in the published facsimiles available as of 1987.

13. M. E. Smith (1973:166) discusses the cartographic conventions for displaying running water in both pre-Conquest manuscripts and Colonial manuscripts. The standard pre-Conquest sign for "stream" or "river" was a stream of blue with wavy lines on the interior and projections ending in shells or circles. Streams with no interior wavy lines and no projections are considered to be a European convention.

14. It should be noted that the figures represented in the murals at Malinalco are depicted with differentiated left and right feet.

15. The discussion of the change in linear style in the early Colonial period by Donald Robertson (1959:65–66) is the most complete treatment of the subject.

16. Fray Toribio de Benavente Motolinía, in *Historia de los indios de la Nueva España* (1951:244), recorded the rapidity with which the native people taught themselves European arts and crafts, primarily by making copies. The rapid acquisition of pictorial conventions among North American indigenous people was also noted by John Ewers (1957). Interestingly enough, the examples cited by Ewers are primarily changes in the representation of human figures.

CHAPTER 4

The Aztec Pictorial History
of the *Codex Mendoza*

Elizabeth Hill Boone

CONTENT AND INTERNAL FEATURES

The first sixteen folios of the *Codex Mendoza* constitute one of the best known of the Aztec pictorial histories.[1] Presented pictorially, and accompanied by amplifying texts and glosses, are the founding of the Aztec-Mexica capital of Tenochtitlan prior to the year Two House (1325) and the fifty-one-year rule of Tenoch (folio 2v). This is followed by the reigns and conquests of the nine Mexica *hueytlatoque* (great rulers), beginning with Acamapichtli, the founder of the dynasty, and ending with Motecuhzoma Xocoyotzin, who died during the Spanish Conquest. As an early Colonial example of a *xiuhamatl* (year book) or *xiuhtlapohualamatl* (year-count book; Nicholson 1971a:45), part 1 of the *Mendoza* shows the progression of time from year to year, with all the years recorded in a continuous sequence. Information in this historical section, however, is organized into discrete units, which are each composed of a glossed illustration and a text, so that the founding of Tenochtitlan is one unit and each reign forms another. As is to be expected in early sixteenth-century manuscripts of this kind, which show minimal acculturation, the paintings carry most of the information, and the writings offer confirmation in a general sense and provide some qualifying details not easily represented pictorially.

Within each unit the material is presented across facing pages—the text pertaining to Acamapichtli's reign, for example, was written on folio 3r facing the corresponding illustration on 2v—and the units themselves begin on the verso sides of folios. As I have indicated in my work on the manuscripts of the Magliabechiano Group (Boone 1983:22), this use of the verso side as a point of beginning bespeaks an indigenous mentality, fundamentally different from the European view of a recto side of a folio as the most appropriate place to begin books, chapters, and other major sections in writings of fiction and nonfiction.[2] In part 1 of the *Codex Mendoza* the verso-recto connection was apparently considered so important that the painter and scribe never began one unit on a page opposite another unit, preferring instead to leave a page blank. With the rule of the fourth *hueytlatoani* Itzcoatl, for example, the painting showing his reign and conquests begins on 5v and spans the facing folio 6r; the text for Itzcoatl is written on the following verso, and the facing page, 7r, is left blank. The illustration for the fifth Mexica ruler, Motecuhzoma Ilhuicamina, then begins on the next verso side, 7v; it also spans the facing page, 8r, and the pertinent text follows on the next verso side. In this manner pages 7r, 9r, 11r, 14r, and 17r have remained blank.

As Donald Robertson (1959:99) has noticed, the illustrations pertaining to the first five Mexica rulers precede the accompanying texts and either begin or are entirely painted on the verso sides of folios, continuing onto the facing rectos if the conquests are many and the paintings must be large. But for the last four Mexica rulers, beginning with Axayacatl on 9v, the texts precede the illustrations, and it is the texts rather than the illustrations which begin on the verso sides. Robertson has attributed this rearrangement to a directive given the artist by his Spanish patron, who wished the Spanish text to precede the native pictures; regardless of the reason for the change, the importance of the versos is still preserved.

The historical part of the *Mendoza*, like the rest of the manuscript, was created in two stages; first the illustrations were painted, and then the manuscript was turned over to a scribe for annotation. In his text on the final page of the document (71v), the *Mendoza* scribe complained that he was given the manuscript to annotate only ten days before the fleet (which presumably was to take it to Spain) left and that he had to have the pictures interpreted for him. This implies that the scribe did not himself commission the paintings, and that the painter was not in the vicinity for consultation and explanation. Although James Cooper Clark (1938 1:1) thought the *Mendoza* scribe perhaps to be Martín Jacobita, Federico Gómez de Orozco (1941:50–51) has disputed this identification and instead has proposed Juan González, an informant of Sahagún, as the scribe. Gómez de Orozco (1941) also advanced the theory that the *Mendoza* artist was Francisco Gualpuyogualcal, a master painter who was mentioned by the conquistador Jerónimo López as creating a manuscript that, from López's description, was similar to the first two parts of the *Mendoza*. This attribution has been accepted by Donald Robertson (159:97, 106), but H. B. Nicholson (chapter 1 in this volume) has cautioned that López's reference does not fit the *Mendoza* exactly and could instead refer to a similar pictorial used by Antonio de Herrera for some vignettes on two title pages to his *Historia general* (see Ballesteros Gaibrois 1973:245–247). Since we know nothing more about Gualpuyogualcal, however, the attribution of the *Mendoza* paintings specifically to him adds little to our understanding of the manuscript.

Parts 1 and 2 of the codex have generally been accepted as stemming from earlier sources (Paso y Troncoso and Galindo y Villa 1925:vii; Clark 1938 1:1; Robertson 1959:73, 97; Borah and Cook 1963; Glass and Robertson 1975: no. 196), and the existence of a pictorial prototype for the historical section would be consistent with the features of this part. Such an earlier version, which was painted but may or may not have been annotated, seems also to be the source for passages in the *Leyenda de los Soles*, as discussed below.

The Painted History

The *Mendoza* painter controlled the structure and the detail of the history. He determined how the story would be organized and what elements would be included, and he must have known that his work would be annotated, because he left blank pages for the inclusion of texts. Before illustrating the founding of Tenochtitlan, he painted on the bottom of folio 1v a series of thirteen years, from One Rabbit to Thirteen Rabbit, as a pictorial preface. These years are not sequent to the years painted around the founding on 2r, for Thirteen Rabbit does not directly precede One House in the count. Instead, the painter most probably added the thirteen years on 1v to coordinate with a textual explanation of the Aztec system of counting the years, and indeed such a text was written above them.

The history proper begins on 2r with the founding of Tenochtitlan,[3] its place glyph being an eagle perched upon a flowering *nochtli* (prickly pear) cactus that grows from a rock. The scene is encompassed by stylizations of the canals and lake of Texcoco; blue *tules* or sedges and green reeds grow in the marshy land. The painter depicted Tenoch, the first ruler of Tenochtitlan, seated just to the left of the place sign, and he differentiated Tenoch from the nine captains who elected him as their leader by his seat (a *petlatl* or mat rather than a bundle of reeds), his speech scroll (indicating his status as speaker or *tlatoani*), his black priestly face and body paint, his fringed cloak, and his hair (which lacks the warrior's topknot of the other captains). All ten men have their name glyphs attached. Above the central place sign appears the temple of Huitzilopochtli or, as Clark (1938 1:21) has suggested, a *cabildo* or townhouse.[4] To the right appears a *tzompantli* or skull rack, and below is a shield crossed by spears or darts, a motif that is repeated for the reign of each successive ruler. Below the area of Tenochtitlan are the place signs of the towns Colhuacan and Tenayucan, conquered with Mexica aid during Tenoch's rule. The beginning, length, and end of his reign are marked by the progression of the years, beginning with Two House in the upper left corner and continuing counterclockwise around the central images until they reach Thirteen Reed at the top. At the bottom of the page, a New Fire Ceremony is indicated for the year Two Reed.

The continuing history is arranged according to the reigns of the following nine rulers in a rigidly standardized visual presentation. For each ruler the painter represented the individual, the years of his reign, the symbol for warfare, and the towns conquered during that reign. The ruler is consistently seated on an *petlatl*, wearing a cloak and his turquoise *xiuhuitzolli* or royal headdress, and shown with a speech scroll and his name glyph. Only Motecuhzoma Xocoyotzin is without a speech scroll (15v), and this is probably an oversight. Roughly in the middle of the page, the emblem for warfare is composed of a shield, *atlatl*, and darts or small spears called *mitl*, the latter being glossed *flechas* or arrows but identifiable as spears because of the presence of the *atlatl* or spear-thrower. This emblem varies from the more usual war symbols, composed of a shield and a *macquahuitl* (the obsidian-edged club), depicted in such histories as the *Códice Aubin*, *Codex Boturini*, *Fonds mexicain 40*, and *Fonds mexicain 217*.[5] Conquest or, perhaps more accurately, subjection or victory in the *Mendoza* is always represented by a burning temple (the roof of which is disarrayed), to which the place sign is attached.

The years are depicted sequentially, beginning at the upper left with the first full year a ruler is in office and continuing in a column down the left side and, if needed, across the bottom of the page to end on the year of the ruler's death. Only the Two Reed years of the New Fire Ceremonies are distinguished, these by a cord knotted around the reed year sign and by the image of a smoking fire drill. The New Fire Ceremony in the year 1455, during the reign of Motecuhzoma Ilhuicamina (7v), is marked only by the knotted cord. The omission of the fire drill here may possibly reflect an actual or believed disturbance in the cyclical ceremony because this Two Reed year followed the great famine of One Rabbit (1454), but since other sixteenth-century sources mention or illustrate the New Fire Ceremony in this year, the lack of a fire drill in the *Mendoza* is more probably another oversight by the artist. An auxiliary gloss in the *Codex Telleriano-Remensis* (folio 41v) states that in 1506–1507 Motecuhzoma Xocoyotzin had the binding of the years and consequent New Fire Ceremony changed from One Rabbit to Two Reed because the One Rabbit years were always marred by famine (and indeed famines became so mentally linked to Rabbit years that Chimalpahin [1965:99–100, 200] said that during the famine of 1454, "la gente se aconejó" [the people One-Rabbited]). The pattern of the *Mendoza* years would seem to disprove this, however, because the *Mendoza*, as with all other pictorials, has the New Fire Ceremony being held consistently on Two Reed even before this alleged change was instituted; no other source mentions such a change.[6]

To this established presentation of ruler, years of rule, and towns conquered, other information is only occasionally added. Acamapichtli is depicted twice (2v), once when he assumes office and is bearing the title Cihuacoatl (represented by a woman's head attached to a serpent body) and again seven years later when he initiates the military campaign against Quauhnahuac, Mizquic, Cuitlahuac, and Xochimilco, by which time he has earned a warrior's topknot and the Cihuacoatl title no longer applies; also added to this scene are the faces of sacrificial victims from the four towns. The third *hueytlatoani* Chimalpopoca also appears twice (4v), when he is seated in office and upon his death, the latter indicated pictorially by Chimalpopoca's posture and closed eyes. His conflict with Chalco is embellished by representations of the cause of war—the Chalcan destruction of four Mexica canoes and killing of five citizens of Tenochtitlan. It is likely that both Acamapichtli and Chimalpopoca are illustrated twice because of the special circumstances of their rule. Acamapichtli was an untried youth imported from the Acolhua town of Coatlichan to found a dynasty, and Chimalpopoca's murder contributed to the Tepanec war in which Tenochtitlan gained its sovereignty.

Few individuals other than the Mexica rulers populate the *Mendoza* history. The rulers of conquered areas are shown in only three exceptional cases, for the important cities of Coayxtlahuacan and Tlatelolco. On 6r Quauhtlatoa, the third lord of Tlatelolco, is painted dead above his place sign, representing his conquest by Itzcoatl, and on 7v Atonal, the deceased ruler of Coayxtlahuacan, is similarly rendered. The death of Moquihuiztli, fourth lord of Tlatelolco, is presented more dramatically (10r); he plummets dead from the heights of the twin temples of Tlatelolco after the final defeat of this city by Axayacatl, and the text describes his suicidal leap from the pyramid where he had fled for sanctuary.

The *Mendoza* place glyphs are concise and standardized, with the exception of two ethnic or political references, both involving Texcoco. During the reign of Huitzilihuitl (3v), the place sign of Texcoco is augmented by a bent arm from which water pours, a visual reminder that its inhabitants are Acolhua (and this is the only polity in the historical section that the scribe later glossed as a city [*ciudad*] rather than a town [*pueblo*]). Then, two reigns later (5v), the sign of Acolhuacan is amplified by the symbol for Texcoco, a reference to Acolhuacan's political affiliation. These few additions are embellishments to the basic history, however, and the artist clearly considered only three kinds of data essential: the rulers, the dates and duration of their reigns, and the towns they subjected.

The *Mendoza* painter initially ended his history on folio 15v in the year Thirteen Reed (1518), the year before the arrival of Cortés. This breaks with the pattern of depicting the year of a ruler's death as the last in the sequence for each reign, and it suggests that the prototype of the *Mendoza* was painted in Thirteen Reed. Motecuhzoma Xocoyotzin lived until Two Flint, and the two years of One Reed and Two Flint were later drawn in place, but not painted. These year signs are sufficiently similar to the others to have been added by the artist himself as an afterthought to make his record current, and the scribe included them in his tally of the sixteen years of Motecuhzoma's reign, mentioned in his gloss beside the years and in his text on 15r. A third year, Three House (1521), was then added by someone other than the painter, probably by the scribe, to bring the count through to the final conquest, but the scribe did not count this as part of Motecuhzoma's reign. The scribe glossed it "fin y pacificación y conquista de la Nueva España" (end and pacification and conquest of New Spain), ignoring the reigns of Cuitlahuac and Cuauhtemoc. According to the *Mendoza*, therefore, the Mexica dynasty ended with Motecuhzoma Xocoyotzin.

Texts and Glosses

The text to the historical section begins on folio 1r with an introductory statement, the general description of the founding of Tenochtitlan and the rule of Tenoch, and the explanation of the Aztec year count. The scribe here dated the arrival of the Mexica at Tenochtitlan to 1324 (One Flint), a year prior to Two House (1325), which is painted as the first full year on 2r. A general discussion of the Mexica wanderings and a description of Tenochtitlan follows, and the scribe named the ten tribal leaders pictured in the following illustration and outlined Tenoch's election and rule. Since the scribe assigned a fifty-two-year rule to Tenoch, and the associated painting on 2r records only fifty-one years (as does the accompanying gloss), the scribe has seemingly added 1324 (One Flint) to the count, apparently knowing that the first painted year (Two House) represented Tenoch's first full year in office rather than his actual accession date.

In three paragraphs on folio 1v, the scribe then digressed into a prefatory explanation of the Aztec year signs and numbers, the workings of the fifty-two-year cycle (which will allow his readers to understand the passage of time in the history that follows), and the New Fire Ceremony at the onset of each cycle. He named the thirteen years previously painted by the artist on this page, identifying them first in Nahuatl, using red ink, and then in Spanish, using his usual black ink. His informants perhaps failing him here, the scribe erred in naming Eight House as *chicnahui calli* or Nine House, and continued to assign the Nahuatl numbers ten through fourteen (one larger than accurate) to the remaining years Nine Rabbit through Thirteen Rabbit; his Spanish glosses, however, are correct (Clark 1938 1:20).

On 2r the scribe identified by glosses the ten Aztec leaders, the site of Tenochtitlan, the subjugated towns of Culhuacan and Tenayuca, and the number of years portrayed. In naming the founders,

however, he glossed the captain seated just to the left of Tenoch as "teçineuh," although the name glyph is composed of a maguey (*metl*) and a rump (*tzintli*), which would read Metzintli (Clark 1938 1:21). Perhaps in a hurry to annotate the codex, he also confused the names of the two captains seated above Tenoch; he glossed Oçelopan, whose glyph is composed of a jaguar-spotted banner (*ocelotl* and *pantli* or banner), as "Acaçitli"; and he glossed Acaçitli, whose glyph combines the elements reed (*acatl*) and hare (*citli*), as "oçelopan." This confirms the scribe's own admission later in the manuscript (71v) that he lacked a full understanding of the images and was relying on informants.

The writings that accompany the rest of the illustrations in this first section of the *Mendoza* are as standardized as the paintings. For each reign, glosses name the ruler; identify the shield, darts, and *atlatl* as instruments of war; give the name of each conquered town, followed by "pueblo" or simply "pu°" (with the exception of Texcoco on 3v, which is called "ciudad"); and give the length of the reign in years. Where the artist had added extra features, the scribe described or identified most of these: he explained the heads of the sacrificial victims on 2v, discussed the conflict with Chalco on 4v, and named the three vanquished enemy rulers painted by the artist on 6r, 7v, and 10r. The glosses follow the paintings closely, without conveying extra information.

The scribe's individual texts for the reigns have the nature of formal recitations, and he used almost the identical phrasing for each, as follows:

> In the year of (Christian year), years of the before-mentioned lordship of Mexico, after the death of (name of previous ruler), (name of new ruler), who was the (son/uncle/brother of . . . [facts of genealogy]), succeeded to the before-mentioned lordship, and during the time of his rule he conquered and took by force of arms (number) towns as are (previously/successively) represented and named. (The scribe then wrote generally about the ruler's virtues and whether he had many wives and children.) His rule lasted (number) years at the end of which he died and passed from this present life.

The scribe used the same phrases throughout, digressing from his formula only if special aspects of a ruler's reign were illustrated. He also added, in a script smaller than his usual, two paragraphs to the bottom of 15r describing the conquest of Mexico.

When the scribe dated the accession of each ruler, he initially gave the wrong year in the Christian count (table 1). He placed the first three members of the Aztec dynasty (Acamapichtli, Huitzilihuitl, and Chimalpopoca) seventy-four years too early (and seventy-five years earlier than the painted count), as indicated by dates A in table 1. He then changed these dates so that the years were two years too late (and one year later than the painted count), as shown by dates B in table 1, and he continued to date the accessions thusly. Only after he completed his texts did he notice this discrepancy and correct all the dates (except for the death date of Acamapichtli) to agree with the One Reed=1519 correlation, as indicated by dates C in table 1. These final dates are a year earlier than the first of the year signs painted for the rulers, because the textual dates record the years of actual accession to office, and the initial painted signs record the first year the rulers are in office. In what must be a simple clerical error, however, he misdated the accession of Tizoc to 1482 (table 1). To clarify his corrections, the scribe returned to each text and added a line or two at the bottom saying that "those dates that are crossed out should not be considered," and he often restated the correct and final number.

TABLE 1. THE SUCCESSION DATES FOR THE AZTEC RULERS
ACCORDING TO THE *MENDOZA* TEXTS AND THE REIGN DATES
ACCORDING TO THE *MENDOZA* PAINTINGS

Ruler & (Reign Length)[a]	Text Dates			Paintings
	A	B	C	
1. Acamapichtli (21)	1305 ⟨1326⟩[b]	1377 ⟨1398⟩[b]	1375	1 Flint (1376)– 8 Flint (1396)
2. Huitzilihuitl (21)	1326	1398	1396	9 House (1397)– 3 House (1417)
3. Chimalpopoca (10)	1347	1419	1417	4 Rabbit (1418)– 13 Reed (1427)
4. Itzcoatl (13)		1429	1427	1 Flint (1428)– 13 Flint (1440)
5. Motecuhzoma Ilhuicamina (29)		1442	1440	1 House (1441)– 3 House (1469)
6. Axayacatl (12)		1471	1469	4 Rabbit (1470)– 2 House (1481)
7. Tizoc (5)		1483	1482[c]	3 Rabbit (1482)– 7 Rabbit (1486)
8. Ahuitzotl (16)		1488	1486	8 Reed (1487)– 10 Rabbit (1502)
9. Motecuhzoma Xocoyotzin (18)		1504	1502	11 Reed (1503)– 2 Flint (1520)

[a] The reign lengths recorded by the texts, glosses, and paintings are consistent for each ruler and are given here in years. The exception is the gloss for Motecuhzoma Ilhuicamina, which incorrectly gives his reign a thirty-year duration.

[b] These are death dates. Acamapichtli is the only ruler whose death was dated by the *Mendoza* scribe.

[c] This year should be 1481 if it is to follow the patterns of being two years earlier than date B and of being one year earlier than the first painted year; the 1482 date additionally conflicts with the given reign lengths of Axayacatl and Tizoc.

COGNATE SOURCES

Like many other sixteenth-century manuscripts compiled under Spanish patronage to explain aspects of Aztec culture, part 1 of the *Codex Mendoza* can be linked to a number of other lost and existing manuscripts of the early Colonial period. It was copied from a now-lost prototype (which served as the source for at least one other document), and its text was the basis of information included in a later chronicle. In particular, parts of two textual documents—Mendieta's *Historia eclesiástica indiana* (see extract 1) and the *Leyenda de los Soles* (see extract 2)—are sufficiently similar in content to part 1 of the *Codex Mendoza* that these manuscripts are undoubtedly related. Mendieta had access to a copy of the *Mendoza* text, and the *Leyenda de los Soles* apparently stems from the *Mendoza* prototype. One of the vignettes in a title page of Antonio de Herrera's *Historia general* is probably also derived from the prototype of *Mendoza* part 1, or a later copy. Sahagún's *Manuscript of Tlatelolco* has additionally been linked to the *Codex Mendoza*, although this connection seems very doubtful.

Mendieta

The Mendieta connection with part 1 of the *Codex Mendoza* is fairly well established (Glass 1975: no. 196; Gibson and Glass 1975: no. 1052). In book 1, chapters 34–36 of his *Historia*, Geró-

nimo de Mendieta (1945 1:162–168) discusses the founding of Tenochtitlan and the lords who ruled the Mexica capital until the coming of the Spaniards (see extract 1), and much of his text seems to be derived not from the pictorial portion of the *Mendoza* (or a prototype) but from the *Mendoza* text. In describing the founding of Tenochtitlan, Mendieta lists the ten Mexica captains in the same order as does the *Mendoza* text, including the erroneous name Teçineuh and the transposition of Oçelopan and Acaçitli, and he dates the founding to 1324 (One Flint) in accordance with the *Mendoza* text instead of the year Two House (1325), which is the first year pictured (Mendieta 1945 1:162–163). Mendieta also gives the same dates and reign lengths for the Mexica rulers as are found in the *Mendoza* glosses and final text (table 1, dates C), he identifies the same conquered towns or (when the conquests are many) gives the same total number of conquests, and he uses several of the descriptive phrases for the rulers found in the *Mendoza* text. This close textual correspondence indicates that Mendieta had access either to the *Codex Mendoza* after it was written or to a nearly exact copy of the final text.

Since the *Codex Mendoza* seems to have left Mexico on the fleet a few days after it was completed, Mendieta could not have seen the codex itself. There must, therefore, have been a transcript of the Mendoza text (at least the text to part 1) made just before the codex was sent, which was used later by Mendieta. Nicholson (this volume) has speculated on the possibility that this transcript could have formed a part of the lost *Suma* of Andrés de Olmos, because Mendieta said that he relied on the writings of Motolinía and on the *Suma* of Olmos for information on pre-Conquest culture, and because the passage in Mendieta's *Historia* that precedes the *Mendoza*-related material almost certainly comes from the *Suma*. The possibility that Olmos copied or obtained a copy of the *Mendoza* text must remain open, however, for, as Nicholson indicates, it is also possible that the transcript of part 1 of the *Codex Mendoza* reached Mendieta independently of Olmos's *Suma*.

Leyenda de los Soles

The relationship of the *Leyenda de los Soles* to the *Mendoza* is less direct and has not, to my knowledge, been previously established. A short textual document that forms part 3 (folios 39r through 43v) of the *Codex Chimalpopoca* (Velázquez 1975:119–128), the *Leyenda* exists as a seventeenth-century copy of an earlier text that has the internal date of May 22, 1558 (Velázquez 1975:119). It briefly describes the four previous suns or ages, gives the mythic history of the Nahuatl speakers since the creation of the present fifth sun, and on the final page (folio 43v) tells of the founding of Tenochtitlan and the rules of the first six Mexica lords (see extract 2). The existing *Leyenda* manuscript is incomplete, for the text breaks off at the end of this page (43v), and a subscript indicates that another page once followed. As Velázquez (1975:ix) has already pointed out, the sixteenth-century text of the *Leyenda* was itself derived from an earlier pictorial source; the text is phrased as if it were describing painted images and, in the final section relating to Tenochtitlan and the Mexica monarchy, the narration is interrupted by what seem to be annotations copied or derived from a pictorial (e.g., for the founding: "51. 2 calli. Colhuacan. Tenayocan").

The last seven paragraphs of the *Leyenda* (folio 43v; Velázquez 1975:127–128), which describe the founding of Tenochtitlan and the reigns and conquests of six Mexica rulers (Acamapichtli through Axayacatl), contain the same information found in the *Mendoza*, without further amplification. For each ruler, the *Leyenda* gives his name, his genealogical relationship to previous rulers, the duration of his reign, the beginning date of his rule in the Aztec count, and the towns he conquered. The dates and reign lengths in the *Leyenda* are identical to those painted in the *Mendoza*, and all the *Leyenda* conquests are also pictured there. For the first four rulers (Acamapichtli, Huitzilihuitl, Chimalpopoca, and Itzcoatl) the towns in the *Leyenda* agree exactly with those painted in the *Mendoza*, although they are listed in a different order. For the fifth ruler, Motecuhzoma Ilhuicamina, the *Leyenda* names twenty-five of the thirty-three towns included in the *Mendoza*, and for Axayacatl it names thirteen of his thirty-seven conquests before the text breaks off; these, too, are listed in the *Leyenda* in a sequence different from that found in the *Mendoza*. Since no other extant manuscript contains the same detailed conquest list found in the *Codex Mendoza*, these correspondences between the *Mendoza* and *Leyenda* reign lengths, dates, and conquests show that the manuscripts must be cognate.

Moreover, the *Leyenda* passage is phrased as if it were a simplified reading of the *Mendoza* paintings, as can be seen by comparing the following *Leyenda* paragraphs with the paintings on *Mendoza* folios 2v and 3v (see extract 2).

> There, afterwards, the lord Acamapichtli was enthroned; he reigned twenty-one years. 20 [*sic*]. 1 Flint. Xochimilco, Cuitlahuac, Cuauhnahuac, Mizquic. Here are his conquests: he conquered Xochimilco, Cuitlahuac, Mizquic, and Cuauhnahuac. Acamapichtli conquered four places.
>
> Here reigned the son of Acamapichtli, his name [was] Huitzilihuitl; he ruled twenty-one years. 21. 9 House. Xaltocan, Acolman, Otompan, Chalco, Tetzcoco, Tollantzinco, Cuauhtitlan, and Toltitlan: here are his conquests. Huitzilihuitl conquered eight towns.

The *Leyenda* text was not derived directly from the *Mendoza*, because there are small inconsistencies between the *Mendoza* and *Leyenda* texts and differences in the sequences of conquests for each ruler, which show the *Leyenda* must instead stem from an earlier painted version of the *Mendoza*. The *Leyenda* text is much closer to the *Mendoza* paintings than the *Mendoza* glosses and text. For example, the *Leyenda* dates each reign according to the native count (as painted in the *Mendoza*), but it does not include the dates in the Christian count which are included in the *Mendoza* texts. In two instances, also, the *Leyenda* assigns variant names to conquered towns. Under Itzcoatl's reign, the Acolhuan town pictured in the *Mendoza* (5v) with the place signs of both Acolhuacan and Texcoco is glossed in the *Mendoza* as Acolhuacan and listed in the *Leyenda* as Texcoco. Under Motecuhzoma Ilhuicamina's reign, the town pictured in the *Mendoza* (8r) with "snake" (*coatl*) and "teeth" (*tlan*) elements is glossed in the *Mendoza* as Chontalcoatlan and in the *Leyenda* as Cohuatlan. The *Leyenda* author would not likely have replaced one name for another if he were copying the *Mendoza* glosses.

It is conceivable, but highly unlikely, that the *Leyenda* text was derived from the *Codex Mendoza* after the latter was painted but before it was glossed. This is unlikely, because the sequence of conquests given in the *Leyenda* for each ruler bears no apparent relation to the pattern of conquered towns painted in the *Mendoza*. Instead, the *Leyenda* sequence strongly suggests that there was an earlier pictorial version of the *Mendoza* which had the conquered towns arranged differently on the pages, and that this version served as the model for the *Leyenda*. This might also explain why eight towns are not included in the *Leyenda* list for Motecuhzoma Ilhuicamina's conquests, for these towns could all have been painted in the earlier version on a single page that was missing or out of its proper order when the *Leyenda* text was written.

The existence of a pictorial prototype for part 1 of the *Codex Mendoza* is also supported by certain features of the codex. As I have previously mentioned, the *Mendoza* artist initially ended his year count in Thirteen Reed (1518), two years before the death of Motecuhzoma Xocoyotzin, which suggests that he was copying a prototype that had Thirteen Reed as the last year in the count—a prototype that was probably therefore painted in 1518. Borah and Cook (1963) have established that part 2 of the *Mendoza* was copied from an earlier source, which they believe to have been a pre-Conquest screenfold (see also Berdan 1976a: 135). Although parts 1 and 2 of the *Mendoza* may have derived from separate sources, it is also possible that the prototype of part 1 additionally included the painted tribute list from which part 2 was copied.

Herrera

Nicholson (this volume) has noted a similarity between one of the title-page vignettes in Antonio de Herrera's *Historia general* and a painting in part 1 of the *Codex Mendoza*, suggesting that the engraver of Herrera's title pages had access to a pictorial manuscript similar to part 1 of the *Mendoza* (Nicholson stops short of saying related to the *Mendoza*). The vignette in question appears on the title page to the "Descripción de las Indias," published as part of Herrera's *Historia* (fig. 1). Although most of the vignettes on this page were derived from a lost manuscript of the Magliabechiano Group (Boone 1983: 47–51), the scene of Acamapichtli in the lower left is indeed strikingly similar to the *Mendoza*. In the vignette, Acamapichtli is pictured seated, with his name sign attached to the back of his head by a line, and he is surrounded by the war shield and spears and by the place glyphs of the four towns he conquered—Xochimilco, Mizquic, Cuauhnahuac, and Cuitlahuac—all of which are pictured together on folio 2v of the *Mendoza*. Although the images in the vignette have been Europeanized, they are so similar to those in the *Mendoza* that they must be related.

It is also possible that the image of the bird appearing in one of the vignettes on the title page of Herrera's *Década segunda* is related to part 1 of the *Mendoza*, although this association is much less certain (fig. 2). The bird on the title page stands on a rounded form that suggests an identification with a prickly pear cactus, and it may be that this bird is derived from the emblem of Tenochtitlan—an eagle on a prickly pear—like that pictured on 2r in the *Mendoza*; the grasslike plant next to the Herreran bird may then relate to one of the *tules* surrounding the emblem of Tenochtitlan in the *Mendoza* scene. I should also mention, however, that the Herreran avian has outstretched wings that make it nearly identical to the quetzal painted in the tribute list of the *Mendoza* (46r) as part of a warrior's costume. The presence of a warrior's costume on the Herrera title page might also suggest a link with the *Mendoza* tribute list, but since this particular costume is not found in the *Mendoza*, there is not really sufficient evidence to associate the title page with part 2 of the *Mendoza*. Only the Acamapichtli scene in the title page to the *Descripción* (fig. 1) can be said with any assurance to stem from a *Mendoza*-related pictorial.

Since Herrera's engraver could not have had access to the *Codex Mendoza* itself, he must therefore have used the earlier prototype of part 1 or an early Colonial copy of it, which had arrived in Spain by the late sixteenth century.

Fig. 1. The title page for the *Descripción de las Indias Occidentales*, published as part of Herrera's *Historia* (1601–1615). The Acamapichtli scene is in the lower left (see detail).

Fig. 2. The title page for *Década segunda* of Herrera's *Historia* (1601–1615). The image of the bird that is possibly related to the *Codex Mendoza* appears in the vignette to the left of the central coat of arms (see detail).

Sahagún

A connection between Sahagún's writings and the *Codex Mendoza* was first proposed by Wigberto Jiménez Moreno (1938:xlvii, note 88), who felt that, in Sahagún's *Manuscript of Tlatelolco*, some of the additions to the text that discusses the reigns of the Mexica rulers are derived from the *Codex Mendoza*. The first three folios of the *Códice Matritense de la Real Academia de la Historia* (Paso y Troncoso 1905–1907 8:2r–4r) contain passages in Nahuatl that describe the rules of the Mexica lords from Acamapichtli to Motecuhzoma Xocoyotzin (these were later incorporated verbatim into the *Florentine Codex* [Sahagún 1950–1982 8:1–3]). After the Nahuatl passages were completed, Sahagún added a few sentences in Spanish to some of them, amplifying the text passage or changing the reign lengths of the rulers. In the amendment to the rule of Axayacatl, he said that "these additions were taken from the painted and written relation given by the Tenochcas to Juan González." Jiménez Moreno (1938:xlvii, note 88) believed this relation to be the *Codex Mendoza*, because he felt the reign lengths adjusted in the additions corresponded approximately with those in the *Mendoza*. Federico Gómez de Orozco (1941:50–51) subsequently agreed with this linking of the Sahagún additions and the *Codex Mendoza* and used this as the major evidence to support his identification of Juan González as the interpreter of the *Mendoza* codex. Although Gibson and Glass (1975:365) have doubted that the amended reign lengths in the Sahagún manuscript are sufficiently similar to those in the *Mendoza* to link the two documents, other writers have seemingly accepted this idea or the identification of Juan González as the *Mendoza* interpreter (e.g., Robertson 1959:96; Echeagaray 1979:13, 15; Jiménez Moreno 1980:213, 216; Nicholson, this volume), so that the matter is worth considering here.

The reign lengths for the Mexica rulers that are given in the Nahuatl passages in the *Manuscript of Tlatelolco*, in the Spanish additions to these passages, and in the *Codex Mendoza* are shown below (see also table 1 for a more detailed presentation of the *Mendoza* dates).

	Manuscript Tlatelolco Nahuatl	Spanish additions	Codex Mendoza
Acamapichtli	21	nc	21
Huitzilihuitl	21	nc	21
Chimalpopoca	10	11	10
Itzcoatl	14	12½	13
Motecuhzoma Ilhuicamina	30	—	29
Axayacatl	14	12	12
Tizoc	4	—	5
Ahuitzotl	18	15½	16
Motecuhzoma Xocoyotzin	19	—	18

Sahagún's Nahuatl reign lengths originally differed considerably from those in the *Mendoza*, and only for the first three Mexica rulers do the two documents agree. When Sahagún then amended this section of his *Manuscript of Tlatelolco*, he added Spanish comments for all the rulers except Motecuhzoma Ilhuicamina, Tizoc, and Motecuhzoma Xocoyotzin. For the first two rulers, his additions do not mention a change in the reign lengths, but for Chimalpopoca, Itzcoatl, Axayacatl, and Ahuitzotl, he gave new reign lengths. These bring the reign lengths in the *Manuscript of Tlatelolco*

closer to those in the *Mendoza*, but they are still not very close. Sahagún changed the reign of Axayacatl to agree with the *Mendoza*, and he brought the reign lengths of Itzcoatl and Ahuitzotl to within a half year of the *Mendoza* information; but since the *Mendoza* presents the reigns in durations of only whole years, I do not feel the 12½ and 15½ years given in Sahagún's additions necessarily equal the thirteen and sixteen years in the *Mendoza*. Moreover, Sahagún actually changed the duration of Chimalpopoca's rule to differ from that in the *Mendoza*, and he did not change three of the reign lengths that already did differ from those in the *Mendoza* (those of Motecuhzoma Ilhuicamina, Tizoc, and Motecuhzoma Xocoyotzin). These three latter, unchanged reign lengths vary from those in the *Mendoza* by only a year each, but since Sahagún changed the Chimalpopoca length, he was apparently sensitive to differences of only a year. This implies that these unchanged reign lengths already agreed with those in the *Relation*. The *Relation* given to Juan González by the Tenochcas thus seems to have agreed exactly with the *Codex Mendoza* only for the reigns of three of the nine Mexica rulers. To my mind, this variation would support the case that González's *Relation* was probably not the *Mendoza*, rather than that it probably was. In disputing the Sahagún-*Mendoza* connection, of course, one disputes most of the evidence that Juan González was the interpreter of the *Mendoza*, and indeed Borah and Cook (1963) have felt that the interpreter may have been a man whose name begins with Q rather than G.

In summary, part 1 of the *Codex Mendoza* can be directly or indirectly linked to Mendieta's *Historia eclesiástica*, the *Leyenda de los Soles*, and one of Herrera's title-page vignettes, but probably not to the *Manuscript of Tlatelolco* of Sahagún.

THE PRESENTATION OF HISTORY IN THE *CODEX MENDOZA* AND IN OTHER AZTEC MANUSCRIPTS

Part 1 of the *Codex Mendoza* shares many features with other Aztec pictorial histories, but it also has important differences that set it apart from the others, and these differences relate to its function as a record specifically of the reigns and conquests of the Mexica rulers. Motolinía (1971:390) has said that the Aztec histories depicted conquests, wars, dynastic successions, plagues, storms, and noteworthy signs in the skies, and the *Mendoza* history clearly lacks this full range of information. In its manner of presenting the ingredients of history the *Mendoza* stands out too. In order to understand the nature of the *Mendoza* more fully, therefore, it is useful to review the kinds of information included in the other extant histories and the ways these elements are arranged, to see how the *Mendoza* fits within the classifications of Aztec recorded history.

Donald Robertson and H. B. Nicholson have provided the most successful typologies of Aztec pictorial histories. Robertson (1959:62–65), who based his classification on organizational principles for the depiction of history, identified three types, which he called styles, and saw these as forming a developmental sequence. The first encompasses "time-oriented" histories, where "history is a series of events ordered according to time," in this case an unbroken stream of time, as for example with the *Tira de Tepechpan* and the *Codex Boturini*. "Place-oriented" histories, histories organized around geography, as in the *Codex Xolotl* and the *Mapa Tlotzin*, form a second style; and "event-oriented" histories, in which the narrative moves from event to event as in the Mixtec manuscripts, form the third. Robertson (1959:64) saw the stream-of-time form as the basic and oldest form, which he felt was imported to Texcoco from the Mixteca. According to his sequence, the Texcocan painters then developed the "place-oriented" style, but not before they transferred the "time-oriented" style to the Mexica, who continued using it until the Spanish Conquest; in the Mixteca, the event-oriented style evolved from the earlier form. While I disagree with Robertson's developmental sequence for these styles and his suggestions that the art of manuscript painting was brought to central Mexico by Mixtec painters (Robertson 1959:13, 64), I find Robertson's basic typology especially useful in classifying the major body of historical manuscripts according to the arrangement of data. John Glass (1975:32) has also followed Robertson's classification.

The question of content, however, fell to Nicholson (1971a: 45–52), who, in what he said was a preliminary attempt, established an extensively detailed and exampled typology of the extant central Mexican pictorial histories, based both on the kinds of information recorded in the histories and on the manner of presentation. He defined five kinds of histories (in which he also included some textual manuscripts), as follows: (1) continuous year-count annals, which are "distinguished by the recordation of a continually sequent record of years with picto-ideographic notations of events usually assigned to particular years" (Nicholson 1971a:45), such as the codices *Boturini, Aubin,* and *Mendoza,* to name three of his nineteen pictorial examples; (2) sporadically dated or undated annals, such as the second section (imperial history) of the *Códice Azcatítlan;* (3) cartographic layouts combined with historical, dynastic, and/or genealogical depictions, which parallel Robertson's place-oriented histories, with the inclusion of the *Mapa Sigüenza* and others; (4) genealogies, of which he gives fifteen examples; and (5) dynastic lists, which are related to genealogies but consist of dynastic sequences without the specification of genealogical connections. Nicholson (1971a:47) further divided the first category, the continuous year-count annals, according to the organization or arrangement of the years, into (a) continuous stream (in a row or column) of sequent year dates (e.g., *Codex Mexicanus, Tira de Tepechpan*), (b) meander arrangement of the year cartouches (e.g., *Codex Boturini, Codex Vaticanus A* section 1), (c) page frame arrangements (e.g., codices *Mendoza* and *Telleriano-Remensis*), (d) block formats (e.g., codices *Aubin* and *Azcatítlan*), and (e) cross layout (*Códice en Cruz*); here I cite only a few of his examples for each division.

In a published commentary on Nicholson's 1971 article, Robertson (1971:91–92) disagreed with two of Nicholson's categories, feeling that dynastic lists are a subcategory of genealogies and that sporadically dated or undated annals are also a subcategory, of the dated annals, and come from compressed Colonial documents. Edward Calnek (1978:243) likewise accepted Nicholson's classification of continuous year-count annals but not his sporadically dated or undated annals.

I agree with Nicholson that dynastic lists and genealogies belong to separate categories, but I agree with Robertson and Calnek that his examples of sporadically dated or undated annals might successfully be treated in another manner. Nicholson's typology uses the mixed criteria of content or function, the existence of dates, and the arrangement of data; and some of the disagreements with his typology seem to stem from this mixture.

As a manner of organizing the Aztec historical codices, in order to put the special features of the *Codex Mendoza* into sharper focus, I propose an integration of the Robertson and Nicholson typologies, a reshuffling of some categories, and a separation of classifications based on different criteria. In this synthetic typology, the Aztec historical manuscripts can first be organized according to

their content or function—what information they actually contain and what they were intended to contain; the histories can then be classed according to the manner in which they present these data.

Historical Manuscripts, Classed According to Content

By content the manuscripts separate easily into four categories: secular histories (of which there are two types), dynastic lists, genealogies, and victory chronicles.

The secular histories, which carry the adjective "secular" to distinguish them from myths or cosmogonic histories that more properly belong in a classification of religious manuscripts, are those about which Motolinía spoke, and most of the information they contain is indeed secular in nature. They often, but not always, record such events as the birth, succession to office, and death of rulers; some of the towns they conquered; programs of construction and dedications of important buildings or monuments; and such natural or climatic phenomena as solar eclipses, earthquakes, floods, and famines. Generally the episodes are dated and, if so, the New Fire Ceremonies are marked, but the consistent use of dates is not a requirement. This category includes all of Robertson's three styles and Nicholson's first three types: the continuous year-count annals, sporadically dated or undated annals, and cartographic layouts.

There are two distinct types of secular histories: migration histories, which record all or part of the Mexica migration from Aztlan to Tenochtitlan and have as their subject the Mexica people; and imperial histories, which present events of the Aztec state from the founding of Tenochtitlan up to (and often after) the Spanish Conquest and focus more particularly on the Mexica monarchy. As is indicated below, the narration of events and the passage of time are often presented and arranged in the migration histories differently than in the imperial histories, so much so that, in a single manuscript containing both types, the elements and structure of the narrative may change markedly when the Mexica migration ends and the dynasty is established (for example, *Códice Azcatítlan, Códice Aubin,* codices *Telleriano-Remensis* and *Vaticanus A/Ríos, Fonds mexicain 40*).

Migration histories, because they are concerned principally with the Mexica tribe and its wanderings, tend not to contain the wider range of data included in imperial histories. The places where the Mexica stayed are shown, as are significant (often religious or military) events along the route and New Fire Ceremonies, but named individuals are few and natural and climatic phenomena are lacking. Two of the fuller pages of part 1 of the *Códice Aubin* (fig. 3), for example, depict the Mexica stopover at Tecpayoacan, which was accompanied by warfare and which lasted from Twelve Flint to Two Reed, when a New Fire Ceremony was held; then in Three Flint the Mexica arrived at Pantitlan for an apparently uneventful stay of another four years. Here only the fundamental events are accommodated pictorially.

Imperial histories record lesser as well as major happenings, and the events are more densely rendered. Part 2 of the *Códice Aubin* (fig. 4) is a good example because it is more detailed than most other imperial histories, and it is a strict continuous year-count annual, as are the vast majority of both the migration and imperial histories.[7] With an economy of form and presentation, the *Aubin* painter succinctly aligned events to the right of individual years in his continuous stream of dates, which were arranged in columns because of the limitations of his pages. On folio 39v (fig. 4, left side) he recorded that the year Four Flint was marked by an earth-

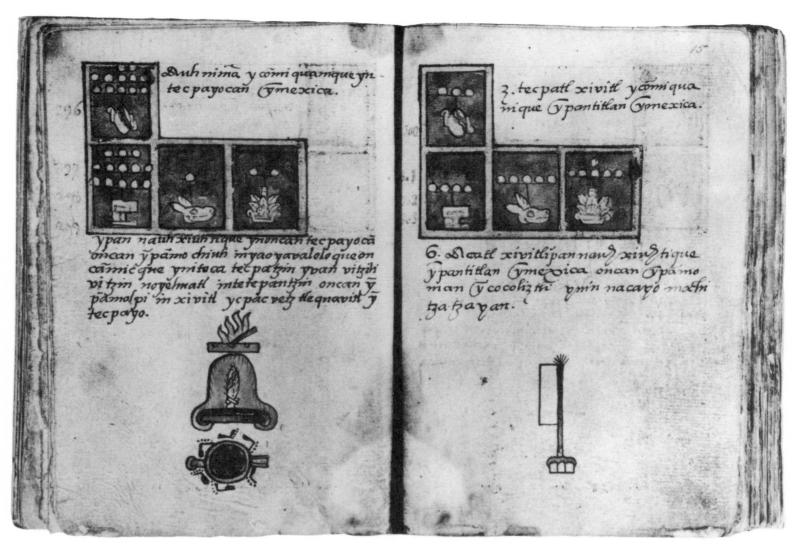

Fig. 3. *Códice Aubin* part 1, folios 14 verso and 15 recto, showing
the Mexica migration to Tecpayoacan and Pantitlan (after Lehmann
and Kutscher 1981:229).

quake, the towns of Xochitlan and Amaxtlan were conquered in
the years Five House and Six Rabbit respectively, and the great
flood from the Coyoacan aqueduct occurred in Seven Reed. On
40r (fig. 4, right side) he indicated that in Nine House rock was
quarried at Malinalco and Ahuitzotl died, to be succeeded by
Motecuhzoma Xocoyotzin in the year Ten Rabbit; in Eleven Reed
the Malinalco quarries were again worked, in Twelve Flint cacao
was imported, and in Thirteen House *tzitzimime* (demons of death)
descended. As Calnek (1978) has pointed out, the painter of the
secular history could not record very much about each happening,
because his medium hindered the presentation of qualifications or
determinants, but he could present a wide range of events.

Dynastic lists contain only one class of data found in the broader
histories, this being the succession of the rulers, which is often accompanied by the duration of their reigns and occasionally by the
specific dates of their accession and death. The king list in the back
of the *Códice Aubin* (folios 70r–79r; fig. 5) gives, for the pre-
Conquest rulers, the order of their succession and the length of
their reigns, and additionally dates some of the later Colonial
rulers according to the European count. It is without genealogical
implications, however. Figure 5 does not, for example, indicate
that Tizoc and Ahuitzotl are brothers, sons of Motecuhzoma Ilhuicamina. Other pictorial dynastic lists, mentioned by Nicholson
(1971:52), are found in the *Codex Cozcatzin* and Sahagún's *Primeros Memoriales* and *Florentine Codex*.

The third class of pictorial manuscript with a historical content
is composed of genealogies. As Nicholson (1971a:50–52) has said,
genealogies often include historical data and record land ownership as well, but they are rarely dated. Genealogies were popular in
pre-Conquest times and were used especially in the Colonial period in land litigations. Glass (1975:33) has named fifty-four genealogies in the census of native-style pictorial manuscripts in volume 14 of the *Handbook of Middle American Indians*, twelve percent
of the total, and he has listed twenty of these as coming specifically
from the State, Federal District, and Valley of Mexico (Glass
1975:47).

Based on its content, part 1 of the *Codex Mendoza* fits well
within none of these three categories of Aztec histories. Although
the texts of the *Mendoza* give genealogical information on the
Aztec rulers, the manuscript was clearly not conceived as a genealogy. Neither is it a true secular history, for the *Mendoza* painter
does not inform of secular (or even religious) events, of natural or
climatic phenomena, or of the birth of rulers as do the fuller histories, and it is far from containing the type of detail relating to the
quarrying of stone or the introduction of foreign produce found in
the *Códice Aubin* and other manuscripts. It contains, however, more
information than is found in a dynastic list, and rather than being
treated as a truncated secular history, it should be considered as
falling between these two categories. The *Mendoza* takes from the
secular histories the use of a continuous year-count sequence,
the marking of the beginning of the fifty-two-year cycles, and the
recordation of conquest, and it can be compared to a dated dynas-

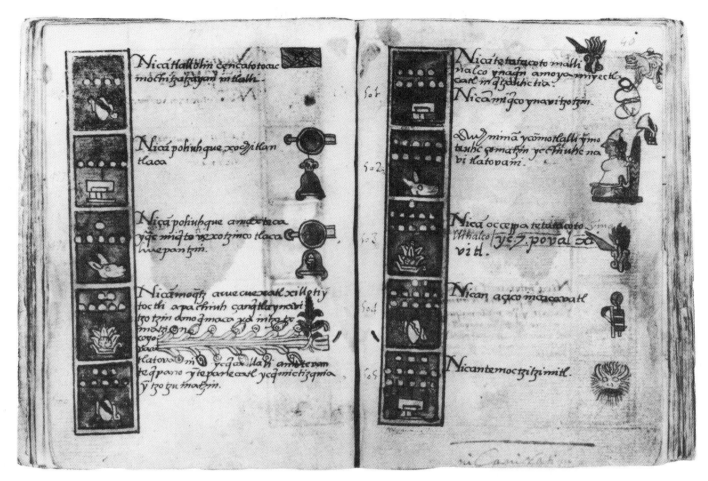

Fig. 4. *Códice Aubin* part 2, folios 39 verso and 40 recto, showing
Mexica imperial history from 4 Flint (1496) through 13 House
(1505) (after Lehmann and Kutscher 1981:254).

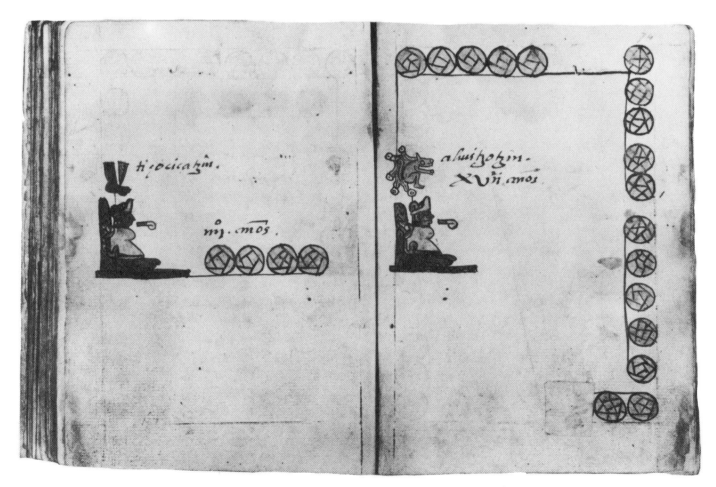

Fig. 5. *Códice Aubin* part 3, folios 73 verso and 74 recto, showing
the portion of the king list pertaining to Tizoc and Ahuitzotl (after
Lehmann and Kutscher 1981:288).

tic list to which the identities of subjected towns have been added.

Part 1 of the *Codex Mendoza* is a victory chronicle, and as such falls into the fourth class of pictorial history. It apparently had pre-Conquest antecedents, because this section of the *Mendoza* was copied from an earlier pictorial prototype, which may have been painted in 1518, the year before the arrival of Cortés. The *Mendoza*, however, seems to be the only one of this type to survive. As a victory chronicle it has some parallels with the lists of conquests found in Mixtec manuscripts like the *Codex Zouche-Nuttall* (1987: 71–74), although there are major structural differences. Victory chronicles are well known in the Old World—they were commonly compiled for Roman emperors—and like its Old World counterparts, the *Mendoza* records perceived as well as actual victories. The conquests of Colhuacan and Tenayucan during the rule of Tenoch, for example, were less Aztec-Mexica conquests than victories of the Tepanecs, under whom the Mexica served. The perception of victory must also have been such that the *Mendoza* painter could depict the destruction of the Chalcan temple four times (a subjugation each for Huitzilihuitl, Chimalpopoca, Itzcoatl, and Motecuhzoma Ilhuicamina) without finding this repetitive conquest inconsistent.

In format, the victory chronicle of the *Codex Mendoza* relates more closely to the secular histories than to dynastic lists and genealogies. Dynastic lists are generally arranged in a tabular or restrictively sequential fashion, and genealogies are presented diagramatically; in neither category are all the years presented to date an event or show duration, as they are in the *Mendoza* and in most of the secular histories. The structure of part 1 of the *Mendoza*, then, can best be understood in relation to the organizational structures of these secular histories.

Organizational Structures of Secular Histories

Histories must record four things: participant(s), event, location, and time—the who, what, where, and when. One of these classes of information generally dominates and provides the foundation or structure around which the narrative is presented, and the other three classes are then arranged to fit the format provided by the governing class. Each organizational structure requires that sacrifices be made in the other areas. Most histories are ordered chronologically, and places, events, and participants are discussed within a temporal framework. Antonio de Herrera's *Historia general de los hechos de los castellanos* (1934–1957, first published 1601–1615), however, is an example of a chronologically ordered history treated too strictly, for Herrera divided his history of the Spanish empire in the New World (from 1492 to 1554) into eight *décadas*, within which he grouped events that happened in widely scattered locations, abruptly halting a particular narrative at the end of a *década* to resume it much later in the next *década*. But generally in temporally arranged histories, time is simultaneously adjusted to accommodate factors of location and event, so that a historian of the conquest of Mexico might present the whole of Cortés's stay in Veracruz before relating the confusion his landing caused in the Mexican capital.

The secular histories painted in late Postclassic Mexico fall into three basic groups according to the kind of information that governs the presentation of history; there are continuous year-count annals, in which time provides the armature for the narrative; cartographic histories, which are governed by geography; and *res gestae* (literally, "deeds done"), in which time and place are arranged around the combination of event and participant. Also painted were histories combining the qualities of annals and *res gestae*,

where time is occasionally interrupted to accommodate the narrative requirements of an event. There were no biographies, except in a dynastic framework.

Continuous year-count annals, like their medieval European counterparts, present, without comment or interpretation, seemingly unconnected events that are subordinated to the radical linearity of time, and this rigidity of time is itself hostile to detailed explanations or descriptions of process. The count of the years provides the structure around which are painted events that must be made to fit within the space left available; the place and participants may either be implied or directly stated. All the years, whether or not they are accompanied by events, are depicted in sequence. The *Codex Mexicanus* (fig. 6), *Tira de Tepechpan, Codex Saville*, reconstructed *Codex La Magdalena Mixiuca*, and *Anales de Tula*[8] all show the year-count progressing in an uncut and undeviating line. The artist of the *Codex Mexicanus* (fig. 6), for example, presents an earthquake, the conquest of Xochitlan, the conquest of Amaxtlan, the Coyoacan aqueduct flood, and the working of quarries at Malinalco, respectively attached to the specific years Four Flint through Eight Flint in his uninterrupted count. In other annals the file of years is broken by the limitations of the painting surface, as in part 2 of the *Códice Aubin* (fig. 4), where each page of European paper can effectively accommodate only five years in a single column. In the *Códice en Cruz*, the years are disposed in rows of thirteen years with every four rows arranged cross-fashion to complete a fifty-two-year cycle. But in none of the annals, as I define them strictly, is the year-count sequence broken by other factors of the narrative (by place, participant, or event).

In all the continuous year-count annals, the location and ethnicity of the main protagonists of the narration are considered to be understood and not in need of depiction. Since the *Codex Mexicanus* and part 2 of the *Códice Aubin* record Mexica history only, the reader, who assumes that the events happen in Tenochtitlan to the Mexica, is given only those place signs that indicate conquest or other action outside the capital.[9] In the *Códice en Cruz*, almost all events without place signs connected to them are assumed to pertain to Texcoco, and when Mexica history is represented the place sign of Tenochtitlan is generally attached.

The second kind of secular histories is the cartographic histories, in which geography provides the organizational structure, with time and event arranged around location. Many of the *lienzos* and *mapas* fall into this category, as do the Texcocan pictorials *Mapa Quinatzin, Mapa Tloltzin,* and *Códice Xolotl,* and the Mexica *Mapa Sigüenza* (fig. 7). Cartographic histories readily present sequence and thus provide an ideal format for the recordation of migrations, where the narrative is told through a people's wanderings; the *Quinatzin, Tloltzin, Xolotl,* and *Sigüenza* manuscripts are all wholly or partially migration histories. Upon an often-stylized geographic panorama, persons and events are depicted, specific locations are identified, and the progression of time is indicated by a directional line or footprints, or merely implied by the direction in which the figures face, but actual dates are only occasionally given. In the *Mapa Sigüenza* (fig. 7), for example, the Mexica tribe leaves Aztlan in the upper left corner to follow a sinuous route to Chapultepec and eventually to Tenochtitlan in the lower right; years of duration for the tribe's residence in various places are indicated by enumerating discs attached to the place signs, but no year signs define time more precisely.

Far fewer pictorial histories are *res gestae*, where the deeds or events of specific individuals or groups outline the story, and time and place are often given but are subsumed. The intersection of

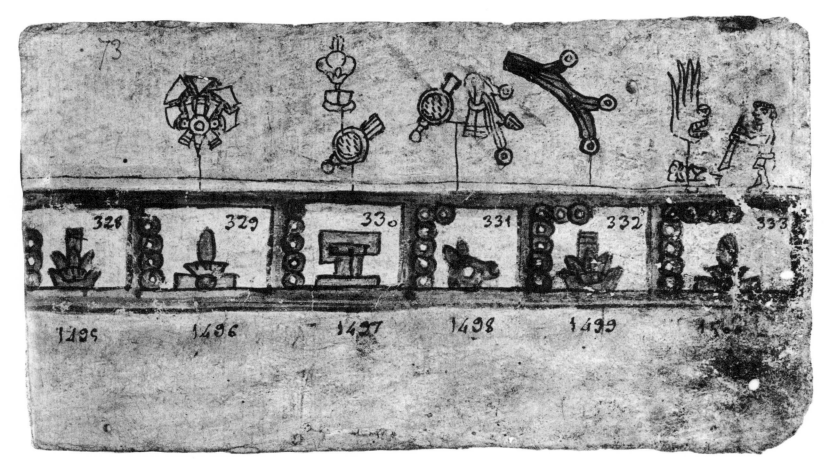

Fig. 6. *Codex Mexicanus*, page 73, showing Mexica imperial history
from 3 Reed (1495) through 8 Flint (1500) (after *Codex Mexicanus*
1952: pl. LXXIII).

participant and event is the fundamental component of history in Western European thought, and most contemporary histories are structured in this manner; but in Late Postclassic and early Colonial central Mexico, pictorial *res gestae* are rare. In southern Mexico the Mixtec historical codices can be considered *res gestae*, for their narratives follow the important deeds and events in the lives of major Mixtec rulers, with place and time depicted where appropriate.

Among the Aztec secular histories, however, only parts 2 and 3 of the *Códice Azcatítlan* can be considered *res gestae* histories. But since they retain some of the structure of year-count annals, I see them as Colonial derivations of the pre-Conquest annal form. Part 2 of the *Códice Azcatítlan* (fig. 8) is the imperial history, and part 3 the conquest and Colonial record. In part 2, history is presented not by date, for there are no dates given, but by the reigns of the Mexica rulers, these reigns being the larger events of some temporal duration within which the lesser happenings are clustered. Although each unit begins with the accession of the ruler on the left and ends with his death on the right, events within the reigns are not always ordered chronologically, for it was apparently less important in this manuscript that an event may have occurred on a certain date than that it happened during the reign of a particular ruler. In figure 8 the second Mexica ruler, Huitzilihuitl, is named and shown acceding to office. He is followed by depictions of the conquest of Texcoco, the birth of Nezahualcoyotl (of Texcoco), the death of the Tlatelocan ruler Cuacuauhpitzahuac and the seating of his successor Tlacateotl, a New Fire Ceremony, and the apparent conquest of a Tepanec town and the death of the usurper Maxtla; lastly, the deceased Huitzilihuitl is depicted on the far right. The chronology of this reign is somewhat confused, for the Mexica were not victorious over the Tepaneca and Maxtla was

not killed until the reign of Itzcoatl. Moreover, even the other events, which properly belong to Huitzilihuitl's reign, are not chronologically sequential. Important here is not a strict adherence to time but rather a pictorial listing of deeds and events within the particular temporal range. Discounting the instances of chronological confusion, which reflect the manuscript's Colonial date, part 2 of the *Azcatítlan* is ordered like an annal, having a continuous sequence of events presented through time. The year count that normally accompanies this kind of historical presentation has been removed, and the flow of time has been divided according to the reigns.

A number of other Aztec secular histories fall between the basic annalistic and *res gestae* types, their structure arising from a combination of the two modes. In them, all the years are presented in a sequence, but time halts for event. All are migration histories: the *Codex Boturini* (fig. 9), part 1 of the *Códice Azcatítlan*, part 1 of the *Códice Aubin* (fig. 3), part 1 of *Fonds mexicain 40*, and all of *Fonds mexicain 85*. These histories are arranged around sequent year counts, the years of which are often clustered in blocks, but the flow of the count is interrupted to accommodate the presentation of events. In the *Codex Boturini* (fig. 9) the Mexica migration progresses incident by incident (or place by place), and the years represent the duration of the Mexica tribe's stay in a particular place. In figure 9 the Mexica arrive in Xaltocan in the year Seven Flint, remain there for four years (through Twelve Reed), and proceed to Acalhuacan, where they settle for another four years. The mixed structure of these histories provides an efficient manner of presenting migrations, especially when it is important to show all the years, because the Mexica migration is characterized by long peri-

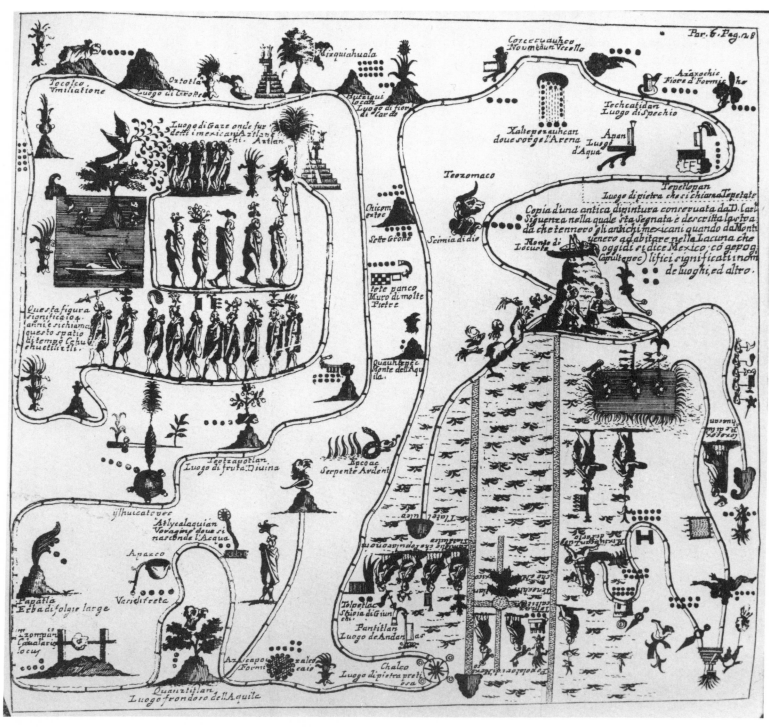

Fig. 7. *Mapa Sigüenza*, showing the Mexica migration from Aztlan to Tenochtitlan (after Gemelli Careri 1976: op. p. 24).

ods during which nothing noteworthy occurred and other times of important and intense activity. In comparison, the migration records of those pictorials that are structured strictly as unbroken year-count annals (like the *Codex Mexicanus* and the *Tira de Tepechpan*) have pages that are blank, or nearly so, and others crowded with detail. With a modified annal form, which clusters the count of time and breaks its flow to depict events, migrations can be recorded both with a fullness of detail and a compactness of space.

As a victory chronicle, part 1 of the *Codex Mendoza* also combines the features of an annal with a *res gestae* history. The *Mendoza* is a year-count annal in the sense that all the years are given from the founding of Tenochtitlan to the Spanish Conquest. The years provide an armature for the sequence of the reigns of the Mexica rulers, for they date the seating and death of these rulers and locate each ruler in the temporal continuum of the Aztec monarchy. The year count does not function, however, to date specifi-

cally any of the events within the reigns, with the exception of the New Fire Ceremonies and the single incident of Acamapichtli's campaign against the four towns he conquered. None of the other internal events in the reigns—the conquests—is tied specifically to the year count; rather, the conquests are loosely grouped according to the rulers responsible for their subjection. In this way, the *Codex Mendoza* has the same structure as the imperial history given in part 2 of the *Códice Azcatítlan*, although the *Mendoza* has retained the year count.

Like many of the migration histories, the *Mendoza* victory chronicle manipulates time to separate and distinguish major events, these events in the *Mendoza* being the reigns of the Mexica rulers. Time in the *Mendoza* is divided into the different reign lengths, so that the sequent reigns, rather than the year count, govern the structure of the presentation, as in a *res gestae* mode. This particular structure fits the subject matter of part 1 of the *Mendoza* well,

Fig. 8. *Códice Azcatítlan*, folios 14 verso and 15 recto, showing
Mexica imperial history during the reign of Huitzilihuitl (after
Códice Azcatítlan 1949: pl. XV).

Fig. 9. *Codex Boturini*, page 11, showing the Mexica migration
to Xaltocan and Acalhuacan (after *Codex Boturini* 1964–1967:
lá-mina XI).

for as a victory chronicle it is necessarily concerned with the conquests of the Aztec rulers rather than with the history of the people. It breaks the year count to assure that the focus remains on the individual rulers, their reigns, and their conquests.

AZTEC CHRONOLOGY AND THE REIGNS OF MEXICA RULERS IN THE *CODEX MENDOZA*

Part 1 of the *Codex Mendoza* presents the "official Tenochtitlan" version of Aztec history. For several centuries its historical information, and particularly the dates it gives for the reigns of the Mexica rulers, was simply accepted as broadly valid. Since the 1940s and 1950s, however, the universality of Aztec chronology has been brought into question, and the existence of a number of separate but contemporaneous year counts operating in central Mexico in the Late Postclassic period has been proposed. In this light, the *Mendoza* has been considered to contain the most prominent of the different year counts.

The theory of the simultaneous use of different year counts or of different systems of naming the years was introduced in 1940 when Wigberto Jiménez Moreno (1940), in his study of the *Codex of Yanhuitlan*, pointed out that the Aztec-Mexica year One Reed (1519) correlated with the year Thirteen Reed among the Mixtec and Popoloca speakers of western Oaxaca and southern Puebla. Alfonso Caso (1946, rpt. 1967:226–240) later argued that the Matlatzincas also had a separate count, with the Mexica year One Reed equaling Three Reed in the Toluca Basin.

Jiménez Moreno and Paul Kirchhoff especially have been proponents of the existence of differing year counts both within and outside the Basin of Mexico. After encountering discrepancies in dates given for the Aztec migrations, Kirchhoff began investigating the possibility that there existed different systems of naming the years, which culminated in his postulating the existence of thirteen different systems in simultaneous use (Kirchhoff 1949, 1950). Working along similar lines, Jiménez Moreno (1956, 1961) more cautiously proposed nine separate systems, as follows:

Mexica 1 Reed equals:			
Mixteca	13 Reed	Colhua I	12 Reed
Texcocan	7 Reed	Colhua II	2 Reed
Matlatzincan	3 Reed	Cuauhtitlan	10 Reed
Cuitlahuacan	8 Reed	Metztitlan	6 Reed

Finding what he considered to be three different counts in the *Anales de Cuauhtitlan* (Cuitlahuacan, Colhua I, and Cuauhtitlan), for example, Jiménez Moreno indicated that many historical sources used dates from a variety of ethnic groups (and thus a variety of naming systems) and that these dates are occasionally translated as if they were all part of the Mexica system. More recently Nigel Davies (1973:193–210, chart) has likewise delineated nine separate counts that partially correspond to those of Jiménez Moreno and Kirchhoff and that he has identified as Cuitlahuaca, Tenochtitlan, Historia de los mexicanos por sus pinturas, Tetzcoco-Culhua, 1 Tecpatl-Ascención de Acamapichtli, 4 Acatl-5 Tochtli, Anales de Cuauhtitlan V, Anales de Cuauhtitlan VI, and Ixtlilxochitl. According to Davies, most of the historical sources use more than one system or count, and some single counts are found in a large number of sources. He has found six different counts within the *Anales de Cuauhtitlan* and seven being used by Alva Ixtlilxochitl.

The evidence for different Mixtec and Matlatzinca counts, as well as for the use of different year bearers in Guerrero (as seen in the *Códices Azoyu*) has been generally accepted,[10] but the arguments in favor of the other counts are considered more problematic. Caso (1967:48) has flatly disagreed that there could have been significant calendrical variation within the Valley of Mexico, and Nicholson (1971a:70; 1976:290–291) cautions against accepting differing year counts for the Nahua groups in the Basin of Mexico, at least after the conquest of Tenayuca by Azcapotzalco, in approximately 1370. Indeed, during the Tepanec empire and later the Mexica empire, it would seem unduly cumbersome both administratively and ceremonially to have different year counts in use around the lake network of the valley. For example, in the early Colonial sources for central Mexico the New Fire Ceremonies fall consistently in the year Two Reed; the use of differing counts would thus mean that the ceremony was celebrated by the Tenochtitlan Mexica in one year, by the Tlatelolcans in another, by the Texcocans in yet another, and so forth. This seems unworkable and contradicts the chroniclers, who describe the ceremony as being celebrated simultanously throughout the region (e.g., Sahagún 1950–1982 7:29). The use of differing year counts would also cause chaos with respect to the divinatory system(s), because the day counts would differ from place to place, and an auspicious day for commerce in Tenochtitlan might be unsuitable in Texcoco. It is possible that individual tribes in the Basin of Mexico could have once had separate year counts, which they might have brought with them during their migrations, and these could have been standardized when the basin was politically unified, but I find it highly unlikely that the twin cities of Tenochtitlan and Tlatelolco, which were founded by factions of the same (Mexica) tribe, could have had differing counts at any time in their history.

Although a full discussion of the problems of Aztec chronology and the correlation of the native and Christian calendars is outside the scope of this article, I think that most of the discrepancies found in Aztec period dates can be attributed to confusions in the sources, particularly where these sources were copied from one or more earlier records. Nicholson (1971a:66) has mentioned that "pattern history," where similar or significant events are assigned to years that have the same names but belong to different fifty-two-year cycles, often operates in migration legends and may have been present in pre-empire times. Religious and cosmological ties, actual or desired, may also have influenced the dating of events. Prem (1982) has indicated that distortions in chronology can also occur by "temporal telescoping," where the events in a single fifty-two-year cycle are spaced over two or more cycles; the events either keep their same order but unavoidably change their dates and year names or retain their relative position (date and year name) in each cycle but lose their relative sequence. There is also the simple transcriptional error, where an artist paints an event next to the wrong date or a writer simply records the wrong number. Where several of these factors are operating in a single source, the chronology may seem hopelessly confused.

The studies that have led to the proposition of differing year counts were based largely on the analysis of the dates of a relatively few individual events, most of which happened before the consolidation of the Mexica empire. With the fourteenth century, however, Aztec chronology, as recorded in the early Colonial pictorial and textual sources, is surprisingly accurate. Appendix A shows the dates of the founding of Tenochtitlan and the seatings and deaths of the Mexica rulers, plus their reign lengths, as these are given in the *Codex Mendoza* and in thirty-eight other sources from central Mexico. Since almost all the dates in the *Mendoza* pertain to the accession and deaths of the rulers of Tenochtitlan, these events rather than individual conquests or natural phenomena are used to make the correlations between sources. The rulers are listed across the top of the table, and the dates and reign lengths recorded in each document are listed beneath. To aid in making comparisons, the Christian years (in the One Reed=1519 correlation) are presented below each native year; numbers or dates in parentheses are reconstructed.

The appendix indicates how closely the sources agree and how well they correspond to the *Codex Mendoza*. There is great consistency in the reign lengths, and beginning with the accession of Itzcoatl, the hard dates given for the rulers are within a three-year range (except for the *Codex Saville*). The range in dates broadens as one moves back in time, Acamapichtli's accession being placed as early as 1220 by Alva Ixtlilxochitl and as late as 1376 by the *Codex Mendoza* and seven others. Within the individual sources, patterns also emerge; for example, Alva Ixtlilxochitl's veracity must be questioned if only because he assigns reign lengths of fifty-one, eighty-six, and seventy-two years for the first three rulers.

Pattern history is clearly a factor that should be taken into account. The year One Flint, the anniversary of the start of the Aztec migration, is a popular year for the accession of rulers; nine sources give One Flint for the accession of Acamapichtli, and some give One Flint in later cycles for the accession of Itzcoatl and Tizoc. Acamapichtli's reign is generally said or implied to have lasted twenty or twenty-one years, but the *Codex Aubin* king list and the *Crónica X* group (Durán et al.) assign it forty years, perhaps because of a ritual or calendric association.

The one- to three-year inconsistencies in the hard dates of the reigns and the reign lengths are not as problematic as they might first appear, because it is not always clear whether a history is presenting, for a ruler, his accession year or the first full year he is in office, and his death year or the last full year he is in office.[11] Most of the pictorial manuscripts and the chronicles record the death of one ruler and the accession of the next as occurring in the same year. The *Codex Mendoza* does not, however; it gives us pictorially the first full year a ruler is in office and the actual year of his death. With such pictorials as the *Codex Aubin*, reconstructed *Codex of La Magdalena Mixiuca*, and *Fonds mexicain 40*, and with the *Historia de Tlatelolco*, it is difficult to tell whether the actual accession year or the first full year is recorded, except by comparison with the other sources. In some cases the stated reign lengths include both the year of accession and the year of death; Sahagún generally seems to have counted them both, because most of the reign lengths he

gives are a year longer than the norm, and Chimalpahin counted them both in his seventh *Relación* and his *Historia* (Durand-Forest 1976:268).

The monarchical chronology of the *Codex Mendoza*, in addition to being the "official" Tenochtitlan version, agrees, within an acceptable one- to three-year range, with the pattern of reign dates of most other central Mexican sources. Where there are significant variances, these almost always occur with the dates of rulers before Itzcoatl, and many can be explained by a better understanding of the variant sources. Although one cannot completely discount the possibility that some differing year counts may have been functioning in the general region of central Mexico in the Postclassic period, such separate counts seem not to have affected the chronology of the Mexica rulers.

SUMMARY

In summary, part 1 of the *Codex Mendoza* is a victory chronicle rather than a fully detailed secular history. It presents only the reigns of the Mexica rulers and the towns they claimed to have subjugated, omitting mention of other events—such as natural and climatic phenomena, building programs, religious celebrations, and the births of rulers—found in other pictorial histories. This focus on the monarchy and its conquests may have been selected for the first *Mendoza* section as a way of preparing the reader of the codex for the tribute list that follows, for the dynastic conquests were fundamental in creating the tribute empire; either tribute-bearing provinces entered the empire by conquest or they entered voluntarily but under the threat of conquest. Certainly part 1 stresses the strength of the Aztec empire.

In its organizational structure, part 1 of the *Mendoza* combines the features of a year-count annal with a *res gestae*, or event-oriented history, where the reigns of the Mexica rulers are the larger events within which lesser events (the individual conquests) are loosely clustered. The *Mendoza* artist painted for each reign a sequential count of the years from the first full year a ruler was in office through the year of his death (although the scribe recorded the actual years of accession), and these painted counts function to date the reigns rather than the separate conquests. In its chronology the *Mendoza* agrees with most other early Colonial annals and chronicles, so that while part 1 of the *Codex Mendoza* may be the only surviving example of an Aztec victory chronicle in painted form, it fits with the other histories in its sequence and dates for the Mexica monarchy.

EXTRACT 1.
Gerónimo de Mendieta's *Historia eclesiástica*,
chapters 34–36, pertaining to the history of the Mexica
(Mendieta 1945 1:162–168).

CAPÍTULO XXXIV

De los señores que reinaron en México, antes que los españoles viniesen.

Ya queda arriba dicho cómo los chichimecos fueron los primeros que vinieron de otras partes a poblar en esta Nueva España, y tras ellos, al cabo (según dicen) de treinta años, llegaron los de Culhua, que son los tezcucanos, y después algún tiempo vinieron los mexicanos. Por donde parece llevar camino lo que un indio viejo de Tezcuco dijo al P. Fr. Toribio Motolinia, uno de los primeros doce, que inquiría de la venida de los indios que poblaron esta tierra, y concuerda con lo que el otro mesmo

pueblo dijo al P. Olmos, y es que le dijo que todos vinieron de una misma parte, sino que como salieron con escuadrones, o capitanías distinctas, unos se adelantaron más que otros, y no vinieron como gente que caminaba para cierto y conocido lugar, sino con mucho espacio, deteniéndose número de años en algunas partes donde hallaban buen cómodo, aunque por no les contentar del todo, pasaron adelante hasta llegar al lugar y asiento donde agora está la ciudad de México, en el año (según se cuenta) de nuestra redempción de mil y trescientos y veinticuatro. Y este asiento les cuadró mucho por hallarlo abundante de cazas de aves y pescados y marisco con que se poder sustentar y aprovechar en sus granjerías entre los pueblos comarcanos, y por el reparo de las aguas con que no les pudiesen empecer sus vecinos. Y luego se hicieron fuertes en este sitio, tomando por muralla y cerca las aguas y emboscadas de la juncia y carrizales y matorrales de que estaba entonces poblada y llena toda la laguna, que no hallaron el agua descubierta sino en sola una encrucijada de agua limpia desocupada de los matorrales y carrizales, formada a manera de una aspa de S. Andrés. Y casi al medio de la encrucijada hallaron un peñasco, y encima de él un tunal grande florido, donde una águila caudal tenía su manida y pasto, porque aquel lugar estaba poblado de huesos y de muchas plumas de aves. Y por causa de aquel tunal dicen algunos que llamaron aquella población Tenuchtitlan, que en nuestro castellano se interpreta "junto al tunal o en el tunal producido sobre piedra." Aunque también pudo ser (y aun lleva más camino) que le pusiesen este nombre del primer señor que eligieron cuando poblaron en aquel sitio, que se llamó Tenuch, como de nuestra vieja España unos dicen que se llamó Iberia, del famoso río Ebro llamado en latín *Iber*, y otros que se nombró así del rey que primeramente lo pobló, llamado también Ibero. Por otro nombre llamaron a esta ciudad y población México (según algunos dicen), porque la mesma gente que la pobló se llamaban antes Meciti o Mexiti, aunque podría ser también que la denominasen del mastuerzo silvestre, que lo llaman *mexixin*, y hay mucho por el campo en esta tierra. Dicen que el ejército mexicano trajo por caudillos o capitanes diez principales que los regían, y estos se llamaron Ocelopan, Quahpan, Acacitli, Auexotl, Tenuch, Tecineutl, Xomimitl, Xocoyol, Xiuhcaqui, Atototl. Entre estos eligieron, luego como hicieron su asiento, por rey y principal señor a Tenuch, que sería el hijo o descendiente del viejo Iztacmixcohuatl, de quien ellos toman el principio y origen de su genealogía, en cuyo tiempo (que fueron cincuenta y un años de su reinado) subjetaron por fuerza de armas, y hicieron sus vasallos y tributarios a dos pueblos sus comarcanos, que fueron Colhuacan y Tenayuca. En el año de mil y trescientos y setenta y cinco, sucedió en el señorío Acamapichli, en cuyo reinado se conquistaron cuatro pueblos nombrados Cuernavaca, Mizquic, Cuitlahuaca y Xuchimilco. Tuvo este señor por grandeza muchas mujeres, y de ellas hubo muchos hijos, que fué causa de haber muchos caciques y capitanes de la casa real, belicosos en guerras. Según otros dicen, este Acamapichtli tuvo el padre de su mismo nombre que reinó algunos años entre él y Tenuch, y parece lo más cierto, porque dar a Tenuch cincuenta y un años de reinado, es mucho tiempo. Y cuéntanlo de esta manera: que reinando el dicho Acamapichtli primero de este nombre, se levantó un tirano que lo mató a traición, y también quiso matar al hijo que era del mismo nombre, sino que su madre o la ama que lo crió lo escapó de noche, metiéndose con él en una canoa o barco, y llevólo a Coatlichan, cuasi como se escribe de Josaba, que cuando la cruel Athalía por reinar mató a todos los que eran de la sangre real, escondió a Joas, heredero hijo del rey muerto, que después reinó en Jerusalem, sobrino de la misma Josaba. Así acaeció del Acamapichtli segundo de este nombre, que siendo niño fué escapado de las manos del tirano, y se crió algunos años en Coatlichan, y despúes que era grande fué llevado a México, y reconocido por los mexicanos, le dieron el señorío, y tuvo mejor dicha que su padre, porque en su tiempo fué muy ennoblecida la cuidad [sic] de México.

CAPÍTULO XXXV

*En que se prosigue la materia de los señores
que reinaron en México.*

En el año de mil y trescientos y noventa y seis sucedió a Acamapichtli en el señorío, en su hijo llamado Huitzilihuitzin. Este amplió mucho el señorío mexicano, porque en su tiempo conquistó ocho pueblos o provincias, que fueron Tultitlan, Cuauhtitlan, Chalco, Tulancingo, Xaltocan, Otumba, Tezcuco, Aculma, y también siguiendo el estilo de su padre, tuvo muchas mujeres y hijos. En el año de mil y cuatrocientos y diez y siete, muerto Huitzilihuitzin sucedió en el reino Chimalpopocatzin, hijo suyo, según algunos, y según otros, hermano. Este reinó solo diez años, porque le atajaron la vida y lo mataron los de Culhua que eran sus contrarios. Y también mataron con él al señor que entonces era de Culhuacan, por ser del linaje de los señores mexicanos, que lo habían ellos puesto de su mano

cuando conquistaron a Culhuacan. Y esto no fué en guerra, sino que los tomaron desapercibidos. Este ganó a Tequixquiac, y conquistó segunda vez a Chalco, que se había rebelado. En el año de mil y cuatrocientos y veintisiete sucedió en el señorío Izcoatzin, hermano de Chimalpopocatzin y hijo de Acamapichtli. Y según esto, todos tres los que reinaron tras él eran sus hijos, porque era la costumbre de estos indios, que muerto el señor, sucedíanle los hermanos (si los tenía), y a los tíos sucedía después el hijo del mayor hermano, aunque en algunas partes sucedía el hijo al padre. Mas lo de los hermanos era lo más común. Este Izcoatzin fué valiente por su persona y venturoso en armas, subjetó al señorío de México muchos pueblos y provincias, y entre ellas a Tacuba, Azcapuzalco, Cuycacan, y en ellas edificó muchos templos, y amplió los de México como hombre devoto en las cosas de su religión. Tuvo también muchas mujeres y hijos, y murió al cabo de trece años de su reinado. En el año de mil y cuatrocientos y cuarenta, sucedió en el señorío de Moctezuma el viejo, llamado así: *huehue* Moteczuma, que quiere decir "viejo," nieto de Acamapichtli, hijo de Huitzilihuitzin: fué belicoso en armas y conquistó treinta y tres pueblos. Muerto Moteczuma el viejo, sin hijos varones, heredó el reino una su hija que estaba casada con un muy cercano pariente suyo, llamado Tezozomotli, y de él hubo tres hijos, el primero, llamado Axayacatzin, padre de Moteczuma el mozo. El segundo, Tizocicatzin. El tercero, Ahuizotzin, que todos tres reinaron sucesivamente uno tras otro. En el año de mil y cuatrocientos y sesenta y nueve entró en el señorío el primero de estos hermanos, dicho Axayacatzin. Este conquistó treinta y siete pueblos, y entre ellos al Tlatelulco, su convecino, siendo señor de él Moquihuix, hombre poderoso: y por ser bullicioso, dando ocasión al señor de México de trabar guerra con él, hubo entre ellos grandes batallas en que el Moquihuix, yendo huyendo de vencida, se retrujo a un templo, y porque un sacerdote se lo reputó a cobardía, se despeñó de despecho de un pináculo alto, de que murió. El señor de México consiguió la victoria, y desde entonces fueron los de Tlatelulco vasallos del señor de México, pagándole sus tributos. Fué Axayacatzin valientísimo en armas, y vicioso en mujeres, y así tuvo muchos hijos. Fué soberbio, y por ende temido y no amado de sus vasallos. Aprobó y guardó las leyes de Huehue Moteczuma, y el discurso de su señorío fueron doce años. En el año de mil y cuatrocientos y ochenta y dos, sucedió en el señorío Tizocicatzin, hermano de su antecesor. Conquistó durante su señorío catorce pueblos. Fué por extremo valiente y bellicoso en guerras, y antes que sucediese en el señorío, hizo en armas cosas señaladas, por donde alcanzó título y estado de Tlacatecatl, habiendo sido capitán general de los ejércitos mexicanos, que fué medio propincuo para conseguir el señorío de México. Porque era punto y escalón el de Tlacatecatl para en vacando el señorío suceder en él, como también lo fué en sus antecesores, porque sin preceder semejantes méritos, no podían subir al señorío. Tuvo por estado tener muchas mujeres, en las cuales hubo muchos hijos; fué hombre grave en su gobierno, temido y acatado. Era de buen natural, inclinado a cosas virtuosas, y buen republicano. Mandó enteramente guardar las leyes de sus antecesores, y fué celoso de hacer castigar los malos vicios, y con esto tuvo bien regida su república y vasallos todo el discurso de su señorío, que fueron cinco años. En el año de mil y cuatrocientos y ochenta y seis, sucedió en el señorío el último de los tres hermanos, llamado Ahuizotzin, hombre valeroso y gran guerrero, por donde alcanzó el título de Tlacatecatl, que es como gran capitán, y tras él el señorío supremo, y en su tiempo conquistó cuarenta y cinco pueblos. Fué virtuoso y celoso de la guarda de las leyes de sus antecesores. Vino a encumbrarse en gran majestad, porque tenía la mayor parte de la Nueva España debajo de su señorío, que le reconocían vasallaje y pagaban tributos, mediante los cuales vino su estado a tanta cumbre y alteza: ca como poderoso y magnánimo hacía grandes mercedes y franquezas a los suyos. Fué de templada y benigna condición, por lo cual sus vasallos y capitanes lo amaban grandemente, y le acataban con gran reverencia. Y por ser él muy alegre de condición, y aficionado a música, por darle contento le festejaban cuotidianamente con diversas músicas y otros pasatiempos sin vacar las noches. Tuvo por autoridad de su estado y grandeza muchas mujeres, y de ellas muchos hijos. Reinó diez y seis años, al cabo de los cuales murió de muerte natural.

CAPÍTULO XXXVI

Del último señor que tuvieron los mexicanos de su nación.

En el año de mil y quinientos y dos, sucedió en el señorío Moteczuma el segundo de este nombre, hijo de Axayacatzin, en la cual sazón estaba ya el señorío de México en gran potestad, y él por su mucha y demasiada gravedad y severidad lo engrandeció en grado supremo. Y antes de lo alcanzar tuvo méritos de Tlacatecatl, como capitán que fué valentísimo, mediante lo cual y sus buenas habilidades vino a señorearse de cuasi toda la Nueva España, y ser como emperador en ella, teniendo reyes y muchos grandes señores por vasallos y tributarios. Y como hombre sabio, y astuto, y entendido en las artes de astrología y nigromancia (según ellos las alcanzaban), fué muy temido de los suyos; tanto, que cuando le hablaban, por el mucho temor que le tenían, no le osaban mirar a la cara, teniendo la cabeza inclinada y los ojos en el suelo, por la gran majestad que les representaba, y por el trono en que le veían puesto. Fué algo cruel, aunque buen republicano. Y no solo aprobó y guardó las leyes y fueros de sus antecesores, mas aun añadió otras que le pareció faltaban. Y para la guarda de ellas puso grandes y graves penas, y fué irremisible en la ejecución de ellas. Dió principio y orden de poner jueces ordinarios y supremos como alcaldes, de los cuales, por vía de agravio, apelaban para su consejo: y en él tenía sus oidores, hombres de buen gobierno y prudentes, y para ellos diputada su sala en su propio palacio. Tenía otra sala de consejo de guerra donde se determinaban las cosas de la milicia, y se proveían capitanes para sus ejércitos en las conquistas que hacía. Y de estas salas había suplicación para la misma persona real de cosas calificadas; pero todas ellas se determinaban en muy breve tiempo. Por su mucha majestad tuvo muchas casas y grandes, llenas de mujeres, hijas de señores; y las más de las que así eran señoras tuvo por legítimas mujeres, según sus ritos y ceremonias, y de ellas tuvo muchos hijos; pero los más respetados fueron los legítimos. Proveyó Moteczuma en cada pueblo de las provincias a él subjetas, gobernadores y calpixques que servían como corregidores y justicias, y los gobernadores predominaban a los demás; y todos ellos eran hombres principales mexicanos, y según sus méritos más o menos, se les daban los cargos; y tenían por oficio el mantener justicia a los tales pueblos, y cobrar los tributos reales, y hacer guarda para que no se rebelasen. Durante el señorío de este Moteczuma, conquistaron los mexicanos cuarenta y cuatro pueblos. A los diez y seis años de su señorío tuvo nueva, por vía de ciertos españoles que aportaron a la costa, de cómo los navíos en que venía Hernando Cortés habían de ser allí dentro de tantos meses, en lo cual los mexicanos tuvieron cuenta y aviso, y así se cumplió. Y a los diez y siete años de su señorío llegó el marqués que después fué del Valle, con su gente a la ciudad de México; y otro año siguiente, que fué a los diez y ocho del dicho señorío, murió, siendo de edad de cincuenta y tres años; porque al tiempo que sucedió en el señorío, tenía treinta y cinco; y luego el año siguiente, después de su muerte, se ganó y conquistó la ciudad de México por el dicho Hernando Cortés. Y porque de las grandezas y majestad del Moteczuma está mucho escripto por otros autores (a los cuales me remito), basta lo aquí referido de su reinado y persona.

EXTRACT 2.

Leyenda de los Soles, folio 43v,
pertaining to the history of the Mexica
(Velázquez 1975:127–128, Spanish translation).

He aquí que llegaron a la tierra, aquí a Tenochtitlan, que no era más que tular y cañaveral, donde padecieron trabajos cincuenta años. Nadie era su rey, sino que aun por sí solos entendían los mexicanos en lo que les tocaba. 51. *2 calli*. Colhuacan. Tenayocan. He aquí lo que fué la conquista de los mexicanos: solamente dos lugares, Colhuacan y Tenayocan.

Allí después se entronizó el señor Acamapichtli; reinó veintiún años. 29. *1 tecpatl*. Xochmilco, Cuitláhuac, Cuauhnáhuac, Mízquic. He aquí su conquista: conquistó a Xochmilco, Cuitláhuac, Mízquic y Cuauhnáhuac. Cuatro lugares conquistó Acamapich.

He aquí que reinó el hijo de Acamapichtli, su nombre Huitzilíhuitl; reinó veintiún años. 21. *9 calli*. Xaltocan, Acolman, Otompan, Chalco, Tetzcoco, Tollantzinco, Cuauhtitlan y Toltitlan: he aquí lo que fué su conquista. A ocho pueblos conquistó Huitzilíhuitl.

He aquí que reinó el hijo de Huitzilíhuitl, su nombre Chimalpopocatzin; reinó diez años. Chalco, Tequixquiac. 20 años. *4 tochtli*. He aquí su conquista. Dos pueblos conquistó Chimalpopocatzin.

He aquí que reinó el hijo de Acamapichtli, su nombre Itzcohuatzin; reinó trece años. 13. *1 tecpatl*. La conquista de Itzcohuatzin fué de todos estos lugares: Azcapotzalco, Tlacopan, Atlacuihuayan, Coyohuacan, Mixcóhuac, Cuauhximalpan, Cuahuacan, Teocalhuiyacan, Tecpan, Huitzitzillapan, Cuauhnáhuac, Tetzcoco, Cuauhtitlan, Xochmilco, Cuitláhuac, Mízquic, Tlatilolco, Itztépec, Xiuhtépec, Tzaqualpan, Chalco, Yohuallan, Tepequacuilco y Cueçallan.

He aquí que reinó el hijo de Huitzilíhuitl, su nombre Ilhuicaminatzin Moteucçomatzin el viejo; reinó veintinueve años que estuvo. 29. *1 calli*. He aquí lo que fué la conquista de Moteucçomatzin el viejo: Coaixtlahuacan, Chalco, Chiconquiyauhco, Tepoztlan, Yauhtépec, Atlatlauhcan, Totollapan, Huaxtépec, Tecpatépec, Yohualtépec, Xiuhtépec, Quiyauhteopan, Tlalcoçauhtitlan, Tlachco, Cuauhnáhuac, Tepequacuilco, Cohuatlan, Xillotépec, Itzcuincuitlapilco, Tlapacoyan, Chapolicxitla, Tlatlauhquitépec, Yacapichtlan, Cuauhtochco y Cuetlaxtlan.

He aquí que reinó el nieto de los dos reyes Moteucçomatzin el viejo e Itzcohuatzin, su nombre Axayacatzin; reinó doce años. 12. *4 tochtli*. Estos son todos los lugares de la conquista de Axayacatzin: Tlatilolco, Matlatzinco, Xiquipilco, Tzinacantépec, Tlacotépec, Tenantzinco, Xochiyacan, Teotenanco, Caliimayan, Metépec, Ocoyácac, Capolloac, Atlapolco, Qua . . .

NOTES

1. A gloss on the bottom of folio 18r states that part 1 ends on this folio, but the note was written by someone other than the principal *Mendoza* scribe; and the historical material effectively ends on 16v with the conquests of the last ruler, Motecuhzoma Xocoyotzin. Folios 17v and 18r, which are separated from the historical section by the blank page 17r, record conquered towns ruled by Mexica-appointed lords.

2. Although it was brought to my attention at the 44th International Congress of Americanists (held in Manchester, September 5–10, 1982, where a preliminary version of this article was presented) that ledgers and economic documents have traditionally commenced on the verso sides of folios, it would seem unlikely that the format of such numerical records would influence the arrangement of chronicles and essays.

3. Although Robertson (1959:98) has referred to this illustration as a frontispiece, thus implying that it is extraneous and introductory, I see the painting as the first substantive part of the history. Mexica imperial history effectively begins with the founding of Tenochtitlan.

4. Van Zantwijk (1958:65) called it a *tecpan* (lord's house).

5. See Glass and Robertson (1975) for the bibliography of the pictorial manuscripts mentioned in this article.

6. See Umberger (1987:442–444) for an argument in support of the idea that the New Fire Ceremony was changed from One Rabbit to Two Reed.

7. See Nicholson (1971a:45–50) for an extensive listing and discussion of other secular histories.

8. The continuous year count in the *Anales de Tula* is segmented by small breaks, but these breaks do not correspond to known events or reign lengths.

9. This holds true also for the *Tira de Tepechpan*, which records both Te-pechpan and Tenochtitlan history. Events related to Tepechpan appear above the continuous horizontal line of years, and those of Tenochtitlan are painted below. The ethnic group and location of the events is understood to be Tepechpan (above) and Tenochtitlan (below), except when place signs indicate other peoples or towns.

10. Hanns J. Prem (1982), who is conducting a computer-assisted analysis of the chronological problem, has recently denied the existence of a separate Matlatzinca count.

11. John Glass (1974:14–15) has pointed out this problem in his reconstruction of the *Codex of La Magdalena Mixiuca*.

CHAPTER 5

The Imperial Tribute Roll
of the *Codex Mendoza*

Frances F. Berdan

The second section of the *Codex Mendoza* is an accounting of Aztec imperial tribute. As reflected in part 1 of this same document, warfare and military conquest were activities central to the Aztec way of life. With each successful conquest, the Aztecs gained territory, subjects, and economic resources. All of these were placed in the service of the conquerors through the institution of tribute.

Specifically, tribute refers to revenue collected by a militarily dominant state from its conquered regions. The payment of tribute serves symbolically to express the dominance of one political entity over another, provides revenue for the dominant state (thus underwriting its complex political structure), stimulates production of specified goods in conquered areas, and may also involve certain contractual agreements such as protection of the subjugated region from invasion by other groups.

The management of tribute is facilitated by a formal accounting system—ideally, to communicate tribute demands, to register "resources on hand," and to keep track of dispersals. Part 2 of the *Codex Mendoza* represents a tribute tally serving at least one of these accounting functions (see below). As such, what exactly does the *Codex Mendoza* reveal about Aztec tribute, and how does this information coincide with the data contained in other tribute documents?

These questions are approached by first considering part 2 of the *Codex Mendoza* as a document—by studying its format and content, and by comparing it to other similar tribute documents. The institution of tribute in the Aztec empire is then discussed, followed by an analysis of three persistent problems associated with the *Codex Mendoza* part 2: the extent of imperial control over the tribute collected, whether assessments or receipts were recorded, and the usable "life span" of a document such as the *Codex Mendoza* tribute tally.

CODEX MENDOZA, PART 2: THE DOCUMENT
Format and Content

Part 2 of the *Codex Mendoza* consists of thirty-nine leaves of European paper (see essay by Ruwet, this volume). With the exception of the first three pictorial pages, the format follows a standardized pattern: the name glyphs of tributary towns line the left-hand margin, marching from top to bottom, and continue along the bottom of the page if necessary. The tribute required of those towns by their Aztec overlords fills the remainder of the page, with articles of clothing (cloaks, loincloths, and women's tunics and skirts) at the top[1] and elaborate warrior costumes next.[2] These are followed by bins of foodstuffs[3]—maize, beans, perhaps chia and amaranth seeds—and then miscellaneous items such as paper, honey, gourd bowls, feathers, or woven mats.

The first four major provinces listed—Petlacalco, Acolhuacan, Quauhnahuac, and Huaxtepec—gave a wide variety of warrior costumes.[4] Since each style had to be depicted separately, this required a good deal of illustrative space on each of those folios. For these four provinces, the tribute, and in some cases the towns, spills over onto another page.[5] In two other cases, more than one province is listed on a single folio (Malinalco/Xocotitlan and Tlalcoçauhtitlan/Quiauhteopan/Yoaltepec).[6] Otherwise, the document settles into a one-province-per-page listing of towns and tribute.

All the pictorial pages are annotated in Spanish, typically providing the indigenous names of towns as well as descriptions of specific tribute items. With the exception of the first and last pictorial folios (17v and 55r), each provincial tribute tally is accompanied by a Spanish commentary describing, usually in some detail, the pictorial material. The comments and explanations are frequently helpful, although the reader should heed the cautions expressed by the commentator himself. On folio 71v he makes some general corrections, complains about the short time he had for the task (blaming his problems on the tardiness of the "Indians, who came to agreement late"),[7] and apologizes for his style. Since the commentator himself is somewhat insecure, and indeed errors can be found in both the annotations and the commentary, some care should be taken in glamorizing these written additions as "facts."

Probably the most perplexing folios of the second section of the *Codex Mendoza* are the first two: folios 17v and 18r. In the first place, it is difficult to determine whether they belong "officially" in part 1 or part 2. The Spanish annotator wrote quite clearly, at the bottom of folio 18r, "end of the first part of this history," certainly meaning that these two folios were to be included with the "history of conquests." Yet both Clark (1938 1 : 55, 58–59) and Barlow (1949a : 126–130) group these folios with the tribute section. In this determination, Barlow may have been influenced by the fact that these two folios also appear in the related *Matrícula de Tributos* (a tribute record, not a military history), although he does suggest the possibility that the *Matrícula* may at one time have included a history section, and only these two remnants remain (Barlow

1949a: 127). Clark may have drawn his inference from the Spanish notation associated with folio 18r:

> The towns drawn and named on this and the preceding page were governed by caciques and chiefs from Mexico appointed by the lords of Mexico for the protection, and good conduct, of the natives. These chiefs, besides being held responsible for suppressing revolt, had entire charge of collecting, and forwarding, the rentals and tribute which these towns were obliged to render to the State of Mexico. (Clark 1938 1:58)

The implication of the Spanish comment is that the folios illustrate sustained obligations; they do not appear to reference a one-time historical event, but rather an event (or series of events) which developed ongoing, institutionalized relationships. If that is indeed the case, then these folios are more consistent with the tribute section of the *Mendoza* than with the event-oriented historical section (see map 2 and page descriptions for folios 17v and 18r).

The balance of the *Codex Mendoza* part 2 is more straightforward. With only three exceptions (Tlatelolco, Tepeacac, and Xoconochco) the towns are neatly and predictably listed, and the tribute is orderly and in recognizable material items.

The page for Tlatelolco (folio 19r) makes pictographic mention of the conquest of Tlatelolco by Tenochtitlan, an event of signal importance to the Mexica.[8] The portraits at the bottom of the page with their accompanying place glyphs, according to the Spanish commentary, indicate when, by whom, and to whom the tribute was first paid—Quauhtlatoa and Moquiuixtli to Itzcoatl and Axayacatl. These juxtaposed glyphs probably indicate separate historical events with some lasting consequences—the intervening Tenochtitlan reign of Motecuhzoma Ilhuicamina is not illustrated, thus suggesting a temporal discontinuity. While it is well documented that Tlatelolco fell to Tenochtitlan in 1473, Barlow (1945: 208) presents suggestive evidence that Tlatelolco may have paid tribute to Tenochtitlan as early as 1431; however, the payments may not have been formalized, or even continuous, until its "official" conquest under Axayacatl.

Like the hypothesized tribute of the Citlaltepec communities (see volume 2, page descriptions), some of the Tlatelolco tribute was in the form of services. The Tlatelolcans were to maintain (in repair) the temple of Huitznahuac; this is specified as a continuous, rather than one-time, obligation. Periods of tribute collection are indicated pictographically (as four glyphs together signifying eighty days); this occurs for only one other province, Xoconochco, where the two periods of tribute collection (for the months of Ochpaniztli and Tlacaxipehualiztli) are drawn.

The second rather deviant page, Tepeacac (folio 42r), is the only page to specify warrior captives as tribute even though Tepeacac was not the only center responsible for such tribute.[9] Nonetheless, these were rather special prisoners, since the appetites of the Mexica solar gods especially preferred the hearts of the valiant warriors from Tlaxcala and Huexotzinco (Berdan 1982:114). Perhaps these offerings constituted a major portion of the tribute due from Tepeacac province.

While at first glance the page representing the province of Xoconochco (folio 47r) appears similar to the other tribute pages, it may in fact have been designed quite differently (see Gasco and Voorhies 1989). In the *Matrícula de Tributos*, glyphs for the months of Ochpaniztli and Tlacaxipehualiztli stand in the upper left and upper right corners, respectively. The page is visually divided into vertical halves, each half associated with one of the month glyphs

MAP 1: The Valley of Mexico, 1519

Map 1. Towns listed on folio 17v as probable tribute-paying communities. Towns shown in parentheses are provisionally located.

(fig. 1). Nearly identical items of tribute are represented on each half, although this division is more distinct in the *Matrícula de Tributos* than in the *Mendoza*. Does this mean that half of the tribute on the page was rendered during Ochpaniztli, and the other half during the month of Tlacaxipehualiztli? Or was the entire tribute listed due on each of those months? Interpretation of these glyphs is further complicated by the omission of the usual "This tribute was given every eighty days" formula; presumably that sort of information was contained in the month glyphs. Furthermore, in the *Matrícula*, the strings of jade beads are annotated for delivery every twenty days, an unusual demand and perhaps an error. Nonetheless, the arrangement of tribute for Xoconochco province is certainly suggestive of a variation in tribute period designation: that each half of the page represented the tribute payable during the appropriate month. If this is the case, the usual tribute totals for this province would need to be halved, and I have followed this procedure in tabulating tribute totals (appendices B and C).

Comparisons with Other Tribute Tallies

It is difficult, if not impossible, to discuss the second section of the *Codex Mendoza* without reference to the *Matrícula de Tributos*, a pictographic record of the towns and tribute goods of thirty-three provinces of the Aztec empire in the early sixteenth century.[10] Likewise, the textual *Información of 1554* of Velasco and Quesada, based on a pictorial book, or *libro de pinturas* (Scholes and Adams

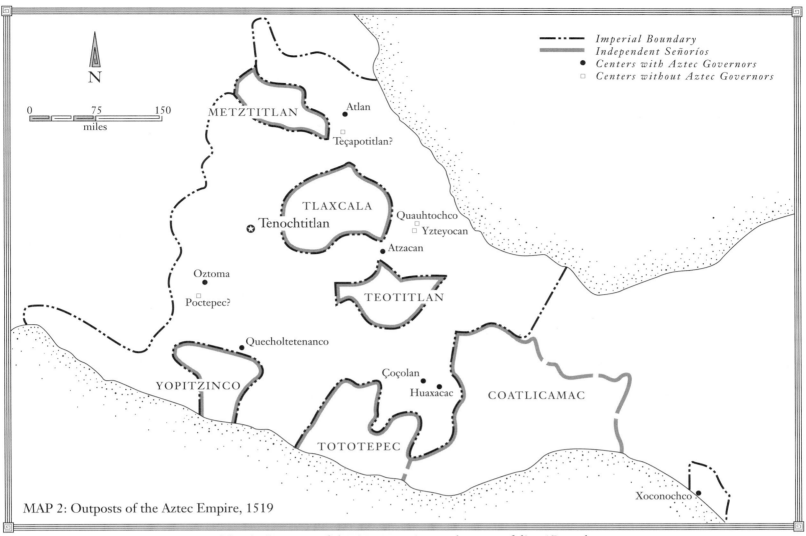

Map 2. Outposts of the Aztec empire, as shown on folios 17v and 18r of the *Codex Mendoza*.

1957:61), provides similar province-by-province tribute tallies.[11]

The *Codex Mendoza* part 2 has been considered by some scholars to be a direct copy of the *Matrícula de Tributos* (see especially Barlow 1949a:4–5; Scholes and Adams 1957:9; Robertson 1959: 99–100). Borah and Cook (1963) feel there is no such direct relationship between the two documents, but that both were copies from a single indigenous prototype, which they label "Prototype A." They propose that this lost pre-Conquest document was in screen-fold form, and that both the *Matrícula de Tributos* and the *Codex Mendoza* part 2 are post-Conquest documents. While this is indisputably true for the *Mendoza*, there is no definitive evidence for labeling the *Matrícula* a post-Conquest pictorial.[12]

Although in most respects the documents are remarkably similar and often identical, there are important differences in the pictorial representations, and even more dramatic disagreements in the annotations of the two tribute tallies.

The sequence of town glyphs on each page is essentially the same in the two documents. Although in the *Mendoza* they begin in the upper left corner and proceed down the left-hand side and along the bottom, their order of presentation is virtually identical to that of the *Matrícula*, which begins the listing in the bottom left corner, proceeding along the bottom and up the right-hand side if necessary. Stylistically, most glyphs that have any horizontal orientation are shown facing left in the *Matrícula*, and right in the *Mendoza*. Robertson (1959:105) considers that the *Matrícula* scribe composed these figures "against the direction of reading," while

the *Mendoza* scribe wrote them *with* or toward the direction of the reading.[13] He also observes that the *Matrícula* pattern is the same as that found in the *Codex Borbonicus tonalamatl*.[14]

More significantly, the order in which classes of goods are presented in the *Mendoza* is reversed from their manner of presentation in the *Matrícula*. While indigenously the codex would be read from bottom to top, this has been altered in the *Mendoza* so that reading proceeds from top to bottom (in the European manner), at the same time maintaining the same general order and sequence of tribute (i.e., first, clothing; second, military insignia; third, bins of foodstuffs and miscellaneous items; fig. 2).[15] This reversal is doubtless an artifact of acculturation—that is, an adaptation to the European style of writing and reading. More telling examples of this process of reversal are found on folios 35r and 40r of the *Codex Mendoza* and their corresponding folios in the *Matrícula*, 8r and 10v. In both documents, these represent the only cases where more than one province was assigned to a single page. In the case of the *Matrícula*, the divisions between the provinces are made by distinct vertical lines; in the *Mendoza*, the division in the one case is not distinctly made (35r), while in the second case (40r) the divisions are indicated by horizontal lines, orienting the reading of the toponymic glyphs and tribute goods from left to right rather than from bottom to top (fig. 3).

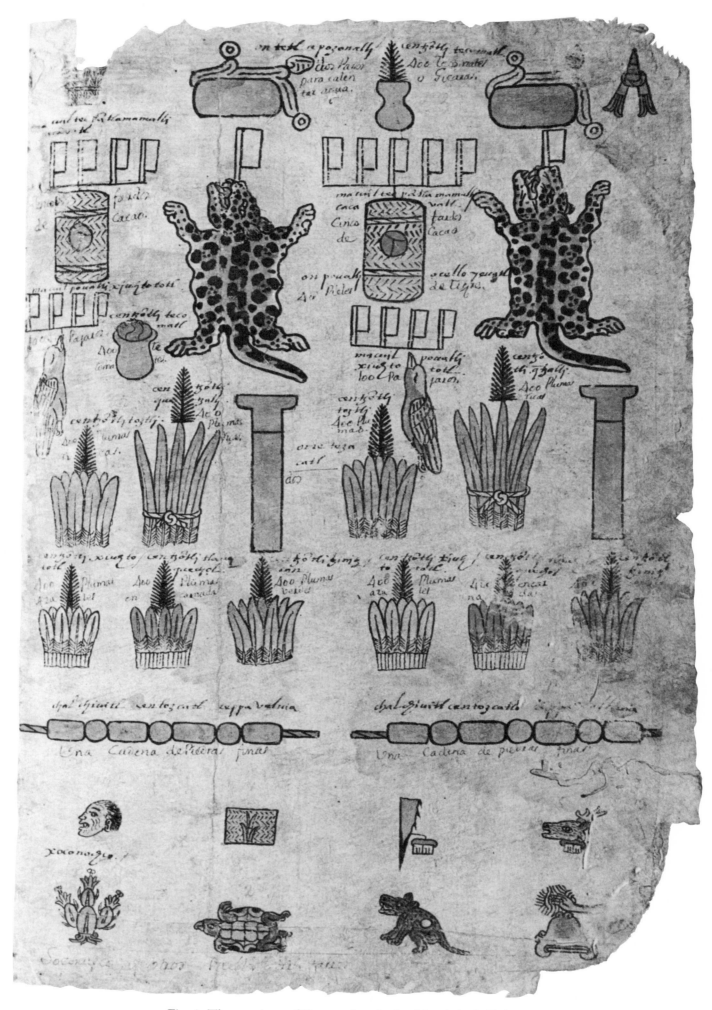

Fig. 1. The province of Xoconochco in the *Matrícula de Tributos.*
The arrangement into halves is clearer here than in the *Mendoza*
(*Matrícula de Tributos* 1980: folio 13r).

Fig. 2. Tribute from the province of Huaxtepec, as recorded in
the *Matrícula de Tributos* (1980: folio 4r).

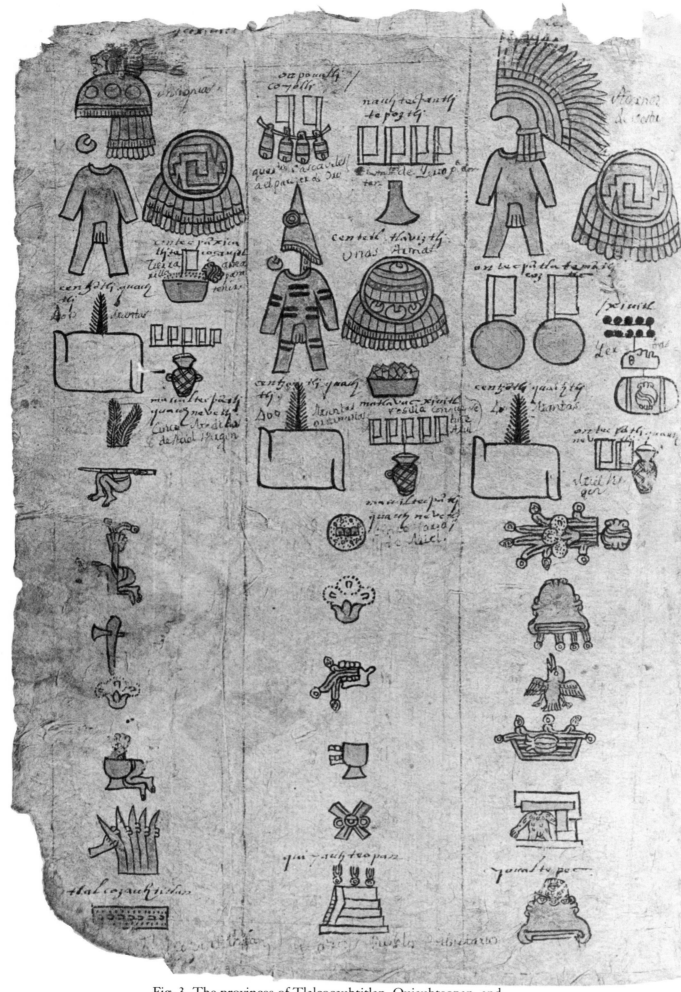

Fig. 3. The provinces of Tlalcoçauhtitlan, Quiauhteopan, and Yoaltepec as seen in the *Matrícula de Tributos*. The vertical arrangement is in contrast to the horizontal orientation in the *Codex Mendoza* (*Matrícula de Tributos* 1980: folio 10v).

It is these same pages that provide important clues to the format of the *libro de pinturas* consulted by the informants of the 1554 tribute document. In both the *Mendoza* (40r) and the *Matrícula* (10v), the initial town glyphs indicate the three provincial capitals: Tlalcoçauhtitlan, Quiauhteopan, and Yoaltepec. These glyphs are found at the extreme left on the page (*Mendoza*) and at the bottom (*Matrícula*). The *Información of 1554*, however, lists no such provinces. In their place it lists Çacatlan, Tequisquitlan, and Ichcaatoyaque. Two of these, Çacatlan and Ichcaatoyaque, are included among the *Mendoza* and *Matrícula* town glyphs, but as the final entries of the first and third provinces mentioned above. If the *libro de pinturas* had been in the format of the *Matrícula*, the informants could have easily read the vertical column of town glyphs from top to bottom in the European manner (after all, it *is* 1554). It would be illogical to assume that they would read from right to left, as would have been necessary if they were copying from a European-style document such as the *Mendoza*. It would seem, therefore, that the 1554 informants were deriving their information from an indigenous-style document, one less influenced by European patterns than the *Codex Mendoza*.

The third provincial capital in the 1554 document, Tequisquitlan, does not appear in either codex. There are two possibilities for its inclusion: it could have been present in a document other than the *Matrícula* as the final town glyph, or, more likely, it is an alternative interpretation of the glyph which does appear in the codices. The glyph, a circle with small dark dots and a set of teeth,[16] is annotated as Xala in the *Mendoza*, and not annotated at all in the *Matrícula*. It is possible that a different indigenous informant could have interpreted the same glyph differently, perhaps as Tequisquitlan.[17] Indeed, Barlow (1949a:84) could not identify or locate this Xala in his pioneering study of Aztec imperial geography.

That the elusive *libro de pinturas* was an indigenously styled document is also supported by the order in which tribute goods are presented. This order is reversed from that of the *Matrícula*, but consistent with the notion that the interpreters were reading an indigenous pictorial in the European manner, from top to bottom. Cloaks, for example, are regularly listed as the final items.[18]

Pictorially, the *Codex Mendoza* part 2 may be compared to the more indigenous *Matrícula de Tributos* according to (1) omissions in the *Mendoza* (items found in the *Matrícula* but absent in the *Mendoza*), (2) additions in the *Mendoza* (items not included in the *Matrícula*), and (3) variations on items found in both documents.

1. Omissions in the *Mendoza*: Although parts of several items are lacking in the *Mendoza*, there is only one case of an entire object being omitted. For the province of Hueypochtlan, one entire warrior costume and shield are missing from the six shown in the *Matrícula*. Furthermore, of the five that do appear in the *Mendoza*, one is a *coyotl* (coyote) type, not found for this province in the *Matrícula*.[19]

2. Additions in the *Mendoza*: The *Mendoza* frequently represents more bins of foodstuffs than are found in the *Matrícula*. This occurs only when the *Matrícula* illustrates a single bin of mixed grains. In the eleven provinces where this occurs, the *Mendoza* shows two bins, one annotated as maize and amaranth, the other as beans and chia (or maize and chia, beans and amaranth).[20] In the nine other cases where staple foodstuffs are shown, the number of bins is identical, but in only one of these instances are the pictographs an exact copy (folio 41r: Chalco). In three of the remaining cases two bins of combined maize, beans, and seeds (*Matrícula*) are transformed into two bins, one each of maize (and amaranth or chia) and beans (and chia or amaranth) in the *Mendoza* (folios 30r,

32r, and 34r in the *Mendoza*). A further case involves three combined bins in the *Matrícula*, represented by three bins in the *Mendoza*, one of beans (and amaranth) and two of maize (and chia; folio 33r in the *Mendoza*).

Another instance involves the usual combined bin in the *Matrícula*, corresponding to a single bin of maize (and chia) in the *Mendoza* (folio 36r in the *Mendoza*). Finally, there are three *Mendoza* provinces (Petlacalco, Axocopan, and Atotonilco de Pedraza: folios 20v, 27r, and 28r) which each offered two bins of mixed foodstuffs; presumably, these would have been represented by a single bin in the *Matrícula*. Although it at first appears that the foodstuff tribute represented in the *Mendoza* is substantially greater than that listed in the *Matrícula*, the annotations (discussed below) suggest different conclusions.

3. Variations: There are a number of cases where similar objects are illustrated, but with some variations. The greatest number of these are in the area of quantities and measures. Number symbols are missing in the *Mendoza* on some warrior costumes and shields[21] but added on a costume (folio 26r: Quauhtitlan) and a jar of honey (folio 40r: Yoaltepec).[22] Measures of cloak length are present in the *Matrícula* but absent or reduced in the *Mendoza* for the provinces of Malinalco and Coayxtlahuacan (folios 35r, 43r). For Tlatlauhquitepec (folio 51r), measures of cloak length are added in the *Mendoza* where they are lacking in the *Matrícula*. Other differences include the substitution of a plain cloak figure in the *Mendoza* for a decorated (apparently quilted) one in the *Matrícula* (folio 24v: Huaxtepec) and numerous variations in designs of cloaks, bowls, and warrior costumes.[23]

Most of these discrepancies are of such a nature that they could have occurred in the process of copying, especially the omission of an item in the later pictorial (*Mendoza*) and variations in order, number symbols, and specific styles. The inclusion of additional bins of foodstuffs in the *Mendoza* is more troublesome, and is considered below.

There are numerous *Mendoza* and *Matrícula* tribute items that are entirely absent in the *Información of 1554*: lime, chile, salt, mats and seats, pottery jars, arrows, smoking canes, firewood, and certain precious stones. On the other hand, the *Información* occasionally adds items, notably rubber, *pinolli*, a bird, and some luxury items. Major tribute items, such as foodstuffs, clothing, and military costumes, however, are well represented. Appendix C provides a comparison of these three documents in terms of total tribute rendered.

Such differences seem significant enough to rule out the possibility that the 1554 document was derived from the extant *Matrícula de Tributos*, suggesting that another similar pictorial must have been in existence recording empirewide tribute, listing the provinces in the same order, and agreeing generally, though not specifically, with the information presented in the *Matrícula*.

The *Matrícula de Tributos* is annotated in both Nahuatl and Spanish. The Spanish annotations are, in at least one indisputable case, translations of the Nahuatl ones rather than direct descriptions of the pictographs.[24] They are also very general in character, while the Nahuatl annotations are rich in detail. These annotations, Nahuatl and Spanish, take the form of statements on types of goods, quantities of goods, and periods of tribute collection. Spanish annotations of the *Mendoza* and the *Información of 1554* provide comparable types of information.

The most nagging problem with the annotations lies in the realm of foodstuffs. Bins of foodstuffs are annotated infrequently in Nahuatl. The *Matrícula* lists only maize and beans, the *Mendoza* adds chia and amaranth. The pictographic symbol for such tribute in the *Matrícula* is generally a wooden bin with a kernel of corn, a bean, and several small dots surrounding them. As already discussed, the *Mendoza* generally illustrates maize and beans in separate bins, adding the small dots to each of these. The differences between the documents could possibly be tied to differing sixteenth-century interpretations of the pictographic symbols. One *Matrícula* annotation (folio 6r) efficiently makes reference to *cuezcomatli in etl cintli* (bin of beans and maize).[25] As plurals are not marked in Nahuatl for inanimate objects, this could be ambiguous: a single bin including both beans and maize (as in the *Matrícula*) or a bin each of maize and beans (as annotated in the *Mendoza*). If the latter interpretation were made, perhaps relying more on oral transmission than strict visual copying, two separate bins as seen in the *Mendoza* could have resulted, corresponding to the single mixed bin in the *Matrícula*. The annotations of the *Mendoza* further complicate matters, however; they generally indicate two bins for each one represented, doubling that tribute.

The Spanish annotations of the *Mendoza* mention four foods: maize, beans, chia, and amaranth. Borah and Cook (1963) accept these annotations and apply them directly to the *Matrícula*, although there is nothing conclusive in the *Matrícula* to indicate the presence of these two additional seeds. They suggest that the single bin shown represents all four food staples, the chia and amaranth both included in the small black dots. They also suggest that each bin in the *Matrícula* represents four bins, one of each foodstuff. Logically and realistically, it would seem likely that separate bins are meant, rather than a single bin of combined foodstuffs. It is possible that bins of each were offered in alternation, based on seasonal or regional availability. It is also possible that only one of the small seeds is meant, and that the addition of the other is a result of the *Mendoza* scribe's penchant for illustrating separate bins.

If a choice of foodstuffs is to be made, the most likely candidate is the chia.[26] This item is mentioned more frequently than the amaranth in these and other documents, although both chia and amaranth were stored in Motecuhzoma's *petlacalco* or storehouse (Sahagún 1950–1982 8:44). In the 1554 *Información*, amaranth is dropped as a tribute item after the first four provinces, and only maize, beans, and chia are then listed. Whether the amaranth was intended to be included with the chia in later provinces is difficult to ascertain. There are indications that, as the *Información* progresses, it gets more and more concise: cloaks are no longer described in detail, and the daily tribute of a great deal of household goods is finally reduced to simply *gallinas* or chickens. This same trend toward conciseness may have affected the tribute in foodstuffs.

Significant discrepancies also appear in the annotations in terms of amounts of goods given in tribute. This is especially true of the cloak tribute. Figures always illustrate single cloaks, typically with the number symbol for 400 attached. The Nahuatl annotations of the *Matrícula* minimally describe such a unit as *400 tilmatli*. The Spanish annotations of the *Mendoza* regularly describe the same unit as "400 loads of cloaks."[27] However, the term *carga* (load) is unmistakably added after the initial Spanish annotations were written. For the latter part of the annotations and for the commentary, this term is incorporated normally into the statements. This seems to be an afterthought on the part of the annotator. Borah and Cook (1963) feel it is attributable to a problem in the designation of the periods of tribute collection; where the *Matrícula* and the *Información* indicate that the clothing tribute was to be rendered every eighty days, the annotations of the *Mendoza* state that

this was to occur twice yearly. Borah and Cook believe that, partway through the writing, the annotator realized that the amount of tribute was far too small and tried to correct for this by adjusting the actual number of cloaks. However, I should note that such an adjustment in the numbers of cloaks would cause even greater deviation from the total numbers recorded in the *Matrícula* and the *Información*.[28]

There are other indications that tend to discourage the notion that each cloak figure was meant to represent a load. There exists in Nahuatl a numerical classifier that is used specifically to count cloaks by twenties, or loads (*-quimilli*). In only two cases is this used in the *Matrícula*, and in both cases the numbers of cloaks are under the customary four hundred (folios 49r, 52r: provinces of Cuetlaxtlan and Tuchpa).[29] It appears that the number glyphs, rather than their sixteenth-century Spanish interpretation, provided the correct actual number.

A similar problem is found with the feather tribute: bunches of feathers are always illustrated, never a single feather.[30] Here, the Nahuatl annotations state "feathers," and the *Mendoza* indicates bunches or bundles (*manojos*). The term *manojo* is added in the same manner as *cargas* is for the cloaks, as an afterthought. While bunches are illustrated, this is unquestionably a vague quantity; the *tlacuilo* or scribe probably intended only "400 red feathers," or the like, but to illustrate a single feather would probably not have done artistic justice to such a precious luxury.

Periods of tribute collection are indicated pictographically for only two provinces, Tlatelolco[31] and Xoconochco. The glyphs for Xoconochco are particularly revealing, since they portray the symbols for two monthly ceremonies, Ochpaniztli and Tlacaxipehualiztli—this implies a twice-yearly payment from the distant province of Xoconochco.

For all other provinces, the only clue to periods of tribute collection is found in the annotations and comments. The annotations of the *Matrícula* mention only two periods: every eighty days and annually. The tribute to be paid every eighty days is stated at the bottom of the page (i.e., where the reading begins) and frequently says "all this" or "this tribute." I understand this to refer to all tribute on the page unless otherwise specifically stated. Infrequently, individual items are singled out to be paid every eighty days (usually cloaks).

The other period of tribute in the *Matrícula* is annual. Warrior costumes are the most regularly mentioned items for annual payment, and they are always given annually. The only other annual item is strings of jadeite stones from the province of Coayxtlahuacan. Only two other periods are specifically stated: paper given every eighty days by Quauhnahuac, and strings of greenstone beads every twenty days by Xoconochco.

The annotations in the *Codex Mendoza* on periods of tribute collection are quite different. The period designated for clothing is consistently twice yearly. Foodstuffs, warrior costumes, turquoise, greenstone, gold, cotton, cacao, chiles, feathers, liquidambar, cochineal, eagles, and so on are usually specified as annual tribute (see Berdan 1976: appendix). Various other items are listed for twice yearly or every eighty days, and include honey, wood objects, bowls, copper bells, copper axes, and salt. Interestingly, some items are listed for different periods for different provinces, including cacao, cotton, copper axes, lime, and amber. Distance from the Aztec capitals does not seem to be a determinant here, since in some cases the more distant provinces were required to deliver their tribute more frequently.[32] One pattern does stand out: cotton and cacao from the Pacific coast regions were demanded semi-annually in the *Mendoza*, but those from the Gulf coast only annually (see maps 7 and 11). This may reflect different schedules of production in the two coastal areas.[33]

Twice yearly is not necessarily a viable time period for Aztec tribute deliveries, with the possible exception of distant Xoconochco. This time period is rarely mentioned in other documents (including the *Información*). The eighty-day period, on the other hand, is mentioned frequently and for many administrative and religious purposes (e.g., Zorita 1963b: 54, 55; Durán 1967 2:300, 412, 474; Torquemada 1969 1:168). In addition, early Spanish colonial tribute assessments frequently called for tribute every eighty days, an unnatural time period in the European calendar. Therefore, with the exception of the warrior costumes and the tribute from the distant province of Xoconochco (and perhaps some bulky tribute, such as cotton and cacao, from coastal areas), virtually all tribute may have been demanded every eighty days.[34] This may be generalized to refer to four times annually, during the months of Tlacaxipehualiztli, Etzalcualiztli, Ochpaniztli, and Panquetzaliztli, creating actual intervals of eighty or one hundred days.[35]

These problem areas all address specific types and quantities of goods given in tribute, and stated periods of tribute delivery; that is, they refer to the internal content of the tribute documents and details of the tribute process. But there are broader unresolved questions as well, questions that bear on the imperial context of these tribute tallies.

THE INSTITUTION OF TRIBUTE IN THE AZTEC EMPIRE: PERSISTENT PROBLEMS OF THE *CODEX MENDOZA* PART 2
Your Petlacalco or Mine?

Tribute took many forms under Aztec administration, and it is reasonable to ask, "What aspect of the tribute system does the *Codex Mendoza* part 2 represent?" "Who received these great quantities of tribute, and by what right?" Barlow (1949a:1) feels that this tribute list applies to the Triple Alliance, with the "Culhua Mexica" as dominant partner; Clark's commentary on the *Codex Mendoza* part 2 refers to Motecuhzoma as the recipient of the tribute recorded (1938 1:55). The *Mendoza* commentary itself refers only to "the State of Mexico" or "the lords of Mexico" as recipients.[36] Broda (1978:116) directs the tribute "to Tenochtitlan," and in previous works I have either rather generously offered this tribute to the three Triple Alliance capitals (Berdan 1975, 1976b), or studiously avoided the problem (Berdan 1980a). The most thorough and insightful discussion of the allocation of tributes is provided by Gibson (1971). Yet, to date, this question remains unresolved: just whose coffers did this extraordinary tribute fill?

Unraveling this is no simple matter, for the tribute system was both complex and variable. The documentary record tells us that the tribute of some towns was divided equally among the three Triple Alliance capitals (Motolinía 1903:353–356); of other towns it was divided on a ⅖, ⅖, ⅕ basis, with Tlacopan as the junior partner (Alva Ixtlilxochitl 1965 2:154; Motolinía 1903:353–356; Zorita 1963b:89); of yet others it was destined solely to Tenochtitlan, or to Texcoco, or to Tlacopan (Lehmann 1938; Orozco y Berra 1960 2:171–174; Motolinía 1903:353–356).[37] Zorita (1963b:37, 89) suggests that all three forms existed simultaneously.

The labor and production of some commoners (*macehualtin*) were geared toward fulfilling "state" needs, while those of other commoners (*mayeque*) were the privilege of individual nobles (see Berdan 1976b, 1978). Some tribute went into general state storehouses; some was directed to royal palace maintenance (Alva Ixtlilxochitl 1965 2:209–210), to the maintenance of temples (Berdan 1975), or to the support of military outposts and activities (ibid.).[38] Some of the tribute was in goods (as illustrated by the bulk of the *Codex Mendoza* part 2 and the *Matrícula de Tributos*), some was in service (Alva Ixtlilxochitl 1965 2:209–210; Berdan 1975). Sometimes the tribute schedules were strictly defined (e.g., every eighty days, annually), sometimes goods and services were required "at times" or "as needed" (e.g., PNE 5:59; PNE 4:185). And then there was special purpose tribute, levied on extraordinary occasions such as a coronation, a royal funeral, or the dedication of an important temple (Berdan 1975, 1976b, 1987b). When Gibson supplies us with the complicated example of the tribute obligations of Quauhtitlan, we might despair of ever deciphering the rules of the system:

> A single town was subject to many services and tribute demands, and its leaders received tribute from many other towns as well. Cuauhtitlan paid tribute in different amounts and principally from separate lands to its own tlatoani, to the tlatoani of Tlacopan, to Montezuma II (who had ten "private" lands in the vicinity of Cuauhtitlan and maintained calpixque [tribute collectors] in two of them as well as in Cuauhtitlan itself), and to other owners in Tlatelolco, Culhuacan, Ixtapalapa, Mexicalzingo, Azcapotzalco and Texcoco. (1971:390)

So, what are the possibilities for the *Codex Mendoza* tribute tally? First of all, the internal evidence places it as a strictly Tenochca document. The historical section commemorates Mexica rulers and their conquests, the "garrison towns" were governed by Mexica officials, the very Mexican conquest and control of Tlatelolco is related, Texcoco is included among the vanquished in part 1 (folio 3v), and the Spanish commentary mentions only the state and lords of Mexico (although the possibility of informant bias could apply here). If, as the document itself suggests, this tribute was destined for Tenochtitlan alone, how are the claims by Texcoco and Tlacopan on many of these same towns to be explained? There are two reasonable possibilities, and they are not mutually exclusive. Gibson phrases it nicely:

> The *Codex Mendoza* does include towns whose tributes were claimed both by the Acolhua and the Tepaneca, but these could still have been Tenochca calpixque stations, either simultaneously, in a system of divided tribute, or in sequence, as the Tenochca took over tributes of the other two members, or both. (ibid.:388)

"Divided tribute" may take two forms: in the first, the town or area (city-state) is not being assessed as a monolithic entity, but rather specific land and labor capabilities are divided, and then tributes are derived from the production of these basic resources. This would result in a situation resembling that of Quauhtitlan (quoted above) and would account for the records of rulers and nobles possessing lands in one another's territories (e.g., ibid.: 389–390).

A second form of divided tribute would involve a division farther along in the process: instead of dividing the basic resources and then assessing tributes accordingly, specific tributes in goods are levied on whole communities or domains. Upon being delivered, these are divided according to an agreed-upon formula. Alva Ixtlilxochitl (1965 2:198) discusses such a procedure and, even with his Texcoco inclinations, admits that the joint tribute was delivered to Tenochtitlan and there divided among the agents of the three rulers, that of Nezahualcoyotl of Texcoco being retained in the palaces of Tenochtitlan. This fails to explain the simultaneous presence of Quauhnahuac and Chalco tributes on the *Codex Mendoza* tally, and tributes from the same domains housed in the Texcocan palace of Nezahualcoyotl (*Mapa Quinatzin:* Robertson 1959: plate 47). It may be that those tribute stores were derived from the first form of divided tributes.

If tributes were divided along so many dimensions, then the town listings in the *Codex Mendoza* part 2 may not be quite as incomplete as suspected. There were certainly many more communities recorded elsewhere as having tribute obligations to "Motecuhzoma," but many of these were subject to the Aztecs as "strategic provinces," paying tribute or giving "gifts" by virtue of special commercial or military relationships with the empire. Barlow's penchant for adding on to the *Codex Mendoza* tribute list other communities in a provincial area should be eyed with caution—the tributes of those communities appear to have been paid on an altogether different basis than that recorded in the *Mendoza* (Berdan et al., n.d.).[39]

Other discrepancies in the documentary record may reflect the dynamic nature of the imperial political and economic system. Gibson (1971) offers ample evidence to support the view that there was considerable shifting of rights, transfer of lands, and reallocation of properties among the three imperial *tlatoque*, or rulers. It may be that many of the documentary discrepancies are artifacts of "collapsed historical time": while Alva Ixtlilxochitl (1965 2:196–199) claims exclusive Texcoco tribute rights over four major provinces (Tuchpa, Tzicoac, Tochtepec, Tlalcoçauhtitlan), later in the history of the empire the Mexica must have made inroads into these areas. There are abundant examples of this phenomenon (see Gibson 1971:385), and they lead to the general conclusion that Tenochtitlan was acquiring rights and properties at the expense of its two allies. The appearance of such provinces in the *Codex Mendoza* tribute roll, claimed in other sources by Texcoco, should therefore offer no necessary contradiction. It does, indeed, alert us to the very dynamic, even fluid, political and economic environment of Aztec Mexico.

In sum, suffice to say there is no extant evidence to claim the *Codex Mendoza* part 2 (or the *Matrícula de Tributos*) as a Triple Alliance tribute tally. Rather, the evidence weighs in favor of Tenochtitlan alone.

Assessments or Receipts?

There is some question whether the *Codex Mendoza* tribute list is a record of assessment (i.e., what was asked or demanded) or a record of collection (i.e., what was sent by the provinces). There is, indeed, no evidence suggesting there was even a discrepancy between the two, although it would be hard to believe that there was not, no matter how efficient the system.[40]

Bernal Díaz del Castillo (1956:211) provides a rather abbreviated clue:

> I remember that at that time his [Motecuhzoma's] steward was a great Cacique to whom we gave the name of Tapia, and he kept the accounts of all the revenue that was brought to Montezuma, in his books which were made of paper which they call amal, and he had a great house full of these books. Now we must leave the books and the accounts for it is outside our story.

If Díaz's observations and memory were accurate, then the major-domos did keep account books of receipts; whether they kept books of assessments remains a question.

Given the structure of the *petlacalco* (storehouses), it would be logical for such account books to be produced on individual, separate sheets of paper; indeed, the tribute from the different provinces was collected and stored separately.[41] And quite obviously, the *Matrícula de Tributos* was composed by three separate scribes and may have been a fully operational account book.[42]

How do these pictorial tribute tallies measure up to the documented contents of the state storehouses (*petlacalco*)? Sahagún (1950–1982 8:44, 51, 52, 58) makes specific mention of the types of goods actually stored in the *petlacalco*, or of dispersals implemented by *petlacalco* officials.[43]

Stored in the *petlacalco* itself were foodstuffs: maize (*tlaolli*), beans, chia, amaranth, salt, chiles, and squash seeds (ibid.:44). A cage for detaining "evildoers" was also located there (ibid.). But the tribute officials were in charge of more than food staples: they were called upon by the ruler when he required "costly articles—insignia of gold, and with quetzal feathers, and all the shields of great price" (ibid.:51) to be distributed prior to a military campaign; the *calpixque* also carried "valuable capes" to the battlefield, to be distributed there (ibid.:52).[44] The more lethal equipment of war, spears and arrows, was kept in other structures, specifically the *Tlacochcalco Acatl Yiacapan* and the *Tezcacoac Tlacochcalco* (Sahagún 1950–1982 2:169, 179). The *calpixque* even supplied the ruler's gaming wagers—cloaks, loincloths, lip plugs, earplugs, necklaces, wristbands, and precious cloaks and cloth (ibid.:58). In addition to these specific references to the goods stored and distributed by the tribute overseers, there is also frequent reference to the ruler offering valuable gifts to visiting rulers (e.g., ibid.:65; Durán 1967 2:414) and to successful warriors (e.g., Sahagún 1950–1982 2:115–116, 8:76–77, 87–88). Where specific styles of cloaks or warrior costumes are mentioned in the textual sources, they at times coincide with items on the *Codex Mendoza* tribute roll (such as the Huaxtec warrior costumes and the *tlilpapatlauac* [black-striped] cloaks; see Anawalt essay in this volume.)[45]

So there is some correlation between the *Codex Mendoza* tally and Sahagún's recorded contents of the Mexica *petlacalco*—and the jurisdictions of the tribute officials. In other words, barring a few discrepancies from our small sample,[46] the *Codex Mendoza* (or better, *Matrícula de Tributos*) could have served as an account of goods-on-hand. Then there is the perhaps surprising absence of spears and arrows at the *petlacalco*—they apparently were not under the watchful eye of the *petlacalcatl* and *calpixque*. We do know that they were stored in at least two other, quite separate buildings (see above). Yet there are some, albeit spotty, notices of tribute payments in weaponry (e.g., PNE 7:8, 28). While such tribute may have been recorded in an assessment book, it would not be included in the *petlacalcatl*'s accounts, and is in fact absent from the *Codex Mendoza* tally. Certainly all the evidence is not yet in. But it is, at the moment, weighing in favor of the *Matrícula de Tributos* and *Codex Mendoza* part 2 as accounts of received tribute payments. The geographic distribution of payments of major types of goods (clothing, cotton, warrior costumes, foodstuffs, cacao, fine stones, precious metals, and feathers) is indicated on maps 3–14.

Historical Moment or Long-term Record?

Barlow (1949a:4) brackets the composition date of the *Matrícula de Tributos* at between 1511 and the 1520s. Does this imply that the same tribute roll applied to those many years? Or was the document, or parts of it, renewed on a regular or situational basis? If so, for what kind of time period did a tribute tally such as the *Matrícula de Tributos* or *Codex Mendoza* apply? The gloss "every eighty days," or "every six months," implies repeated deliveries of the goods portrayed—suggestive of a document that would apply for at least a year. Barring any untoward circumstances, perhaps a year was the usual life span for these registers. But there *were* untoward circumstances: rebellions resulted in an increase in tribute demands (Berdan 1975:246–247), new communities and their resources were incorporated into the realm (Gibson 1971), and the tribute demands in general increased over time (see Gibson 1971; Berdan 1975:247–254). All of this points to an obviously dynamic political and economic system to which the imperial account books would have been keenly sensitive. The rather fleeting utility of these registers may help explain the discrepancies between their content and textual descriptions of tribute demands. For example, the textual accounting of the Cuetlaxtlan tribute, either before or after its rebellion and reconquest, bears little resemblance to the *Codex Mendoza* record (Durán 1967 2:199; *Codex Mendoza*, folio 49r). Each may be accurate, but apply to different times in the province's conquest history. Overall, I suspect that, given the dynamics of empire building, these pictorial tallies reveal only a historical moment rather than an extended, long-term set of repeated tribute deliveries.

If this is true, what "moment" is the best candidate for the *Matrícula–Mendoza* tribute tally? Barlow (1949a:4) observes that this tribute roll was probably composed after 1511 or 1512, given the inclusion of the town of Tlachquiauco (folio 45r), which was not conquered until that time. But to what period, between the years 1512 and 1519, might the document have applied? A small clue does exist in the document, embedded in the tribute requirements of the province of Tepeacac (folio 42r). The tribute of this province included, as already mentioned, the somewhat unusual rendering of enemy warriors from nearby Tlaxcala, Huexotzinco, and Cholula. But Mesoamerican political and military history is a continuous story of shifting alliances, and the period just prior to the

Spanish arrival was no exception. So it appears that, from approximately 1512 until 1516, Huexotzinco was a part of the Triple Alliance; under those circumstances, it would be unlikely that its warriors would be sought as tribute by its own allies. But in 1516 Huexotzinco rejoined Tlaxcala and Cholula: the tribute list could apply to that year. During 1517–1518, Tlaxcala, Huexotzinco, and Cholula remained separate from the Triple Alliance, in a state of open hostilities. However, during those years it appears that Cholula, being rather marginally attached to either the Triple Alliance or the Tlaxcala-Huexotzinco alliance, leaned more and more toward association with the former (Isaac 1983:416). By the time the Spaniards arrived, it appears that Cholula may have been more closely associated with the Triple Alliance, while still maintaining some of its neutrality (Berdan 1985:354). As relations warmed between Cholula and the Triple Alliance, Cholulan prisoners may have still been appropriate and valuable to the Mexica and their allies, but it might have been somewhat impolitic to demand them as tribute. If this tribute demand in enemy prisoners can be taken seriously, and literally, then the years 1516–1518 seem to be the best candidates for the composition of this tribute tally.

The Aztec imperial tribute system was extremely complex and dynamic. Its management was facilitated by the use of accounting registers, of which the *Codex Mendoza* part 2 is but one example. Efficient administration of the system would require documents that recorded assessments, goods-on-hand, and dispersals. Yet the tribute tally of the *Codex Mendoza* probably represents but one of these functions. It also appears to tally only a portion of the total tribute levied, only that received by Tenochtitlan, and for a relatively short period of time. The *Codex Mendoza* part 2 (along with the *Matrícula de Tributos*) is unquestionably the most valuable Aztec tribute document still available; yet, like our other documentation on Aztec Mexico, it must be interpreted within a specific temporal and spatial context. In so doing, it becomes an even more valuable, and understandable, record.

NOTES

1. All but two of the thirty-eight *Codex Mendoza* provinces (Tepeacac and Xoconochco) gave clothing in tribute. For an extended discussion of these articles of tribute, see Anawalt's essay in this volume.

2. Of the thirty-eight provinces, twenty-nine gave one or more varieties of warrior costumes (*tlahuiztli*). Anawalt, in this volume, discusses these costumes in detail.

3. Twenty provinces were required to deliver bins of staple foodstuffs; all but one of these provinces were in relatively close proximity to the island capital of Tenochtitlan.

4. Each of these provinces gave eight different styles of warrior costumes. The next largest number is five, given by three provinces: Quauhtitlan, Atotonilco (de Pedraza), and Hueypochtlan.

5. For Petlacalco, the towns on the additional page line the left-hand margin; for Acolhuacan, they border the bottom of the second page and continue a bit up the right-hand margin; for Quauhnahuac, no additional space was required for the town listing; and for Huaxtepec, the listing is continued along the bottom of the additional page. The different patterns may be explained by the placement of the pages. In the cases of Acolhuacan and Huaxtepec, the artist was composing the towns and tribute on facing pages (21v/22r and 24v/25r respectively) and is merely continuing the bottom row of town glyphs on the facing page. In the case of Petlacalco, the artist continued his town and tribute information on the reverse side of the folio (20r/20v) and hence was inclined to begin his list anew, at the top left, as he had begun it on the recto side.

6. Indeed, the items and towns listed are brief enough to allow this col-

lapsing; yet the question does emerge why these and not other "sparsely endowed" provinces were so grouped. One possibility is ethnic association. Malinalco and Xocotitlan were not geographically contiguous, yet they both apparently contained Matlatzinca peoples (see Barlow 1949a:30–31; Alva Ixtlilxochitl 1965 2:256). Yet Tlalcoçauhtitlan, Quiauhteopan, and Yoaltepec, grouped on a single page and contiguous geographically, apparently contained considerable cultural and linguistic diversity. Little association can be seen, especially between Tlalcoçauhtitlan and Yoaltepec (Barlow 1949a:83, 85, 105). Another possibility may be that the grouped provinces were conquered in the same campaign and the tribute assessed in the same motion. The evidence is unclear and incomplete, but Tlalcoçauhtitlan, Quiauhteopan, and Yoaltepec are all listed as conquests of Motecuhzoma Ilhuicamina (1440–1468) in the *Códice Chimalpopoca* (1975:66–67) and in part 1 of the *Codex Mendoza* (folio 8r). Alva Ixtlilxochitl (1965 2:201) mentions the conquest of Quiauhteopan in association with other conquests, but neither Tlalcoçauhtitlan nor Yoaltepec is among them. As for the Malinalco/Xocotitlan grouping, while the "Matlatzincas" or "Matlatzinco" are frequently referenced as a conquest of Axayacatl (1468–1481), Xiquipilco rather than Xocotitlan or Malinalco seems to have been the prize (see Kelly and Palerm 1952:296–300 and page description for Malinalco, volume 2). Neither ethnicity nor military history seems to serve as an adequate explanation; perhaps an "administrative-efficiency" decision on the part of a well-organized *petlacalcatl* (tribute overseer) was at play.

7. See Gómez de Orozco (1941:49–50) and Berdan (1976a:133). This statement also implies that the "committee of Indians" may not always have

agreed on the meanings of the pictographs. For some possible errors in interpretation, see Berdan et al. n.d.

8. The great prizes were mercantile: closer association with the professional merchants centered in Tlatelolco and control over the grand Tlatelolco marketplace.

9. According to Durán (1967 2:264–265) and Alvarado Tezozomoc (1975a:394–397), Tlatelolcans were also responsible for war captives: this may be somehow indicated on the *Codex Mendoza* tribute roll by the four *flores*. See also note 32 and volume 2 page descriptions for folios 17v and 18r.

10. Five provinces, included in the *Codex Mendoza* tribute roll, are missing from the *Matrícula de Tributos*: Axocopan, Atotonilco (de Pedraza), Tlachquiaco, Tochtepec, and Oxitipan. The *Matrícula de Tributos* currently resides in the Museo Nacional de Antropología in Mexico City.

11. The *Información* omits the provinces of Tlatelolco, Malinalco, and Xocotitlan, but adds the unlocated province of Apan. This analysis is a refinement of the discussion in Berdan 1976a.

12. The only characteristic of the *Matrícula* which is considered to preclude it as a pre-Conquest document is its manner of binding. Robertson (1959:72–77) strongly feels that, to be pre-Conquest in origin, the document must appear in screen-fold form. I have argued against that position (see Berdan 1980:9), and even Robertson (1959:33) presents evidence that not all pre-Conquest writings were in screen-fold books.

13. One hopes that this does not simply reflect a left-handed versus right-handed scribe.

14. A good deal of disagreement surrounds the dating of the *Codex Borbonicus*; it may indeed be pre-Conquest in origin (see Nicholson 1974 and Robertson 1959:105).

15. In "copying" the individual members of categories, if they were indeed copied from the *Matrícula*, the *Mendoza* scribe followed no clear pattern. In some cases he displayed a penchant for taking all cloaks as a group, proceeding from top to bottom and left to right within that group (e.g., for Petlacalco, Huaxtepec, Cihuatlan). At other times he would take each row of cloaks separately, while on the same page treating the warrior costumes as a group (e.g., Acolhuacan, Quauhnahuac, Xilotepec, Tepequacuilco). For Cuetlaxtlan, the *Mendoza* scribe strangely began his second row of cloaks with the two on the far right in the *Matrícula*, and for Tuchpa the first two rows of cloaks are reversed while the third maintains its position, the three rows of cloaks taken as a group. Sometimes the items within a category are frustratingly jumbled, revealing no pattern of, or evidence for, direct copying of the *Mendoza* from the *Matrícula* (e.g., warrior costumes of Quauhtitlan, Hueypochtlan, Atotonilco). Similarly, miscellaneous items are frequently jumbled (e.g., for Tepeacac, Coayxtlahuacan, Tuchpa). It is possible that strict sequential order was not an important ideal.

16. In the *Codex Mendoza* there are two shining white teeth; in the *Matrícula*, three rather red ones.

17. *Xala: xalli* (sand) and *tlan* (abundance of). *Tequixquitlan*: nitrous, or saltpeter bed. Realistically, the glyph could be interpreted either way.

18. Some small details of the *libro* can also be gleaned from the 1554 testimonies. As in the *Mendoza* and the *Matrícula*, shields regularly accompany warrior costumes. However, the symbol for twenty (*pantli*) is obviously present on numerous shields, but omitted from their corresponding costumes. For example, the *Información* lists seven warrior costumes and forty-five shields—although only seven of each would be pictured, two of the accompanying shields would carry the *pantli* symbol for twenty, yielding a total of forty-five shields.

19. The two warrior insignia found for this province in the *Matrícula* and not in the *Mendoza* are the *cueçalpatzactli* and the *momoyactli*. One of these is worn with an *ehuatl* (see Anawalt essay in this volume).

20. The maize and beans are clearly distinguished, but the representations of chia and amaranth are indicated by identical small black dots. The folios in the *Mendoza* which represent two bins for each single bin in the *Matrícula* are 22v, 23v, 25r, 26r, 29r, 31r, 35r (two provinces), 37r, 42r (although chia and amaranth are omitted), and 44r (lacking amaranth).

21. Folios 21v, 31r, 26r: Acolhuacan and Xilotepec, and on shields only for Quauhtitlan.

22. For the latter, only two *pantli* (20) symbols are shown in the *Matrícula*, while five are illustrated in the *Mendoza*.

23. These variations are distributed over several provinces and correspond to the following folios in the *Mendoza*: 21v, 23r, 23v, 24v, 25r, 26r, 29r, 30r, 32r, 36r, 40r, 49r.

24. This is apparent in the tribute for the province of Yoaltepec. Turquoise is clearly pictured, and the Nahuatl annotation accurately states *xiuitl*. *Xiuitl*, however, has various other meanings, including a type of herb, and the Spanish annotator indeed translated this *xiuitl* as *yerbas*, apparently disregarding the pictograph.

25. It should be admitted, however, that in Nahuatl reference to maize frequently meant sustenance in general, and might include such foods as chia and amaranth. This does not explain the explicit mention of beans in this context.

26. Chia may have been more significant to the Aztecs as a foodstuff than previously thought (see Truman n.d.).

27. One load equals twenty cloaks.

28. If loads of cloaks were given, an annual tribute total of 2,584,000 cloaks would result.

29. *Chicuiquimilli*: $8 \times 20 = 160$ (folio 49r: Cuetlaxtlan). *Matlacquimilli omome*: $12 \times 20 = 240$ (folio 52r: Tuchpa). These are the exact amounts indicated by the number glyphs.

30. Bunches of quetzal feathers (the most prized) are always tied, while the others are not. The quetzal feathers pictured for the province of Tochtepec (folio 46r) are wrapped, tied, and held by a hand.

31. The Tlatelolco tribute intervals are illustrated as four *flores* or flowers, each representing twenty days. Similar *flores* are found on ritual cloaks linked to the god Macuilxochitl (Five Flower; *Codex Magliabechiano* 1970:4v, 5v). Warrior slaves (*maltequime*) were sacrificed in his honor (Sahagún 1950–1982 1:31–32), and indeed Tlatelolco was required to supply such captives (Alvarado Tezozomoc 1975a:394–397, Durán 1967 2:264–265). Alvarado Tezozomoc (ibid.) and Durán (ibid.) affirm that the Tlatelolco tribute was demanded on an eighty-day schedule. See also Barlow (1945:211–212).

32. Xoconochco, the most distant imperial province, was required to deliver its tribute semi-annually; many of the same types of goods were delivered only annually by less distant provinces, such as Tochtepec, Quauhtochco, and Cuetlaxtlan. Similarly, distant Cihuatlan cacao was required to appear in Tenochtitlan semi-annually, according to the *Mendoza*, while the more nearby provinces of Quauhtochco, Atlan, and Tzicoac gave the same produce annually. For the delivery of lime, copper axes, and amber, the distance differential is negligible.

33. The *Matrícula* is of little help here, since all these items are subsumed under the "all this tribute is due every eighty days" blanket statement. The one exception, of course, is again the detached province of Xoconochco.

34. This would include the foodstuff tribute. Although it was not harvested that frequently, there is extensive information on the presence and maintenance of large storehouses in the provinces for tribute purposes (see especially Durán 1967 2:241–242; Zorita 1963b:123, 198; Torquemada 1969 1:168). Carrasco observes that Etzalcualiztli and Panquetzaliztli coincide with harvest times (1976c:280). These four months also mark the solstices and equinoxes (ibid.:274–279).

35. Clark (1938 1:60) places these intervals at 80–100–80–105 days. Carrasco (1976c:280–281) argues persuasively for the logic of these periods of collection, citing a corresponding imperial distribution of tribute items at the same or nearly the same times. The *Información* repeatedly mentions "every eighty days" as well as these four months, especially for special tribute payments. Nonetheless, other periods of tribute payment probably existed (see PNE 4:260).

36. The commentator excuses himself from *always* making such a statement, in the interest of brevity (see folio 41v).

37. An excellent discussion of these various sources and levies is in Gibson (1956). Zorita (1963b:37), in describing the process of tribute collection, refers to the tribute collectors sent by the rulers of Tenochtitlan, Texcoco, *or* Tlacopan—he seems to be implying the lack of a joint tribute system.

38. See page descriptions for folios 17v and 18r, volume 2.

39. Such city-states were often located along hostile borderlands or important trade routes, and their incorporation into the empire seems to have been more informal than for the provinces recorded in the *Mendoza*.

40. In a realm of such ethnic and linguistic diversity, the discrepancies may have been great, although the information about outlying regions was extensive (see Robertson 1959:31–32). For an analysis of the relationship between tribute demands and local histories see the Anawalt essay in this volume, and Berdan 1987a.

41. Sahagún (1950–1982 8:51) makes it quite clear that there were separate *calpixque* (tribute collectors) overseeing the tributes from each individual province.

42. Their individual efforts correspond to folios 2r–5v, 6r–11v, 12r–16v. The first recorded the tributes from the central and northern portion of the empire; the second accounted for the west and southwest (plus Chalco); the third, for the east and southeast.

43. These include the *petlacalcatl* (apparently the head overseer), the *aztacalcatl* (perhaps a Tenochtitlan "quartermaster"—see Siméon 1963:45), and various *calpixque* (tribute collectors).

44. *Calpixque* were also in charge of guarding military captives, caring for the birds in the *totocalli* (bird house), and tending the wild animals. Luxury artisans worked at the *totocalli*, where fresh materials were readily available (Sahagún 1950–1982 8:45).

45. Huaxtec (*cuextecatl*) warrior costumes were distributed during the Ochpaniztli ceremonies (Sahagún 1950–1982 2:115) and are found in abundance on the *Codex Mendoza* tribute roll. *Tlilpapatlauac* cloaks, although only of one, two, or four lengths, were provided by five different *Codex Mendoza* provinces. The Sahagún texts specify eight lengths (ibid., 8:87).

46. The following items, found in Sahagún's listings of storehouse contents, are not included in the *Codex Mendoza* part 2: squash seeds, one type of cloak (*xomoiuitilmatli:* duck feather), one type of loincloth, greenstone lip plugs (although lip plugs of other materials are included), golden earplugs, and perhaps wristbands with jade on them (although numerous greenstone strings of apparently different sizes are represented). There are, of course, many more types of goods on the tribute rolls than available in Sahagún's abbreviated *petlacalco* listings.

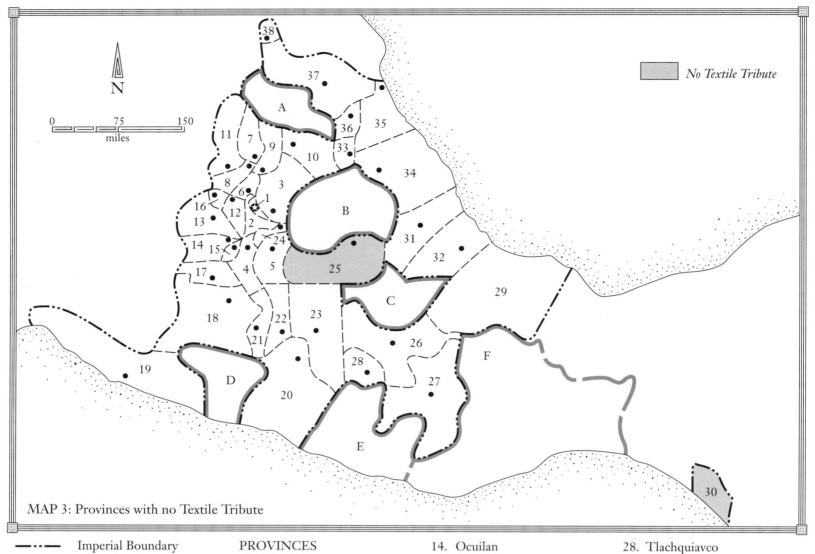

MAP 3: Provinces with no Textile Tribute

No Textile Tribute

—··— Imperial Boundary
— — — Provincial Boundary
▬▬▬ Independent Señoríos
  • Provincial Cabecera
  ✪ Tenochtitlan

INDEPENDENT SEÑORÍOS
A. Metztitlan
B. Tlaxcala
C. Teotitlan del Camino
D. Yopitzinco
E. Tototepec
F. Realm of Coatlicamac

PROVINCES
1. Tlatelolco
2. Petlacalco
3. Acolhuacan
4. Quauhnahuac
5. Huaxtepec
6. Quauhtitlan
7. Axocopan
8. Atotonilco (de Pedraza)
9. Hueypuchtla
10. Atotonilco (el Grande)
11. Xilotepec
12. Quahuacan
13. Tuluca

14. Ocuilan
15. Malinalco
16. Xocotitlan
17. Tlachco
18. Tepequacuilco
19. Çihuatlan
20. Tlapan
21. Tlalcoçauhtitlan
22. Quiauhteopan
23. Yoaltepec
24. Chalco
25. *Tepeacac*
26. Coayxtlahuacan
27. Coyolapan

28. Tlachquiavco
29. Tochtepec
30. *Xoconochco*
31. Quauhtochco
32. Cuetlaxtlan
33. Tlapacoyan
34. Tlatlauhquitepec
35. Tuchpa
36. Atlan
37. Tzicoac
38. Oxitipan

Map 3. Provinces paying no tribute in textiles to the Aztec empire.
Tribute in textiles was the most widespread over the empire's
provinces.

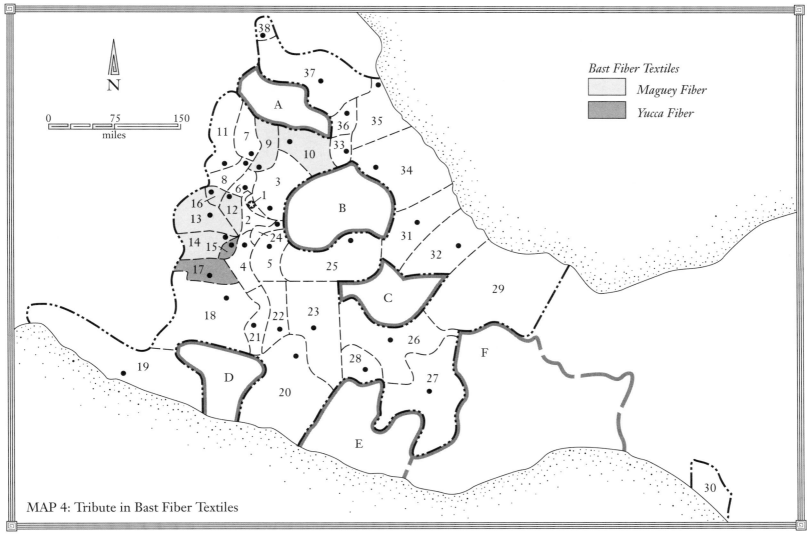

Bast Fiber Textiles

Maguey Fiber

Yucca Fiber

MAP 4: Tribute in Bast Fiber Textiles

–··–··– Imperial Boundary
– – – – Provincial Boundary
▬▬▬ Independent Señoríos
• Provincial Cabecera
✪ Tenochtitlan

INDEPENDENT SEÑORÍOS
A. Metztitlan
B. Tlaxcala
C. Teotitlan del Camino
D. Yopitzinco
E. Tototepec
F. Realm of Coatlicamac

PROVINCES
1. Tlatelolco
2. Petlacalco
3. Acolhuacan
4. Quauhnahuac
5. Huaxtepec
6. Quauhtitlan
7. Axocopan
8. Atotonilco (de Pedraza)
9. *Hueypuchtla*
10. *Atotonilco (el Grande)*
11. Xilotepec
12. *Quahuacan*
13. *Tuluca*

14. *Ocuilan*
15. *Malinalco*
16. *Xocotitlan*
17. *Tlachco*
18. Tepequacuilco
19. Çihuatlan
20. Tlapan
21. Tlalcoçauhtitlan
22. Quiauhteopan
23. Yoaltepec
24. Chalco
25. Tepeacac
26. Coayxtlahuacan
27. Coyolapan

28. Tlachquiavco
29. Tochtepec
30. Xoconochco
31. Quauhtochco
32. Cuetlaxtlan
33. Tlapacoyan
34. Tlatlauhquitepec
35. Tuchpa
36. Atlan
37. Tzicoac
38. Oxitipan

Map 4. Tribute in bast fiber textiles. Only provinces to the north and west of the Valley of Mexico, where maguey and yucca plants flourished, provided textiles of these materials.

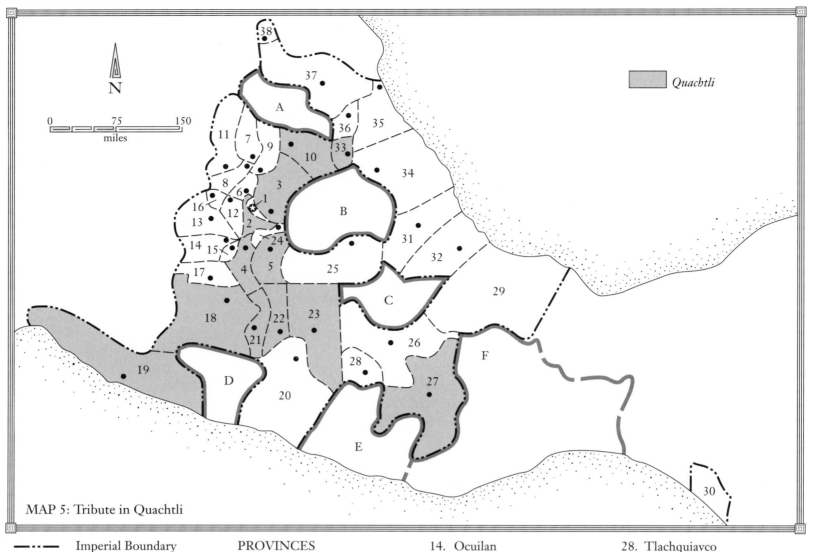

MAP 5: Tribute in Quachtli

| Quachtli |

| --- |

| Imperial Boundary |
| Provincial Boundary |
| Independent Señorios |
| • Provincial Cabecera |
| ✪ Tenochtitlan |

INDEPENDENT SEÑORÍOS
A. Metztitlan
B. Tlaxcala
C. Teotitlan del Camino
D. Yopitzinco
E. Tototepec
F. Realm of Coatlicamac

PROVINCES
1. Tlatelolco
2. *Petlacalco*
3. *Acolhuacan*
4. *Quauhnahuac*
5. *Huaxtepec*
6. Quauhtitlan
7. Axocopan
8. Atotonilco (de Pedraza)
9. Hueypuchtla
10. *Atotonilco (el Grande)*
11. Xilotepec
12. Quahuacan
13. Tuluca

14. Ocuilan
15. Malinalco
16. Xocotitlan
17. Tlachco
18. *Tepequacuilco*
19. *Çihuatlan*
20. Tlapan
21. *Tlalcoçauhtitlan*
22. *Quiauhteopan*
23. *Yoaltepec*
24. Chalco
25. Tepeacac
26. Coayxtlahuacan
27. *Coyolapan*

28. Tlachquiavco
29. Tochtepec
30. Xoconochco
31. Quauhtochco
32. Cuetlaxtlan
33. *Tlapacoyan*
34. Tlatlauhquitepec
35. Tuchpa
36. Atlan
37. Tzicoac
38. Oxitipan

Map 5. Tribute in *quachtli*. These large, undecorated white cotton *mantas* served a variety of purposes, including a medium of exchange in trade. The identification of *quachtli* in the tribute roll is based on the annotations in the *Matrícula de Tributos*.

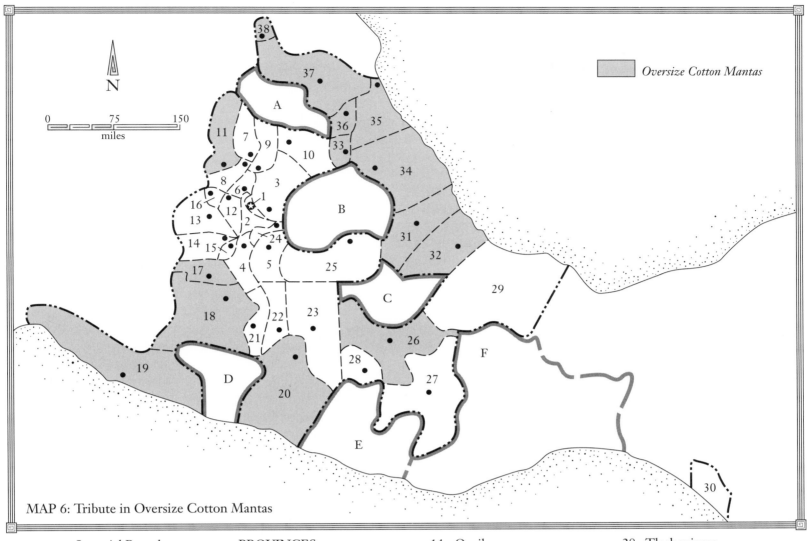

MAP 6: Tribute in Oversize Cotton Mantas

Oversize Cotton Mantas

-----·--- Imperial Boundary
- - - - - Provincial Boundary
━━━━━ Independent Señoríos
• Provincial Cabecera
✪ Tenochtitlan

INDEPENDENT SEÑORÍOS
A. Metztitlan
B. Tlaxcala
C. Teotitlan del Camino
D. Yopitzinco
E. Tototepec
F. Realm of Coatlicamac

PROVINCES
1. Tlatelolco
2. Petlacalco
3. Acolhuacan
4. Quauhnahuac
5. Huaxtepec
6. Quauhtitlan
7. Axocopan
8. Atotonilco (de Pedraza)
9. Hueypuchtla
10. Atotonilco (el Grande)
11. *Xilotepec*
12. Quahuacan
13. Tuluca

14. Ocuilan
15. Malinalco
16. Xocotitlan
17. *Tlachco*
18. *Tepequacuilco*
19. *Çihuatlan*
20. *Tlapan*
21. Tlalcoçauhtitlan
22. Quiauhteopan
23. Yoaltepec
24. Chalco
25. Tepeacac
26. *Coayxtlahuacan*
27. Coyolapan

28. Tlachquiavco
29. Tochtepec
30. Xoconochco
31. *Quauhtochco*
32. *Cuetlaxtlan*
33. Tlapacoyan
34. *Tlatlauhquitepec*
35. *Tuchpa*
36. Atlan
37. *Tzicoac*
38. *Oxitipan*

Map 6. Tribute in *mantas* of 2, 4, or 8 *brazas* in length. These oversize *mantas* are concentrated in cotton-growing areas (compare with map 7). Provinces providing the longest *mantas* (8 brazas) were Xilotepec and Tuchpa, in the northern part of the empire.

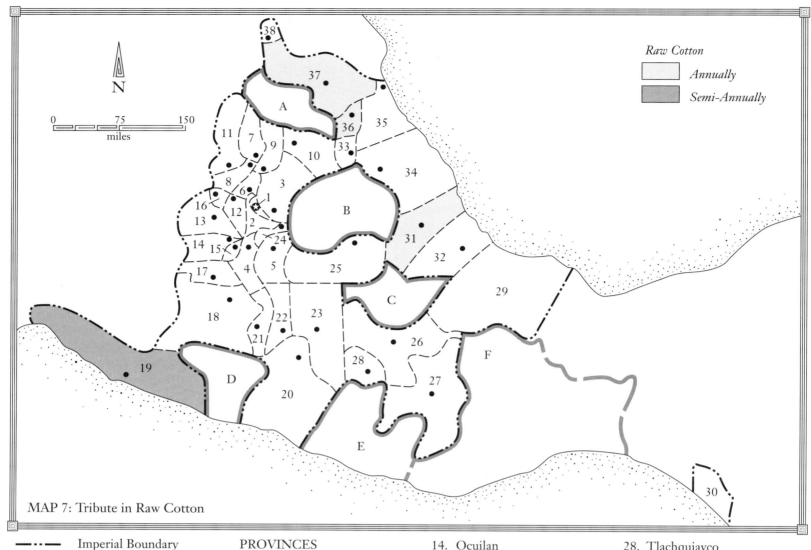

MAP 7: Tribute in Raw Cotton

Raw Cotton

☐ *Annually*

▨ *Semi-Annually*

— ·· —	Imperial Boundary	
— — —	Provincial Boundary	
▬▬▬	Independent Señoríos	
•	Provincial Cabecera	
✪	Tenochtitlan	

INDEPENDENT SEÑORÍOS
A. Metztitlan
B. Tlaxcala
C. Teotitlan del Camino
D. Yopitzinco
E. Tototepec
F. Realm of Coatlicamac

PROVINCES
1. Tlatelolco
2. Petlacalco
3. Acolhuacan
4. Quauhnahuac
5. Huaxtepec
6. Quauhtitlan
7. Axocopan
8. Atotonilco (de Pedraza)
9. Hueypuchtla
10. Atotonilco (el Grande)
11. Xilotepec
12. Quahuacan
13. Tuluca

14. Ocuilan
15. Malinalco
16. Xocotitlan
17. Tlachco
18. Tepequacuilco
19. *Çihuatlan*
20. Tlapan
21. Tlalcoçauhtitlan
22. Quiauhteopan
23. Yoaltepec
24. Chalco
25. Tepeacac
26. Coayxtlahuacan
27. Coyolapan

28. Tlachquiavco
29. Tochtepec
30. Xoconochco
31. *Quauhtochco*
32. Cuetlaxtlan
33. Tlapacoyan
34. Tlatlauhquitepec
35. Tuchpa
36. *Atlan*
37. *Tzicoac*
38. Oxitipan

Map 7. Tribute in raw cotton. The cotton that arrived from the Gulf coast provinces was rendered annually, that from the Pacific coast paid twice a year. According to the *Matrícula de Tributos*, all the cotton tribute was paid "every eighty days."

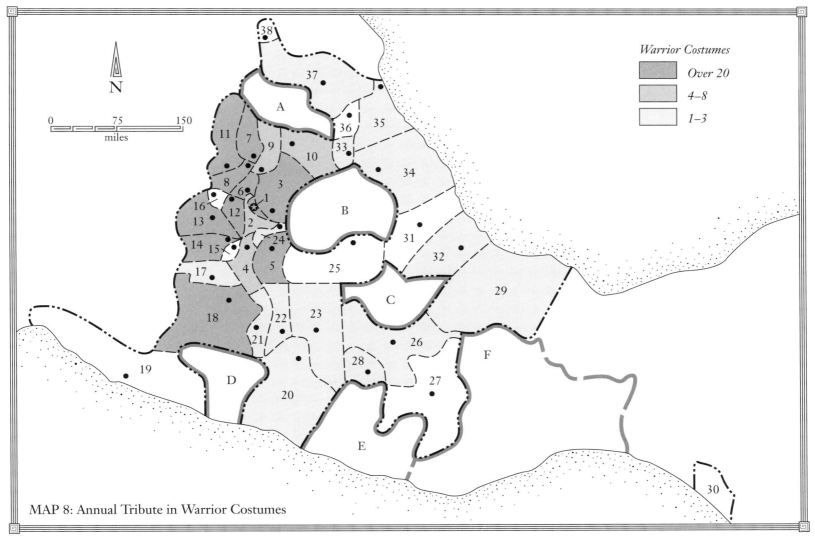

MAP 8: Annual Tribute in Warrior Costumes

Warrior Costumes

- ▓ Over 20
- ▒ 4–8
- ░ 1–3

—··—··— Imperial Boundary
— — — — Provincial Boundary
━━━━━ Independent Señorios
● Provincial Cabecera
✪ Tenochtitlan

INDEPENDENT SEÑORÍOS
A. Metztitlan
B. Tlaxcala
C. Teotitlan del Camino
D. Yopitzinco
E. Tototepec
F. Realm of Coatlicamac

PROVINCES
1. *Tlatelolco*
2. *Petlacalco*
3. *Acolhuacan*
4. *Quauhnahuac*
5. *Huaxtepec*
6. *Quauhtitlan*
7. *Axocopan*
8. *Atotonilco (de Pedraza)*
9. *Hueypuchtla*
10. *Atotonilco (el Grande)*
11. *Xilotepec*
12. *Quahuacan*
13. *Tuluca*

14. *Ocuilan*
15. *Malinalco*
16. *Xocotitlan*
17. *Tlachco*
18. *Tepequacuilco*
19. *Çihuatlan*
20. *Tlapan*
21. *Tlalcoçauhtitlan*
22. *Quiauhteopan*
23. *Yoaltepec*
24. *Chalco*
25. Tepeacac
26. *Coayxtlahuacan*
27. Coyolapan

28. *Tlachquiavco*
29. *Tochtepec*
30. Xoconochco
31. Quauhtochco
32. *Cuetlaxtlan*
33. *Tlapacoyan*
34. *Tlatlauhquitepec*
35. *Tuchpa*
36. Atlan
37. *Tzicoac*
38. Oxitipan

Map 8. Tribute in warrior costumes. The greatest quantities were paid by provinces geographically close to the Valley of Mexico, with heavy concentrations to the west. All but six provinces provided these devices in tribute.

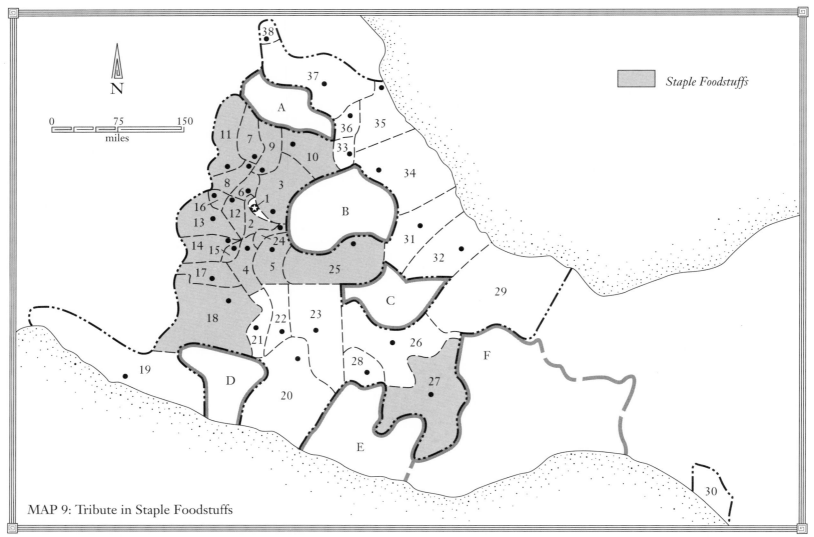

MAP 9: Tribute in Staple Foodstuffs

Imperial Boundary	PROVINCES	14. *Ocuilan*	28. Tlachquiavco
Provincial Boundary	1. Tlatelolco	15. *Malinalco*	29. Tochtepec
Independent Señoríos	2. *Petlacalco*	16. *Xocotitlan*	30. Xoconochco
● Provincial Cabecera	3. *Acolhuacan*	17. *Tlachco*	31. Quauhtochco
✪ Tenochtitlan	4. *Quauhnahuac*	18. *Tepequacuilco*	32. Cuetlaxtlan
	5. *Huaxtepec*	19. Çihuatlan	33. Tlapacoyan
	6. *Quauhtitlan*	20. Tlapan	34. Tlatlauhquitepec
INDEPENDENT SEÑORÍOS	7. *Axocopan*	21. Tlalcoçauhtitlan	35. Tuchpa
A. Metztitlan	8. *Atotonilco (de Pedraza)*	22. Quiauhteopan	36. Atlan
B. Tlaxcala	9. *Hueypuchtla*	23. Yoaltepec	37. Tzicoac
C. Teotitlan del Camino	10. *Atotonilco (el Grande)*	24. *Chalco*	38. Oxitipan
D. Yopitzinco	11. *Xilotepec*	25. *Tepeacac*	
E. Tototepec	12. *Quahuacan*	26. Coayxtlahuacan	
F. Realm of Coatlicamac	13. *Tuluca*	27. *Coyolapan*	

Map 9. Tribute in staple foodstuffs. In the *Codex Mendoza*, this usually
consists of maize, beans, chia, and amaranth. For the province of
Chalco, only maize and chia are indicated; for Tepeacac, only maize
and beans; and for Coyolapan, only maize, beans, and chia are listed.
Other variations are found in Tolocan with an extra bin of maize
and chia; in Chalco with two extra bins of maize; and in Quauhnahuac,
where the dots for chia have been omitted, the annotation includes chia.

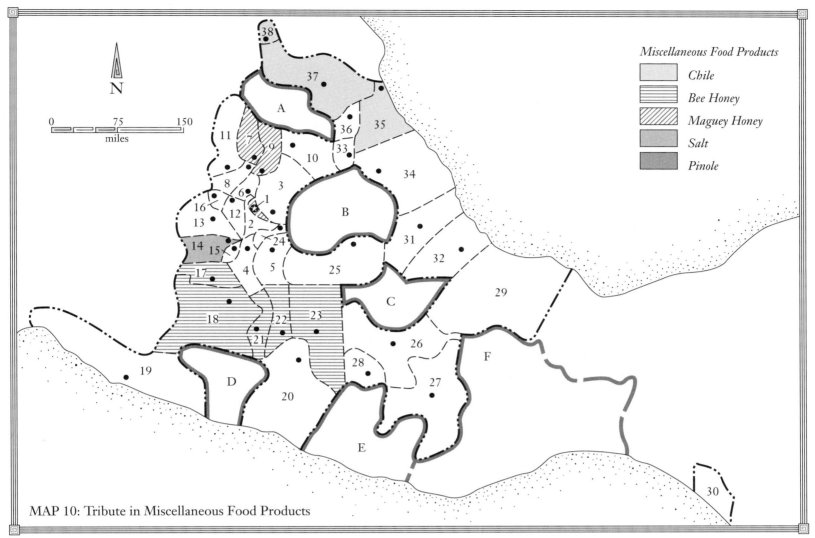

MAP 10: Tribute in Miscellaneous Food Products

Miscellaneous Food Products

☐	Chile
☰	Bee Honey
▨	Maguey Honey
▨	Salt
▨	Pinole

---·· Imperial Boundary
--- Provincial Boundary
▬▬ Independent Señoríos
• Provincial Cabecera
✪ Tenochtitlan

INDEPENDENT SEÑORÍOS
A. Metztitlan
B. Tlaxcala
C. Teotitlan del Camino
D. Yopitzinco
E. Tototepec
F. Realm of Coatlicamac

PROVINCES
1. *Tlatelolco*
2. Petlacalco
3. Acolhuacan
4. Quauhnahuac
5. Huaxtepec
6. Quauhtitlan
7. *Axocopan*
8. Atotonilco (de Pedraza)
9. *Hueypuchtla*
10. Atotonilco (el Grande)
11. Xilotepec
12. Quahuacan
13. Tuluca

14. *Ocuilan*
15. Malinalco
16. Xocotitlan
17. *Tlachco*
18. *Tepequacuilco*
19. Çihuatlan
20. Tlapan
21. *Tlalcoçauhtitlan*
22. *Quiauhteopan*
23. *Yoaltepec*
24. Chalco
25. Tepeacac
26. Coayxtlahuacan
27. Coyolapan

28. Tlachquiavco
29. Tochtepec
30. Xoconochco
31. Quauhtochco
32. Cuetlaxtlan
33. Tlapacoyan
34. Tlatlauhquitepec
35. *Tuchpa*
36. Atlan
37. *Tzicoac*
38. *Oxitipan*

Map 10. Tribute in miscellaneous food products. These products tend to be concentrated in specific regions, with chiles to the northeast, maguey honey just to the north of the Valley of Mexico, bee honey to the south, and salt to the southwest of the Valley of Mexico. *Pinole*, or ground toasted maize to be mixed with water (and, optionally, cacao or other flavoring), was part of the tribute of nearby Tlatelolco.

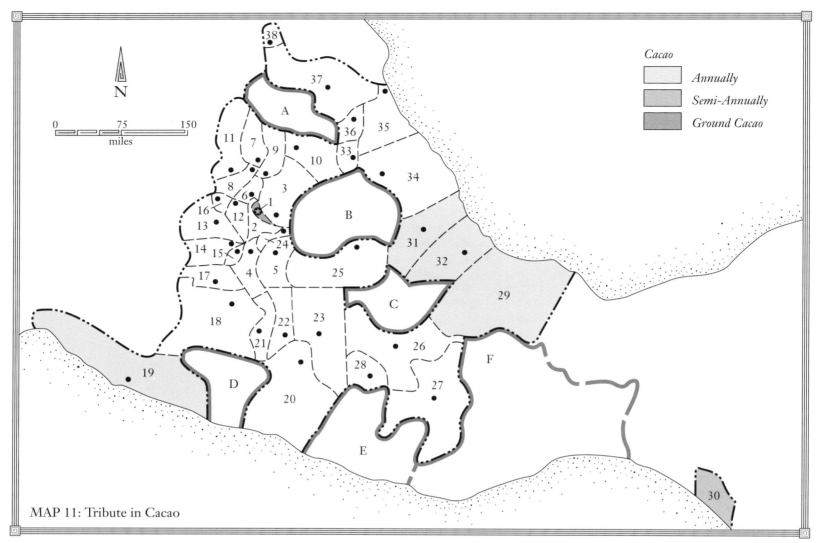

MAP 11: Tribute in Cacao

Cacao

	Annually
	Semi-Annually
	Ground Cacao

—··— Imperial Boundary
– – – Provincial Boundary
▬▬ Independent Señoríos
● Provincial Cabecera
✪ Tenochtitlan

INDEPENDENT SEÑORÍOS
A. Metztitlan
B. Tlaxcala
C. Teotitlan del Camino
D. Yopitzinco
E. Tototepec
F. Realm of Coatlicamac

PROVINCES
1. *Tlatelolco*
2. Petlacalco
3. Acolhuacan
4. Quauhnahuac
5. Huaxtepec
6. Quauhtitlan
7. Axocopan
8. Atotonilco (de Pedraza)
9. Hueypuchtla
10. Atotonilco (el Grande)
11. Xilotepec
12. Quahuacan
13. Tuluca

14. Ocuilan
15. Malinalco
16. Xocotitlan
17. Tlachco
18. Tepequacuilco
19. *Çihuatlan*
20. Tlapan
21. Tlalcoçauhtitlan
22. Quiauhteopan
23. Yoaltepec
24. Chalco
25. Tepeacac
26. Coayxtlahuacan
27. Coyolapan

28. Tlachquiavco
29. *Tochtepec*
30. *Xoconochco*
31. *Quauhtochco*
32. *Cuetlaxtlan*
33. Tlapacoyan
34. Tlatlauhquitepec
35. Tuchpa
36. Atlan
37. Tzicoac
38. Oxitipan

Map 11. Tribute in cacao. Like cotton, Gulf coast cacao was paid in tribute annually, while the Pacific coast product was rendered semi-annually. As with *pinole* (see map 10), Tlatelolco was required to present in tribute processed (ground) cacao.

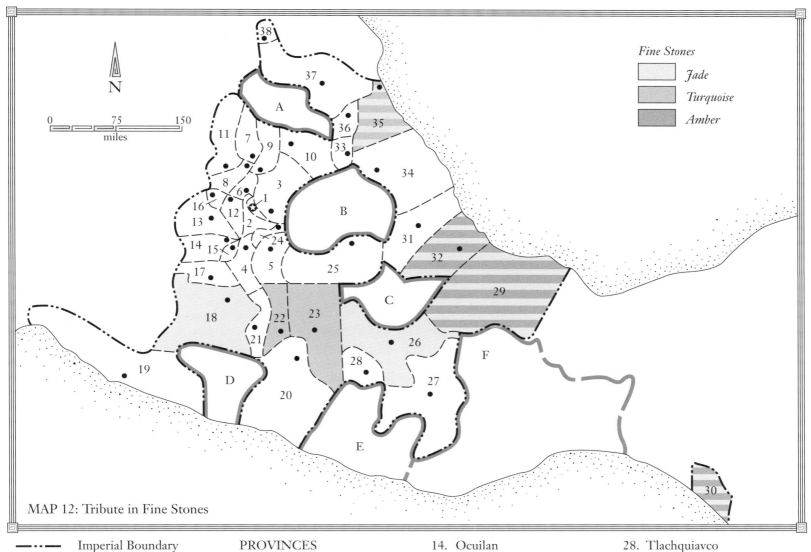

MAP 12: Tribute in Fine Stones

Fine Stones

Jade

Turquoise

Amber

–··–··– Imperial Boundary

– – – – Provincial Boundary

▬▬▬ Independent Señoríos

● Provincial Cabecera

✪ Tenochtitlan

INDEPENDENT SEÑORÍOS

A. Metztitlan
B. Tlaxcala
C. Teotitlan del Camino
D. Yopitzinco
E. Tototepec
F. Realm of Coatlicamac

PROVINCES

1. Tlatelolco
2. Petlacalco
3. Acolhuacan
4. Quauhnahuac
5. Huaxtepec
6. Quauhtitlan
7. Axocopan
8. Atotonilco (de Pedraza)
9. Hueypuchtla
10. Atotonilco (el Grande)
11. Xilotepec
12. Quahuacan
13. Tuluca
14. Ocuilan
15. Malinalco
16. Xocotitlan
17. Tlachco
18. *Tepequacuilco*
19. Çihuatlan
20. Tlapan
21. Tlalcoçauhtitlan
22. *Quiauhteopan*
23. *Yoaltepec*
24. Chalco
25. Tepeacac
26. *Coayxtlahuacan*
27. Coyolapan
28. Tlachquiavco
29. *Tochtepec*
30. *Xoconochco*
31. Quauhtochco
32. *Cuetlaxtlan*
33. Tlapacoyan
34. Tlatlauhquitepec
35. *Tuchpa*
36. Atlan
37. Tzicoac
38. Oxitipan

Map 12. Tribute in fine stones. All of these highly desired stones were available only from the more distant provinces.

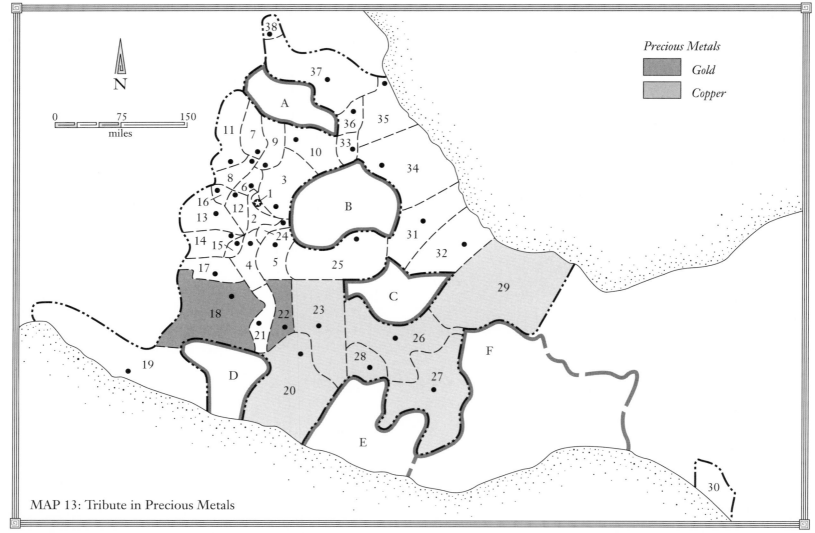

MAP 13: Tribute in Precious Metals

Precious Metals

■ Gold
▨ Copper

---·-- Imperial Boundary
------ Provincial Boundary
━━━ Independent Señoríos
• Provincial Cabecera
✪ Tenochtitlan

INDEPENDENT SEÑORÍOS
A. Metztitlan
B. Tlaxcala
C. Teotitlan del Camino
D. Yopitzinco
E. Tototepec
F. Realm of Coatlicamac

PROVINCES
1. Tlatelolco
2. Petlacalco
3. Acolhuacan
4. Quauhnahuac
5. Huaxtepec
6. Quauhtitlan
7. Axocopan
8. Atotonilco (de Pedraza)
9. Hueypuchtla
10. Atotonilco (el Grande)
11. Xilotepec
12. Quahuacan
13. Tuluca
14. Ocuilan
15. Malinalco
16. Xocotitlan
17. Tlachco
18. *Tepequacuilco*
19. Çihuatlan
20. *Tlapan*
21. Tlalcoçauhtitlan
22. *Quiauhteopan*
23. *Yoaltepec*
24. Chalco
25. Tepeacac
26. *Coayxtlahuacan*
27. *Coyolapan*
28. *Tlachquiavco*
29. *Tochtepec*
30. Xoconochco
31. Quauhtochco
32. Cuetlaxtlan
33. Tlapacoyan
34. Tlatlauhquitepec
35. Tuchpa
36. Atlan
37. Tzicoac
38. Oxitipan

Map 13. Tribute in precious metals. As with fine stones, precious metals were demanded from provinces at some distance from the imperial capitals.

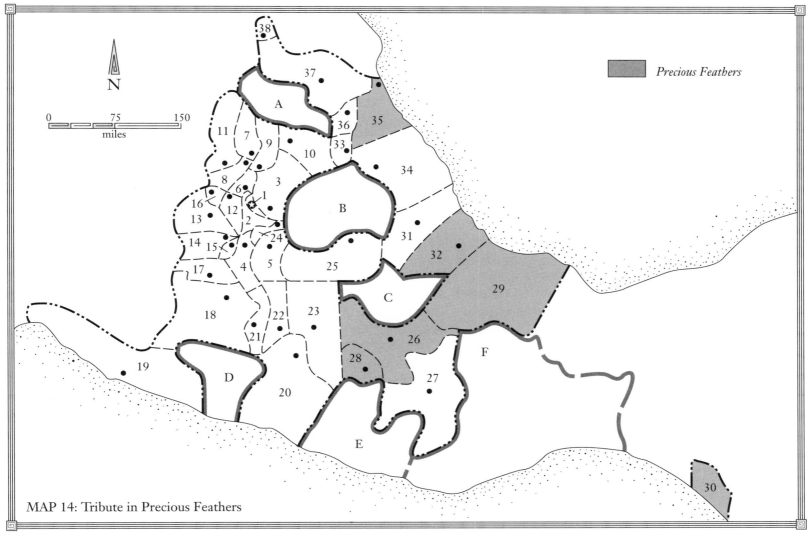

MAP 14: Tribute in Precious Feathers

Precious Feathers

- — ·· — Imperial Boundary
- — — — Provincial Boundary
- ▬▬▬ Independent Señoríos
- ● Provincial Cabecera
- ✪ Tenochtitlan

INDEPENDENT SEÑORÍOS
A. Metztitlan
B. Tlaxcala
C. Teotitlan del Camino
D. Yopitzinco
E. Tototepec
F. Realm of Coatlicamac

PROVINCES
1. Tlatelolco
2. Petlacalco
3. Acolhuacan
4. Quauhnahuac
5. Huaxtepec
6. Quauhtitlan
7. Axocopan
8. Atotonilco (de Pedraza)
9. Hueypuchtla
10. Atotonilco (el Grande)
11. Xilotepec
12. Quahuacan
13. Tuluca

14. Ocuilan
15. Malinalco
16. Xocotitlan
17. Tlachco
18. Tepequacuilco
19. Çihuatlan
20. Tlapan
21. Tlalcoçauhtitlan
22. Quiauhteopan
23. Yoaltepec
24. Chalco
25. Tepeacac
26. *Coayxtlahuacan*
27. Coyolapan

28. *Tlachquiavco*
29. *Tochtepec*
30. *Xoconochco*
31. Quauhtochco
32. *Cuetlaxtlan*
33. Tlapacoyan
34. Tlatlauhquitepec
35. *Tuchpa*
36. Atlan
37. Tzicoac
38. Oxitipan

Map 14. Tribute in precious feathers. All these provinces, except Tuchpa, gave the prized quetzal feathers as tribute; Tochtepec and Xoconochco also rendered a variety of other precious tropical feathers. Tuchpa, in the northeast, gave white down.

CHAPTER 6

The Ethnographic Content of the Third Part of the *Codex Mendoza*

Edward E. Calnek

The last part of *Codex Mendoza* has been the least studied of the three sections, possibly because it was thought to contain few points of ethnographic documentation not pursued in more elaborate detail in the somewhat later *Florentine Codex* (Sahagún 1950–1982). Robertson (1959) describes its main stylistic characteristics, but devotes only passing attention to its informational content.

Although *Mendoza* part 3 deals with several topics also covered in the *Florentine Codex*, it does so in a distinct way, and from the point of view of an entirely different social class. Sahagún relied primarily on elite or semi-elite informants (Calnek 1974). As discussed below, the Indian authors of part 3 were almost certainly *tolteca* or skilled craftsmen, who expressed the social perspective of Tenochtitlan's commoner population.

The works of Sahagún, like those of Durán, Motolinía, Alvarado Tezozomoc, and other early Colonial-period writers, were prose texts, in some cases with pictorial illustrations. *Codex Mendoza* part 3 is a pictorial-glyphic text with prose annotations and is therefore based on substantially different rules of narrative content and composition.

In this essay, I attempt a provisional identification of the social backgrounds of the authors of this highly distinctive ethnographic source, outline its main structural characteristics, and provide a relatively detailed outline of its ethnographic content.

The pictorial text itself consists of fifteen illustrated pages, with notes and comments in Spanish interspersed with the pictorial text or written out on a facing page. To facilitate identification of pertinent segments discussed below, I have divided part 3 as a whole into eighty-two numbered scenes positioned in the original manuscript as indicated in table 1. Individual scenes commonly depict the involvement of one or more individuals in some thematically distinct act, interaction, or state of being, and in most cases form part of larger or more inclusive narrative segments of the general type indicated in appendix D (see below).

The glosses and commentaries in Spanish for the most part identify the individuals or objects shown in the pictorial text or explain the significance of actions that would have been otherwise unintelligible to Europeans with little or no prior knowledge of Mesoamerican culture. In a few cases, however, the commentaries include significant information that is neither contained in nor implied by the pictorial text. Unfortunately, it cannot be determined with certainty whether this was supplied by the indigenous authors or other knowledgeable informants, or whether it derived from the annotator's own familiarity with the Nahuatl language and Aztec culture. Conversely, certain apparently significant elements appearing in the pictorial text, such as the counterclockwise footprints in scene 2, are neither mentioned nor explained in the commentaries.

THE AUTHORS

The question of authorship must be considered briefly, since it bears directly on the social field to which the manuscript's ethnographic content may be validly applied. Unlike parts 1 and 2, which were copied from earlier texts, part 3 was a substantially new composition. Robertson (1959:97) observes that "there was no na-

TABLE 1. LOCATION OF NUMBERED SCENES IN *MENDOZA* PART 3

Folio	Scene				Folio	Scene		
57r	1			2	64r	51		52
		3				53		54
58r	4			5		55	56	57
	6			7		58	59	60
	8			9	65r	61	62	63
	10			11		64	65	66
59r	12			13		67a	<–>	67d
	14			15		68a	<–>	68d
	16			17	66r		69	
	18			19		70		71
60r	20			21			72	
	22			23	67r		73	
	24			25			74	
	26			27	75a	<–>		75d
61r		28a			68r		76	
		28b					77	
		29b					78	
		29a			69r		79a	
62r	30	31 32		33			79b	
	34	35 36		37	70r	80a	<–>	80o
	38			39	71r	81a	<–>	81d
	40			41			82a	
63r	42	43		44			82b	
	45			46				
	47			48				
	49			50				

tive tradition for this part of the manuscript and that it was created especially for *Codex Mendoza*." Although a single *tlacuilo* is believed to have painted the entire codex, *tlacuiloque* were primarily scribes and copyists rather than the authors of pictorial texts. This, at least, was their pre-Conquest role, but it might have been at least partly suspended in the composition of so unusual a text as *Mendoza* part 3.

In his final remarks, the Spanish *ynterpretador* complained that because *los yndios* had been late in reaching agreement, he received the completed text for annotation only ten days before the scheduled departure of the fleet ("diez dias antes de la partida de la flota se dio al ynterpretador esta ystoria para que la ynterpretase *el qual descuydo fue de los yndios que acordaron tarde*" [folio 71v, emphasis added]). This brief comment establishes two key points: (1) that more than one individual was responsible for delaying the manuscript's delivery for annotation, and (2) that the Indians themselves controlled the process of composition, working with little or no direct Spanish supervision.

Clark (1938 1:98) suggests that the delay was caused by disagreements about the meaning of certain glyphs, but these would have arisen only in connection with the annotator's attempt to create reliable transcriptions in European script. Since the first two parts must have been copied from earlier prototypes, they are the least likely to have provoked debate. The nontraditional subject matter of part 3, on the other hand, might well have given rise to prolonged controversy on any number of points.

According to Robertson (1959:107), the *tlacuilo* himself "was not trained in native style before the Conquest but was rather trained following 1519–21, enough later so his style is not completely native in feeling." If so, he might have felt obliged to consult a group of knowledgeable elders—perhaps similar in composition to that recruited for the more ambitious projects of Fray Bernardino de Sahagún a few years later (López Austin 1974)—with respect to the content of *Mendoza* part 3.

Two scenes (S2 and S80i–m), both alluding to craft specialization, supply clues to the Indian authors' social if not personal identities. The first (fig. 1) depicts certain tools or instruments used by carpenters (*cuauhxinque*), manuscript painters (*tlacuiloque*), featherworkers (*amanteca*), and metalsmiths (*teocuitlahuaque*) in emblematic fashion. The written text identifies these as "insignia" representing the father's profession (*ofiçio*), which were placed in a male child's hand at the time of his ceremonial postnatal bathing by a midwife ("y al prinçipio de quando la criatura sacavan a bañar si era varon le sacauan con su ynsinia puesta en la mano de la criatura y la ynsinia era el ystrumento con que su padre de la criatura se exerçitaua" [folio 56v]).

The second scene (fig. 2) portrays fathers instructing their sons in basic craft skills (lapidaries [*tlatecque*] have been added to the original group), which will be used after reaching adulthood ("los ofiçios de carpintero y lapidario y pintor y platero y guarneçedor de plumas segun que estan figurados e yntulados [*sic*] signyfican que los tales maesos enseñavan los ofiçios a sus hijos luego desde muchachos para que syendo onbres se aplicasen por sus ofiçios" [folio 69v]).

This singling out of only five of Tenochtitlan's several dozen occupational specializations in these contexts is highly suggestive. The scenes just discussed indicate that the text as a whole is primarily concerned with life-cycle events as exemplified in the lives of the sons and daughters of *tolteca* or skilled craftsmen. It is highly probable that this was the case because its Indian authors were themselves members of these groups. Because of the great respect

Fig. 1. Craftsmen's insignia (scene 2): a. carpenter, b. featherworker, c. manuscript painter, d. goldsmith.

accorded to age and authority, responsibility for determining the actual content would have rested primarily with influential elders.

NARRATIVE STRUCTURE OF THE PICTORIAL TEXT

The third part of *Codex Mendoza* provides a highly synoptic narrative account of the main phases of male and female life cycles as understood by its Indian authors. Although individual scenes have been frequently utilized as illustrations in modern studies of Aztec social organization, there has been no previous attempt to identify and describe the more complex structural characteristics of the text as a whole.

Robertson's insightful description of the pictorial format includes the following critically important observations, which provide the basis for the analysis pursued below:

> The third section of Codex Mendoza is characterized by a layered page. The composition is divided either by a line into four horizontal zones (except those pages done as large single panels) or cast in the form of small evenly distributed items. *Action and meaning of the forms depends on a narrative, not on a unifying device of either time or place signs. . . .* The laminated pages of the third section suggest that even when the artist of the Mendoza was not working from a tira or a copy of a tira, the single long sheet of paper was the organizing element in his work. This third section suggests strongly that the artist conceived his design in a single, continuous strip rearranged to fit the pages of the codex as we have it now. (1959:101, emphasis added.)

To show more clearly what the artist had in mind, an approximation to the *tira* format exemplified by the *Tira de la Peregrinación* (*Codex Boturini* 1964–1967) and *Tira de Tepexpan* was prepared as figure 1 of appendix D. Figure 2 (appendix D) is a simplified flow chart highlighting interconnections between the scenes and segments identified in figure 1.

It will be observed that the pictorial text splits into separate lines for males and females after scene 2, and that the male line subsequently splits to represent separate careers linked with the *calmecac* and *cuicacalli* (scenes 3 and 28). This was achieved by the following means. Scene 1 on the first page depicts a newborn child of indeterminate sex. A dotted line from the infant's toe leads through four rosettes (signifying the passage of four days) to a midwife holding the same child in scene 2, just before performing the crucially important bathing and naming ceremony. At this point, separate lines from the infant's finger lead upward to a set of male emblems (shield and arrows and craft tools) and downward to female emblems (broom, spindle, and workbasket). If the child were male, the next significant act, according to this Spanish text, would be his ritual presentation to either a senior priest (*alfaqui mayor*) or a master of youths (*maeso de muchachos y moços*), as indicated by dotted lines in scene 3. This determined whether he would enter the

Fig. 2. The training of young craftsmen by their fathers (scene 80): 1. carpenter, m. lapidary, n. manuscript painter, o. goldsmith, p. featherworker.

calmecac, to be trained as a priest, or the *cuicacalli*, for noneclesiastical training, beginning with scene 28.

The interrelationships between individual scenes and segments are sometimes difficult to grasp when displayed in European page format, because visual continuities were seriously disrupted when "rearranged to fit the pages of the codex as we have it now." The artist's intent is, however, readily understood within the reconstructed *tira* format of figure 1 in appendix D. This applies without significant complications from scene 1 through scene 68, where contrasting male-female careers and the distinction between *calmecac* and *cuicacalli* are easily discerned.

The *tira* format yields to somewhat different visual arrangements on the next pages, dealing with military operations, judicial procedures, moral issues, and old age. Scenes 69–79 and 82 continue the overall progression from youth though adulthood to old age. The complex arrangement of vignettes in scene 80, occupying the whole of folio 70r, serves a somewhat different purpose, since they relate primarily to moral choices made in adolescence or early adulthood.

Despite these complications, there is an overarching narrative structure linking the first and last scenes in a particularly striking way. If the first scene introduces a newborn child to the Aztec world, the final page (folio 71r) illustrates two sharply contrasting ways in which the same child's life might come to an end. Young men and women executed for drunkenness, theft, and adultery occupy the upper third of the page, while just below we observe the privileges enjoyed by the very old after lifetimes of virtuous conduct (S81). The juxtaposition of early death and privileged old age on a single page highlights the importance assigned this specific thematic opposition. The penalty for intoxication, theft, or adultery while young was death. A reward for temperance and good conduct was the "freedom to drink wine [*pulque*] in public or private and intoxicate themselves because they were very old and had children and grandchildren" ("tenya liçençia asi en publico como en secreto de poder beuer vino y enbeodarse por ser de tanta edad y tener hijos y nietos").

The pictorial text as a whole thereby identifies two, and only two, ways in which the lives commenced in the first scene of its first page might be brought to an end. The intervening pages illustrate the nature and consequences of the choices by means of which the individual could, and within the framework of *Mendoza* part 3 inevitably would, arrive at one of these destinations.

The eighty-two scenes of the pictorial text are a fairly small number given the actual complexity of individual lives. The expository technique just described nonetheless served to multiply the number of possible life scenarios with maximum economy of means. The same scene, for example, frequently serves a number of distinct functions. Scene 1 depicts mother and child, a single speech scroll, a crib, and secondary features such as hairstyle and clothing, which, like adjectives in speech, contribute significantly to contextual definition. The speech scroll suggests a mother addressing her newborn child. This is certainly correct, but speech scrolls in pre-Hispanic pictorial texts almost never allude to incidental or indiscriminate speech events (although they may in certain contexts), but serve to indicate that highly specific oral texts should be introduced at that point (see Calnek 1978). Sahagún's account of birth-related ceremonials contains several formal orations of this type (e.g., 1950–1982 6, chapters 32–34). A full understanding of the pictorial scene accordingly requires knowledge of what was being said. Unfortunately, this was not transcribed by the annotator, even though it is likely to have been in the minds of the authors of *Mendoza* part 3.

The choice of birth rather than some other event to begin the pictorial text, while by no means illogical, requires brief comment in its own right. Book 6 of Sahagún's *Florentine Codex* describes childbirth at much greater length, but as the culmination of a very detailed account of matchmaking, marriage, and pregnancy (chapters 23–39). The rearing and education of children is described in greatest detail in books 3 (appendix: chapters 4–8) and 8 (chapters 16, 20). Sahagún's primary objective in these books was to describe customary practice as understood by Indian informants responding to his own precisely formulated questionnaires. In *Mendoza* part 3, however, birth introduces a series of events that might culminate in either death by execution or the privileged status of the very old. Either possibility, moreover, could be realized by individuals of either sex. Viewed from this standpoint, *Mendoza* part 3 is less a generalized account of Aztec life than a map outlining possible routes leading from birth to one or the other of the denouements portrayed in the final scenes.

Comparison of this scene with parallel sections of the Sahagún texts reveals still more significant details. The infant discussed here appears to have been both swaddled and placed in a boxlike cradle. The cradle itself is identical to those shown in the *Florentine Codex* (6: figs. 27, 31), but according to Sahagún, neither male nor female infants were placed in a cradle until bathed and named during a ceremony held at daybreak, usually four days after birth (ibid.: 205). Sahagún (ibid.: 197–199) devotes an entire chapter to the role of the calendar priests in selecting a child's name. No such event is recorded in *Codex Mendoza*, which says that the midwife chose a name for the child ("y el nonbre que le ponían era qual la partera le queria poner" [folio 56v]).

Both sources agree that a male child's umbilical cord was bound to the small shield crossed with four arrows shown in the second scene of *Mendoza* part 3, after which it was taken away to be buried in a battlefield location (folio 55v; Sahagún 1950–1982 4:3–4). Sahagún does not, on the other hand, refer to the placing of instruments symbolizing the transmission of hereditary occupational specializations, described as follows in *Mendoza* part 3: "when they took the creature for bathing, if he were male, they took him with his insignia placed in his hand, and the insignia was the instrument which his father used . . . such as that of the goldsmith [*platero*] or that of the wood carver [*entallador*], or of any other profession" ("quando la criatura sacavan a bañar si era varon le sacauan con su ynsinia puesta en la mano de la criatura y la ynsinia era el ystrumento con que su padre de la criatura se exerçitaua . . . o ofiçios asi de platero como de entallador o otro qualquier ofiçio" [folio 56v]). The first ritual, signifying a future commitment to war, was performed for males of all social ranks; the second, signifying commitment to specific craft specializations, reflects both class and occupational distinctions.

These brief examples indicate something of the density and economy with which information could be expressed and stored in relatively simple pictorial scenes. The same parsimonious approach also characterizes much larger narrative units, in which straightforward portrayals of acts and events were combined to form narrative texts of much greater complexity.

The first scenes of part 3 (folio 57r) again provide an exceptionally clear illustration of the differing ways in which a single scene, or even a part of a single scene, could be incorporated in two or more otherwise discrete narrative sequences. The sex of the newborn child in scene 1, as previously noted, is undefined, but should not therefore be regarded as undetermined. Scene 2 resolves this apparent ambiguity in the following way. The scene is a composite

in the sense that while some of its elements allude to ceremonial procedures that were the same for both males and females, other important features are quite distinct. This is an ethnographic datum that may be legitimately inferred from the pictorial text, but a choice must be made before the scene can be accurately read.

The correct narrative sequence is unambiguously defined by a dotted line extending from the infant in the first scene to the midwife in the second, and thereafter toward either the male insignia above or the female insignia below. If we choose to follow male careers, we must, as remarked earlier, proceed from scene 2 to scene 3, where the male child must be dedicated to either an ecclesiastical or a secular career, and thereafter to the child-rearing scenes on the left side of the next three pages (up to S26). If we choose to examine female careers, the sequence moves from scene 2 directly to scene 5, and from this through scenes on the right-hand side (up to S27). The only indicated option thereafter was to marry at age fifteen (S29).

The basic ramifying structure of part 3 just discussed persists through most of the fifteen pages of the pictorial text. This is based, for the most part, on very simple binary oppositions: male-female, secular-ecclesiastical, virtue-vice, success-failure, death-life, and the like.

It should be emphasized that what has been described to this point is the skeletal design of *Mendoza* part 3, rather than its sometimes highly dramatic pictorial content. Although part 3 was unquestionably created especially for *Codex Mendoza*, its design was almost certainly modeled on that of certain categories of pre-Spanish historical texts such as the *Tira de la Peregrinación* or *Tira de Tepexpan*, but perhaps even more closely on *mapas históricos* similar to the *Mapa de Sigüenza* or *Códice Xolotl*. Each of these is based on sequentially ordered pictorial scenes similar in type to those just described, with individual scenes depicting specific events similar in structural type to those under discussion here (see Calnek 1978). The principal difference is that historical events are conventionally regarded as entirely unique (even if any given historical pattern may be indefinitely repeated), whereas the events portrayed in *Mendoza* part 3, while uniquely experienced by a given individual, conform to replicable patterns realized any number of times in actual practice.

As indicated in figures 1 and 2 of appendix D, a logical connection may well link scenes that are widely separated in the manuscript. Marriage rites (S29b), for example, are placed as if they were a continuation of the female child-rearing sequence. Females, according to this source, were married at age fifteen (S29); males married only after several years of further training and military experience. Since the marriage scene appears in the manuscript only once, it must be assumed to be insertable—at least in imagination—at a later point in the text. Scene 76 does show a young man taking leave from others with whom he has lived for several years. The presence of his wife (engaged in spinning) in the same scene implies that he had previously participated in the marriage ceremony figuring only in scene 29b.

THEMATIC CONTENT

Mendoza part 3 encapsulates several alternative life histories in a single text by the means just described. Any complete analysis would require both the dissection of each scene into its component semantic units and the tracing out of individual lives in each category (male-female; secular-religious, and so on) from the first to the last scenes. Strict logical procedure would also demand that attempts to compare part 3 with other sources be undertaken only when the relationship between individual scenes and the manuscript as a whole has been clearly and explicitly defined.

It must be emphasized that the *Mendoza's* third section, although relatively brief, is a complete pictorial text in itself, and by no means a simplified version of parallel chapters in the *Florentine Codex* or any other source. Although it probably contains occasional errors of the kind likely to occur in any pictorial or prose text composed *de novo* and with great haste, it must be assumed to provide valid representations of Aztec ritual, educational practice, life aspirations, moral beliefs, and the like, as experienced by the groups discussed in connection with the question of authorship. If these differ significantly from parallel accounts in the Sahagún texts, it must be at least provisionally assumed that we deal with actual variations in belief and practice within Tenochtitlan's highly complex urban population.

Fray Diego Durán indicates that this was indeed the case when he contrasts upper- and lower-class practice in the following sharply stated and self-consciously elitist terms:

> We can affirm that for people so remote and lacking contact with polished Spanish lands there has been no people on earth, who lived in their paganism with such harmony, good organization, and social order as this nation. *I speak of the illustrious and noble people because I must confess that there was a coarse lower class.* . . . It is my opinion that, no matter how beastly, they practiced their religion and its precepts well, though not with the refinements of the noblemen and lords. (1971:287 emphasis added.)

Sahagún occasionally makes very similar distinctions, for example, when he contrasts the expensive clothing worn by the sons of lords and rich persons when entering the *calmecac* with that worn by the sons of the poor (1946 1:325), or remarks on the inferior resources displayed when "poor people" conducted the bathing and naming rituals (1950–1982 6:201).

It may be usefully recalled at this point that the social stratum composed of petty artisans, most of whom were full-time nonagricultural occupational specialists, was by far the largest single component of Tenochtitlan's large and highly urbanized population (Calnek 1972). By the mid-fifteenth century or earlier, urban craftsmen, together with the *pochteca* or merchants responsible for maintaining a steady flow of exotic raw materials to Tenochtitlan as well as for reselling finished goods at market centers throughout Mesoamerica, enjoyed a relatively privileged position within the commoner population.

Although reliable figures cannot be obtained, we know that there were at least six merchant *barrios* in Tenochtitlan and its sister city, Tlatelolco, and several times that number occupied by specialized craftsmen, including those represented in *Codex Mendoza.* The *amanteca* or featherworkers, for example, occupied at least one *barrio* named Amantlan (Place of the Featherworkers) in Tlatelolco, and at least two more in Tenochtitlan (Sahagún 1950–1982 9:88; AGN Tierras 20-1-1 and 35-6). Metalsmiths lived in the *barrio* of Yopico in Tenochtitlan, where they worshiped Xipe Totec—one of the most powerful and prestigious gods of the Aztec pantheon (Sahagún 1950–1982 2:2, 5, 44, 49, 50, 199; 9: 69–71). Carpenters and woodcarvers must have been numerous, but cannot yet be linked with identifiable pre-Conquest or Colonial-period *barrios.*

These and other similarly constituted craft groups were organized into corporate, localized, guildlike units called *calpultin* (sing. *calpulli,* literally "large house"). Although there is no specific reference to the *calpulli* system in the *Mendoza's* third section, the practice of placing an implement signifying a boy's father's occupation in his hand during the bathing ceremony as depicted in this codex may well have involved the ritual assignment of *calpulli* membership, while also acknowledging the hereditary nature of craft specializations.

In fact, and perhaps unfortunately, *Mendoza* part 3 tells us remarkably little about the actual practice of craft specializations. It does, nonetheless, provide a graphic portrayal of a life-style evidently considered typical by its authors. To judge from the three pages dealing with a male child's early years (folios 58r–60r, S4-27; see below for a review of female careers), the future artisan was routinely trained in frugality, severely disciplined, and incessantly lectured until he left his natal household to continue his training at either the *calmecac* or the *cuicacalli.*

He began to carry small basins of water and was assigned other forms of light work as early as age four. At age five, he carried firewood and other small items to the market. Aged six, he scavenged for grains of maize, beans, and what the Spanish commentary (folio 57v) calls "otras myserias," and at seven, he received a first lesson in the use of a fishnet.

The five scenes that follow (ages 8–12) shift to the depiction of increasingly severe punishments meted out, according to the Spanish text (folios 58v–60r), to children who were negligent, rebellious, or lazy, or who refused to accept verbal correction ("que no Reçebia correçion de palabra"). The punishments themselves commenced with simple threats (S14), followed (at yearly intervals) by pricking with maguey thorns (S16), beating with a stick (S18), forced inhalation of smoke from burning red chile peppers (S18), and prolonged exposure on cold damp ground (S20).

That the examples of Aztec child-rearing practices from age three to twelve given here were intentionally paradigmatic is suggested by their suspiciously symmetrical division into two equivalent five-year segments. The purpose of these illustrations, I suspect, was to highlight parental responsibility for instructing, admonishing, and disciplining children, together with the child's reciprocal obligation to contribute, however modestly, to the economic well-being of the domestic group. Instruction during the first five years (ages three to seven) was designed to inculcate basic norms of virtuous conduct; the increasingly serious consequences of deviating from these norms were set forth during the next five-year period. The final scenes, which show boys of thirteen and fourteen bringing wood from the mountain, collecting reeds in canoes, and catching fish in the lagoon without the least trace of adolescent rebellion, tell us that these lessons had been well learned.

Female training closely paralleled that of males up to age fifteen, differing primarily in that the girl was bound to the domestic milieu from the moment of birth. Where males were dedicated from birth to both military service and craft specialization, the only insignia utilized in the girl's bathing and naming ritual were broom, spindle, and workbasket (S2). Her umbilical cord was buried under a *metate* ("su obligo le enterravan debaxo del metate piedra de moler tortillas [folio 56v]), signifying her lifetime commitment to domesticity. Sahagún (1950–1982 6:171) expresses the same attitude when he writes that the umbilical cord of a female infant was buried near the hearth, "which signified that the woman was to go nowhere. Her very task was the home life, life by the fire, by the grinding stone."

Once again, five years of relaxed instruction, primarily concerned with using the spindle to prepare thread, were followed by five years of increasingly stringent punitive sanctions, similar in type but less rigorous than those applied to boys of the same age. The last two scenes (S25 and S27) depict mothers teaching daughters aged thirteen and fourteen to cook and weave—indispensable skills, since each girl will, as indicated in the next scene (S29), be available for marriage at age fifteen.

The ethnographic significance of the child-rearing scenes is by no means exhausted by a recounting of their evident moralizing intent. The activities in which young males engaged—at least when not being actively punished—might be thought to suggest that craftsmen and their families lived in the shadow of economic destitution. Why else employ young boys, the sons of specialized artisans, to scavenge grains of maize and other nearly valueless items left behind in the market? Berdan (1982:85) relates this scene (S10) to Sahagún's (1950–1982 5:184) reference to the practice of quickly gathering up "dried grains of maize lying scattered on the ground" lest they (the maize grains) "suffer" and "weep"— to him just another instance of the deluded thought characteristic of all pre-Conquest religion—in which case the motivation would have been primarily religious. She plausibly suggests (personal communication) that moral training rather than economic need explains the inclusion of this and similar scenes.

Although definitive answers to questions of this type are not easily found, it may be pointed out that highly complex craft skills could have been acquired only in the course of long and meticulously supervised apprenticeships. The instructional process itself is shown in only five vignettes on the next to last page (folio 70r, S80 l–p), which illustrate "the professions of carpenter, lapidary, [manuscript] painter, goldsmith, and feather-worker . . . [and] signify that the said masters taught these professions to their children from childhood, so that in becoming men they should apply themselves to these professions and occupy [their] time with virtuous things" ("los oficios de carpintero y lapidario y pintor y platero y guarneçedor de plumas . . . signyfican que los tales maesos enseñavan los oficios a sus hijos luego desde muchachos para que syendo onbres se aplicasen por sus oficios y ocupasen el tiempo en cosas de virtud" [folio 69v]).

In sharp contrast to the highly authoritarian parent-child relationships just discussed, these illustrations convey a sense of intense mutual involvement in the learning process. Speech glyphs emerging from the mouths of both sons and fathers suggest that the artist here means to represent conversation rather than formal orations. The son of the featherworker (*maeso de guarneçer con plumas*) holds a feather and cutting tool in his own hand, while carefully observing their use by his father (S80m). The goldsmith blows through a long tube to increase the heat of his fire; the son appears to be commenting on some aspect of this delicate procedure (S80o).

When the message of this page is considered in its entirety, however, we find that it is, after all, still another repetition of the familiar sermon favoring virtuous conduct and condemning the usual vices. Although the pictorial text is perfectly clear on this point, the commentary provides an uncharacteristically detailed account of the actual kinds of good advice offered by fathers to sons, "giving them as an example that those who achieve every virtue come to the attention of the rulers and lords, who will assign to them honorable responsibilities, employ them as messengers, and the musicians and singers will admit them to their festivals and weddings, because of the special regard in which they are held" ("ponyendole por ejemplo que los que llegan a toda virtud vyenen despues a valer con los señores y caçiques en que les dan cargos

horrosos [*sic*] y los ocupan por sus mensajeros. y que los musicos y cantores los admyten en sus fiestas y bodas por la priuança que tyenen" [folio 69v]).

CLASS POSITION OF URBAN CRAFT GROUPS

Despite the wealth and prestige awarded to skilled craftsmen in pre-Conquest Tenochtitlan, their status as *macehualtin* (sing. *macehualli*, commoner) rather than *pipiltin* (sing. *pilli*, nobleman) is not in dispute. The term *macehualli* was applied to all persons of non-royal descent, and also to *pipiltin* stripped of noble status by judicial process or royal decree. It is thus defined by the absence of those social and genealogical qualifications associated with noble status. Depending on the size and internal composition of any specific city-state, the commoner population might or might not be divided into class or castelike subgroups.

The system of social stratification was complicated by the fact that most commoners, regardless of status, relied on full-time non-agricultural occupational specializations for their incomes, and by the fact that mercantile and craft specializations were the most prosperous and highly ranked among these (Calnek 1972, 1976, 1978). In this source, however, allusions to class stratification are subdued and invariably upward rather than downward looking. In the passage quoted at the end of the last section, the right of *señores y caciques* (lords and rulers) to control the distribution of rewards for virtuous conduct is simply taken for granted.

The inferior standing of part 3's protagonists vis-à-vis the nobility is further indicated in the portrayal of religious architecture and titled noblemen. Thus pyramids and temples, drawn in a small scale, figure in only three scenes in the *Mendoza*'s third section, where they are glossed respectively as *ayauhcali* (house of mist, S51), *çihuateocali* (temple of women, S53), or simply *mezquita* (literally, "mosque," but here designating a small pyramid-temple, S50). They figure, not as the focal points of socially crucial ceremonial events, but as places where young commoners worked out their labor obligations (*coatequitl*).

Facing the third temple (*cihuateocalli*), a *tecuhtli* (lord) and his assistant (*mandón*) supervise repairs to nearby streets and bridges (S53; "anda ocupado en reparar las calles y puentes que van a parar a la mezquita" [folio 64r]). The small size of these temples contrasts sharply with that of the *calmecac* and *cuicacalli*, which are represented at a significantly larger scale (S28).

The corveé system figures again toward the end of the manuscript (S80d; fig. 3). Here the *petlacalcatl* or high steward gives "good advice" to two young men, weeping because they had been called up to provide personal (labor) services ("llorando por se les aver ofreçido de que los ocupe en seruyçios personales que Representan las coas y guacales" [folio 69v]). The *petlacalcatl* sits on a reed stool in a building named *texancalco*, "where they meet to discuss and organize public works" ("donde se junta a tratar y proveer para las obras publicas" [folio 69v]). The *texancalli* (also called *calpixcacalli*) is described by Sahagún (1950–1982 8:44) as the place where "all the majordomos and tribute gatherers" assembled to await the ruler's commands. The *petlacalcatl* was an extremely important official, responsible for supervising the procurement of tributes in goods and labor throughout the Aztec empire in its entirety (Sahagún 1950–1982 8:51; Alvarado Tezozomoc 1944:149, 162, 256).

In real life, the young men would probably have been lectured by a *calpixqui* or steward of considerably lower rank. The vignette

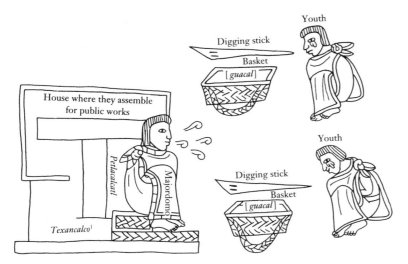

Fig. 3. *Coatequitl* (corvée).

(S80d) discussed here may depict the *petlacalcatl* instead in order to stress the subordination of young men of artisan class and therefore *macehual* status to the powerful administrative apparatus headed by the high steward of Motecuhzoma. The crucial point is that the *tetecuhtin*, the judges, and the very few other high officials depicted are the wielders of governmental authority, whereas commoners, who are the actual protagonists of *Mendoza* part 3, either obey or are punished for their disobedience.

At the same time, we see nothing of groups ranking below the artisan class such as porters (*tlameme*), slaves (*tlacotin*), or others engaged in menial labor. The young men with whom we have been concerned might fish in the lagoon to augment household incomes, but they would become craftsmen, priests, or warriors rather than professional fishermen. Similarly, the females could spin and weave, but this was an adjunct to domestic life rather than a professional skill.

FEMALE CAREERS

Female lives as viewed by the presumably male authors of *Mendoza* part 3 are portrayed in highly schematic fashion (57r–61r). From the moment of birth, we learn, the properly reared girl must aspire to the purely domestic career symbolized by the broom, spindle, and workbasket used in the postnatal bathing rite (S2) and by the burial of her umbilical cord under a grinding stone (*metate*) near the hearth.

Accordingly, and as represented in *Mendoza* part 3, the young girl was trained primarily in basic domestic skills (cooking, spinning, weaving, child care, etc.) After this, she was carried to the groom's house for the elaborately conducted marriage ceremony shown on folio 61r. Her life thereafter is summed up by returning to the first scene of the pictorial (S1), by substituting the newly married girl after the birth of her first child for her own mother.

But what else could a woman do? According to Sahagún (1950–1982 6:209–218), both male and female infants were promised to the *calmecac* or *telpochcalli-cuicacalli* at birth, but no such reference exists in *Mendoza* part 3. Similarly, Sahagún's informants describe the key role played by female *amanteca* in the featherworker's craft (ibid. 9:88), but this role passes without explicit notice in *Codex Mendoza*. the meager repertoire of nondomestic options actually represented in this source includes the roles of matchmaker, curer, and midwife, discussed below, together with a few less praiseworthy options.

Two scenes (S46 and S48) allude to the involvement of young women in illicit sexual unions with novice priests and apprentice warriors. That neither was married is indicated by hairstyle. Both are shown in kneeling postures, arms crossed, simply dressed, and seemingly contrite. The purpose of these scenes is not, however, to depict female roles, but to illustrate the severe punishments (being beaten with sticks or stabbed with maguey spines) meted out to their male partners.

The pictorial text otherwise documents very few positively evaluated female careers. The first is that of the *partera* or midwife, who presides at the bathing and naming ceremony in scene 2. The second involves a woman somewhat perplexingly glossed with the word *amanteca* (S29a), which refers to featherworkers, but which is here glossed as a "female physician" (*médica*) who carried the bride on her back to the house of the groom ("la desposada la lleuaba a cuestas . . . vna amanteça [sic] que es medica . . . y llegada a casa del desposado," etc.). Conceivably the annotator, working hastily, wrote *amanteça* rather than *tiçitl*. Since women were, as mentioned above, active participants in the featherworkers' craft, she may indeed have been an *amanteca* who was also a *tiçitl*—a word that meant, according to Sahagún, a (female) curer, midwife, or matchmaker (see, for example, 1950–1982 6, chapters 23–38, for several examples).

Also interesting is the appearance of women with men while engaged in vigorously contested court litigation (S78 and S79b). Significant here is that both in first hearing and later appeal, men and women appear to speak with the same freedom, and the latter with considerably greater élan.

Although the bathing-and-naming ritual shown in scene 2 differs slightly from that described by Sahagún (see above), the midwife's overall role is substantially the same in both accounts. Similarly, Sahagún's description of marriage rites (1950–1982 6:130–131) differs from that portrayed in scene 29 only in a few minor details. He writes that the bride's face was colored with "pyrites" (reddish pigment) and that after sunset she was carried to the groom's house on the back of "a woman whose task it was, one already strong," accompanied by torch-bearing female relatives. Once in the groom's house, "they placed the woman to the left, and they placed the man to the right of the woman. . . . And the elderly matchmakers [*in titici*] then tied them together. They took the corner of the man's cape; also they drew up the woman's shift; then they tied these together" (ibid.:131–132). The *Florentine Codex* provides a great deal more information than can be inferred from the corresponding scene in *Codex Mendoza*, but many of the points noted in the preceding citations are readily identifiable in the latter. The only readily noted distinction is that the first source says that the bride was carried in a sling made of black cloth (*manta*), whereas the latter shows this as white.

In short, the only legitimate female professions other than marriage and motherhood illustrated in this source were those of midwife and curer. Judged by content alone, it could be argued that the principal thrust of *Mendoza* part 3 as a whole was didactic and moralizing, and that the lives of women are dealt with just so far as was required to illustrate the authors' views on the question of female virtue. This may explain why the total number of explicitly portrayed female roles—even if the drunken wife of a drunken thief (S80), the *muger moça* (young woman) executed for drunkenness (S81), and the elderly female tipplers (S82) shown on the last two pages (folios 70r and 71r) are included—is so extremely reduced.

That there was a much wider range of male career options should be clear from the preceding discussion. It must be observed, nonetheless, that male lives were in no sense less rigidly controlled. Whatever their social rank or occupational status, Aztec males were committed from birth to training for and participation in hand-to-hand combat. It was primarily parental choice that dictated whether a boy would enter the priesthood or learn basic occupational skills from his father.

In either case, boys remained at home until age fifteen. The father's primary responsibility for discipline and moral training through a series of activities analogous to those in which females engaged has been previously discussed. But where girl and mother are shown in exclusively domestic settings, father-son activities took place in such varied locales as the countryside (S8), the marketplace (S10), or the open lake surrounding Tenochtitlan (S24, 26). The greater versatility involved in the early education of males seems to have forced the artist sometimes to represent the same adult male as if he were father of two sons of the same age in three scenes (S8, 10, 24), although only one child appears in the others. No comparable device was required to depict the evidently more stereotyped training of a young girl.

The most important distinction, however, was that while a girl moved directly from childhood to social adulthood when she married at age fifteen, boys simply commenced a new course of training at the *calmecac* or *cuicacalli* (S28a, b; indistinguishable in function in this text from the *telpochcalli* [young men's house] described by Sahagún; see Calnek 1988), so that marriage and fatherhood, at least for those who did not become priests, was necessarily deferred for several years.

Although the time period involved was little more than a half dozen years, the next scenes are among the most detailed and valuable in this part of the codex. The main thrust of the text is to highlight the possibilities for social advancement available to *macehualtin*, whether priests or craftsmen, by taking live prisoners of war in hand-to-hand combat. Warriors advanced from rank to rank with each such conquest, donning the increasingly prestigious military-religious costumes so splendidly illustrated in scenes 55–60 and 62–68 at each stage (see analysis by Anawalt in this volume).

The *calmecac*'s function was to train noblemen and certain socially qualified commoners to assume high office within the Aztec state, as well as for routine ecclesiastical careers. At the *cuicacalli*, an institution closely linked with the *telpochcalli* (young men's house; see below), training in military skills was combined with more routine service to the religious establishment and the state.

The Calmecac

The word *calmecac* meant "a rope of houses" (*cal[li]*, house + *meca[tl]*, rope + *c*, within), or possibly "a corridor" as Andrews (1975:424) suggests. Sahagún identifies a total of eight *calmecac*— seven apparently located within Tenochtitlan's ceremonial precinct (1950–1982 2:165ff.). The eighth was located in a barrio named Amantlan (ibid. 9:88). Alvarado Tezozomoc (1944:271) lists a total of eleven *calmecac*, five of which also appear in Sahagún's list (see table 2). The *calmecac*, it may be remarked, was attended by most males of noble rank (*pipiltin*), although the sons of poor men could also be admitted and might aspire to the highest ecclesiastical ranks. Sahagún (ibid. 3:69) writes that "no lineage was considered; only a good life was noted" when it was a question of se-

TABLE 2. CALMECAC IN TENOCHTITLAN

Sahagún	Alvarado Tezozomoc
Tlillan Calmecac*	Tlilancalco (Calmecac)
Mexico Calmecac*	—
Huitznahuac Calmecac*	Huitznahuac (Calmecac)
Tetlanman Calmecac*	—
Tlamatzinco Calmecac*	Tlamatzinco (Calmecac)
Yopico Calmecac*	Yupico (Calmecac)
Tzonmolco Calmecac*	Tzomnolco [sic] (Calmecac)
(Amantlan) Calmecac†	—
	Tlacatecpan (Calmecac)
	Atempan (Calmecac)
	Coatlan (Calmecac)
	Molloco (Calmecac)
	Izquitlan (Calmecac)
	Tezcacoac (Calmecac)

*Sahagún 1950–1982 2:165ff.   Alvarado Tezozomoc 1944:271.
†Sahagún 1950–1982 9:88.

lecting priests of the highest rank holding the title *Quetzalcoatl* ("either Totec Tlamacazqui or Tlaloc").

With the exception of Mexico Calmecac, the names of each of the above-listed *calmecacs* are also the names of *barrios* (*calpullis* or *tlaxillacallis*) in Tenochtitlan. Two of these—Yopico and Amantlan—were occupied by craft specialists (goldworkers and featherworkers respectively; Sahagún 1950–1982 2:2, 5, 44, 49, 50, 199; 9:69, 71, 88); two more—Tlamatzinco and Tzonmolco—were merchant *barrios* (ibid. 9:12). Sahagún documents the presence of a *calmecac* in one of the *barrios* figuring in *Mendoza* part 3, highlighting its role in the actual training of skilled craftsmen: "The inhabitants of Amantlan pledged all their children as offerings. If it were a boy, one asked that he might serve as a priest, to grow up there in the priests' house [*calmecac*], and that when matured he would acquire understanding, artisanship [*tultecaiotl*] (ibid. 9:88).

This seems to mean that *all* males from Amantlan served as priests while learning basic craft skills, rather than that parents had the right to choose between *calmecac* and *cuicacalli* as indicated by *Mendoza* part 3. All that can be said at this point is that the artisan authors of part 3 appear to have taken it for granted that some fifteen-year-old males went to the *calmecac* while others were routinely assigned to the *cuicacalli*. Whatever the reason for this apparent conflict between the two sources, the lists appearing in table 2 show that *calmecac* existed in at least some *barrios* occupied by *macehualtin*—in this case, *barrios* occupied by *pochteca* and *amanteca*. Pending further investigation, we may reasonably assume that these, as was certainly the case with the *calmecacs* attended by hereditary elites (*pipiltin*), provided religious education to young males who might eventually hold high office in secular life, as well as to those who chose to serve as full-time priests.

Whatever the case, the pertinent scenes in *Mendoza* part 3 commence by portraying the personal services routinely assigned to a novice priest (*alfaqui noviçio*) such as sweeping, carrying reeds and branches to decorate his temple, and fetching maguey spines for bloodletting rituals (S30–33). He could be severely punished for negligence or rebellious behavior (S38–39) or for the previously described sexual offenses (S48). On the positive side, more important priestly responsibilities were learned, such as the conducting of nighttime penitential rites in the *sierra* (S42), use of the *teponaztli* (wooden drum; S43), timekeeping by observing the nighttime sky (S44), and other temple-related functions.

The series culminates, however, with a series of six scenes dealing with war. The first shows the novice carrying baggage for a priest-warrior going to war "to encourage and animate the warriors and conduct other ceremonies in the war" ("alfaqui mayor que va a la guerra para esforçar y animar a los guerreros y hazer otras ceremonias en la guerra"; S52). The next five scenes illustrate the military dress and insignia awarded to warrior priests by the Aztec kings each time they seized a live prisoner for sacrifice on the battlefield (S61–S66; see commentary in Spanish on folio 64v).

The Cuicacalli

The word *cuicacalli* (*cuica*[*tl*], song + *calli*, house) means "house of song." According to Durán (1971:289), these were "large houses which were the residence of teachers who taught dancing and singing. . . . Nothing was taught there to youths and maidens but singing, dancing, and the playing of musical instruments." He goes on to state that in Mexico Tenochtitlan "this house stood in the place where today [ca. 1580] are found the Portales de Mercaderes" (ibid.:291) located on the west side of the modern Plaza de la Constitución (Zócalo), directly opposite the pre-Conquest site of the palace of Motecuhzoma shown in scene 79 of part 3.

In *Codex Mendoza* part 3, the *cuicacalli* is represented as the place where young men who did not attend the *calmecac* lived and were trained from age fifteen until they married. The building glossed as *cuicacalli* in scene 28b is specifically identified as the "house where young men were raised and educated" ("casa donde criavan y enseñaban a los moços"). When presented there by his father, the fifteen-year-old boy was received by an official glossed as *teachcauh* (elder brother) and *maeso* (master; the commentary to scene 3 on folio 56v refers to the "maeso de muchachos y moços, [el qual] llamavan teachcauh o telpuchtlato").

Sahagún and most other early Colonial writers, however, agree that young men, whether nobles or commoners, who were not assigned to the *calmecac* went to live at the *telpochcalli* rather than the *cuicacalli*. Referring specifically to *macehualtin*, Sahagún (1950–1982 3:51) writes,

> When a boy was born, then they placed him in the *calmecac* or in the young men's house. That is to say, [the parents] promised him, gave him as a gift, made an offering of him in the temple, in the *calmecac* in order that [the boy] would become a priest or a young [warrior].

The original Nahuatl text employs the words *calmecac* and *telpuchcali* for "priests' house" and "young men's house" respectively, in a passage that very accurately describes the event so vividly depicted in scene 3 of the *Mendoza*'s third section. Elsewhere, Sahagún states that there was a *telpochcalli* in each of the city's *barrios* or *tlaxilacallis* (ibid. 8:58).

The question, then, is why does *Codex Mendoza* part 3 seemingly insist that young commoners who were not pledged to the *calmecac* entered the *cuicacalli* rather than the *telpochcalli* at age fifteen? It might be thought that the Spanish *ynterpretador* of the codex simply erred in writing *cuicacalli* when he ought to have written *telpochcalli* in scene 28b. There is, however, a similar pairing of *calmecac* and *cuicacalli* in Sahagún's remark that, when they reached the age of ten, twelve, or thirteen, the sons of lords and noblemen might be placed either in the *calmecac*, where "they delivered him

into the hands of the fire priests and [other] priests" (*tlenamacaque* and *tlamacazque*), or in the *cuicacalli*, where "they left him in the hands of the masters of the youths" (*tiachcaoan*; 1950–1982 8:71–72).

Although the relationship between the *cuicacalli* and the *telpochcalli* is not entirely clear, Durán (1971:290–291) describes the conducting of young boys from their own barrios to the *cuicacalli* an hour before sunset so that they could be taught dance and song. In the Spanish version of his *Historia general*, Sahagún wrote that "it was customary that at sunset each night, all of the young men [from the *telpochcalli*] went to sing and dance at the house that was called *cuicacalco*" ("Era costumbre que a la puesta del sol, todos los mancebos iban a bailar y danzar a la casa que se llamaba *cuicacalco* cada noche" [1954:319]). Again according to Sahagún (1950–1982 8:43), the *cuicacalli* was also a council chamber where one found "the masters of the youths [*tiachcahoan*] and the rulers of the youths [*telpuchtlatoque*], there established in order to oversee what was by way of work." When the sun had set "they turned their attention to dances" until late in the night, after which the young men "went straight to the young men's houses [*telpuchcalli*], which were everywhere" in order to sleep (ibid.:43).

If any consistent interpretation can be ventured at this point, it is that the *cuicacalli*—at least in Tenochtitlan—coordinated a variety of activities in which young men who lived and slept in *telpochcalli* located in each of the urban barrios were engaged on a day-by-day basis. These evidently included labor obligations of the type portrayed in scenes 34–37, 50, and 53, as well as the teaching of song and dance. In this case, the authors of *Mendoza* part 3 may have chosen to simplify their account of the training of young men who did not attend the *calmecac* by focusing their presentation on the *cuicacalli*'s organizing role vis-à-vis the *telpochcallis* located in each and every urban *barrio*.

The course of training offered young men under the auspices of the *cuicacalli* differed from that associated with the *calmecac* in several important characteristics. The first four scenes deal with the performing of menial tasks—the carrying of firewood and branches to be used in the temples (S34–37)—similar to those assigned novice priests (S30–33). The youth in the *cuicacalli* was also subject to extremely rigorous punishments for sexual offenses (S46) or vagabondage (S49). The salient distinction was that a young man assigned to the *cuicacalli* could, if his parents so desired, be placed in the hands of an experienced warrior (*tequihua*) for military training (S40–41) and go into battle himself (S45) at an earlier age than the novice priest.

Sahagún (1950–1982 3:53) describes the *telpochcalli* in very similar terms, adding that the young man was taken to the forest and made to carry one or two logs on his back to test "whether perhaps he might do well in war when, still an untried youth, they took him into battle."

The last scenes in the series resemble those previously discussed in connection with the priest-warrior (S54–59). The overriding theme involves advancement in rank, signified by progressively more elaborate forms of military dress, insignia, and ornamentation, associated with the seizing of enemy warriors in hand-to-hand combat. The Spanish gloss states that after taking five or six prisoners, the warrior achieved the grade of *Otonti* (Otomí; S58). He advanced to the grade of *Quachic* if he took a captive "in the war of Huexotzinco, after having taken many other enemy captive in other wars" ("demuestra aver cautiuado en la guerra de Guexoçingo demas de que en otras guerras a cautiuado a otros muchos de sus enemigos"; S59), and to the office of *Tlacatecatl* if he demonstrated valor and achievement exceeding those leading to the aforementioned ranks (S60).

In this case, part 3 of *Codex Mendoza* diverges rather sharply from Sahagún's discussion of the military careers of males trained at the *telpochcalli*. According to Sahagún (1950–1982 3:53), a warrior who took only four captives could attain the office of *Tlacatecatl*, *Tlacochcalcatl*, or *Quauhtlato*, or "also [in those days] one rose to be called constable [*achcauhtli*]." But once again, there is no clear evidence for determining which, if either, of the two accounts is more likely to be correct on this—from my standpoint—relatively minor point.

Rank, Title, and High Office

As noted above, the title of *Tlacatecatl* was awarded to commoners who demonstrated particular valor and merit in military campaigning over and above the taking of numerous war prisoners for sacrifice. *Codex Mendoza* makes it clear that both novice priests and ordinary warriors advanced in rank each time they took a new captive on the field of battle. Each such advance was marked by the adoption of new dress and insignia, the predominantly religious significance of which is discussed in detail by Anawalt in this volume.

The distribution of the highest titles between priests and non-priests is, however, somewhat unclear in the pictorial text. A sequence of six scenes (S54–59) portraying the advancement from rank to rank of nonecclesiastical warriors is followed by the depiction of a warrior who had achieved the rank of *Tlacatecatl* (S60). The next six scenes (S61–66) deal with priest-warriors and are followed by representations of eight richly garbed individuals together with glyphs that identify titled offices awarded for particularly meritorious service. The first four (S67) are glossed as "mandones y executores de lo que los Señores de Mexico mandaban y determinaban"; the next four (S68) are described as military commanders ("capitanes de los exerçitos mexicanos, y personas que exerçían cargos de generales de los exerçitos Mexicanos").

Unfortunately, neither the pictorial nor the written text makes it entirely clear whether this group relates specifically to the immediately preceding scenes depicting priest-warriors, in the same way that the office of *Tlacatecatl* appears to represent the highest rank open to men trained at the *cuicacalli* (or *telpochcalli*). It is entirely possible that a wider range of titled offices was reserved for commoners who had undergone the more rigorous and esoteric teachings provided only through the *calmecac*. On the other hand, the passage from the *Florentine Codex* cited above clearly states that the office of *Tlacochcalcatl*, which appears in scene 68, could be attained by males trained at the *telpochcalli*. This problem evidently cannot be resolved on the basis of internal evidence alone.

A MILITARY CAMPAIGN

The narrative focus shifts from social mobility to affairs of state at this point. Folios 66r and 67r depict the principal events involved in what appears to have been a routine military campaign undertaken to avenge the murder and robbing of Aztec merchants (*pochteca*) in a distant town or province. The written commentary (folios 65v and 66v) accuses the local ruler of having rebelled against the sovereignty of Mexico Tenochtitlan, thus bringing about his own ultimate destruction.

In this case, the technique of visual composition is in many ways of greater interest than the factual content. The account consists of a total of seven more or less distinct but interrelated scenes. The first (S69) represents the last event in the series, namely the execution of a rebel lord and the apparent enslavement of his wife and son, who appear with wrists bound and long wooden yokes attached to their necks.

The next scenes explain this culminating event: (1) traveling merchants (*pochteca*) are robbed and killed by subjects of the local *cacique* (ruler; S70) but according to the Spanish commentary, without his knowledge or consent (folio 69v); (2) emissaries from Tenochtitlan present the rebel lord with a shield, symbolizing war, and an ointment, signifying his own future death (S71; text on folio 69v); (3) the emissaries are pursued by defiant enemy warriors as they depart (S72); (4) vanguard troops from a punitive imperial force reconnoiter the rebel town during the night (S73); (5) envoys from the latter sue for peace (S74); and (6) four high-ranking military commanders (a *Tlacatecatl*, *Tlacochcalcatl*, *Huitznahuacatl*, and *Ticocyahuacatl*, identified in the written text as "capitanes de los exerçitos mexicanos" [folio 66v]), appear on the scene (S75). Precisely why such high-ranking commanders suddenly appear in this situation is unfortunately not explained.

The pictorial narrative displayed on these two pages relates a simple but pointed and coherent story. By placing the denouement (i.e., the *cacique*'s execution) at the beginning, the artist anticipates his message, namely, that any challenge to the military might of the Aztec empire was an exercise in futility. In the end, the originally defiant enemy warriors were obliged to plead for their lives (S74)—not because they had been overcome in battle, but because defeat would have been a predetermined outcome of any attempt at armed combat.

RETURN TO CIVIL LIFE

A typical wedding ceremony appears earlier in the text (folio 61r, S29). This is positioned so that it appears to refer primarily to the changed status of a fifteen-year-old girl at marriage and the threshold of motherhood. The upper half of the same page (S26) shows fifteen-year-old boys entering the *calmecac* and *cuicacalli* for further education and military training. The groom who appears in the marriage scene must be assumed on this basis to have been older than his bride.

The authors of *Mendoza* part 3 chose to clarify this aspect of social life in a later folio by representing a young man, glossed as "young married man" (*telpochtli casado*), taking leave from his former companions of the *telpochcalli*, with his wife spinning in the background (S76). The ceremonial leave-taking portrayed in part 3 is similar to that described by Sahagún (1950–1982 6:127–128) with respect to the presentation of gifts (food, drink, copper axes), a ceremonial discourse, and the like. It differs in that according to Sahagún's informants a young man first requested separation from the *telpochcalli* and married only when the request had been granted. The Spanish commentary, however, refers to the young man's married status as an accomplished fact, and the principal reason for asking that he be allowed to rest after his past service ("hazeles el casado vn Razonamyento sobre que se desiste del cargo y ofiçio de ser mandon por Razon de su casamyento y que quyere descansar del seruyçio pasado" [folio 67v]).

The next scene (S77) depicts three recently married males raised to the rank of *tequihua* (seasoned warrior) by the Aztec ruler (*señor de mexico*). The text states that they were then qualified to serve as royal emissaries and as military leaders in future wars. The main point, however, is that the young man achieved full adult status only at this point in his life. He might thereafter, depending on

JUDICIAL INTERLUDES

The three and a half pages remaining in the pictorial text (folios 68r–71r) lack a clearly defined unifying principle, but nonetheless convey a sense of the complexity of life in pre-Conquest Tenochtitlan. Two scenes, one occupying an entire page, deal with judicial procedures (S78–S79). In the first, three couples of indeterminate social status face four titled judges, each with an assistant holding the rank of *tectli* (*tecuhtli*, lord) seated just behind. In the next scene, two men and two women appear before Motecuhzoma's highest judicial council at the royal palace. The commentary (folio 68v) states that they are appealing the decision issued by the judges of the preceding scene. Motecuhzoma himself sits in a chamber on the second level of the palace, where he will hear further appeals involving legal cases of more than usual importance.

Although the scene was drawn to illustrate judicial procedures, it also provided an opportunity to illustrate salient features of the royal palace (*tecpan*), including the rooms or suites reserved for allied rulers and for councils of war.

CONCLUDING REMARKS

The information contained in the last two illustrated pages (folios 70r and 71r) was briefly summarized and evaluated in connection with earlier sections of this essay. It remains to comment on the overall value of *Codex Mendoza* part 3 as a source of valid ethnographic documentation relating to Aztec society in the last years of the pre-Conquest era.

We can reasonably surmise that part 3 was prepared at the request of some high-ranking member of the Spanish Colonial administration. As discussed in the section dealing with authorship, however, there seems to have been little or no direct Spanish oversight during the actual process of composition. The authors evidently chose to portray carefully selected aspects of the worldview of their own social class, a group composed of highly skilled artisans who were technically commoners or *macehualtin*, but who nonetheless enjoyed a somewhat privileged status within Tenochtitlan's urban population as a whole.

The most important quality of their presentation lies in the fact that it was created specifically for the edification of Spaniards living in Spain. The subject matter chosen for representation apparently reflects those aspects of pre-Conquest life that were most highly valued, or most vigorously disavowed, by the authors of *Mendoza* part 3, and that were therefore regarded as particularly suitable for the expression of Aztec culture in a favorable light.

The authors faced a formidable problem when they chose to emphasize upward mobility based on military valor, when valor itself was defined by the seizure of prisoners of war in hand-to-hand combat for later sacrifice to the Aztec gods. The point is finessed by stressing militaristic virtues similar to those valued by the conquistadors themselves, while refraining from overt representation of actual sacrificial rites.

Pre-Conquest religiosity was, nonetheless, smuggled in by devoting the most precise attention to detail when portraying the insignia and accoutrements awarded to Aztec warriors who successfully met the highest standards of military valor, because the costumes themselves, as Anawalt demonstrates elsewhere in this volume, were a powerful expression of Aztec religiosity.

When attempting to evaluate and validate specific points of information contained in the third part of *Codex Mendoza*, it is essential that ethnic and class distinctions be taken into account. As previously discussed, certain features of the birth and marriage rituals portrayed in part 3 differ from those described in the *Florentine Codex*. Unless specific evidence to the contrary exists, the *Mendoza*'s account should probably be taken as valid for urban craft groups, while Sahagún's account is likely to be correct when he writes about social elites.

When it is a question of whether promotion to the rank of *Tlacatecatl* or *Tlacochcalcatl* occurred when a warrior of commoner status had taken only four prisoners, or whether six or more such conquests were required, no definitive solution can be proposed. All that can be stated with any certainty is that Sahagún's informants proposed the first interpretation, while the authors of *Mendoza* part 3 believed the second to be correct.

The last point to be addressed relates to the overall design of part 3 and its implications for further investigations of *Codex Mendoza* and other similarly structured pictorial manuscripts. In composing the pictorial text, the artist and his collaborators were obliged to adopt or devise a format suitable for the presentation of a completely nontraditional corpus of information. If the argument developed in the earlier sections of this essay is correct, a narrative structure typical of certain kinds of pre-Conquest historical texts was consciously or unconsciously adapted to the radically distinct requirements of self-appraisal and self-presentation to an alien cultural group, the Spanish.

Whether or not *Codex Mendoza* part 3 proves to contain valid ethnographic documentation not found in the Sahagún texts or other early Colonial period sources, the process of semiotic transfer from pre-Conquest to post-Conquest modes of thought and visual representation which must have been involved in its composition will surely provide a fertile field for future investigation.

CHAPTER 7

Glyphic Conventions
of the *Codex Mendoza*

Frances F. Berdan

The *Codex Mendoza* contains a wealth of information on the glyphic writing system of early sixteenth-century central Mexico. The variety of cultural features portrayed is unparalleled in any other single Mesoamerican codex. The *Mendoza* represents calendrics, conquests, places, persons and their names, and material goods (included in a tribute-paying context, in name glyphs, and in scenes of daily life). This codex also traces a Mexica's life history from birth to death through experiences of education, warfare, crime and punishment, political glamour, and everyday drudgery. Largely absent from the *Mendoza*, however, is information of an explicitly religious or ritual nature.[1]

Several meticulous, detailed, and insightful studies have been made of the glyphic content of the *Codex Mendoza* (see especially Nicholson 1973; Nowotny 1959; Peñafiel 1885; Dibble 1971; Galarza 1988; Robertson 1959; M. E. Smith 1973; Whittaker 1980; Berdan 1979). In particular, works of Nicholson (1973) and Nowotny (1959) have elucidated much about the rules, conventions, and patterns of glyphic usage—that is, the internal construction and content of the writing system.[2]

I have no wish to repeat the fine work that has been done on this front. Rather, the thrust of this commentary leans more toward an analysis of *Codex Mendoza* glyphic usages as they relate to the cultural context in which they were produced, with the specific goal of understanding the extent to which standardized conventions affected the formulation of glyphs, and the extent to which stylistic license was allowed. To this end, I should like to present the *Codex Mendoza* in the context of the central Mexican writing tradition; discuss the major categories of glyphs included in the document; analyze the conventions, patterns, and anomalies of glyphic construction; and explore the variation in glyphic usage employed by the artist or artists of the three parts of the *Codex Mendoza*.

THE CENTRAL MEXICAN
WRITING TRADITION

Books[3] in pre-Spanish Mesoamerica were typically produced in long strips and folded, accordion-style, into a screen-fold format called a *tira* (see essay by Calnek, this volume). They were then often painted on both sides. Peter Martyr, enthralled with the native books he encountered in the New World, wrote,

> They do not bind them as we do, leaf by leaf; but they extend one leaf to the length of several cubits, after having pasted a certain number of square leaves one to the other with a bitumen so adhesive that the whole seems to have passed through the hands of the most skilful bookbinder. And whichever way the book is opened, it will always present two sides written; and two pages appear, and as many folds, unless you extend the whole of it. (von Hagen 1944:28–29)

Some leaves, however, may well have been left unattached "one to the other." Accounts of tribute holdings or assessments, for example, may have been more effectively rendered on individual sheets of paper (see Berdan 1976a, 1980).

This paper (*amatl*) was made from the inner bark of the *amaquahuitl* and, undoubtedly, other related fig-tree species.[4] Anderson and Dibble (Sahagún 1950–1982 11:111) identify this paper-yielding tree as *Ficus benjamina* or *Ficus involuta*, members of the vast genera of fig trees which grow throughout Mexico. To produce paper, the bark was apparently stripped, soaked, beaten, and then dried.

On this paper, and on a variety of other media as well (such as stone, wood, and animal hides), the Aztec scribes blended artistic expression and glyphic conventions to produce meaningful writings. Scribal or painting skills apparently passed from father to son, as depicted on folio 70r of the *Codex Mendoza*. These craftsmen, for so they were considered, may have shared some unity in organization, residence, and perhaps ritual; to insure success in their work, they took special care to honor, with ritual offerings, the especially propitious day Seven Flower. Robertson (1959:27) suggests that the scribes, or painters, were members of the priesthood, or at least trained under priestly guidance. The *calmecac*, or school for noble boys under the direction of priests, was certainly the most likely setting for the transmission of reading and writing skills. Yet, according to Sahagún (1950–1982 10:28), the scribe learned more than specific content; he also learned proper form:

> The scribe: writings, ink [are] his special skills. [He is] a craftsman, an artist, a user of charcoal, a drawer with charcoal; a painter who dissolves colors, grinds pigments, uses colors.
>
> The good scribe is honest, circumspect, far-sighted, pensive; a judge of colors, an applier of the colors, who makes shadows, forms feet, face, hair. He paints, applies colors, makes shadows, draws gardens, paints flowers, creates works of art.
>
> The bad scribe [is] dull, detestable, irritating—a fraud, a

cheat. He paints without luster, ruins colors, blurs them, paints askew—acts impetuously, hastily, without reflection.

It is possible that, while the content of writing and reading were learned in a school such as the *calmecac*, the skills of form and design were taught and honed in the home, or perhaps in a guildlike setting.

Many of these scribes served the royal palace and its numerous requirements, for imperial administration necessitated an almost constant production of the written glyph, whether it be census records, tribute tallies, astrological writings, or any of the myriad other accounts helpful in sustaining a broad and diverse empire. Some scribes, however, may have been more "personally employed." This was probably the case with those scribes who assisted the featherworkers by initially drawing the design on which the feather artisans would then meticulously apply their colorful plumes (ibid. 9:93).

It was a group of such scribes, primarily trained and experienced in the pre-Hispanic writing traditions, who composed the pictorial portions of the *Codex Mendoza* some twenty years after the Spanish Conquest.

THE *CODEX MENDOZA* IN THE CENTRAL MEXICAN WRITING TRADITION

The *Codex Mendoza* is unquestionably a post-Conquest document (probably composed in the early 1540s: see Nicholson essay, this volume), produced on European paper, usually drawn on one side only, but displaying indigenous glyphic writing forms and conventions. Each of the three sections of the *Mendoza* contains a different repertoire of glyphs. In glyphic content and form, parts 1 and 2 are similar, while part 3 is quite a different matter altogether.

The second, or tribute, part of the document may be a direct copy of the extant *Matrícula de Tributos*, unless both were copies from yet another document.[5] Books containing tribute data were undoubtedly numerous in imperial bookkeeping; Bernal Díaz del Castillo provides an abbreviated but definite statement:

> he [Tapia, Motecuhzoma's steward] kept the accounts of all the revenue that was brought to Montezuma, in his books which were made of paper which they call amal, and he had a great house full of these books. (1956:211)

The other two sections of the *Codex Mendoza* have no direct analogue, although Barlow (1949a:5, 126) has suggested that the *Matrícula de Tributos* may have at one time been preceded by a "history of conquests" section. Conquest history records, or books, probably were drawn in pre-Conquest Mexico; Motolinía (1969:2) mentions such accounts in his preliminary letter to the *Historia de los indios de la Nueva España*.[6] Statements by Durán (1964:70, 80, 217, 276, 293) strongly suggest that historical events of note were painted in books, as well as the "lives and deeds" of important individual personages. The conquests of successive Mexica rulers, as seen in part 1 of the *Codex Mendoza*, may be of this genre (see also essay by Boone, this volume).

The third part of the *Codex Mendoza* was probably a novel effort (see Robertson 1959:97; Barlow 1949a:5), but the capabilities and conventions for its execution were certainly available in the native writing repertoire. A variety of "everyday life" circumstances and events were indigenously recorded on paper: testimonies in judicial proceedings (Sahagún 1950–1982 8:55); accounts of crimes (Robertson 1959:31); military strength (ibid.); relatively small-scale maps depicting travel routes, enemy positions, and even geographic information beyond the imperial domain (Sahagún

1950–1982 8:51; Díaz del Castillo 1963:266); larger-scale "tract" maps detailing census-type information, including land rights and inheritance (Zorita 1963b:110; *Plano en Papel de Maguey*) and genealogies (Durán 1964:43, 84). Even such unusual subjects as the bearded Spaniards with their odd equipment were faithfully illustrated using indigenous styles and conventions (Durán 1964:268–270).[7] While the specific content of the third part of the *Codex Mendoza* does not conform well to any of these "types," the individuals, materials, and events were available in their repertoire of pictorial images.

Whereas the content and style of the third section of the *Codex Mendoza* may have fallen prey to some Spanish influence, that of the first two sections seems to exhibit an indigenous character. The second section of the document is at least cognate with the *Matrícula de Tributos*, which is indisputably indigenous in style and content, and perhaps in fact an indigenous document (see Berdan 1976a, 1980; Nicholson 1973; Robertson 1959). The place glyphs in part 1 of the *Codex Mendoza* deviate somewhat from those found in the second section (see below) and may display more Spanish influence.

The compilation of these three topics into a single book was surely a Spanish request. As apparently used in pre-Spanish times, books were useful devices for conveying information or storing knowledge. As such, histories, genealogies, tribute tallies, religious and ritual almanacs, maps, and so on may have been compiled and housed separately. Religious and ritual volumes may have reposed in or near temples (Díaz del Castillo 1963:105); instruction manuals at the *calmecac* or noble schools (see note 7); local census maps with the *calpullec* (headman) of each *calpulli* (Zorita 1963b:110); tribute tallies with the tribute overseers (see Berdan 1982); and genealogies and histories in royal or state archives, where claims to titles, territories and legitimacy could be safely guarded (see also Robertson 1959:29–33).

TYPES OF GLYPHS IN THE *CODEX MENDOZA*

If only parts 1 and 2 of the *Codex Mendoza* are taken into account, we need concern ourselves only with a fairly limited set of glyphic types: calendar notations, numerical glyphs, personal names and titles, place-names, and a variety of pictured materials (such as clothing, foodstuffs, and feathers) due in tribute. Some few events, such as conquest and New Fire Ceremonies, are also noted glyphically.

But part 3, in addition to containing many of the same types of glyphs as parts 1 and 2, includes numerous persons, indeed persons in distinct relationships with one another. In some cases, these individuals are in definable settings and are undertaking specific actions. Nonetheless, the glyphic conventions used to convey this information are not so different from those used in the other two sections of the *Mendoza*.

Calendrics

Calendar notations appear most prominently in the form of year glyphs in part 1 (fig. 1). These sequences of glyphs are uniformly painted blue, with the exception of the three year glyphs added to include the conquest years (folio 15v). The year glyphs, marching along the margins of the pages, illustrate the four year names (House, Rabbit, Reed, and Flint Knife) combined with the numbers 1–13. Occasionally a special event, notably a New Fire Ceremony celebrated once every fifty-two years (folios 2r, 3v, 15v; see Nicholson 1971b: table 4), the succession of a ruler to the highest office of the land (folios 2v, 4v), the beginnings of a ruler's conquests (folio 2v), and the death of a ruler (folio 4v), are also noted calendrically. In the *Codex Mendoza*, only part 1 exhibits these year glyphs. However, such calendrical notations, variably drawn, are common in the central Mexican pictorials (see, for example, the *Codex Telleriano-Remensis*, *Mapa de Tepechpan*, and *Codex Boturini*). Years, as designating ages for individuals, are represented by blue dots in part 3 of the *Mendoza* (e.g., folio 71v).

Left: Fig. 1. Glyph representing the year Five Rabbit (*Codex Mendoza* folio 15v). Right: Fig. 2. A rosette, in this instance representing twenty days (*Codex Mendoza* folio 19r).

Beyond year counts, the *Codex Mendoza* also contains, in four places, glyphs designating days (fig. 2). In one case, the large, colorful rosettes are glossed as each meaning twenty days (folio 19r); in the second (folio 57r), the smaller rosettes are said to stand for one day each. With the exception of size, there is no pictorial difference between the two depictions; and each translation makes perfect sense. It may be that the symbols indeed indicate single days, and the artist failed to attach the banner (*pantli*) symbol for twenty atop (as he did on occasion, especially with shields in part 2). Or, as is often the case in Aztec glyphic writing, these symbols were known to stand for "days," but one interpreted the symbol "sensibly" (e.g., it would not be usual to render tribute in intervals shorter than eighty days; it would be out of the question for a midwife to bathe an infant for more than four successive days after birth). The symbol gave the clue, the culture provided the guidelines for the interpretation. Days are indicated in two other spots in the *Mendoza*, on folio 62r, where three days (or, perhaps, three nights) are shown by three small black dots; and on folio 7v, where four red dots make up part of the name glyph for Atonal (*tonalli* = day).

Numerical Glyphs

Number values in the *Codex Mendoza*, conforming to the vigesimal system of counting (by twenties), were drawn in typical Mesoamerican fashion: dots or circles for single units, banners (*pantli*) for twenties, hairs (*tzontli*) for units of 400, and the ritual priestly bag (*xiquipilli*) representing the number 8,000 (see fig. 3). These number glyphs were either attached directly to the top, bottom, or side of the object or linked to the item by a line. The latter method was most commonly used for warrior costumes and shields, and where several number glyphs were combined, additive-style, on a single object (see, for example, folios 28r, 42r, 47r). Single units were simply implied by the presence of the pictograph and were given no special numerical sign. On occasion, as on folio 4v, figures themselves are repeated to indicate the total number (rather than drawing one figure with a number glyph attached).[8]

Fingers (*mapilli*) are occasionally drawn on *manta* figures in part 2, apparently to indicate length of cloth (e.g., folio 38r). They always occur in even numbers (2, 4, or 8), and a variety of lengths have been hypothesized for this symbol.[9] However, there is none of the additional glyphic symbolism, such as the heart and the

Fig. 3. Glyphs representing the numbers 1, 20, 400, and 8,000 as seen in the *Codex Mendoza*.

hand, used to designate dimensions (particularly of land; see especially Harvey and Williams 1980).

In only one case did the *Codex Mendoza* artist combine different numerical notations: on folio 71r three mosaic-style disks, with attached banners, are combined with ten small dots, the total equaling seventy. The disks with the twenty-symbols are larger than the single year symbols. We may be seeing a pun here, with a mosaic, the usual sign for turquoise (*xihuitl*) used to represent year (also *xihuitl*). In all other cases in the *Mendoza*, where the scribe wished to indicate a number other than the standard units (20, 400, 8,000), he simply added more symbols (so 40 = two banners, 4,000 = ten hairs, and so on). Fractions were not noted glyphically; the number 200 is designated by ten banners rather than half a hair. Only in the third part of the *Mendoza* do we see fractions appear, and this in the form of half a tortilla (e.g., folio 58r). This use of fractions may be a result of Spanish influence.

The only noticeable variation in numerical representations can be seen in the singles (dots or circles). In part 1 the circles as counters appear only with the blue year glyphs. While not entirely consistent, circles representing small totals (usually 1–4 or 5) contain a small dot in the center; those of larger numbers are plain circles. In part 2, single units are shown as black dots (folio 40r), red dots (folio 45r), or red and white dots (folio 18r); in part 3, single units designating age are shown as blue dots (folios 58r–61r, 71r), while those representing days or nights are drawn as black dots (folio 62r).

Personal Names and Titles

The *Codex Mendoza* contains only a few glyphic representations of personal names and titles. A name is always attached to a person's head or clothing by a short line; a title usually has such a line, but may also rise directly from the head (as in the *Tezcacoacatl* of folio 18r), or rest just above the head (as with the several *Tlacatectli* and *Tlacochtectli* on folios 17v and 18r).[10] The largest single grouping of personally named individuals is found at the very beginning of the codex, on folio 2r. Here ten persons are shown with actual names. Beyond this "founding" scene, only the exalted rulers of Tenochtitlan and Tlatelolco (with but three exceptions) deserve personal naming. The three exceptions involve also high-ranking personages, one the defeated ruler of Coaxtlahuacan (Atonal: folio 7v); the others powerful governors of Xoconochco, Omequauh and, perhaps, Acueyotl (folio 18r).[11]

Glyphs for titles are slightly more common, but also more repetitive than personal names. In the four examples of *Tlacatectli* (folios 17v, 18r), the glyphic indication is simply a *xiuhuitzolli*, or noble diadem, uniformly an ideographic indication for *tecutli* or chief (fig. 4).[12] For the four cases of *Tlacochtectli* (folios 17v, 18r), a spear (*tlacochtli*) is pictographically added to the diadem (fig. 5). And for the two instances of *Tlacochcalcatl* (folios 18r, 65r), a house (*calli*) is combined with two spears (fig. 6).[13] In all these repetitive cases, there is no variation in glyphic forms, although the individuals to whom these glyphs are attached do exhibit some differences (e.g., facial body paint, hairstyle). The glyphs for *Tlilancalqui*, *Tezcacoacatl*, and *Ezhuahuacatl* each appear twice (folios 18r, 65r, 68r), with only minor variations.

Left: Fig. 4. Glyphic designation for the title Tlacatecuhtli, represented by the noble diadem, *xiuhuitzolli* (*Codex Mendoza* folio 17v). Center: Fig. 5. Glyph for Tlacochtecuhtli (*Codex Mendoza* folio 17v). Right: Fig. 6. Glyph for Tlacochcalcatl (*Codex Mendoza* folio 18r).

In a slightly different vein, the "gossiper" on folio 70r is shown with two curled appendages on his head; these represent a "two-headed snake" (*maquizcoatl*), part of the name of a gossip (*maquizcoatl chiquimolin*: Molina 1970:52v). Similarly, the thief (*ichtecqui*) on folio 71r displays a glyph composed of a hank of hair being cut by an obsidian blade (*itztli* = obsidian, *tequi* = to cut).[14]

As often occurs with place-name glyphs, part of a personal name or title may be left to the reader's prior knowledge or culturally based interpretation. So the title *Atenpanecatl* (folio 65r) requires only the notation of water (*atl*) and lips (*tentli*), leaving -*panecatl* to a general understanding. A similar case occurs on folio 68r, where the -*panecatl* of *Acatl Iyacapanecatl* again goes unillustrated. Clark (1938 3: overleaves to folios 65r, 68r) adds *pani* (on) to his glyphic interpretation. However, relative position of glyphic elements was rarely used in central Mexico (see below) and, in the particular case of *Atenpanecatl*, an identical "water-lips" glyph is used for *atenco* in the place-name glyph for Chalco Atenco (folio 17 v).

In good part, personal name and title glyphs involve direct pictographic depictions: a spear for *tlacoch*-, an eagle for *quauh*-, a shield for *chimal*-, and so on. While some of these are vividly graphic, such as the reed in the nose of the judge *Acatliyacapanecatl*, others are highly stylized, requiring considerable involvement with the culture to be understood. Such are the layers of the night sky as the *Ilhuica* part of the name glyph for Motecuhzoma Ilhuicamina (fig. 7), the obsidian blades as part of Itzcoatl's name glyph (fig. 8), and the variously drawn name glyphs for Tizoc (see volume 2, page descriptions for a more detailed discussion).

Left: Fig. 7. The name glyph for Motecuhzoma Ilhuicamina; prominent is the representation of the night sky (*ilhuicatl*; *Codex Mendoza* folio 7v). Right: Fig. 8. Name glyph for the ruler Itzcoatl (*Codex Mendoza* folio 5v).

Ideographic conventions are also used in titles, such as the noble diadem, *xiuhuitzolli*, to stand for *tecutli* (*tectli* in the *Mendoza* glosses). Footprints, used for a wide variety of purposes in central Mexican pictorials, may also be considered as standing for something besides themselves; thus the title *Myxcoatlaylotlac* (folio 68r)

uses footprints to indicate movements, the *tlaylo-* (to return) component of the name.

Phonetic usage is not widely found in this small corpus of personal names and titles, but it is present. *Atl* (water) is found in several cases to convey the vowel sound *a*, as in, for example, Atonal (folio 7v), Axayacatl (folio 10r) and, redundantly, in Ahuitzotl (folio 13r). A further discussion of these different glyphic conventions is provided below. Translations of the personal names and titles appearing in the *Codex Mendoza* are provided in the individual page descriptions in volume 2, and in appendix E.

Place-Names

Place-name glyphs are found only in parts 1 and 2 of the *Codex Mendoza*, but there they are extremely prevalent, totaling 612 glyphs (although some repeat). Indeed, for the study of place-name glyphs, the *Codex Mendoza* provides the single most valuable corpus among the Mesoamerican pictorials.

While a more detailed discussion of the place-name glyphs follows (and an alphabetically arranged compendium of the glyphs and their translations is to be found in appendix E), it is important to consider that these glyphs combine a variety of conventions of glyphic formation: pictographic, ideographic, phonetic, and relative position.

In the numerous place-names contained in the *Codex Mendoza*, pictographs encompass a wide range of the physical world of animal, vegetable, mineral, and landforms; the cultural world of temples, clothing, ethnic groups, and mummy bundles; and the action world of dividing, washing, pouring, and twisting about. Straightforward as they may seem, pictographic representations conformed to cultural dictates of symbolism and artistic design—so to the sixteenth-century reader, the god Opochtli[15] of Hueypuchtla is readily identifiable (folio 29r; fig. 9), as well as a stylized cave (folios 11r, 21v, 24v, 37r, 42r, and 46r; fig. 10) and a glyphic symbol for night (Yoallan: folios 37r and 39r; fig. 11).

Left: Fig. 9. Glyph for the town Hueypuchtla (*Codex Mendoza* folio 29r). Center: Fig. 10. Glyph for the town Oztoma (*Codex Mendoza* folio 37r). Right: Fig. 11. Yoallan, represented by the night sky (*Codex Mendoza* folio 37r).

The ideographic principle as seen in the place-name glyphs was somewhat more abstract. Certain qualities or attributes of an object or action were selected and served to represent the entirety: so a stylized speech scroll indicated speech (*nahua*), a speech scroll with flowers represented song or poetry (as in Cuicatlan, folio 43r; fig. 12), a noble's headband (*xiuhuitzolli*) symbolized a lord or *tecutli* (as in the place-name Tecmilco in fig. 13), a *quemitl* or cape represented the gods in Teteutlan (folio 46r) and Teteuhtepec (folio 7v; see fig. 35 in Anawalt essay), and Xipe Totec's headgear stood for Yopico (folio 20r; also seen on a Yope personage on folio 39r; fig. 14).

There are numerous examples of phoneticism in the *Codex Mendoza* (and *Matrícula de Tributos*) place glyphs, where phonetic ele-

Left: Fig. 12. Cuicatlan: the elaborate speech scroll signifies "song" (*Codex Mendoza* folio 43r). Center: Fig. 13. Tecmilco, with the noble headband providing the ideograph for *tecuhtli* (*Codex Mendoza* folio 41r). Right: Fig. 14. Yopico (*Codex Mendoza* folio 20r).

ments are commonly combined with pictographic or ideographic images (see especially Nicholson 1973; Nowotny 1959; León-Portilla 1982). Briefly, the phoneticism was in the form of phonetic transfer (Gelb 1952:67), more commonly known as rebus writing. In this system, homonyms were employed; the one more capable of being represented pictorially was drawn to symbolize its more abstract mate. In English, for example, a flying insect (bee) can symbolize a state of existence (be), and a part of the body (eye) can represent the personal pronoun "I."

In the central Mexican pictorials, place-name locatives (e.g., "place of," "near") were frequently indicated pictorially by this technique:[16]

tlan, tla (where there is an abundance of)	teeth (*tlantli*) (fig. 15)
pan (on, over, above)	banner (*pantli*) or footprint (*pano*) (figs. 16, 17)[17]
nahua(c) (adjacent to, beside)	speech scroll (*nahua*: speech) (fig. 18)
icpa(c) (on top of)	ball of thread (*icpatl*)
ix(co) (in front of)	face (*ixtli*)
man (where something extends)	hand (*maitl*)
yaca(c) (where begins . . .)	nose (*yacatl*)

Upper left: Fig. 15. Glyph for Coatlan, with the teeth standing for -*tlan* (*Codex Mendoza* folio 23r). Upper right: Fig. 16. Glyph for Oxitipan, with the banner standing for the -*pan* locative (*Codex Mendoza* folio 55r). Lower left: Fig. 17. Glyph for the town of Yztapan, with the footprint providing the -*pan* locative (*Codex Mendoza* folio 38r). Lower right: Fig. 18. Glyph for Quauhnahuac, with the speech scroll standing for speech, -*nahua* (*Codex Mendoza* folio 23r).

And, while not a locative per se, the common -*tzin* suffix, a diminutive, is illustrated by human buttocks, also called *tzintli* (fig. 19). As Nicholson (1973:9) has observed, the locative -*co* is often represented by *comitl*, "pot," in many post-Conquest central Mexi-

can documents. In the *Matrícula* and *Mendoza*, however, phoneticism for this locative is not present. The -*co/-c* locative may not have developed the *comitl* (pot) pictorial representation in pre-Conquest times due to its variable usage. That is, while *comitl* would be a reasonable transfer for -*co*, it would be quite inadequate for the -*c* form of the locative. It is also notable that the locatives without pictorial substitutes are all bound morphemes: -*can*, -*nal*, and -*yan*. Unlike locatives such as -*tlan* and -*pan*, they are not discrete morphemes and hence cannot stand alone as phonetic substitutes.

Relative position as a glyphic convention occurs rarely in the place-name glyphs. The one obvious and consistent application of this convention is the use of the *calli* (house) element to represent -*chan* (home). This occurs in two cases in the *Codex Mendoza*, in the place-names for Quauhtinchan ("Home of the Eagles") and Oxichan (perhaps "Home of the Iguana";[18] folios 42r and 49r)—in both instances the primary figure is situated in front of the house (figs. 20 and 21). These are the only examples of such placement, and -*chan* is otherwise absent from the *Codex Mendoza* place-names.

Left: Fig. 19. Tecpatzinco, with the -*tzin* diminutive provided by the human element (*Codex Mendoza* folio 8r). Center: Fig. 20. Quauhtinchan (*Codex Mendoza* folio 42r). Right: Fig. 21. Oxichan (*Codex Mendoza* folio 49r).

Action and Events

Events and activity are sparsely recorded in parts 1 and 2 of the *Mendoza*. The event of conquest does appear repeatedly in part 1, symbolized by a flaming, smoking, toppling temple. Other types of activities are occasionally embodied in name glyphs (either personal or place), such as the act of washing (Tlapacoyan, folios 8r and 50r; fig. 22), of building a house (Tepepulan, folio 20r; fig. 23), of extracting stone (Tetlapanaloyan, folio 29r; fig. 24), or of speaking (Quauhtlatoa, folios 6r and 19r; fig. 25).

Actions are far more prevalent in part 3 of the *Mendoza*, where individuals are repeatedly shown in relationships with one another,

Upper left: Fig. 22. Glyph for the town of Tlapacoyan (*Codex Mendoza* folio 8r). Upper right: Fig. 23. Tepepulan (*Codex Mendoza* folio 20r). Lower left: Fig. 24. Glyph for Tetlapanaloyan (*Codex Mendoza* folio 29r). Lower right: Fig. 25. Quauhtlatoa, name of a ruler of Tlatelolco (*Codex Mendoza* folio 19r).

from birth through old age. Information concerning these persons is conveyed by a variety of artistic means. For example, the size of the human figures was important: the larger represented more important or dominant individuals, the smaller ones indicated subservient or less significant persons from the point of view of the artist (see folios 2r, 64r, 65r; see also essay by Howe, this volume). Color also provided valuable information on persons: priests are portrayed in a black/gray hue with a red smear at the temple, other men as "peach," and women as yellow. Other details, such as the prominent wrinkles on an old man's or old woman's face (folios 57r, 61r, 71r), a blue tear descending from an eye (e.g., folio 60r), or special hair arrangements, served to enhance the writing system and allow it to record and transmit a great variety of detailed information.

While devices such as these, along with posture, special equipment (such as an ax, drum, or staff), and relative personal position, offer clues to interactions in part 3, glyphic symbols were also used. One such prominent symbol was the speech scroll, found repeatedly throughout this section to indicate instruction or discussion. In some cases, where the speech act is quite profuse, multiple scrolls indicate this intensity (as with the father to his son, the majordomo issuing public work orders, or the singer-drummer, all seen on folio 70r). Footprints are also another common device found in part 3 of the *Mendoza*, indicating direction or movement (as, for example, the two boys entering schools on folio 61r, or the battle scene on folio 67r). Dotted lines are also used, primarily to link persons with objects or persons with persons. Such is the case, for example, on folio 64r, with the boy paddling his canoe to the *ayauhcalli* temple, the constable involved in repairs to temple and road, and the warriors earning their fancy *mantas* through success in battle. As another example, on folio 57r, an infant is attached by such lines not to his father and mother, but to the head priest and teacher to whom he has been dedicated. In a further example, a dotted line connects a priest's face with an eye, both face and eye oriented toward the night sky, which he is studying; the line and the detached eye provide the needed information to interpret this action correctly.

Beyond calendrics, numerical notations, personal names and titles, place-names, and actions and events, there is a vast array of objects portrayed pictographically in all three sections of the *Codex Mendoza*. As a small sampling, these include items such as gourd bowls, warriors' costumes, ballcourts, copper axes, maize kernels and beans, trees, fish, shells, and rocks. Such objects frequently form part of a personal or place name, and sometimes indicate action or events (such as the feathers and feathermaking equipment on folio 70r or the burning temples throughout part 1). They are also employed in the year glyphs (as House, Rabbit, Reed, and Flint Knife are all "things") and as part of the number glyphs (as with the *xiquipilli*, serving double duty as a priestly bag itself on folio 63r and as the number 8,000 in part 2). And, as throughout the tribute section, they simply denote the objects themselves.

One aim of this commentary is to bring into sharper focus the rules and conventions used in the formation of *Codex Mendoza* glyphs. While these conventions have already been mentioned, their variable use and perplexing inconsistencies warrant further discussion.

GLYPHIC RULES AND CONVENTIONS IN THE *CODEX MENDOZA*

The central Mexican writing system was based on a great number of glyphs that served, largely, as mnemonic (memory-jogging)

devices. Being fundamentally nonalphabetic, the glyphs provided only guides or clues to the entire message. Learning to read, therefore, involved much more than just learning the glyphic symbols: it was essential to have learned, or memorized, the messages themselves. In other words, reader and writer required a good deal of knowledge not directly expressed in the glyphs.

The degree of specific linguistic information included in the glyphs probably varied according to the content of the pictorial. As Dibble (1971:330) has observed, ritual and calendric books were adjuncts to a rather stiff oral tradition: songs and prayers (such as found in book 2 of the *Florentine Codex*) were committed to memory—instruction and assistance in recitations would have been provided by the pictorials. These types of codices in particular, but also perhaps certain books containing historical or "everyday life" content, could rely heavily on general pictographic devices to store or relate the desired meanings. However, where sets of single words serve as the content of the pictorial, and the content has not been memorized as a kind of "litany," more specific means are necessary to eliminate possible ambiguities. Especially in personal and place names, which are typically composed of two or more syllabic elements, direct expression of each element is often found. Pictographic means are not always sufficient in these cases and are supplemented by ideographic, phonetic, or positional devices.

Pictographs

The pictographic principle predominated in composing glyphs, whether as ritual reminders or in names of persons and places. A picture of the item or action was merely drawn: a deer for *maçatl*, as in *Maçatlan* (fig. 26), a flint knife for *tecpatl*, in Tecpatepec (fig. 27), a temple with a ball of cotton atop for Ychcateopan (fig. 28), or spears and a house representing the title *Tlacochcalcatl* (fig. 6).

Left: Fig. 26. Maçatlan (*Codex Mendoza* folio 47r). Center: Fig. 27. Glyph for the town Tecpatepec (*Codex Mendoza* folio 27r). Right: Fig. 28. Ychcateopan (*Codex Mendoza* folio 37r).

Nonetheless, the interpretations of some pictographs were apparently open to moderate disagreement and were confusing even in the sixteenth century: this was particularly true where a given pictographic element indeed had several possible representations.

Left: Fig. 29. The glyph for Nextitlan (*Codex Mendoza* folio 20v). Center: Fig. 30. Xala, the small dots representing sand (*Codex Mendoza* folio 40r). Right: Fig. 31. Coçohuipilecan, with an *ehuatl*, not a *huipilli* (*Codex Mendoza* folio 38r).

Small dots are an obvious example here—they represented sand, saltpeter, ashes, chia, and perhaps amaranth (see Berdan 1982). Thus the glyphs for Nextitlan (folio 20v; fig. 29) and Xala (folio 40r; fig. 30) are very similar, and Xala is probably not Xala at all, but rather Tequisquitlan (see Berdan 1979). Furthermore, if the *Codex Mendoza* annotations are to be believed, some of the pictographs may not be quite what they seem: as an example, the place-name *Coçohuipilecan* is represented not by a yellow *huipilli* but a yellow *ehuatl* (folios 13r and 38r; fig. 31; see Anawalt essay, this volume).

Ideographs

Ideographic representations are interesting culturally, since the specific qualities selected to represent the whole were based on patterned cultural criteria. For example, an enemy was considered vanquished when its main temple was burned; it is no surprise that a burning temple glyphically symbolized conquest. Likewise, the noble headband was an item of attire restricted to men of high rank and guarded by sumptuary laws; its visible and exclusive association with nobility itself is evidenced by its use as a glyphic symbol.

Ideographic usages, while not especially common, were applied most notably to place-names and to personal names and titles. Thus a particular item may be pictured, but with an aim of representing more than just itself. As already mentioned, such was the use of the noble headband, which was not to be translated as *xiuhuitzolli* (noble diadem), but rather as *tecutli* (chief, noble, or judge). Also, inverted eyes, to represent *ixtlapal* (reverse or inverted) serve as ideographs for *ixtlauatl* (plain or flatland) when combined with the pictograph for field (see folio 36r, Acamilyxtlahuacan: "Place of the Plain of Cultivated Fields of Reeds"). Other notable examples have been cited above (and see figs. 12–14 and appendix E).

Phoneticism

As noted above, phoneticism as a glyphic convention was used most frequently in the formation of place and personal names. The rebus style of phoneticism was often applied to the locatives of place-names (as in *-pan*, *-tlan*, and so on). Additionally, an element was occasionally included in a place-name glyph to reduce ambiguity. Thus, the town of Coyoacan (folio 47r; fig. 32) is represented by a coyote with a hole in its body; both *coyotl* (coyote) and *coyoctic* (hole) are illustrated, to leave no doubt as to the name involved. A similar redundancy appears in the place-name glyph of Quahuacan (fig. 33), where both an eagle (*quauhtli*) and tree (*quauitl*) perch atop a hill; only one element is really needed, but two eliminate any ambiguities (in, for instance, reading the bird as *tototl* instead of *quauhtli*). The glyph for Acolhuacan, or Acolman, seen in the

Fig. 34. Glyph sculpted onto the front of the Acolman monastery (photo courtesy of Xavier Noguez).

Mendoza (folios 3v, 21v) and on the Acolman monastery (fig. 34), also contains this feature; the *a*, as represented by water in the glyph, is superfluous when combined with *acolli*, shoulder. However, in this case, it may be that the arm is actually representing the verb *coloa*, to bend, in which case the water glyph is essential.

Some glyphic usages correspond to the vowels *o*, *a*, and *e*. The vowel *o* was derived from *ohtli* (road) and represented by a line of footprints, as in the place glyph Ocpayucan on folio 23r or Tiçayucan on folio 22r (fig. 35; the footprints provide the *-yo* or *yu* element). The vowel *a* was derived from *atl* (water) and was represented by the common stylized stream of water. The *e* vowel appears less frequently, but can be seen in the glyph for Miquetlan in Tuchpa province (folio 52r; fig. 36)—the annotator of the *Codex Mendoza* has omitted the *e* or *etl* (bean) element in his reading of this sign (see also Whittaker 1980:77–78).

Left: Fig. 35. Tiçayucan, with its footprints for the sound *o* or *yo* (*Codex Mendoza* folio 22r). Right: Fig. 36. Miquetlan, glossed as Mictlan (*Codex Mendoza* folio 52r).

Phoneticism is found not only in place and personal names but in other parts of the writing system as well. An interesting example is found in part 2 of the *Codex Mendoza* (and in the *Matrícula de Tributos*). Cloaks of yucca fiber, *ycçotilmatli* (*ycçotl*: yucca fiber; fig. 37), are shown pierced with a bone perforator (*ço*: to bleed). To distinguish these from other plain white cloaks, a phonetic convention was applied which is also found in the place-name glyphs. The bone provides the phonetic clue *ço*, hence the overall meaning of the item. Its redundant use on a place-name glyph (Çoçolan: folios 15r and 17v) is interesting: while only one perforator is shown, several perforations are illustrated, providing the reduplicative (*çoço-*) information (fig. 38).

Relative Position

These three principles, pictographic, ideographic, and phonetic transfer, account for the vast majority of the glyphic representations in the *Codex Mendoza*. There remain some glyphic elements, however, that have no phonetic or other realization in the glyphs. Position, to indicate *-chan*, has already been mentioned.

Left: Fig. 32. Coyoacan, with its redundant "hole" (*Codex Mendoza* folio 47r). Right: Fig. 33. Quahuacan, with both eagle and tree (*Codex Mendoza* folio 32r).

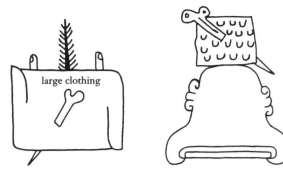

Left: Fig. 37. Yucca fiber mantas, or *ycçotilmatli* (*Codex Mendoza* folio 36r). Right: Fig. 38. Glyph for the town of Çoçolan (*Codex Mendoza* folio 17v).

Glyphs for a number of towns, for example Mizquic, Coçotlan, and Tepechpan (all in Petlalco province, folios 20r and 20v), contain a house or *calli* element, as, for example, in Caltepec, which is represented as a house on a hill (folio 51r). Elsewhere (Berdan 1979) I have argued that these *calli* elements may function as a background or point of reference against which the locative postpositions of the place-names could be interpreted. That is, the positional relationship between the house and the other elements of the glyph represents the locative.

Of the nine place-names with the untranslated *calli* glyphic element, four contain the postposition -*c*/-*co*. As a postposition, it is most commonly translated as "on" or "in." In three of the four cases the glyphs indicate a serpent, water, or a bone perforator partially inside a house; their placement suggests "in" (Tezcacoac, Toyac, and Tlaçoxiuhco: folio 20v; fig. 39). The fourth example illustrates mesquite branches protruding from the top, either in or on a house (Mizquic: folio 20v; fig. 40).

Left: Fig. 39. Tlaçoxiuhco (*Codex Mendoza* folio 20v). Right: Fig. 40. Glyph for Mizquic (*Codex Mendoza* folio 20v).

There is another somewhat similar case with an untranslated *calli* in the glyph of the place-name Coçotlan ("Place of the Turtle-doves"). This is represented with feathers emerging from the top of a house (folio 20r). Interpretation of the *calli* glyph as a spatial representation of the postposition -*tlan* is somewhat less satisfying, however. The possible meanings of -*tlan* as "abundance of," "near," "next to," or "among" are less apparent from the construction of the glyph (León-Portilla 1982:62). The other four cases with untranslated houses show the *calli* twice situated on top of a rock (Teticpac: folios 36r and 44r), on top of a "rock mat" (Tepechpan: folio 20r), and on top of a mound of sand (Xaxalpan: folio 20r). The postpositions -*icpac* and -*pan* both indicate the general spatial relationship "on" or "on top of," completely consistent with the glyphs as interpreted here. In these cases, however, the house glyph is the active agent rather than the background. Of all nine instances, seven are from a single province, Petlalco, on the southern shores of Lake Chalco. The two remaining examples are from diverse southern provinces. It may be that the use of this glyphic principle was a regional developme   that was used only sparingly elsewhere. This, of course, opens u.e distinct possibility that, while some rules for glyphic construction were uniform throughout central Mexico, others were created and used in more restricted geographical areas.

VARIATION IN GLYPHIC USAGE

Armed with these conventions and a wide array of pictographic symbols, the central Mexican scribe composed readable manuscripts. In some cases, he had at his disposal symbols that could be used in a variety of ways to convey a variety of meanings. For example, the speech scroll indicated speech acts (*Codex Mendoza*, part 3, *passim*); was part of the symbolism of the ruler, or *tlatoani*, to indicate his function as "speaker" (*Codex Mendoza*, part 1, *passim*); and was also used as a phonetic substitute for -*nahua(c)*, "adjacent to" or "beside" (see fig. 18). Even more variably used, footprints indicated actual movement (as commonly seen throughout part 3) or could convey the meaning "road" (folio 64r, and commonly on maps of sixteenth-century Mexico) or "bridge" (as in Quauhpanoayan, where *quauhpantli* means bridge, but the footprints also may indicate *pano*, to cross a river on foot [folio 10r]). The footprint is used in place-name glyphs to indicate movement of water (Alahuiztlan: folio 37r), and as a locative to indicate -*pan* (see above), as an alternative to the more usual banner (*pantli*).[19] The footprint also conveyed the vowel sound "o" (from *ohtli*: road) in several glyphs.[20] And, apparently for the place-name glyph for Tlapan (folios 12r, 13r, 39r), the scribe used the ubiquitous footprint to mean *pa*, to dye or tint, again drawing on the pun with *pano*.

In using these and other symbols, how much "free play" could the scribe exercise in the rendering of glyphs, so as to convey the correct meaning with a minimum of confusion and ambiguity? There are several approaches to this question.

A particularly promising avenue is a comparison of the place-name glyphs in parts 1 and 2 of the *Codex Mendoza*. All three parts of this pictorial were supposedly composed by a single artist (Roberston 1959:96; Gómez de Orozco 1941; Howe in this volume); yet there are striking contrasts in the appearance of many place glyphs in parts 1 and 2. While some of these may indicate merely the use of alternative conventions by a single artist, other differences are more dramatic and suggest the work of perhaps another artist, or the possibility that section 1 was copied from a document rather unlike the *Matrícula de Tributos* (associated with part 2 of the *Mendoza*). Particularly notable is the general fact that figures with a horizontal attitude face left in part 1 and right in part 2.

What are some of the more specific contrasts?

1. *Mizquic*: As a tributary community contained in the province of Petlalco (folio 20v), the glyph for this locale consists of a house with mesquite branches atop. While the element -*calli* is not contained in the town name, it may serve a positional function (-*c*: "on"; fig. 40). The glyph for this same community in the conquest history of the *Mendoza*, however, omits the -*calli* element (fig. 41). Other part 2 communities identified with the use of "relative position" are not included in part 1; nor does there seem to be any other use of "relative position" in part 1 of the *Mendoza*.

Fig. 41. Mizquic, as drawn in part 1 of the *Codex Mendoza* (folio 6r).

2. *Malinaltepec:* In part 2 of the *Mendoza*, the symbolic day sign for *malinalli* is used in the place glyphs for Malinalco (folio 35r) and Malinaltepec (folios 39r and 41r; fig. 42). This ritual sign, however, is replaced in part 1 by twisted grass (folio 16r; fig. 43), the sign used for this place glyph in the *Códice Xolotl* (McGowan and Van Nice 1979:42). There are insufficient data to go so far as to suggest that the first part of the *Mendoza* uses less religious symbolism than the second part, but there are indeed only a few cases of its use in part 1 (e.g., Teteuhtepec, Yztactlalocan).

Left: Fig. 42. Glyph for Malinaltepec in part 2 of the *Codex Mendoza* (folio 41r). Right: Fig. 43. Malinaltepec as seen in part 1 of the *Codex Mendoza* (folio 16r).

3. *Coyucac:* This is a case where additional, redundant linguistic information is presented in part 1 where it is lacking in part 2. With Coyucac, in part 1 (folio 13r) this name is "spelled out" as well as illustrated pictographically (fig. 44). Perhaps the artist did not feel that the rather undistinguished head (fig. 45) was sufficient to identify this community unambiguously (folio 38r). Similarly, the diagnostic *tecutli* headband sits on an identifiable *tecpan* in part 1 (folio 5v; fig. 46), but was not felt necessary for the same town glyph in part 2 (folio 32r; fig. 47). On the other hand, in some few cases the part 2 glyphs provide more information: for Quauhtitlan, the head of a *Chichimeca*, lacking in part 1 (Peñafiel 1885:96), poses beside the obligatory tree; for Miquiyetlan (folio 11r) or Miquetlan (folio 12r) in part 1, the single reposing figure is represented by the classic mummy bundle with a bean added (-*e*, or -*ye*) in part 2. In these cases, the information presented in part 2 is more elaborate and less ambiguous.

4. *Xalapan:* This glyph is quite literally rendered in part 1 (folio 16v; fig. 48), somewhat more vaguely in part 2 (folio 26r; fig. 49), and it is easily confused with Xalac, also in part 2 (folio 28r; fig. 50). While there is little additional evidence to suggest that part 1 is a more "literal" document, this is consistent with the statements about Coyucac and Tecpan already made.

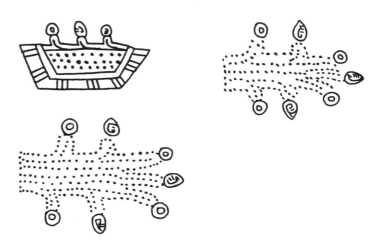

Upper left: Fig. 48. Xalapan as drawn in part 1 of the *Codex Mendoza* (folio 16v). Upper right: Fig. 49. Xalapan, in part 2 of the *Codex Mendoza* (folio 26r). Lower left: Fig. 50. Xalac (*Codex Mendoza* folio 28r). Note the similarity with Xalapan.

5. *Tuchpa:* The sixteenth-century scribe unquestionably had a considerable repertoire of conventions for alternate use—and indeed used them alternately. The usual sign for the locative -*pan* is a *pantli* or banner, as in the Tuchpa of part 2 (folio 52r; fig. 51); yet this same place-name is presented in part 1 with a footprint (for *pano*) replacing the classic banner (folio 10v; fig. 52). Of the most commonly used locatives, -*pan* seems to be most irregular—most frequently omitted, and sometimes alternating banner and footprint. That scribal preference is involved is suggested by the use of both signs for the same name (Tuchpa), and also by the variable use of these signs in two sequential place glyphs: Tuchpa and

Upper left: Fig. 44. Coyucac, as seen in part 1 of the *Codex Mendoza* (folio 13r). Upper right: Fig. 45. Coyucac, as seen in part 2 of the *Codex Mendoza* (folio 38r). Lower left: Fig. 46. Tecpan, in part 1 of the *Codex Mendoza* (folio 5v). Lower right: Fig. 47. Tecpan as rendered in part 2 of the *Codex Mendoza* (folio 32r).

Upper left: Fig. 51. Glyph for the town of Tuchpa in part 2 of the *Codex Mendoza* (folio 52r). Upper center: Fig. 52. Tuchpa, as drawn in part 1 of the *Codex Mendoza* (folio 10v). Upper right: Fig. 53. Tuchpa and Tlaltiçapan, with different glyphic conventions for the locative -*pan* (*Codex Mendoza* folio 52r). Lower left: Fig. 54. Huehuetlan, in part 1 of the *Codex Mendoza* (folio 13v). Lower right: Fig. 55. Huehuetlan, in part 2 of the *Codex Mendoza* (folio 47r).

Tlaltiçapan (folio 52r; fig. 53). The locative *-tlan*, while less variable overall, seems to be found with somewhat greater frequency in part 1 than in part 2. This is true, for example, in the glyphs for Huehuetlan (folios 13v and 47r; figs. 54 and 55), Quauhtlan (folios 13v and 24v), and Nochiztlan (folios 15v and 43r; figs. 56 and 57). Considerable variation is sometimes evident, as with the two renderings of Achiotlan (folios 15v and 45r): in part 1 the conventional incisors are drawn; in part 2 a jaw full of teeth is drawn for the *-tlan* element, with water atop for phonetic duplication of the initial *a-* sound.

Left: Fig. 56. Nochiztlan, in part 1 of the *Codex Mendoza* (folio 15v).
Right: Fig. 57. Nochiztlan, in part 2 of the *Codex Mendoza* (folio 43r).

Overall, this comparison between parts 1 and 2 of the *Codex Mendoza* suggests that the part 1 glyphs may provide greater elaboration of linguistic information, be more literal, and lack some use of religious symbolism and the convention of relative position. All these variations could be attributed to scribal preference, if a rather flexible system was the norm (as, for example, Prem and Riese [1983] suggest). The different horizontal orientations of the two parts of the document are more bothersome, and suggest either a completely different scribe or the copying of another scribe's work. However, this still argues for some writing flexibility—but between scribes rather than by a single scribe. Thus, while the written efforts in composing religious and ritual codices may have attended to rather strict rules and conventions, in the realm of "single words," the scribe seems to have had at his disposal a variety of symbols and conventions that were only more or less standardized in use. A single scribe might omit, embellish, duplicate, or vary the content of his glyphic signs; different scribes would exercise these "freedoms" differently. This may have been the case with the first two sections of the *Codex Mendoza*.

In using variable forms of glyphic expression, the scribe (or scribes) of the *Codex Mendoza* was undoubtedly not behaving in a unique or even unusual manner—this was probably the norm in the Late Postclassic central Mexican writing tradition. The *Codex Mendoza*, in glyphically expressing so many aspects of Aztec culture, is a particularly valuable document in our understanding of this writing system.

NOTES

1. The *Codex Borbonicus*, a ritual-calendrical almanac from Tenochtitlan, serves as a nice complement to the *Codex Mendoza* (and the *Matrícula de Tributos*) in this regard.

2. Nowotny focuses directly on the *Codex Mendoza*; Nicholson, although not at all restricted to the *Codex Mendoza*, draws heavily on its material in his authoritative analysis. Other important works on Mesoamerican writing include Dibble (1940, 1960, 1973), Marcus (1980), and Prem (1968). Place-names have received special attention from M. E. Smith (1973), Dykerhoff (1984), Brand (1948), and León-Portilla (1982).

3. In Nahuatl, *amoxtli* (book) and *amatl* (paper) served as the basic terms for "book." See, for example, the many derivatives of both of these terms in Molina (1970) and Siméon (1963).

4. According to von Hagen (1944), the term *amatl* also refers to the various species of fig trees themselves. A drawing of one such tree, the *tex-calamacoztic*, appears in the Badiano herbal (Gates 1939: folio 38v). A number of these species are described and drawn in Francisco Hernández's *Historia natural de Nueva España* (1959 1:83–90).

5. The *Matrícula de Tributos* currently resides in the Museo Nacional de Antropología in Mexico City. For discussion on the relationships between the two tribute documents, see Berdan (1976a), Barlow (1949a:1–7), Scholes and Adams (1957:9), and Robertson (1959:72–77, 95–107).

6. Motolinía's statement reads, "las hazañas e historias de vencimientos y guerras": "the deeds and histories of conquests and wars."

7. Other types of books also existed, especially ritual, calendric, and divinatory almanacs. Some of these were used as "instruction manuals": "Carefully they were taught the songs which they called the gods' songs. They were inscribed in the books. And well were all taught the reckoning of the days, the book of dreams, and the book of years" (Sahagún 1950–1982 3:65). Alva Ixtlilxochitl (1965 2:179) mentions that the royal archives (*archivos reales*) of Texcoco were spatially associated with the "universidad." While it appears that great libraries existed which housed the vast quantities of books, there are suggestions that scribes, or perhaps organized groups of scribes, also maintained stores of books—this certainly would have been useful in training neophytes to the profession (Durán 1964:268–270; 1967:513–516).

8. Harvey (1982:195–196) suggests that the circles depicted on the large bins of foodstuffs represent the item plus one (=2 for each bin, consistent with the *Mendoza*'s Spanish glosses). He observes the two cases in the *Matrícula de Tributos* that show a square in place of a circle, and posits that this sign indicates the number 4.

9. In the *Matrícula*, these are at times annotated as *omatl*, *onmatl* (two hands, or lengths), or *nanmatl* or *nananmatl* (four hands, or lengths). For a discussion of various possible "lengths," see Berdan (1980b:33) and Castillo (1972). Barlow (1949a), erroneously I think, interprets these fingers as additional quantities.

10. For translations of personal names, titles, and place-names, see appendix E.

11. Clark (1938 1:59) interprets this unglossed name glyph as "Wave": Acueyotl (*atl*: water, and *cuechtli*: shell).

12. These were high-ranking nobles, usually occupying important administrative positions—judges, military officers, or the like. See Berdan 1982:51–54.

13. The *Tlacochcalcatl* on folio 18r was incorrectly glossed as *Tlacochtectli*.

14. Clark (1938: folio 71r overleaf) suggests the glyph consists of teeth and dark marks, combining to yield *tlanamoyani*, thief. See volume 2 page descriptions for folios 70r and 71r for details on these names.

15. Clark (1938 2:33) identifies this figure as Opochtli; Peñafiel (1885:118) feels it represents a *pochtecatl* or professional merchant. See Hueypuchtlan in appendix E.

16. See also León-Portilla 1982:62–68.

17. Although *pano* itself does not appear in either Molina or Siméon, compounds of it do: *calpanoa*, *calpanuia* ("andar de casa en casa"); Molina 1970:10.

18. Peñafiel (1885:157) was unable to identify firmly the animal portrayed, although he suggests it to be an iguana and notes its similarity to the *ahuitzotl*.

19. Examples of this use include Yztapan (folio 38r), Tlaltiçapan (folio 52r), and Texopan (folio 43r).

20. Examples include Tiçayucan (folio 22r), Ocpayucan (folio 32r), Xomeyocan (folio 29r), Quachqueçaloyan (folio 30r), Ytzucan (folio 42r), and Ytzteyocan (folio 48r).

CHAPTER 8

A Comparative Analysis
of the Costumes and Accoutrements
of the *Codex Mendoza*

Patricia Rieff Anawalt

The ethnographic section of *Codex Mendoza* provides a rare glimpse into the Aztecs' pre-Hispanic world. Almost every facet of their life cycle is portrayed: a new baby is ritually bathed, willful children are properly reared, youths dutifully submit to arduous training, brave warriors rise through illustrious ranks, litigants appeal in courts of law, and, finally, both heedless and meritorious lives reach their destined end. Throughout these folios exemplary behavior is consistently reinforced and the Aztecs' emphasis on warfare is all-pervasive.

Thanks to the scope of the ethnographic scenes, we learn a great deal about the inhabitants of Tenochtitlan prior to the Spaniards' arrival. There is, however, a puzzling aspect to these fascinating and informative vignettes. Aside from warrior paraphernalia, all the costumes are strangely lacking in color and decoration. Something is amiss here. Other sources testify that the Aztecs wore far livelier garments than *Codex Mendoza* indicates.

Clothing depictions in this sixteenth century pictorial vary according to context. The nineteen pages of part 1, the historical section, contain only a few garment illustrations and hence contribute sparse costume information. Almost all the clothing, textiles, and warrior costumes discussed here come from part 2, the thirty-eight tribute tallies, and part 3, the fifteen folios devoted to an ethnographic account of Mexican life.

A comparison of this apparel with analogous material in other pictorials demonstrates the disparities between *Codex Mendoza*'s clothing depictions and what we know was actually worn by the Aztecs. The following analysis of these data involves three steps: (1) *Codex Mendoza* apparel is contrasted with analogous examples from other early Colonial pictorials; (2) the implications of the revealed disparities are explored; and (3) the selective costume repertory of *Codex Mendoza* is considered in terms of what it indicates about the document itself.

CODEX MENDOZA WEARING APPAREL CONTRASTED WITH THAT IN OTHER COLONIAL SOURCES

Mexico, unlike Peru or Egypt, did not have the combination of burial practices and dry climate that preserves ancient cloth. Nonetheless, the area's pictographic writing system performed its own unique form of textile conservation. The Mesoamerican pictorials contain hundreds of images of pre-Hispanic garments, many of them drawn in remarkable detail. Whether worn by deities or humans, pictured in tribute tallies or displayed as offerings, this clothing reflects a wide array of social contexts. These varied depictions occur in both pre- and post-Conquest documents.

Only two of the Aztec codices, *Codex Borbonicus* and *Matrícula de Tributos*, are regarded as possibly being pre-Hispanic.[1] Following the Spanish Conquest, the native writing system sometimes continued to be used. As a result, there are early Colonial Mexican pictorials whose depictions of indigenous dress have sufficient validity to serve in reconstructing the Aztec costume repertory.[2]

In addition to these visual data, there is written information on Aztec clothing in sixteenth-century Spanish textual records. The eyewitness accounts of the conquistadors include observations on the indigenous dress, as do some administrative documents.[3] The greatest source of information on Indian costume, however, comes from the work of the early Spanish missionary friars discussed below.

Aztec clothing reflected the restraints imposed by the indigenous weaving technology, the backstrap loom (fig. 1). The same weaving equipment was and is used by Indian women throughout the entire Mesoamerican area. This assemblage of simple parts restricts the width of each piece of woven cloth to the breadth of the loom, which produces webs of cloth finished on all four sides. As a result, a textile can be worn draped on the body just as it comes from the loom without further processing, or unfitted garments can be created by sewing together the selvages of two or more pieces of material.

Most Aztec clothing was draped or tied about the body. The predominant garments were the male loincloth, hip-cloth, and cape; females wore a simple wrap-around skirt and a nonfitted tunic. With the exception of the warrior/ceremonial costumes—special-purpose garments worn only a small percentage of the time—clothing did not encase the limbs or conform to the lines of the body. Also, aside from warrior costumes, Aztec clothing had no sleeves. Despite what appears to be contradictory pictorial evidence—the result of wide garments that drape over the shoulder in a sleevelike manner—comparative analysis indicates that pre-Hispanic Mesoamerican clothing was basically sleeveless.[4]

According to certain of the early missionary accounts, particularly those of Fray Diego Durán, Aztec clothing reflected the sharply stratified society from which it came. Although the various classes wore the same basic garments, rigidly enforced sumptuary laws supposedly guaranteed that nobles' and commoners' apparel

Fig. 1. The backstrap loom on which the Indian women weavers produced the textiles of Mesoamerica (Clark 1938 3: folio 60r).

varied markedly in fabric and design.[5] Recent research seriously challenges this contention, suggesting that the post-Conquest descriptions of the severity of the reported sumptuary edicts represent an idealized image of the military and political order of pre-Hispanic Tenochtitlan.[6] As such, these vaunted laws reflected a creed far more than a reality.

What is incontestably apparent in both missionary and conquistador accounts is the splendor of pre-Hispanic textiles. Durán speaks of the nobles' magnificent cloaks, resplendent in varying colors and designs and shimmering featherwork.[7] In reference to Aztec women's apparel, he mentions the detailing, featherwork, and intricate motifs.[8] Durán's observations are confirmed by Fray Bernardino de Sahagún, who devotes considerable attention to the impressive clothing of the rulers and nobles. He lists sixty-seven different garments; the vast majority are described as having colorful and highly decorative designs.[9] Another of Sahagún's chapters is devoted to the "adornments of women." Fifteen blouses and nine skirts are listed, all of which are characterized as being colorfully ornamented.[10]

The conquistadors were also greatly impressed by the Mesoamerican textiles. Cortés highly praised the extensive range of color, design, and variety of the weavings, as well as the high quality of the cloth and clothing of Tenochtitlan.[11] The Anonymous Conqueror also commented most favorably on Aztec apparel, mentioning particularly men's capes with their finely worked and richly decorated bands and borders.[12]

The clothing of Tenochtitlan's daily round obviously created a stunning pageant of color and decoration, a panoply that appropriately reflected the riches and multiformity of a mighty empire. It is thus particularly intriguing that *Codex Mendoza* is so at variance with this documented reality: (1) in the secular scenes, almost all the garments are undecorated; (2) ritual attire is virtually ignored, despite the Aztecs' obsession with matters religious; (3) the tribute tallies do not include the full range of Aztec warrior costumes; (4) scenes of the military hierarchy are at variance with analogous data; and finally, (5) the depicted tribute textiles represent only a portion of the wide range of the Aztecs' decorated cloth. Each of these categories is examined in turn, the better to understand the limited scope of the Aztec world as reflected in the costumes of *Codex Mendoza.*

Before considering how *Codex Mendoza* depicts the secular dress of Tenochtitlan, it is helpful first to set part 3, the ethnographic

section, in context. While part 1, the history, and part 2, the tribute section, appear to have been copied from earlier manuscripts, part 3 has no known pre-Hispanic analogue and hence it is almost certainly post-Conquest, drawn up specifically for export to Spain.

The purpose of this ethnographic material was to inform Charles V of the inhabitants of his exotic new land. It therefore might be anticipated that the diversity, wealth, and stratification of the powerful Aztec empire purposely would be reflected in the apparel worn in scenes dealing with various stages and aspects of the Indians' life cycle. Such is not the case. Certainly the native scribes who drew the vignettes used the proper native conventions, and, from what we know from Spanish eyewitness reports and missionary accounts, the content of the scenes is ethnographically valid. The depicted clothing, however, is strangely lacking in embellishment. The result is an image of the Aztec world at variance with what we know from other Colonial sources, particularly the extensive work of Fray Bernardino de Sahagún, the Aztecs' most encyclopedic chronicler.

In order to convert the Indians, the early Spanish missionaries had to preach in the indigenous languages. Sahagún not only mastered Nahuatl, the Aztec language, but also went on to compile the most detailed account for any of the newly discovered peoples in the Age of Discovery. He spent almost four decades—apparently from 1547 to 1585—carefully recording, cross-checking, and transcribing all that his native informants told him about almost every aspect of Mexican life.[13] When Sahagún died at ninety-one, his magnum opus was contained in what has come down to us as the twelve books of the *Florentine Codex.* This corpus encompasses detailed drawings and information on a kaleidoscope of topics covering natural history, religion, secular life, and the stratified levels of Aztec society. Scattered throughout these books are long lists of Aztec apparel for various classes and occasions, some with accompanying drawings that record the range and detailing of the society's costumes and accoutrements. As a result, Sahagún provides a logical source against which to contrast the clothing of the *Codex Mendoza* ethnographic scenes.

Secular Dress

FEMALE CLOTHING

A variety of life stages and social contexts for both sexes are represented in part 3 of *Codex Mendoza.* A girl of three years (fig. 2) is depicted wearing only a blouse with no skirt. This blouse, or *huipilli,*[14] has the ubiquitous *Codex Mendoza* red hem and red decorative design square at the garment's neck. At age five (fig. 3), the girl has added a simple wrap-around skirt, or *cueitl.*[15] It is unbordered, as is her *huipilli.* However, by the time a young woman marries (fig. 4) she is shown wearing the standard female attire of part 3: white skirt and *huipilli,* both bordered in red with a red design square at the neck. This same costume is depicted at all stages of a woman's life, be she child, maiden, young mother, or revered grandmother who has earned the right to drink unlimited pulque (fig. 5).

Despite the sharply stratified and puritanical nature of Aztec society, females whom fate had placed on the darker side of life are shown in *Codex Mendoza* wearing exactly the same kind of clothing as their more exemplary sisters. For example, a woman who, so the gloss informs us, had "carnal connections" with a novice priest (fig. 6) wears precisely the same standard attire. This is also true of a female drunkard, whose vice of excessive drinking had led her to thievery (fig. 7). Rather than being shown in garish clothing or disheveled garments, she is depicted exactly like the most re-

Left to right, top row: Fig. 2. An Aztec mother and her three-year-old daughter, who wears only a red-bordered *huipilli* (Clark 1938 3: folio 58r). Fig. 3. An Aztec girl of five years who wears a *huipilli* and skirt, both unbordered (Clark 1938 3: folio 58r). Fig. 4. An Aztec wedding scene. The bride wears a red-bordered white skirt and *huipilli* with a red design square at the neck. The groom wears an undecorated white *tilmatli* (Clark 1938 3: folio 61r). Center row: Fig. 5. A respected older Aztec woman whose advanced age entitles her to become intoxicated when she wishes. Her costume is the white blouse and skirt with red trim (Clark 1938 3: folio 71r). Fig. 6. An Aztec woman who had "carnal connections" with a novice priest. She wears the same skirt and *huipilli* as all the other females in *Codex Mendoza* (Clark 1938 3: folio 63r). Fig. 7. An Aztec woman whose vice of excessive drinking has led to thieving. She too wears the same white *huipilli* and a skirt with red trim (Clark 1938 3: folio 70r). Bottom row: Fig. 8. The place glyph for Cahualan ("Place of Many Forsaken Women") shows a weeping woman dressed in white *huipilli* and skirt; the borders and rectangular design at the neck are not depicted in red (Clark 1938 3: folio 13v). Fig. 9. The wife of a disobedient *cacique* wears a white *huipilli* with red design trim and a white skirt (Clark 1938 3: folio 66r).

spected of Aztec matrons. This same, ever-present white clothing, sans red trim, also appears in the place glyph in part 1 for Cahualan ("Place of Many Forsaken Women"; fig. 8).[16] Even women of power and influence, such as the wife of the disobedient *cacique*

(fig. 9), wear precisely the same simple garments as all other *Codex Mendoza* females.

This homogeneity of simple attire is not at all the picture of Aztec clothing which Sahagún, our most detailed source, conveys

Upper left: Fig. 10. Eight upper-class women wearing richly patterned attire (Sahagún 1979 8: folio 30v). Upper right: Fig. 11. Decorated *huipilli* and skirts of upper-class Aztec women (Sahagún 1979 8: folio 31r). Center left: Fig. 12. Noblewomen of Tenochtitlan wearing richly decorated *huipilli* (*Códice Azcatítlan* 1949: planche XXVI). Lower left: Fig. 13. A seller of capes displaying a *huipilli* and skirt with specific design motifs (Sahagún 1979 10: folio 46r). Lower right: Fig. 14. A harlot wearing a *huipilli* and skirt similar to the garments displayed by the cape seller (Sahagún 1979 10: folio 39v).

in his descriptions and drawings of female garments in the *Florentine Codex*, compiled at least twenty years after *Codex Mendoza*. In book 8, *Kings and Lords*, Sahagún gives us an idea of the interesting design detail on the garments of upper-class women (figs. 10 and 11). *Códice Azcatítlan* shows similar rich apparel in a scene (fig. 12) which Barlow speculates may represent the removal of Indian noblewomen from besieged Tenochtitlan.[17]

It might be argued that the lack of design detail on the female

attire of *Codex Mendoza* is a reflection of the social strata portrayed—that no upper-class women are depicted. However, a review of the range of contexts presented in the ethnographic section demonstrates that is not the case. The captured *cacique*'s wife certainly is no commoner,[18] nor perhaps is the young wife spinning cotton, the status fiber, at a feast given by her new husband (see fig. 32).

Moreover, other sources make it clear that the female clothing

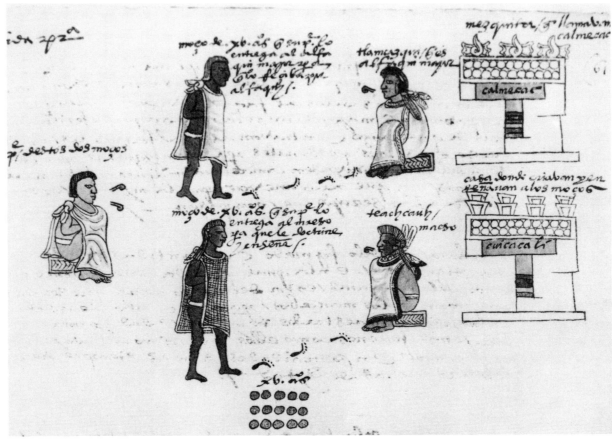

Left to right, top row: Fig. 15. An Aztec boy of three years wears only an undecorated cape (Clark 1938 3: folio 58r). Fig. 16. A thirteen-year-old Aztec boy wears a loincloth tied in the "Aztec knot" style: both ends of the loincloth are brought forward and tied in a distinctive knot (Clark 1938 3: folio 60r). Fig. 17. An old man of seventy is allowed to drink *pulque* for pleasure. Note that he still wears the same standard male clothing illustrated throughout part 3 (Clark 1938 3: folio 70r). Fig. 18. The gossip wears a white cape with a multicolored border (Clark 1938 3: folio 70r). Fig. 19. The "Master of Youths" wears a netted cape with a narrow red border (Clark 1938 3: folio 57r). Bottom: Fig. 20. Two fifteen-year-old boys being presented to their respective schools. In the upper register is the temple school, the *calmecac*, where the upper-class youths were trained by priests. Below is the school for the lower-class youths, the *telpochcalli* (glossed *cuicacalli*), where the Masters of Youths taught. Note that the two teachers wear white cloaks with differentiated borders; the lower-class boy wears a net cape with a narrow white border (Clark 1938 3: folio 61r).

of the lower rungs of the Aztec social ladder was not lacking in individuality. Sahagún illustrates a cape seller with a *huipilli* and skirt (fig. 13) remarkably similar to the clothing of a bona fide member of the *hoi polloi*, the harlot (fig. 14). Also, in book 9, *The Merchants*, Sahagún depicts a woman of the merchant class wearing clothing with interesting design motifs (see fig. 31).

MALE CLOTHING

Returning to *Codex Mendoza*, the ethnographic section also reflects the varying life stages and social contexts of Aztec males. A three-year-old boy needs only a cape (fig. 15), but by the time he reaches puberty—man's estate—he always wears the mandatory loincloth,

the *maxtlatl* (fig. 16).[19] Here, as elsewhere throughout *Codex Mendoza*, both ends of this garment are brought forward and tied in a style that has been designated the "Aztec knot."[20] This loincloth, combined with a white *tilmatli* (translated *manta*, cloak, or cape),[21] is the standard male apparel of *Codex Mendoza*, worn throughout a man's life from bridegroom (see fig. 4) to respected, aged tippler, a veteran of over seventy years (fig. 17). Aside from *Codex Mendoza*'s scenes of hierarchical warrior grades, the norm is to present male attire as white and undecorated. The exceptions are two white cloaks with narrow multicolored borders worn by the Gossip (fig. 18) and the Keeper of the Storehouse[22] and netted capes worn by Masters of Youths (fig. 19) and their young charges (fig. 20).[23]

Aside from the warrior hierarchical scenes and a few military and political functionaries (see folios 64r, 65r, 66r, 67r), the *Codex Mendoza* ethnographic section denies elaborate clothing to even the most prestigious members of the Aztec society. For example, the judges on folio 68r are attired in unadorned white capes (e.g., fig. 21), yet these dignitaries belong to the highest class; all are shown wearing a symbol of nobility, the *xiuhuitzolli*, the turquoise diadem.[24] Although the emperor Motecuhzoma is clothed in a blue-green *tilmatli* (fig. 22), it too is an undecorated garment. In contrast, other Colonial pictorials present quite a different picture of Aztec imperial attire.

Left: Fig. 21. All the judges depicted in *Codex Mendoza* wear plain white capes. These officials were members of the nobility, as is indicated by the wearing of the turquoise diadem (Clark 1938 3: folio 68r). Right: Fig. 22. Emperor Motecuhzoma, shown seated in his palace, wears a plain turquoise cloak completely devoid of design motif (Clark 1938 3: folio 69r).

In book 8 of the *Florentine Codex*, *Kings and Lords*, Sahagún depicts the successive rulers of Tenochtitlan.[25] From Itzcoatl to Cuauhtemoc (e.g., fig. 23), each emperor wears the *xiuhtlalpilli tenixyo tilmatli* (the blue knotted cloak with the *tenixyo* [eyes on the edge] border).[26] *Codex Ixtlilxochitl* makes the lavishness of these royal cloaks far more explicit in a magnificent depiction of Nezahualpilli (fig. 24). This ruler of Texcoco, with his *quetzallalpiloni* pom-pom headgear,[27] jade lip plug, jade necklace and bracelets, gold leg bands, and turquoise sandals, presents a picture of the raiment of kings that agrees with the eyewitness accounts of the conquistadors as to degree of imperial grandeur.

Codex Ixtlilxochitl also indicates how great lords were arrayed. Tocuepotzin, a Texcocan noble, wears a carmine-colored *tilmatli* with the prestigious *tenixyo* "eyes on the edge" border, together with gold armbands and an elaborate gold necklace (fig. 25). Another lord of Texcoco, Quauhtlatzacuilotl, is adorned in a cream-colored cloak with a repeat design of conch shells, jaguar-skin sandals, and a labret of crystal (fig. 26).

Just as rulers and nobles actually dressed far more elegantly than *Codex Mendoza* indicates, so too did judges. Sahagún illustrates eight magistrates, each wearing a unique cloak design (e.g., fig. 27). But judges, of course, either were of the nobility or had achieved their honored position through military prowess. Was such elaborated clothing restricted only to the noble class, as the Aztec sumptuary laws would have us assume? Not according to Sahagún, whose accounts reveal that not even commoners always went about in undecorated clothing.

Book 10 of the *Florentine Codex*, *The People*, contains a section that discusses the activities of various humble occupations: sellers of foodstuffs, medicines, utilitarian objects, and clothing.[28] Among the latter is a seller of coarse maguey-fiber capes, garments restricted to the lower classes.[29] The way these "coarse" capes are described is very revealing. Sahagún enumerates seven of the cloaks, all of which sound decidedly elaborated: "the whirlpool design, as if with eyes painted; with the turkey having the mat-designed interior; with the small face; . . . the one with broken cords, with husks outlined in black—in wide black lines, with the interior diagonal design; the cape with the ocelot design; . . . those with flowers."[30] These particular coarse maguey cloaks were obviously decorated.

There is additional evidence that commoners wore elaborated clothing. Sahagún illustrates a quintessential man of the people, the Procurer (fig. 28), wearing a cape bearing designs. Also, in book 9, *The Merchants*, there are repeated illustrations of decorated cloaks. For example, merchants shown receiving *tilmatl* from the emperor Ahuitzotl wear cloaks with designs (fig. 29). In another scene, Tenochtitlan and Tlatelolco merchants clad in elaborated cloaks are shown convened on business and/or ceremonial matters (fig. 30). These men of commerce obviously had access to decorated clothing, although they seldom wore their fine garments in public.

The Aztec merchants had an intermediate social position between the free commoners and the aristocratic ruling lineages. The upper classes were threatened by the growing power of the merchants; as a result, the latter adopted a very low profile. Despite this cautious policy of inconspicuous consumption, successful merchants wore elaborated garments when among themselves (e.g., fig. 31).

The ethnographic scenes of part 3 of *Codex Mendoza* present a costume repertory at odds with the evidence gathered by Sahagún some twenty years later. This paradox is particularly evident in the upper register of *Codex Mendoza*'s folio 68r, a scene in which a newly married man, desirous of relinquishing some of his duties so as to attain more leisure, hosts a feast in order to influence his peers (fig. 32). All the participants wear plain white clothing for this festive event. Even the two *mantas* given as gifts are virtually undecorated and completely colorless, almost identical to most of the clothing in the ethnographic scenes.

SUMMARY

We know from evidence in Colonial pictorials and Spanish accounts that Aztec secular clothing was colorful and well decorated. For some reason this pre-Hispanic reality is not reflected in *Codex Mendoza*. In addition, there is another entire category of Aztec costume that is greatly underrepresented: ritual ceremonial dress.

Ritual Attire

One of the distinctive hallmarks of pre-Hispanic Mesoamerica was the all-pervasive nature of religious belief, a force that permeated every aspect of daily life. In a world where the ceremonial round paced the activities of each individual, the ritual attire associated with the great ceremonies was an indispensable and memorable part of the culture. This clothing category receives scant attention in *Codex Mendoza*.

In the Aztec costume repertory there were three special-purpose garments that appear only in a ritual-ceremonial context, the *quechquemitl*, *quemitl*, and *xicolli*.[31]

Left to right, top row: Fig. 23. A highly stylized portrayal of Motecuhzoma the Younger (1502–1520) wearing the *xiuhtlalpilli* (blue-knotted cape), the official blue cloak worn by Aztec rulers (Sahagún 1979 8: folio 2v). Fig. 24. The ruler of Texcoco, Nezahualpilli, wearing another version of the *xiuhtlalpilli* (blue-knotted) cloak, similar (note that the border differs) to that illustrated in figure 23 (*Codex Ixtlilxochitl* 1976: folio 108r). Fig. 25. Tocuepotzin, a lord of Texcoco, wears a richly decorated *tilmatli* (*Codex Ixtlilxochitl* 1976: folio 105r). Fig. 26. Quauhtlatzacuilotl, a lord of Texcoco, wears richly decorated attire (*Codex Ixtlilxochitl* 1976: folio 107r). Center row: Fig. 27. Four Aztec judges, each of whom wears a cloak with a distinctive design motif (Sahagún 1979 8: folio 36v). Fig. 28. The Procurer, a man of the people, wears a patterned cloak over his Colonial shirt and pantaloons (Sahagún 1979 10: folio 24v). Bottom row: Fig. 29. Merchants wearing decorated capes receive cloaks from Emperor Ahuitzotl as reward for valor (Sahagún 1979 9: folio 8r). Fig. 30. Merchants from Tenochtitlan and Tlaltelolco shown in conference; each wears a cloak with a distinctive design motif (Sahagún 1979 9: folio 7v). Fig. 31. Members of the merchant class listening to the admonitions of an elder; each wears a garment with specific design motifs (Sahagún 1979 9: folio 25v).

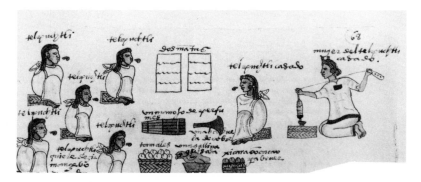

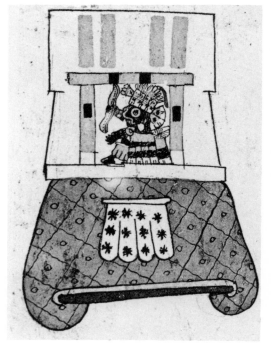

Fig. 32. A feast scene where all the depicted garments, excepting the two gift mantles, are completely undecorated (Clark 1938 3: folio 68r).

Left: Fig. 33. The rain deity Tlaloc wears the *quemitl*, the godly bib or chest cape, around his neck. A *quemitl* also appears as part of the place glyph on the mountain beneath him (*Codex Borbonicus* 1974:32). Center: Fig. 34. The place glyph for Aztaquemeca ("The Place of the White Heron Feather Capes") contains a feathered *quemitl*, the godly bib of the deities (Clark 1938 3: folio 21v). Right: Fig. 35. In the place glyph for Teteuhtepec ("On the Hill of the Gods") the *quemitl* has become the symbol for the gods themselves (Clark 1938 3: folio 7v).

QUECHQUEMITL

The *quechquemitl*, a triangular chest cape, was worn—in the Mexica world—only by goddesses and their impersonators.[32] Since no deities appear in all of *Codex Mendoza*, it follows that there are no depictions of *quechquemitl*.

QUEMITL

The *quemitl* was a small chest cape that tied under the chin of idols; Seler translates it "deity bib."[33] The *quemitl* occurs frequently in Late Postclassic pictorials.[34] In *Codex Borbonicus* the garment appears in several contexts, most often in association with Tlaloc.[35] There the *quemitl* not only is worn by this rain god but also serves as part of the name glyph for the mountain on which Tlaloc's temple rests (fig. 33).

The *quemitl* appears in *Codex Mendoza* only as a glyphic element in place-names, occurring once in part 1, the historical section, and five times in part 2, the tribute tallies.[36] In five of these place glyphs, the *quemitl* is employed for its phonic value: for example, in the name Aztaquemeca ("The Place of the White Heron Feather Capes";[37] fig. 34). In the sixth case, however, the religious implication of the garment is utilized. The place glyph for Teteuhtepec ("On the Hill of the Gods";[38] fig. 35) contains only two elements: the hill, *tepetl*, and the deity bib, *quemitl*. Note that this latter sound does not occur in the place-name. In this instance, *quemitl* plays an ideographic role, representing the concept of *teotl*, god. With this sole exception, the *quemitl* of *Codex Mendoza* convey no apparent religious significance.

XICOLLI

Of the Aztecs' three special-purpose ritual garments, only the *xicolli* appears in the ethnographic section of *Codex Mendoza*. This sleeveless jacket is recognizable by its diagnostic fringe at the hem and, when depicted *en face*, by a central vertical line denoting the opening of the jacket (fig. 36).[39] Among the Aztecs, the *xicolli* was worn only by males: idols, deity impersonators, priests—sometimes when performing a human sacrifice (fig. 37)—rulers acting in a priestly capacity, sacrificial slaves and their merchant sponsors, and constables carrying out imperial decrees.[40]

Codex Mendoza contains seven *xicolli* depictions; six of these are worn by constables on folio 66r (fig. 38). This scene illustrates the punishment of a rebellious *cacique* who has defied the power of the Aztec empire. The Spanish glosses identify the *xicolli*-clad males in the second register simply as "officers," but their face paint, hairstyle, and duties all indicate that they are constables.[41] The gloss for each of the four *xicolli*-clad officials in registers 3 and 4 reads "officer and ambassador of the lord of Mexico." Each carries the symbols of imperial investiture, a fan and staff.

A seventh *xicolli* depiction occurs on folio 63r (fig. 39), worn by a priest performing an incensing ceremony. He carries the necessary accoutrements for this ritual: an *incensario*, an incense pouch, and a gourd filled with a stimulant containing tobacco to reinforce him during his exhausting round.

SUMMARY

Although *Codex Mendoza* illustrates the *xicolli* in association with official government missions and as a part of ritual paraphernalia, the potent religious implications of the garment are ignored (e.g., worn by sacrificing priests and deity-impersonator victims in human sacrifice ceremonies). As for the Aztecs' two other ritual costumes, the *quechquemitl* does not appear at all in *Codex Mendoza*, and the *quemitl* occurs only as an element of glyphic notation in place-names.

Upper left: Fig. 36. A close-up of the *xicolli*, showing a vertical line denoting the central opening of the jacket (Clark 1938 3: folio 66r). Upper right: Fig. 37. Two Aztec priests, each of whom wears a *xicolli*, perform a human sacrifice (*Codex Magliabechiano* 1970: folio 70r). Lower right: Fig. 38. Six *xicolli*-clad Aztec officials wear the special-purpose jacket while performing imperial functions (Clark 1938 3: folio 66r). Lower left: Fig. 39. A *xicolli*-clad Aztec priest performing an incense ritual (Clark 1938 3: folio 63r).

Despite the downplaying of Aztec ritual and ceremonial life in part 3, *Codex Mendoza* does inadvertently contain repeated illustrations of pre-Hispanic religious symbolism in its warrior costumes. These martial talismans appear prominently among the tribute paraphernalia. The resplendent feathered suits and insignia shown in the tribute tallies each embody a complex iconography, indicating that these garments and devices served a profound and essen-tial purpose beyond that of impressive visual display. It is in this flamboyant military apparel that *Codex Mendoza* reveals the all-pervasive religious nature of Aztec life.

By comparing these warrior costumes with analogous martial attire from other Aztec pictorials, it is possible to judge the degree to which *Codex Mendoza* reflects the full range of Aztec military attire.

Left: Fig. 40. A *momoyactli* back device and bodysuit. The latter clearly depicts the feathers with which it was covered (*Matrícula de Tributos* 1980: folio 6v). Center: Fig. 41. A coyote-costumed warrior. The hatch marks on his suit indicate that the garment was constructed of feathers (Seler 1960–1961 2:576). Right: Fig. 42. A warrior costume showing the covering of feathers and also the back closure (Durán 1967 2: *lámina* 22).

Warrior Costumes (See Appendix F)

There is both pictorial and written evidence that the Aztecs' battle suits and insignia were made of feathers. The Aztec tribute document cognate, *Matrícula de Tributos*, contains a detailed depiction of a warrior suit that clearly illustrates the feathers from which it was made (fig. 40). The *Codex Mendoza*'s Spanish commentary identifies most of the warrior costumes that appear in the tribute tally as being made of either "rich feathers" or "ordinary feathers."[42] In Sahagún's initial work, *Primeros Memoriales*, he illustrates over sixty articles of warrior apparel, including bodysuits, headdresses, back devices, and shields. In addition to each insignia's Nahuatl name, many also have an accompanying explanation of how they were constructed; feathers are mentioned repeatedly in these descriptions.[43] In the case of four of the seven coyote costumes, hatch marks indicate the use of feathers (fig. 41). An illustration of Durán's provides further evidence that these flamboyant warrior suits were made of feathers, and also that they tied in the back (fig. 42).

One of Cortés's original conquistadors, the Anonymous Conqueror, describes some of these magnificent costumes. After explaining that quilted cotton armor was worn beneath the feathered warrior costumes, he continues:

> Over these [cotton armor] they [the warriors] wear suits all of one piece and of a heavy cloth, which they tie in back; these are covered with feathers of different colors and look very jaunty. One company of soldiers will wear them in red and white, another in blue and yellow, and others in various ways.[44]

The conquistadors' eyewitness accounts also make it clear that the Aztecs' remarkable feather warrior costumes and towering back devices are actually worn in combat. The powerful role played by such insignia is attested to in an account concerning one of the most crucial battles of the Spanish Conquest.

The *xopilli* or "claw"[45] back device (fig. 43) played a critical role at a decisive point in Hernán Cortés's career, the battle of Otumba, which took place on July 7, 1520. The conquistadors had suffered a devastating defeat at the hands of the Mexicans and had been driven out of Tenochtitlan in the famous rout of *Noche Triste*. Wounded and exhausted, the Spaniards were attempting to make their way back to their Indian allies in Tlaxcala. However, when they reached the plains of Otumba near the great pyramids of Teotihuacan, the massed military forces of the Aztec empire were awaiting them.

Woefully outnumbered, Cortés realized the Spaniards' only hope lay in an unexpected move. He scanned the battlefield and identified the Aztecs' commanding officer. This leader was easily recognizable not only by the rich panoply of his entourage and his own magnificent costume but particularly by the huge, distinctive feather and silver crest strapped on his back, an elaborated version of *Codex Mendoza*'s claw device (see appendix F, column 9).

Under Cortés's direction, the remaining Spanish troops and cavalry drove through the tightly grouped Indian forces and succeeded in reaching and killing their conspicuous commanding officer. Panic immediately spread among the Indians, even though they vastly outnumbered the Europeans. The loss of the Aztec leader and his symbolic emblem caused demoralization among the warriors, and the tide of battle quickly turned. Thus, by capturing the Aztec imperial standard, the conquistadors survived the battle of Otumba and were able to reach Tlaxcala, where they mounted the final devastating assault on Tenochtitlan.[46]

There is a depiction of the Otumba battle in a Tlaxcalan pictorial, *Lienzo de Tlaxcala*, which includes the local place-name of the battlefield, Tonan ixpan (fig. 44). The net claw device is prominently featured on this page, emphasizing that it had just been captured by Cortés. In the same pictorial, several pages later, the Tlaxcalan noble Maxixcatzin is shown standing before Cortés with the Aztecs' insignia in his hand (fig. 45). Torquemada confirms that the Spaniards presented the Tlaxcalans with the Aztecs' *matlaxopilli* (net claw device), captured on the Otumba battlefield.[47]

Left: Fig. 43. A warrior wearing the *xopilli* (claw) back device (Clark 1938 3: folio 64r). Upper right: Fig. 44. The capturing of the *xopilli* back device by Cortés at the battle of Otumba (*Lienzo de Tlaxcala* 1892:25). Lower right: Fig. 45. The presentation by Cortés of the captured *xopilli* to the Tlaxcalans (*Lienzo de Tlaxcala* 1892:28).

Obviously, the key to understanding the Aztecs' unique feathered battle array is to recognize it as a tremendous source of psychological reinforcement.[48] Each warrior costume had connected with it an elaborate religious symbolism; to don this apparel was to tap into the power and protection of the deity involved.

Before examining the various warrior costumes that appear in *Codex Mendoza*, it first must be explained how we know their Nahuatl names. The thirty-eight tribute folios of *Codex Mendoza* are almost identical to an earlier cognate document, *Matrícula de Tributos*.[49] Records of five provinces that appear in *Mendoza* are missing from *Matrícula*, but the remaining tallies match item for item, with only a few minor exceptions.[50] *Matrícula de Tributos* is particularly valuable for research because, unlike *Mendoza*, its folios contain sixteenth-century notations—glosses—which provide the Nahuatl names for various of the tribute items, including many warrior costumes and certain textile designs.

As already mentioned, in Sahagún's initial work, *Primeros Memoriales*, glosses also accompany illustrations of warrior gear. Thanks to these notations, and those of *Matrícula*, we know the Aztec names for most of the depicted warrior paraphernalia. As an aid to further research, appendix K contains the Nahuatl terms, with English translations, for the *Primeros Memoriales* warrior insignia shown on figures 53, 54, 62, 63, 64, and 70.

Now that the role served by the warrior costumes, their construction of feathers, and how their names are known have been explained, each of these garment styles that appear in *Codex Mendoza* will be discussed in turn.

CUEXTECATL (APPENDIX F, COLUMN 1)

The battle attire most frequently pictured on the imperial tribute rolls was the *cuextecatl*, the Huaxtec warrior costume (fig. 46a). *Matrícula de Tributos* provides this costume's name (fig. 46b).[51] The *cuextecatl* warrior costumes were sent in tribute by twenty culturally and geographically diverse provinces but, strangely, not from the Huaxtec region.[52]

Perhaps the *cuextecatl* was popular among the Aztecs because it was the "entry-level" elaborated warrior costume. According to *Codex Mendoza*, the Huaxtec suit was the initial feather attire awarded a warrior after he had taken his second captive in battle.[53]

Folio 64r (fig. 47) shows the successive ranks through which a warrior advanced in the course of his career. He is first shown wearing only the basic Mesoamerican martial attire, the *ichcahuipilli*.[54] This thickly padded, quilted cotton armor was worn for protection under all the more elaborate feathered attire. It was so effective against arrows that even the Spaniards adopted it as battle

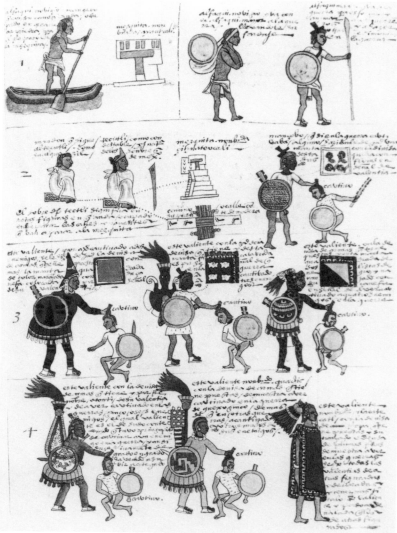

Upper left: Fig. 46a. The *cuextecatl* (Huaxtec) warrior costume and *cuexyo chimalli* (Huaxtec shield). Note the diagnostic conical hat, the cotton ear ornaments, the Huaxtec nose ring (*yacametztli*), and, on the surface of the costume, the short, black parallel lines (Clark 1938 3: folio 22r). Upper right: Fig. 46b. The *cuextecatl* costume and attendant *cuexyo* shield (*Matrícula de Tributos* 1980: folio 3v). Bottom: Fig. 47. The successive ranks through which a *telpochcalli*-trained warrior passed in the course of his career (Clark 1938 3: folio 64r).

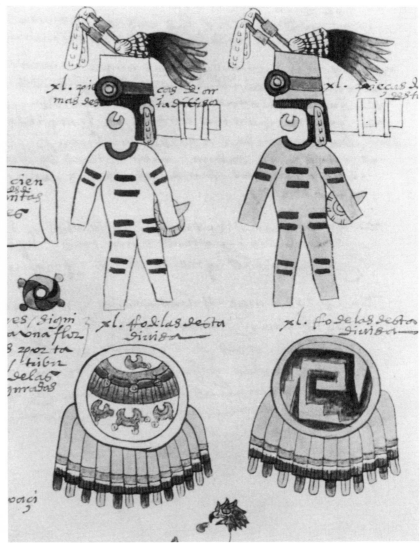

Left: Fig. 48. The Aztec goddess Tlalzolteotl wearing a *copilli*, the conical hat associated with the Huaxtec region. Fillets of unspun cotton encircle her head and serve as the pendulous portions of her ear ornaments (*Codex Borbonicus* 1974:13). Right: Fig. 49. Two *cuextecatl* costumes, each with a truncated *copilli* hat with cotton spindles serving as its crest. To the left, the white suit is accompanied by a variant of the *cuexyo* shield: water symbolism has been added to the four *yacametztli* nose ornaments and the top blue band. The yellow warrior suit on the right is accompanied by a yellow and green *xicalcoliuhqui* (step-fret) shield (Clark 1938 3: folio 19r).

gear.[55] Note that all the war prisoners on folios 64r and 65r (fig. 47; fig. 74) wear this same garment.

In the warrior hierarchy of folio 64r (fig. 47), only after a warrior has taken two prisoners is he pictured wearing a feather costume, the *cuextecatl*. His accompanying shield is a variation on the *cuexyo* (Huaxtec) design, designated Variant 2 in appendix G (column 3). All the *Codex Mendoza* shields are discussed in detail below.

The choice of the *cuextecatl* costume as the first full warrior attire bestowed—and hence the most prevalent on the tribute lists—is intriguing because of its iconographic implications. This regalia apparently was adopted by the Mexica after the emperor Axayacatl's victories in the Huaxtec region during his reign (1469–1481). One of the diagnostic costume traits of that area is the *copilli*,[56] the pointed, cone-shaped cap often seen on ancient Huaxtec stone sculpture.[57] This headgear is also part of another *cuextecatl* costume style, the "starry sky" variant.[58] Additional Huaxtec traits of the *cuextecatl* warrior costume are the rosette attached to the *copilli*,[59] the band of unspun cotton hanging from the ear ornament, the *yacametztli* nose ornament,[60] and the twin black lines that decorate the body of the garment. Sahagún refers to these parallel bars as "hawk scratches."[61]

The Huaxtec region was a lowland area that held a particular fascination for the highland Aztecs and their central plateau neighbors.[62] One of the most powerful and venerated deities among the Huaxtec was their mother goddess, whom the highland cultures subsequently adopted from the tropical region.[63] When this goddess later appears in the Mexica pantheon, she is called Tlazolteotl and is associated with spinning and weaving. Indeed, the Aztec ritual pictorial *Codex Borbonicus* depicts Tlazolteotl (fig. 48) wearing a *quemitl* decorated with Huaxtec nose ornaments, a Huaxtec conical hat also ornamented with *yacametztli*, fillets of unspun cotton about her head, and unspun cotton as her ear drop ornaments.

Emphasis on Tlazolteotl's weaving symbolism is highlighted on two particularly elaborate *cuextecatl* costumes, which appear on the tribute tally from Tlatelolco (fig. 49). The usually pointed caps here have been truncated, and two spindle whorls of raw cotton serve as crests. Each of these costumes has a different shield. The white *cuextecatl* costume on the left is accompanied by a variant of the *cuexyo* shield; note that this shield's four nose ornaments and top cross band are elaborated with water symbols. The yellow *cuextecatl* suit to the right has a *xicalcoliuhqui* (stepped-fret) shield.[64] Both costumes are also accompanied by an unidentified gold disklike object with a cone protruding from its center.

Upper left: Fig. 50a. The *tzitzimitl* (frightful specter) warrior suit, accompanied by a *cuexyo* shield. Note that both the bodysuit and the headgear have distinctive markings (*Matrícula de Tributos* 1980: folio 3v). Upper right: Fig. 50b. The *tzitzimitl* warrior costume accompanied by a *cuexyo* shield (Clark 1938 3: folio 20r). Lower left: Fig. 51a. The *ocelotl* (jaguar) warrior costume, whose bodysuit and headgear each have distinctive markings. The accompanying shield is the *cuexyo* design (Clark 1938 3: folio 20r). Lower right: Fig. 51b. The *ocelotl* warrior attire and *cuexyo* shield (*Matrícula de Tributos* 1980: folio 3v).

In addition to the *cuextecatl* style with its Tlazolteotl-Mother Goddess fertility symbolism, ten other warrior suits appear in the tribute tallies of *Codex Mendoza*. The religious implications of these insignia are not all as accessible as those of the *cuextecatl* costume, but each is interesting in itself. The warrior costumes on row 1 of appendix F are arranged in the approximate order of their numerical representation in the tribute tallies, but they are discussed below according to construction similarities.[65]

TZITZIMITL (APPENDIX F, COLUMN 3)

This costume, which is glossed in *Matrícula de Tributos* as the *tzitzimitl* ("frightful specter"; fig. 50a), is connected with the fearful phenomenon of a solar eclipse.[66] Seler describes the *tzitzimime*, the namesakes of this warrior attire, as "demons of the darkness," or star gods. This refers to the stars that appear in the sky during an eclipse. It was then that the *tzitzimime* would descend to earth to bring about the end of the world.[67]

In *Primeros Memoriales* only the *tzitzimitl*'s death head appears,[68] worn as a helmet (see fig. 62; also appendix F, row 3, column 3). Sahagún describes this insignia: "The quetzal [feather] demon of the dark [insignia]: a frame is fashioned resembling a death's head. It is covered entirely of quetzal [feathers]. Its head is as if unkept."[69] As in *Matrícula de Tributos*, in *Codex Mendoza* both the

skeletal helmet and the *tzitzimitl* bodysuit have their own iconography (fig. 50b). In the case of the latter, a sacrificial cut appears across the chest. Although this wound implies a heart sacrifice, the emerging organ is now believed to represent the liver.[70] In *Codex Mendoza*, the full *tzitzimitl* warrior suit, complete with helmet, appears in white, red, blue, and yellow.[71]

OCELOTL (APPENDIX F, COLUMN 6)

Another warrior costume whose iconographic message appears on both bodysuit and helmet is the *ocelotl* (fig. 51a); a *Matrícula de Tributos* depiction of a jaguar costume (fig. 51b) supplies the identifying gloss.[72] This battle attire obviously draws its inspiration from the jaguar, a powerful and much revered feline.[73] The jaguar knights were particularly beloved by both the populace and the rulers because of the courage and valor of these warriors on the battlefield. The high esteem in which they were held transferred over into the councils of war, where they had great influence.[74] The comrades in arms of the jaguar warriors were the eagle knights, who, strangely, are nowhere to be found in *Codex Mendoza*.

Jaguar costumes appear in the tribute rolls of *Codex Mendoza* ten times: four in yellow, three in blue, two in red, and one in white. Given the differing colors of this warrior suit, plus evidence that feathers were used in making all the other martial costumes, it

Upper left: Fig. 52a. The *coyotl* (coyote) warrior suit, composed of an undecorated yellow bodysuit and a distinctive headgear, accompanied by the *cuexyo* shield (*Matrícula de Tributos* 1980: folio 3v). Upper right: Fig. 52b. The coyote costume and Huaxtec shield (Clark 1938: 3: folio 25r). Lower left: Fig. 53. Warrior costumes and accoutrements from the *Primeros Memoriales* (1926: *estampa* XXVII); see appendix K for English translations. Lower right: Fig. 54. Warrior costumes and accoutrements from the *Primeros Memoriales* (1926: *estampa* XXIV); see Appendix K for English translations.

seems most probable that these garments were made of feathers rather than actual jaguar skins.

The popularity of the jaguar costume is attested by its appearance in five other Aztec pictorials.

COYOTL (APPENDIX F, COLUMN 8)

Like the *cuextecatl*, *tzitzimitl*, and *ocelotl* styles, the *coyotl* costume has a distinctive headpiece and an identifying gloss in the *Matrícula* (fig. 52a).[75] Unlike them, however, the coyote costume's bodysuit is perfectly plain; it has no identifying insignia. The suit always appears in the same color as its helmet. Although the *Codex Mendoza* coyote costumes (fig. 52b) appear only in yellow, *Primeros Me-*

moriales depicts this same warrior apparel in eight different styles, some solid colors—yellow, blue, white, red, black, and purple—and two variegated: the fire and star-studded coyote costumes (fig. 53, 54; see also fig. 70).

Coyote costumes appear in two additional Aztec pictorials.

PATZACTLI (APPENDIX F, COLUMN 5)

The *patzactli* devices (figs. 55a, b), which appear in different styles and colors, constitute a category in themselves. The common feature of almost all these insignias is a wiglike element that frames the face of a warrior when worn on the head. Although some of these *patzactli* insignia are also shown as back devices, the "wig" is

Left: Fig. 55a. The *patzactli* (compressed feather) headpiece, worn with an undecorated bodysuit, accompanied by the *cuexyo* shield (Clark 1938 3: folio 24r). Right: Fig. 55b. A *patzactli* headgear and *cuexyo* shield (*Matrícula de Tributos* 1980: folio 4r).

almost always part of the configuration (note rows 3, 4, 5, and 7 of appendix F, column 5).

The term *patzactli* translates "compressed" or "bursting."[76] This could refer either to the compressing of the device's many long and full feathers into the "wig" element or to the resulting expansive burst of plumes of this magnificent insignia. The *Florentine Codex* contains an illustration of a *patzactli* being constructed.[77] The arranging of the many feathers required would certainly call for tightly compressing their quill ends.

Five styles of this insignia type are identified in *Primeros Memoriales* by name; two appear in *Codex Mendoza*. The first of these, the red *cueçalpatzactli* (fig. 55a), is glossed in both *Primeros Memoriales*[78] and *Matrícula de Tributos*.[79] This device, made of the feathers of the scarlet macaw,[80] appears five times on *Mendoza* tribute pages. *Primeros Memoriales* also provides the gloss for the green *quetzalpatzactli*.[81] Nine of these magnificent quetzal feather head ornaments appear in *Codex Mendoza*, where they are always accompanied by a yellow bodysuit.[82] The scarlet macaw *patzactli*'s suit is usually red.[83]

The remaining three *patzactli* styles are illustrated and glossed in *Primeros Memoriales*, the *cacalpatzactli* ("compressed crow feather insignia";[84] see fig. 63), the *tlacochpatzactli* ("compressed arrow insignia";[85] see fig. 63), and the *aztapatzactli* ("compressed heron feather insignia";[86] see fig. 70).[87] *Patzactli* devices appear in three other Aztec pictorials.

MOMOYACTLI (APPENDIX F, COLUMN 7)

This dramatic red, black, and white back device can be found only in the cognate pictorials *Codex Mendoza*, where seven examples appear (e.g., fig. 56a),[88] and *Matrícula de Tributos* (figs. 56b, c),[89] where a gloss provides the name.

In Herman Beyer's article on the *momoyactli*, he translates the term "the dispersed feather headdress."[90] Beyer suggests that the red-and-black fan of the *momoyactli* device was constructed as a single unit, mainly of scarlet macaw feathers. Only after this central section was completed were the diagnostic white feather tips—probably heron feathers—added. Beyer also speculates that such fanlike emblems as the *momoyactli* were originally worn at the nape of the neck. Only later, when these insignia had grown too large and heavy to be supported in this manner, were they placed on lightweight frames to be worn as back devices.[91]

In the *Codex Mendoza* depictions there is a resemblance between the *patzactli* and *momoyactli* insignia; both feature a huge fan of tightly packed feathers.[92] The *Matrícula de Tributos* versions of the *momoyactli*, however, show a greater differentiation in the placement of each feather (figs. 56b, c).[93] Also, as mentioned above, the *momoyactli* was worn only as a back device—note the supporting frame—whereas the *patzactli* also appears as a head ornament, as in the *Codex Mendoza* examples.

The greatest distinction between the two insignia is that the *momoyactli* is always a white-black-red feather fan,[94] whereas *patzactli* devices come in a variety of colors. Further, in *Codex Mendoza* all the warrior suits worn with *patzactli* insignia—although color coordinated to their particular device—are undecorated, while four of the seven *momoyactli* bodysuits have contrasting cuffs of red and white. This emphasis on red may be what encouraged Seler to suggest that the *momoyactli* warrior attire is affiliated with Chantico, the fire deity.[95]

PAPALOTL (APPENDIX F, COLUMN 10)

There is one other warrior costume that—like the *momoyactli*—has contrasting cuffs but depends on its back device to convey the iconographic message. In this case the insignia is the *papalotl* (butterfly) device, so identified by a gloss in *Matrícula de Tributos* (fig. 57a).[96] *Codex Mendoza* includes three butterfly devices in its tribute list (e.g., fig. 57b), each a different color combination. This particular insignia must have been very popular; *Primeros Memoriales* includes five additional examples, none of which duplicates *Mendoza*.[97] Butterflies are connected with the fertility god Xochipilli, "Flower Prince," associated with solar warmth, flowers, feasting, and pleasure.[98]

The remaining four warrior costumes from the *Codex Mendoza* tribute section have unadorned bodysuits in a variety of colors. However, the color of each costume is not necessarily correlated with its accompanying insignia. As a result, the iconographic message of these interchangeable feathered suits is conveyed only by their back devices.

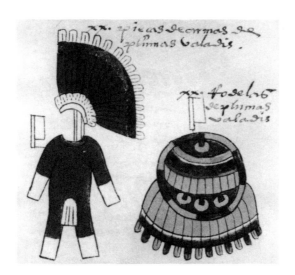

Left to right, top row: Fig. 56a. The *momoyactli* back device and contrasting-cuff bodysuit accompanied by a Huaxtec shield (Clark 1938 3: folio 27r). Fig. 56b. The *momoyactli* (dispersed feather) back device, whose bodysuit has contrasting cuffs, is accompanied by a *cuexyo* shield (*Matrícula de Tributos* 1980: folio 4r). Center: Fig. 56c. A variant of the *momoyactli* warrior costume accompanied by a *quauhtetepoyo* shield (*Matrícula de Tributos* 1980: folio 3v). Bottom: Fig. 57a. The *papalotl* (butterfly) device and a *cuexyo* shield. The contrasting-cuffs bodysuit is similar to the *momoyactli* costume, figures 56a,b (*Matrícula de Tributos* 1980: folio 3v). Fig. 57b. A *papalotl* back device and contrasting-cuff bodysuit. The accompanying shield is the *quauhtetepoyo chimalli* (eagle's foot shield; Clark 1938 3: folio 22r).

Upper left: Fig. 58a. The *quaxolotl* warrior costume, composed of an undecorated bodysuit and distinctive back device, is accompanied by a *xicalcoliuhqui* shield (*Matrícula de Tributos* 1980: folio 3v). Upper right: Fig. 58b. The umbrellalike *quaxolotl* and a *xicalxoliuhqui* shield (Clark 1938 3: folio 20r). Lower left: Fig. 59a. The *xopilli* (claw device) warrior costume, composed of an undecorated bodysuit and distinctive back device, accompanied by a *xicalcoliuhqui* shield (*Matrícula de Tributos* 1980: folio 4r). Lower right: Fig. 59b. The *xopilli* back device and a *xicalcoliuhqui* shield (Clark 1938 3: folio 20v).

QUAXOLOTL (APPENDIX F, COLUMN 4)

Matrícula de Tributos provides a gloss that identifies the *quaxolotl* back device (fig. 58a).[99] The distinctive feature of the umbrellalike insignia is the dog's head that rests atop it, as also can be seen in *Codex Mendoza* (fig. 58b). This is Xolotl, the canine deity associated with ballcourts, twins, and monstrosities. *Primeros Memoriales* illustrates three of these insignia, in red, white, and yellow (see figs. 63, 70).[100] Sahagún describes the latter, the *tozquaxolotl:* "The Xolotl head of yellow parrot feathers, with balls of quetzal feathers, was ornamented with gold."[101] Elsewhere he notes that the feather artisans of Amatlan made the *quaxolotl* insignia.[102] Undecorated bodysuits in three colors are worn with this device: seven yellow, two blue, and three green.[103]

Two additional Aztec pictorials depict *quaxolotl* devices.

XOPILLI (APPENDIX F, COLUMN 9)

The *xopilli* ("claw" device) appears glossed in *Matrícula de Tributos* (fig. 59a).[104] This insignia is the back device of the Otomí rank warrior on folio 64r (see fig. 43).[105] Like the Otomí's costume, two of four *xopilli* warrior suits from the *Codex Mendoza* tribute tallies are green (fig. 59b); the other two are red and blue. As discussed earlier, a *xopilli*-style insignia played a crucial role in the Spanish conquest of Mexico.

TOZCOCOLLI (APPENDIX F, COLUMN 11)

Primeros Memoriales provides the Nahuatl name for this intriguing back device,[106] which may be imitating an umbilical cord. Seler translates *tozcocolli* as "ein hinundhergewundenes Gestell," or "a

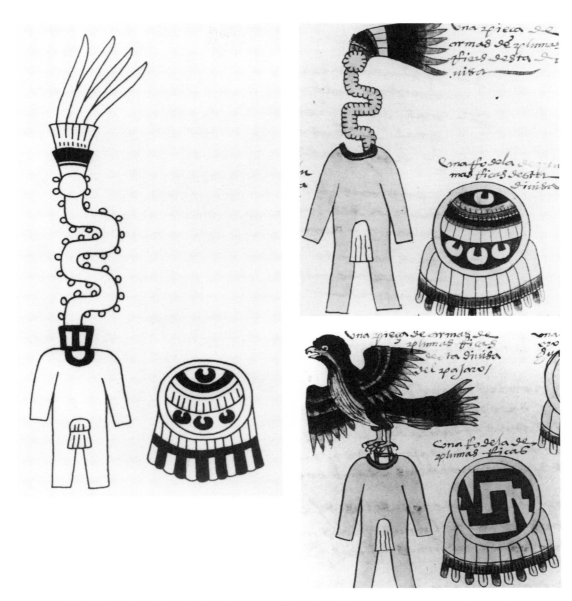

Left: Fig. 60a. The distinctive *tozcocolli* back device, worn with an undecorated bodysuit and accompanied by a *cuexyo* shield (*Matrícula de Tributos* 1980: folio 12r). Upper right: Fig. 60b. The *tozcocolli* and *cuexyo* shield (Clark 1938 3: folio 43r). Lower right: Fig. 61. The *quetzaltototl* (quetzal bird) back device worn with an undecorated bodysuit and accompanied by a *xicalcoliuhqui* shield (Clark 1938 3: folio 46r).

twisted-to-and-fro frame."[107] Clark calls the insignia a "winding navel-string," which seems most plausible considering analogous depictions.[108] This same convention of using a yellow, crinkled line to indicate drying human skin appears on flayed sacrificial skin worn by both Xipe Totec, "Our Lord the Flayed One,"[109] and the Huaxtec-Aztec goddess Tlazolteotl (see fig. 48). The *tozcocolli* of *Matrícula de Tributos* and *Codex Mendoza* (figs. 60a, b) apparently were made of yellow parrot feathers; the insignia is worn with a yellow bodysuit. The device appears only once in the tribute section, sent by the province of Coayxtlahuacan, located in the southeastern section of the Aztec empire.

This distinctive insignia appears in three other Aztec pictorials.

QUETZALTOTOTL (APPENDIX F, COLUMN 12)

The *Codex Mendoza* example of this lifelike "quetzal bird" back device (fig. 61) correctly depicts the bird's crimson chest and long, luxurious green tail feather.[110] Although the analogous tribute page (Tochtepec) is missing from *Matrícula de Tributos*, fortunately

there is a gloss in *Primeros Memoriales* which provides the insignia's Nahuatl name (fig. 62).[111]

The natural habitats of the quetzal bird are the high cloud forests, an environment particularly associated with the southeastern highlands of Chiapas, which are adjacent to the Aztec province of Xoconochco.[112] However, that region is not the section of the empire from which this device comes. Only one province sent the *quetzaltototl* insignia: Tochtepec, located along the lowland Gulf coast but encompassing adjacent, temperate higher lands. This province sent 80 handfuls of quetzal feathers, which are identical to the tail feathers of this back device, as well as lesser amounts of yellow, blue, and red feathers.

The *Lienzo de Tlaxcala* also contains examples of the *quetzaltototl*.

SUMMARY

Of the eleven warrior costume styles represented in the tribute tallies, six have completely undecorated, interchangeable body-suits.[113] Although three of these—the *coyotl*, *patzactli*, and *quaxo-lotl*—have suits that are color coordinated with their insignia, the iconographic message of all six of these feather-covered costumes is conveyed only by their accompanying insignia. These emblems are worn sometimes as headgear but more often as a back device supported by a lightweight frame.

The visual impact of the flamboyant, dramatic warrior costumes derived in part from the unique design of each insignia but, equally, from the rainbow-hued feathers with which they were covered. And of all the magnificent tropical birds represented, none was more highly valued, or more magnificent, than the quetzal. Its long, supple tail feathers shaded from a deep blue through green to gold, so that the slightest breeze caused the elongated plumes to vary slightly in color as they undulated, creating a shimmering effect. Little wonder that the Aztecs wore them whenever possible; note that a panache of these prestigious quetzal feathers adorns the crests of over half of the *Codex Mendoza* warrior suits.

When one compares the warrior costumes in the *Codex Mendoza* tribute tallies with those of the other Aztec pictorials (see appendix F), one contrast becomes apparent. The *momoyactli* style (appendix F, column 7) occurs only in *Codex Mendoza*, as do the contrasting-cuffs bodysuits (appendix F, columns 7 and 10).

One other back device style, the *pamitl* (banner)[114] insignia (see appendix F, column 13), appears in the ethnographic section but not the tribute tallies of *Codex Mendoza*. The *pamitl* styles are discussed in detail in the "Military Hierarchy" section of this essay.

As for *Codex Mendoza* omissions, *Primeros Memoriales* depicts eight different styles of coyote costumes (see figs. 53, 54, 70), whereas *Mendoza* shows only one, made of yellow parrot feathers. *Primeros Memoriales* also includes twenty-four back devices absent from *Codex Mendoza* (figs. 62, 63, 64).[115] But the most peculiar omission of all in *Codex Mendoza* is the *quauhtli* (eagle)[116] costume, a warrior attire well documented elsewhere in both ethnohistorical and archaeological sources. Not only do eagle warriors appear in five other Aztec pictorial sources (see appendix F, column 14) but an eagle costume also adorns a clay warrior discovered in the recent Templo Mayor excavation (fig. 65).

Obviously, *Codex Mendoza* does not reflect the full range of warrior paraphernalia that was being worn in the pre-Hispanic Aztec world. This fact is further underscored by a survey of the shields that accompanied these costumes. The *Codex Mendoza* shields are illustrated in appendix G, which also includes analogous examples from seven other Aztec pictorials.

SHIELDS (APPENDIX G)

Cuexyo Shield and Its Variants (Appendix G, Columns 1–5)

Just as the *cuextecatl* warrior costume was the most commonly given in tribute, so too was the *cuexyo chimalli*, which translates "Huaxtec shield."[117] We know the name of this design because a Nahuatl gloss accompanies it in *Primeros Memoriales*.[118] In the *Codex Mendoza* tribute tallies, there are twenty-two *cuextecatl* costumes; all but two are accompanied by one of the five *cuexyo*-related shields.

The most common of the shields (appendix G, column 1) has the Huaxtec nose crescent in its design, once at the top and three times below the cross bands. In addition, appendix G illustrates

four variants of this shield (see columns 2, 3, 4, and 5); all of these occur only with *cuextecatl* warrior costumes. Variant 1 of the *cuexyo* shield, which has water symbols on the Huaxtec nose ornaments, appears only once in the tribute section (folio 19r) and again, once, in the ethnographic section (folio 64r). The two-prisoner warrior on folio 64r (see fig. 47) carries Variant 2 of this design, which has the "hawk scratches" motif of the *cuextecatl* warrior suit (appendix G, column 3). Four of the *cuextecatl* costumes in the tribute section (folios 20v, 25r, 34r, 37r) are also accompanied by this "hawk scratches" shield. Variant 3 of the *cuexyo* shield design (folio 20r) also has a pair of Huaxtec-related parallel bars in its design; this style appears in the *Lienzo de Tlaxcala* (see appendix G, column 4, row 4). Variant 4 is classified with the *cuexyo* styles because it is carried by the "starry-sky" warrior, who wears a type of Huaxtec costume (see appendix F, row 2, column 2).[119]

The names of the remaining shields of appendix G are known to us because their designs, like the *cuexyo*, have accompanying glosses in *Primeros Memoriales*.

Xicalcoliuhqui (Appendix G, Column 6)

This shield, whose name translates literally "twisted gourd,"[120] is the second most common in the tribute lists. In *Codex Mendoza*, the design appears with a yellow step fret on a green ground. In *Primeros Memoriales*, however, the shield's stepped-fret section is red.[121]

Peñafiel illustrates an extant *xicalcoliuhqui* shield from the collection of the Württembergisches Landesmuseum, Stuttgart, West Germany (fig. 66).

Quauhtetepoyo (Appendix G, Column 7)

The *quauhtetepoyo chimalli* or "eagle's foot shield" is a less common design.[122] It occurs only three times in the *Codex Mendoza* tribute tallies and once again in the ethnographic section (see fig. 74). The *quauhtetepoyo* shield also appears in *Primeros Memoriales*, together with a very similar design, the *ocelotetepoyo chimalli*, "jaguar foot shield."[123] In *Primeros Memoriales*, both of these motifs appear on a solid field as opposed to the diagonally divided backgrounds of the *Codex Mendoza* "eagle foot" shields.

Tlahauitectli (Appendix G, Column 8)

The *tlahauitectli chimalli* (whitewashed shield)[124] is most probably the name of the generic shield of *Codex Mendoza*, carried by all twelve of the captives on the warrior hierarchies.[125] It also appears elsewhere in the ethnographic section. This shield is usually shown with a blue border—as is the glossed depiction in *Primeros Memoriales*[126] (see fig. 53)—but sometimes the *Mendoza* shields are outlined in white or red. Of the thirty-nine shields that appear in the ethnographic section of *Codex Mendoza*, twenty-two are this completely undecorated style.

Teocuitlaxapo (Appendix G, Column 9)

This shield, the *teocuitlaxapo chimalli* (gold disk shield),[127] appears in *Primeros Memoriales*, carried by a captain.[128] Although we have little information on this simple design, it must have been quite popular. Note that "gold disk" shields appear in four other Aztec pictorials.

Ihuiteteyo (Appendix G, Column 10)

The *ihuiteteyo chimalli* (down ball shield)[129] also occurs with a gloss in *Primeros Memoriales*.[130] This shield, drawn with either seven or eight down balls, appears regularly in part 1 of the *Codex Mendoza*,

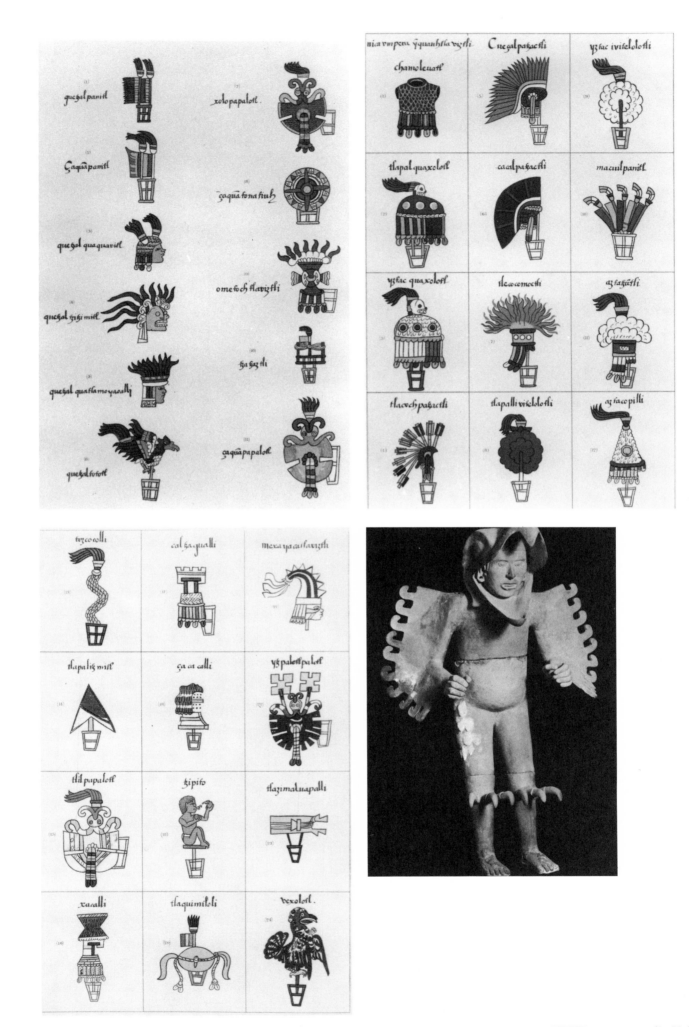

Upper left: Fig. 62. Back devices and headgear from the *Primeros Memoriales* (1926: *estampa* XXIII); see appendix K for English translations. Upper right: Fig. 63. Eleven back devices plus an *ehuatl* costume that appear in *Primeros Memoriales* (1926: *estampa* XXV); see appendix K for English translations. Lower left: Fig. 64. Back devices from *Primeros Memoriales* (1926: *estampa* XXVI); see appendix K for English translations. Lower right: Fig. 65. An eagle costume adorns a clay warrior figure discovered in recent Templo Mayor excavations (Nicholson 1983:84).

Fig. 66. An extant *xicalcoliuhqui* shield in the Wurttembergisches Landesmuseum, Stuttgart, Austria. (Peñafiel 1977: *lámina* 21).

the historical section. There it occurs in association with the city of Tenochtitlan, backed by arrows. The shield is the symbol of Mexica conquest. It is drawn in front of each of the successful Aztec emperors who are seated facing glyphs of the towns they have conquered.[131]

Shield of Appendix G, Column 11

The name of this shield is unknown. It appears in *Codex Mendoza* only in the ethnographic section (see fig. 74), carried by the third-rank priest warrior. Judging from the shield's appearance in four other Aztec pictorials, it was not uncommon.

Shield of Appendix G, Column 12

This final shield also lacks a name. It occurs three times in *Codex Mendoza*, twice in the ethnographic section, and again on folio 42r, a tribute tally page. However, here the shield does not appear to be part of the listed tribute of the folio. Instead, it apparently is an element of a glyph indicating conquest; note that on folio 42r a war club appears behind it. The shield/war club combination indicate the capturing of war prisoners from the three independent city-states symbolized by the three head glyphs that face the shield.

Summary

The *xicalcoliuhqui* (step-fret) and the *cuexyo* (Huaxtec) shields are the most common of the designs illustrated in the *Codex Mendoza* tribute tallies (see appendix G). However, because four examples of the *cuexyo* shield are illustrated (see appendix G, columns 1, 2, 3 and 4), actually only three identifiable iconographic concepts are represented on shields in *Codex Mendoza*'s tribute section: the *cuexyo* design (fifty-nine examples), the *xicalcoliuhqui* (thirty-one examples), and the *quauhtetepoyo* (three examples; see appendix G, column 7).

Only one shield appears in the tribute tallies without a warrior suit. It is a *tlahauitectli chimalli*, an undecorated yellow shield that is part of the tribute of the province of Tochtepec (see appendix G, row 1, column 8). This shield, as well as all the others that appear in *Codex Mendoza*, can also be found in other Aztec pictorials, as appendix G indicates.

The geographical distribution of provinces by shield type reveals that the *cuexyo* design dominates in those provinces closest to Tenochtitlan. Nearby Acolhuacan, for example, sent six *cuexyo* shields, but only one *xicalcoliuhqui* and *quauhtetepoyo*. On the other

hand, provinces further removed from the capital frequently sent a mixture of both warrior suits and accompanying shields.[132]

The color of a shield apparently carried meaning. Thirty-two of the *cuexyo* have green backgrounds, twenty-one have red, and the elaborated *cuexyo* shield from Tlatelolco—Variant 1—has a white ground. There is an extant *cuexyo* shield on display in the Chapultepec Museo Nacional de Historia in Mexico City, but its feathers are now too faded to determine the original colors (see fig. 67). In contrast to the range of color in the *cuexyo* shields, the *Codex Mendoza xicalcoliuhqui* styles are all the same: a yellow step meander imposed on a green field. Similarly, the design of the three *quauhtetepoyo* shields always appears on a field of red and white.

Judging from the depictions in the cognates *Matrícula de Tributos* and *Codex Mendoza*, shields with feather fringes seem to have been *de rigueur* for tribute. However, in the ethnographic section of *Codex Mendoza* and in other Aztec pictorials, some shields are shown without this fringe (see appendix G).[133] Because of the contrast between the fringed shields of the tribute lists and fringeless examples in the ethnographic folios, we can assume that the more elaborate shield style was required in tribute.

Several revelations emerge concerning *Codex Mendoza*'s range of shields when comparing them with those of other Aztec pictorials. *Codex Mendoza* omits a major shield that appears thirty-four times in *Lienzo de Tlaxcala* (fig. 68)[134] and at least once in *Codex Telleriano-Remensis*[135] and the *Florentine Codex*.[136] Further, there are at least twenty shield designs carried by Indian warriors in *Lienzo de Tlaxcala* that do not appear in *Codex Mendoza*. Also, the shields of *Codex Mendoza* are scarcely duplicated by the deity shields in *Primeros Memoriales*;[137] in only one instance out of twenty-six is there a correlation: the god Yacatecuhtli carries the *xicalcoliuhqui* shield.

A third disparity between *Codex Mendoza* and other Aztec pictorials involves the warrior equipment depicted in *Primeros Memoriales*: fourteen shields are shown which do not appear in *Codex Mendoza*. These include an intriguing variety of iconographic motifs, many with their accompanying Nahuatl names (see figs. 53, 54, 70).[138] Finally, no correlation can be found in the Aztec pictorials between a shield design and a particular warrior costume; apparently no shield motif was firmly linked to a specific costume.

In addition to the limb-encasing warrior suit already discussed, the Aztecs had another class of feathered battle costume, the *ehuatl*.

EHUATL (APPENDIX H)

The *ehuatl* was a sleeveless, tuniclike garment, made of feather-covered cloth, whose diagnostic feature was a short skirt of feathers (fig. 69).[139] The term *ehuatl* is variously translated by modern scholars as "shirt," "doublet," and "tunic." Molina defines *ehuatl* as an animal pelt for tanning or as the peel and rind of fruit,[140] and Sahagún used the word *eoatl* (*ehuatl*) with reference to human skin.[141] The essential meaning of the word is "outer layer," and according to Sahagún that was the function of this garment. As already mentioned, his *Primeros Memoriales* depicts a wide assortment of arms and insignia, each with an accompanying gloss. This corpus of military attire includes both pictures and descriptions of the entire raiment of six noble warriors, five of whom wear an *ehuatl* (fig. 70). The first item described for each of these lords is his padded cotton armor (*ichcahuipilli*), followed by the feathered tunic (*ehuatl*); only then are the remaining accoutrements listed. What is clear is that the *ehuatl* itself was not a protective garment but rather a beautifully colored, shimmering feather outer costume.[142]

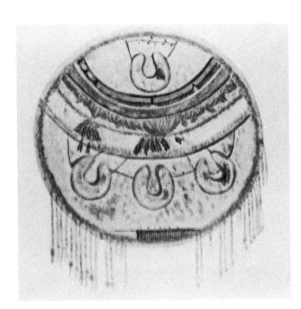

Upper left: Fig. 67. An extant *cuexyo* shield in the Museo Nacional de Historia, Mexico, D. F. (Peñafiel 1977: *lámina* 18). Upper right: Fig. 68. A shield that appears twenty-eight times in *Lienzo de Tlaxcala*, but never in *Codex Mendoza* (*Lienzo de Tlaxcala* 1892:33). Lower left: Fig. 69. A detailed depiction of an *ehuatl* (*Primeros Memoriales* 1926: *estampa* XXV). Lower right: Fig. 70. Five examples of the *ehuatl* costume; see appendix K for a thorough description of the accoutrements of each warrior (*Primeros Memoriales* 1926: *estampa* XXII).

In *Codex Mendoza*, the *ehuatl* appears only twice in the tribute lists (appendix H, row 1). Such sparse representation is strange, because this garment occurs four times in *Mendoza's* older cognate, *Matrícula de Tributos* (appendix H, row 2).[143] In both documents, the *ehuatl* is worn only with a *patzactli* insignia. Despite these occurrences of the *ehuatl*, in neither of the related pictorials do the Indian artists seem to understand the garment fully. Note the inconsistent treatment of sleeves.[144] It would seem that the Valley of Mexico scribes were not too familiar with this costume. Yet the four provinces depicted in the *Matrícula de Tributos* which sent the *ehuatl* in tribute were all close to the imperial capital: Hueypochtlan was located to the north, Quauhtitlan and Quahuacan to the west, and Acolhuacan nearly directly to the east. It is in this latter, easterly direction that clues concerning the costume's possible ethnic origin can be found.

As the *ehuatl* examples in appendix H demonstrate, the garment appears most frequently in the pictorial codices of people living on the east side of Lake Texcoco. The Texcocans are depicted in *Códice Xolotl*, the Tlaxcalans are the protagonists of *Lienzo de Tlaxcala*, and *Primeros Memoriales* deals with the inhabitants of Tepepulco, located close to the Tlaxcalan border (fig. 71). This east-of-Tenochtitlan geographical concentration suggests an affinity either between Tlaxcala and the *ehuatl* or between this martial costume and the Acolhuacan centers of Texcoco and Tepepulco. It is this latter association that seems most valid.

There is pictorial evidence for a connection between the *ehuatl* and the Acolhuacan region, homeland of the ancient thirteenth-century Acolhua kingdom, which preceded the Aztecs. Strangely, the clue to this association comes from a region quite removed from central Mexico. The province of Çihuatlan was located on the Pacific coast (see fig. 78, province 19). Its tribute is recorded on folio 38r of *Codex Mendoza* (fig. 72), along with the place glyphs of the towns that made up that province. One of these, Coçohuipilecan, the ninth glyph, contains a section of the word *huipilli* in its written gloss, yet the garment depicted for the place glyph is an *ehuatl* almost identical to that of *Primeros Memoriales* (see fig. 69). Although the Coçohuipilecan glyph does not function phonetically, the inclusion of an *ehuatl* instead of a *huipil* in the drawing suggests that this Pacific coast region may have been colonized from Acolhuacan, an area where the *ehuatl* was frequently worn battle attire. This hypothesis is further supported by comparing another place glyph of the Cihuatlan province, Colima (fig. 72, second place glyph), which is an extended arm with water emerging from the shoulder joint. This glyph is almost identical to that of Acolhuacan (fig. 73).

Political expansion by the more powerful peoples of central Mexico along both seacoasts occurred repeatedly in pre-Hispanic times, for both economic and military purposes.[145] Perhaps a prior Acolhua colonization is what is reflected in the highland *ehuatl* and Acolhuacan-like glyph on the tribute page of a Pacific coast province.[146]

Returning to the five *ehuatl*-clad warriors of *Primeros Memoriales* (see fig. 70; also appendix H, row 3), while their insignia and three of their shields have counterparts in *Codex Mendoza*, two shields do not. Such examples of unusual military gear are not uncommon. Warrior insignia appear in *Primeros Memoriales* that occur nowhere else in the Aztec pictorial corpus. This intriguing martial anomaly is better understood by considering the circumstances surrounding the compilation of *Primeros Memoriales* and the area of Tepepulco, the region from which it comes.

Tepepulco

Tepepulco is located some fifty miles northeast of Mexico City. It was never one of the major centers of the Valley of Mexico; Tepepulco's pre-Hispanic population was probably around 40,000, in contrast to Tenochtitlan's estimated population of up to 200,000.[147] Fray Bernardino de Sahagún began his investigation into pre-Conquest Aztec culture in Tepepulco, working there between 1558 and 1561.[148] As already noted, one hallmark of this "first study" is the illustrations of a surprisingly large array of military attire. Since so many of these items are unique to *Primeros Memoriales*, a number of questions arise. If a smaller, subsidiary community such as Tepepulco had, for example, eight variants of the coyote costume (see figs. 53, 54, 70), it seems odd that only one such style appears in *Codex Mendoza* (see fig. 52b), a document recording tribute from thirty-eight far-flung provinces to the empire's capital. *Primeros Memoriales* also contains at least twenty-four back devices and fourteen shield designs completely missing from the thirty-eight tribute tallies of *Codex Mendoza*. How is such disproportionate representation to be explained? It may have something to do with geographical location.

Although situated within the Aztec empire, Tepepulco was located near the Tlaxcalan border (see fig. 71). In fact, one of the *xochiyaoyotl* "flowery war" battlefields—areas where the Aztecs and Tlaxcalans carried out their prearranged, deadly serious military engagements—was on its eastern boundary.[149] Even allowing for Tepepulco's strategic location, it seems strange that a subsidiary community one-fifth the size of the imperial capital would have a greater diversity of certain types of martial attire than Tenochtitlan. Given the Aztecs' propensity for incorporating other peoples' deities into their own crowded pantheon,[150] it is surprising that the Mexica did not adopt much of nearby Tepepulco's impressive warrior gear. In contrast, the neighboring Tlaxcalans took full advantage of the Tepepulco martial styles; some of the same costumes and insignia appear in both *Primeros Memoriales* and *Lienzo de Tlaxcala*.[151]

As discussed earlier, the Aztec warrior costumes and accoutrements worn into battle embodied a guardian function that rendered them indispensable. Given this religious imperative, it could be anticipated that the wider the range of insignia, the more effective the force involved. The smaller number of military costumes shown in the *Codex Mendoza* suggests that only a partial range of the highly symbolic warrior paraphernalia that actually existed in Tenochtitlan is depicted.

Part 2 of *Codex Mendoza*, however, is not the only section that shows martial apparel. The ethnographic section, part 3, also illustrates warrior costumes, focusing particularly on the clothing of the graded warrior ranks.

Hierarchical Warrior Apparel (Appendix F, Row 2)

Folios 64r (fig. 47) and 65r (fig. 74) of part 3 of *Codex Mendoza* each illustrate six grades of warriors and their captives.

FOLIO 64R WARRIOR RANKS

One-Captive Warrior Rank

The initial warrior on folio 64r of *Codex Mendoza* (fig. 47) does not wear a feather costume; indeed, he is shown in exactly the same unadorned cotton armor as that of his captive. Both of their *ichcahuipilli* bear marks of quilting. The victorious warrior's hair is bound in the *temillotl* (pillar of stone) style.[152] According to Sa-

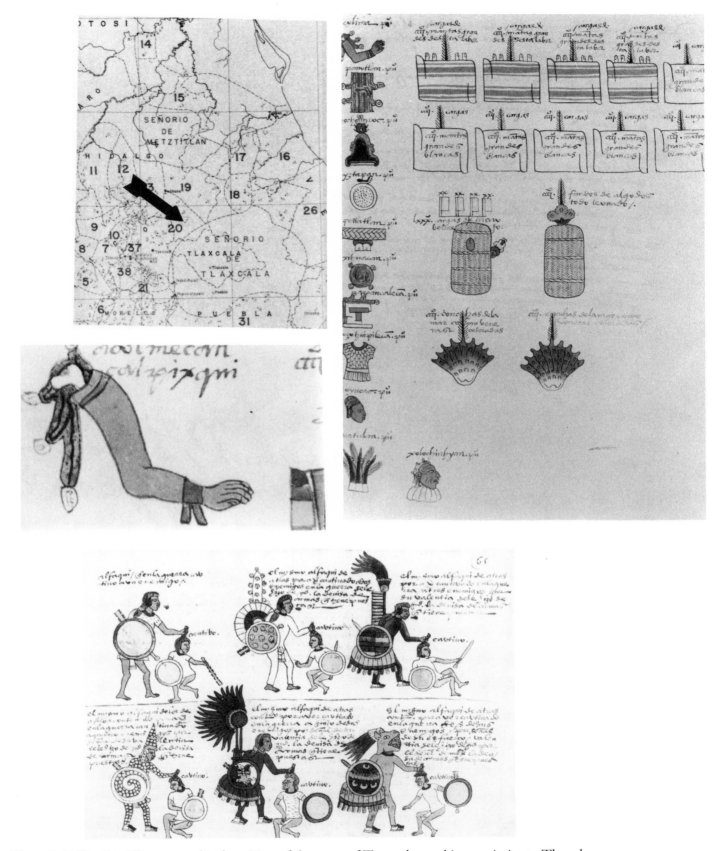

Upper left: Fig. 71. The geographical position of the town of Tepepulco and its proximity to Tlaxcala (Barlow 1949a). Right: Fig. 72. Tribute page of Cihuatlan province; for geographical location of the province see figure 80 (Clark 1938 3: folio 38r). Center left: Fig. 73. Place glyph of Acolhuacan (Clark 1938 3: folio 4r). Bottom: Fig. 74. The military attire worn during the successive stages of a priest warrior's career (Clark 1938 3: folio 65r).

hagún, this honor was reserved only for those valiants who had taken four captives in battle.[153] Note, however, that the *Codex Mendoza temillotl*-coiffed novice has just taken his first prisoner.

The shields of the victor and vanquished are also of interest. The former looks like a series of tightly bound reeds, almost as though it were viewed from the back.[154] His captive's shield and those of the rest of the prisoners consist of an undecorated circle surrounded by a plain band. This is the *Codex Mendoza*'s generic style; it probably is the *tlahauitectli chimalli*, "whitewashed shield" (see fig. 53; also appendix G, column 8).

Returning to folio 64r (fig. 47), to the right of the first warrior is an illustration of a *tilmatli*—a cape with a design of four flowers—which is part of the award to a warrior after taking his initial captive. This cloak is puzzling, because a flowered *tilmatli* is at variance with Sahagún's account of the cloaks awarded for a first captive. He says they were an orange cape with a striped border, the *camopaltenuahuanqui*, and the scorpion-colored tie-dye cape, the *colotlalpilli*.[155] These prestigious cloaks, which warriors were awarded for meritorious acts, obviously served a very important function in Aztec society. In Sahagún's discussion of warrior ranks, he never mentions the feathered costumes or back devices; only the capes bestowed on the valiant warriors are described.

Two-Captive Warrior Rank

The second-rank warrior (3d register, left side) in figure 47 wears a red *cuextecatl* feathered suit and carries the Huaxtec-related shield with cone-shaped symbol and parallel bars, discussed in the shield section. The warrior's accompanying cloak is an undecorated orange with a red border. Could this be a variant of the orange cloak mentioned above by Sahagún? It is impossible to know; Sahagún makes no other correlations between cloaks and warrior ranks until he mentions three prestigious capes awarded five-captive warriors.[156] As a result, we have no further comparisons between Sahagún and *Codex Mendoza*, because folio 64r illustrates no cloak accompanying the fifth warrior rank.

Three-Captive Warrior Rank

Returning to the third-ranked warrior, he is attired in unusually long cotton armor, carries the undecorated "whitewashed" shield, and wears his hair in the "pillar of stone" style. His insignia is the *papalotl* (butterfly) device in red with a white border. This same color combination occurs once in the tribute lists, but there it is worn with a white bodysuit with red cuffs. Although the Tepepulco warrior paraphernalia shown in *Primeros Memoriales* contains five different butterfly devices,[157] this particular style is not included. The three-prisoner warrior's accompanying cloak is the *yecacozcayo* (jewel of Ehecatl)[158] design, discussed below in the tribute textile section.

Four-Captive Warrior Rank

The adjacent, four-captive warrior wears a red jaguar suit and carries a red-ground *cuexyo* shield. His cloak is a black and orange, diagonally divided design with the important *tenixyo* border, discussed below. Capes with diagonal divisions were called *nacazminqui*, "diagonally divided."[159] It is this type of cloak, "a cape of two colors divided diagonally," that Sahagún says was given to particularly valiant warriors who had taken five prisoners from the independent polity of Atlixco, Huexotzinco, or Tliliuquitepec.[160] Captives from these areas were particularly valued.[161] Note that folio 64r of *Codex Mendoza* (fig. 47) pictures the captives of the three

highest ranks as wearing the curved labrets associated with the Huexotzinco area.

Five- and Six-Captive Warrior Rank
Otomí Warrior

The Spanish gloss on folio 64r says the next warrior (bottom register, left side), "surnamed *otonti*," had taken five or six enemies. He wears the *xopilli* (claw) device (see fig. 59a, b) with an undecorated green warrior suit, a gold ear ornament, and a gold labret. He carries an elaborated version of the *cuexyo* shield with a crescent-shaped water symbol replacing the Huaxtec nose ornament. This same design, the decorated *yacametztli*, also occurs on one of the shields given in tribute from Tlatelolco (folio 19r; see fig. 49 and appendix G, column 2).

Quachic Warrior

The sixth warrior of folio 64r is identified in the gloss as *quachichictli* and is said to have taken "many captives." The term Quachic means "the shorn one."[162] Durán contends this rank was attained only after performing more than twenty deeds and brave acts;[163] these warriors, like the Otomí, had a reputation for becoming almost crazed in battle.[164] The Quachic warrior, whose hair is shorn in this rank's unique manner, wears a necklace of what appears to be shells and carries the *xicalcoliuhqui* shield with the familiar yellow-fret-on-green-ground combination. Note that both this warrior and the Otomí are depicted without attendant cloaks.

The valiant Quachic warrior wears a back device whose near duplicate appears on folio 67r, worn there by a high official of Tenochtitlan (fig. 75). This insignia is a *pamitl* style, which Seler identifies as either a *youalpamitl* (night banner) or *citlalpamitl* (star banner).[165]

Pamitl (Appendix F, Column 13)

Some of the most prevalent of the Aztecs' martial insignia were the *pamitl* (banner)[166] styles, all of which featured a stiff, short banner attached to a tall pole with a luxuriant array of quetzal feathers spilling from its top. In *Codex Mendoza* these devices appear only in the ethnographic section, and there only four times (see fig. 74 for one example; fig. 75 for three examples). *Primeros Memoriales* contains illustrations of *pamitl* (figs. 61, 63, 70). This particular device also appears in four other Aztec pictorials, which indicates its frequent use by the Aztecs (see appendix F, column 13 for examples). The degree of variance among the *pamitl* styles may be reflecting a means of recognizing meritorious feats on the field of battle.

Tlacatecatl

The final figure of folio 64r is a particularly distinguished warrior who has reached the esteemed position of *Tlacatecatl* (Commanding General).[167] He wears the *quetzallalpiloni* hair ornament, gold earplugs, a labret, and a red cloak with the *tenixyo* "eyes on the edge" border. His prestigious cape with its decorated border is discussed in this chapter under "Tribute Textiles."

FOLIO 65R: PRIEST-WARRIORS

The subsequent page of *Codex Mendoza*, folio 65r (fig. 74), contains a second hierarchical scene dealing with successive grades of priest warriors. Note that each valiant wears a priestly smear of blood in front of his ear and binds his long hair back in a simple manner. These six priest-warrior grades lack the accompanying cloaks of the preceding group.

Fig. 75. Four high-ranking Aztec commanders in military attire. Note that three of them wear variants of the *pamitl* (banner) device (Clark 1938 3: folio 67r).

One-Captive Priest-Warrior

Like his counterpart on folio 64r, the first priest-warrior is dressed in the same basic martial attire as his captive.

Two-Captive Priest-Warrior

The costume of the second rank is an anomaly. Neither the white, limb-encasing suit nor its back device has any equivalent in other Aztec pictorials; hence this insignia does not appear on appendix F. Seler speculates that the red-and-white back device may have to do with the goddess associated with fire, Chantico.[168] The shield of this rank, the *ihuiteteyo*, occurs elsewhere in *Codex Mendoza*, as well as in other Aztec pictorials (see appendix G, column 10).

Three-Captive Priest-Warrior

The third rank features a *pamitl*-style back device. The attendant shield, whose name is unknown to us, appears neither on the *Codex Mendoza* tribute rolls nor in the Tepepulco data. It does occur, however, in other Aztec pictorials (see appendix G, column 11).

Four-Captive Priest-Warrior

The fourth warrior of folio 65r wears a variant of the *cuextecatl* costume; note the conical hat and cotton ear ornaments. Seler calls this apparel *cicitlallo cuextecatl* (starry-sky Huaxtec warrior costume).[169] Because this warrior's shield accompanies a *cuextecatl*-type costume, it has been designated a variant of the *cuexyo* design. This same motif also appears on shields in other Aztec pictorials (see appendix G, column 5).

Five-Captive Priest-Warrior

The fifth rank warrior of folio 65r carries the *quauhtetepoyo* (eagle's foot) shield, which occurs only three times in the tribute lists; there it is always with the butterfly device. This warrior's insignia, however, is a variant of the *momoyactli* back device. Also, note that

this warrior's captive, together with the prisoner of the adjacent coyote warrior, wears the tusklike labret of Huexotzinco. The latter captive also has a red band around his head, another hallmark of Huexotzinco.[170]

Six-Captive Priest-Warrior

The final warrior wears a yellow coyote suit identical to that already discussed in the tribute section. He carries the familiar *cuexyo* shield.

There are four additional warrior costume depictions in *Codex Mendoza* on folio 67r (fig. 75), each worn by a high-ranking captain.

FOLIO 67R: FOUR AZTEC CAPTAINS

Tlacatecatl

The first of these Aztec captains dressed in battle attire is the *Tlacatecatl*; his official cloak of office is depicted in the lower right of folio 64r (see fig. 47). Here this commander wears a red limb-encasing costume together with a *quaxolotl* back device.[171] The *Codex Mendoza* tribute section illustrates the *quaxolotl* device only with a yellow, green, or blue bodysuit; this red costume is the sole example of the device worn with a red suit. *Tlacatecatl* carries the *teocuitlaxapo* "gold disk" shield.

Tlacochcalcatl

The second captain of figure 75 has reached the high rank of *Tlacochcalcatl* (Keeper of the House of Darts).[172] He wears a style of the *tzitzimitl* (frightful specter) warrior suit that appears in the tribute section and a *pamitl*-style back device that does not. Seler identifies the latter as the *teocuitlapamitl* (banner of gold or silver plate).[173] The shield of this important general is the *ihuiteteyo*, a style that also occurs in other Aztec pictorials (see appendix G, column 10).

Fig. 76. Priest-warriors who have been elevated to positions of power; each wears his official cloak of office. Those in the upper register are constables; below are military commanders (Clark 1938 3: folio 67r).

Huiznahuatl

The third captain is designated *Huiznahuatl*, "Thorn Speech";[174] he appears in his cloak of office in the upper register of folio 66r. Here *Huiznahuatl*'s warrior costume includes the most common shield of the tribute lists, the *cuexyo*. His back device is a further variant of the *pamitl* insignia class, none of which appears in the tribute section of *Codex Mendoza*. However, a device very similar to this one is worn by the third priest-warrior rank of folio 65r (see fig. 74).

Ticocyahuacatl

The fourth captain of this group has attained the rank of *Ticocyahuacatl*, "Keeper of the Bowl of Fatigue."[175] He carries the second most common shield of the tribute list, the *xicalcoliuhqui*, and wears an almost identical *citlalpamitl* (star banner) back device[176] to that of the Quachic of folio 64r (see fig. 47). In fact, except for hairstyle and earplug color, the Quachic and *Ticocyhuacatl* are identical.

SUMMARY

This detailed analysis of *Codex Mendoza*'s three military scenes reveals additional interesting features about Aztec military attire. First, it again confirms that a wider range of warrior apparel was actually worn in Tenochtitlan than the tribute rolls indicate: paraphernalia missing from the tallies appear in the warrior hierarchical scenes. For example, a variant of the Huaxtec costume, the *cicitlallo* (starry-sky) *cuextecatl*, suggests that there may have been several styles of the basic Huaxtec apparel, variations similar to the range of coyote costumes recorded from Tepepulco. Second, four *pamitl*-style back devices and five shield designs not found in the tribute lists appear in these warrior scenes.[177] These shield insignia are not anomalies; analogues appear in other sources (see appendix

G). As for three of the four *pamitl* insignia, similar devices also appear in other Aztec pictorials (appendix F, column 13).

This review of the pictorial information on warrior attire suggests that the Aztec military was composed of many different fighting units, each with its own ranking system and graded apparel. Although part 3, folios 64r and 65r of *Mendoza* illustrates only two of these warrior hierarchies (see figs. 47 and 74), the collective Aztec pictorial data contain clues that many more must have existed. For example, Tepepulco may well have had a unit whose members wore only the *ehuatl* and perhaps others that featured coyote and butterfly insignia. Note that the Anonymous Conqueror stated that "one company of soldiers will wear them [feather suits] in red and white, another in blue and yellow, and others in various ways."[178]

The lower half of folio 65r (see fig. 76) contains a third hierarchical scene depicting a series of eight officials. Here a further aspect of the Aztec military world is revealed: later career stages of distinguished and achieved warriors. Cloaks of office are featured rather than military apparel.

FOLIO 65r: HIERARCHICAL SCENE OF GOVERNMENT OFFICIALS

The upper register of figure 76 shows four priest-warriors who have become imperial officers. All wear undecorated capes with contrasting plain borders; three of these *mantas* are orange, identical to the cloak that accompanied the second-ranked *cuextecatl* warrior costume of folio 64r (see fig. 47).

In the lower register are four "commanders of the army." One, *Tezcacoacatl*, wears an undecorated cloak with the prestigious *tenixyo* "eyes on the edge" border,[179] discussed below. The other three, however, wear capes whose motifs offer insight into the way the Aztecs made use of the preexisting religious iconography of their conquered provinces.

Tlacochcalcatl

The official *tilmatli* worn by the figure on the far left, *Tlacochcalcatl* (Keeper of the House of Darts),[180] and the capes of two other commanders bear design motifs associated with specific regions of the ethnically diverse Aztec empire. Of the thirty-eight provinces, thirty-six sent textiles in tribute. The *Tlacochcalcatl*'s cloak is the *yecacozcayo* (jewel of Ehecatl).[181] This mantle style was sent in tribute by two Gulf coast conquests, the contiguous provinces of Atlan and Tuchpa.

Tocuiltecatl

The cloak of the commander to the far right, the *Tocuiltecatl* (Keeper of the Worm on Blade of Maize),[182] is identified by Seler as the *temalacayo tilmatli*.[183] Seler describes this as a shoulder covering with large disks of a sort of sun design, presumably executed in featherwork, and links the motif to the sacrificial ritual in which warriors fight a captive tied to a round stone (*temalacatl*).[184]

Ticocyahuacatl

The third commander rank is the *Ticocyahuacatl* (Keeper of the Bowl of Fatigue),[185] whose name glyph contains the symbol for *pulque*. This is the fermented drink that played such an important role in Aztec ceremonial life. Appropriately, the *tilmatli* that the "Keeper of the Bowl of Fatigue" wears is the *pulque* jug mantle, the *ometochtecomayo*.[186] This *manta* (fig. 77) was given in tribute from two east coast provinces, Tochtepec (folio 46r) and Tuchpa (folio 52r; fig. 78), both of which have a rabbit in the name glyph of their provincial capitals (fig. 79, 80). The *tochtli*, "rabbit," element is associated with the *pulque* deities. This emphasis on the rabbit was most appropriate, for in the Gulf coast area *pulque* gods were particularly revered, as is explained below.

Analysis of the *pulque* jug motif, as well as other designs used on tribute textiles, provides additional understanding of the costumes and accoutrements of *Codex Mendoza*.

Tribute Textiles (Appendices I and J)

The reappearance of some of the *Codex Mendoza*'s part 2 tribute textiles worn by important officials in the part 3 ethnographic scenes is very instructive. As already mentioned, the Mexica used the *ometochtecomayo* "pulque jug" and *yecacozcayo* "jewel of Ehecatl" *mantas* as cloaks for their official bureaucracy (see fig. 76). This indicates that certain provincial cape designs were utilized at the highest imperial level. As is discussed below, the implications of this use suggest how the distribution system of the empire worked.

OMETOCHTECOMAYO "PULQUE JUG" DESIGN
(FIGURE 77 AND APPENDIX I, ROW 1, COLUMN 9)

Understanding Aztec utilization of provincial textile motifs for official use is aided by plotting the geographic distribution of certain relevant provinces. In this way both the cultural-historical depth of these regional designs and the extent of control exercised by the empire over provincial textile production are better understood. In the case of the *pulque* jug *manta*, although the provinces of Tochtepec and Tuchpa were separated geographically (see fig. 78), the rabbit motif in both their place glyphs (see figs. 79, 80) suggests that they shared an important religious focus. The rabbit (*tochtli*) was the Mesoamerican symbol for ritual inebriation; its use indicates an emphasis on the *pulque* gods. The existence of a Gulf coast *pulque* cult is further attested by the design of the *ometochtecomayo*, "pulque jug" on a cloak (see fig. 77), a *manta* both provinces sent in imperial tribute.

The appearance of a cult of the *pulque* gods along the Gulf coast is particularly intriguing, because the type of maguey from which the fermented drink was made does not grow at low altitudes. Sahagún's lively account of the mythical beginnings of *pulque* sheds light on this puzzling relationship between an intoxicating drink from a highland plant and its deification in a lowland region. The beverage was supposedly first fermented in the Morelos area of highland central Mexico. Once it was brewed, rulers and important men from far and wide were invited to partake of the powerful new beverage. Cuextecatl, the leader of the Gulf coast region that would be named Cuextlan after him, overindulged and disgraced himself by impetuously flinging off his loincloth. As a result, he and his people returned home in disrepute but nonetheless firmly committed to *pulque*.[187]

Tuchpa and Tochtepec's emphasis on *pulque*-associated designs implies an ancient, pre-Aztec time depth for these motifs. The use of the *pulque* jug cloak by the Mexica official hierarchy (see fig. 76) suggests that the relatively new Aztec empire sought additional validity through incorporation of an older culture's iconographic tradition. This practice of utilizing provincial motifs on the official clothing of some of the most powerful members of Aztec society can be further documented. In this second case, the geographic distribution of a provincial design motif is again involved.

XIUHTLALPILLI "BLUE KNOTTED" TIE-DYE DESIGN
(APPENDIX I, TIE-DYE, COLUMNS 1–3)

Eleven of the thirty-eight Aztec provinces sent tribute textiles that contained a shared motif, a blue-and-white diaper design composed of evenly spaced squares, each with a dot in the middle (fig. 81). These small, repeating units are the hallmark of a tie-dye technique known today as *plangi*.[188]

Five of the eleven provinces sent textiles displaying the blue tie-dye design and a solid yellow field. These cloaks are divided diagonally, hence the Nahuatl name *nacazminqui*, "diagonally divided." The five provinces formed a contiguous north-south band that stretched on either side of Tenochtitlan, the Aztec capital (fig. 82).

The two provinces that gave textiles containing the same blue tie-dye design but combined with solid red (fig. 83) were located to the northwest of Tenochtitlan (fig. 84). The four provinces that sent textiles combining blue tie-dye with red and yellow (fig. 85)[189] were immediately adjacent to the above two provinces (fig. 86). Collectively, these eleven provinces adjoined one another (fig. 87).

Out of the Aztec empire's thirty-eight provinces, only eleven sent textiles that incorporated the blue tie-dye design in one of two fields, and all eleven of these provinces were located immediately adjacent. There has to be more to this grouping than mere coincidence. Certainly these were not the only provinces that had access to the lowland cotton needed to weave the cloaks or the ability to obtain the necessary materials for dyeing them. Appendix I illustrates tribute textiles that came from all over the Aztec empire (see appendix J for attributions); the colors involved in the blue tie-dye group also appear on weavings from other provinces. Is the common denominator of the blue tie-dye textiles a response to an imperial mandate? Were these cloaks all "made to order"? The *pulque* jug cloak argues against this. In that case, the rulers in Tenochtitlan took advantage of a prestigious regional motif already long in place. The tie-dye textiles provide additional evidence that the Aztecs sometimes made use of older provincial designs for their official clothing.

(Text continued on page 139.)

Above: Fig. 77. The *ometochtecomayo* (*pulque* jug) *manta* given in tribute by Tochtepec and Tuchpa (Clark 1938 3: folio 52r). Right: Fig. 78. The geographic distribution of the two provinces that gave the *ometochtecomayo manta* in tribute.

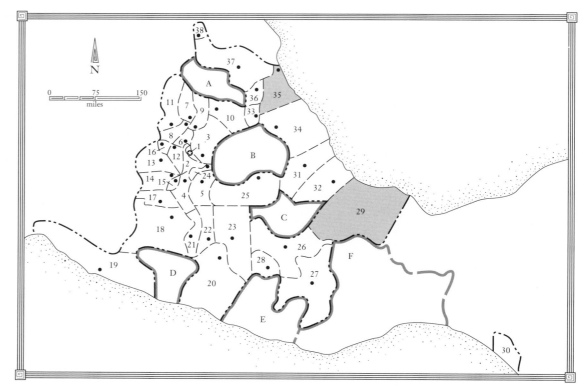

- - - · - Imperial Boundary
- - - - Provincial Boundary
——— Independent Señoríos
  ● Provincial Cabecera
  ✪ Tenochtitlan

INDEPENDENT SEÑORÍOS
A. Metztitlan
B. Tlaxcala
C. Teotitlan del Camino
D. Yopitzinco
E. Tototepec
F. Realm of Coatlicamac

PROVINCES
1. Tlatelolco
2. Petlacalco
3. Acolhuacan
4. Quauhnahuac
5. Huaxtepec
6. Quauhtitlan
7. Axocopan
8. Atotonilco (de Pedraza)
9. Hueypuchtla
10. Atotonilco (el Grande)
11. Xilotepec
12. Quahuacan
13. Tulucan
14. Ocuilan
15. Malinalco
16. Xocotitlan
17. Tlachco
18. Tepequacuilco
19. Çihuatlan
20. Tlapan
21. Tlalcoçauhtitlan
22. Quiauhteopan
23. Yoaltepec
24. Chalco
25. Tepeacac
26. Coayxtlahuacan
27. Coyolapan
28. Tlachquiavco
29. *Tochtepec*
30. Xoconochco
31. Quauhtochco
32. Cuetlaxtlan
33. Tlapacoyan
34. Tlatlauhquitepec
35. *Tuchpa*
36. Atlan
37. Tzicoac
38. Oxitipan

Left: Fig. 79. The place glyph for the town and province of Tochtepec features the rabbit, *tochtli*, associated with the *pulque* gods (Clark 1938 3: folio 46r). Right: Fig. 80. The place glyph for the town and province of Tuchpa features the rabbit, *tochtli*, associated with the *pulque* gods (Clark 1938 3: folio 52r).

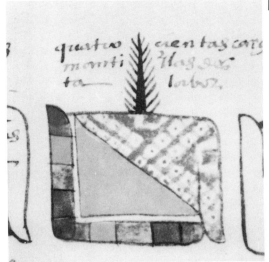

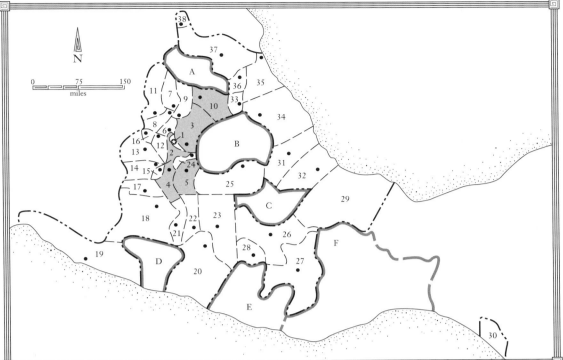

Above: Fig. 81. A yellow with blue-and-white tie-dye *nacazminqui* (diagonally divided) *manta* given in tribute by the provinces of Petlacalco, Acolhuacan, Quauhnahuac, Huaxtepec, and Atotonilco el Grande (Clark 1938 3: folio 20r). Right: Fig. 82. The geographic distribution of the provinces that sent the yellow with blue-and-white tie-dye *nacazminqui* cloaks in tribute.

‑‑‑‑	Imperial Boundary
‑ ‑ ‑	Provincial Boundary
▬▬	Independent Señoríos
•	Provincial Cabecera
✿	Tenochtitlan

INDEPENDENT SEÑORÍOS
A. Metztitlan
B. Tlaxcala
C. Teotitlan del Camino
D. Yopitzinco
E. Tototepec
F. Realm of Coatlicamac

PROVINCES
1. Tlatelolco
2. *Petlacalco*
3. *Acolhuacan*
4. *Quauhnahuac*
5. *Huaxtepec*
6. Quauhtitlan
7. Axocopan
8. Atotonilco (de Pedraza)
9. Hueypuchtla
10. *Atotonilco (el Grande)*
11. Xilotepec
12. Quahuacan
13. Tulucan

14. Ocuilan
15. Malinalco
16. Xocotitlan
17. Tlachco
18. Tepequacuilco
19. Çihuatlan
20. Tlapan
21. Tlalcoçauhtitlan
22. Quiauhteopan
23. Yoaltepec
24. Chalco
25. Tepeacac
26. Coayxtlahuacan
27. Coyolapan

28. Tlachquiavco
29. Tochtepec
30. Xoconochco
31. Quauhtochco
32. Cuetlaxtlan
33. Tlapacoyan
34. Tlatlauhquitepec
35. Tuchpa
36. Atlan
37. Tzicoac
38. Oxitipan

Above: Fig. 85. A *manta* combining the yellow with blue-and-white tie-dye diagonal and a solid red section given in tribute from the provinces of Quauhtitlan, Hueypuchtla, Xilotepec, and Quahuacan (Clark 1938 3: folio 26r). Right: Fig. 86. The geographical distribution of the four provinces that sent in tribute the *manta* combining the yellow with blue-and-white tie-dye diagonal and solid red section.

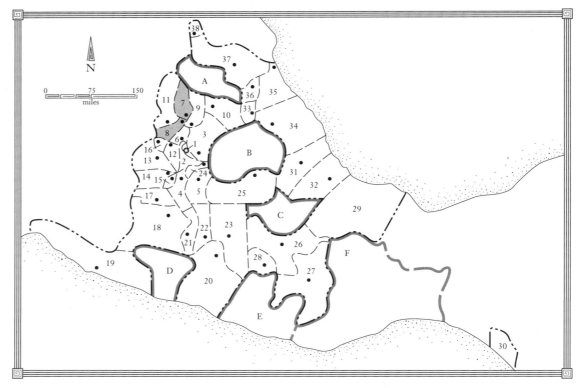

– · – · –	Imperial Boundary
– – –	Provincial Boundary
▬▬▬	Independent Señoríos
•	Provincial Cabecera
✿	Tenochtitlan

INDEPENDENT SEÑORÍOS
A. Metztitlan
B. Tlaxcala
C. Teotitlan del Camino
D. Yopitzinco
E. Tototepec
F. Realm of Coatlicamac

PROVINCES
1. Tlatelolco
2. Petlacalco
3. Acolhuacan
4. Quauhnahuac
5. Huaxtepec
6. Quauhtitlan
7. *Axocopan*
8. *Atotonilco (de Pedraza)*
9. Hueypuchtla
10. Atotonilco (el Grande)
11. Xilotepec
12. Quahuacan
13. Tulucan
14. Ocuilan
15. Malinalco
16 Xocotitlan
17. Tlachco
18. Tepequacuilco
19. Çihuatlan
20. Tlapan
21. Tlalcoçauhtitlan
22. Quiauhteopan
23. Yoaltepec
24. Chalco
25. Tepeacac
26. Coayxtlahuacan
27. Coyolapan
28. Tlachquiavco
29. Tochtepec
30. Xoconochco
31. Quauhtochco
32. Cuetlaxtlan
33. Tlapacoyan
34. Tlatlauhquitepec
35. Tuchpa
36. Atlan
37. Tzicoac
38. Oxitipan

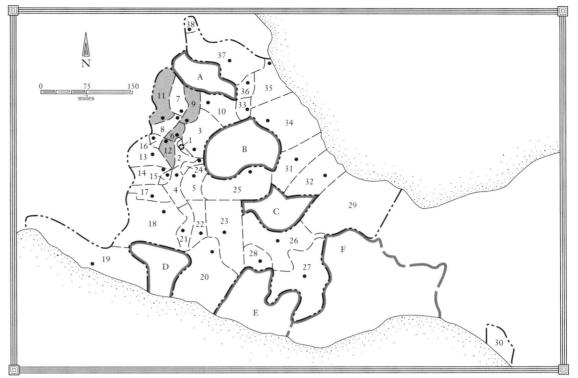

Above: Fig. 85. A *manta* combining the yellow with blue-and-white tie-dye diagonal and a solid red section given in tribute from the provinces of Quauhtitlan, Hueypuchtla, Xilotepec, and Quahuacan (Clark 1938 3: folio 26r). Right: Fig. 86. The geographical distribution of the four provinces that sent in tribute the *manta* combining the yellow with blue-and-white tie-dye diagonal and solid red section.

----·--- Imperial Boundary
----- Provincial Boundary
----- Independent Señoríos
• Provincial Cabecera
✪ Tenochtitlan

INDEPENDENT SEÑORÍOS
A. Metztitlan
B. Tlaxcala
C. Teotitlan del Camino
D. Yopitzinco
E. Tototepec
F. Realm of Coatlicamac

PROVINCES
1. Tlatelolco
2. Petlacalco
3. Acolhuacan
4. Quauhnahuac
5. Huaxtepec
6. *Quauhtitlan*
7. Axocopan
8. Atotonilco (de Pedraza)
9. *Hueypuchtla*
10. Atotonilco (el Grande)
11. *Xilotepec*
12. *Quahuacan*
13. Tulucan

14. Ocuilan
15. Malinalco
16 Xocotitlan
17. Tlachco
18. Tepequacuilco
19. Çihuatlan
20. Tlapan
21. Tlalcoçauhtitlan
22. Quiauhteopan
23. Yoaltepec
24. Chalco
25. Tepeacac
26. Coayxtlahuacan
27. Coyolapan

28. Tlachquiavco
29. Tochtepec
30. Xoconochco
31. Quauhtochco
32. Cuetlaxtlan
33. Tlapacoyan
34. Tlatlauhquitepec
35. Tuchpa
36. Atlan
37. Tzicoac
38. Oxitipan

Legend:

- · - · - Imperial Boundary
- - - - - Provincial Boundary
────── Independent Señoríos
- • Provincial Cabecera
- ✪ Tenochtitlan

INDEPENDENT SEÑORÍOS
A. Metztitlan
B. Tlaxcala
C. Teotitlan del Camino
D. Yopitzinco
E. Tototepec
F. Realm of Coatlicamac

PROVINCES
1. Tlatelolco
2. *Petlacalco*
3. *Acolhuacan*
4. *Quauhnahuac*
5. *Huaxtepec*
6. *Quauhtitlan*
7. *Axocopan*
8. *Atotonilco (de Pedraza)*
9. *Hueypuchtla*
10. *Atotonilco (el Grande)*
11. *Xilotepec*
12. *Quahuacan*
13. Tulucan

14. Ocuilan
15. Malinalco
16 Xocotitlan
17. Tlachco
18. Tepequacuilco
19. Çihuatlan
20. Tlapan
21. Tlalcoçauhtitlan
22. Quiauhteopan
23. Yoaltepec
24. Chalco
25. Tepeacac
26. Coayxtlahuacan
27. Coyolapan

28. Tlachquiavco
29. Tochtepec
30. Xoconochco
31. Quauhtochco
32. Cuetlaxtlan
33. Tlapacoyan
34. Tlatlauhquitepec
35. Tuchpa
36. Atlan
37. Tzicoac
38. Oxitipan

Fig. 87. The geographic distribution of the eleven provinces that sent in tribute *mantas* that all share the blue-and-white tie-dye element (Anawalt 1990).

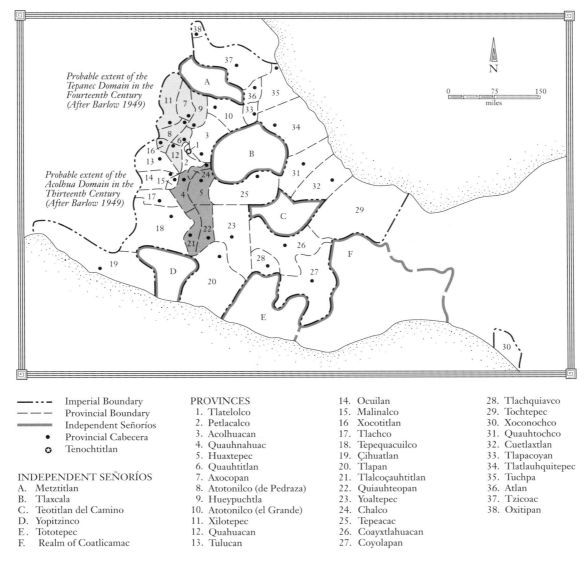

Probable extent of the
Tepanec Domain in the
Fourteenth Century
(After Barlow 1949)

Probable extent of the
Acolhua Domain in the
Thirteenth Century
(After Barlow 1949)

N

0   75   150
miles

——·—·— Imperial Boundary
— — — Provincial Boundary
———— Independent Señoríos
• Provincial Cabecera
⊙ Tenochtitlan

INDEPENDENT SEÑORÍOS
A. Metztitlan
B. Tlaxcala
C. Teotitlan del Camino
D. Yopitzinco
E. Tototepec
F. Realm of Coatlicamac

PROVINCES
1. Tlatelolco
2. Petlacalco
3. Acolhuacan
4. Quauhnahuac
5. Huaxtepec
6. Quauhtitlan
7. Axocopan
8. Atotonilco (de Pedraza)
9. Hueypuchtla
10. Atotonilco (el Grande)
11. Xilotepec
12. Quahuacan
13. Tulucan

14. Ocuilan
15. Malinalco
16 Xocotitlan
17. Tlachco
18. Tepequacuilco
19. Çihuatlan
20. Tlapan
21. Tlalcoçauhtitlan
22. Quiauhteopan
23. Yoaltepec
24. Chalco
25. Tepeacac
26. Coayxtlahuacan
27. Coyolapan

28. Tlachquiavco
29. Tochtepec
30. Xoconochco
31. Quauhtochco
32. Cuetlaxtlan
33. Tlapacoyan
34. Tlatlauhquitepec
35. Tuchpa
36. Atlan
37. Tzicoac
38. Oxitipan

Fig. 88. Geographic boundaries of the thirteenth-century Acolhuacan and the
fourteenth-century Tepanec domains (Anawalt 1990).

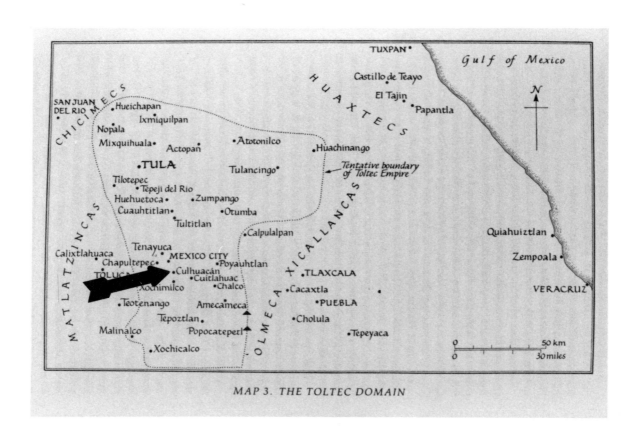

MAP 3. THE TOLTEC DOMAIN

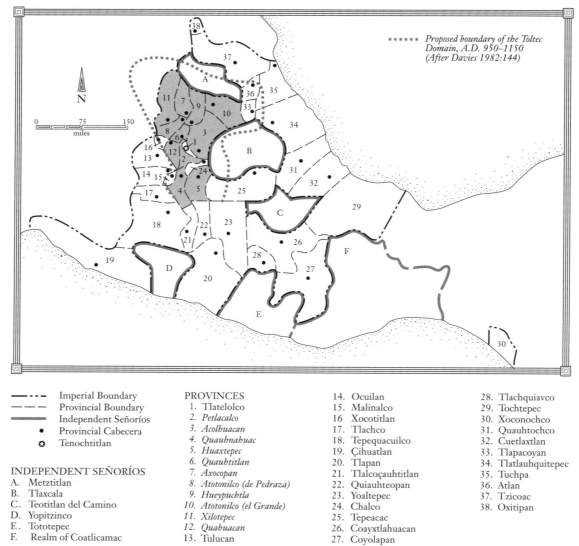

······· Proposed boundary of the Toltec
Domain, A.D. 950–1150
(After Davies 1982:144)

— · — · —   Imperial Boundary
— — —   Provincial Boundary
————   Independent Señoríos
●   Provincial Cabecera
✪   Tenochtitlan

INDEPENDENT SEÑORÍOS
A. Metztitlan
B. Tlaxcala
C. Teotitlan del Camino
D. Yopitzinco
E. Tototepec
F. Realm of Coatlicamac

PROVINCES
1. Tlatelolco
2. *Petlacalco*
3. *Acolhuacan*
4. *Quauhnahuac*
5. *Huaxtepec*
6. *Quauhtitlan*
7. *Axocopan*
8. *Atotonilco (de Pedraza)*
9. *Hueypuchtla*
10. *Atotonilco (el Grande)*
11. *Xilotepec*
12. *Quahuacan*
13. Tulucan

14. Ocuilan
15. Malinalco
16. Xocotitlan
17. Tlachco
18. Tepequacuilco
19. Çihuatlan
20. Tlapan
21. Tlalcoçauhtitlan
22. Quiauhteopan
23. Yoaltepec
24. Chalco
25. Tepeacac
26. Coayxtlahuacan
27. Coyolapan

28. Tlachquiavco
29. Tochtepec
30. Xoconochco
31. Quauhtochco
32. Cuetlaxtlan
33. Tlapacoyan
34. Tlatlauhquitepec
35. Tuchpa
36. Atlan
37. Tzicoac
38. Oxitipan

Top: Fig. 89. Geographical configuration of the old Toltec empire
(after Davies 1982:144, map 3). Bottom: Fig. 90. Provinces located within the boundaries
of the old Toltec empire (Anawalt 1990).

(Text continued from page 131.)

Fig. 91. Tlaxcalan noblewomen wearing skirts with the tie-dye motif (*Lienzo de Tlaxcala* 1892 : 19).

What is suggested by the contiguous grouping of the eleven tie-dye provinces is a common heritage. The clue to this shared bond rests, again, in geographic distribution. The solid yellow and blue tie-dye textiles all fall within the southeastern portion of the ancient Acolhua kingdom, located on the eastern side of the Valley of Mexico. The solid red and blue tie-dye provinces, however, collectively conform to the boundaries of the fourteenth-century Tepanec domain (fig. 88).

What meaning could this blue tie-dye motif have conveyed to the thirteenth-century Acolhua and fourteenth-century Tepanec? What was it about this design that inspired continuity? Why did these regions, which were later absorbed into the sixteenth-century Aztec empire as eleven provinces, continue to feature it? What common heritage does this tie-dye motif reflect?

The Aztecs' Acolhua and Tepanec predecessors—like the later Mexica themselves—had been nomadic invaders into the settled Valley of Mexico after the fall of the mighty Toltecs in A.D. 1150. The attaining of legitimacy for these parvenues was through marriage into the royal house of the small city-state of Colhuacan, located just south of Tenochtitlan (fig. 89). Colhuacan claimed an unbroken heritage back to the ruling Toltec line. Note that the eleven tie-dye provinces are all located within the confines of the ancient Toltec imperial boundaries (fig. 90).

What the eleven provinces were stating, via their blue tie-dye motif tribute textiles, was a claim to the Toltec bloodline. The right to use the design, a Toltec genealogical marker, was passed down by the nobility to both female (fig. 91; see also fig. 12) and male descendants. Indeed, it is a stylized version of the blue tie-dye motif that appears on the official cloak worn by the most powerful males of Late Postclassic Mesoamerica, the Aztec emperors. No matter which of these successive rulers is depicted (fig. 92), his imperial cape always displays this same diaper pattern. Obviously, the convention of using the design served an essential purpose: the ruler's cape was a genealogical statement, an heraldic device that declared the Aztecs' claim to a genealogical heritage (see figs. 23 and 24).[190]

Just as the blue tie-dye motif provides new understanding of Aztec culture history, so too does the iconography that adorns all the *tenixyo*-bordered textiles of the tribute tallies.

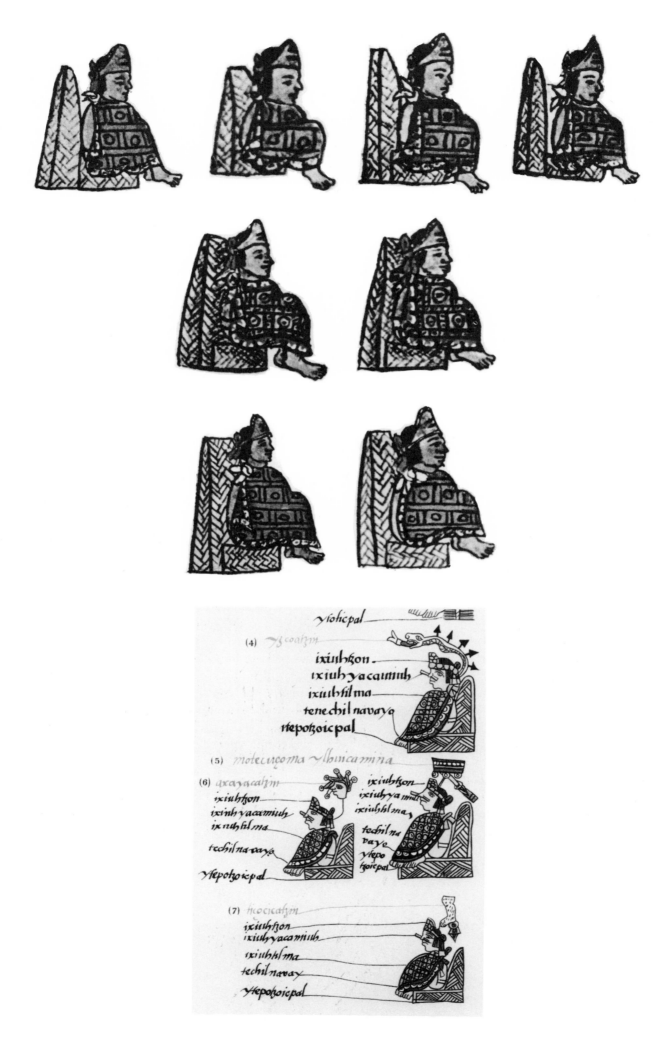

Fig. 92. Examples of the emperors' blue cloaks of office. Left
to right, top row: (a) Sahagún 1979 8: folio 1r. second row:
(b) Sahagún 1979 8: folio 1v. third row: (c) Sahagún 1979 8:
folio 2r. bottom: (d) *Primeros Memoriales* 1926: *estampa* XVIII.

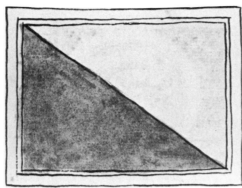

Left to right, top row: Fig. 93. A ritual *manta* with a single shell motif from *Codex Magliabechiano* (1970: folio 3v). Fig. 94. Diagonally divided cloak from among the forty-six ritual *mantas* of *Codex Magliabechiano* (1970: folio 6v). Fig. 95. Tlaloc ritual *manta* from among the forty-six ritual *mantas* of *Codex Magliabechiano* (1970: folio 6r). Bottom row: Fig. 96. Eagle ritual *manta* from among the forty-six ritual *mantas* of *Codex Magliabechiano* (1970: folio 6v). Fig. 97. A conch shell cross-section design *manta* from among the forty-six ritual *mantas* of *Codex Magliabechiano* (1970: folio 3v).

TENIXYO "EYES ON THE EDGE" BORDERED TEXTILES (APPENDIX I, ROW I)

The seven tribute textiles in row 1 of appendix I all have an identical border, the *tenixyo*, "eyes on the edge," which is discussed below. But first, in order to understand the symbolism involved in the central motifs found on these cloaks, it is helpful to compare them with the forty-six ritual *mantas* from another Aztec pictorial, *Codex Magliabechiano*. A one-on-one correlation occurs only with the *ocelotilmatli*,[191] the jaguar design cape (appendix I, row 8, column 5). Nonetheless, it is possible to compare these two sets of cloaks by recognizing the minimalist nature of the *Codex Magliabechiano* ritual *mantas*. They are a succinct presentation of the same iconographic messages contained in the ornate *Codex Mendoza* textiles.

The first analogous motif to be compared is the single shell (see appendix I, row 1, column 1). This *manta* meets the definition of the *tecucizyo tilmatli tenixyo*, which Anderson and Dibble translate as "the cape with the conch shell design, bordered with eyes";[192] Seler calls it "the conch shell cloth with the red eyes border."[193] Its analogue among the *Magliabechiano* group is the ritual *manta* featuring a single shell (fig. 93). An example of this motif used as a recurring pattern appears on a *tilmatli* worn by a Texcocan lord in *Codex Ixtlilxochitl* (see fig. 26).

The next of the seven *tenixyo*-bordered *mantas* (appendix I, row 1, column 2) is identified by a gloss in *Matrícula de Tributos* as *nacazminqui*, "diagonally divided" cloak.[194] This is a puzzling name, because the textile also features the familiar profile of Tlaloc, with his unmistakable goggle eyes and prominent fangs. The *Codex Mendoza* manta has two analogues in *Codex Magliabechiano*, whether viewed as a diagonally divided (fig. 94) or as a Tlaloc cloak (fig. 95).

The next four *mantas* of appendix I (row 1, columns 3, 5, 7, 8)

differ in their central motif but share very similar overall backgrounds of swirling, complex, and detailed patterns. It is tempting to read these designs as featherwork. Sahagún speaks of capes of colored feathers,[195] "rulers' capes, feathered in cup-shaped designs,"[196] and also cloaks of "eagle face designs, and striped on the borders with feathers."[197]

The feathered border reference is discussed below; here it is interesting to note how closely the eagle motif *tenixyo*-bordered textile of appendix I (row 1, column 3) meets Sahagún's description of the *xahualquauhio tilmatli tenixyo*, which Anderson and Dibble translate "the cape with an eagle's face painted on it, bordered with eyes."[198] Unfortunately, this description provides no clues as to the nature of the background patterns, but it does certainly emphasize the central eagle motif, which has its analogue within the *Magliabechiano* group (fig. 96).

Despite the temptation to regard these four complex-background *mantas* as feathered, at least the central motif was probably painted. This "eagle" pattern textile in *Codex Mendoza*'s cognate, *Matrícula de Tributos*, has an accompanying gloss that reads *ixnextlacuilolli*, "painted textile."[199] The custom of naming a textile not for its recognizable design motif but rather for the technology involved in creating it is still in use today in Nahuatl-speaking communities in the Sierra Norte de Puebla, Mexico.[200]

Returning to the textiles of appendix I, row 1, the second of the four complex-background *tenixyo mantas*, column 5, may be the *apalecacozcayo tilmatli ihuitica tentlayahualo*, which Anderson and Dibble translate "the light blue cape with a wind jewel design, which had a border of feathers with spirals."[201] The gloss accompanying the *Codex Magliabechiano* ritual-*manta* analogue (fig. 97) associates the shell design with the Aztec deity Tezcatlipoca.[202] This is a strange attribution, because the motif resembles the spiral-shaped pectoral made from a sliced conch shell, an orna-

Left to right, top row: Fig. 98. A butterfly design *manta* from among the forty-six ritual *mantas* of *Codex Magliabechiano* (1970: folio 8v). Fig. 99. The *oyohualli* motif *manta* from among the forty-six ritual *mantas* of *Codex Magliabechiano* (1970: folio 8r). Fig. 100. A ritual *manta* with the nose ornament motif from among the forty-six ritual *mantas* of *Codex Magliabechiano* (1970: folio 4v). Left: Fig. 101. Rabbit design *manta* from among the forty-six ritual *mantas* of *Codex Magliabechiano* (1970: folio 7v).

ment of the god Quetzalcoatl.[203] Whatever this shell's implications, it obviously was very popular. There are three additional *mantas* from the tribute tallies (appendix I, row 2, columns 4, 5, 6) that feature this same motif. One of these capes (column 4) served as the official cloak of office for *Tlacochcalcatl*, a leading functionary of Aztec imperial government (see fig. 76).

Returning to appendix I, the third of the similar, swirling-background *tenixyo*-bordered *mantas* (row 1, column 7) features the butterfly as its central motif and thus meets Sahagún's description of the *papaloyo tilmatli tenixyo*, "the cape with butterfly design, bordered with eyes."[204] Once again, an analogue can be found among the forty-six ritual mantles of *Codex Magliabechiano* (fig. 98). The butterfly, with its strong floral associations, is connected with the Xochipilli complex of deities who signify solar warmth, beauty, pleasure, and sensual delights.[205]

The fourth of the appendix I detailed-background *tenixyo mantas* (row 1, column 8) has as its central motif what appears to be the perforated, egg-shaped device—sometimes called the *oyohualli*—which is also associated with the Xochipilli complex, specifically with the pleasure-loving god, Macuilxochitl. This oval motif also appears on one of the ritual *mantas* of *Codex Magliabechiano* (fig. 99). The design is also in a decorative panel on the cloak worn by a noble of Texcoco who appears in *Codex Ixtlilxochitl* (see fig. 25).

The last of the seven *tenixyo*-bordered *mantas* (appendix I, row 1, column 9) meets the description of the *ometochtecomayo*, "pulque jug" design.[206] This *manta* has two conceptual analogues among the ritual *mantas* of *Codex Magliabechiano*, both connected with ritual drunkenness. One bears the *yacametztli*, the crescent-shaped nose ornament worn by the *octli*—pulque—deities and those allied with them (fig. 100). The second analogue is with the rabbit, symbol of ritual intoxication and hence *pulque* (fig. 101).

The feature shared by all seven of the diverse *mantas* of appendix I, row 1, is their border. A review of the *tenixyo* border on garments that appear in central Mexican pictorials emphasizes the aristocratic associations of this motif as well as its appearance in unexpected and contradictory contexts.

Tenixyo Border

The *tenixyo* border was commonly used on garments worn by rulers and the nobility. The motif is seen repeatedly on *mantas* worn by the emperors and lords shown throughout the Aztec pictorial corpus (e.g., figs. 23, 25, and 27). Research reveals that this design element appears on garments in the ritual sections of eleven codices that deal with religious matters. Ten of these are Aztec: *Codex Borbonicus*, Durán, *Codex Ixtlilxochitl*, *Codex Magliabechiano*, *Primeros Memoriales*, *Codex Telleriano-Remensis*, *Codex Vaticanus A*, *Tonalamatl Aubin*,[207] and books 1 and 2 of the *Florentine Codex*. The only non-Aztec pictorial that depicts costumes with the *tenixyo* border is *Codex Borgia*, also a central Mexican pictorial.[208]

Sixty examples of clothing decorated with the *tenixyo* border can be found in the eleven religious codices.[209] Twenty-six of these *tenixyo* examples occur in connection with ten of the eighteen annual veintena ceremonies. For example, a god impersonator of Xochipilli is borne by litter bearers who wear *mantas* with the border during the festival of Tecuilhuitl (fig. 102). However, the strongest of these ceremonial correlations is with the feast day Hueytecuilhuitl, where the border occurs four times.[210]

In terms of the deities themselves, the strongest correlation is between the *tenixyo* border and the capricious god Tezcatlipoca. In *Codex Borbonicus* the god impersonator wears a *tenixyo*-bordered hip-cloth (fig. 103), and in *Codex Magliabechiano* a *xicolli* (fig. 104). Both images symbolize the monthly ceremony of Miccailhuitontli. Tezcatlipoca impersonators also appear in *tenixyo*-bordered clothing twice in that final section of *Codex Magliabechiano* devoted to miscellaneous rites.[211] In Durán's *The Book of the Gods and Rites* Tezcatlipoca is only shown once, and there he is wearing a net *manta* with the *tenixyo* border (fig. 105). In *Codex Borgia*, a non-Aztec pictorial, the *tenixyo* border occurs five times; in three of these it is worn by the Black Tezcatlipoca (e.g., fig. 106).[212]

The majority of the evidence from pictorial sources indicates that *tenixyo*-bordered garments were associated with high-status males—gods, rulers, or nobles. However, in the *Florentine Codex*

Upper left: Fig. 102. An impersonator of the god Xochipilli carried by litter bearers who wear *mantas* with the *tenixyo* border (*Codex Magliabechiano* 1970: folio 35r). Upper right: Fig. 103. An impersonator of the god Tezcatlipoca depicting the veintena ceremony Maccuilhuitontli. He wears a hip-cloth decorated with the *tenixyo* border (*Codex Borbonicus* 1974:28). Center left: Fig. 104. An impersonator of the god Tezcatlipoca depicting the veintena ceremony of Maccuilhuitontli. He wears a *xicolli* with a *tenixyo* border (*Codex Magliabechiano* 1970: folio 37r). Lower right: Fig. 105. An impersonator of the god Tezcatlipoca wearing a *manta* with a *tenixyo* border (Durán 1967 1: *lámina* 8). Lower left: Fig. 106. The Black Tezcatlipoca wearing a hip-cloth with a *tenixyo* border (*Codex Borgia* 1976:21).

Upper left: Fig. 107. A woman wears a *huipilli* with a *tenixyo* border (Sahagún 1979 1: folio 50r). Upper right: Fig. 108. Judges wear *mantas* with the *tenixyo* border (Sahagún 1979 8: folio 276r). Lower left: Fig. 109. An imprisoned judge wears a *manta* with the *tenixyo* border (Sahagún 1979 8: folio 277r). Center right: Fig. 110. Both Emperor Ahuitzotl and a merchant presenting him with gifts wear *mantas* with *tenixyo* borders (Sahagún 1979 9: folio 326r). Lower right: Fig. 111. A *manta* with a *tenixyo* border being sold in the marketplace (Sahagún 1979 10: folio 43r).

four women wear *tenixyo*-bordered garments (e.g., fig. 107).[213] Also, the Tezcatlipoca correlation is weakened when *Primeros Memoriales* illustrates this god wearing a *manta* without the *tenixyo* border. However, the border itself does occur in the *Primeros Memoriales;* it appears on the raiment of four deities: Omacatl, Yacatecuhtli, Tlacochcalco Yautl, and Paynal.[214]

Despite these anomalies, there are strong correlations between the *tenixyo* border, ruling-class male ritual garments, and ceremonial robes of office. It is therefore not surprising to find the border on the robes of judges who were of the aristocracy, as their *xiuhuitzolli*—the headgear of nobles—indicate (fig. 108). Even the occurrence of the *tenixyo* on the border of the cape of an unworthy, imprisoned judge does not negate its aristocratic association (fig. 109). However, when the border also appears repeatedly on garments in book 9, *The Merchants*, the exclusivity of the motif becomes questionable. The *tenixyo* design occurs on both the cloaks of a merchant who presents gifts to Emperor Ahuitzotl (fig. 110) and on the cape of the ruler himself. This prestigious border associated with gods and emperors appears again on *tilmatli* worn by merchants involved in a legal dispute (see fig. 30) and listening to the admonitions of an elder (see fig. 31).

The pictorial evidence indicates that not only the aristocracy but also wealthy merchants were wearing cloaks adorned with the prestigious *tenixyo* border. How did these men of commerce acquire such aristocratic clothing? In contrast to what the vaunted Aztec sumptuary laws suggest—that the dress of each class was zealously restricted—book 10, *The People*, illustrates such capes being sold in the marketplace (fig. 111).[215]

Sahagún further confirms the public sale of prestige capes in book 9, *The Merchants*. He describes the emperor Ahuitzotl giving a gift of 1,600 *quachtli*—the large cotton capes that sometimes served as mediums of exchange—to merchants of Tenochtitlan and the adjoining city of Tlatelolco. These merchants used their *quachtli* to buy luxury merchandise in the marketplace for future resale. In those marts of trade they often bought "rulers' capes, feathered in cup-shaped designs, and those of eagle face designs, and striped on the borders with feathers" (see appendix I, row 1, column 3).[216] Here, then, is proof that the most elegant and prestigious of Aztec apparel, even that bordered with what may have been the *tenixyo* design, was for sale in the marketplace.

Although *Codex Mendoza* depicts seven prestigious, *tenixyo*-border tribute capes, we know from Sahagún that a far greater variety of such richly decorated, high-status cloaks existed. He lists fifty-four *tilmatli* that adorned rulers and noblemen.[217] Obviously, *Codex Mendoza* tribute textiles, like the pictorial's other apparel, present only a limited view of the pageantry, diversity, and grandeur that was the essence of imperial Tenochtitlan.[218]

IMPLICATIONS OF THE *CODEX MENDOZA* COSTUME ANALYSIS
The Degree of State Control over Warrior Costumes and Tribute

The foregoing comparative analysis of *Codex Mendoza* secular dress, ritual attire, warrior costume, hierarchial clothing, and tribute textiles indicates that there was a far wider range of garments and design motifs utilized in Tenochtitlan than is represented in the pictorial. This realization bears on an issue in Mesoamerican economic ethnohistory: the degree to which the Aztec state controlled and standardized the manufacture of provincial goods.[219]

The above analysis of *Codex Mendoza*'s costumes and accoutrements challenges the concept of an imperial overlay standardizing provincial tribute. This argument is valid only if (1) the warrior costumes used in Tenochtitlan were restricted to those of the tribute rolls, (2) this martial attire was supplied solely through tribute, (3) the state was the only distributor of warrior costumes, and (4) the tribute rolls reflect a regularly recurring, long-term record. Only when one accepts these premises does the state control argument have merit. However, from the findings of this study it is evident that there was a wider range of martial apparel used by the Aztecs than is reflected in the tribute rolls. This diversity suggests that warrior attire was also provided outside tribute channels, no doubt moving through the society via both trade and market networks.

The analysis of tribute textiles further challenges the imperial-overlay argument. What emerges from the distribution maps is not state standardization but rather archaic substructure. For certain official cloaks, the empire chose to make use of provincial textile designs containing symbols that existed prior to Triple Alliance hegemony. The Aztecs' display of these cloaks in bureaucratic contexts constituted a form of charter, an attempt at legitimization aimed at linking the *nouveaux* Aztecs not only to their respected Acolhuaque, Tepanec, and Gulf coast predecessors but also, more importantly, back to the revered Toltecs themselves.

In addition to revealing the scope of Tenochtitlan's costume repertory, this study has highlighted the puzzling variation in clothing elaboration in the ethnographic section of *Codex Mendoza;* only the garments of the hierarchical warrior scenes are drawn with any design motif elaboration. How is this anomaly to be understood?

An Explanation for the Contrast in Clothing Detail Within the Ethnographic Section

A key to understanding the anomaly of undecorated clothing in part 3 of *Codex Mendoza* can be found in a vignette involving indigenous priests, one of whom wears an Aztec ritual garment, the *xicolli*. Folio 63r, on which the *xicolli* appears, contains two scenes (figs. 112 and 113) involving Aztec priests, all of whom are recognizable by the diagnostic smear of blood in front of the ear. Each of the six is involved in a priestly chore: one sweeps a temple, two punish a wayward novice, another observes the stars, a fifth plays a drum, and the sixth, who is doing penance, carries an *incensario*. It is this last priest who wears the *xicolli*, the Aztecs' "godly jacket."[220]

Each of these depictions would pictographically answer the question, "What duties did Aztec priests perform?" Given the vigilant proselytizing of the Spanish clergy who oversaw the *Codex Mendoza*'s compilation, the Indian scribes could not include human sacrifice as an Aztec priestly chore (see fig. 37 for *xicolli*-clad sacrificing priests). Incensing as a religious act, however, was certainly within the range of Catholic sanction; hence, this duty of *xicolli*-clad priests was acceptable. The pre-Hispanic association between the *xicolli* and human sacrifice may have been unknown to these particular Spanish friars. If so, there would be no objection to including a depiction of this ritual-associated jacket.

The undecorated apparel of the ethnographic scenes can also be understood as a pictorial response to specific questions. This explains why the undecorated ethnographic clothing contrasts so markedly with the detailed garments of the military hierarchies. If the native scribes were asked, "What did women/men do at the various stages of their lives?" emphasis would be on activities involving gender and age, not on recording class or rank via ornamentation of dress. If, however, the question was, "How were war-

Top: Fig. 112. Three Aztec priests—note the diagnostic smear of blood in front of the ear—involved in priestly chores. One sweeps a temple; two punish a novice (Clark 1938 3: folio 63r). Bottom: Fig. 113. Three Aztec priests—note the diagnostic smear of blood in front of the ear—involved in priestly chores. One observes the stars, the second plays a drum under a night sky, and the third, who wears a *xicolli*, performs an incensing ceremony (Clark 1938 3: folio 63r).

rior ranks designated?" the pictographic response would involve careful detailing of the achieved status-marker clothing.

A subsidiary aspect of the warrior-rank hierarchical scenes of folios 64r and 65r (see figs. 47 and 74) also bears out this conclusion. Note that in each case the captives are depicted in a standardized, simplified manner; there is no detailing of wearing apparel or shield. The request to the native artist must have been solely to provide pictorial information on the Mexica warrior ranks of Tenochtitlan. As a result, the captives emerge as twelve almost identical standardized notations.

The semantic function of Aztec pictorial writing[221] explains the undecorated clothing anomalies of *Codex Mendoza*. However, the contrasts between *Codex Mendoza* and the more detailed illustrations of the later Colonial pictorials, particularly those from Sahagún's *Florentine Codex*, require further discussion.[222]

WHAT THE SELECTIVE COSTUME REPERTORY OF *CODEX MENDOZA* REVEALS ABOUT THE DOCUMENT

The noticeable difference between the lack of clothing detail in the ethnographic section of *Codex Mendoza* and the design motif elaboration of garments in similar scenes of later pictorials can be explained by the acculturation process. The artistic canon brought by the Spanish was that of sixteenth-century Europe, a convention that involved conveying a visual message by evoking reality through emphasis on detailing. Even in such completely imaginary scenes as those painted by Hieronymus Bosch (d. 1516), landscape, architecture, and clothing are richly detailed, thus adding verisimilitude to Bosch's inspired flights of fancy. In contrast, such uncontestably pre-Hispanic pictorials as *Codex Fejérváry-Mayer*,[223] *Codex Laud*,[224] and *Codex Zouche-Nuttall*[225] include only that degree of detailing needed to impart the intended information. Even in that most elaborated of pre-Conquest Mesoamerican books, *Codex Borgia*, only those details of architecture or costume which serve to convey the esoteric pictorial's ritual message are included.

In the case of Sahagún and the other Spanish clerics who supervised pictorials in the native style, the demands made on Indian scribes must have included requests for increasing degrees of European-style detailing, the better to impart "how it really was" prior to the Conquest.

In the ethnographic section of *Codex Mendoza*, compiled only some twenty years after the arrival of the Spanish, the Indian scribes were asked to depict a theme new to their artistic canon, the life cycle. This they did, but within their own pre-Hispanic mode. As a result, many aspects of the material culture of Tenochtitlan are presented in a minimal manner because the questions asked of the artists required no more. However frustrating this paucity of detail is for us after almost half a millennium, we must gratefully acknowledge that as a result *Codex Mendoza* represents a double treasure: not only is invaluable pre-Conquest ethnographic information preserved, but it is recorded in the still-extant indigenous tradition.

1. *Codex Borbonicus* (1974; Glass and Robertson 1975: census no. 32); *Matrícula de Tributos* (1980: census no. 368).

Glass and Robertson (1975) offer detailed information on pre- and post-Hispanic Mesoamerican pictorial manuscripts. Census numbers are included here to assist the reader with further references.

2. The following Colonial codices were utilized to reconstruct the Aztec costume repertory in Anawalt 1981, a detailed study of Late Postclassic Mesoamerican costume: *Códice Azcatítlan* (1949: census no. 20); *Códice Xolotl* (1951: census no. 412); *Codex Ixtlilxochitl* (1976: census nos. 171 and 172); *Codex Magliabechiano* (1970: census no. 188); *Codex Mendoza* (1938: census no. 196); *Codex Telleriano-Remensis* (1964–1967: census no. 308); *Codex Vaticanus A* (1979: census no. 270); *Florentine Codex* (Sahagún 1950–1982, 1979: census no. 274); *Primeros Memoriales* (n.d. [Thelma D. Sullivan translation], 1926: census no. 271).

3. The following eyewitness conquistador accounts were used in Anawalt 1981 to reconstruct the Aztec costume repertory: Anonymous Conqueror (1858); Cortés (1971); Díaz del Castillo (1967); Aguilar (1954). The administrative documents utilized were Cline (1972); Harvey (1972); PNE (1905–1948); Zorita (1963a).

4. Anawalt 1981: 42, 214.

5. Durán 1967 2: 211–214.

6. Anawalt 1980.

7. Durán 1967 2: 206.

8. Ibid.: 207.

9. Sahagún 1950–1982 8: 23–27.

10. Ibid. 8: 47.

11. Cortés 1971: 101, 104.

12. Fuentes 1963: 170–171.

13. Nicholson 1974: 146.

14. Molina 1977: folio 157v "Vipilli. camisa de india" (blouse of an Indian woman). To the present day, the term *huipil* is used to designate the variety of sleeveless tunics worn by the Indian women of Middle America.

The Aztec *huipilli* was a sleeveless tunic or shift that came to a little below the hips or top of the thighs. It was the woman's basic upper-body garment, and as such was worn by women of all classes. The *huipilli* often had a specially decorated rectangle over the chest and back which may have served the practical purpose of strengthening the neck slit to protect it from tearing. There was also sometimes a differentiated area over each shoulder.

For more detailed information on the *huipilli*, see Anawalt 1981: 52–55.

15. Molina 1977: folio 26r "Cueitl. faya, faldellin, faldillas., o naguas" (overskirt or petticoats).

For more information on the *cueitl*, see Anawalt 1981: 33–35.

16. See appendix E this volume.

17. Barlow 1949b: 130.

18. Aztec *caciques* were members of the upper class and hence had access to the finer clothing of society. The disobedient *cacique*'s wife (fig. 9), although shown in fetters, should have been attired in a manner befitting her husband's station in life.

19. Molina 1977: folio 54v "Maxtlatl. bragas, o cosa semejante" (breeches, or similar thing).

For more information on the *maxtlatl*, see Anawalt 1981: 21–24.

20. Anawalt 1984.

21. Molina 1977: folio 113r "Tilmatli. manta" (cape).

For more information on the *tilmatli*, see Anawalt 1981: 27–33.

22. *Codex Mendoza:* folio 70r.

23. The net cape of the Master of Youths on folio 57r (fig. 19) has a red border; the cloak of the Master of Youths on folio 61r (fig. 20) lacks net cross-hatching but does have the red border.

24. Siméon 1963: 699 "Xiuhuitzolli, Couronne, mitre, diadème garni de pierres précieuses" (crown, miter, diadem garnished with precious stones).

25. In *Primeros Memoriales* (1926: estampa XVIII), the royal diadem and blue cloak of office are worn only by the Mexica emperors, Itzcoatl through Cuauhtemoc; the earlier rulers, Acamapichtli, Huitzilihuitl, and Chimalpopoca, all wear the *cozoyahualolli* (yellow rosette) Chichimec hair ornament and deerskin cloaks.

26. Molina 1977: folio 159v "Xiuitl. año, cometa, turquesa e yerua." (year, comet, turquoise and herb); folio 124v "Tlalpilli. cosa atada, o añudada, o prisionero de otro" (something tied, or knotted, or prisoner of another). Thus *xihuitl* (turquoise) + *tlalpilli* (knotted) + *tenixyo* (eyes on the edge) + *tilmatli* (cape) = *xiuhtlalpilli tenixyo tilmatli*, or "the blue knotted cape with the *tenixyo* [eyes on the edge] border."

Both this cape design motif and the *tenixyo* border are discussed under Tribute Textiles.

27. See volume 2, "Image Descriptions," folio 64r, for information on the *quetzallalpiloni* headgear.

28. Sahagún 1950–1982 10: 63–94.

29. Upper-class males are sometimes referred to as wearing cloaks of bast fibers, but their mantles are always described as finely woven (e.g., ibid. 9: 7).

30. Ibid. 10: 73.

31. Anawalt 1984.

32. Anawalt 1982a.

33. Seler 1901–1902: 123.

34. Anawalt 1984: 166–167.

35. *Codex Borbonicus* 1974: 8, 23–26, 31, 32, 35, 36.

36. *Codex Mendoza:* folios 7v, 20r, 21v (twice), 22r, 37r.

37. See appendix E this volume. Note that the place glyph in figure 34 shows a *quemitl* made of white feathers, probably those of the heron.

38. See appendix E this volume.

39. Anawalt 1981: 42. The sleevelike look of the *Codex Mendoza xicolli* reflects the width of the garment across the shoulders and the manner in which the cloth drapes under the arm. This style of garment is still woven and worn today in the Sierra Norte de Puebla, where it is now called a *cotorina*.

40. Anawalt 1976.

41. The two constables in register 2 of folio 66r are seen from the side, hence the opening of the *xicolli* is not apparent. The vertical line indicating the jacket's opening for the four remaining *xicolli* is clearly visible.

See volume 2, folio descriptions, folio 66r, for a discussion of the *xicolli*-clad constables.

42. Mention of warrior costumes and shields constructed of feathers can be found on the following *Codex Mendoza* tribute tally folio commentaries: 18v, 19v, 21r, 22v, 24r, 25v, 26v, 27v, 28v, 29v, 30v, 31v, 32v, 33v, 35v, 36v, 38v, 39v, 40v, 42v, 44v, 45v, 48v, 49v, 50v, 51v, and 53v. See volume 4 for transcriptions and translations of the Spanish commentary. See also the folio descriptions of these pages (vol. 2) for a discussion of costumes made of both ordinary and rich feathers.

43. *Primeros Memoriales* n.d.: chap. 4, par. 8, Thelma D. Sullivan translation.

44. Fuentes 1963: 168–169. Also, Peñafiel (1977: láminas 104, 105) illustrates both the front and back side of a feathered cloak, showing how the feathers were attached.

45. Molina 1977: folio 161r "Xopilli. dedo de pie" (claw).

46. See Anawalt 1977 for a fuller account of the battle of Otumba.

47. Torquemada 1969 1: 508–510.

48. See Anawalt 1977 for a fuller description of the role of pageantry in Aztec warfare.

49. *Matrícula de Tributos* 1980: 10–11.

50. The *Matrícula de Tributos* record for the province of Yoaltepec (folio 10v) shows an unadorned warrior suit with feathered *patzactli* device accompanied by a shield with a *xicalcoliuhqui* design; for the same province, *Mendoza* (folio 40r) shows the identical suit accompanied by a shield with the *cuexyo* design. The significance of this variance is not yet understood.

51. *Matrícula de Tributos* 1980: folio 3v (*cuextecatl* gloss). Sahagún (1950–1982 10: 185) identifies *cuextecatl* as the singular form of *Cuexteca* [Huaxteca], meaning the people from the Huaxtec region. Berdan (*Matrícula de Tributos* 1980: 30, note 12) gives the meaning of the suffix -*catl* as "native of . . ."; hence *cuextecatl* refers to a costume characteristic of the people of Cuextlan (i.e., the Huaxtec region).

Because the images in *Matrícula de Tributos* do not photograph as clearly as those of *Codex Mendoza*, tracings of the analogous *Matrícula* warrior costumes have been used.

52. Broda 1978.

53. *Codex Mendoza:* folio 64r.

54. *Primeros Memoriales* n.d.: chap. 4, par. 8 "ychcavipilli." From Molina 1977: folio 32r "Ichcatl. algodon, o oueja" (cotton, or sheep); folio 157v "Vipilli. camisa de india" (blouse of Indian woman). Thus, *ichcatl* (cotton) + *huipilli* (shirt) = *ichcahuipilli* or "cotton shirt." See Anawalt 1981: 46–49 for a detailed discussion of quilted cotton armor.

55. *Codex Vaticanus A* 1979: folio 57v.

56. See Sahagún 1950–1982 8: 35 for descriptions of several *copilli*.

Seler (1960–1961 2: 435–436) considers the term *copilli* to be derived from *com(itl)* + *pilli*, or "small pot." He also mentions that Clavigero and Torquemada confuse this headgear with the *xiuhuitzolli*, or turquoise diadem, and that many Mexican scholars follow their example. Although Siméon (1963:111) erroneously follows Clavigero's definition, he nonetheless describes the Huaxtec's pointed hat correctly and clearly: *"Copilli . . . Elle était haute et pointue sur le devant; le derrière pendait sur le cou"* (it was tall and pointed on the front; the back fell on the neck).

Codex Mendoza's tribute section contains one *cuextecatl* warrior suit that has a panache of quetzal feathers rising from the top of the *copilli* headgear. This yellow costume appears on folio 50r, the tribute sent from the province of Tlapacoyan.

57. For examples of the *copilli* on ancient Huaxtec stone sculpture see Seler 1960–1961 2:175–180.

58. See appendix F, column 2, for the "starry-sky" variant and appendix G, Variant 4, for that costume's accompanying shield.

59. Seler 1960–1961 2:606–607.

60. Molina 1977: folio 30v "Yacatl. nariz, o punta de algo" (nose, or point of something); 55v "Metztli. luna, o pierna de hombre o de animal, o mes" (moon, or leg of man or animal, or month). Thus *yacatl* (nose) + *metztli* (moon [crescent]) = *yacametztli* or "nose crescent."

For information on the Huaxtec nose ornament, *yacametztli*, see volume 2, folio descriptions, folio 61r ("Image Descriptions"), note 69.

61. Sahagún 1950–1982 8:35.

62. Anawalt 1982a.

63. Ibid.

64. Molina 1977: folio 158v "Xicalli. vaso de calabaça" (gourd vessel); 24r "Coliuhqui. cosa torcida, o acostada" (twisted or leaning thing). Thus *xicalli* (gourd) + *coliuhqui* (twisted) = *xicalcoliuhqui* or "twisted gourd." This is apparently a reference to the stepped-fret design of this shield.

65. The warrior suits are represented in the *Codex Mendoza* tribute tallies in the following numbers: twenty-two *cuextecatl*, fourteen *patzactli*, thirteen *tzitzimitl*, twelve *quaxolotl*, ten *ocelotl*, seven *momoyactli*, six *coyotl*, four *xopilli*, three *papalotl*, one *tozcocolli*, and one *quetzaltototl* (in a pear tree).

66. *Matrícula de Tributos* 1980: folio 3v (*tzitzimitl* gloss).

From Molina 1977: folio 153r "Tzitzimitl. nombre de demonio" (the name of a demon [god]).

Seler (1960–1961 2:562) translates *tzitzimitl* as "Schreckgestalt," or "frightful specter." Berdan chooses to call this the "death" warrior costume (*Matrícula de Tributos* 1980:30, note 10); Anderson and Dibble translate it "demon of the air" (Sahagún 1950–1982 8:34–35). Sullivan uses the term "demon of the dark" (*Primeros Memoriales* n.d.: chap. 4, par. 8). These titles are all references to the *tzitzimime* deities' appearance in the sky during an eclipse, a dreaded omen foretelling the destruction of mankind.

67. Seler 1967:520.

68. *Primeros Memoriales* 1926: estampa XXIII.

69. *Primeros Memoriales* n.d.: chap. 4, par. 8, Thelma D. Sullivan translation.

70. See *Codex Mendoza*: folio 10v, where a red and yellow liver identical to the one on the *tzitzimitl* warrior costume appears (atop a hill) as part of the place glyph for Tanpatel.

71. In *Codex Mendoza* the *tzitzimitl* appears in white on folios 20r, 27r, and 67r, in red on folio 30r, in blue on folios 21v, 24v, 26r, 28r, 33r, and 41r, and in yellow on folios 23r, 29r, 36r, and 50r.

72. *Matrícula de Tributos* 1980: folio 3v (*ocelotl* gloss). Also, Siméon 1963: 314 "Ocelotl, Tigre; au. fig. guerrier, homme brave" (tiger; figuratively, warrior, brave man).

73. Despite its name, the *ocelotl* warrior suit does not resemble the ocelot, a medium-sized American wildcat (*Felis pardalis*) with a tawny yellow or grayish coat dotted and striped with black (*Webster's New Collegiate Dictionary* 1980:788). The Aztec *ocelotl* costume has the distinctive pattern of spots common to the jaguar (*Felis onca*), another, larger New World feline. For this reason the conventional English translation of "jaguar" is used here.

This confusion of feline names arises from the fact that *ocelotl* is a general term encompassing a variety of Mesoamerican large cats, much like the word *tigre* usually employed by Spanish chroniclers.

74. Durán 1971:187–188, 197.

75. *Matrícula de Tributos* 1980: folio 3v; *Primeros Memoriales* 1926: estampa XXIV.

76. Molina 1977: folio 80r "Patzaua. machucar, o estrujar fruta, o cosa semejante, o deshincharse el encordio, o la hinchazon" (to bruise, or to squeeze/press fruit, or something similar, or the bursting of a blister, or the swelling).

77. Sahagún 1950–1982 9: plate 82 (1979 9: folio 62r). For a written description of the construction of a *patzactli* device, see *Primeros Memoriales* n.d.: chap. 4, par. 8, Thelma D. Sullivan translation.

78. *Primeros Memoriales* 1926: estampa XXV. See appendix K for translations of *Primeros Memoriales* glosses.

79. *Matrícula de Tributos* 1980: folio 4r.

80. See Sahagún 1950–1982 11:23 for a description of the scarlet macaw.

81. *Primeros Memoriales* 1926: estampa XXII. See appendix K for translations of *Primeros Memoriales* glosses.

Sahagún (1950–1982 11:85) provides a description of the *quetzaltototl*, or quetzal bird.

82. For examples of the *quetzalpatzactli* in *Codex Mendoza* see folios 30r, 34r, 37r, 40r, 43r, 45r, 49r, 52r, 54r.

83. There is one yellow *ehuatl* tunic worn with a red *patzactli* (folio 32r).

84. *Primeros Memoriales* 1926: estampa XXV. See appendix K for translations of *Primeros Memoriales* glosses.

Sahagún (1950–1982 11:43) provides a description of the *cacalotl*, or crow, identified by Anderson and Dibble more specifically as a raven.

85. *Primeros Memoriales* 1926: estampa XXV. See appendix K for translations of *Primeros Memoriales* glosses.

From Molina 1977: folio 118r "Tlacochtli. flecha" (arrow, or dart).

86. *Primeros Memoriales* 1926: estampa XXII. See appendix K for translations of *Primeros Memoriales* glosses.

Sahagún (1950–1982 11:28) provides a description of the *aztatl*, or heron, identified by Anderson and Dibble more specifically as a snowy egret.

87. Peñafiel 1977 provides additional depictions of the *patzactli*. See *láminas* 46–48 for a statue of the deity Xipe Totec wearing what appears to be a *patzactli*. See *lámina* 77 for a painted figure wearing this insignia. Also, see *láminas* 147–148 for a nineteenth-century statue of Cuauhtemoc wearing a *patzactli* device.

88. For examples of *momoyactli* in the *Codex Mendoza* see folios 20v, 23v, 24v, 26r, 27r, 28r, 32r.

89. *Matrícula de Tributos* 1980: folio 3v.

90. Beyer 1969:413.

91. If Beyer's speculation on the evolution of back devices is correct, the increased complexity and size of the insignia may have reflected the Aztecs' successful campaigns of expansion. Control of the tropical "hot lands" resulted in increased access to costly colored feathers, the better to enhance further the most flamboyant of Aztec apparel, the warrior costumes.

92. There is one aberrant *momoyactli* depiction (see *Codex Mendoza*: folio 20v). To the device's central white section—from which the red feathers radiate—the "curls" of the *patzactli* wig insignia have been added. Perhaps the scribe confused these two styles.

93. In depicting the *momoyactli*, the scribe of the *Matrícula de Tributos* delineated each feather separately on the back device, while the *Codex Mendoza* artist blended the feathers into a more tightly packed, heavier design resembling that of the green and red *patzactli*.

94. The *momoyactli* back device from the province of Quauhnahuac (folio 23v) has a design curiously divergent from the other *momoyactli* illustrated in *Codex Mendoza*. Just below the fan of feathers appears a yellow pom-pom (possibly a huge, composite down ball) with a short fringe of decorated red feathers. In the *Matrícula de Tributos* analogue, although the yellow pom-pom also appears (fig. 56c), the fringe of feathers is missing. The only analogous *momoyactli* occurs in the ethnographic section of *Codex Mendoza*, where a priest-warrior is shown wearing a back device with a similar red pom-pom but without the fringe of feathers (folio 65r). See figure 74 and appendix F, row 2, column 7.

95. Seler 1960–1961 2:614.

96. *Matrícula de Tributos* 1980: folio 3v (*papalotl* gloss). Also, Molina 1977: folio 79v "Papalotl. mariposa" (butterfly).

97. *Primeros Memoriales* 1926: estampas XXII, XXIII, XXVI (figs. 70, 62, 64). These examples of the *papalotl* insignia are identified as "quetzal feather," "dark yellow parrot feather," "black and yellow troupial feather," "black," and "obsidian." This latter device is described as being made of sheets of beaten copper (Sullivan 1972; see also appendix K).

98. Nicholson 1971b: table 3.

99. *Matrícula de Tributos* 1980: folio 3v.

100. *Primeros Memoriales* 1926: estampas XXII, XXV.

101. Sahagún 1950–1982 8:34.

102. Ibid. 9:89.

103. There is one aberrant *quaxolotl* costume that appears on folio 30r. Across the chest of this suit is a sacrificial cut with the liver emerging. This iconography appears elsewhere only on the *tzitzimitl* warrior suits. As with the divergent *momoyactli* insignia of folio 20v (see note 92), there is the possibility that the recording Indian scribe may have become confused.

104. *Matrícula de Tributos* 1980: folio 3v.

105. The device of the Otomí warrior—like the four *xopilli* that appear in *Codex Mendoza*'s tribute section—is most probably the *matlaxopilli*, "net claw" device. This was the insignia involved in the battle of Otumba (Torquemada 1969 1:508–510). From Molina 1977: folio 102v (Spanish-Nahuatl section) "Red generalmente. matlatl" (net in general). Thus *matlatl* (net) + *xopilli* (claw device) = *matlaxopilli* or "net claw device."

106. *Primeros Memoriales* 1926: estampa XXVI (*tozcocolli* gloss). In *Primeros*

Memoriales n.d.: chap. 4, par. 8 (Thelma D. Sullivan translation), the word appears as "tozcocolli" and "tozcoloi." Here the spelling which accompanies the *tozcocolli*'s depiction will be used.

From Siméon 1963 : 658 "Toztli, Espèce de perroquet au plumage jaune" (species of parrot with yellow feathers). This was probably a reference to the feathers from which the back device was made.

107. Seler 1960–1961 2 : 587.

108. Clark (1938 1 : 78, note 2) suggests that this should be *toxicocolli*, or "winding navel-string."

109. *Codex Borbonicus* 1974 : 24.

110. Clark (1938 2 : 79, note 6) mistakenly identifies this quetzal bird as a Mexican green macaw.

111. *Primeros Memoriales* 1926: *estampa* XXIII.

112. *Codex Mendoza*: folio 47r.

113. The six costumes with undecorated, feather-covered bodysuits are the *coyotl, patzactli, quaxolotl, xopilli, tozcocolli,* and *quetzaltototl.*

114. See note 166.

115. See appendix K for Nahuatl names and English translations of all the warrior attire depicted on the *Primeros Memoriales* folios.

116. Molina 1977: folio 87v "Quauhtli. aguila" (eagle).

117. Note the four Huaxtec *yacametztli* nose ornaments that decorate this shield.

118. *Primeros Memoriales* 1926: *estampa* XXII; Sullivan 1972 : 160–161 "quetzalcuexyo chimalli." From Molina 1977: folio 89r "Quetzalli. pluma rica, larga y verde" (rich, large, and green feather [the feather of the quetzal bird]); folio 21r "Chimalli. rodela, adarga paues, o cosa semejante" (shield, round target, or similar thing). Thus *quetzal* (quetzal feather) + *cuexyo* (Huaxtec) + *chimalli* (shield) = *quetzalcuexyo chimalli* or "quetzal feather Huaxtec shield."

119. Peñafiel (1977: *lámina* 29) associates this *cuexyo* variant (appendix G, column 5, row 7) with Quetzalcoatl, because Durán (1967 1 : *lámina* 12) shows the deity carrying the shield. Note that in this depiction of Quetzalcoatl he also wears the pointed Huaxtec headpiece, the *copilli.*

120. See note 64.

121. *Primeros Memoriales* 1926: *estampa* XXII.

122. From Molina 1977: folio 87v "Quauhtli. aguila" (eagle); 107r "Tetepuntli. rodilla de la pierna, o tronco de arbol" (knee, or tree trunk).

123. *Primeros Memoriales* 1926: *estampa* XXIV.

124. *Primeros Memoriales* 1926: *estampa* XXVII. Molina 1977: folio 114v "Tlaauitectli. cosa enxaluegada assi" (thing whitewashed in this manner). Thus *tlahauitectli* (whitewashed) + *chimalli* (shield) = *tlahauitectli chimalli* or "whitewashed shield."

125. See *Codex Mendoza*: folios 64r, 65r for captives carrying *tlahauitectli chimalli.*

126. *Primeros Memoriales* 1926: *estampa* XXVII. The *tlahauitectli chimalli* is usually shown with a white center, whereas the similar, equally plain shields of *Mendoza* have yellow interiors. However, what is indicated is that some sort of plain covering was applied to the exterior surface of these reed shields; this may be to what the term "whitewashed" is referring.

Peñafiel (1977: *lámina* 15) contends any shield painted a single color was a *tlahauitectli chimalli.*

127. From Molina 1977: folio 100v "Teocuitlatl. oro o plata" (gold or silver).

128. *Primeros Memoriales* 1926: *estampa* XXII.

129. From Molina 1977: folio 44r "Ihuitl. pluma menuda" (tiny feather [down]); 107v "Tetl. piedra, generalmente" (rock, in general). In this case, *tetl* means a round thing like a rock. It has been reduplicated to form the plural. Thus, *ihuiteteyo,* or "down ball shield."

130. *Primeros Memoriales* 1926: *estampa* XXVII.

131. *Codex Mendoza*: folios 2v, 3v, 4v, 5v, 7v, 10r, 12r, 13r, 15v.

132. According to *Codex Mendoza,* four provinces—Quahuacan, Quiauhteopan, Yoaltepec, and Coayxtlahuacan—sent shields with only the *cuexyo* design, and three provinces—Tlachco, Tlalcofauhtitlan, and Tlachquiauco—sent shields with only the *xicalcoliuhqui* motif.

133. Examples of these simpler, fringeless shields can be seen on folio 64r of *Codex Mendoza* (see fig. 47), where the valiant and attendant at the top of the page, the lowest-ranking warrior, and the warrior who had captured three prisoners, as well as all the captives, lack feather fringes on their shields. Likewise, in folio 65r (see fig. 74) three priest-warriors are shown with fringeless shields, as are all their prisoners. Sahagún 1979, *Primeros Memoriales, Lienzo de Tlaxcala, Codex Telleriano-Remensis,* Durán 1967, and *Códice Xolotl* all include some fringeless shields, examples of which can be seen in appendix G.

134. *Lienzo de Tlaxcala* 1892 : 14 (twice), 15, 16, 17, 18 (twice), 19 (three times), 20, 21, 22, 26 (three times), 27, 31, 33 (twice), 34 (twice), 36, 38, 40 (twice), 45, 46 (three times), 47, 50, 74, 75 (census no. 350).

135. E.g., *Codex Telleriano-Remensis* 1964–1967: folio 37v.

136. E.g., Sahagún 1950–1982 12: plate 116 (1979 12: folio 54r).

137. *Primeros Memoriales* 1926: *estampas* VII, VIII, IX, X.

138. Ibid.: *estampas* XXII, XXIV, XXVII. See appendix K for the Nahuatl names and English translations of all these insignia.

Research funded by the John Simon Guggenheim Memorial Foundation will correlate and analyze Aztec design motifs found on wearing apparel with their Nahuatl names (Anawalt n.d.).

139. See Peñafiel 1977: *láminas* 9–12 for a Colonial depiction of an Aztec warrior wearing an *ehuatl.* See *lámina* 144 for a nineteenth-century bronze relief for another such depiction.

140. Molina 1977: folio 29v "Euatl. cuero por curtir, o mondadura y caxcara de fruta" (leather for tanning, or peel and rind of fruit).

141. Sahagún 1950–1982 10 : 95.

142. Anawalt 1981 : 50.

143. Note that rows 1 and 2 of appendix H are constructed so each *ehuatl* example of *Codex Mendoza*'s tribute section is matched with the *ehuatl* example from the corresponding folio in *Matrícula de Tributos.* The provinces of Acolhuacan (Acolman in the *Matrícula*; column 1) and Quahuacan (column 4) each show an *ehuatl* in both manuscripts. However, in *Codex Mendoza,* the *patzactli* attire paid in tribute from Quauhtitlan (column 2) is represented with a full bodysuit rather than an *ehuatl,* and the folio for Hueypochtlan (column 3) is missing the *Matrícula de Tributos*'s *ehuatl*-accompanied *patzactli* completely.

144. *Primeros Memoriales* 1926 clearly depicts the *ehuatl* as sleeveless (appendix H, row 3).

145. See the page descriptions for folios 17v–18r, volume 2, and chapter 5 by Berdan in volume 1, which deal with garrison towns.

146. See Anawalt n.d. for a more detailed analysis of the *ehuatl* warrior attire.

147. H. B. Nicholson: personal communication 1983.

148. Nicholson 1974.

149. Ibid.

150. See Anawalt 1982a for a discussion of the incorporation of foreign deities into the Aztec pantheon.

151. See *Lienzo de Tlaxcala* 1892 for the impressive range of warrior costumes that the Tlaxcalans wore into battle.

152. Seler 1960–1961 2 : 454, 497, 521, 536. From Molina 1977: folio 97v "Temimilli. coluna redonda de piedra" (round column of stone). Seler also gives the terms *ixquatzontli* (forehead hair) and *ixquatecpilli* (forehead prince) for this hairstyle. *Primeros Memoriales* n.d.: chap. 1, par. 5 (Thelma D. Sullivan translation) uses the terms *temillotl* and *ixquatzontli.*

153. Sahagún 1950–1982 8 : 77.

154. For a description of how shields were made with tightly bound reeds see Seler 1960–1961 2 : 551–552.

155. Sahagún 1950–1982 8 : 76. For more information on the *colotlalpilli* tie-dye design see Anawalt 1990.

156. The three capes mentioned as awarded to a five-captive warrior are the *chichiltic cuechintli* (bright red, rich, netting cape), the *chicoapalnacazminqui tilmatli* (the cape of two colors divided diagonally), and the *cuetlastilmatli* (leather cape). Sahagún 1950–1982 8 : 77, Anderson and Dibble translation.

157. *Primeros Memoriales* 1926: *estampas* XXII, XXIII, XXVI (figs. 70, 62, 64).

158. *Matrícula de Tributos* 1980: folios 15v, 16r "yecacozcayo." Also, Molina 1977: folio 28r "Eecatl. viento, o ayre" (wind, or air; Ehecatl was also the deity associated with the wind); folio 27v "Cuzcatl. joya, piedra preciosa labrada de forma redonda, o cuenta para rezar" (jewel, precious stone polished into round form, or beads for praying). Thus *eecatl* (wind) + *cuzcatl* (jewel or ornament) = *yecacozcayo,* or "jewel of Ehecatl," sometimes referred to as the "wind ornament design."

159. *Matrícula de Tributos* 1980: folio 3v; passim.

160. Sahagún 1950–1982 8 : 77.

161. See volume 2, "Image Descriptions," folio 64r for a discussion of the desirability of captives from Atlixco, Huexotzinco, and Tliliuquitepec.

162. Durán 1971 : 198. From Molina 1977: folio 84r "Quachichictli. corona de clerigo" (crown of the head of a priest). Stevens (1726) defines "corona de religioso" as "the crown that is shaved on a religious man's head." This Nahuatl term no doubt refers to the shaved hairstyles of the Quachic warriors.

163. Durán 1971 : 198.

164. Sahagún 1950–1982 10 : 23.

165. Seler 1960–1961 2 : 571.

166. Siméon 1963 : 330 "Pamitl, Drapeau, étendard, bannière" (flag, standard, banner). Also, ibid.: 332 "Pantli, Drapeau, bannière, mur, ligne, rangée" (flag, banner, wall, line, rank [of soldiers]).

167. For more detailed information on the Tlacatecatl, see page descriptions for folios 64r and 67r, volume 2; see also appendix E.

168. Seler 1960–1961 2:614.

169. Ibid.:609.

170. Nicholson 1967:74–75.

171. Note that three of these four mighty warriors wear undecorated bodysuits that differ only in color.

172. *Tlacochcalcatl:* Durán 1964:72, also in Durán 1967 2:103. From Molina 1977: folio 118r "Tlacochtli. flecha" (arrow); 11v "Calli. casa . . ." (house). Thus *tlacochtli* (dart) + *calli* (house) + *catl* (signifying affiliation) = *tlacochcalcatl,* or "Keeper of the House of Darts."

Sahagún (1950–1982 10:24) uses the less literal and far more succinct translation "General."

For more information on the stem *(ca)-tl signifying national, tribal or civic affiliation, see Andrews 1975:332–333.

173. Seler 1960–1961 2:566.

174. *Huiznahuatl:* Molina 1977: folio 157v "Vitzli. espina grande, o puya" (large spine, or point); folio 63v "Nauatl. cosa que suena bien, assi como campana &c. o hombre ladino" (thing which sounds well, like a bell etc. or "a stranger that speaks Spanish perfectly well" [from Stevens 1726]).

Also, Seler 1967:532 "Uitznaua 'die an den Dornen,' die Götter des Südens, feindliche Brüder Uitzilopochtli's . . ." ("they of the thorns," the gods of the South, fiendish brothers of Uitzilopochtli).

Siméon 1963:688 "Uitznauatl, Dieu des esclaves detinés à mourir" (god of slaves destined to die).

For more information on the *Huiznahuatl* warrior see page descriptions for folio 66r in volume 2.

175. *Ticocyahuacatl:* From Molina 1977: folio 93r "Tecomatl. vaso de barro, como taça honda" (vessel of clay, like deep cup [to drink out of]); 22r "Ciaui. cansarse" (to be fatigued). Thus *tecomatl* (drinking vessel) + *ciaui* (to be fatigued) + *catl* (signifying affiliation) = *ticocyahuacatl,* or "Keeper of the Bowl of Fatigue."

Clark (1938 3: folio 65r overleaf, note 15) suggests that *Ticocyahuacatl* is derived from *teço,* "blood-letter," and *ciaua,* "he is imbrued." This translation seems unlikely; it is not supported by the glyph. Also, while *i's* and *e's* are often exchanged in Nahuatl spelling, a cedilla would not be dropped (and the *Codex Mendoza* scribe was consistent on this point), because the word would then necessarily be pronounced very differently. As a result, *Teço* is an unlikely prefix.

176. Seler 1960–1961 2:571.

177. See appendix F, row 2, column 2 for the *cicitlallo cuextecatl;* column 13 for an example of a *pamitl* device; appendix G, row 2, columns 5, 9, 10, 11, 12 for the shield designs not in the tribute tallies.

178. Fuentes 1963:169.

179. Seler 1960–1961 2:514. Also, Molina 1977: folio 99v "Tentli. los labrios, o el borde, o orilla de alguna cosa" (lips, or border, or edge of something); 48v "Ixtli. la haz o la cara" (face; also used to mean eye). Thus *tentli* (edge) + *ixtli* (eye) = *tenixyo* or "eyes on the edge" design.

180. See note 172.

181. *Matrícula de Tributos* 1980: folio 16r. A gloss provides the name for this design (*yecacozcayo*).

182. *Tocuiltecatl:* From Molina 1977: folio 148v "Toctli. porreta o mata de mayz, antes q̄espigue" (young leek or bush/shrub of maize, before growing ears); 76r "Ocuilin. gusano, generalmente, o ceuo para pescar" (worm, in general, or bait for fishing). Thus *toctli* (blade of maize) + *oculin* (worm) + *tecatl* (signifying affiliation) = *tocuiltecatl* or "lord of the worm on blade of maize."

183. Seler 1960–1961 2:974.

184. See Sahagún 1950–1982 2:50–53, 190 for a description of the "gladiatorial sacrifice" and the part played by the *temalacatl.*

185. See note 175.

186. Sahagún 1950–1982 8:23. Molina 1977: folio 76r "Ome. dos" (two); 148r "Tochtli. conejo" (rabbit); 93r "Tecomatl. vaso de barro, como taça honda" (vessel of clay, like deep drinking bowl). Thus *ome* (two) + *tochtli* (rabbit) = Ometochtli, or "Two-Rabbit," one of the *pulque* deities, + *tecomatl* (*pulque* vessel) = *ometochtecomayo,* "Two-Rabbit *pulque* vessel," or, more simply, the *pulque* jug design.

Two-Rabbit is also a calendrical name.

187. Sahagún 1950–1982 10:193. See page descriptions for folio 61 in volume 2 for more details on the Gulf coast *pulque* cult.

188. This same bound resist pattern is known in Japan as *yokobiki kanoko,* "square ring dot" (Wada, Rice, and Barton 1983:62).

189. Note that both this textile and the red/tie-dye design are divided vertically rather than diagonally. To date, the meaning of these contrasting ways of dividing the two fields is not known.

190. See Anawalt 1990 for a fuller description of the Aztec emperors' blue tie-dye cloak.

191. Sahagún 1950–1982 8:23 gives us the name *ocelotilmatli; Codex Magliabechiano* 1970: folio 6r depicts the design of the jaguar design cape.

192. Sahagún 1950–1982 8:23.

193. Seler 1960–1961 2:522.

194. *Matrícula de Tributos* 1980: folio 3v.

195. Sahagún 1950–1982 8:25.

196. Ibid. 9:8.

197. Ibid.

198. Ibid. 8:23.

199. *Matrícula de Tributos* 1980: folio 7v "ixnextlacuillolli." Molina 1977: folio 48v "Ixtli. la haz o la cara, o el ñudo de la caña" (surface or face, or knot of cane); 71v "Nextli. ceniza" (ashes); 120r "Tlacuilolli. escriptura, o pintura" (manuscript, or painting). Thus *ixtli* (face) + *nextli* (ash [the blacking agent of scribes' inks]) + *tlacuilolli* (painting) = *ixnextlacuilolli* or "painting in ink on the face [of the cloth]," or simply "painted textile."

200. See Anawalt and Berdan field notes, 1983, 1985, 1988, 1989, for "Cloth, Clothing, and Acculturation: Textile Traditions of Middle America," research funded by the National Geographic Society.

201. Sahagún 1950–1982 8:23.

202. *Codex Magliabechiano* 1970: folio 3v.

203. Nicholson 1983:95.

204. Sahagún 1950–1982 8:23.

205. Nicholson 1971b: table 3.

206. Sahagún 1950–1982 8:23.

207. Seler 1900–1901 (*Tonalamatl Aubin,* census no. 15).

208. Codex Borgia 1976 (census no. 33).

209. Sixty examples of clothing decorated with the *tenixyo* border can be found in the ritual sections of the following codices:

  8 - *Codex Borbonicus* 1974:3, 6, 26 (twice), 27, 28, 31 (twice)

  1 - Durán 1967 1: *lámina* 8

  3 - *Codex Ixtlilxochitl* 1976: folios 97r, 98r, 99r

  10 - *Codex Magliabechiano* 1970: folios 35r (twice), 37r, 39r, 63r, 71r (three times), 89r, 92r

  5 - *Primeros Memoriales* 1926: *estampas* V, VII (twice), X (twice)

  5 - *Codex Telleriano-Remensis* 1964–1967: folios 1v, 5r, 6v, 22r, 24r

  6 - *Codex Vaticanus A* 1979: folios 31v, 35r, 37r, 46r, 49v, 51r

  1 - Seler 1900–1901:10 (*Tonalamatl Aubin*)

  8 - Sahagún 1950–1982 1: plates 2, 15, 19, 32, 38, 39 (twice), 41; 1979 1: folios 10r, 11v, 12r, 22v, 34v, 38r (twice), 39v (*Florentine Codex*)

  6 - Sahagún 1950–1982 2: plates 13, 21, 27, 28 (twice), 38; 1979 2: folios 28r, 32r, 58v (three times), 103r (*Florentine Codex*)

  7 - *Codex Borgia* 1976:7, 9, 17, 21, 42, 50, 60

210. The *tenixyo* border appears on male garments worn in association with the annual veintena ceremony Hueytecuilhuitl in *Codex Borbonicus* (1974: 27), *Codex Telleriano-Remensis* (1964–1967: folio 1v), *Codex Vaticanus A* (1979: folio 46r), and *Florentine Codex* (Sahagún 1950–1982 2: plates 27, 28 twice [1979: folio 58v]).

211. *Codex Magliabechiano* 1970: folios 89r, 92r.

212. In *Codex Borgia* 1976, the black Tezcatlipoca wears a hip-cloth with a *tenixyo* border three times: pages 17, 21, 42.

213. There are four depictions of women wearing *huipilli* decorated with the *tenixyo* border in the *Florentine Codex* (Sahagún 1950–1982 1: plate 39; 2: plates 13, 38; 10: plate 139 [1979 1: folio 38r; 2: folios 28r, 103r; 10: folio 65v]).

214. *Primeros Memoriales* 1926: *estampa* VII (Yacatecutli and Paynal), X (Omacatl and Tlacochcalco Yautl). Nicholson (personal communication 1984) points out that these four deities all have associations with Tezcatlipoca.

215. See Anawalt 1980 for information on the Aztec sumptuary laws.

216. Sahagún 1950–1982 9:7–8.

217. Ibid. 8:23–25.

218. For a more detailed analysis of the *tenixyo* border see Anawalt n.d.

219. See Offner 1981, Carrasco 1978, and Brumfiel 1980 as examples of the two sides of this controversy, and see Berdan 1983 and Berdan et al. n.d. for a compromise model.

220. Anawalt 1976.

221. I am indebted to Diana Fane, Curator, Department of African, Oceanic, and New World Cultures, The Brooklyn Museum, for calling my attention to the semantic function of Aztec pictorial writing.

222. Joaquín Galarza (1988) and Marc Thouvenot (1980, 1982), among others, are working on "reading" the Colonial manuscripts, maintaining that despite a European overlay, the pre-Hispanic notation system survived many decades following Conquest.

223. *Codex Fejérváry-Mayer* 1971 (census no. 118).

224. *Codex Laud* 1966 (census no. 185).

225. *Codex Zouche-Nuttall* 1987 (1975: census no. 240).

PART II

Appendices

APPENDIX A: The Founding of Tenochtitlan and the Reign Dates of the Mexica Rulers According to Thirty-Nine Central Mexican Sources, by Elizabeth Hill Boone

		Acamapichtli			Huitzilihuitl			Chimalpopoca			Itzcoatl		
Source	Founding	seat	length	death	seat	length	death	seat	length	death	seat	length	death
Codex Mendoza paintings	2 House (1325)	1 Flint (1376)	21	8 flint (1396)	9 House (1397)	21	3 House (1417)	4 Rabbit (1418)	10	13 Reed (1427)	1 Flint (1428)	13	13 Flint (1440)
Codex Aubin	2 Flint (1364)	1 Flint (1376)	20	7 Reed (1395)	8 Flint (1396)	(21)	2 Flint (1416)	3 House (1417)	(8)	10 Flint (1424)	11 House (1425)	(13)	10 House (1437)
Codex Aubin king list		40			22			12			13		
Codex Mexicanus	2 House (1325)	1 Flint (1376)	(20)	8 Flint (1396)	8 Flint (1396)	(21)	3 House (1417)	3 House (1417)	(11)	1 Flint (1428)	1 Flint (1428)	(13)	1 House (1441)
Tira de Tepechpan	c. 4 Rabbit (c. 1366)	1 Flint 1376	(20)	8 Flint 1396	8 Flint 1396	(21)	3 House 1417	3 House 1417	(9)	12 Rabbit 1426	1 Flint 1428	(12)	13 Flint 1440
Codex en Cruz				2 Reed (1403)	3 Flint (1404)	(10)	13 Rabbit (1414)	13 Rabbit (1414)	(13)		13 Reed (1427)	(13)	13 Flint 1440
C. Telleriano-Rem.				5 Rabbit 1406	5 Rabbit 1406	(8)	13 Rabbit 1414	13 Rabbit 1414	(12)	12 Rabbit 1426	12 Rabbit 1426	(14)	13 Flint 1440
C. Vaticanus A				5 Rabbit (1406)						12 Rabbit (1426)	12 Rabbit (1426)		
Anales de Tula		4 Rabbit 1366	(38)	3 Flint 1404	3 Flint 1404	(13)	3 House 1417	3 House 1417	(10)	13 Reed 1427	13 Reed 1427	(13)	13 Flint 1440
C. Magdalena Mixiuca				8 Flint 1396	9 House 1397								13 Flint 1440
Aubin-Goupil 40	2 Flint (1364)	1 Flint (1376)	(21)	8 Flint (1396)	9 House (1397)	(21)	3 House (1417)	4 Rabbit (1418)	(9)	12 Rabbit (1426)	13 Reed (1427)	(14)	13 Flint (1440)
Aubin-Goupil 85		1 Flint 1376		10 Rabbit (1398)	11 Reed (1399)								
Aubin-Goupil 217					3 House (1417)			3 House (1417)	(10)	13 Reed (1427)	13 Reed (1427)	(14)	13 Flint (1440)
Codex Saville							8 Rabbit (1422)	8 Rabbit (1422)	(10)	5 Flint (1432)	5 Flint (1432)	(13)	5 House (1445)
Codex Huichapan		2 Reed 1403	(14, 21)	1417 & 1424				1417 & 1424	(9, 2)	1426	1427	(13, 22)	1440 & 1449
Hist. de los Mexicanos	(1322)	53 (1375)	(20)	73 (1395)	73 (1395)	(21)	94 (1416)	94 (1416)	(11)	c. 105 (1427)	c. 105 (1427)	(13)	118 (1440)
Lista de los Reyes (*Anales Tlatelolco 2*)		1 Flint (1376)	21 (20)		8 Flint (1396)	22 (21)		3 House (1417)	11		1 Flint (1428)	13 (12)	
Hist. de Tlatelolco (*Anales Tlatelolco 5*)	2 House (1325)	5 Reed (1367)	21	12 Reed (1387)	3 Reed (1391)	22	11 Flint (1410)	1 Reed (1415)	(12)	12 Rabbit (1426)	13 Reed (1427)	13	12 Reed (1439)
A. de Tecamachalco													
Anales Tepanecas									12	12 Rabbit 1426	13 Reed 1427	14 (13)	13 Flint 1440
Anales Cuauhtitlan I	8 Rabbit (1318?)	1 Rabbit (1350)	(54)	3 Flint (1404)	3 Flint (1404)	(13)	3 House (1417)	3 House (1417)	(11)	1 Flint (1428)	1 Flint (1428)	(12)	13 Flint (1440)
A. Cuauhtitlan king list	2 House	1 Flint	54		9 House	10		4 Rabbit	13			12	
Leyenda de los Soles	2 House (1325)	1 Flint (1376)	21		9 House (1397)	21		4 Rabbit (1418)	10		1 Flint (1428)	13	
Chimalpahin Rel. 3	2 House (1325)	7 House (1369)	21 (20)	1 House (1389)		(26)	4 Rabbit (1418)	4 Rabbit (1418)	10 (9)	13 Reed (1427)	13 Reed (1427)	14	1 House (1441)
Chimalpahin Rel. 7	2 House (1325)	5 Reed (1367)	21	12 Reed (1387)	3 Reed (1391)	25 (24)	1 Reed (1415)	1 Reed (1415)	12	12 Rabbit (1426)	13 Reed (1427)	14 (13)	13 Flint (1440)
Chimalpahin Hist.	1325	5 Reed (1367)	21	12 Reed (1387)	3 Reed (1391)	25 (24)	1 Reed (1415)	1 Reed (1415)	12	12 Rabbit (1426)	13 Reed (1427)	14 (13)	13 Flint (1440)
Chimalpahin Compend.		7 House (1369)	(24)		5 House (1393)	(25)		4 Rabbit (1418)	(10)		1 Flint (1428)	(13)	
Crónica mexicayotl	2 House (1325)	5 Reed (1367)			3 Reed (1391)	25 (24)	1 Reed (1415)	1 Reed (1415)	12	12 Rabbit (1426)	13 Reed (1427)	14 (13)	13 Flint (1440)
Sahagún, Bk. 8			21			21			10			14	
Mendieta	1324	1375	(21)	(1396)	1396	(21)	1417	1417	10	(1427)	1427	13	(1440)
Durán, *Historia*		(1364)	40	1404	1404	13					1424	14	1440
Tovar, JCBL & C. Ramírez		1318	40		1404/1359	13					1404/1424	12	
Acosta		40			13						12		
Torquemada		21			(3 Reed)	22			13				
Alva Ixtlilxochitl		1 Flint (1220)	51	13 Reed (1271)	13 Reed (1271)	86	8 House (1357)	8 House (1357)	72	13 Reed (1427)	13 Reed (1427)	14	1 House (1441)
Relación de los Señores		19.5			21			10			11		
Pablo Nazareo		21/19.5			22/21			10/11			13/11		
Juan Cano *Relación*		46?			33?			21?			13		
Juan Cano *Origen*		46?			33?			21			13		

Motecuhzoma I			Axayacatl			Tizoc			Ahuitzotl			Motecuhzoma II			Source
seat	length	death	seat	length	death	seat	length	death	seat	length	death	seat	length	death	
1 House (1441)	29	3 House (1469)	4 Rabbit (1470)	12	2 House (1481)	3 Rabbit (1482)	5	7 Rabbit (1486)	8 Reed (1487)	16	10 Rabbit (1502)	11 Reed (1503)	18	2 Flint (1520)	C. Mendoza
11 Rabbit (1438)	(33)	5 Reed (1471)	5 Reed (1471)	(9)		1 Flint (1480)	(4)		5 Flint (1484)	(18)	9 House (1501)	10 Rabbit (1502)	(18)	1 Reed (1519)	C. Aubin
	29			14			4			17			19		C. Aubin list
1 House (1441)	(29)	4 Rabbit (1470)	4 Rabbit (1470)	(13)	4 Reed (1483)	4 Reed (1483)	(3)	7 Rabbit (1486)	7 Rabbit (1486)	(16)	10 Rabbit (1502)	10 Rabbit (1502)	(19)		C. Mexicanus
13 Flint 1440	(28)	2 Flint 1468	2 Flint 1468	(13)	2 House 1481	2 House 1481	(4)	6 House 1485	6 House 1485	(17)	10 Rabbit 1502	10 Rabbit 1502	(19)	2 Flint 1520	T. Tepechpan
13 Flint 1440	(28)	2 Flint (1468)	2 Flint (1468)	(13)	2 House (1481)	2 House (1481)	(5)	7 Rabbit (1486)	7 Rabbit (1486)	(16)	10 Rabbit (1502)	10 Rabbit (1502)	(19)	2 Flint (1520)	C. en Cruz
13 Flint 1440	(29)	3 House 1469	3 House 1469	(14)	4 Reed 1483	4 Reed 1483	(3)	7 Rabbit 1486	7 Rabbit 1486	(16)	10 Rabbit 1502	10 Rabbit 1502			C. Tell.-Rem.
					4 Reed (1483)	4 Reed (1483)					10 Rabbit (1502)	10 Rabbit (1502)			C. Vat. A
13 Flint 1440	(29)	3 House 1469	3 House 1469	(12)	2 House 1481	2 House 1481	(5)	7 Rabbit 1486	7 Rabbit 1486	(17)	11 Reed 1503	11 Reed 1503	(18)	2 Flint 1520	A. de Tula
1 House 1441					2 House 1481	3 Rabbit 1482					10 Rabbit 1502	11 Reed 1503			C. Magdalena M.
1 House (1441)	(27)	1 Reed (1467)	2 Flint (1468)	(13)	1 Flint (1480)	3 Rabbit* (1482)	(4)	6 House (1485)	7 Rabbit (1486)	(17)	10 Rabbit (1502)	11 Reed (1503)	(17)	1 Reed (1519)	A-Goupil 40
															A-Goupil 85
1 House (1441)	(28)	2 Flint (1468)	3 House (1469)	(13)	2 House (1481)	3 Rabbit (1482)	(4)	7 Rabbit (1486)	7 Rabbit (1486)	(16)	10 Rabbit (1502)	10 Rabbit (1502)	(19)	2 Flint (1520)	A-Goupil 217
5 House (1445)	(22)	1 Reed (1467)	1 Reed (1467)	(14)	2 House (1481)	2 House (1481)	(5)	7 Rabbit (1486)	7 Rabbit (1486)	(16)	10 Rabbit (1502)	10 Rabbit (1502)			C. Saville
1441	(27, 28)	1468 & 1469	1469	(12)	1481	1481	(5)	1486	1486	(16, 17)	1502 & 1503	1502 & 1503			C. Huichapan
118 (144)	(29)	147 (1469)	147 (1469)	(12)	159 (1481)	159 (1481)	(5)	164 (1486)	164 (1486)	(16)	180 (1502)	180 (1502)	(18)	198 (1520)	Hist. Mex.
13 Flint (1440)	27 (28)		2 Flint (1468)	13		2 House (1481)	5		1 Reed (8 Reed)	18		10 Rabbit (1502)	18		Lista de Reyes
13 Flint (1440)	29	2 Flint (1468)	3 House (1469)	13	2 House (1481)	3 Rabbit (1482)	4	6 House (1485)	7 Rabbit (1486)	17	10 Rabbit (1502)			2 Flint (1520)	Hist. Tlatelolco
		2 Flint (1468)													A. Tecamachalco
13 Flint (1440)	29	2 Flint (1468)	3 House (1469)	(12)	2 House (1481)	2 House (1481)	6	7 Rabbit (1486)	7 Rabbit (1486)	17	10 Rabbit (1502)	10 Rabbit (1502)	(18)	2 Flint (1520)	A. Tepanecas
13 Flint (1440)	29	2 Flint (1468)	3 House (1469)	(12)	2 House (1481)	2 House (1481)	(5)	7 Rabbit (1486)	7 Rabbit (1486)	(17)	11 Reed (1503)	11 Reed (1503)			A. Cuauhtitlan
	29			9			5			14			18.5		Cuauhtitlan list
1 House (1441)	29		4 Rabbit (1470)	12											Leyenda Soles
1 House (1441)	29 (28)	3 House (1469)	3 House (1469)	12	2 House (1481)	2 House (1481)	(5)	7 Rabbit (1486)	7 Rabbit (1486)	(17)	11 Reed (1503)	11 Reed (1503)			Chimalpahin 3
13 Flint (1440)	29	2 Flint (1468)	3 House (1469)	13 (12)	2 House (1481)	2 House (1481)	6 (5)	7 Rabbit (1486)	7 Rabbit (1486)	17 (16)	10 Rabbit (1502)	10 Rabbit (1502)	(18)	2 Flint (1520)	Chimalpahin 7
13 Flint (1440)	29	2 Flint (1468)	3 House (1469)	13 (12)	2 House (1481)	2 House (1481)	5	7 Rabbit (1486)	7 Rabbit (1486)	17 (16)	10 Rabbit (1502)	10 Rabbit (1502)	19 (18)	2 Flint (1520)	Chimalpahin Hist.
1 House (1441)	(28)		3 House (1469)	(12)	2 House (1481)	2 House (1481)	(5)		7 Rabbit (1486)	(16)	10 Rabbit (1502)	10 Rabbit (1502)	(18)	2 Flint (1520)	Chimalpahin Comp.
13 Flint (1440)	29	2 Flint (1468)	3 House (1469)	13	2 House (1481)	2 House (1481)	6	7 Rabbit (1486)	7 Rabbit (1486)	(16)	10 Rabbit (1502)	10 Rabbit (1502)	19	2 Flint (1520)	Cr. mexicayotl
	30			14			4			18			19		Sahagún
1440	(29)	(1469)	1469	12	(1482)	1482	(4)	(1486)	(1486)	16	(1502)	1502	18	(1520)	Mendieta
	30	1469	(1469)	13	1481	(1481)	4/5	1486	(1486)			1503	16.5	1519	Durán
	28			11			4			15			15		Tovar
	28			11			4			11					Acosta
(13 Flint)	29														Torquemada
1 House (1441)	27+	2 Flint (1468)	2 Flint (1468)	12	2 House (1481)	2 House (1481)	4.5	6 House (1485)	6 House (1485)	19.4	13 House (1505)	13 House (1505)	16.5	3 House (1521)	Alva Ixtlilxochitl
	29			12			4			15			17		Relación de los Señores
	28/29			15			4/5			16			17/18		Pablo Nazareo
	29			12			4			17			(18)		J. Cano Relación
	29			12			4			17			(18)		J. Cano Origen

*The seating of Tizoc is drawn beside 2 House, but a line reassigns it to 3 Rabbit.

APPENDIX B: Annual Tribute in *Codex Mendoza* Part 2

Tribute	Period(s) of Delivery [a]	Annual Quantity	Folios
MANTAS (*TILMATLI*)[b]		Total: 128,000[c]	
White, cotton[d]	quarterly, semi-annual	53,600[e]	19r, 20r, 21v, 23r, 24v, 26r, 27r, 28r, 37r, 38r, 39r, 40r, 41r, 44r, 45r, 48r, 49r, 50r, 52r, 53r, 54r, 55r
White, maguey fiber	semi-annual	9,600	29r, 30r, 32r, 33r, 34r
White, yucca fiber	semi-annual	4,800	35r
White, with border	semi-annual	5,600	20r, 24v, 26r, 27r, 28r, 49r, 54r
White, with border (maguey)	semi-annual	1,600	29r, 33r
Red, with border	semi-annual	1,600	21v, 23r
Diagonally divided[f]	semi-annual	11,200	20r, 21v, 23r, 26r, 27r, 28r, 29r, 30r, 31r, 32r, 37r
Quilted[g]	semi-annual	5,600	21v, 23r, 27r, 37r, 43r, 44r, 49r
Striped	semi-annual	18,400	37r, 38r, 39r, 43r, 46r, 49r, 50r, 51r, 52r, 55r
Richly decorated, cotton	semi-annual	8,000	34r, 36r, 46r, 49r, 52r, 53r
Decorated, maguey	semi-annual	3,200	33r, 34r, 35r
Miscellaneous designs	semi-annual	4,800	31r, 43r, 52r
LOINCLOTHS (*MAXTLATL*)	semi-annual	7,200	20r, 21v, 23r, 24v, 43r, 52r, 53r, 54r
WOMEN'S TUNICS (*HUIPILLI*) AND SKIRTS (*CUEITL*)[h]	semi-annual	10,400	20r, 21v, 23r, 24v, 27r, 35r, 37r, 39r, 43r, 46r, 49r, 52r, 54r
WOMEN'S TUNICS/SKIRTS	semi-annual	800	31r
WOMEN'S SKIRTS	semi-annual	800	31r
WARRIOR COSTUMES AND SHIELDS[i]		Total: 665	
Cuextecatl	annual	252	19r, 20r, 22r, 23r, 25r, 27r, 28r, 29r, 30r, 31r, 32r, 33r, 34r, 35r, 37r, 39r, 40r, 43r, 50r, 51r
Quaxolotl	annual	12	20r, 21v, 23r, 24v, 26r, 28r, 29r, 30r, 33r, 40r, 49r, 52r
Momoyactli	annual	80	24v, 26r, 28r, 32r
Patzactli[j]	annual	150	20v, 22r, 23v, 24v, 26r, 27r, 28r, 30r, 32r, 34r, 37r, 40r, 43r, 45r, 49r, 52r, 54r
Tzitzimitl (Death)	annual	13	20r, 21v, 23r, 24v, 26r, 27r, 28r, 29r, 30r, 33r, 35r, 41r, 50r
Ocelotl	annual	28	20r, 21v, 23v, 25r, 29r, 31r, 37r, 51r, 54r
Coyotl	annual	64	21v, 23r, 25r, 26r, 27r, 29r, 39r
Xopilli	annual	23	20r, 22r, 23v, 25r
Papalotl (Butterfly)	annual	41	20r, 22r, 23v
Tozcocolli	annual	1	43r
Quetzaltototl	annual	1	46r
STAPLE FOODSTUFFS, bins[k]			
Maize	annual	28	20r, 22r, 23v, 25r, 26r, 27r, 28r, 29r, 30r, 31r, 32r, 33r, 34r, 35r, 36r, 37r, 41r, 42r, 44r
Beans	annual	21	20r, 22r, 23v, 25r, 26r, 27r, 28r, 29r, 30r, 31r, 32r, 33r, 34r, 35r, 37r, 41r, 42r, 44r
Chia	annual	21	20r, 22r, 23v, 25r, 26r, 27r, 28r, 29r, 30r, 31r, 32r, 33r, 34r, 35r, 36r, 37r, 41r, 44r
Amaranth	annual	18	20r, 22r, 23v, 25r, 26r, 27r, 28r, 29r, 30r, 31r, 32r, 33r, 34r, 35r, 37r, 41r
MISCELLANEOUS ITEMS			
Chile, loads	annual	1,600	52r, 54r, 55r
Honey, pots or jars			
maguey honey	semi-annual	1,600	27r, 29r
bees' honey	quarterly, semi-annual	2,200	36r, 37r, 40r
Salt, "loaves"	semi-annual	4,000	34r
Pinolli, baskets	quarterly	160	19r

Tribute	Period(s) of Delivery [a]	Annual Quantity	Folios
Cacao, loads	semi-annual, annual	680	38r, 46r, 47r, 48r, 49r
Cacao, ground, in baskets	quarterly	160	19r
Cotton, loads	semi-annual, annual	4,400	38r, 48r, 53r, 54r
Lime, loads	quarterly, semi-annual	16,800	28r, 42r
Cochineal, bags	annual	65	43r, 44r, 45r
Beams, large wooden	quarterly	4,800	32r
Planks, broad wooden	quarterly	4,800	32r
Planks, narrow wooden	quarterly	4,800 [l]	32r
Carrying frames	quarterly	800 [m]	42r
Firewood, loads	quarterly	4,800	32r
Mats, reed	semi-annual	8,000	26r
Seats, reed	semi-annual	8,000	26r
Paper [n]	semi-annual	32,000	23v, 25r
Canes	quarterly	16,000	42r
Canes for spears	quarterly	32,000	42r
Smoking canes	quarterly	32,000	42r
Gourd bowls (xicalli)	quarterly, semi-annual	17,600	23v, 25r, 36r, 37r
Pottery bowls (tecomatl)	semi-annual, annual	2,400	39r, 47r
Rubber, balls	annual	16,000	46r
Copal, unrefined balls	quarterly	64,000	36r, 37r
Copal, baskets of white incense	quarterly	3,200	36r, 37r
Yellow ocher, pans	semi-annual	40	40r
Seashells	semi-annual	1,600	38r
Live eagles	annual	2 or more	31r, 55r
Enemy warriors	unspecified	unspecified	42r
Deerskins	quarterly	3,200	42r
Liquidambar, jars	annual	100	46r
Liquidambar, cakes	semi-annual	16,000	51r
Jaguar skins	semi-annual	40	47r
Lip plugs	semi-annual, annual	82	46r, 47r, 49r
Amber	annual	2	47r
Turquoise			
beads, strung	annual	1	52r
disks	annual	2	52r
stones, bowl of	annual	1	40r
stones, packet of	annual	1	40r
masks	annual	10	40r
Jade			
beads, strung [o]	semi-annual, annual	19	37r, 43r, 46r, 47r, 49r, 52r
stones	annual	3	46r
Copper			
bells	semi-annual	80	40r
axes	quarterly, semi-annual	560	37r, 40r
Gold			
dust, in bowls	annual	60	39r, 43r, 45r
bars or tablets	annual	10	39r
disks [p]	annual	60	40r, 44r
beads, strung	annual	1	46r
beads with bells, strung	annual	1	46r
diadem	annual	1	46r
headband	annual	1	46r
shield	annual	1	46r

Tribute	Period(s) of Delivery [a]	Annual Quantity	Folios
Feathers [q]			
quetzal	semi-annual, annual	2,480	43r, 45r, 46r, 47r, 49r
blue feathers	semi-annual, annual	8,800	46r, 47r
red feathers	semi-annual, annual	8,800	46r, 47r
green feathers	semi-annual, annual	8,800	46r, 47r
yellow feathers	semi-annual	800	47r
"bunches" of rich green and yellow feathers	annual	4	46r
feathered headpieces	annual	2	43r, 49r
back device of yellow feathers	annual	1	46r
feather down, bags	annual	20	52r
bird skins	semi-annual	160	47r

a. In the vast majority of cases, information on periods of tribute delivery is contained only in the annotations and commentary.

b. The great variety of *mantas* displayed in this part of the codex are reduced, in this table, to just a few manageable categories. There is considerable variation within each category, and for these details, the reader is referred to the facsimile and to chapter 8 by Anawalt.

c. If these were bundles of twenty, rather than individual *mantas*, the total would climb to 2,560,000. Overall, I prefer the total of 255,360, utilizing the "single *manta*" figure but applying quarterly payments, as indicated in the *Matrícula de Tributos*.

d. Even with the plain white cotton *mantas*, there was some variation: some are annotated as large, some as small; in the *Matrícula de Tributos*, some of these are also glossed as narrow or fine.

e. On folio 55r, the white *mantas* display no number symbol for 20 (they do, however, each have two finger glyphs, indicating extra length). In my calculations, I am assuming that the artist, in haste, simply failed to include the customary number sign for 400. A number of *mantas* in this tribute section were oversized: there were 6,800 of two *brazas* in length, 5,200 of four *brazas*, and 1,600 of eight *brazas*.

f. These *mantas* often contain other important elements, such as borders, coloring, or tie-dyed segments. I have chosen to subsume all these variations under the category "diagonally divided," since this seems to have had special diagnostic value to the Aztecs: these *mantas* are consistently described as *nacazminqui* (diagonally divided) in the *Matrícula de Tributos*. I have also, quite arbitrarily, included two *manta* styles that are divided vertically rather than diagonally (folios 27r and 28r). Unfortunately for comparative purposes, these same folios are missing from the *Matrícula de Tributos*.

g. All the *mantas* in this category are black and white. The Spanish annotations, and the corresponding Nahuatl glosses in the *Matrícula de Tributos*, describe these as "quilted." There remains a remote possibility that they may

have been tie-dyed (see especially folio 44r). See chapter 8 by Anawalt in this volume for a discussion of tie-dying and quilting. One of the examples included here is only *half*-decorated or quilted (folio 49r).

h. The glyphs and annotations indicate tunics and the skirts accompanying them. I have separated out the one case where tunics and skirts are pictured side by side.

i. The quantities given conform to those indicated for the warrior costumes. On occasion, the number symbols are omitted from the accompanying shields.

j. Two of the warrior costumes worn with this back device are *ehuatl*.

k. In quantities and types of foodstuff, I am following the annotations included on the illustrated bins.

l. The quantity is not specified on the document; I am "assigning" these planks the same quantities as the other planks and beams associated with it— in the name of consistency.

m. The number glyph is not included with the illustration of the carrying frame. The annotation indicates "200."

n. The unit in the codex is "pliego," a "sheet of paper," according to Stevens (1726). As this term also means "a fold in a garment," these may have been screenfold sheets.

o. These strings of beads appear to be of various sizes.

p. These gold disks are of varying sizes.

q. As with "cargas of *mantas*," there is some debate whether individual feathers are meant, or bunches of feathers. I prefer to think of these as individual feathers, with the exception of the green and yellow feather combination, which appears to be of some special workmanship.

Tribute Totals in the *Codex Mendoza,*
Matrícula de Tributos,
and *Información* of 1554

The *Codex Mendoza, Matrícula de Tributos,* and *Información* of 1554 all provide roughly comparable material on empire-wide tribute assessments. Individual assessment totals and calculated annual totals are tabulated in this appendix. The common eighty-day assessment period is considered to involve four payments annually.

The *Matrícula de Tributos* lacks five provinces found in the *Codex Mendoza,* and information for these has been taken from its close associate, the *Codex Mendoza.* Some adjustments in periods of collection have been made to conform to the *Matrícula* patterns (e.g., *mantas* listed as semi-annual tribute in the *Mendoza* are considered as eighty-day tribute in the *Matrícula*). The *Información* of 1554 adds the province of Apan, but omits Tlatelolco, Malinalco, and Xocotitlan.

Major discrepancies in the totals are primarily due to differences in periods of tribute collection, and in units of the items collected (e.g., single *mantas* versus loads of *mantas*). Unfortunately, there is little pictographic verification for either periods or units. For actual quantities of goods in the *Matrícula* and *Mendoza,* the pictographs have been followed rather than the annotations.

	Codex Mendoza				Matrícula de Tributos					Información of 1554		
Tribute	80-day	semi-annual	annual	annual total	80-day	semi-annual	annual	from Mendoza	annual total	80-day	annual	annual total
Mantas	800	62,400		128,000	53,840			10,000	255,360	81,100	47,400	371,400
Loincloths		3,600		7,200	3,600				14,400	1,600		6,400
Women's tunics/skirts		6,000		12,000	5,200			800	24,000	2,000		8,000
Warrior costumes/shields			665	665			396	251	647		91	91
"Mixed foodstuffs"			36	36	23			3	104		4	4
Bins maize			4	4	2				8		22	22
Bins beans			2	2					—		15	15
Bins chia				—					—		7	7
Chile, loads			1,600	1,600	1,200			400	6,400			—
Honey, pots or jars	400	1,900		5,400	1,040			400	5,760		100	100
Salt, "loaves"		2,000		4,000	2,000				8,000			—
Pinolli, baskets	40			160				40	160		4,000	4,000
Cacao, loads		280	420	980	300	200		200	1,800		560	560
Cacao, ground	40			160				40	160			—
Cotton, loads		400	3,600	4,400	4,000				16,000		20	20
Lime, loads	4,000	400		16,800	4,000			400	17,600			—
Cochineal, bags			65	65	60			5	260		65	65
Beams, large wooden	1,200			4,800	1,200				4,800		1,200	1,200
Planks, broad wooden	1,200			4,800	1,200				4,800		1,200	1,200
Planks, narrow wooden	1,200			4,800	1,200				4,800		2,400	2,400
Carrying frames	200			800	200				800		4,000	4,000
Firewood, loads	1,200			4,800	1,200				4,800			—
Mats, reed		4,000		8,000	4,000				16,000			—
Seats, reed		4,000		8,000	4,000				16,000			—
Paper		16,000		32,000	16,000				64,000	2,000	2,000	10,000
Canes	4,000			16,000	4,000				16,000		200	200
Canes for spears	8,000			32,000	8,000				32,000			—
Smoking canes	8,000			32,000	8,000				32,000			—
Gourd bowls (*xicalli*)	2,400	4,000		17,600	7,200				28,800		1,600	1,600
Pottery bowls (*tecomatl*)		1,200		2,400		800			1,600			—
Rubber, balls			16,000	16,000				16,000	16,000		6,000	6,000

Tribute	Codex Mendoza				Matrícula de Tributos					Información of 1554		
	80-day	semi-annual	annual	annual total	80-day	semi-annual	annual	from Mendoza	annual total	80-day	annual	annual total
Copal, unrefined balls	16,000			64,000	16,000				64,000		2,000	2,000
Copal, baskets	800			3,200	800				3,200		16,000	16,000
Yellow ocher, pans		20		40	20				80		8,000	8,000
Seashells		800		1,600	800				3,200		800	800
Live eagles			2+	2+	10			1+	41+		11	11
Enemy warriors				?					?			—
Deerskins	800		.	3,200	800				3,200			—
Liquidambar, jars			100	100				100	400		8,000	8,000
Liquidambar, cakes		8,000		16,000	8,000				32,000			—
Jaguar skins		20		40		20			40		40	40
Lip plugs		2	80	84	40	2		40	324		82	82
Amber		1		2	1				2		2	2
Turquoise												
strings (of beads)			1	1	1				4			—
disks			2	2	2				8			—
stones, bowl of			1	1	10				40		10	10
stones, packet of			10	10	10				40		10	10
masks			10	10	10				40		10	10
Jade												
beads, strung		1	17	19	8	2	10		46		17	17
stones			3	3				3	12			—
Copper												
bells		40		80	40				160	100		400
axes	100	80		560	180				720	400		1,600
Gold												
dust, in bowls			60	60	20			20	160		60	60
bars or tablets			10	10	10				40	2		8
disks			60	60	60				240		60	60
beads, strung			1	1				1	4		1	1
beads w/bells, strung			1	1				1	4			—
diadem			1	1				1	4		1	1
headband			1	1				1	4		1	1
shield			1	1				1	4			—
"pieces"				—					—		10	10
Feathers												
quetzal		400	1,680	2,480	1,200	800		480	8,320		2,401	2,401
blue feathers		400	8,000	8,800		400		8,000	32,800			—
red feathers		400	8,000	8,800		400		8,000	32,800		8,800	8,800
green feathers		400	8,000	8,800		400		8,000	32,800		8,800	8,800
yellow feathers		400		800		400			800		800	800
green/yellow			4	4				4	16			—
feathered headpieces			2	2	2				8		3	3
back device:												
yellow feathers			1	1				1	4		1	1
feather down, bags			20	20	20				80			—
bird skins		80		160		80			160		8,801	8,801
"Estatuas de hombres de hule"				—					—		1,200	1,200
string of "stones"				—					—		3	3

APPENDIX D: Reconstructed Tira of the Codex Mendoza Part 3, by Edward E. Calnek

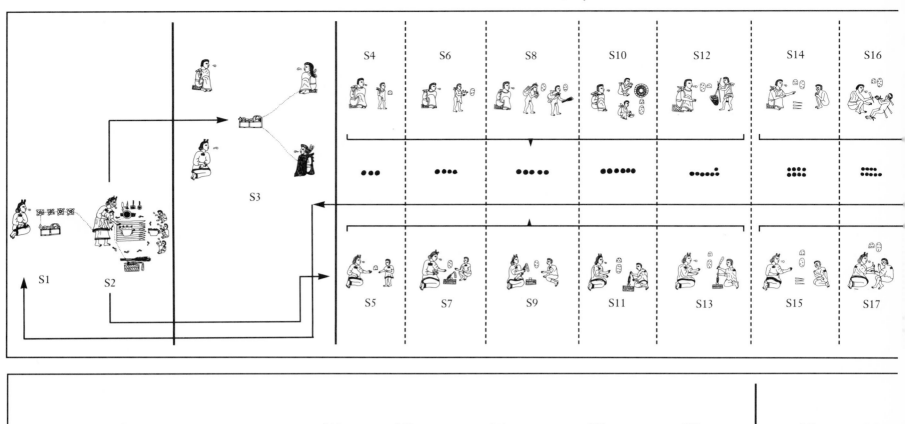

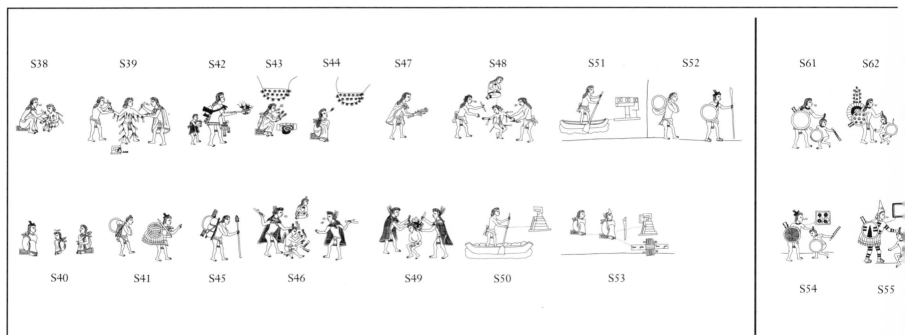

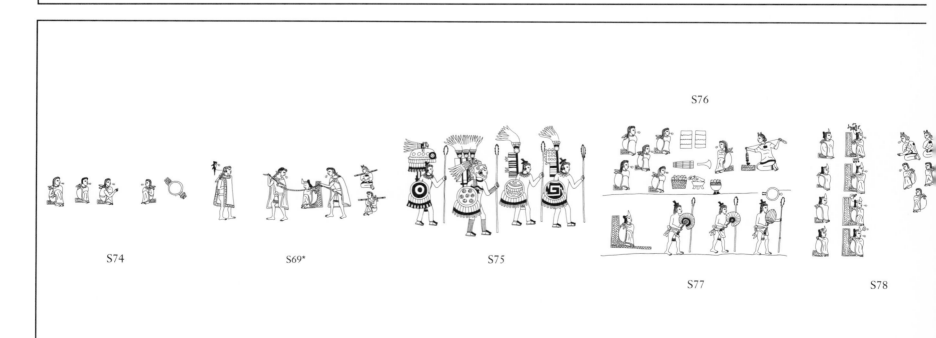

*Repositioned to agree with
implied event sequence.

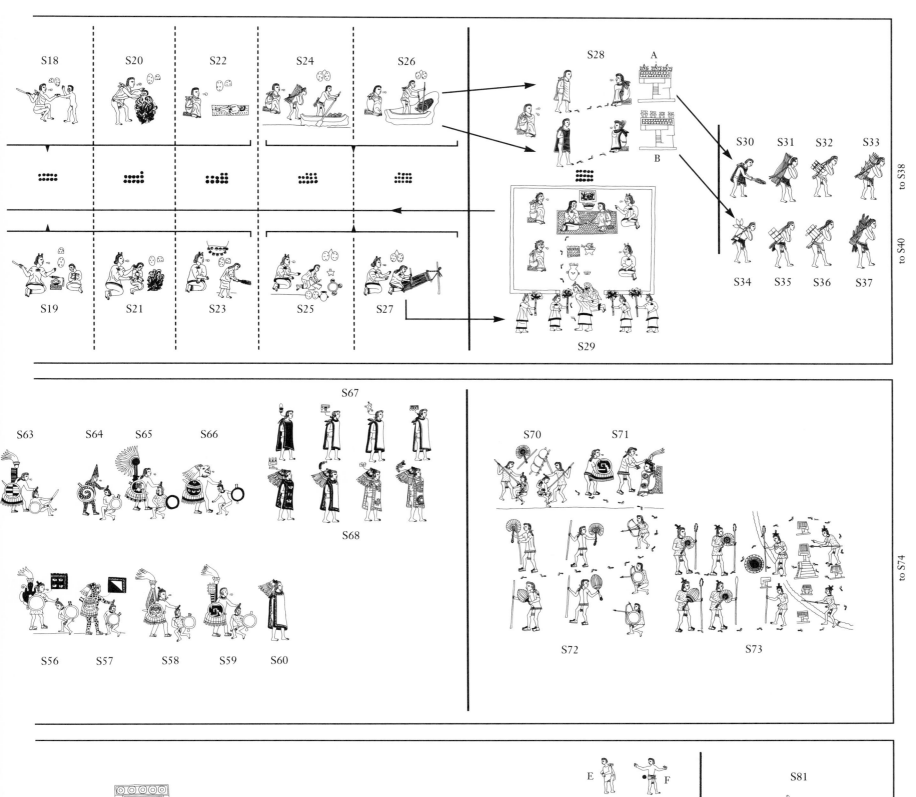

to S38

to S40

to S74

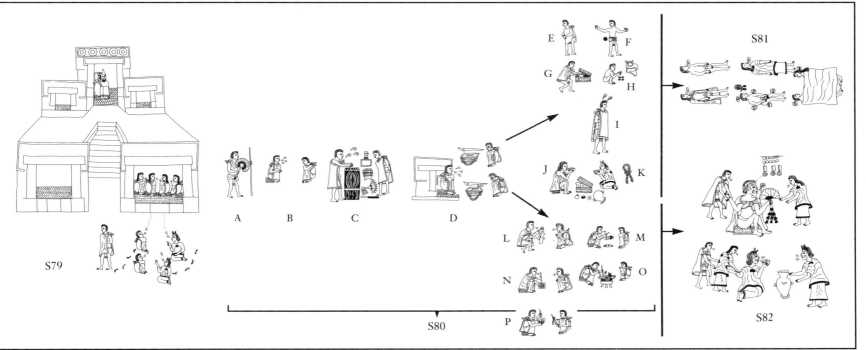

The Place-Name, Personal Name, and Title Glyphs of the *Codex Mendoza:* Translations and Comments

A SHORT GUIDE

The *Codex Mendoza* is well known for its impressive inventory of Aztec name glyphs; indeed, it is one of the finest and most basic sources for studies of the central Mexican glyphic writing system. The codex contains a total of 612 place-name glyphs as well as glyphs for 25 personal names and 16 titles. Adding to their value is the fact that all the place-name and title glyphs, and most of the personal name glyphs, are accompanied by glosses in Nahuatl.

This appendix translates and documents all these glyphs, cataloged according to their glosses. These few introductory pages are included as a brief guide to the procedures used in compiling the appendix, linguistic peculiarities, and additional information contained in the entries. In short, it is designed to make your journey through these translations both efficient and enjoyable.

The appendix is divided into three categories: place-names, personal names, and titles. Within each category, the names appear in alphabetical order, according to their Nahuatl glosses. The spelling of the glosses, as they appear in the *Mendoza*, has been strictly followed. If the spelling is quite eccentric according to the standards of Classical Nahuatl, a more usual spelling is included in the discussion of the name. If a name appears more than once and is spelled differently in its additional appearance(s), the alternate spelling is included in parentheses.

There are a number of ways such an index could be organized. We have chosen to combine all variants of the same gloss into a single entry, even if they represent obviously different towns (this is, however, always noted in the entry). In some cases the names in a single entry exhibit small spelling variations; these differences represent typical variations in spelling conventions of the period (e.g., *tz/ç, tz/z,* omission of final *n*). A discussion of these conventions and spelling alternatives is included in the introduction to the Spanish translations, volume 4 of this publication. There are a few special cases where towns with the same name but different glyphs were given separate entries (e.g., Tecalco, Atenco, Mictlan, Tepechpan). This was done usually due to radically different renderings of the glyphs or to unusual problems with the glosses.

Each entry contains the name of the place (or person, or title), the folio(s) on which it appears, its translation, a description of the glyph, linguistic analysis of the name, and any other pertinent or interesting information. The translations of these names, and their glyphic correspondences, are not always straightforward; difficul-

ties in interpretation and translation are also discussed where relevant. In addition, as a further aid, an illustration of each glyph accompanies its entry in the appendix.

In the translations, each name has been parsed into its component parts. Absolutive suffixes of nouns (*-tl* or *-tli*) and some verbal endings (such as *-a*) are in parentheses; linguistically, these endings drop off when combined with other elements. For instance, *Coatepec* derives from *coatl + tepetl + c.*

As is common with translations across radically different languages, translation correspondences are not always neat, and alternate interpretations may be equally reasonable. One readily obvious linguistic problem is the matter of singular versus plural. In Nahuatl, only animates carry plural markers. So, for example, whether one banner or several are intended is not expressed linguistically; both are called *pantli.* Sometimes context helps, but often either option would be possible. In those cases, we have simply chosen one alternative (frequently preferring the singular).

The other notable interpretation dilemma lies in the degree of literalness in the meaning of a name. For example, in the name *Nantzintlan,* is "Where There Are Many Revered Mothers" intended, or do these elements represent a plant known by the name of *nantzinxocotl* but not represented glyphically? Or, as other examples, does the name *Huehuetlan* represent "Place of Many Old Men," or "Place of the Old God"; should *Cuicatlan* be translated as "Place of Song" or as "Place of the Cuicateca"? In his translations, Clark (1938 vol. 2) often prefers to make extended rather than literal interpretations. We have leaned more toward the literal, although we do note where extended translations are possible.

This appendix would have taken even longer than it did had it not been for the pioneering work of others who have provided a background of information on glyphic translations. These include Peñafiel (1885), Clark (1938 vol. 2), Orozco y Berra (1960 vol. 1), Nicholson (1973), Barlow and MacAfee (1949), Macazaga Ordoño (1979), and others who have undertaken translations of individual place-names, personal names, and titles. While these sources have provided an invaluable basis for the present work, this appendix does not duplicate earlier efforts. In many cases only one interpretation of a name is reasonable, and we along with the other sources listed above will agree on a single translation (e.g., *Coatzinco, Tlatlauhquitepec*). However, there are several cases where we disagree with prior interpretations (and where these earlier authors also disagree among themselves). We have made a special effort in such cases to discuss these controversial interpretations. In addition, we have used these translations as an entree into the world of nature, food preparation, housing, agriculture, body decoration, gods, beliefs, and myriad other intriguing details of Aztec lifeways and worldviews.

Nahuatl names and English translations for each of the tributary towns are included in the page descriptions of the tribute folios (part 2 of *Codex Mendoza*). Translations of personal names and titles appear in the page descriptions for parts 1 and 3, which include thorough analyses of the Nahuatl.

PLACE-NAMES
List of Place-Names

ACAÇACATLA (f. 50r)
ACALHUACAN (f. 17v)
ACAMILYXTLAHUACAN (f. 36r)
ACAPAN (f. 20r)
ACAPETLATLAN (f. 47r)
ACAPULCO (f. 13r)
ACATEPEC (f. 13r)
ACATL YCPAC (f. 23r)
ACATZINCO (f. 42r)
ACAXOCHIC (f. 32r)
ACAXOCHITLA (fs. 30r, 31r)
ACAYOCAN (f. 29r)
ACHIOTLAN (fs. 15v, 45r)
ACOCOLCO (f. 28r)
ACOCOZPAN (f. 39r)
ACOLHUACAN (fs. 5v, 21v)
ACOLMAN (f. 3v)
ACOLNAHUAC (f. 17v)
ACOZPAN (f. 49r)
ACUITLAPAN (f. 39r)
AHUACATLA (f. 39r)
AHUAÇIÇINCO (f. 40r)
AHUATEPEC (f. 21v)
AHUEHUEPAN (f. 24v)
AHUILIZAPAN (fs. 10v, 48r)
ALAHUIZTLAN (f. 37r)
ALHUEXOYOCAN (f. 26r)
AMACOZTITLA (f. 23r)
AMATLAN (f. 16r)
AMAXAC (f. 39r)
AMAXTLAN (f. 13r)
AMEYALCO (fs. 22r, 32r)
AMILÇINCO (f. 25r)
ANENECUILCO (f. 24v)
AOCHPANCO (f. 20v)
APANCALECAN (fs. 13r, 38r)
ATENANCO (f. 37r)
ATENCO (f. 27r)
ATENCO (ATEMPAN) (f. 51r)
ATEPEC (f. 16v)
ATEZCAHUACAN (fs. 12r, 42r)
ATLACUIHUAYAN (f. 5v)
ATLAN (fs. 18r, 53r)
ATLAPULCO (f. 10r)
ATLATLAUHCA (ATLATLAVCA)
 (fs. 7v, 25r)
ATL HUELIC (f. 25r)
ATLICHOLOAYAN (f. 23r)
ATOCPAN (f. 29r)
ATOTONILCO (fs. 8r, 28r, 30r)
ATZACAN (f. 18r)

AXOCOPAN (fs. 8r, 27r)
AYAUHTOCHCUITLATLA (f. 13v)
AYOÇINTEPEC (f. 46r)
AYOTLAN (f. 47r)
AYOTZINTEPEC (TZAQUALTEPEC) (f. 46r)
AYOXOCHAPAN (f. 24v)
AYUTUCHCO (f. 51r)
AZCAPUÇALCO (f. 5v)
AZTA APAN (f. 50r)
AZTAQUEMECA (f. 21v)
CACALOMACA (f. 33r)
CAHUALAN (f. 13v)
CALIXTLAHUACAN (f. 33r)
CALIYMAYAN (fs. 10r, 33r)
CALTEPEC (fs. 16r, 51r)
CALYAHUALCO (f. 22r)
CAMOTLAN (f. 44r)
CAPULTEOPAN (f. 33r)
CAPULUAC (f. 10r)
CHALCO (fs. 3v, 4v, 6r, 7v, 41r)
CHALCO ATENCO (f. 17v)
CHAPOLMOLOYAN (f. 32r)
CHAPOLYCXITLA (f. 8r)
CHIAPAN (f. 13r)
CHICHICQUAVTLA (f. 32r)
CHICHIHUALTATACALA (f. 15v)
CHICONQUIAUHCO (f. 7v)
CHIETLAN (f. 42r)
CHILACACHAPAN (f. 37r)
CHILAPAN (f. 37r)
CHILTECPINTLAN (f. 42r)
CHIMALCO (f. 23r)
CHINANTLAN (f. 46r)
CHIPETLAN (f. 39r)
CHONTALCOATLAN (fs. 8r, 36r)
CHULULA (f. 42r)
COACALCO (f. 24v)
COAPAN (f. 50r)
COATEPEC (fs. 32r, 34r)
COATITLAN (f. 17v)
COATLAN (f. 23r)
COATLAYAUHCAN (f. 17v)
COATZINCO (f. 42r)
COAXOMULCO (f. 43r)
COAYXTLAHUACAN (fs. 7v, 43r)
COCOLAN (f. 37r)
COÇAMALOAPAN (f. 46r)
COÇOHUIPILECAN (fs. 13r, 38r)
COÇOTLAN (f. 20r)
COLHUACAN (f. 2r)
COLHUAÇINCO (f. 20r)
COLIMA (f. 38r)
COMALTEPEC (f. 16v)
COMITLAN (f. 13v)

CONTLAN (f. 21v)
COYOLAPAN (fs. 13v, 44r)
COYUACAN (COYOACAN) (fs. 5v, 47r)
COYUCAC (fs. 13r, 38r)
COZCAQUAUHTENANCO (f. 13r)
COZCATECUTLAN (f. 54r)
CUEÇALAN (fs. 6r, 37r)
CUEÇALCUITLAPILA (f. 13v)
CUEÇALOZTOC (f. 10v)
CUETLAXTLAN (fs. 8r, 10v, 49r)
CUEZCOMAHUACAN (f. 26r)
CUEZCOMATITLAN (f. 46r)
CUEZCOMATL YYACAC (f. 10v)
CUEZCOMAYXTLAHUACAN (f. 16r)
CUICATLAN (f. 43r)
CUITLAHUAC (fs. 2v, 6r, 20v)
ÇACATEPEC (f. 16r)
ÇACATLA (f. 40r)
ÇACATULAN (f. 38r)
ÇAPOTLAN (fs. 13r, 45r)
ÇAQUALPAN (f. 6r)
ÇAQUANTEPEC (f. 16r)
ÇENÇONTEPEC (f. 16r)
ÇENPOALAN (f. 21v)
ÇIHUANTEOPAN (CIHUATEOPAN) (f. 52r)
ÇIHUATLAN (f. 38r)
ÇILAN (f. 12r)
ÇINACANTEPEC (f. 10r)
ÇINACANTLAN (f. 15v)
ÇINCOZCAC (f. 34r)
ÇITLALTEPEC (f. 17v)
ÇOÇOLAN (fs. 15v, 17v)
ÇONPAHUACAN (f. 35r)
ÇONPANCO (f. 24v)
ÇOQUITZINCO (f. 33r)
ÇTZIHUINQUILOCAN (f. 30r)
ÇULAN (f. 15v)
ECATEPEC (fs. 12r, 22r)
ECATL YQUAPECHCO (f. 12r)
EHUACALCO (f. 40r)
EPAÇUYUCAN (f. 22r)
EPATLAN (f. 42r)
ETLAN (f. 44r)
GUAPALCALCO (f. 28r)
HUAXACAC (GUAXACAC) (fs. 17v, 44r)
HUAXTEPEC (fs. 7v, 24v)
HUEHUETLAN (fs. 13v, 42r, 47r)
HUEXOLOTLAN (fs. 13r, 16r)
HUEXOTZINCO (f. 42r)
HUEYAPAN (fs. 16r, 30r)
HUEYPUCHTLAN (HUEYPUCHTLA)
 (fs. 8r, 29r)
HUIÇIÇILAPAN (HUITZIÇILAPA)
 (fs. 6r, 32r)

HUIÇILAN (fs. 21v, 24v)
HUIÇILAPAN (f. 23r)
HUIÇILOPUCHCO (f. 20r)
HUILOTEPEC (f. 15v)
HUIPILAN (f. 13v)
HUITZAMOLA (f. 39r)
HUITZOCO (f. 37r)
HUIXACHTITLAN (f. 17v)
HUIZNAHUAC (f. 19r)
HUIZQUILOCAN (f. 32r)
HUIZTLAN (fs. 13v, 15v, 47r)
MACUILXOCHIC (f. 44r)
MAÇATLAN (fs. 12r, 13v, 47r)
MALINALCO (f. 35r)
MALINALTEPEC (fs. 16r, 39r, 41r)
MAMALHUAZTEPEC (f. 7v)
MAPACHTEPEC (fs. 13v, 47r)
MATIXCO (f. 21v)
MATLATLAN (f. 10v)
METEPEC (fs. 10r, 33r)
MIACATLA (f. 23r)
MIAHUA APAN (f. 52r)
MICHAPAN (f. 46r)
MICHMALOYAN (f. 31r)
MICHTLAN (f. 46r)
MICTLAN (f. 16v)
MICTLAN (fs. 43r, 52r)
MICTLAN QUAUHTLA (f. 49r)
MIQUIYETLAN (MIQUETLAN) (fs. 10v, 12r)
MITEPEC (f. 33r)
MITZINCO (f. 40r)
MIXCOAC (f. 5v)
MIXTLAN (fs. 10v, 46r)
MIZQUIC (fs. 2v, 6r, 20v)
MIZQUITLAN (f. 13v)
MOLANCO (fs. 13r, 16r, 54r)
MOLOTLA (f. 23r)
MYZQUIYAHUALA (f. 27r)
NACOCHTLAN (f. 42r)
NANTZINTLAN (f. 13v)
NEPOPOALCO (f. 25r)
NEXTITLAN (f. 20v)
NOCHCOC (f. 38r)
NOCHIZTLAN (fs. 15v, 43r)
NOCHTEPEC (f. 36r)
OCOAPAN (f. 39r)
OCOTEPEC (f. 32r)
OCOYACAC (f. 10r)
OCPAYUCAN (f. 23r)
OCTLAN (f. 44r)
OCUILAN (fs. 10v, 34r)
OÇELOTEPEC (f. 52r)
OHUAPAN (f. 37r)
OLAC (f. 20r)
OLINALAN (f. 40r)
OLINTEPEC (f. 24v)
OTLATITLAN (f. 46r)
OTLAZPAN (f. 28r)
OTUNPA (f. 3v)
OXICHAN (f. 49r)
OXITIPAN (f. 55r)
OXITLAN (f. 46r)
OZTOMA (fs. 10v, 18r, 37r)
OZTOTICPAC (f. 10v)

OZTOTLAPECHCO (f. 42r)
PANOTLAN (f. 38r)
PANTEPEC (f. 16r)
PAPANTLA (f. 52r)
PATLANALAN (f. 40r)
PETLACALCATL (PETLACALCO) (f. 20r)
PETLATLAN (f. 38r)
PIAZTLAN (f. 15v)
PIPIYOLTEPEC (f. 16r)
POCTEPEC (f. 17v)
PUCTLAN (f. 46r)
PUPUTLAN (f. 17v)
PUXCAUHTLAN (f. 10v)
QUACHQUEÇALOYAN (f. 30r)
QUAGUACAN (QUAHUACAN) (fs. 5v, 32r)
QUAHUITL YXCO (f. 24v)
QUALAC (f. 40r)
QUATLATLAUHCAN (f. 42r)
QUATZONTEPEC (f. 44r)
QUAUHNACAZTLAN (f. 13v)
QUAUHNAHUAC (fs. 2v, 6r, 7v, 23r)
QUAUHPANOAYAN (fs. 10r, 32r)
QUAUHPILOLAN (f. 13v)
QUAUHQUECHULAN (f. 42r)
QUAUHQUEMECAN (f. 22r)
QUAUHTECOMAÇINCO (f. 40r)
QUAUHTECOMATLA (f. 40r)
QUAUHTETELCO (f. 48r)
QUAUHTINCHAN (f. 42r)
QUAUHTITLAN (fs. 3v, 5v, 26r)
QUAUHTLAN (fs. 10v, 13v, 24v)
QUAUHTOCHCO (fs. 8r, 17v, 48r)
QUAUHXAYACATITLAN (f. 13v)
QUAUHYOCAN (f. 22r)
QUAUXIMALPAN (f. 5v)
QUAVXILOTITLAN (f. 44r)
QUAVXUMULCO (f. 41r)
QUECHULAC (f. 42r)
QUEÇALMACAN (f. 28r)
QUETZALTEPEC (f. 16r)
QUIMICHTEPEC (f. 16r)
QUIYAUHTEOPAN (QUIAUHTEOPAN)
     (fs. 8r, 40r)
TAMAÇOLAN (f. 43r)
TAMAÇOLAPAN (f. 43r)
TAMAPACHCO (f. 12r)
TAMUOC (f. 10v)
TANPATEL (f. 10v)
TEACALCO (f. 21v)
TECALCO (fs. 10v, 42r)
TECALCO (f. 20v)
TECAMACHALCO (f. 42r)
TECAXIC (fs. 12r, 15v)
TECMILCO (f. 41r)
TECOÇAUHTLA (TECOÇAUHTLAN)
     (fs. 16r, 31r)
TECOLOAPAN (f. 20r)
TECPAN (TECPA) (fs. 5v, 32r)
TECPATEPEC (fs. 13r, 27r)
TECPATLAN (f. 16r)
TECPATZINCO (TECPAÇINCO) (fs. 8r, 24v)
TECUTEPEC (f. 15v)
TEÇIUTLAN (f. 51r)
TEÇOYUCAN (f. 22r)

TEHUEHUEC (f. 28r)
TEHUILOYOCAN (f. 26r)
TEHUIZCO (f. 24v)
TELOLOAPAN (f. 37r)
TEMAZCALAPAN (f. 21v)
TEMOHUAYAN (f. 27r)
TENANCO (f. 7v)
TENANÇINCO (TENANTZINCO)
     (fs. 10v, 34r)
TENAYUCAN (f. 2r)
TENEXTICPAC (f. 10v)
TENOCHTITLAN (TENUXTITLAN)
     (fs. 2r, 4v, 19r)
TEOAÇINCO (f. 16r)
TEOCALÇINCO (f. 23r)
TEOCALHUEYACAN (f. 5v)
TEOCHIAPAN (f. 16r)
TEOCUITLATLAN (fs. 13v, 44r)
TEOÇIOCAN (f. 49r)
TEONOCHTITLAN (f. 42r)
TEOPANTLAN (f. 42r)
TEOTENANCO (fs. 10r, 33r)
TEOTLALPAN (f. 51r)
TEOTLILAN (f. 46r)
TEOTLIZTACAN (f. 36r)
TEPECHIAPAN (f. 13r)
TEPECHPA (f. 21v)
TEPECHPAN (f. 20r)
TEPEMAXALCO (f. 33r)
TEPEPULAN (f. 20r)
TEPEQUACUILCO (fs. 6r, 8r, 37r)
TEPETITLAN (f. 31r)
TEPETLACALCO (f. 20r)
TEPETLAOZTOC (f. 21v)
TEPETLAPAN (f. 22r)
TEPETL HUIACAN (f. 33r)
TEPEXAHUALCO (f. 36r)
TEPEXIC (f. 42r)
TEPEYACAC (TEPEACAC) (fs. 10v, 42r)
TEPOXACO (f. 26r)
TEPOZTITLAN (f. 40r)
TEPUZCULULAN (f. 43r)
TEPUZTLAN (TEPOZTLAN)
     (fs. 8r, 24v, 41r)
TEQUALOYAN (f. 34r)
TEQUANTEPEC (f. 13v)
TEQUEMECAN (f. 20r)
TEQUIXQUIAC (fs. 4v, 29r)
TETENANCO (fs. 17v, 36r, 39r, 42r)
TETEPANCO (f. 27r)
TETEUHTEPEC (f. 7v)
TETEVTLAN (f. 46r)
TETICPAC (fs. 36r, 44r)
TETLAPANALOYAN (f. 29r)
TETZAPOTITLAN (TEÇAPOTITLAN)
     (fs. 10v, 18r, 53r)
TEUHÇOLTZAPOTLAN (f. 48r)
TEXOPAN (f. 43r)
TEZCACOAC (f. 20v)
TEZCATEPEC (f. 27r)
TEZCATEPETONCO (f. 29r)
TEZCUCO (f. 3v)
TIÇATEPEC (f. 21v)
TIÇAYUCAN (f. 22r)

TLAAHUILILPAN (f. 27r)
TLACHCO (fs. 8r, 31r, 36r)
TLACHINOLTICPAC (f. 15v)
TLACHMALACAC (f. 37r)
TLACHQUIYAUHCO (TLACHQUIAVCO)
   (fs. 16r, 45r)
TLACHYAHUALCO (f. 21v)
TLACOPAN (f. 5v)
TLACOTEPEC (fs. 10r, 13v)
TLACOTLALPAN (f. 46r)
TLAÇOXIUHCO (f. 20v)
TLALATLAVCO (f. 32r)
TLALCOÇAUHTITLAN (fs. 8r, 40r)
TLALCUECHAHUAYAN (f. 44r)
TLALLACHCO (f. 32r)
TLALTIÇAPAN (fs. 24v, 52r)
TLAMACAZAPAN (f. 36r)
TLANIZTLAN (f. 15v)
TLAOLAN (f. 10v)
TLAPACOYAN (fs. 8r, 50r)
TLAPAN (TLAPPAN) (fs. 12r, 13r, 39r)
TLAPANICYTLAN (f. 49r)
TLAQUILPAN (f. 22r)
TLATILULCO (fs. 6r, 10r, 19r)
TLATLAUHQUITEPEC (fs. 8r, 51r)
TLAXCALA (f. 42r)
TLAXIMALOYAN (f. 10v)
TLAYACAC (f. 24v)
TLAYACAPAN (f. 24v)
TLILTEPEC (f. 16v)
TOCHTEPEC (f. 46r)
TOLIMANI (f. 40r)
TOLTITLAN (f. 3v)
TONALI YMOQUEÇAYAN (f. 12r)
TONANYTLA (f. 21v)
TONATIUHCO (f. 34r)
TOTOLAPA (TOTOLAPAN) (fs. 7v, 25r)
TOTOLÇINCO (f. 21v)
TOTOMIXTLAHUACAN (f. 39r)
TOTOTEPEC (fs. 13r, 46r)
TOTOTLAN (f. 48r)
TOXICO (f. 12r)
TOYAC (f. 20v)
TOZTLAN (f. 46r)
TUCHÇONCO (f. 48r)
TUCHPAN (TUCHPA) (fs. 10v, 52r)
TUCHTLAN (f. 50r)
TULAN (f. 8r)
TULANÇINCO (TULANÇINGO) (fs. 3v, 30r)
TULUCAN (TULUCA) (fs. 10v, 12r, 33r)
TZAPOTITLAN (f. 20v)
TZAYANALQUILPA (f. 31r)
TZICAPUÇALCO (f. 36r)
TZICCOAC (ÇTZICOAC) (fs. 13r, 54r)
TZILACA APAN (f. 40r)
TZINACANOZTOC (f. 46r)
TZONPANCO (f. 17v)
XALA (f. 40r)
XALAC (fs. 28r, 29r)
XALAPAN (fs. 16v, 26r)

XALATLAUHCO (f. 10r)
XALOZTOC (f. 24v)
XALTEPEC (fs. 13r, 43r)
XALTIANQUIZCO (f. 16v)
XALTOCAN (fs. 3v, 17v)
XAXALPAN (f. 20r)
XAYACO (f. 46r)
XICALHUACAN (f. 29r)
XICALTEPEC (fs. 33r, 46r)
XICO (f. 20v)
XICOCHIMALCO (f. 13r)
XILOÇINCO (f. 26r)
XILOTEPEC (fs. 8r, 31r)
XILOXOCHITLAN (f. 50r)
XIQUIPILCO (f. 10v)
XIUHHUACAN (XIHUACAN) (fs. 13r, 38r)
XIUHTECÇACATLAN (f. 13r)
XIUHTEPEC (fs. 6r, 7v, 23r)
XOCHIACAN (f. 10r)
XOCHICHIVCA (f. 27r)
XOCHIMILCAÇINCO (f. 24v)
XOCHIMILCO (fs. 2v, 6r)
XOCHIQUAUHTITLAN (f. 50r)
XOCHITEPEC (f. 23r)
XOCHIYETLA (f. 12r)
XOCHTLAN (f. 13r)
XOCONOCHCO (fs. 15v, 18r, 47r)
XOCOTITLAN (fs. 10v, 35r)
XOCOTLA (f. 39r)
XOCOYOCAN (f. 54r)
XOCOYOLTEPEC (f. 41r)
XOLOCHIUHYAN (fs. 13r, 38r)
XOLOTLAN (f. 13v)
XOMEYOCAN (f. 29r)
XONOCTLA (XONOTLA) (f. 51r)
XOXOVTLA (f. 23r)
YACAPICHTLAN (YACAPICHTLA)
   (fs. 8r, 24v)
YANCUITLAN (fs. 12r, 43r)
YAONAHUAC (f. 51r)
YAOTLAN (f. 46r)
YAUHTEPEC (fs. 8r, 24v)
YAYAVQUITLALPA (f. 51r)
YCÇOCHINANCO (f. 42r)
YCHCA ATOYAC (f. 40r)
YCHCATEOPAN (fs. 37r, 39r)
YCHCATLA (f. 40r)
YCHCATLAN (fs. 40r, 54r)
YCPATEPEC (f. 15v)
YOALAN (YOALLAN) (fs. 6r, 37r, 39r)
YOALTEPEC (fs. 8r, 40r)
YOLOXONECUILA (f. 16v)
YOPICO (f. 20v)
YTZUCAN (f. 42r)
YXCOYAMEC (f. 51r)
YXICAYAN (f. 40r)
YXMATLATLAN (f. 46r)
YXQUEMECAN (f. 21v)
YZAMATITLA (f. 24v)
YZCUINCUITLAPILCO (f. 8r)

YZCUINTEPEC (f. 16r)
YZHUATLAN (f. 13v)
YZMIQUILPAN (f. 27r)
YZTACALCO (f. 17v)
YZTAC TLALOCAN (fs. 13v, 15v)
YZTAPAN (f. 38r)
YZTATLAN (f. 13v)
YZTEPEC (YTZTEPEC) (fs. 6r, 23r, 51r)
YZTEYOCAN (YTZTEYOCAN) (fs. 17v, 48r)
YZTITLAN (f. 16v)
YZTLA (f. 23r)

PERSONAL NAMES
List of Personal Names

ACAÇITLI (f. 2r)
ACAMAPICH (f. 2v, twice)
ACUEYOTL (f. 18r)
AGUEXOTL (f. 2r)
AHUIÇOÇIN (f. 13r)
ATONAL (f. 7v)
ATOTOTL (f. 2r)
AXAYACAÇIN (AXAYACAÇI) (fs. 10r, 19r)
CHIMALPUPUCA (f. 4v, twice)
HUEHUE MOTECÇUMA (f. 7v)
HUIÇILYHUITL (f. 3v)
MIXCOATL (f. 17v)
MOQUIHUIX (fs. 10r, 19r)
MOTECÇUMA (f. 15v)
OÇELOPAN (f. 2r)
OMEQUAUH (f. 18r)
QUAP (f. 2r)
QUAUHTLATOA (fs. 6r, 19r)
TEÇINEUH (f. 2r)
TENUCH (f. 2r)
TIÇOÇICATZIN (f. 12r)
XIUHCAQUI (f. 2r)
XOCOYOL (f. 2r)
XOMIMITL (f. 2r)
YZCOAÇI (fs. 5v, 19r)

TITLES
List of Military and Political Titles

ACATL IYACAPANECATL (f. 68r)
ATENPANECATL (f. 65r)
EZGUAGUACATL (fs. 65r, 68r)
HUIZNAHUATL (HUITZNAHUATL)
   (fs. 66r, 67r)
MYXCOATLAYLOTLAC (f. 68r)
PETLACALCATL (f. 70r)
QUAUHNOCHTLI (f. 65r)
TEQUIXQUINAHUACATL (f. 68r)
TEZCACOACATL (fs. 18r, 65r)
TICOCYAHUACATL (f. 65r)
TLACATECATL (f. 18r)
TLACATECTLI (fs. 17v, 18r)
TLACOCHCALCATL (fs. 18r, 65r)
TLACOCHTECTLI (fs. 17v, 18r)
TLILANCALQUI (fs. 18r, 65r)
TOCUILTECATL (f. 65r)

ACAÇACATLA (folio 50r):
"Land Full of Reed-Grass"

The glyph is formed by yellow grass overlain by blue reeds. In the *Matrícula* (folio 14v), the grass and reeds are more entwined. The name is formed from:

aca(tl): reed
çaca(tl): grass
tla(n): abundance of

The locative *tla(n)* is not glyphically portrayed.

Molina (1970: folio 1r) defines *acaçacatla* as "carrizal" (land full of reed-grass), and this is undoubtedly what is meant here. Hernández (1959 1:34) describes *acazacatl* as a reed-grass that grows in a variety of climates (including the highlands, where today's Zacatlán de las Manzanas, descendant of Acaçacatla, is located). He also notes that this reed-grass could be used to relieve fevers (ibid.).

ACALHUACAN (folio 17v):
"Place of Those Who Have Canoes"

The glyph is a canoe with two black vertical lines. In the *Codex Boturini* (*lámina* XI), the glyph for this town appears as an unmarked canoe with paddle. The name is formed from:

acal(li): canoe (itself a combination of *a(tl):* water and *cal(li):* house)
hua: possessive
can: place of

Only the *acalli* element is glyphically shown.

Peñafiel (1885:37) gives the name "Place That Has Canoes." Orozco y Berra (1960 1:421) translates the name as "lugar en que hay dueños de canoas" (Place Where There Are Owners of Canoes).

ACAMILYXTLAHUACAN (folio 36r):
"Place of the Plain of Cultivated Fields of Reeds"

The glyph consists of a cultivated field, two blue reeds, and three inverted eyes. In the *Matrícula* drawing of this glyph (folio 8v), the field is only one color. The name is derived from:

aca(tl): reed
mil(li): cultivated field
yxtlahua(tl): plain (flat land)
ixtlapal: reverse, or inverted
can: place of

The inverted eyes serve as ideographic cues that the land is not just *milli* (cultivated land) or *tlalli* (land), but a special kind of land. Peñafiel (1885:37–38) interprets the reeds as maize and translates the whole as "Plain of the Cultivated Fields of Maize."

ACAPAN (folio 20r): "On the Reeds"

The glyph is composed of three elements: the year and day sign for reed alongside a banner, both perched atop a horizontal yellow cane. The name is formed from:

aca(tl): reed
pan(tli): banner, on

The *acatl* glyph is actually presented twice, once symbolically and once naturalistically. Clark (1938 2:24) describes the symbolic *acatl* as "the nock-end of an arrow with its wings, in a red-painted bowl of water." The yellow reed represents the canes from which arrows were made; Hernández (1959 1:397) mentions *acatl* as one of four indigenous varieties of canes (*otlatl*). This glyph does not appear in the *Matrícula* due to document disintegration.

ACAPETLATLAN (folio 47r):
"Place of Many Reed Mats"

The glyph is a green reed inside a rectangular yellow woven mat. The name is formed from:

aca(tl): reed
petla(tl): woven mat
tlan: abundance of

The locative *tlan* is not glyphically expressed.

Molina (1970: folio 1r) includes an entry for *acapetlatl:* cane mat. Peñafiel (1885:39) identifies the cane as *Phragmites communis*.

ACAPULCO (folio 13r):
"In the Place of Destroyed (or Tall) Reeds"

The glyph consists of the nock end of an arrow and two hands (with lower arms) among a dismembered reed. The name is formed from:

aca(tl): reed
poloa: to destroy
co: in, or on

The particle *-pol* attached to a noun conveys an excessive or augmented state; hence *acapul* would mean a large or tall reed. Peñafiel (1885:39) translates this glyph as "Place Conquered or Destroyed." Clark (1938 2:14) prefers a "tall canes" translation. In their love of puns, perhaps the Nahua intended both meanings.

ACATEPEC (folio 13r):
"On the Hill of Reeds"

The glyph is a hill from which protrude two reed plants and an arrow cane between them. The name derives from:

aca(tl): reed
tepe(tl): hill
c: on, or in

Reeds and arrow canes are discussed under Acapan.

ACATL YCPAC (folio 23r):
"On Top of the (Arrow) Reeds"

The glyph is the nock end of a reed arrow flanked by two reeds. This assemblage sits on top of a hill. The name derives from:

acatl: reed
icpac: on top of

ACATZINCO (folio 42r):
"In the Small Reeds"

The glyph is a green reed on top of the lower part of a loincloth-clad man. The name derives from:

aca(tl): reed
tzin(tli): rump
tzin: small
co: on, or in

ACAXOCHIC (folio 32r):
"On the *Acaxochitl*"

The glyph is a bright red multi-petaled flower. The name derives from:

acaxochi(tl): acaxochitl flower
c: on, or in

The "chile-red" flower of the *acaxochitl, Lobelia sp.,* was also called *acaxochitl* (Sahagún 1950–1982 11:211). This plant is illustrated in Hernández (1959 1:31). See also the glyphs for Acaxochitla (folios 30r, 31r).

ACAXOCHITLA (folios 30r, 31r):
"Where There Is Much *Acaxochitl*"

The glyph is a chile-red flower with many petals. The glyph on folio 30r also contains a yellow arrow cane. See the discussion of arrow canes under Acapan. The name derives from:

aca(tl): reed
acaxochi(tl): acaxochitl plant or flower
tla(n): abundance of

The glyph on folio 31r is virtually identical to that of Acaxochic on folio 32r. In all three cases, locative glyphs are absent.

ACAYOCAN (folio 29r):
"Place Full of Reeds"

The glyph shows reeds growing gracefully on a hill. The name is formed from:

aca(tl): reed
acayo: full of reeds
can: place of

ACHIOTLAN (folios 15v, 45r):
"Where There Is Much *Achiotl*"

Both glyphic illustrations show a brown bowl filled with a red substance. On folio 15v the *tlantli* glyph is shown with the usual two teeth and red gums; on folio 45r a lower jaw with four teeth conveys the same information, with water cascading over the teeth. The name is formed from:

a(tl): water
achio(tl): a light red coloring (*Bixa orellana* L.)
tlan(tli): tooth, abundance of

The water on the folio 45r glyph provides the phonetic clue that the name will begin with an "a" sound. This identifies the substance in the bowl as *achiotl* (or, more likely, *achiotetl,* the material in its unground form). These are seeds from the *achiotl* tree, used for face paint (Santamaría 1974:28). The name for this town in Mixtec is *Ñuundecu* (M. E. Smith 1973:176).

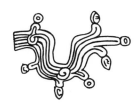

ACOCOLCO (folio 28r):
"On the Twisting River"

The glyph is a twisting stream of water. The name derives from:

>   *a(tl):* water
>   *cocol(oa):* to go somewhere by twists and turns
>   *co:* on, or in

ACOCOZPAN (folio 39r):
"On the Very Yellow Water"

The glyph is a canal containing yellow water with black bands. The name derives from:

>   *a(tl):* water
>   *cocoz(tic):* very yellow
>   *pan(tli):* canal
>   *pan:* on

ACOLHUACAN (folios 5v, 21v):
"Place of the *Acolhua*"

The glyphs on both folios show a bent arm with water spilling from its broken shoulder. On folio 21v the arm is embellished with a wristband; on folio 5v a tripeaked rocky hill with a single flower on top is added (see the glyph for Tezcuco). The name is formed from:

>   *a(tl):* water
>   *coloa:* to bend
>   *Acolhua:* a group inhabiting the eastern side of Lake Texcoco
>   *can:* place

On folio 21v the gloss adds *acolmecatl calpixqui:* "man of Acolman, tribute collector." The glyph for Acolman is on folio 3v.

ACOLMAN (folio 3v):
"Place Captured by the *Acolhua*" or "Place Where the *Acolhua* Extend"

The glyph consists of a bent arm, shoulder to fingertips. A shoulder bone is exposed. A small stream of water gracefully spills over the arm. The name derives from:

>   *a(tl):* water
>   *coloa:* to bend
>   *Acolhua:* a group living on the eastern side of Lake Texcoco
>   *ma(itl):* hand
>   *ma:* to capture
>   *man:* where something extends

See also the similar glyphs for Tezcuco and Acolhuacan, folios 3v, 5v, and 21v.

ACOLNAHUAC (folio 17v):
"Beside the Shoulder" or "Beside the Acolhua"

The glyph is an arm (from shoulder to fingers, with a bone showing at the shoulder-end); a blue speech scroll emerges from an opening in the biceps. The name derives from:

>   *acol(li):* shoulder
>   *nahua(tl):* good sound
>   *c:* on, or in
>   *nahuac:* beside

The Acolhua people predominated on the eastern side of Lake Texcoco in the Valley of Mexico.

ACOZPAN (folio 49r):
"On the Yellow Water"

The glyph is a swirling circle of yellow water outlined with black. The name is formed from:

>   *a(tl):* water
>   *coz(tic):* yellow
>   *pan:* on

The locative banner or footprint, homonym for *-pan* (on), is not included in this glyph, nor in its mate in the *Matrícula de Tributos.*

ACUITLAPAN (folio 39r):
"On the Water Dung Heap"

The glyph consists of a canal full of water, and excrement. The name is formed from:

>   *a(tl):* water
>   *cuitla(tl):* excrement
>   *apan(tli):* canal
>   *pan:* on
>   *cuitlapan:* pile of dung

AHUACATLA (folio 39r):
"Where There Are Many Avocados"

The glyph is a green tree with green fruits and red roots. Two rows of teeth are set into the trunk. The name derives from:

>   *ahuaca(tl):* avocado fruit
>   *tla(ntli):* tooth, abundance of

Hernández (1959 1:29) describes the avocado tree in detail, including its broad leaves seen in this glyph.

AHUAÇIÇINCO (folio 40r):
"On the Very Small Oak Trees"

The glyph consists of the lower half of a man's body attached to a tree. The tree has two branches; flowers and spilling water adorn the tops of the branches. The name derives from:

> *ahua(cho):* dewed
> *ahua(tl):* oak
> *tzin(tli):* rump
> *tzin:* small
> *co:* on, or in

Sahagún (1950–1982 11:108) describes the *auatl* as a tree with crotched branches. In both the *Mendoza* and the *Matrícula* (folio 10v), the tree clearly shows its bifurcated quality. The water glyph also provides a clue that the name of this tree begins with *a*. Since the *tzin* is reduplicated in the name (-*çiçin*-), these must have been *very* small oaks.

AHUATEPEC (folio 21v):
"On the Hill of the Oak Tree"

The glyph consists of a three-branched tree with water instead of flowers spilling from its leaves. The tree grows from the middle of a green hill. The name is formed from:

> *a(tl):* water
> *ahua(tl):* oak tree
> *tepe(tl):* hill
> *c:* on, or in

Since trees are often drawn in a generic style and not readily identifiable, the water in this case alerts the reader that the name of the tree begins with an *a* sound.

AHUEHUEPAN (folio 24v):
"On the Cypress" or "On the Drum"

The glyph is a tree emerging from a vertical drum. The name derives from:

> *ahuehue(tl):* cypress tree
> *huehue(tl):* drum
> *pan:* on

The *ahuehuetl* tree (*Taxodium mucronatum*) is described by Sahagún (1950–1982 11:108).

AHUILIZAPAN (folios 10v, 48r):
"On the Irrigation Canals"

The glyph shows a cheerful man with raised arm and half-immersed in a canal full (indeed overflowing) with water. The figure on folio 10v is rather less enthusiastic than that on folio 48r. The name is formed from:

> *ahahuializ(tli):* joy
> *ahuilia:* to irrigate fields
> *apan(tli):* canal
> *apan:* on the water

In this place glyph the joyful person provides the phonetic prompt leading to *ahuilia*. The glyph for this town is also found on Tizoc's immodest stone. Over time and under Spanish influence, this name eventually became transformed to Orizaba.

ALAHUIZTLAN (folio 37r):
"Where There Are Many Gliding Swimmers"

The glyph is an arm bent at the elbow, with water flowing through the hand. Two teeth rest on the water flow, and a single footprint lies at the side. The name is formed from:

> *ala(hua):* to glide
> *ahuitz(oa):* to swim
> *tlan(tli):* tooth, abundance of

The footprint is not used for phonetic purposes here, but rather to convey the sense of movement. Peñafiel (1885:54) emphasizes the notion of *huiztlan* (south) in his interpretation.

ALHUEXOYOCAN (folio 26r):
"Place Full of Water Willows"

The glyph is a tree growing in a swirl of water. The name derives from:

> *a(tl):* water
> *huexo(tl):* willow tree
> *ahuexo(tl):* water willow
> *ahuexoyo:* full of water willows
> *can:* place

Sahagún (1950–1982 11:110) discusses the *huexotl* and *ahuexotl*, presenting them as synonyms. The willow is a tall, fast-growing tree, frequently planted along the edges of *chinampas*. Hernández (1959 1:46–47) provides a detailed discussion of this tree.

AMACOZTITLA (folio 23r):
"Among the *Amacoztic* Trees"

The glyph consists of a yellow piece of paper with two teeth above and a stream of water below. The name is formed from:

> *a(tl):* water
> *ama(tl):* paper
> *coz(tic):* yellow
>> *amacoztic:* the *amacoztic* tree
> *tla(ntli):* tooth
>> *titla(n):* among

The water provides the phonetic prompt that the yellow rectangle is a sheet of paper, *amatl.* The *amacoztic* (yellow paper) tree is described and illustrated by Hernández (1959 1:84). It is identified as *Ficus petiolaris* by Clark (1938 2:29).

AMATLAN (folio 16r):
"Where There Is Much Paper"

The glyph is a bound cylinder of white paper. The name derives from:

> *ama(tl):* paper
> *tlan:* abundance of

Paper was produced from the inner bark of the fig tree (*amaquahuitl*).

AMAXAC (folio 39r):
"On the River That Divides into Channels"

The glyph is a pair of legs separated by a stream of water. The name derives from:

> *a(tl):* water
> *maxac:* between my legs
>> *amaxac:* where the river divides into many parts
> *c:* on, or in

AMAXTLAN (folio 13r):
"Where There Are Many Paper Loincloths"

The glyph shows water spilling over a tied loincloth. The name is formed from:

> *a(tl):* water
> *ama(tl):* paper
> *maxtla(tl):* loincloth
> *tlan:* abundance of

There is much overlapping of syllables here, and it is possible that water rather than paper was actually meant.

AMEYALCO (folios 22r, 32r):
"On the Spring"

The glyph shows water flowing out of a hole. The name is formed from:

> *a(tl):* water
> *meya:* to flow
>> *ameyal(li):* a spring
> *co:* on, or in

AMILÇINCO (folio 25r):
"On the Small Irrigated Lands"

The glyph consists of a maize plant (with yellow and red ears) growing on a plot of ground. Both rest on top of the lower half of a man's body. The name is formed from:

> *amil(li):* irrigated land
> *tzin(tli):* rump
>> *tzin:* small
> *co:* on, or in

ANENECUILCO (folio 24v):
"On the Water That Twists Back and Forth"

The glyph is a stream of water with a whirlpool; the stream is bent at a gentle right angle. The name derives from:

> *a(tl):* water
> *nenecuil(oa):* to sway or twist back and forth
> *co:* on, or in

AOCHPANCO (folio 20v):
"On the Water Highway"

This glyph consists of three stacked elements: a stream of water on the bottom, a brown rectangle with two footprints next, and a banner on top. The name is formed from:

> *a(tl):* water
> *o(htli):* road
> *pan(tli):* banner
>> *ochpan(tli):* broad, royal road; a highway
> *co:* on, or in

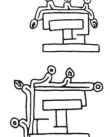

APANCALECAN (folios 13r, 38r):
"Place of House Canals"

The glyph shows water flowing over the top and back of a house. On folio 13r the water also spills over the front of the house. The name is formed from:

apan(tli): canal
cal(li): house
can: place of

Clark (1938 2:41) suggests that "drains" is intended here.

ATENANCO (folio 37r):
"On the Wall of Water"

The glyph is a blue and red wall with water running along its ramparts and off the wall. Four blue circles decorate the wall. The name derives from:

a(tl): water
tenam(itl): wall
co: on, or in

Clark (1938 2:40) observes that it was common for such a name to be given to towns on unfordable rivers. This Atenanco apparently was located on a river (Barlow 1949a:16).

ATENCO (folio 27r):
"On the Shore"

The glyph is a set of lips in a canal full of water. The name derives from:

a(tl): water
ten(tli): lips
    aten(tli): shore
co: on, or in

ATENCO (ATEMPAN) (folio 51r):
"On the Shore"

The glyph is formed by water flowing behind a mouth (lips). The name derives from:

a(tl): water
ten(tli): lips (or border, edge)
(*atentli:* shore)
co: on, or in
(*pan):* on

This glyph was probably glossed incorrectly, for the only logical referent is Atempan, in the present-day Sierra Norte de Puebla. Since no locative glyph was included, *pan* is just as likely as *co*. The combination of water and lips (or edge, border) yield the word for shore, *atentli*.

ATEPEC (folio 16v):
"On the Hill of Water"

The glyph shows a stream of water gracefully flowing off the top of a hill. The name is formed from:

a(tl): water
tepe(tl): hill
c: on, or in

The conventional name for an inhabited place or town in Nahuatl is *altepetl* (*in atl in tepetl:* "water, hill").

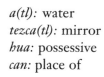

ATEZCAHUACAN (folios 12r, 42r):
"Place That Has a Pool of Water"

The glyph on folio 42r consists of a large round swirl of water above a black mirror with a red border. On folio 12r the mirror is incorporated into the whirlpool, which is much more elaborate than that on folio 42r. The name derives from:

a(tl): water
tezca(tl): mirror
hua: possessive
can: place of

In the *Matrícula* version of this glyph (folio 11v) the mirror element is quite simplified.

ATLACUIHUAYAN (folio 5v):
"Place Where They Draw Water"

The glyph is a one-handled pitcher filled with water. The name derives from:

atlacuihua(ni): water pitcher
atlacui: to draw water
hua: possessive
yan: place where

The *Codex Aubin* 1576 presents an *atlatl* as this town's place glyph; Alvarado Tezozomoc (1975b:48–49) mentions that, following the death of Huitzilihuitl el Viejo, the Mexica went from Chapultepec to Acuezcomac, where they acquired (or invented?) the *atlatl*, naming the place Atlacuihuayan after that momentous event. Clark (1938 2:3) observes that this town, the modern Tacubaya, rests in the foothills and has an aqueduct for bringing abundant stream water into the town.

ATLAN (folios 18r, 53r):
"Place of Much Water"

The glyph is a canal with two or four teeth inside. On folio 53r the four teeth are inverted, as they are in the *Matrícula de Tributos*. The name is derived from:

a(tl): water
apan(tli): canal
tlan(tli): tooth, abundance of

ATLAPULCO (folio 10r): "In the Very Deep Gorge"

The glyph consists of two hills with a stream of water rushing from between them. The name is formed from:

atlauh(tli): deep *barranca* (gorge)
pol-: an excessive or augmented state
co: on, or in

This glyph closely resembles that for the town of Xalatlauhco (folio 10r).

ATLATLAUHCA (ATLATLAVCA) (folios 7v, 25r): "Place of Red Water"

Both glyphs show a yellow-bordered canal filled with red water. On folio 25r the water lacks its usual waves. The name derives from:

a(tl): water
tlatlauh(qui): red
ca(n): place

ATL HUELIC (folio 25r): "On the Pleasant Potable Water"

The glyph is a man drinking water. The name derives from:

atl: water
huelic: something tasty and enjoyable
c: on, or in

ATLICHOLOAYAN (folio 23r): "Place Where Water Spurts"

The glyph shows water spilling from a deer's foot. The name is formed from:

atl: water
choloa: to flee or jump
  atl ichololiz: spurt or stream of water
yan: place where

Clark (1938 2:29) translates the name as "Place Where the Water Overflows and Irrigates the Fields." Today, *acholole* refers to the overflow of irrigation waters through a field's furrows. The term and practice survive especially in the present-day state of Morelos, where this town is located (Santamaría 1974:29).

ATOCPAN (folio 29r): "On the Heavy Damp Fertile Land"

The glyph is a maize plant growing from a lump of brown soil with numerous black dots. The name derives from:

a(tlalli): irrigated land
toc(tli): maize plant
  atoc(tli): heavy, damp, fertile soil
pan: on

ATOTONILCO (folios 8r, 28r, 30r): "On the Hot Water"

All four glyphs (two on folio 8r) consist of a clay pot resting on two hearthstones; water spills out of the top of the pot. The glyphs on folios 28r and 30r have handles; those on folio 8r lack that embellishment. The name is formed from:

a(tl): water
totonil(ia): to heat
co: on, or in

ATZACAN (folio 18r): "Place of the Sluice"

The glyph shows a hand holding the lid of a sluice; the boxy container is full of water. The name is formed from:

atza(qualoni): lid for closing off water; sluice
can: place of

AXOCOPAN (folios 8r, 27r): "On the Bitter Water" or "On the Creeping Wintergreen"

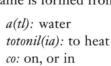

The glyph shows a tree with generous green leaves and round yellow fruits. The tree emerges from a canal full of water. The name is formed from:

a(tl): water
xoco(tl): fruit (bitter fruit)
pan(tli): canal
  pan: on

Xocotl refers to fruits with a bitter taste. The *Relación geográfica* for this town (PNE 6:14) states that Axocopan means "Bitter Water" because of the presence of such water in the town. Clark (1938 2:32) observes that *axocopac* is the creeping wintergreen.

AYAUHTOCHCUITLATLA (folio 13v): "Where There Is Much Armadillo Excrement"

The glyph shows an armadillo (represented as half-rabbit, half-tortoise) and some small droppings. The name derives from:

ayo(tl): tortoise
toch(tli): rabbit
　ayotoch(tli): armadillo
cuitla(tl): excrement
tla(n): abundance of

Another armadillo is pictured on folio 51r of *Codex Mendoza* (for Ayutuchco). This animal and its habits are discussed by Sahagún (1950–1982 11:61) and Hernández (1959 2: 296–297).

AYOÇINTEPEC (folio 46r): "On the Hill of the Little Turtle"

The glyph is the underside of a turtle shell on top of a hill. The name derives from:

ayo(tl): turtle
tzin: little
tepe(tl): hill
c: on, or in

The *tzin(tli)* glyph, a person's backside, is not expressed in this place glyph. Clark (1938 2:50) suggests that this complex of elements stands for the *ayotzin,* a plant resembling a gourd.

AYOTLAN (folio 47r): "Where There Are Many Turtles"

The glyph shows an upside-down turtle with yellow shell and brown appendages. The name derives from:

ayo(tl): turtle
tlan: abundance of

The Pacific coastal region of the Xoconochco was known generally to the Aztecs as Anahuac Ayotlan, surely referring to an abundance of turtles.

AYOTZINTEPEC (TZAQUALTEPEC) (folio 46r): "On the Pyramid Hill"

The glyph is a temple platform resting atop a hill. The annotator has misglossed this glyph as Ayotzintepec, a place glyph that actually appears later on this same folio as Ayoçintepec. The name derives from:

tzaqual(li): step pyramid
tepe(tl): hill
c: on, or in

There is some room for interpretation in this name. The stepped platform resembles the one for the place-name Çaqualpan (folio 6r), but it is also similar to Quauhtetelco on folio 48r. In the latter case the platform part of the glyph is translated as *tetelli,* "mound." Clark (1938 2:49) prefers *tzaqualli,* but either would be possible. Peñafiel (1885:185–186), recognizing the annotator's error, elected to translate the name as Teopantepec, but temples (*teopantli* or *teocalli*) are drawn quite differently (see, for example, folios 5v, 8r, 23r, 37r).

AYOXOCHAPAN (folio 24v): "On the Water of the Gourd Flower"

The glyph is a green squash with a yellow flower. Water spills off the side of the gourd. The name derives from:

ayo(tli): gourd
xoch(itl): flower
　ayoxoch(itl): gourd flower
a(tl): water
pan: on
　apan: on the water

Two varieties of *ayotli* and their flowers are described by Sahagún (1950–1982 11:288–289). Hernández (1959 1:50–51) discusses several types of gourds.

AYUTUCHCO (folio 51r): "On the Armadillo"

The glyph shows an armadillo with water emerging from its body. The name derives from:

a(tl): water
ayotoch(tli): armadillo
co: on, or in

Ayotochtli is composed of *ayotl* (tortoise) and *tochtli* (rabbit); the glyph does have the appearance of a rabbit with a tortoise shell. This is especially clear in the *Matrícula de Tributos* rendering of this glyph (folio 15r). The inclusion of *atl* as a phonetic reduplicator alerts the glyph-reader that the name of this beast begins with an "a" sound.

AZCAPUÇALCO (folio 5v):
"On the Ant Heap"

The glyph is a large red ant poised among small black dots (probably sand) and pebbles. The name derives from:

azca(tl): ant
putzal(li): sand heap
co: on, or in

Clark (1938 2:2) suggests that in this case "ant heap" refers to "dense population."

AZTA APAN (folio 50r):
"On the Canal of the White Heron"

The glyph is an ornament of heron feathers in a canal. The name is derived from:

azta(tl): white heron
apan(tli): canal
apan: on, or in

Anderson and Dibble (Sahagún 1950–1982 11:28) identify this bird as the snowy egret, *Leucophoyx thula.* Clark (1938 2:53) identifies it as *Ardea occidentalis.*

AZTAQUEMECA (folio 21v):
"Place of the Snowy Egret Feather Capes" or "Place of the White Heron Feather Capes"

The glyph is a heron's head atop a hill; a white feathered cape adorns the hill. The name derives from:

azta(tl): snowy egret or white heron
quemi(tl): deity cape
can: place

The *aztatl* is variously identified as the snowy egret or white heron (Anderson and Dibble in Sahagún 1950–1982 11:28; Hernández 1959 2:319–320; Clark 1938 2:26).

CACALOMACA (folio 33r):
"Place Where They Hunt Ravens"

The glyph consists of a bent arm hovering over a gray bird with a large open beak. The name is formed from:

cacalo(tl): common raven
ma(itl): hand
　ma: to hunt or capture
ca(n): place where

Anderson and Dibble (in Sahagún 1950–1982 11:43) identify the *cacalotl* as *Corvus corax sinuatus.* It was a black bird with glistening feathers (ibid.).

CAHUALAN (folio 13v):
"Place of Many Forsaken Women"

The glyph shows a seated woman with her hands crossed in front of her. She is weeping. The name derives from:

cahua: to leave or forsake
(t)lan: abundance of

Peñafiel (1885:80) notes the similarity between this image and that of the goddess Cihuacoatl in Durán's history, and extends his translation of this place-name to "Near the Goddess Cihuacoatl." The tooth locative is absent in this glyph.

CALIXTLAHUACAN (folio 33r):
"Place of the Plain of Houses"

The glyph consists of two inverted eyes inside a rectangular plot of ground. A house rests on the ground. The name is formed from:

cal(li): house
ixtla(pal): inverted
　ixtlahua(tl): a plain
can: place of

As elsewhere in the *Mendoza* and *Matrícula,* eyes are used as the background to demonstrate the notion of "inverted."

CALIYMAYAN (folio 10r, 33r):
"Place Where They Put Houses in Order"

Both glyphs show two houses set front-to-back. The name is formed from:

cal(li): house
ima(ti): to put in order
yan: place where

CALTEPEC (folios 16r, 51r):
"On the House on the Hill"

The glyph is a house perched atop a hill. The name is formed from:

cal(li): house
tepe(tl): hill
c: on, or in

CALYAHUALCO (folio 22r):
"In the Circle of Houses"

The glyph is a house inside a circle. The name derives from:

cal(li): house
yahual(tic): something round
co: on, or in

CAMOTLAN (folio 44r):
"Place of Many Sweet Potatoes"

The glyph consists of a gray root with green branches; upper and lower jaws with teeth extend from the side of the tuber. The name derives from:

camo(tli): sweet potato
tlan(tli): tooth, abundance of

The *camotli* is a round but twisted root, with creeping foliage (Sahagún 1950–1982 11:125), and is described in detail by Hernández (1959 1:173). The town of Camotlan was called *Ñuundihi* in Mixtec (M. E. Smith 1973:176).

CAPULTEOPAN (folio 33r):
"On the Temple of the *Capulin*"

The glyph shows two bunches of red berries or fruits in front of a tall temple. The name is formed from:

capul(lin): capulin tree fruit
teopan(tli): temple
pan: on

Anderson and Dibble (in Sahagún 1950–1982 11:121) identify the *capulin* tree as *Prunus capuli;* it has small red, brown, or black fruits. Several varieties of *capulin* are described by Hernández (1959 1:301–302).

CAPULUAC (folio 10r):
"In the Water Full of Cherry Trees"

The glyph shows a tall tree overburdened with red berries; the tree grows in a canal full of water. The name is formed from:

capul(in): cherry: the tree or the fruit
capulo: full of cherries
a(tl): water
c: on, or in

Both Hernández (1959 1:301–302) and Sahagún (1950–1982 11:121–122) discuss several varieties of *capulin*, mentioning that its fruits can be quite bitter and recommending that they be eaten only in moderation.

CHALCO (folios 3v, 4v, 6r, 7v, 41r):
"On the Greenstone" or "In the Place of the Chalca"

The glyph on all five folios is a greenstone jewel with a red border and decorative white setting. The name derives from:

chal(chihuitl): greenstone
    Chal(ca): the people of Chalco
co: on, or in

On folios 4v, 6r, and 7v this glyph is set against a plain square background.

CHALCO ATENCO (folio 17v):
"On the Water's Edge in the Place of the Chalca"

The glyph consists of two attached parts: the upper part is a greenstone jewel in a setting; the lower part is water curling around the backside of a set of lips. The name is formed from:

chal(chihuitl): greenstone
    Chalca: people of Chalco
co: on, or in
        +
a(tl): water
ten(tli): lips
    tentli: border or edge
co: on, or in

CHAPOLMOLOYAN (folio 32r):
"Place Where They Catch Grasshoppers"

The glyph consists of an arm bent over a grasshopper. The scribe took considerable pains in his drawing of the grasshopper. The name is formed from:

chapul(in): grasshopper
ma: to catch
malo: the act of catching
yan: place where

The act of catching, represented by the arm and hand, is more vividly portrayed in the *Matrícula de Tributos* (folio 6v).

CHAPOLYCXITLA (folio 8r):
"Where There Is Much *Chapolicxitl*"

The glyph shows the hairy leg of a grasshopper. The name is formed from:

chapol(in): grasshopper
ycxi(tl): foot
    chapolicx(itl): a plant
tla(n): abundance of

Hernández (1959 1:286) calls this plant *pata de cigarra* (leg of the locust, or cicada), a name reminiscent of its glyph. The roots of the plant had medicinal qualities.

CHIAPAN (folio 13r): "On the Water of the *Chinampa*"

The glyph is an unbordered canal rimmed with water and containing a plot of a land. The name derives from:

> *chi(namitl): chinampa*, an enclosure of cultivated land
> *a(tl):* water
> *pan:* on

CHICHICQUAVTLA (folio 32r): "Where There Are Many *Chichiquauhtla* Trees"

The glyph is a spotted dog crouching below a tree. The name derives from:

> *chichi:* dog
> *chichic:* bitter
> *quahu(itl):* tree
> *chichiquahuitl:* "bitter tree"
> *tla(n):* abundance of

The *chichiquahuitl*, according to Hernández (1959 1:269), had no notable characteristics or redeeming qualities. The *tlantli* locative is absent.

CHICHIHUALTATACALA (folio 15v): "Place Where Breasts Are Punctured"

The glyph is a woman's shoulders, arms, and breasts; the breasts are covered with numerous small red dots, and the body is colored yellow. The name derives from:

> *chichihual(li):* breast
> *tatacal(oa):* to make small holes
> *(t)la(n):* abundance of, place of

Peñafiel (1885:107) proposes the translation "Population of Wet Nurses." Clark (1938 2:17) mentions the Otomí custom of decorating women's arms and breasts by painting them and then cutting into them with a knife. However, Kelly and Palerm (1952:311) tentatively locate this town in southern Oaxaca, some distance from Otomí country.

CHICONQUIAUHCO (folio 7v): "In the Place of Seven-Rain" or "In the Place of *Chiconquiauitl*"

The glyph consists of a hill with three raindrops inside. Above the hill are arranged seven black dots. The name is formed from:

> *chicom(e):* seven
> *quiahu(itl):* rain
> *Chiconquiahuitl:* "Seven-Rain," a goddess
> *co:* on, or in

The combination "Seven Rain" also served as a day name in the 260-day ritual calendar. Chiconquiahuitl was an earth and water goddess revered by merchants (Sahagún 1950–1982 1:43; 2:213).

CHIETLAN (folio 42r): "Where There Is Much Chia" or "Where There Are Many *Chinampas*"

The glyph is a rectangular cultivated field below a hand; water and a sizable black dot spill from the hand. The name derives from:

> *chi(namitl): chinampa*, an enclosed cultivated area
> *a(tl):* water
> *chie(n)* or *chia(n):* chia, a plant with edible seeds
> *tlan:* abundance of

Clark (1938 2:45) feels that this glyph has been misglossed and should be switched with Molanco (folios 13r, 16r, and 54r). However, Barlow (1949a:100) finds and maps the town of Chietlan in its appropriate province (Tepeacac), which suggests that the gloss is correct. Also supporting this view are two other glyphs with the *chia-* element: Chiapan and Tepechiapan, both on folio 13r. Tepechiapan has further information on chia. Peñafiel (1885: 106) misinterprets the name as Chictlan.

CHILACACHAPAN (folio 37r): "On the Water of the *Chilacaxtli*"

The glyph is a red-bordered canal with a red chile pepper floating on top of the water. Inside the canal are three small yellow leaves. The water in the canal lacks its characteristic "waves." The name derives from:

chil(li): chile pepper
acaxi(tl): pond
　chilacax(tli): a small aquatic plant
apan(tli): canal
apan: on the water

This glyph is completely obliterated in the Matrícula (folio 9r). Clark (1938 2:40) identifies the aquatic plant as *Azolla caroliniana.* Peñafiel (1885:107–108) tentatively suggests that *acachatl,* lobster or locust, is meant here.

CHILAPAN (folio 37r): "On the Water of the Chile"

The glyph is a red chile pepper floating in a canal. The name derives from:

　chil(li): chile pepper
　apan(tli): canal
　　apan: on the water

CHILTECPINTLAN (folio 42r): "Place of Many Small Red Peppers"

The glyph is a brown bowl with a load of five red chile peppers. Two teeth form the base of the bowl. The name derives from:

　chiltecpin(tli): small red pepper
　tlan(tli): tooth, abundance of

The red pepper is identified by Clark (1938 2:46) as *Capsicum microcarpum* DC. *Chiltecpin* are described by Hernández (1959 1:138) as resembling mosquitoes in their color and small size.

CHIMALCO (folio 23r): "In the Shield"

The glyph is a round shield with a banner inside. The name derives from:

　chimal(li): shield
　co: on, or in

　Clark (1938 2:28) observes that the *pantli* (banner) glyph refers to the name *Panchimalco.*

CHINANTLAN (folio 46r): "Where There Are Many Chinanteca"

The glyph shows a cultivated field; a stalk of maize with ears and flowers emerges from the top of the field, while two teeth lie below. The name derives from:

chinam(itl): chinampa, an enclosed irrigated field
Chinan(teca): a group living in south-central Mexico
tlan(tli): tooth, abundance of

A place glyph strongly resembling this one is shown twice in the *Codex Telleriano-Remensis* (folios 37v and 41r), although the interpreter (José Corona Núñez) identifies it as Atocpan. This town would be located in the region inhabited by the Chinanteca.

CHIPETLAN (folio 39r): "Place of Xipe"

The glyph shows a head of the god Xipe Totec, "Our Lord the Flayed One." He wears his characteristic red and white pointed cap, which elsewhere stands alone as an ideograph for the god (see the glyph for Yopico, folio 20r). He wears a divine ear ornament; his face is yellow (suggesting its flayed condition) with a streak of blood through the eye. The name derives from:

　xipe: flayed
　tlan: abundance of

Xipe Totec was an important god to the peoples of this southern Mexican region. Images similar to this one are drawn on the Humboldt Fragment 1 (Seler 1904a).

CHONTALCOATLAN (folios 8r, 36r): "Where There Are Many Strange Snakes"

The glyph is a yellow and brown rattlesnake. On folio 8r the snake's rattles are blue and prominent, and a set of four teeth are attached to the snake's underbelly. The name derives from:

　chontal(li): stranger
　coa(tl): snake
　tlan(tli): tooth, abundance of

CHULULA (folio 42r) "Where There is Much Fleeing"

The glyph shows a deer's foot with blue hooves. The name is formed from:

　cholo(a): to flee or jump
　(t)la(n): abundance of

While the place-name itself is not glossed, the glyph is attached by a thin black line to the head of a man representing the Chuluteca. He wears a red headband and two feather tufts on top of his head.

COACALCO (folio 24v): "In the House of the Snake"

The glyph consists of a house with a yellow snake peering out its entrance. The name derives from:

coa(tl): snake
cal(li): house
co: on, or in

COAPAN (folio 50r): "On the Canal of the Snake"

The glyph is a snake in a canal. The name derives from:

coa(tl): snake
apan(tli): canal
pan: on

The locative *pan* (usually as a banner) is not represented, but is "buried" in the word for "canal."

COATEPEC (folios 32r, 34r): "On the Hill of the Snake"

The glyph shows a yellow snake emerging from the top of a green hill. The name is formed from:

coa(tl): snake
tepe(tl): hill
c: on, or in

COATITLAN (folio 17v): "Among the Snakes"

The glyph is a yellow rattlesnake with extended tongue; below the serpent's curving belly lie four teeth. The name derives from:

coa(tl): snake
tlan(tli): tooth
titlan: among

COATLAN (folio 23r): "Where There Are Many Snakes"

The glyph is a yellow rattlesnake curled over two teeth. The name derives from:

coa(tl): snake
tlan(tli): tooth, abundance of

Clark (1938 2:28) mentions that a large sculpture of a snake adorned this town's plaza.

COATLAYAUHCAN (folio 17v): "Place of the Coiling Snake"

The glyph is a coiled gray rattlesnake, poised to strike. The name derives from:

coa(tl): snake
tlayaua: to make gestures (as in a dance)
can: place of

COATZINCO (folio 42r): "On the Small Snake"

The glyph is a slithering rattlesnake atop the lower half of a man's body. The name is formed from:

coa(tl): snake
tzin(tli): rump
tzin: small
co: on, or in

COAXOMULCO (folio 43r): "On the Corner of the *Coatli* Tree"

The glyph consists of a three-legged bowl with a heap of black dots on top; the bowl sits on an *L* (probably of wood) which has water spilling off it. The name derives from:

co(mitl): bowl
a(tl): water
coa(tli): a tree (*Eysenhardtia polystachya*)
xumul(li): corner
co: on, or in

Since a place-name combining "bowl," "water," and "corner" seems unlikely, the reference to the *coatli* tree seems reasonable. Sahagún (1950–1982 11:110, 144) describes this large but slender tree: it apparently stored water and was used for medicinal purposes. The glyph is partially obscured in the *Matrícula* (folio 12r). The reason for including the mound of black dots is unclear.

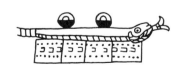

COAYXTLAHUACAN (folios 7v, 43r): "Place of the Plain of Snakes"

The glyphs on both folios are composed of a rectangular plot of ground with a long rattlesnake and inverted eyes on top. The name derives from:

coa(tl): snake
ixtla(pal): inverted
ixtlahua(tl): a plain
can: place of

The inverted eyes are included as a homonym for "plain," somewhat more difficult to express glyphically. Coayxtlahuacan was *Yodzocoo* in Mixtec (M. E. Smith 1973:176).

 COCOLAN (folio 37r): "Place of Many Disputes"

The glyph shows a coiled, twisted quagmire. The name is formed from:

col(tic): twisted
  cocol(li): dispute
(t)lan: abundance of

 COÇAMALOAPAN (folio 46r): "On the Water of the Captive Weasels"

The glyph shows a weasel poised on water in a canal. The weasel is yellow with a black band across its eye. The name is formed from:

coça(tli): weasel
mallo(tl): captivity
coçamalo(tl): rainbow
apan(tli): canal
apan: on the water

While Molina (1970: folio 23r) identifies a *coçatli* as a weasel, Macazaga Ordoño (1979:53) feels it may be a weasel or an opossum. Peñafiel (1885:85) translates this name literally as "In the River or Water of Weasels," while Clark (1938 2:49) prefers the more interpretive "On the Water of the Rainbow." Macazaga Ordoño (1979:53) pairs *coçatli* with *mallotl* to yield "River of the Captive Weasels."

 COÇOHUIPILECAN (folios 13r, 38r): "Place of the Yellow *Huipilli*" or "Place of the Yellow *Ehuatl*"

The glyph shows a yellow feathered *ehuatl,* or short warrior costume. The *ehuatl* has a red neckline. The name is formed from:

 coçauh(qui): yellow
huipilli: woman's tunic
can: place of

Although *huipilli* is included in the town's name, the glyph clearly shows an *ehuatl.* This glyph is glossed in the *Matrícula* (folio 9v), again as *coçohuipilecan. Ehuatl* appear as items of tribute on *Mendoza* folios 22r and 32r; see also appendix H, this volume.

 COÇOTLAN (folio 20r): "Where There Are Many Turtledoves"

The glyph is four yellow feathers emerging from the top of a house. The name derives from:

coçauh(qui): yellow
  coco(tli): turtledove
tlan: abundance of

Peñafiel (1885:79–80) presents the "turtledove" interpretation. Clark (1938 2:24) translates this simply as "Place of Yellow Feathers." He considers the house to represent the home of a *calpixqui,* or tribute collector.

 COLHUACAN (folio 2r): "Place of the Colhua"

The glyph is a gracefully curved hill. The name derives from:

col(tic): curved
hua: possessive
  Colhua: a group living in the
    southern Valley of Mexico
can: place of

 COLHUAÇINCO (folio 20r): "On the Little Place of the Colhua"

The glyph is a large, gracefully curved hill sitting atop the bottom half of a man's body. The name derives from:

col(tic): curved
hua: possessive
  Colhua: a group living in the
    southern Valley of Mexico
tzin(tli): rump
  tzin: small
co: on, or in

 COLIMA (folio 38r): "Place Taken by Acolhuas"

The glyph consists of an arm, bent at the elbow, with water spilling out of the upper arm. A blue band decorates the wrist. The name is formed from:

a(tl): water
col(oa): to bend
  acol(hua): Acolhua peoples
ma(itl): hand
  ma: to capture or take

The name and its glyph are somewhat enigmatic. The initial *a* is present in the glyph but not in the town's name. The glyph is very similar to that for Acolhuacan on folio 21v.

COMALTEPEC (folio 16v): "On the Hill of the *Comalli*"

The glyph consists of a large yellow disk inside a green hill. The name is formed from:

> *comal(li):* griddle, flat earthenware cooking dish
> *tepe(tl):* hill
> *c:* on, or in

The *comalli* was (and still is) used primarily for cooking tortillas.

COMITLAN (folio 13v): "Where There Are Many Pots"

The glyph is a plain brown water pot with two handles for a carrying cord. The name derives from:

> *comi(tl):* pot
> *tlan:* abundance of

CONTLAN (folio 21v): "Where There Are Many Pots"

The glyph is an *olla* (water pot) with two handles. The pot sits on two teeth. The name derives from:

> *com(itl):* pot
> *tlan(tli):* tooth
> *tlan:* abundance of

COYOLAPAN (folios 13v, 44r): "On the Water of the Bell"

The glyph on both folios consists of a yellow bell (most elaborate on folio 44r) resting in a canal. The name is formed from:

> *coyol(li):* large bell
> *apan(tli):* canal
> *apan:* on the water

The earlier Mixtec name for this town was *Saha yucu* ("At the Foot of the Hill"; M. E. Smith 1973:50).

COYUACAN (COYOACAN) (folios 5v, 47r): "Place of the Lean Coyotes"

The glyph is a furry coyote with a hole in his body. The coyote's mouth is open; his tongue protrudes noticeably on folio 5v. The name derives from:

> *coyo(ctic):* hole
> *coyo(tl):* coyote
> *huacqui:* lean, hungry
> or
> *hua:* possessive
> *can:* pertaining to a place

While these place glyphs refer to two different places, the glyphs themselves are essentially the same. The hole (*coyoctic*) provides the phonetic clue that identifies this animal indisputably as a coyote and yields the appropriate place-name. The "a" element is more ambiguous. Clark (1938 2:51) feels the element refers to the animal's leanness. Macazago Ordoño (1979:52) prefers the possessive *-hua*. Orozco y Berra (1960 1:410) and Peñafiel (1885:83) present both options. It seems a bit unlikely, though, to be speaking of "owners of coyotes," which are rather independent creatures.

COYUCAC (folios 13r, 38r): "In the Place of the Coyuca"

The glyphs of Coyucac on these two folios are very different. The glyph on folio 38r shows a person's long head in profile. On folio 13r the glyph is a complex of three elements: a coyote's head, a sandal, and a seated woman with a head much like that on folio 38r. The name derives from:

> *coyo(tl):* coyote
> *cac(tli):* sandal
> *c:* on, or in

> ---
> *coyu:* elongated
> *ca:* people (of)
> *Coyuca:* Coyuca people
> *c:* on, or in

The glyph on folio 13r "spells out" the name, while that on folio 38r relies on the elongated shape of the head, and especially its hairstyle, to convey the intended meaning. The glyph in the *Matrícula* (folio 9v) resembles that on *Mendoza* folio 38r.

COZCAQUAUHTENANCO (folio 13r): "On the Wall of the Vulture"

The glyph is a colorful vulture's head above a blue wall with ramparts. The name derives from:

> *cozcaquauh(tli):* vulture
> *tenam(itl):* wall
> *co:* on, or in

Both Hernández (1959 2:325) and Anderson and Dibble (in Sahagún 1950–1982 11:42) identify the bird as the king vulture; Hernández provides a great deal of detail on the bird's appearance and habits.

COZCATECUTLAN (folio 54r): "Where The Nobles' Beads Abound"

The glyph is formed by a ring of greenstone beads paired with a *xiuhuitzolli* (nobleman's diadem), the ideogram for *tecuhtli*, or noble. Enough of this glyph still remains in the *Matrícula de Tributos* to see its similarity with the *Mendoza* glyph. The name derives from:

cozca(tl): bead, jewel
tecuh(tli): noble
tlan: abundance of

The *tlantli*, or tooth glyph providing the locative, is missing from this place-name glyph (its use appears optional in any case, and it is difficult to imagine where the scribe might have neatly placed it here).

CUEÇALAN (folios 6r, 37r): "Where There Are Many Scarlet Macaw Feathers"

The glyph on folio 37r shows four resplendent red plumes with green tips resting atop a pair of teeth. The *Matrícula* (folio 9r) shows five plumes; only alternate feathers have green tips. On folio 6r the glyph consists of five red plumes tied with a rope; two rows of teeth are inserted into the bundle. The name derives from:

cueçal(in): scarlet macaw feathers
(t)lan: tooth, abundance of

The scarlet macaw is called *alo* in Nahuatl; its red feathers, of "well-textured, even color" are called *cueçalin* (Sahagún 1950–1982 11:19). These should not be confused with the shimmering green feathers of the quetzal bird.

CUEÇALCUITLAPILA (folio 13v): "Where There Are Many Scarlet Macaw Tail Feathers"

The glyph is a bunch of long red feathers with blue tips. The name derives from:

cueçal(in): wing and tail feathers of the scarlet macaw
cuitlapil(li): tail
(t)la(n): abundance of

These prized feathers are discussed by Sahagún (1950–1982 11:23) and Hernández (1959 2:345).

CUEÇALOZTOC (folio 10v): "In the Cave of the Scarlet Macaw Feathers" or "In the Precious Cave"

The glyph shows four red plumes in the mouth of a stylized cave. The name is formed from:

cueçal(in): scarlet macaw tail and wing feathers
quetzal(li): precious (also feathers of quetzal bird)
ozto(tl): cave
c: on, or in

The scarlet macaw (*alo*) and its elegant feathers are described by Sahagún (1950–1982 11:23) and Hernández (1959 2:345).

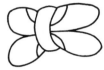

CUETLAXTLAN (folios 8r, 10v, 49r): "Where the Dressed Leather Knots Abound"

The glyph is a red leather knot in all three *Codex Mendoza* images, and in the *Matrícula de Tributos* (folio 14r). The name derives from:

cuetlax(tli): dressed leather
cuetlax(uia): to tie up something with dressed leather
tlan: abundance of

The tooth glyph, for the locative *tlan*, is absent in these glyphs. A very similar version of this glyph is also found on the Tizoc Stone. The *Codex Telleriano-Remensis* (folio 37r) includes a simplified Cuetlaxtlan glyph, red in color but lacking the knot.

CUEZCOMAHUACAN (folio 26r): "Place Where They Have Granaries"

The glyph is a food storage bin sitting on two stones. The name derives from:

cuezcoma(tl): granary or bin
hua: possessive
can: place

CUEZCOMATITLAN (folio 46r): "Among the Granaries"

The glyph shows a storage bin for maize. The name is formed from:

cuezcoma(tl): maize bin or granary
titlan: among

These bins, according to Clark (1938 2:50), were constructed of willows covered with a mud plaster; this was set on a wooden platform and raised off the ground on stones. The glyph does an admirable job of replicating this construction.

CUEZCOMATL YYACAC (folio 10v): "In the Beginning of the Granaries"

The glyph is a gray storage bin resting on a wooden platform; a nose protrudes from the side of the bin. The name derives from:

>*cuezcomatl:* granary or storage bin
>*y:* its
>*yaca(tl):* nose; point or beginning
>*c:* on, or in

CUEZCOMAYXTLAHUACAN (folio 16r): "Place of the Plain of Granaries"

The glyph consists of a gray storage bin sitting atop a rectangular plot of ground. On top of the land, and on either side of the bin, sit two inverted eyes. The name is formed from:

>*cuezcoma(tl):* storage bin or granary
>*ixtla(pal):* inverted
>*ixtlahua(tl):* a plain
>*can:* place

As used throughout the *Mendoza*, the eyes provide the backdrop against which the notion of "inverted" is presented (see, for example, Coayxtlahuacan on folios 7v and 43r).

CUICATLAN (folio 43r): "Place of Song" or "Place of the Cuicateca"

The glyph shows a face in profile with a flamboyant red and white speech scroll. The name derives from:

>*cuica(tl):* song
>*Cuica(teca):* a group in Oaxaca
>*tlan:* abundance of

The elaborate speech scroll represents singing or song. As Clark (1938 2:47) observes, the scroll is divided into five segments, the first consisting of a glyph for "painting," the next with a glyph representing Venus, and the remaining three with seashells. The corresponding five divisions in the *Matrícula* glyph (folio 12r) do not clearly relate to these representations. The *tlantli* locative is absent in both *Matrícula* and *Mendoza* renderings of this glyph.

CUITLAHUAC (folios 2v, 6r, 20v): "On the Water-Excrement"

The glyph consists of the element representing excrement inside a canal full of water. The water on folio 2v lacks the traditional "waves." The name is formed from:

>*cuitla(tl):* excrement
>*cuitlahu(ia):* to fertilize land, to take care of others (or things), or to invite oneself to an event (banquet)
>*a(tl):* water
>*c:* on, or in

Usual practice in the *Mendoza* is to use the canal (*apantli*) to indicate *apan* (on the water). This would yield the name Cuitlapan, however, an option noted by Peñafiel (1885:101–102). Clark (1938 2:24) presents only the first meaning of *cuitlauia*.

ÇACATEPEC (folio 16r): "On the Hill of Grass"

The glyph shows five blades of yellow grass growing on a green hill. The name is formed from:

>*çaca(tl):* grass
>*tepe(tl):* hill
>*c:* on, or in

The grass (*çacatl*) is discussed under Acaçacatla.

ÇACATLA (folio 40r): "Where There Is Much Grass"

The glyph is three stems of yellow grass. Only two stems are drawn in the *Matrícula* version of this glyph (folio 10v). The name derives from:

>*çaca(tl):* grass
>*tla(n):* abundance of

See the glyph for Acaçacatla (folio 50r) for a discussion of *çacatl*.

ÇACATULAN (folio 38r): "Place Where Grass and Reeds Abound"

The glyph combines blades of yellow grass with spikes of green reeds. The reeds have a white base and yellow flowers. The name is formed from:

>*çaca(tl):* grass
>*tol(lin):* reed
>*(t)lan:* abundance of

The tooth locative is missing on this glyph. *Çacatl* is discussed under the glyph for Acaçacatla (folio 50r). Reeds similar to the one shown here are drawn on *Mendoza* folio 2r.

ÇAPOTLAN (folios 13r, 45r): "Where There Are Many Zapote Trees"

The glyph on both folios is a green tree with red roots. The tree on folio 13r shows more elaborate fruits and flowers, while the glyph on folio 45r adds two teeth for the *tlantli* locative. The name derives from:

tzapo(tl): zapote tree
tlan(tli): tooth, abundance of

Clark (1938 2:49) feels that the zapote tree serves here as an ideograph for the Zapoteca, a Oaxacan Indian group. It may have carried this extended meaning.

ÇAQUALPAN (folio 6r): "On the Enclosure"

The glyph is a step pyramid (with no temple atop); an arm is drawn beside the structure. The name is formed from:

tzaqual(li): enclosure
pan: on

Clark (1938 2:4) mentions that small pyramids such as this were intended to contain especially valuable materials. He also states that the inclusion of the arm and hand mean that the pyramid was constructed by hand; given the place-name, however, it may as well signify the act of depositing "things" in the structure.

ÇAQUANTEPEC (folio 16r): "On the Hill of the Troupial"

The glyph shows two bunches of yellow feathers (with two feathers each) arranged at the base and summit of a hill. The name is formed from:

çaquan: troupial
tepe(tl): hill
c: on, or in

Sahagún (1950–1982 11:20–21) mentions that the "very yellow" tail feathers of this bird are overlain by black ones, and when the troupial spreads its tail the yellow feathers can be seen, "like the gold they show through." Molina (1970: folio 15r) defines a *çaquantototl* as a "bird with rich yellow feathers."

ÇENÇONTEPEC (folio 16r): "On the Hill of the Four Hundred"

The glyph is a tall hair on the summit of a hill. The name derives from:

cen: one
tzon(tli): hair
　centzon(tli): four hundred
tepe(tl): hill
c: on, or in

The hair, as symbol for the number 400, is found repeatedly on objects throughout the tribute section of *Codex Mendoza.*

ÇENPOALAN (folio 21v): "Place of Twenty"

The glyph consists of the head, in profile, of a Totonac. He wears a large white earplug and a prominent blue lip plug, and has his hair tied up in the back with a red cord. This hairstyle is more fully developed in the *Matrícula* (folio 3r). The head rests on the customary green hill. The name is formed from:

cempoal(li): twenty
(t)lan: abundance of

Both Clark (1938 2:26) and Peñafiel (1885:72) mention the possibility that the name derives from the custom of holding a market every twenty days in this town. However, the name may as well derive from its association (through migrants?) with the Totonac town of Cempoalla near the Gulf coast.

ÇIHUANTEOPAN (CIHUATEOPAN) (folio 52r): "On the Woman's Temple"

The glyph consists of a woman's head atop a temple. The woman has her hair twisted (more clearly seen in the *Matrícula de Tributos:* folio 15v) and wears an ear ornament. The name derives from:

cihua(tl): woman
teo(calli): temple
pan: on

Clark (1938 2:54) suggests that the *cihuateopan* (or *cihuateocalli*) were "places where images of the Ciuapipiltin [women who died in childbirth] were kept." Peñafiel (1885:73–74) suggests that the head represents the mother goddess Cihuacoatl. However, the combination of hairdo and earplug more closely resembles Sahagún's depiction of the Cihuapipiltin (1950–1982 1: plate 10).

 ÇIHUATLAN (folio 38r): "Place of Many Women"

The glyph is a woman's head in profile. Her face is colored yellow with two black marks on her cheek, and her hair is arranged in typical Aztec fashion. She wears a large blue ear ornament. The name derives from:

cihua(tl): woman
tlan: abundance of

The tooth glyph is absent here and on this glyph in the *Matrícula* (folio 9v). Clark (1938 2:40) feels that the *cihuatl* serves as an ideograph for *cihuapipiltin,* women who died in childbirth and were transformed into goddesses.

 ÇILAN (folio 12r): "Where There Are Many Small Shells"

The glyph contains six white shells scattered about; they resemble the shells attached to streams of water, usually alternating with water drops. The name is formed from:

cil(in): small shell
(t)lan: abundance of

This spiral seashell, "small and very smooth, very white," is briefly mentioned by Sahagún (1950–1982 11:231).

 ÇINACANTEPEC (folio 10r): "On the Hill of the Bat"

The glyph shows the fierce gray head of a bat on top of a hill. The name is formed from:

tzinacan: bat
tepe(tl): hill
c: on, or in

Clark (1938 2:9) suggests that the bat is used here as an ideograph for the tree *tzinacanquahuitl,* discussed by Hernández (1959 2:143).

 ÇINACANTLAN (folio 15v): "Where There Are Many Bats"

The glyph shows a hungry-looking bat in flight. The name is formed from:

tzinacan: bat
tlan: abundance of

A bat's head is shown on folio 10r (Çinacantepec). Clark (1938 2:18) observes that the bat depicted here resembles a vampire bat.

 ÇINCOZCAC (folio 34r): "On the Maize Jewel"

The glyph consists of three maize ears (two yellow and one red) strung on a tied green cord. In the *Matrícula* (folio 7v) all three ears are red. The name is formed from:

cin(tli): dried maize ears
cozca(tl): jewel
c: on, or in

Clark (1938 2:38) notes that the *cincozcatl* was the necklace of the goddess Mayahuel.

 ÇITLALTEPEC (folio 17v): "On the Starry Hill"

The glyph is a collection of solid white circles on a black background set into the top of a green hill. The name derives from:

citlal(lo): starry
tepe(tl): hill
c: on, or in

 ÇOÇOLAN (folios 15v, 17v): "Where Much Is Old and Worn"

The glyph consists of a square white cloth with a bone perforator passing through it. Numerous dark semicircles suggest that the bone has entered the cloth several times. On folio 17v the cloth sits atop a hill. The name is formed from:

ço: to bleed (to perforate with
  something sharp)
  çoço: to perforate many times
  çoçol(tic): old and worn
  (t)lan: abundance of

The bone is used elsewhere in the
Mendoza to indicate the sound "ço"
(as on folios 20v, 35r, and 36r).

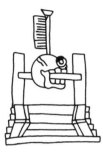

ÇONPAHUACAN (folio 35r):
"Place That Has a Skull Rack"

The glyph consists of a skull rack,
complete with one skull. A banner,
probably of hair, flies above the skull.
The *Matrícula* (folio 8r) shows a
feather tuft in the middle of the banner and glosses the name as *tzonpanco*. The name is formed from:

  tzon(tli): hair
    pan(tli): banner
    tzompan(tli): skull rack or row
  hua: possessive
  can: place of

ÇONPANCO (folio 24v):
"On the Hair" or "On the Skull
Rack"

The glyph is a banner made of hair,
with a small clump of hair on the top
of its staff. In the *Matrícula* (folio 4r)
the tuft of hair is quite prominent.
The name derives from:

  tzon(tli): hair
  pan(tli): banner
    pan: on

Peñafiel (1885:228) suggests that
the glyph represents a *tzompantli*, or
skull rack.

ÇOQUITZINCO (folio 33r):
"On the Little Clay"

The glyph is a lump of gray clay and
the bottom half of a man's body. The
name derives from:

  çoqui(tl): clay
  tzin(tli): rump
    tzin: small or little
  co: on, or in

ÇTZIHUINQUILOCAN (folio 30r):
"Place Full of *Itzihuinquilitl*"

The glyph consists of three elements:
a rectangular plot of ground, a flint
knife with four teeth on its side, and
two leafy branches. The name is
formed from:

itz(tli): obsidian
  ihuin(in): shape
  quil(itl): an edible plant
    itzihuinquili(tl): itzihuinquilitl
      (a cultivated plant)
  itzihuinquilo: full of *itzihuinquilitl*
  can: place

An edible plant glossed as *itzmiquilitl*
is described and illustrated in Sahagún (1950–1982 11:134, ill. 464a).

ÇULAN (folio 15v):
"Where There Are Many Quails"

The glyph consists of a quail with
spotted breast, brown feathers, and
blue feet and bill. The name is formed
from:

  çul(in): quail
  (t)lan: abundance of

The tasty but quick quail is described
by Sahagún (1950–1982 11:49), who
affirms the white-spotted breast and
"chia-spotted" feathers depicted here.

ECATEPEC (folios 12r, 22r):
"On the Hill of Wind" or "On the
Hill of Ehecatl"

The glyph on both folios is a head
representing the god of wind (Ehecatl) atop a hill. The name derives
from:

  eheca(tl): wind or god of wind
  tepe(tl): hill
  c: on, or in

ECATL YQUAPECHCO (folio 12r):
"On Ehecatl's Wooden Platform"

The glyph is the head of the wind
god Ehecatl, resting on a wooden
platform. The name derives from:

  ecatl: Ehecatl, god of wind
  y: his
  quauh(tla)pech(tli): wooden plat-
    form or scaffold
  co: on, or in

EHUACALCO (folio 40r):
"In the House of Skin"

The glyph shows a yellow human
skin (*tlacaehuatl*) in the entrance of
a house. The name derives from:

  ehua(tl): skin
  cal(li): house
  co: on, or in

EPAÇUYUCAN (folio 22r):
"Place Full of *Epaçotl*"

The glyph shows a crouching mammal with a bushy tail and three stripes. Two leafy plants emerge from the animal's back. In the *Matrícula* (folio 3r), the plants are not included. The name is formed from:

> *epa(ntli):* three lines or rows
> *epa(tl):* skunk
> *tzo(tl):* odor
>> *epaço(tl):* epazote, a small green plant
> *yo(tl):* pertaining to, full of
> *can:* place

Epazote (*Chenopodium ambrosioides*) was used to enhance sauces and to cure various ills (Sahagún 1950–1982 11:193; Hernández 1959 1:369).

EPATLAN (folio 42r):
"Where There Are Many Skunks"

The glyph is a furry brown skunk crouched on two teeth. The name is formed from:

> *epa(tl):* skunk
> *tlan(tli):* tooth, abundance of

The *Matrícula* version of this glyph (folio 11v) omits the teeth. Sahagún (1950–1982 11:13–14) describes the skunk in good detail.

ETLAN (folio 44r):
"Where There Are Many Beans"

The glyph is a simple black bean with a white spot. The name is formed from:

> *e(tl):* bean
> *tlan:* abundance of

No tooth locative is included in this place glyph. The Zapotec name for this town was *Loo-uanna*, "Place of Provisions" (Clark 1938 2:49); its Mixtec name was *Ñuunduchi* (M. E. Smith 1973:177).

GUAPALCALCO (folio 28r):
"On the House of Planks"

The glyph is a large and elegant building with wooden pillars and decorated façade and roof. The name derives from:

> *huapalcal(li):* store or house of planks
> *co:* on, or in

Clark (1938 2:33) interprets this as "In the Place of the Storehouse"; Peñafiel (1885:115) suggests that the structure might represent a public building for schooling or the administration of justice. A more conventional spelling of this name would be Huapalcalco.

HUAXACAC (**GUAXACAC**) (folios 17v, 44r):
"Where the *Haxin* Trees Begin"

The glyph on folio 44r is a profile face with two tree branches attached to the nose. The glyph on folio 17v adds a hill and hair on the head; the branches actually emerge from the face. In both cases, long, bright red pods dangle from the branches. The image in the *Matrícula de Tributos* (folio 12v) more closely resembles the former *Mendoza* glyph. The name derives from:

> *huax(in):* huaxin tree
> *yaca(tl):* nose, or beginning
> *c:* on, or in

The *huaxin* tree is described by Sahagún (1950–1982 11:120) as resembling the mesquite with long, chile-red, beanlike fruits. The Mixtec name for this town is *Nuunduvua* or *Ñundungua* (M. E. Smith 1973:177).

HUAXTEPEC (folios 7v, 24v):
"On the Hill of the *Huaxin*"

Both glyphs consist of a hill with a tree growing from its top. The tree has three branches, green leaves, and long red fruit pods. The name is formed from:

> *huax(in):* huaxin tree
> *tepe(tl):* hill
> *c:* on, or in

Sahagún (1950–1982 11:120) describes the *huaxin* tree (*Leucaena esculenta*) as smooth and swaying, with chile-red "fruit like string beans," precisely as depicted in this place glyph.

HUEHUETLAN (folios 13v, 42r, 47r): "Place of Many Old Men" or "Place of the Old God"

On folio 13v the glyph shows the wrinkled face and white hair of an old man; a pair of teeth are below, indicating the locative. Similar heads appear on folios 42r and 47r, though the *tlantli* glyph is omitted. The name is formed from:

> *huehue:* old man
> *tlan:* tooth, abundance of

Clark (1938 2:46) suggests that *huehue* serves here as an ideograph for Huehueteotl, the old god, also the fire god Xiuhtecuhtli. Peñafiel (1885:117) also makes this interpretation.

HUEXOLOTLAN (folios 13r, 16r): "Where There Are Many Turkeys"

The glyph on both folios shows a standing turkey, drawn in colorful and careful detail. The name derives from:

> *huexolo(tl):* turkey
> *tlan:* abundance of

Domesticated and wild turkeys are described by Hernández (1959 2:333–334).

HUEXOTZINCO (folio 42r): "On the Small Willow Tree"

The glyph shows a leafy green tree rooted to the bottom half of a *maxtlatl*-clad man. The name derives from:

> *huexo(tl):* willow tree
> *tzin(tli):* rump
> *tzin:* small
> *co:* on, or in

The place glyph is attached by a black line to the head of a man identified as a Huexotzincatl. The man wears a red headband and the curved labret typical of men from this town.

HUEYAPAN (folios 16r, 30r): "On the Lake"

The glyphs show a circle full of sheets of water. A banner tops the circle on folio 16r, but is absent on the glyph on folio 30r. The name is formed from:

> *hueya(tl):* lake
> *pan(tli):* banner
> *pan:* on

HUEYPUCHTLAN (HUEYPUCHTLA) (folios 8r, 29r): "Place of Great Opochtli"

The glyph is the head of the god Opochtli. The face is painted red, the mouth blue, and the hair yellow. He is decorated with a single tail feather and, on folio 8r, a blue necklace with bells. The name derives from:

> *huey:* great or large
> *(o)poch(tli):* Opochtli, a god
> *tlan:* abundance of

Peñafiel (1885:118) identifies this figure as a professional merchant, or *pochtecatl*, while Clark (1938 2:33) suggests that it represents Opochtli. The drawing of Opochtli in Sahagún only vaguely resembles that shown here (1950–1982 1: plate 17).

HUIÇIÇILAPAN (HUITZIÇILAPA) (folios 6r, 32r): "On the Water of the Hummingbird"

Both glyphs show a green hummingbird with long yellow beak inside a yellow-bordered canal. The name is formed from:

> *huitzitzil(in):* hummingbird
> *apan(tli):* canal
> *apan:* on the water

The hummingbird is described in detail by Sahagún (1950–1982 11:24).

HUIÇILAN (folios 21v, 24v): "Where There Are Many Hummingbirds"

Both glyphs show a green bird with yellow bill. The tooth (*tlantli*) locative is absent on this glyph on folio 24v, but present on folio 21v. The name is formed from:

> *huitzi(tzilin):* hummingbird
> *(t)lan:* abundance of

HUIÇILAPAN (folio 23r): "On the Water of the Hummingbird"

The glyph shows a hummingbird in a canal full of water. The name is formed from:

> *huitzi(tzilin):* hummingbird
> *apan(tli):* canal
> *apan:* on the water

HUIÇILOPUCHCO (folio 20r): "In the Place of *Huitzilopochtli*"

The glyph shows a green hummingbird inside a blue circle. The name is formed from:

> *huitzi(tzilin)*: hummingbird
> *opoch(tli)*: left
> > *Huitzilopochtli*: patron god of the Mexica
>
> *co*: on, or in

Sahagún (1950–1982 11:24–25) describes several varieties of hummingbirds.

HUILOTEPEC (folio 15v): "On the Hill of the Mourning Dove"

The glyph shows a delicate gray bird perched on top of a hill. The name is formed from:

> *huilo(tl)*: mourning dove
> *tepe(tl)*: hill
> *c*: on, or in

This bird acquired its name from its weeping song, "uilo-o-o," and also from a myth in which this lazy bird told all the other birds to go (*uiloa*) to drink water without him (Sahagún 1950–1982 11:51).

HUIPILAN (folio 13v): "Where There Are Many *Huipiles*"

The glyph is a woman's tunic with red trim. The name derives from:

> *huipil(li)*: *huipilli*, woman's tunic
> *(t)lan*: abundance of

Other illustrations of such tunics (worn or bundled for tribute payment) are found throughout parts 2 and 3 of *Codex Mendoza*.

HUITZAMOLA (folio 39r): "Where *Huitzamolli* Abounds"

The glyph is a red and green maguey thorn stuck into a yellow root with green leaves. The name is formed from:

> *huitz(tli)*: large thorn or spine
> *amol(li)*: amole, a root
> > *huitzamol(li)*: a variety of *amole*
> *tla(n)*: abundance of

Amole was a thick, fibrous root used as a soap (Hernández 1959 1:93; Sahagún 1950–1982 11:133). Santamaría (1974:63–64) describes several varieties of *amole*, but not this one. He also mentions that some varieties of yucca and agave had similar roots; given the thorny character of these plants, this may be what is meant by this glyph. Clark (1938 2:42) specifies the thorn in the glyph as "the blood-stained maguey spike jewel" (*chalchiuhuitztli ezço*).

HUITZOCO (folio 37r): "On the Digging Stick"

The glyph shows a long pointed pole with a fringed white cloth across its middle. The name derives from:

> *huitzoc(tli)*: stick used for cultivating
> *co*: on, or in

The cloth shown in the glyph is not included in the glossed name. Peñafiel (1885:123) suggests that the cloth is a *quemitl*, or sacred bib; Clark (1938 2:39) interprets it as a *tetectli*, a cloth hanging. In the former case the name might read *Huitzoquemecan*; in the latter, *Huitzoteteco*.

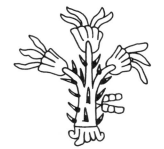

HUIXACHTITLAN (folio 17v): "Among the *Huixachin*"

The glyph is a thorny tree with green leaves and yellow pods. Two rows of teeth lie at the side of the trunk. The name derives from:

> *huixach(in)*: huizache
> *tlan(tli)*: tooth
> > *titlan*: among

Clark (1938 2:21) identifies this thorny plant as *Pithecellobium albicans*, while Santamaría (1974:608) considers it an acacia and describes it at some length.

HUIZNAHUAC (folio 19r): "Beside the Large Maguey Spine"

The glyph consists of a blue and red maguey spine (the red representing sacrificial blood) with a blue speech scroll emerging from a small opening in the spine. The name is formed from:

huitz(tli): large thorn or spine
nahua(tl): good sound
c: on, or in
  nahuac: beside

This glyph is accompanied by a detailed drawing of a temple, representing the temple of Huitznahuac. This temple was located in the city of Tenochtitlan south of the central ceremonial plaza; *huitztlampa* also means "south." Ceremonies celebrated at this temple were especially important during the month of Panquetzaliztli. At that time images of the *Centzonhuitznahua* ("400 southerners") were sacrificed to honor Huitzilopochtli, thus recounting the myth of that god's energetic birth.

HUIZQUILOCAN (folio 32r): "Place Full of *Huitzquilitl*"

The glyph shows three leafy branches emerging from the top of a hill. The name is formed from:

huitz(tli): large thorn or spine
quil(itl): edible plant
  huitzquilo: full of *huitzquilitl*
can: place

The *huitzquilitl (Circum mexicanum)* is a stringy, thorny plant (Sahagún 1950–1982 11:137).

HUIZTLAN (folios 13v, 15v, 47r): "Place of Many Thorns" or "South"

On folios 13v and 47r this glyph consists of a red and blue maguey thorn with a pair of teeth attached at the side. On folio 15v the thorn pierces the teeth from above. The name is formed from:

huitz(tli): large thorn or spine
tlan: tooth, abundance of

This name may also be a pun on *huitztlampa,* meaning "south," as Peñafiel (1885:124) suggests.

MACUILXOCHIC (folio 44r): "Place of the God Macuilxochitl"

The glyph consists of five red circles with an elaborate multicolored flower above. The name derives from:

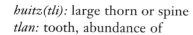

macuil(li): five
xochi(tl): flower
  Macuilxochitl: a maize god, patron of games
c: on, or in

Clark (1938 2:48) suggests that the two symbols stand for the god Macuilxochitl; Peñafiel (1885:135) shares this interpretation.

MAÇATLAN (folios 12r, 13v, 47r): "Place of Many Deer"

The glyph on folios 13v and 47r is a handsome deer head with two teeth attached to its neck. The glyph on folio 12r lacks the two teeth. The name derives from:

maza(tl): deer
tlan(tli): tooth, abundance of

Clark (1938 2:51) extends this interpretation to "Near the Maçateca," a group living in Oaxaca. While the town meant on folios 13v and 47r is situated too far south for this to have significance, the conquest attributed to Tizoc (folio 12r) may have been located in Oaxaca (Kelly and Palerm 1952:301–303). While the presence or absence of locative glyphs is quite freewheeling in this document, in this case it may have served to distinguish between the two towns.

MALINALCO (folio 35r): "On the Grass"

The glyph shows the day sign for grass: a partial skull with gaping mouth, red and white eye, and green and yellow grass blades for hair. The name is formed from:

malinal(li): grass
co: on, or in

Clark (1938 2:38) observes that this type of grass was used in securing mummy bundles. Hernández (1959 2:54) notes that it was used for making nets and was pleasantly edible when mixed with other foods.

MALINALTEPEC (folios 16r, 39r, 41r): "On the Hill of Grass"

The glyphs on these folios are quite different. The one on folio 16r shows twisted grasses with red roots and yellow flowers. The ones on folios 39r and 41r have a white skull with yellow-flowered grass for hair. A green hill provides a base in all three glyphs. The glyphs for Malinaltepec in the *Matrícula* (folios 10r and 11r) resemble those on *Mendoza* folios 39r and 41r. The name is formed from:

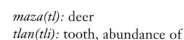

malinal(li): grass
tepe(tl): hill
c: on, or in

Malinalli was one of the twenty day signs in the Aztec 260-day ritual calendar. As such, it is usually represented as the grass-haired skull (see Caso 1971:334).

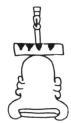

MAMALHUAZTEPEC (folio 7v): "On the Hill of the Fire Drill"

The glyph is an arrow set into a fire stick. This arrangement sits on top of a hill. The name derives from:

mamalhuaz(tli): fire drill
tepe(tl): hill
c: on, or in

As Clark (1938 2:5) observes, *mamalhuaztli* also referred to the constellation of Gemini (Castor and Pollux), as well as to a tall tree with broad leaves (ibid.; Hernández 1959 2:53–54). Fire sticks used to light the ceremonial fire commemorating the completion of each fifty-two-year cycle are shown on *Codex Mendoza* folios 2r, 3v, and 15v.

MAPACHTEPEC (folios 13v, 47r): "On the Hill of the Raccoon"

The glyph is a hand in front of a mass of Spanish moss. On folio 13v the hand and moss are below a hill; on folio 47r they lie above a hill. The name derives from:

ma(itl): hand
pach(tli): Spanish moss
mapach(tli): raccoon
c: on, or in

It is interesting that the scribe chose a compound way of forming this name, in place of a single pictograph of a raccoon.

MATIXCO (folio 21v): "In the Place of Escape"

The glyph consists of an eye poised between two outstretched hands. The name is formed from:

ma(itl): hand
ix(telolotli): eye
maquixtia: to escape
co: on, or in

Barlow (1949a:69) and Clark (1938 2:26) both note the similarity of this name to Maquixco. Barlow bases his observation on the presence of a town by that name in Acolhuacan province; Clark suggests this meaning based on his interpretation of the glyphs, that the hands are actually wrists (*maquechtli*). If the name is Matixco, the *t* is added for euphony.

MATLATLAN (folio 10v): "Where There Are Many Nets"

The glyph consists of an open fishing net above two teeth. The name is formed from:

matla(tl): net, in general
tlan(tli): tooth
tlan: abundance of

METEPEC (folios 10r, 33r): "On the Hill of the Maguey"

On both folios the glyph is a red and blue maguey plant on top of a hill. The red roots of the plant are clearly shown. The name is formed from:

me(tl): maguey
tepe(tl): hill
c: on, or in

MIACATLA (folio 23r): "Where There Are Many Reed Arrows"

The glyph is an arrow flanked by blue reeds. The name derives from:

mi(tl): arrow
aca(tl): reed
tla(n): abundance of

The tooth locative is absent in this glyph.

MIAHUA APAN (folio 52r): "On the Canal of the Maize Flower"

The glyph consists of two flower stalks of maize rising above a canal. The name derives from:

miahua(tl): the maize flower and spike
apan(tli): canal
pan: on

Clark (1938 2:55) suggests that the maize-flower glyph represents Miahuatl, "goddess of the products of the earth." The glyph is very similar in the *Lienzos de Tuxpan* (Melgarejo Vivanco 1970).

MICHAPAN (folio 46r):
"On the Water of the Fish"

The glyph shows a fish swimming in a canal full of water. The name derives from:

mich(in): fish
apan(tli): canal
apan: on the water

MICHMALOYAN (folio 31r):
"Place Where They Catch Fish"

The glyph shows an arm bent over a white fish. The name is formed from:

mich(in): fish
ma(itl): hand
  ma: to catch
  malo: the act of catching
yan: place where

MICHTLAN (folio 46r):
"Where There Are Many Fish"

The glyph consists of a single element: a fish with clearly delineated scales and fins. The name is formed from:

mich(in): fish
tlan: abundance of

As in several cases in the *Mendoza*, the tooth locative is absent from this place glyph.

MICTLAN (folio 16v):
"Where There Are Many Dead"

The glyph consists of long white bones bordering a square plot of dark ground on three sides. The name is formed from:

mic(qui): dead
tlan: abundance of

Mictlan was the "place of the dead" where most deceased were believed to spend their afterlives. Compare this glyph with the "mummy-bundle" glyphs for *Mictlan* on folios 43r, 49r, and 52r, and the "corpse" glyphs for *Miquiyetlan* and *Miquetlan* on folios 10v and 12r.

MICTLAN (folios 43r, 52r):
"Where There Are Many Dead"

On folio 43r the glyph has a gaping skull on the left and a wrapped and tied mummy bundle on the right. Both are unpainted. On folio 52r the glyph is a mummy bundle with a bean perched atop its head. The name derives from:

mic(qui): dead
tlan: abundance of
and
mic(qui): dead
e(tl): bean
  micque(tl): corpse
tlan: abundance of

The tooth locative is omitted from these place glyphs. The glyph on folio 52r might be better glossed as Miquetlan, thus including the bean element. On folio 10v a similar gloss is applied to a defunct-looking individual lacking the bean (for Miquiyetlan). These two may have been confused. In the *Lienzos de Tuxpan* (Melgarejo Vivanco 1970), this place is represented by the head of the god Mictlantecuhtli.

MICTLAN QUAUHTLA (folio 49r):
"Forest (at the) Place of the Dead"

The glyph shows a tied mummy bundle resting against a three-branched tree (two branches in the *Matrícula de Tributos* folio 14r). The name derives from:

mictlan: place of the dead
  mi(qui): die
  tlan: abundance of
quauhtla: forest

MIQUIYETLAN (**MIQUETLAN**) (folios 10v, 12r):
"Where There Are Many Corpses"

The glyph on both folios shows a nude corpse with hair cropped short on top of the head, and a hole for a nose plug. On folio 10v the hair is shown long in back. The name derives from:

micque(tl): corpse
tlan: abundance of

Clark (1938 2:11) suggests that the *y* is included for euphony, and that a bean glyph (for *etlan*) must be missing. He also states that the nose-plug hole indicates that the individual is a Pacific coast inhabitant; however, Kelly and Palerm (1952:297) place this town in Veracruz state. The figure in the place glyph for Tamuoc (folio 10v), a Huaxtec town in northern Veracruz, has a similar hairstyle and nose-plug hole. Three of the glyphs for Mictlan in *Codex Mendoza* (folios 43r, 49r, and 52r) all show more conventional corpses, wrapped in mummy bundles. The remaining Mictlan glyph (folio 16v) consists of bones and a plot of dark ground.

MITEPEC (folio 33r):
"On the Hill of the Arrow"

The glyph is a yellow and red arrow poised on a green hill. The name derives from:

mi(tl): arrow
tepe(tl): hill
c: on, or in

MITZINCO (folio 40r):
"On the Small Arrow"

The glyph is a red and yellow arrow with three eagle-feather tufts; the lower half of a man's body sits below the arrow. The feather tufts are much reduced in the *Matrícula* glyph (folio 10v). The name is formed from:

mi(tl): arrow
tzin(tli): rump
tzin: small
co: on, or in

MIXCOAC (folio 5v):
"On the Cloud-Snake" or "On Mixcoatl"

The glyph is the upper part of a blue snake; four swirls decorate the serpent's back. Both the swirls and the blue color symbolize clouds. The name derives from:

mix(tli): cloud
coa(tl): snake
Mixcoatl: a god of the hunt
c: on, or in

Mixcoatl was a god of war and the hunt who was especially celebrated during the month of Quecholli (Nicholson 1971b: table 4).

MIXTLAN (folios 10v, 46r):
"Where There Are Many Clouds"

The glyph in both instances consists of two teeth above the stylized glyph for a cloud. The name is formed from:

mix(tli): cloud
tlan(tli): tooth, abundance of

The cloud resembles facial symbolism associated with the god Tlaloc. Clark (1938 2:49) extends this name to mean "Near the Mixteca," people living in Oaxaca.

MIZQUIC (folios 2v, 6r, 20v):
"On the Mesquite"

The glyphs on folios 2v and 6r show a complete mesquite plant with roots, stem, leaves, and pods. The glyph on folio 20v shows only the upper branches, leaves, and pods; these rest on top of a house. The name is formed from:

mizqui(tl): mesquite
c: on, or in

Clark (1938 2:25) interprets the house glyph on folio 20v as the residence of a *calpixqui,* or tribute collector. The mesquite (*Prosopis juliflora*) is described by Sahagún (1950–1982 11:120–121).

MIZQUITLAN (folio 13v):
"Where There Are Many Mesquite"

The glyph shows the mesquite plant in detail, with red roots, thorny trunk, green leaves, and red and yellow pods. The name is formed from:

mizqui(tl): mesquite
tlan: abundance of

The mesquite is pictured elsewhere in *Codex Mendoza* on folios 2v, 6r, 20v, and 27r. Sahagún (1950–1982 11:120–121) describes this plant and its uses in some detail.

MOLANCO (folios 13r, 16r, 54r):
"In the Place of Many Rubber Bowls"

The glyph consists of three elements, arranged somewhat differently on the three folios. On folio 13r the glyph contains all three elements: a brown two-legged bowl on the bottom, a black dot with white border in the middle, and two teeth on top. On folio 16r the glyph includes only the dot and teeth. On folio 54r, the bowl (three-legged) and dot appear, but not the teeth. The one constant is the dot. The name is formed from:

mol(caxitl): bowl for grinding, *molcajete*
ol(li): rubber
(t)lan(tli): tooth
tlan: abundance of
co: on, or in

Clark (1938 2:12) feels that the glyph must be misglossed and that it should be switched with Chietlan (folio 42r). However, both Peñafiel (1885:144–145) and Barlow and MacAfee (1949:27, 29) pick up the bowl-and-rubber elements of the name. Furthermore, these circles resemble balls of rubber given in tribute by the province of Tochtepec (folio 46r). Both Barlow (1949a:54) and Kelly and Palerm (1952:311) locate this town geographically within the realm of Tzicoac province. The only unusual aspect of the name's interpretation is the use of the *tlantli* (tooth) element in combination with another locative. In the *Matrícula de Tributos*, the glyph is partially obliterated, with only the circle showing (folio 16v).

MOLOTLA (folio 23r):
"Where There Are Many Common House Finches"

The glyph is a stocky bird with brown feathers and a red crown. The name derives from:

molo(tl): common house finch
tla(n): abundance of

The illustration of this bird in Sahagún (1950–1982 11: plate 157) shows a more fragile-looking avian. Sahagún (ibid.: 48) describes the *molotl* as an ashen and brown bird with a short bill; the male has a red crown. It was easily domesticated and a great singer.

MYZQUIYAHUALA (folio 27r):
"Where There Are Many Mesquite Circles"

The glyph is a thorny but very droopy mesquite trunk. The trunk has red roots, green leaves, and long yellow flowers. The name derives from:

mizqui(tl): mesquite
yahual(tic): circle
(t)la(n): abundance of

Molina (1970: folio 31v) translates *yahualtic* as "something round like the moon or a shield." Sahagún (1950–1982 11:120–121) describes the mesquite (*Prosopis juliflora*) in some detail, indicating that it could be bent and formed "into a circle."

NACOCHTLAN (folio 42r):
"Place of Many Earplugs"

The glyph is an ear; a turquoise-colored ornament passes through a large perforation in the earlobe. The name derives from:

nacoch(tli): earplug
tlan: abundance of

The *tlantli* glyph is absent from this place glyph. Clark (1938 2:46) suggests that the earplug is not of turquoise, but rather of painted wood.

NANTZINTLAN (folio 13v):
"Where There Are Many Revered Mothers" or "Where There Is Much *Nantzinxocotl*"

The glyph is the bottom half of a kneeling woman with yellow feet; a pan full of black dots rests above her body. The name derives from:

nan(tli): mother
tzin(tli): rump
  nantzin(xocotl): fruit of the
    nantzin, or "revered mother"
tzin: small, revered
tlan: abundance of

Clark (1938 2:15) mentions that the small dots symbolize maternity and suggests the reference to the plant (discussed by Hernández 1959 2:30), while Peñafiel (1885:147–148) prefers the more direct translation "Where They Reverence Mothers or Maternity." Hernández indicates that the plant was used to relieve women in labor.

NEPOPOALCO (folio 25r):
"In the Place of the Count"

The glyph shows many small stones spilling from a hand; both are above a hill. The name is formed from:

nepopoal(li): a count, repeatedly
co: on, or in

Peñafiel (1885:148), drawing on Torquemada's historical information, which speaks of Chichimec occupation of this town and its subsequent conquest by the Totonac, translates the place-name as "Place Where the Chichimecs Were Counted."

NEXTITLAN (folio 20v):
"Among the Ashes"

The glyph is a gray circle containing numerous small black dots and two rows of teeth. The name derives from:

> *nex(tli):* ash
> *tlan(tli):* tooth
>> *titlan:* among

NOCHCOC (folio 38r):
"On the Prickly Pear Cactus Fruit"

The glyph consists of a red and yellow prickly pear cactus fruit perched on top of a hill. The name is formed from:

> *noch(tli):* prickly pear cactus fruit
> *co:* on, or in
> *c:* on, or in

Clark (1938 2:40) includes *ço* (to bleed) in his translation, but the annotator was extremely careful with cedillas and it is unlikely that he missed one here. Nonetheless, it is odd to have two locatives in the name.

NOCHIZTLAN (folios 15v, 43r):
"Where There Is Much Cochineal"

The glyph is a brown bowl with a prickly pear cactus and its red fruits. Two teeth provide the *tlantli* locative on folio 15v. The name derives from:

> *noch(tli):* prickly pear cactus fruit
> *ez(tli):* blood
>> *nochez(tli):* cochineal
> *tlan(tli):* tooth, abundance of

The Mixtec name for this town was *Atoco* (M. E. Smith 1973:176).

NOCHTEPEC (folio 36r):
"On the Hill of the Prickly Pear Cactus"

The glyph is a prickly pear cactus on top of a green hill. The name derives from:

> *noch(tli):* prickly pear cactus fruit
> *tepe(tl):* hill
> *c:* on, or in

OCOAPAN (folio 39r):
"On the Pine Water" or "On the Pine Canal"

The glyph is a pine tree, complete with pine cone and needles, standing behind a half-canal. The name derives from:

> *oco(tl):* pine (*Pinus* sp.)
> *apan(tli):* canal
>> *apan:* on the water

The Aztecs valued pine trees for their resin, which was used to make torches (Sahagún 1950–1982 11:107–108).

OCOTEPEC (folio 32r):
"On the Hill of Pines"

The glyph is a pine tree atop a green hill. The name derives from:

> *oco(tl):* pine
> *tepe(tl):* hill
> *c:* on, or in

The pine tree (*Pinus teocote*) was especially valued for its resin, which was used for torches.

OCOYACAC (folio 10r):
"In the Beginning of the Pine Trees"

The glyph is a pine tree, complete with two pine cones, with a nose poking out from the side of the tree's trunk. The name derives from:

> *oco(tl):* pine tree
> *yaca(tl):* nose, point, beginning
> *c:* on, or in

The pine tree is discussed by Sahagún (1950–1982 11:107–108), who emphasizes the value of its resin.

OCPAYUCAN (folio 23r):
"Place Full of *Ocpatli*"

The glyph consists of a bowl with the *pulque* sign on its side and bubbles on top; two roots float above the bubbles, and a tree grows along the bowl's side. Three footprints march along below the bowl. The name is formed from:

> *oc(tli):* pulque
> *ocpa(tli):* pulque-enhancing root
> *o(htli):* road
>> *yo(tl):* pertaining to, full of
> *can:* place

Simple *octli* is represented by the bubbling bowl with its curved sign (*yacametztli*); *ocpatli*, also called *quapatli*, gave the *pulque* an extra kick, and is described by Hernández (1959 2:119–120). As elsewhere in the *Mendoza*, the footprints, as *ohtli* (road), represent the more abstract *yotl* ("pertaining to" or "full of").

OCTLAN (folio 44r):
"Where There Is Much *Pulque*"

The glyph is a bubbling bowl of *pulque* with two teeth on top. The frothy contents are identified as *pulque* by the curved *yacametztli* glyph on the bowl. The *pulque* glyph is considerably different in the *Matrícula*, resembling a reverse *J* (folio 12v). The name is formed from:

oc(tli): pulque
tlan(tli): tooth, abundance of

OCUILAN (folios 10v, 34r):
"Where There Are Many *Ocuilteca*" or "Where There Are Many Caterpillars"

The glyph is a green caterpillar. The name derives from:

ocuil(in): caterpillar
    Ocuil(teca): a group of people living west of the Valley of Mexico
(t)lan: abundance of

No *tlantli* element is drawn in this glyph. In style, the *Matrícula* version of this glyph (folio 7v) closely resembles the glyph on *Mendoza* folio 34r.

OÇELOTEPEC (folio 52r):
"On the Hill of the Jaguar"

The glyph is a jaguar's head perched atop a hill. The name is formed from:

ocelo(tl): jaguar
tepe(tl): hill
c: on, or in

The glyph is very similar in the *Lienzos de Tuxpan* (Melgarejo Vivanco 1970).

OHUAPAN (folio 37r):
"On the Stalk of Green Maize"

The glyph consists of a green maize stalk, complete with red roots, a ripe ear of corn, and yellow tassels. A white banner stands at the top. The name is formed from:

ohua(tl): stalk of green maize
pan(tli): banner
    pan: on

OLAC (folio 20r):
"On the Spring"

The glyph shows a stream of water dividing cultivated land on which two flowers grow. A solid black circle (for rubber) is in the water. The name is formed from:

ol(li): rubber
    ol(inia): to bubble up
a(tl): water
c: on, or in

OLINALAN (folio 40r):
"Place of Much Movement" or "Place of Many Earthquakes"

The glyph is the stylized symbol for movement. The name derives from:

ollin: movement
(t)lan: abundance of

The first *a* is included for euphony. This glyph is also used to indicate "earthquake" (e.g., *Codex Telleriano-Remensis: láminas* IX, XII, XXII) and as one of the twenty day signs in the 260-day ritual calendar.

OLINTEPEC (folio 24v):
"On the Hill of the Earthquake"

The glyph is the sign for "movement" perched atop a hill. The name derives from:

ollin: movement
    (tlal)olin(i): earthquake
tepe(tl): hill
c: on, or in

According to Clark (1938 2:30), Olintepec was indeed destroyed by an earthquake.

OTLATITLAN (folio 46r):
"Among Much Bamboo"

The glyph is a curved yellow stalk of bamboo with a set of upper and lower teeth at the side. The name derives from:

otla(tl): bamboo
tlan(tli): tooth
titlan: among

OTLAZPAN (folio 28r):
"On the Bamboo"

The glyph consists of a cluster of three bamboo shoots. The name is formed from:

otla(tl): bamboo
pan: on

While a banner (*pantli*) or footprint (*pano*) locative could have been included, it was not. The *z* is perhaps added for euphony. Hernández (1959 1:397) describes several varieties of *otlatl.*

OTUNPA (folio 3v):
"On the Otomí"

The glyph is the head of a man on top of a hill. The man's face is painted yellow with horizontal and vertical red lines; he wears a turquoise earplug, and his hair is long and tied at the back. The name derives from:

otom(itl): Otomí
pa(n): on

Sahagún (1950–1982 10:176–181) describes the customs of the Otomí in detail.

OXICHAN (folio 49r):
"Home of Oxomoco"

The glyph is composed of a house with a reptile resembling an iguana in front. The animal has a green body, a knife (*tecpatl*) on its nose, and a row of spines down the length of its back and tail. In the *Matrícula de Tributos* the creature has the knife-nose and spines, but is yellow in color. The name derives from:

ox: Oxomoco?
i: his
chan: home

Clark (1938 2:52) feels the animal is a cayman (*cipactli*), while Peñafiel (1885:157) identifies it as an iguana (*quauhcuetzpalin*). Neither of these alternatives yields the phonetic element *ox-*. Another possibility is that this animal represents a *tecoixin* (a variety of lizard; see Hernández 1959 2:376, 378–379). This would provide some function for the flint knife

(providing the *tec-* element) and leave *oixin* relatively close to *oxi*. But, alas, these lizards lack the spines so characteristic of the glyphic representations. Clark (1938 2:52) suggests that the name may derive from the mythical Oxomoco, an inventor of magic rites in the Huaxteca, a region to the north of this town. For lack of a more interesting option, we tentatively follow his inspired suggestions here. This place glyph is one of only two in *Codex Mendoza* to use the *-chan* (home) element. In both cases the modifier is drawn over the house glyph and the possessive *i* or *in* is present in the name. This placement may indicate the possessive or provide a means of distinguishing between *-chan* (home) and the more usual *-calli* or *-cal* (house).

OXITIPAN (folio 55r):
"Where *Oxitl* Is Used"

The glyph shows a brown bowl complete with a scoop and mounds of *oxitl*, a black ointment. This is topped with a banner. The name is formed from:

oxiuti(a): to use or apply *oxitl*
pan: banner, on

'Oxitl was a black ointment made from turpentine (Molina 1970: folio 78v), called "resina de pino" (pine resin) by Hernández (1959 2:178) and used for medicinal purposes (ibid.: 1:293). Santamaría (1974:770) mentions the presence of large *oxitl* trees in the Huaxteca. The inclusion of a scoop or spatula may provide the sense of action, of working with the ointment.

OXITLAN (folio 46r):
"Where *Oxitl* Abounds"

The glyph is a yellow pan heaped with *oxitl*, a black ointment. A spatula or a scoop is included, and two teeth are attached to the black mound by a vertical line. The name is derived from:

oxi(tl): an ointment
tlan(tli): tooth, abundance of

See the glyph for Oxitipan (folio 55r) above for a discussion of *oxitl*.

OZTOMA (folios 10v, 18r, 37r):
"Cave Made by Hand"

These glyphs consist of a stylized animalistic cave with a hand attached. On folio 10v the cave faces front; on folios 18r and 37r it is shown in profile. The name derives from:

ozto(tl): cave
ma(itl): hand

Caves were believed to be entrances to the underworld.

OZTOTICPAC (folio 10v):
"Above the Cave"

The glyph is a front-facing stylized cave with mouth agape; a rolled ball of thread perches on the top of the cave. The name derives from:

ozto(tl): cave
icpa(tl): thread
c: on, or in
  icpac: above

The *t* is added for euphony.

OZTOTLAPECHCO (folio 42r):
"On the Platform of the Cave"

The glyph is a stylized cave resting on a four-legged platform. The name is formed from:

ozto(tl): cave
tlapech(tli): platform, or scaffold
co: on, or in

Peñafiel (1885:159) suggests that this name may refer to a deity's altar, or perhaps a burial ground. Clark (1938 2:46) feels that *tlapech(tli)* serves here as an ideograph for *tlapachoa,* "to fall in." This would yield "In the Place of the Fallen-In Cave."

PANOTLAN (folio 38r):
"Place of River Fords"

The glyph is a broad river of water with a footprint inside. The name derives from:

pano: to cross a river on foot
tlan: abundance of

The footprint is placed horizontally across the river, directly conveying the intended meaning. The *tlantli* glyph, however, is missing.

PANTEPEC (folio 16r):
"On the Hill" or "On the Hill of Banners"

The glyph shows a white banner waving from atop a hill. The name is formed from:

pan(tli): banner
pan: on
tepe(tl): hill
c: on, or in

PAPANTLA (folio 52r):
"Place of *Papanes*" or "Good Moon"

The glyph is a banner with two tufts of hair, one tied with a knot. The name is derived from:

papa(tli): long, matted hair of priests
pan(tli): banner
tla(n): abundance of

The locative *tlan* is not depicted glyphically. There are many possible meanings for this place glyph. Clark (1938 2:54) suggests that the banner and hair actually represent something more abstract: *papanauia,* "to cross in boats." He translates the name as "Near the Place Where They Crossed the Sea." Peñafiel (1885:162), after some debate with himself, settles on "Place Where There Are Priests." Other suggestions are "Good Moon," of Totonac derivation (Melgarejo Vivanco 1970: 13); and "Place of *Papanes*" (Macazaga Ordoño 1979:118 and Melgarejo Vivanco 1970:111). Santamaría (1974:801) indicates that *papanes* are a type of bird (*Psilorhunus*) more commonly known as "pepe" or "pea." In the *Lienzos de Tuxpan,* the glyph for this place consists of Tezcatlipoca's head (Melgarejo Vivanco 1970).

PATLANALAN (folio 40r):
"Where There Is Much Flying"

The glyph is a green bird with wings extended; the bird appears to be flying upward. The name derives from:

patlan(i): to fly
(t)lan: abundance of

Peñafiel (1885:162) suggests that *alo,* "scarlet macaw," is included in this glyph's name. However, the *alo* had feathers of red, blue, and yellow, not the green illustrated in this glyph (Sahagún 1950–1982 11:23).

PETLACALCATL (PETLACALCO)
(folio 20r):
"On the Woven Reed Coffer" or
"On the Storehouse"

The glyph is a house covered with woven reed matting. The name derives from:

> *petla(tl):* woven reed mat
> *cal(li):* house
>> *petlacal(li):* woven reed coffer; storehouse, especially where tributes were stored
>> *catl:* signifying affiliation
> *co:* on, or in

This glyph and its gloss are rather confusing: at some point someone blacked out the usual "puᵒ" (pueblo), and wrote "governador" above the place-name. The use of the titular form (*petlacalcatl*) may have led the annotator to write "governador." Clark (1938 2:23) feels that it simply refers to a "governor's" residence at the following town, Xaxalpan, and does not consider it a discrete place at all. Nor does Peñafiel (1885) include this town in his compendium. However, Barlow (1949a:132) believes that it must represent an actual town due to its location on the page and its original designation as such; he even locates it on his map of the empire. We tend to agree with Barlow.

PETLATLAN (folio 38r):
"Where There Are Many Mats"

The glyph is a woven yellow mat with two prominent teeth below. The name derives from:

> *petla(tl):* mat
> *tlan(tli):* tooth, abundance of

PIAZTLAN (folio 15v):
"Where There Are Many Sucking Tubes" or "Where There Are Many Long, Narrow Gourds"

The glyph is a long, thin tube, decorated like an arrow cane, through which water is flowing upward. The name derives from:

> *piaz(tli):* long, narrow gourd
> *tlan:* abundance of

The sense here appears to be that of a sucking tube. Clark (1938 2:18) mentions that canes such as these were filled with blood and offered to the gods.

PIPIYOLTEPEC (folio 16r):
"On the Hill of the Mountain Honey Bees"

The glyph is a yellow bee in flight on top of a green hill. The name derives from:

> *pipiyol(in):* mountain honey bee
> *tepe(tl):* hill
> *c:* on, or in

This small yellow bee made its hive underground (Sahagún 1950–1982 11:94).

POCTEPEC (folio 17v):
"On the Hill of Smoke"

The glyph is a hill with four puffs of smoke curling from its summit. The name derives from:

> *poc(tli):* smoke
> *tepe(tl):* hill
> *c:* on, or in

PUCTLAN (folio 46r):
"Where There Is Much Smoke"

The glyph is four roiling puffs of gray and yellow smoke. The name derives from:

> *poc(tli):* smoke
> *tlan:* abundance of

The tooth locative is not included in this place glyph.

PUPUTLAN (folio 17v):
"Where There Is Much *Popotli*"

The glyph shows a tied bundle of yellow grasses. The name is formed from:

> *popo(tli):* a grass used for making brooms
> *tlan:* abundance of

Clark (1938 2:22) observes that the bundle is tied with "the sacred white cord," and that this bundle is "the badge of Tlaçolteotl as the harvest-goddess." He translates the name as "Near Tlaçolteotl." Hernández (1959 2:100–101) describes this grass.

PUXCAUHTLAN (folio 10v):
"Where There Is Much Mold"

The glyph is a flower lying on its side, with varicolored spots covering it. The name derives from:

> *poxcauh(qui):* moldy
> *tlan:* abundance of

Both Clark (1938 2:10) and Peñafiel (1885:165) suggest that plants are involved here. Clark mentions a plant unidentified in Nahuatl, while Peñafiel refers to *camotes;* Hernández (1959 1:173) indeed discusses a variety of *camote* called *puxcauhcamotli.*

QUACHQUEÇALOYAN (folio 30r): "Place Where They Make Fine Cotton *Mantas*"

The glyph is a white rectangle with a footprint inside. The name derives from:

> *quach(tli):* large white cotton *manta*
> *(que)queça:* to tread on
> *quetzal(li):* precious
> *quetzalo:* the act of making something precious
> *yan:* place where

QUAGUACAN (QUAHUACAN) (folios 5v, 32r): "Place Where They Have Trees" or "Place Where They Have Eagles"

The glyph on folio 5r is a tree behind an eagle. On folio 32r a hill is added and only the eagle's head with the tree behind it shows. The name derives from:

> *quahu(itl):* tree
> *quauh(tli):* eagle
> *hua:* possessive
> *can:* place of

Clark (1938 2:35) suggests that *qua-quauhqui,* "woodsman," is intended. Alternatively, the tree could be included to signal the identity of the eagle, or vice versa.

QUAHUITL YXCO (folio 24v): "On the Surface of the Tree"

The glyph is a tree with an eye set sideways. The tree has green leaves and red roots. The name derives from:

> *quahuitl:* tree
> *ix(tli):* face or surface
> *co:* on, or in

The eye (*ixtelolotli*) serves as an ideograph for "face" or "surface."

QUALAC (folio 40r): "In the Place of Good Drinking Water"

The glyph shows water spilling from upper and lower jaws full of teeth. The name is formed from:

> *qua (cua):* to eat
> *qual(li):* good
> *a(tl):* water
> *c:* on, or in

QUATLATLAUHCAN (folio 42r): "Place of Red Heads"

The glyph is a face in profile with a prominent ear and bright red cap. The name derives from:

> *qua(itl):* head
> *tlatlauh(qui):* red
> *can:* place of

QUATZONTEPEC (folio 44r): "On the Hill of Much Hair"

The glyph consists of two teeth and a tied rope, thread, or hair on top of a hill. The name derives from:

> *quatzon(tli):* hair
> *tepe(tl):* hill
> *c:* on, or in
> *tlan(tli):* tooth
> *tlan:* abundance of

Clark (1938 2:48) suggests that the plant *quautzontetl* is intended here; however, Anderson and Dibble (in Sahagún 1950–1982 11:113) define *quauhtzontetl* as part of a tree, its base, rather than a specific plant. A plant of this name is not found in Hernández, although other plants with the *quauhtzon-* prefix are. Peñafiel (1885:90) ventures the interesting hypothesis that two names are embedded in the glyph, Quatzontepec and Quatzontlan. He mentions that the latter was a military mark of Motecuhzoma Xocoyotzin. The former (as Cuatzonteccan) is listed as a conquest of that same Mexica ruler and located tentatively within the confines of Coyolapan province, where it appears in the *Mendoza* (Kelly and Palerm 1952:310, 314). Barlow (1949a: map) does not locate any towns with these names.

QUAUHNACAZTLAN (folio 13v): "Where There Are Many *Quauhnacaztli*"

The glyph consists of a tree with an enormous ear on its trunk. The name is formed from:

quahu(itl): tree
nacaz(tli): ear
   quauhnacaz(tli): quauhnacaztli,
   a tree
tlan: abundance of

This tree is mentioned only in passing by Hernández (1959 2:173).

QUAUHNAHUAC (folios 2v, 6r, 7v, 23r):
"Beside the Trees"

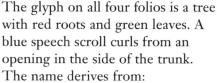

The glyph on all four folios is a tree with red roots and green leaves. A blue speech scroll curls from an opening in the side of the trunk. The name derives from:

quahu(itl): tree
nahua(tl): good sound
c: on, or in
   nahuac: beside

QUAUHPANOAYAN (folios 10r, 32r):
"Place Where the Water Is Crossed by a Wooden Bridge"

The glyph on both folios shows a tree trunk (with branches) crossing a river. On folio 32r the tree appears to be an oak, with its diagnostic diagonal lines. The tree on folio 10r has three footprints, indicating the tree's "bridge" function. The name is formed from:

quahu(itl): tree
pano: to cross a river on foot
   quauhpan(tli): wooden bridge
o(htli): road
a(tl): water
yan: place where

The "road" element in this name is represented by the footprints, shown only on folio 10r.

QUAUHPILOLAN (folio 13v):
"Where Many Eagle Feathers Hang Down"

The glyph shows a brown eagle-feather tuft attached to a looped red cord. The name is formed from:

quauh(tli): eagle (feather)
pilo(a): to hang or suspend
(t)lan: abundance of

It is unclear why the *t* was dropped from the *tlan;* perhaps *yan* was intended, as this more closely resembles the town's modern name (Coapiloloya: Kelly and Palerm 1952:305). *Quauhtli* is surely an abbreviation for an eagle feather, since elsewhere a full bird or at least its head stands for *quauhtli.* A feather tuft (*quechulli*) on an eagle is shown on folio 42r (Quauhquechulan). Sahagún (1950–1982 11:40) names and describes the many kinds of eagle feathers.

QUAUHQUECHULAN (folio 42r):
"Where There Are Many Feather-Tufted Eagles"

The glyph consists of an eagle with a feather tuft on its head. The eagle faces a hill with a flower on its top and five dots to the side of the flower. The name is formed from:

quauh(tli): eagle
quechul(li): feather tuft
(t)lan: abundance of

The glyph for "five flower on a hill," *Macuilxochitepec,* is present in the place-name glyph but not included in the town's glossed name. However, Clark (1938 2:46) translates the entire name as "Quauhquechulan Belonging to Macuilxochitepec." The *quechulli* is discussed with the glyph for Quechulac (folio 42r). Macuilxochitl was a god who presided over games.

QUAUHQUEMECAN (folio 22r):
"Place of the Eagle-Feather Cape"

The glyph consists of an eagle's head atop a green hill. A feather cape is draped over the hill. The name is formed from:

quauh(tli): eagle
quemi(tl): deity cape
can: place

QUAUHTECOMAÇINCO (folio 40r):
"On the Little Gourd Tree"

The glyph consists of a flowered tree branch emerging from a brown gourd bowl. The lower part of a man's body curls up against the cup. The name derives from:

quahu(itl): tree
tecoma(tl): gourd bowl
 quauhtecoma(tl): gourd tree
tzin(tli): rump
 tzin: little or small

The *quauhtecomatl* has large fruits and long, narrow leaves (Hernández 1959 1:141).

 QUAUHTECOMATLA (folio 40r): "Where There Are Many Gourd Trees"

The glyph is a gourd bowl with a set of upper and lower teeth extending from its side. The name derives from:

quahu(itl): tree
tecoma(tl): gourd bowl
 quauhtecoma(tl): gourd tree
tla(n): tooth, abundance of

The *quauhtecomatl* is discussed under the glyph for Quauhtecomaçinco (folio 40r).

 QUAUHTETELCO (folio 48r): "Tree on the Mound"

The glyph is a two-branched tree perched atop a four-tiered platform. The name derives from:

quahu(itl): tree
(tlal)tetel(li): mound (of earth)
co: on, or in

Clark (1938 2:52) suggests that this assemblage of sounds refers to the *quauhteteco*, a tree he identifies as *Heterotheca inuloides*. Peñafiel (1885: 95) prefers a different interpretation, extending "mound" to "pyramid" and "tree" to "wood," yielding "On the Wooden Temple."

 QUAUHTINCHAN (folio 42r): "Home of the Eagles"

The glyph is a house behind an eagle's head. The name derives from:

quauh(tli): eagle
in: their
chan(tli): home

This is one of only two cases where the element *-chan* is used in *Mendoza* place glyphs. The position of the eagle before the house may indicate that *-chan* rather than *cal(li)* is meant.

 QUAUHTITLAN (folios 3v, 5v, 26r): "Near the Trees"

The glyphs on folios 3v and 5v are trees with teeth inserted in their trunks. The glyph on folio 26r shows the same type of tree (with green leaves and red roots), also with teeth. However, this image also includes the black and white mask of the goddess Tlazolteotl ("Filth-Deity"). The mask has a cotton headband with two cotton fillets, a diagnostic characteristic of this goddess (see *Codex Borbonicus* 1974:13). The name is formed from:

quahu(itl): tree
tlan(tli): tooth
titlan: near

 QUAUHTLAN (folios 10v, 13v, 24v): "Where There Are Many Eagles"

The three glyphs representing Quauhtlan are all different. The glyph on folio 10v is a complete and rather animated eagle. The representations on folios 13v and 24v show only the eagle's head; on folio 13v two teeth are added. The glyph for this town in the *Matrícula* (folio 4r) resembles that on *Mendoza* folio 24v. The name is formed from:

quauh(tli): eagle
tlan(tli): tooth, abundance of

 QUAUHTOCHCO (folios 8r, 17v, 48r): "On the Tree-Rabbit"

The glyph consists of a rabbit (rather fierce-looking on folio 8r) with a tree emerging from its back. This glyph is largely obliterated in the *Matrícula de Tributos*. The name is formed from:

quahu(itl): tree
toch(tli): rabbit
co: on, or in

There is some disagreement on the translation of this place-name. Peñafiel (1885:97) feels that the rabbit more closely resembles a mountain cat, *ocotochtli*. Clark (1938 2:52) extends the translation by adding *quauhtochtli* (stake for planting) and suggesting "In the Place of Stakes" for the full place-name. Macazaga Ordoño (1979:76) interprets the animal as a tree-dwelling *ardilla*.

QUAUHXAYACATITLAN (folio 13v): "Among the Wooden Masks"

The glyph is a tree with green leaves and red roots; a front-facing human mask is in front of the tree trunk. The name derives from:

quahu(itl): tree
xayaca(tl): mask or face
titlan: among

QUAUHYOCAN (folio 22r): "Place Full of Trees"

The glyph is a tree growing from the top of a hill. The name derives from:

quahu(itl): tree
yo(tl): pertaining to, full of
can: place

QUAUXIMALPAN (folio 5v): "On the Wood Chips"

The glyph is an ax with a copper head chopping on a broken tree trunk. Pieces of wood fly from the trunk. The name derives from:

quauhximal(li): wood chip
pan: on

The glyph is very similar to that for Tlaximaloyan, folio 10v.

QUAVXILOTITLAN (folio 44r): "Among the *Quauhxilotl* Trees"

The glyph is a brown tree with two branches and red roots. The tree is also adorned with two black stripes and a maize ear with a red tassel. The name derives from:

quahu(itl): tree
xilo(tl): maize ear
    quauhxilo(tl): tree that yields a
        fruit resembling a maize ear
titlan: among

Hernández (1959 1:145) describes the *quauhxilotl* tree in some detail. The Mixtec name for this town was *Ñuundodzo* (M. E. Smith 1973:177).

QUAVXUMULCO (folio 41r): "On the Corner of the Tree(s)"

The glyph is a tree trunk with four branches; the trunk is bent at a 90-degree angle. The name derives from:

quahu(itl): tree
xumul(li): corner
co: on, or in

Clark (1938 2:44) suggests that *quauhtla,* "grove," is intended.

QUECHULAC (folio 42r): "On the Water of the Feather Tuft"

The glyph is a feather tuft floating in a canal. The name derives from:

quechul(li): feather tuft
a(tl): water
c: on, or in

Molina (1970: folio 88v) defines *quechulli* as a richly feathered bird. *Quecholli* was also the fiesta dedicated to Camaxtli, god of the hunt. This god is pictured in Durán (1971: plate 51) adorned with a feather tuft at the back of his head. Participants in this festival decorated their mouths and heads with feathers (ibid.:456) and "tied a bunch of feathers from the eagle and other [birds], which hung down their backs" (ibid.:146). Quechulac is located in a part of central Mexico which especially venerated the god Camaxtli. A *quechulli* is also included, on the head of an eagle, on the glyph for Quauhquechulan (folio 42r).

QUEÇALMACAN (folio 28r): "Place Where Quetzal Feathers Are Captured"

The glyph is a hand grasping a bunch of quetzal feathers. The name derives from:

quetzal(li): quetzal feathers
ma(itl): hand
    ma: to catch or capture
can: place

This is a rather interesting place name, since quetzal birds were not native to this region.

QUETZALTEPEC (folio 16r): "On the Hill of the Quetzal Feathers"

The glyph shows four graceful green plumes on top of a hill. The name is formed from:

quetzal(li): tail feathers of the
    quetzal bird
tepe(tl): hill
c: on, or in

This most prized of all Meso-american birds, the resplendent trogon, inhabited broad reaches of the tropical "cloud forest." The long, shimmering tail feathers of the male were so highly valued that they could be plucked only from live birds; the bird was not to be killed. Sahagún (1950–1982 11:19–20) and Hernández (1959 2:318–319) describe the *quetzaltototl* and the uses of its feathers in considerable detail.

QUIMICHTEPEC (folio 16r):
"On the Hill of the Rats" or "On the Hill of the City Sentries"

The glyph shows a furry gray animal crouched on a hill. The name is formed from:

> *quimich(in):* rat
> > *quimich(tin):* rats, or city sentries
> *tepe(tl):* hill
> *c:* on, or in

QUIYAUHTEOPAN (QUIAUHTEOPAN) (folios 8r, 40r):
"Outside the Temple"

The glyph on both folios consists of three raindrops falling on a stepped-pyramid temple. The name is formed from:

> *quiahu(itl):* rain
> > *quiahu(ac):* outside, away from
> *teopan(tli):* temple

The raindrops provide the homophonous clue for "outside."

TAMAÇOLAN (folio 43r):
"Where There Are Many Frogs"

The glyph is a crouching frog. The name is formed from:

> *tamaçol(in):* frog
> *(t)lan:* abundance of

The tooth locative is not included in this glyph, nor apparently in its partially obscured mate in the *Matrícula* (folio 12r). The name for this town in Mixtec is *Yahua* (M. E. Smith 1973:177).

TAMAÇOLAPAN (folio 43r):
"On the Water of the Frogs"

The glyph shows a frog in a canal. The name is formed from:

> *tamaçol(in):* frog
> *apan(tli):* canal
> *apan:* on the water

The canal in the *Matrícula* (folio 12r) closely resembles the Mixtec style for this element (see M. E. Smith 1973:39). The Mixtec name for this town is *Tequevui* (ibid.:176).

TAMAPACHCO (folio 12r):
"Place of Seashells" of "Place of Palms"

The glyph consists of a hand touching a large red and white seashell. The name is formed from:

> *tapach(tli):* seashell
> > *tam-:* "place of," in Huaxtec
> *ma(itl):* hand
> *co:* on, or in

As with glyphs for Tamuoc and Tanpatel (both on folio 10v), the name-glyph correspondence is not neat. It is clear that the Aztecs retained the local Huaxtec names, making do as well as they could with glyphic correspondences. Shells called *tapachtli* are described by Sahagún (1950–1982 11:60, 230). This shell resembles two shown on *Codex Mendoza* folio 38r, tribute from the Pacific coastal province of Çihuatlan. However, Tamapachco was located in eastern Mexico, in Huaxtec country. The *Lienzos de Tuxpan* includes a glyph of Tamapachco (probably this same town), which Melgarejo Vivanco (1970: foldout) translates as "On the Rock-Raccoon." Nicholson (1973:14–17) provides an analysis of this place-name. He translates the name as "Place of Palms," which more closely resembles the *Lienzo* place glyph, a hill with two palmlike appendages.

TAMUOC (folio 10v):
"Tamuoc, Place Where Things Are Measured"

The glyph consists of a crouching man holding a long rectangle with three footprints on it. The man has a sizable hole in his nose for a nose plug, and his hair is cropped on top but long in back. The name is formed from:

> *tam(achihua):* to measure something
> > *tam-:* "place of," in Huaxtec
> *o(htli):* road
> *c:* on, or in

This town is in Huaxtec country, in the very northeastern corner of the empire. The Huaxtec name of this town was apparently retained by its conquerors, with an appropriate Aztec glyph produced as its place sign. Its interpretation is uncertain (see Nicholson 1973:14–16). Sahagún (1950–1982 10:185) mentions that Huaxtec men wore a tuft of hair at the back of their head.

TANPATEL (folio 10v): "Tampatel, Place of Metal"

The glyph is a red and yellow symbol for liver on top of a green hill. The name derives from:

>*tam-:* "place of," in Huaxtec
>*(el)tapa(chtli):* liver

There is really no Nahuatl derivation for this name, as the Aztecs adopted the local Huaxtec name. In devising a glyph in their style, the Aztecs used symbols that "came close" to the sounds of the name (see also the glyph for the town of Tamuoc, folio 10v, in this regard). Both Clark (1938 2:11) and Peñafiel (1885:171) interpret the glyph on the hill as coral (*tapachtli*), and Peñafiel equates the name of the town with Tamapachco (folio 12r), feeling the name Tanpatel is an error. Kelly and Palerm (1952:297), however, locate this town as modern Tampatel, Veracruz, quite a different place from Tamapachco. See Nicholson (1973:14–16) for an analysis of this place-name.

TEACALCO (folio 21v): "On the Stone Canoe"

The glyph is a canoe-shaped stone full of water. The name derives from:

>*te(tl):* stone
>*acal(li):* canoe (lit. "water house")
>*co:* on, or in

This glyph is a particularly good example of the Aztec scribe's ability to meld several elements into one image.

TECALCO (folios 10v, 42r): "In the Stone House"

The glyphs on both folios consist of a house made of stone. The name derives from:

>*te(tl):* stone or rock
>*cal(li):* house
>*co:* on, or in

TECALCO (folio 20v): "On the Noble's House" or "On the Judge's House"

The glyph is a turquoise *xiuhuitzolli* with red back-tie (a noble's diadem) resting on top of a house. The name derives from:

>*tec(uhtli):* high-ranking noble, or judge
>*cal(li):* house
>*co:* on, or in

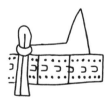

TECAMACHALCO (folio 42r): "On the Stone Jaw"

The glyph is a round stone with an open, toothy mouth. The name is formed from:

>*te(tl):* stone or rock
>*camachal(li):* jaw
>*co:* on, or in

TECAXIC (folios 12r, 15v): "On the Stone Basin"

The glyph on both folios consists of a bowl made of stone and full of water. In both cases the water lacks its characteristic "waves." The name is formed from:

>*te(tl):* stone
>*caxi(tl):* bowl
>   *tecaxi(tli):* stone basin
>*c:* on, or in

TECMILCO (folio 41r): "On the Noble's Cultivated Lands"

The glyph shows a turquoise diadem with its red tie (*xiuhuitzolli*) poised on a rectangular plot of ground. The name is formed from:

>*tec(uhtli):* a high-ranking noble, or judge
>   *mil(li):* cultivated land
>*co:* on, or in

The turquoise diadem was such a hallmark of nobility that it served as an ideograph for that exalted status.

TECOÇAUHTLA (TECOÇAUHTLAN)
(folios 16r, 31r):
"Where There Is Much Yellow
Ocher"

The glyph on both folios consists of
a stone, and dots and circles in a
yellow background. On folio 16r the
yellow circle rests above the stone;
on folio 31r a yellow stone is surrounded by dots and circles. The
name is formed from:

> *te(tl):* stone or rock
> *coçauh(qui):* yellow
> > *tecoçahu(itl):* yellow ocher
> *tlan:* abundance of

The "tooth" element is absent in this
glyph.

TECOLOAPAN (folio 20r):
"On the Water of the Owl"

The glyph is an owl's head in a canal
full of water. The name derives from:

> *tecolo(tl):* owl
> *apan(tli):* canal
> *apan:* on the water

The owl, with shiny eyes "like spindle whorls" and horns of feathers, is
described by Sahagún (1950–1982
11:42). Its name apparently derives
from its hoot: "tecolo, tecolo, o, o."

TECPAN (TECPA) (folios 5v, 32r):
"Place of the Royal Palace"

The glyph on both folios is a palace—a house with diagnostic white
circles on a black background. On folio 5v a nobleman's diadem rests on
top of the palace. Also on folio 5v fire
rages from the place, incorporating
the symbol of conquest. The name
derives from:

> *tec(uhtli):* noble, or judge
> *pan:* on
> > *tecpa(n):* royal palace

The turquoise diadem with red back-
tie (*xiuhuitzolli*) serves as an ideograph for *tecuhtli,* noble or judge.

TECPATEPEC (folios 13r, 27r):
"On the Hill of the Flint Knife"

Both glyphs consist of three red and
white knives on top of a hill. The
name is formed from:

> *tecpa(tl):* flint knife
> *tepe(tl):* hill
> *c:* on, or in

Clark (1938 2:33) indicates that the
red on the knife represents blood; the
white, bone.

TECPATLAN (folio 16r):
"Where There Are Many Flint
Knives"

The glyph is a flint knife, colored
half red and half white. The name
derives from:

> *tecpa(tl):* flint knife
> *tlan:* abundance of

Such knives were used for sacrifice,
the red symbolizing blood (Clark
1938 2:18).

TECPATZINCO (TECPAÇINCO) (folios
8r, 24v):
"On the Little Flints"

Both glyphs consist of a hill, a red
and white knife, and the bottom half
of a man's body. On folio 8r the man
emerges from the base of the hill; on
folio 24v, from a side of the knife.
The name is formed from:

> *tecpa(tl):* flint
> *tzin(tli):* rump
> > *tzin:* little
> *co:* on, or in

The sacrificial knife is drawn in red
to represent blood, and white to represent bone (Clark 1938 2:31).

TECUTEPEC (folio 15v):
"On the Hill of the Lord, or Judge"

The glyph consists of the nobleman's
hallmark, the turquoise diadem with
red back-tie (*xiuhuitzolli*). In this
rendering, the diadem rests on a head
of hair. This assemblage hovers over
a green hill. The name is formed
from:

> *tecu(tli):* high-ranking noble, or
> > judge
> *tepe(tl):* hill
> *c:* on, or in

Clark (1938 2:17), drawing on the
illustration of this town glyph in the
Codex Telleriano-Remensis, translates
its name as "In the Hill of the Lord
Xiuhtecutli, the Fire-God."

TEÇIUTLAN (folio 51r):
"Place of Much Hail"

The glyph consists of a stone at the
bottom of a blue water drop, and a
pair of teeth to the side. The name is
formed from:

> *teçiu(itl):* hail
> *tlan(tli):* tooth, abundance of

The stone in place of the usual water symbols indicates hail.

TEÇOYUCAN (folio 22r):
"Place Full of Black Pumice"

The glyph is a hill composed of gracefully curved lines representing stone or rock. The name derives from:

te(tl): stone or rock
teço(ntli): black pumice stone
yo(tl): pertaining to, full of
can: place

Teçontli is rough of texture and dark in color (Sahagún 1950–1982 11:264).

TEHUEHUEC (folio 28r):
"On the Stone Drum"

The glyph is a vertical drum made of stone. The graceful curves indicating "stone" are shown, as well as the drum's jaguar-skin top. The name derives from:

te(tl): stone
huehue(tl): drum
c: on, or in

The "arrow" design at the bottom is the wooden rattle motif (*chicahuaxtli*). The rattle was used to mark the rhythm of their many dances. A drum with jaguar-skin top and rattle motif at its bottom is drawn on folio 70r of *Codex Mendoza.*

TEHUILOYOCAN (folio 26r):
"Place Full of Crystal Stones"

The glyph is a stone behind a jewel. The name derives from:

te(tl): stone
tehuilo(tl): crystal
tehuiloyo: full of crystal
can: place

TEHUIZCO (folio 24v):
"On the Sharp Rocky Ground"

The glyph is a hill that peaks in three sharp points. The entire hill is made of stone. The name derives from:

te(tl): stone
huitz(o): something that has spines
tehuitz(tla): rocky ground, with sharp rocks
co: on, or in

TELOLOAPAN (folio 37r):
"On the Water of the Pebbles"

The glyph consists of a canal with a black dot in the water. The name is formed from:

telolo(tli): round stone
apan(tli): canal
apan: on the water

TEMAZCALAPAN (folio 21v):
"On the Sweat Baths"

The glyph is a sweat bath, showing smoke pouring from the rear dome. The house part of the sweat bath has two round outlets, from which heat emerges, while water spills from its entrance. The name derives from:

temazcal(li): sweat bath
a(tl): water
pan: on

The two round openings in the "house" are placed prominently at the top of the sweat bath in the *Matrícula* drawing of this glyph. Sahagún shows them there and describes them as "outlets" (1950–1982 11:275, plate 920).

TEMOHUAYAN (folio 27r):
"Place Where Everyone Descends"

The glyph is a pyramid platform with two footprints marching down one side. The name derives from:

temo: to descend
temoa: everyone descends
yan: place where

TENANCO (folio 7v):
"On the Wall"

The glyph shows a wall with three ramparts; the entire glyph is painted blue. The name is formed from:

tenam(itl): wall
co: on, or in

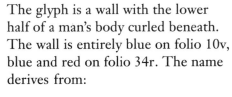

TENANÇINCO (TENANTZINCO)
(folios 10v, 34r):
"On the Small Wall"

The glyph is a wall with the lower half of a man's body curled beneath. The wall is entirely blue on folio 10v, blue and red on folio 34r. The name derives from:

tenam(itl): wall
tzin(tli): rump
tzin: small
co: on, or in

TENAYUCAN (folio 2r):
"Place Full of Walls"

The glyph consists of a blue wall with ramparts stretching across a green hill. The name is formed from:

tena(mitl): wall
yo(tl): full of, pertaining to
can: place of

TENEXTICPAC (folio 10v):
"On Top of the Lime"

The glyph shows a man's head on top of a hill; the head has a prominent nose perforation, and small black dots on a white background in place of hair. The name is formed from:

te(nitl): man from another tribe and language
tenex(tli): lime
icpac: on top of

The *t* is included for euphony. Clark (1938 2:11) feels that the use of the man's head provides the *te-* prompt, thus identifying the dots as lime rather than salt, chalk, or sand.

TENOCHTITLAN (**TENUXTITLAN**) (folios 2r, 4v, 19r):
"Among the Stone-Cactus Fruit"

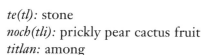

The glyph in all three cases consists of a prickly pear cactus on a rock. On folio 2r the glyph is embellished with a perching eagle. The fruits of the cactus are prominent on all the glyphs. The glyph on folio 4v is not glossed. The name derives from:

te(tl): stone
noch(tli): prickly pear cactus fruit
titlan: among

Clark (1938 2:23) interprets this name as "Place Founded by Tenoch" (name of an early leader, shown on folio 2r). The prickly pear cactus (*nopalli*) and its juicy fruits (*nochtli*) are described by Sahagún (1950–1982 11:122–124, 180, plate 599) and Hernández (1959 1:311–313).

TEOAÇINCO (folio 16r):
"On the Small Sacred Water"

The glyph consists of three stacked elements: a half-sun disk on top, a pool of water contained by stylized reeds in the middle, and the bottom half of a man's body on the bottom. The name is formed from:

teo(tl): god
teoyo(tl): sacred thing
a(tl): water
tzin(tli): rump
tzin: small or little
co: on, or in

TEOCALÇINCO (folio 23r):
"On the Small Temple"

The glyph is a tall temple resting atop the lower half of a man's body. The name derives from:

teocal(li): temple
tzin(tli): rump
tzin: small
co: on, or in

TEOCALHUEYACAN (folio 5v):
"Place of the Tall Temple"

The glyph is a lofty temple resting precariously atop a green hill. The name derives from:

teocal(li): temple (lit. "god's house")
hueyac: long (tall)
can: place

Since a burning temple was the symbol for conquest, the "smoke and fire of conquest" are incorporated into the very place glyph for this town.

TEOCHIAPAN (folio 16r):
"On the Sacred Water Chia" or "On the Sacred *Chinampa*"

The glyph consists of a half-sun disk above a small area surrounded by water. The area enclosed by water has a gray background and contains small black dots. The name is formed from:

teo(tl): god
teoyo(tl): sacred thing
chi(namitl): chinampa, an enclosed area for cultivation; or
chia: a plant with small black edible seeds
a(tl): water
pan: on

The glyph for the town of Chiapan (folio 13r) clearly shows a cultivated field, whereas this glyph does not. The chia may be the more accurate interpretation, following the glyph. Hernández (1959 1:67–68) discusses two varieties of *achian* (water chia) and their medicinal value.

TEOCUITLATLAN (folios 13v, 44r): "Place of Much Gold"

The glyph on folio 44r consists of a stylized disk of gold as the central image, with a hand and arm supporting it on one side and water spilling from it on the other. The glyph on folio 13v shows the disk with only two red flames. The name is formed from:

> *teocuitla(tl):* gold (lit. "godly excrement")
> *tlan:* abundance of

The tooth glyph is missing here and in the *Matrícula* version of this glyph. The addition of the arm and water on folio 44r is somewhat enigmatic. Clark (1938 2:48) suggests that they are included to convey the notion of placer gold. Peñafiel (1885:184–185) feels that perhaps *Teocuitlapan* ("In the River of Gold" or "In the Place Where Gold Is Collected") is meant. Equally curious is the inclusion of flames on the folio 13v glyph.

TEOÇIOCAN (folio 49r): "Place of the Sacred Young Maize Ears"

The glyph is a composite of a stylized half-sun topped by a pair of young maize ears. The name derives from:

> *teo(tl):* god (sun)
> *xilo(tl):* young maize ears
> *can:* pertaining to a place

The correspondence between glyph and name is a near miss. While it is obvious that two *xilotl* are drawn, the name is written without the letter *l*. Perhaps the annotator erred. Alternatively, Peñafiel (1885:184) suggests a derivation from *teocioa* (hunger), but he remains mystified by the relationship between this condition and the colorful, optimistic-looking glyph.

TEONOCHTITLAN (folio 42r): "Among the Sacred Prickly Pear Cactus Fruits"

The glyph is a three-branched prickly pear cactus perched on top of a stylized half-disk, symbol of the sun. The name derives from:

> *teo(tl):* god, or sun
> *teo(yotl):* divine or sacred thing
> *noch(tli):* prickly pear cactus fruit
> *teonoch(tli):* divine prickly pear cactus fruit
> *titlan:* among

The *teonochtli* is discussed by Hernández (1959 2:106, 176). He mentions the red and yellow fruits, prominent in this glyph.

TEOPANTLAN (folio 42r): "Place of Many Temples"

The glyph is a temple base with its steps visible; on top is a stylized half-disk representing the sun. The name derives from:

> *teo(tl):* god, or sun
> *teopan(tli):* temple
> *tlan:* abundance of

The *tlantli* (tooth) glyph is not included here or in the corresponding glyph in the *Matrícula* (folio 11v).

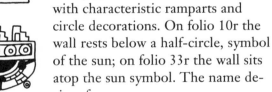

TEOTENANCO (folios 10r, 33r): "On the Sacred Wall"

The glyphs consist of a blue wall with characteristic ramparts and circle decorations. On folio 10r the wall rests below a half-circle, symbol of the sun; on folio 33r the wall sits atop the sun symbol. The name derives from:

> *teo(tl):* god
> *teo(yotl):* sacred thing
> *tenam(itl):* wall
> *co:* on, or in

The stylistic sun symbol in this case stands for the more general "god."

TEOTLALPAN (folio 51r): "On the God's Land"

The glyph consists of a half-sun disk atop a rectangular segment of cultivated land. The name is formed from:

> *teo(tl):* god
> *tlal(li):* land
> *pan:* on

Early in the Colonial period, this name became transformed to Hueytlalpan.

TEOTLILAN (folio 46r):
"Place of the Sacred Ink"

The glyph is composed of a house decorated with black lintel and jamb, both displaying the sign for Venus (Clark 1938 2:49). This house sits on top of a colorful half-sun symbol. The name is derived from:

> *teo(tl):* god
> *tlil(li):* black, or ink
> *(t)lan:* abundance of

Peñafiel (1885:186–187) transcribes this incorrectly as Teotitlan.

TEOTLIZTACAN (folio 36r):
"Place of the White God"

The glyph is the profile head of a white-faced god, wearing a long ear ornament and a headpiece of four red feathers. The head rests on a green hill. In the *Matrícula* (folio 8v) the god also wears a fancy necklace. The name derives from:

> *teo(tl):* god
> *izta(c):* white
> *can:* place of

The *tl* is included in the name for euphony.

TEPECHIAPAN (folio 13r):
"On the Water of the Verbena" or "On the Water-Hill of Chia"

The glyph consists of a hill with a ring of water looped about it. The hill is blacked in above and below the water ring. The name is formed from:

> *tepe(tl):* hill
> *chia:* chia, a plant with tiny black seeds
> *a(tl):* water
> *pan:* on

Both Clark (1938 2:14) and Peñafiel (1885:188) interpret the black areas as spots, suggesting the black seeds of chia (although Peñafiel despairs of a translation). Clark further suggests that an extended meaning of *tepechian*, verbena, is intended (see also Hernández 1959 1:70). The only other alternative for the *chi-* element would derive from *chinamitl*, but that seems to be represented quite differently in the *Mendoza* (see Chiapan, folio 13r). Varieties of chia and their tiny, oily seeds are described by Hernández (ibid.:67–74) and Sahagún (1950–1982 11:285–286).

TEPECHPA (folio 21v):
"On the Stone Foundation"

The glyph is a foot on top of a rectangular stone. The name derives from:

> *te(tl):* stone
> *(pe)pech(otl):* foundation
> *pa(n):* on

TEPECHPAN (folio 20r):
"On the Large Rock"

The glyph is a house resting on a rectangle; the left half of the rectangle is a rock, the right is a woven reed mat. The name derives from:

> *te(tl):* stone
> *(pe)pech(tli):* sleeping mat
> *tepex(itl):* large rock
> *pan:* on

TEPEMAXALCO (folio 33r):
"On the Divided Hill"

The glyph is a wide green hill with a deep cleft in the middle. The name derives from:

> *tepe(tl):* hill
> *maxal(tic):* divided or forked
> *co:* on, or in

TEPEPULAN (folio 20r):
"Where There Are Many Big Hills"

The glyph shows a hand against a small house. The house sits inside a green hill. The name is formed from:

> *tepe(tl):* hill
> *pol(oa):* to make mud
> *pol-:* big
> *(t)lan:* abundance of

TEPEQUACUILCO (folios 6r, 8r, 37r):
"Place Where Faces Are Painted"

The glyph on all three folios, and in the *Matrícula* (folio 9r), shows the head of a Cohuixcatl man on top of a green hill. The head is painted black, and a long rod passes over the ear (especially noticeable on folios 6r and 8r). The name is formed from:

> *tepe(tl):* hill
> *qua(itl):* head
> *cuil(oa):* to paint
> *co:* on, or in

TEPETITLAN (folio 31r):
"Near the Hill"

The glyph is two teeth inside a green hill. The name derives from:

tepe(tl): hill
tlan(tli): tooth
   titlan: near or among

TEPETLACALCO (folio 20r):
"On the Sepulcher"

The glyph is a house sitting on top of three stones. The house itself is composed of woven reed matting and stone. The name derives from:

   te(tl): stone
   petla(tl): woven mat
   cal(li): house
      tepetlacal(li): sepulcher
   co: on, or in

TEPETLAOZTOC (folio 21v):
"In the Lava Cave"

The glyph shows a front-facing stylistic cave, mouth agape, in front of a woven reed mat. The name is formed from:

   petla(tl): woven reed mat
      tepetla(tl): tepetate, a lava stone
   ozto(tl): cave
   c: on, or in

It is a bit of a surprise here to see the omission of the easily drawn *tetl*, or stone glyph, for the first syllable of this name (as in Tepetlapan, folio 22r). Perhaps this was an oversight.

TEPETLAPAN (folio 22r):
"On the Basalt"

The glyph is a rectangle divided in half horizontally: the top is woven like a mat, the bottom bears the glyph for rock or stone. The name derives from:

   te(tl): stone or rock
   petla(tl): mat
      tepetla(tl): basalt
   pan: on

Tepetlatl, a white porous stone, is described by Sahagún (1950–1982 11:265). *Tepetate* soils are discussed by Williams and Ortiz-Solorio (1981).

TEPETL HUIACAN (folio 33r):
"Place of the Tall Mountain"

The glyph is an elongated green hill. The name derives from:

   tepetl: hill
   hueyac: long or tall
   can: place of

TEPEXAHUALCO (folio 36r):
"In the Painted Hill"

The glyph is two parallel black bars inside a green hill. The name derives from:

   tepe(tl): hill
   xahual(li): paint
   co: on, or in

TEPEXIC (folio 42r):
"On the Crag"

The glyph shows a broad green hill with a deep cleft in its middle. The name is formed from:

   tepe(tl): hill
   xi(ni): landslide
      tepexi(tl): crag
   c: on, or in

TEPEYACAC (**TEPEACAC**) (folios 10v, 42r):
"On the Beginning of the Hill"

On both folios the glyph is a hill with a nose peeking out one side. The name derives from:

   tepe(tl): hill
   yaca(tl): nose, or beginning
   c: on, or in

The corresponding glyph in the *Matrícula* (folio 11v) is partly obscured.

TEPOXACO (folio 26r):
"On the Soft Stone"

The glyph is a rock surrounded by small black dots. The name derives from:

   te(tl): stone
   poxac(tic): soft or spongy
      tepoxac(tli): light(weight) stone
   co: on, or in

TEPOZTITLAN (folio 40r):
"Among the Copper"

The glyph is an ax: the brown ax head is inserted through the broad part of the brown handle. The name derives from:

   tepoz(tli): copper
   titlan: among

Axes such as these had copper heads and wooden handles.

TEPUZCULULAN (folio 43r): "Where There Are Many Copper Hooks"

The glyph is a hill with a gracefully curved copper ax. The name is formed from:

> *tepuz(tli):* copper
> *colol(li):* hook
>> *tepuzcolol(li):* copper hook
> *(t)lan:* abundance of

The tooth locative is not included on this glyph. In Mixtec, the name for this town is *Yucundaa* (M. E. Smith 1973:176).

TEPUZTLAN (TEPOZTLAN) (folios 8r, 24v, 41r): "Where There Is Much Copper"

The glyphs on these three folios differ stylistically. All show a brown ax set into a green hill. On the folio 8r glyph the ax head is inserted horizontally into the side of the handle; the handle is dressed in a red-spotted cloth tied with a cord. On folio 24v the copper ax head is set into a wooden club and tied with a "sacred knotted cord" (Clark 1938 2:30). On folio 41r the ax head is tied into the top of a gracefully curved handle. The *Matrícula* glyphs (folios 4r, 11r) closely resemble the latter two styles. The name derives from:

> *tepuz(tli):* copper
> *tlan:* abundance of

The inclusion of the cloth (perhaps a ritually charged *quemitl*) on one of these place glyphs may serve as a reference to the god Tepuztecatl, patron of this community.

TEQUALOYAN (folio 34r): "Place Where There Are Jaguars"

The glyph shows a jaguar consuming a loincloth-clad man. Only the lower half of the man shows. In the *Matrícula* (folio 7v) the jaguar's red tongue is clearly visible. The name is formed from:

> *tequa(ni):* carnivorous beast, jaguar
> *tequalo:* act of eating someone (i.e., being a jaguar)
> *yan:* place where

TEQUANTEPEC (folio 13v): "On the Hill of the Jaguar"

The glyph shows a fierce jaguar's head on top of a hill. A bright red chile pepper sits inside the hill. The name is formed from:

> *tequa(ni):* carnivorous beast, jaguar
> *tepe(tl):* hill
> *c:* on

Clark (1938 2:14) extends the meaning of the glyph to intend "poisonous," an alternate meaning of *tequani*. The inclusion of the chile pepper in the glyph is a mystery. The jaguar, better known as *ocelotl*, is discussed by Hernández (1959 2:301) and Sahagún (1950–1982 11:1–3).

TEQUEMECAN (folio 20r): "Place of Rocky Cultivated Land" or "Place of the Sacred Stone"

The glyph consists of a large stone with a white deity cape inside. The name derives from:

> *te(tl):* stone
> *quemi(tl):* deity cape
>> *cuemi(tl):* cultivated land, property
> *can:* place of

Peñafiel (1885:196) suggests the first translation above. He also observes that the *quemitl* is often used ideographically to represent the god Tlaloc, and he presents the possibility that a god of *pulque*, Tequechmecaniani, is intended here. Clark (1938 2:24) prefers "rough cape" (*tequaqua* = rough). The *Matrícula* version of this glyph shows black splotches (probably rubber) on the cape, a feature associated with Tlaloc and other rain deities (see Sahagún 1950–1982 1: plates 22, 23, 25).

TEQUIXQUIAC (folios 4v, 29r): "On the Saltpeter Water"

The glyph consists of two or three saltpeter lumps inside a canal. The name is formed from:

> *tequixqui(tl):* saltpeter
> *a(tl):* water
>> *tequixquia(tl):* saltpeter water
> *c:* on, or in

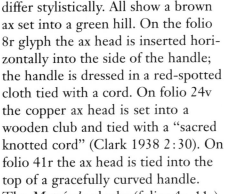

TETENANCO (folios 17v, 36r, 39r, 42r):

"On the Stone Wall"

The glyph on the last three folios is a red and blue stylized stair-stepped wall resting on two stones. On folio 17v, four stones provide the wall's base; this glyph is not glossed.

The name derives from:

te(tl): stone
tenam(itl): wall
co: on, or in

The images on folios 39r and 42r show only the ramparts, not the wall. Wall and ramparts are clearly drawn on two of the corresponding *Matrícula* folios (8v and 11v). On folio 10r (*Matrícula*) only the ramparts show. On folio 17v (*Mendoza*), it is unclear if the feather tuft above the place glyph is meant as a part of the place or its governing official. Clark (1938 2:21) prefers the latter alternative.

TETEPANCO (folio 27r):

"On the Stone Wall"

The glyph is a stone wall resting on two stones. Two teeth separate the stones. The name derives from:

te(tl): stone
tepan(tli): wall
co: on, or in

This name seems to be misglossed or "misglyphed"; the inclusion of the teeth would suggest the name *Tetepantlan.* The *Matrícula* is of no help, as this folio is missing from that document.

TETEUHTEPEC (folio 7v):

"On the Hill of the Gods"

The glyph is a *quemitl* (deity cape) spattered with spots of black rubber. The cape is in front of a green hill. The name derives from:

teo(tl): god
   teteo: gods
tepe(tl): hill
c: on, or in

Elsewhere in the *Mendoza* both plain and rubber-spattered deity capes are used to symbolize gods, specifically those associated with rain (folio 20r: Tequemecan; folio 46r: Tetevtlan).

TETEVTLAN (folio 46r):

"Where There Are Many Gods"

The glyph shows a fringed *quemitl,* or godly neck cloth, atop two shining teeth. The name derives from:

teteo: gods
tlan(tli): tooth, abundance of

In this name, the *quemitl* serves as an ideograph for "god," reflecting its close links with the realm of the sacred. This ideographic usage is also found on the glyph for Tequemecan (folio 20r) and on glyphs directly associated with the god Tlaloc (for example, *Codex Telleriano-Remensis* folio 43r and *Codex Borbonicus* 1974: 24). See Anawalt (1984) for a detailed discussion of the *quemitl*'s godly symbolism.

TETICPAC (folios 36r, 44r):

"On Top of the Rock"

The glyph is a house poised on top of a rock. The name is formed from:

te(tl): rock
icpac: on top of

The house appears to be serving a locative function by virtue of its position ("on top of"), since *calli* (house) is nowhere in the name of these towns. The second *t* serves a euphonic function. The Mixtec name for Teticpac was *Miniyuu* (M. E. Smith 1973:177).

TETLAPANALOYAN (folio 29r):

"Stone Quarry"

The glyph shows a hand holding a stone and breaking a large rock. The name is formed from:

te(tl): rock
tlapana: to break
tlapanalo: the act of breaking
yan: place where
   tetlapanaloyan: stone quarry

Clark (1938 2:34) suggests that the hand is in the act of extracting, not breaking, the rock.

TETZAPOTITLAN (TEÇAPOTITLAN)
(folios 10v, 18r, 53r):
"Among the Zapote Trees on the Rock"

The glyph, on all three folios, shows a three-branched tree atop a stone. On 53r the entire tree is green; on 18r the trunk and round flowers are yellow while the leaves are shades of green. On folio 10v the tree has a brown trunk and green leaves and flowers. In the *Matrícula de Tributos* (folio 16r) the entire tree is yellow. The name is derived from:

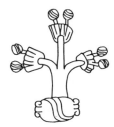

> *te(tl):* rock
> *tzapo(tl):* zapote tree or fruit
> *titlan:* among

Sahagún (1950–1982 11:117) describes the zapote fruit as round, as it is shown glyphically. There were many varieties of zapotes, and the term *tzapotl* was used to refer to sweet fruits in general (Hernández 1959 1:90).

TEUHÇOLTZAPOTLAN (folio 48r): "Where There Are Many *Teçon-tzapotl* Trees"

This rather complex glyph consists of three elements stacked one upon another: a stone at the base, a quail's head in the middle, and a tree on top. The name derives from:

> *te(tl):* stone
> *çol(in):* quail
> *tzapo(tl):* zapote tree
> *tlan:* abundance of

Clark (1938 2:52) feels that this constellation of sounds suggests *texal-tzapotl*, a sweet sop tree. However, if this set of sounds stands for a tree, a better candidate is perhaps the *teçontzapotl*, described by Sahagún (1950–1982 11:118). In the *Matrícula de Tributos*, the tree illustrated (folio 13v) is quite distinct from the zapote tree shown for Teçapotitlan (*Codex Mendoza* folio 53r).

TEXOPAN (folio 43r): "On the Blue Color"

The glyph consists of a blue patch with a footprint above. The name derives from:

> *texo(tli):* blue color
> *pan(o):* to cross a river on foot
> *pan:* on

Clark (1938 2:47) suggests that the blue spot stands for *texouia*, "to put on blue color." The Mixtec name for this town was *Ñuundaa* (M. E. Smith 1973:176).

TEZCACOAC (folio 20v): "In the Mirror-Snake"

The glyph is a snake protruding from the entrance of a house. The snake has an obsidian mirror on its back. The name derives from:

> *tezca(tl):* mirror
> *coa(tl):* snake
> *c:* on, or in

The inclusion of the house may provide a background for the notion "in" or "on," as seems to be the case with several place glyphs from the province of Petlacalco. Clark (1938 2:24) feels that the house stands for *calpixqui* and denotes that official's residence in this town. Peñafiel (1885: 202) interprets the house as a temple (which it clearly is not).

TEZCATEPEC (folio 27r): "On the Hill of the Mirror" or "On the Hill of Tezcatlipoca"

The glyph is a black and red mirror sitting on a hill. The round mirror has four feather down balls around its rim. The name derives from:

> *tezca(tl):* mirror
> *tepe(tl):* hill
> *c:* on

Clark (1938 2:32) suggests that the god Tezcatlipoca, "Smoking Mirror," is intended here. This glyph is almost identical with that of Tezcatepetonco on folio 29r.

TEZCATEPETONCO (folio 29r): "On the Small Hill of the Mirror" or "On the Small Hill of Tezcatlipoca"

The glyph is a red and black mirror on top of a hill. The name derives from:

> *tezca(tl):* mirror
> *tepe(tl):* hill
> *tepeton(tli):* small hill
> *co:* on, or in

This glyph is almost identical to that of Tezcatepec on folio 27r; the four white circles on the mirror on folio 29r should be down feathers like those on 27r. Clark (1938 2:34) interprets this as "In the Little Hill of Tezcatlipoca."

TEZCUCO (folio 3v):

"On the Alabaster Pot, Place of the *Acolhua*"

The glyph consists of two major elements. To the left is an arm bent at the elbow with water spilling from the shoulder. To the right is a rocky hill divided into three peaks; between the peaks grow red and yellow flowers. The name derives from:

> *tex(calli):* rocky place
> > *tetz(caltetl):* alabaster
>
> *co(mitl):* pot
> *co:* on, or in
>
> and
>
> *a(tl):* water
> *coloa:* to bend
> > *Acolhua:* a group living on the eastern side of Lake Texcoco
>
> *can:* place

There is considerable disagreement about the interpretation of this name glyph. Barlow and MacAfee (1949: 37) suggest that *tetzcotli* refers to a "certain plant." Peñafiel 1885:201) and Clark (1938 2:2) both mention the possibility that *texcalli* may stand for *texcotli*, a small jar. This is supported by other glyphic representations of this city (indeed, the only place dignified with *çibdad* in its gloss). The *Mapa Quinatzin* shows a large pot with a flower, both set into a rocky hill. The *Códice Osuna* shows the bent arm on top of a hill, although water spills from the base of the hill (see also Macazaga Ordoño 1979:154). Compare with the glyph for Acolhuacan on folio 5v.

TIÇATEPEC (folio 21v):
"On the Hill of Chalk"

The glyph is a white hill of little black dots. A stone glyph with white bands rests at the base of the hill. The name derives from:

> *tiça(tl):* chalk
> *tepe(tl):* hill
> *c:* on, or in

The reason for the inclusion of the *tetl* (stone) glyph is unclear, unless its phonetic similarity to *ti-* is being used to identify the black dots as chalk as opposed to, say, *iztatl* (salt).

TIÇAYUCAN (folio 22r):
"Place Full of Chalk"

The glyph is a mound with small black dots inside. Three footprints line the base of the mound. The name derives from:

> *tiça(tl):* chalk
> *o(htli):* road, the sound "o"
> *yo(tl):* pertaining to, full of
> > *tiçayotl:* full of chalk
>
> *can:* place

TLAAHUILILPAN (folio 27r):
"On the Irrigated Land"

The glyph shows an *olla* pouring water over a rectangular plot of ground. The name is formed from:

> *tlaahuilil(li):* irrigated land
> *pan:* on

TLACHCO (folios 8r, 31r, 36r):
"On the Ball Court"

All three glyphs show a ball court with side rings. The courts are divided into four colored segments of green, red, yellow, and blue, although the colors are distributed differently in all three glyphs. However, the colors are always arranged with red-yellow and blue-green as diagonal opposites. The name is formed from:

> *tlach(tli):* ball court
> *co:* on, or in

TLACHINOLTICPAC (folio 15v):
"On Top of the Scorched Countryside"

The glyph shows red and yellow flames around a petite circle; the flames and circle rest on top of a hill. The name is formed from:

> *tlachino(a):* to burn the countryside or mountains
> *ol(oltic):* something round
> > *tlachinol(li):* burnt or scorched countryside
>
> *icpac:* above, on top of

This may refer to the customary way of clearing land for cultivation, by controlled burning.

TLACHMALACAC (folio 37r):
"On the Thrown Spindle Whorl" or "On the Ball Court Rings"

The glyph shows a bordered gray ball court with a red spindle shaft across its middle. The spindle has a small whorl and spun and unspun cotton. The name derives from:

tlach(tli): ball court
   tlaça: to throw
malaca(tl): spindle whorl
tlach(te)malaca(tl): ball court ring
c: on, or in

The combination of ball court and spindle whorl may lead to the interpretation that *tlachtemalacatl* is meant. The *tlachtemalacatl* were stone rings placed on either side of the ball court which served as goals (Sahagún 1950–1982 8:29). Molina (1977: folio 97r) defines *temalacatl* as "millstone, or stone wheel."

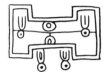

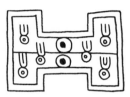

TLACHQUIYAUHCO (TLACH-QUIAVCO) (folios 16r, 45r): "On the Place Outside the Ball Court"

The glyph on folio 45r is a ball court divided into colored sections (red in upper left, blue in upper right, green in lower left, yellow in lower right). The center rings of the ball court are shown, along with six blue and white raindrops. On folio 16r the red and blue colors are reversed, and only four raindrops are illustrated. The name derives from:

tlach(tli): ball court
quiahu(itl): rain
   quiahuac: outside
co: on, or in

Peñafiel (1885:208) feels that this place-name may be related to Tlaloc, god of rain. In contrast, Clark (1938 2:49) suggests that *quiahuitl* (rain) stands for *quiauac,* "outside or away from," and extends his translation to "Place of the Ball Court Outside the Town." This "ball court-raindrop" glyph also appears on *lámina* XXVI of the *Codex Telleriano-Remensis.* The Mixtec name for this town was *Ndisi nuu,* for which M. E. Smith (1973: 59) suggests translations of "visible face," "visible eyes," or "clearly seen." In this case the Mixtec and Nahuatl names seem to have no relationship to each other.

TLACHYAHUALCO (folio 21v): "In the Circle of the Ball Court"

The glyph is a ball court inside a circle. The name derives from:

tlach(tli): ball court
yahual(tic): something round
co: on, or in

Clark (1938 2:26) feels that the glyph represents *tlachicaualli,* "fortified."

TLACOPAN (folio 5v): "On the *Tlacoxochitl*"

The glyph contains three pert red and yellow flowers growing on a narrow white rectangle. The name is formed from:

tlaco(xochitl): tlacoxochitl
pan: on

Hernández (1959 2:127–130) describes several varieties of *tlacoxochitl;* Sahagún (1950–1982 11:208) mentions only one, with red flowers and "in no wise aromatic."

TLACOTEPEC (folios 10r, 13v): "On the Hill of the *Tlacoxochitl*"

The glyph is three colorful flowers on long stems emerging from the top of a hill. The name derives from:

tlaco(xochitl): tlacoxochitl
tepe(tl): hill
c: on, or in

These flowers are discussed under Tlacopan.

TLACOTLALPAN (folio 46r): "On the Divided Lands"

The glyph is a circle divided in half vertically, the left side containing glyphs indicating cultivated land, the right side blank. The name is formed from:

tlaco: half
tlal(li): land
pan: on

Clark (1938 2:51) translates this as "on the half cultivated lands," interpreting *tlalli* as "cultivated land." However, *tlalli* is usually the term for land in general, while *milli* would more precisely indicate cultivated land. We find Peñafiel's interpretation, "On the Divided Lands," more attractive.

TLAÇOXIUHCO (folio 20v): "In the Precious Turquoise"

The glyph consists of a house resting on a woven reed mat; a turquoise bead pierced by a needle sits at the entrance to the house. The name is formed from:

tlaço(tl): something strung
    tlaço(tli): precious
xihui(tl): turquoise
    co: on, or in

Clark (1938 2:25) suggests that the house-on-a-mat represents the residence of a *petlacalcatl,* a high administrative official in charge of tributes. The bone perforator is found elsewhere in the *Mendoza* to represent the sound *ço* (to perforate) (see folios 15v, 17v, 35r, 36r).

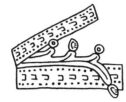

TLALATLAVCO (folio 32r):
"On the Canal"

The glyph is two rectangular plots of ground "hinged" to resemble an open box; water spills from the opening. The *Matrícula* version of this glyph (folio 6v) shows dirt spilling out with the water. The name derives from:

    tlal(li): land
    a(tl): water
    ao(tli): channel of water
      tlalatlauh(tli): canal
    co: on, or in

TLALCOÇAUHTITLAN (folios 8r, 40r):
"Among the Yellow Lands"

The glyph on folio 8r is a rectangular plot of brown and yellow land heaped with a mound of yellow pebbles and sand. The glyph on folio 40r shows only the ground, colored yellow. The image of this place glyph in the *Matrícula* (folio 10v) resembles the one on *Mendoza* folio 40r. The name derives from:

      tlal(li): land
      coçauh(qui): yellow
      titlan: among

TLALCUECHAHUAYAN (folio 44r):
"Place of Damp Land"

The glyph shows a rectangular plot of land; a shell and two raindrops are above. The name derives from:

    tlal(li): land
    cuech(tli): shell
      cuechahua(c): damp or humid
    yan: place where

The notion of dampness is conveyed glyphically by the inclusion of raindrops.

TLALLACHCO (folio 32r):
"On the Cultivated Land"

The glyph is a brown ball court filled with the symbols for land or ground. The name derives from:

    tlal(li): land
    (t)lach(tli): ball court
      tlatlax(tli): cultivated land
    co: on, or in

Clark (1938 2:36) suggests the above interpretation, while Peñafiel (1885: 215) chooses to interpret the glyphic elements more literally as "Place of the Ball Court with an Earthen Floor."

TLALTIÇAPAN (folios 24v, 52r):
"On the Land of Chalk"

On folio 24v the glyph consists of a half-circle filled with small black dots on top of a rectangular plot of ground. Three vague collections of dots surround the half-circle. On folio 52r the glyph is a mound with black dots, with a footprint above. The name is formed from:

    tlal(li): land
    tiça(tl): chalk
    pan(o): to cross a river on foot
    pan: on

Clark (1938 2:54) suggests that the first part of the word derives from *tlaltetl,* "large mound." However, the *-tetl* (stone) element, though easily expressed glyphically, is not present. The glyph for this town (folio 52r), sans footprint, is found in the *Lienzos de Tuxpan* (Melgarejo Vivanco 1970). It may well be the present-day town of Tierra Blanca (ibid.:114).

TLAMACAZAPAN (folio 36r):
"On the Water of the Priest"

The glyph is the profile head of a priest with blackened face, long matted hair, and a smear of blood below the temple. The head rests on a canal full of water. The name derives from:

    tlamacaz(qui): priest
    apan(tli): canal
      apan: on the water

Peñafiel (1885:212) interprets the priest as Tlaloc, while Clark (1938 2:39) feels that *tlamacazqui* stands for the plant *tlamacazcatzotl.*

TLANIZTLAN (folio 15v):
"Where There Is Much Light" or
"Where There Are Many Shin
Bones"

The glyph consists of a leg and foot,
with two rows of teeth attached to
the shin. The name is formed from:

tlanitz(tli): shin bone
tlanex(tli): light, or brightness
tlan(tli): tooth
tlan: abundance of

Peñafiel (1885:212) does not ven-
ture a translation of this name; Clark
(1938 2:17) offers the suggestion that
tlanextli is intended, thus avoiding
the translation "Where There Are
Many Shin Bones."

TLAOLAN (folio 10v):
"Where There Is Much Dried
Maize"

The glyph consists of a woven basket
filled to overflowing with white maize
kernels. The name is formed from:

tlaol(li): dried maize kernels
(t)lan: abundance of

Tlaolli normally refers to dried kernels of maize (off the cob), the form
in which they were stored. *Cintli*
more typically refers to the maize
plant. However, while Sahagún
(1950–1982 11:279–284) presents
the various types of maize as *cintli*,
Hernández (1959 1:288–292) sub-
sumes his discussion of maize under
tlaolli, going into considerable depth
regarding the properties of maize,
planting customs, and recipes.

TLAPACOYAN (folios 8r, 50r):
"Place Where They Wash"

The glyph is a hand over a bordered
white cloth; this sits on water on a
stone. In the glyph on folio 8r, the
water is flowing over the top of the
cloth. In the *Matrícula de Tributos*
(folio 14v), the glyph is constructed
as on folio 50r of the *Mendoza*. The
name derives from:

tlapaco: the act of washing
yan: place where

TLAPAN (TLAPPAN) (folios 12r, 13r,
39r):
"On the Dye" or "Place of the
Tlapaneca"

The glyph is a red disk with a footprint inside. The name derives from:

tlapa(lli): dye
pan(o): to cross a river on foot
(footprint)
pan: on

As Clark (1938 2:41) notes, the
Tlapaneca decorated themselves with
a red dye.

TLAPANICYTLAN (folio 49r):
"At the Foot of the Broken Hill"

The glyph shows a green hill with a
split top and two teeth at its base.
The name derives from:

tlapani: to break something
icxi(tl)?: foot
tlan(tli): tooth, abundance of

To obtain the *icxitl* (foot) element, it
must be assumed that the writer mistakenly omitted the letter *x;* Peñafiel
(1885:214) and Macazaga Ordoño
(1979:162) quite unabashedly add it
to the place-name. While we do it
with somewhat greater reservation,
we see no other option for the *cy*
element.

TLAQUILPAN (folio 22r):
"On the Polisher" or "On the *Tlaquilin* Herb"

The glyph is a plain white polisher
with handle. The name derives from:

tlaquil(li): polisher
tlaquil(in): tlaquilin herb
pan: on

The *tlaquilin*, with green butterfly-
shaped leaves and pale fragile flowers, is described and illustrated in
Sahagún (1950–1982 11:199, plate
676) and Hernández (1959 2:164).
Clark (1938 2:27) identifies the *tlaquilin* as *Mirabilis jalapa L.*

TLATILULCO (folios 6r, 10r, 19r):
"On the Round Earth Mound"

The glyph on all three folios is
an enclosed gray mound with small
black dots inside. The mound sits on
a thin white rectangle. The name derives from:

tlatel(li): earth mound
ol(oltic): round
co: on, or in

In the *Matrícula* (folio 2r) this
glyph contains alternating layers of
dots and hooks.

TLATLAUHQUITEPEC (folios 8r, 51r):
"On the Red Hill"

The glyph is a red hill; on folio 51r a red circle has been added atop the hill (as in the *Matrícula de Tributos* folio 15r). The name is derived from:

tlatla(ctic): red
 tlahu(itl): red ocher
qui: thing
tepe(tl): hill
c: on, or in

The term *tlatlauhqui* appears in Hernández (1959 1:36, 73, 424) several times, denoting various plants.

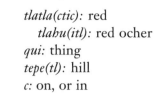

TLAXCALA (folio 42r)
"Place of Many Tortillas"

The glyph is a yellow hand (that of a woman) patting a round tortilla. The name derives from:

tlaxcal(li): tortilla
(t)lan: abundance of

This glyph is attached by a thin black line to the head of a *Tlaxcaltecatl*, a person from Tlaxcala. The place glyph itself is not glossed. The top of the man's head is adorned with two feather tufts.

TLAXIMALOYAN (folio 10v):
"Place Where They Do Carpentry"

The glyph is an ax with a copper head; a partially chopped, felled tree lies below the long-handled ax. The name derives from:

tlaximalo(ni): ax
 tlaximal(li): chips, splinters
 tlaxima: to do carpentry
yan: place where

Clark (1938 2:9) mentions that this was the Nahuatl pronunciation of Taximaroa or Taxgimaroa, an important town in Tarascan territory. This glyph bears close similarity to that for Quauximalpan, folio 5v.

TLAYACAC (folio 24v):
"In Front"

The glyph is a hill with a nose on one side. The name derives from:

tla: something
yaca(tl): nose
 tlayaca(ti): first thing, front
c: on, or in

TLAYACAPAN (folio 24v):
"In Front"

The glyph consists of a hill with a nose on its side. A banner perches on the nose. The name derives from:

tla: something
yaca(tl): nose
 tlayaca(ti): first thing, front
pan(tli): banner
 pan: on

TLILTEPEC (folio 16v):
"On the Black Hill"

The glyph shows a hill painted black or purple. The name is formed from:

tlil(li): black
tepe(tl): hill
c: on, or in

TOCHTEPEC (folio 46r):
"On the Hill of the Rabbit"

The glyph shows a rabbit's head in profile, resting atop a green hill. The name is formed from:

toch(tli): rabbit
tepe(tl): hill
c: on, or in

TOLIMANI (folio 40r):
"Place of the Reed Cutters"

The glyph consists of a hand grasping one of four reed stalks. The name is formed from:

tol(li): reed
ma(itl): hand
 ma: to hunt or catch
ni: doer of

Both Peñafiel (1885:218) and Clark (1938 2:42) interpret the hand, *maitl*, as an ideograph for the verb *ma*.

TOLTITLAN (folio 3v):
"Among the Reeds"

The glyph shows four green reeds, each with yellow tops and yellow flowers, and white roots. The reeds sit on a narrow brown rectangle, and two rows of teeth are set into the side of the plants. The name is formed from:

tol(lin): tule reed
tlan(tli): tooth
 titlan: among

TONALI YMOQUEÇAYAN (folio 12r): "Place Where the Sun's Heat Leaves"

The glyph consists of a human leg (complete with foot pointing downward) standing over four white circles with red centers. The name is formed from:

> *tonalli:* day, heat of the sun, summertime
> *y:* his
> *moquetz(qui):* to stand on tiptoe
> > *quiça:* to finish, to leave
> *yan:* place where

TONANYTLA (folio 21v): "Place of Tonantzin"

The glyph shows an old woman's head atop a green hill. The name is formed from:

> *to-:* our
> *nan(tli):* mother
> > *tonan(tzin):* "our mother," referring to the goddess Tonantzin
> *i:* her
> *tla(n):* abundance of (place of)

TONATIUHCO (folio 34r): "On the Place of the Sun God"

The glyph is the sun disk. The name derives from:

> *tonatiuh:* sun god
> *co:* on, or in

TOTOLAPA (**TOTOLAPAN**) (folios 7v, 25r): "On the Water of the Turkey"

Both glyphs consist of a turkey's head in a canal full of water. The name derives from:

> *totol(in):* turkey
> *apan(tli):* canal
> > *apan:* on the water

TOTOLÇINCO (folio 21v): "On the Small Turkeys"

The glyph consists of a colorful turkey head attached to the bottom half of a man's body. The name is formed from:

> *totol(in):* turkey
> *tzin(tli):* rump
> > *tzin:* small
> *co:* on, or in

TOTOMIXTLAHUACAN (folio 39r): "Place of the Bird-Hunter's Plain"

The glyph shows a bird with a feathered arrow shaft for a body. The bird flies over a rectangular plot of ground. The name is formed from:

> *toto(tl):* bird
> *mi(tl):* arrow
> *ixtlahua(tl):* a plain
> *can:* place of

Clark (1938 2:42) suggests that the bird-arrow combination stands for *totomani,* "bird hunter." This seems a reasonable possibility for this potpourri of glyphs.

TOTOTEPEC (folios 13r, 46r): "On the Hill of the Bird"

The glyph shows a green bird perched on a hill. On folio 46r the green feathers shade into white. The name is formed from:

> *toto(tl):* bird
> *tepe(tl):* hill
> *c:* on, or in

TOTOTLAN (folio 48r): "Where There Are Many Birds"

The glyph is very straightforward: a green bird with yellow beak and legs. In the *Matrícula* (folio 13v) the bird is entirely yellow. The name is formed from:

> *toto(tl):* bird
> *tlan:* abundance of

This place glyph has no *tlantli,* or tooth glyph, to indicate the locative.

TOXICO (folio 12r): "In the Place of Toci" or "On Our Turquoise"

The glyph is a cord strung with nine round beads (all white); the cord ends in two tassels. The name derives from:

> *to:* our
> *xi(huitl):* turquoise
> > *Toci:* "Our Grandmother," a goddess
> *co:* on, or in

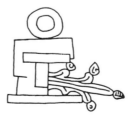

TOYAC (folio 20v): "In the Place of Overflowing Water"

The glyph is a house with a round "doughnut" on top; a stream of water pours from the entrance of the house. The name derives from:

toya(ua): overflowing of water
c: on, or in

Clark (1938 2:25) interprets the house as the residence of a *calpixqui,* or tribute collector. Clark sees no reason for the inclusion of the circle; he suggests that it was a scribal error.

TOZTLAN (folio 46r): "Where There Are Many Yellow-Headed Parrots"

The glyph is a yellow bird. The name derives from:

toz(tli): adult yellow-headed parrot
tlan: abundance of

This bird is described as "very yellow" by Sahagún (1950–1982 11:23) and is illustrated as shown here, though with longer tail feathers (ibid.: plate 56). Peñafiel (1885:223) interprets the name and glyph as *toznene,* a parrot from the Huaxtec region, considerably north of this province of Tochtepec.

TUCHÇONCO (folio 48r): "On the Rabbit's Hair"

The glyph shows a rabbit's head in characteristic profile, with a bunch of hair piled high and contained with red lashings. The name derives from:

toch(tli): rabbit
tzon(tli): hair
co: on, or in

Peñafiel (1885:217) erroneously transcribes this name as Tochconco, identifying the bound hair as a feather and deriving the name from *tochconetl,* "young rabbit."

TUCHPAN (TUCHPA) (folios 10v, 52r): "On the Rabbit"

The glyph on folio 10v is a rabbit with a footprint above; on folio 52v the glyph is a rabbit with a banner atop. The name is derived from:

toch(tli): rabbit
pan(tli): banner
or
pan(o): to cross a river on foot
pan: on

This was, more anciently, called Tabuco in Huaxtec (Melgarejo Vivanco 1970:17) and was located some four kilometers east of today's Tuxpan (Ekholm 1953:414). The glyph for this town in the *Lienzos de Tuxpan* is a temple with a conical roof. Tabuco means "Place of Seven" in Huaxtec.

TUCHTLAN (folio 50r): "Place of Many Rabbits"

The glyph is a rabbit sitting on three teeth. The name is formed from:

toch(tli): rabbit
tlan(tli): tooth, abundance of

TULAN (folio 8r): "Where There Are Many Reeds"

The glyph consists of four reed stalks, each with yellow tips, yellow flower balls, and white bases. They sit on a narrow white rectangle. The name is formed from:

tol(lin): tule reed
(t)lan: abundance of

Glyphs for this town in other codices show little variation: the *Códice Osuna* perches the reeds on top of a hill, as does the *Historia tolteca-chichimeca.* The *Codex Boturini* submerges the reeds' roots in water (in which a fish swims), and the *Codex Aubin* of 1576 displays only the wavy reeds.

TULANÇINCO (TULANÇINGO) (folios 3v, 30r): "On the Small Reed"

The glyphs on both folios consist of a bunch of reeds with the bottom half of a man's body. On folio 3v the man emerges from the base of the reeds; on folio 30r, from the side. The name is formed from:

tol(lin): reed
tzin(tli): rump
tzin: small
co: on, or in

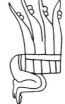

TULUCAN (TULUCA) (folios 10v, 12r, 33r): "Place Where Men Incline Their Heads" and "Place of the Matla-tzinca"

The glyphs on all three folios show a man's head bent atop a green hill. The place glyphs on folios 10v and 12r add a net with the bottom half of a man's body attached. The name derives from:

tolo(a): to incline the head
can: place of

Clark (1938 2:36) suggests that this glyph represents Tolotepetl, the mountain currently known as the Nevado de Toluca.

The net-rump glyph stands for Matlatzinca: "People of the Small Nets."

matla(tl): net
tzin(tli): rump
tzin: small
ca(tl): people of

The Matlatzinca people lived in the Valley of Toluca.

TZAPOTITLAN (folio 20v):
"Among the Zapotes"

The glyph is a green zapote tree with red roots and two rows of teeth set into the trunk. The name derives from:

tzapo(tl): zapote tree
tlan(tli): tooth
titlan: among

Hernández (1959 1:90–93) describes several varieties of zapotes.

TZAYANALQUILPA (folio 31r):
"On the Water of the *Tzayanalquilitl*"

The glyph is a canal from which sprout two leafy branches. The name derives from:

tzayanal(oni): something that splits
quil(itl): herb
tzayanalquil(itl): a plant
(a)pa(ntli): canal
pa(n): on the water

Sahagún (1950–1982 11:136) describes the *tzayanalquilitl* as a tender, tasty plant.

TZICAPUÇALCO (folio 36r):
"On the *Tzicatl* Sand Heap"

The glyph consists of an ant in a background of small dots and circles. The name is formed from:

tzica(tl): large stinging ant
putzal(li): sand heap
co: on, or in

The *tzicatl* especially enjoyed hot, damp environs, swiftly swarming over anything edible (Sahagún 1950–1982 11:91).

TZICCOAC (ÇTZICOAC) (folios 13r, 54r):
"On the Turquoise-Blue Snake"

The glyph is a graceful green, yellow, and red snake with the protruding tongue and rattles of a rattlesnake. On 13r the snake faces left, while on 54r it slithers to the right. This glyph is largely obliterated in the *Matrícula de Tributos.* The name derives from:

xiuh(tic): turquoise-blue color
coa(tl): snake
c: on, or in

This name is spelled in a variety of ways: Tzicoac, Tziccoac, Xiuhcoac, and the rather eccentric Çtzicoac. Clark (1938 2:12) refers to the verb *tzicoa* (to detain anyone) and translates this place-name as "In the Place of Detention." Orozco y Berra (1960 1:418) translates the name as "On the Blue Snake." Glyphs for Tzicoac (as a snake lying atop a hill) are also shown on the *Lienzos de Tuxpan* (Melgarejo Vivanco 1970).

TZILACA APAN (folio 40r):
"On the Water of the *Tzilacayotli* Gourd"

The glyph shows a green gourd floating in a red-bordered canal overflowing with water. The name derives from:

tzilaca(yotli): a smooth, varicolored gourd
apan(tli): canal
apan: on the water

This gourd is described and illustrated in Sahagún (1950–1982 11:288; ill. 965) and mentioned by Hernández (1959 1:50).

TZINACANOZTOC (folio 46r):
"In the Cave of the Bat"

The glyph consists of a bat in the mouth of a stylized cave. The bat is designed with a "conventionalized serpent head, blue supraorbital ridge, red and yellow tongue, red and white fangs and, in the snout, a *tecpatl,* or sacrificial knife, in place of the membranous nose leaf" (Clark 1938 2:50). The name derives from:

tzinacan: bat
ozto(tl): cave
c: on, or in

Clark (ibid.) feels that the bat god is implied here.

TZONPANCO (folio 17v):
"On the Skull Rack"

The glyph is a skull strung on a wooden skull rack. The name derives from:

tzonpan(tli): skull rack
co: on, or in

XALA (folio 40r):
"Where There Is Much Sand"

The glyph is a circle containing numerous dots and small circles. Two teeth with red gums sit in the center of the circle. The name derives from:

xal(li): sand
(t)la(n): tooth, abundance of

XALAC (folios 28r, 29r):
"On the Sandy River"

Both glyphs show white streams of water full of tiny black dots. The name derives from:

xal(li): sand
a(tl): water
c: on, or in

The glyphs are undistinguishable from that on folio 26r, glossed *Xalapan.*

XALAPAN (folios 16v, 26r):
"On the Sandy Water"

The glyph on folio 26r is a stream of water full of small black dots. On folio 16v, dots representing sand are piled below surface water in a canal. The name derives from:

xal(li): sand
a(tl): water
  apan(tli): canal
pan: on

The glyph is identical to those on folios 28r and 29r, both glossed *Xalac.*

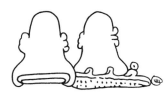

XALATLAUHCO (folio 10r):
"In the Sandy Gorge"

The glyph consists of two green hills with a stream of water flowing from between them. Below the stream rest numerous black dots in a white background. The name is formed from:

xal(li): sand
atlauh(tli): deep *barranca* (gorge)
co: on, or in

With the exception of the glyph for sand, this place glyph is identical with that for Atlapulco (folio 10r).

XALOZTOC (folio 24v):
"In the Cave of Sand"

The glyph is a profile of the stylized cave glyph, with numerous small black dots in the cave's open mouth. The name derives from:

xal(li): sand
ozto(tl): cave
c: on, or in

Clark (1938 2:31) translates this as "In the Sand Pit."

XALTEPEC (folios 13r, 43r):
"On the Sand Hill"

The glyph shows a white hill decorated with numerous black dots. The name is formed from:

xal(li): sand
tepe(tl): hill
c: on, or in

XALTIANQUIZCO (folio 16v):
"On the Sandy Marketplace"

The glyph consists of the symbol for marketplace (a round disk with variously decorated concentric circles within it); small black dots cover the interior of the disk. The name is formed from:

xal(la): sandy
tianquiz(tli): marketplace
co: on, or in

Another depiction of the conventionalized marketplace glyph is drawn on folio 67r of the *Mendoza.*

XALTOCAN (folios 3v, 17v):
"Place of the Sand-Spider"

The glyph on both folios consists of a circle full of black dots, in which a purple spider spins its web. The name derives from:

xal(li): sand
toca(tl): spider
can: place of

XAXALPAN (folio 20r):
"On a Great Deal of Sand"

The glyph is a house sitting atop a mound of little black dots. The name derives from:

xal(li): sand
xaxal(li): a great deal of sand
pan: on

Clark (1938 2:23) suggests that the house represents the residence of a *calpixqui* (tribute collector). However, it may instead signal the locative "on," by virtue of its position in the overall glyph.

 XAYACO (folio 46r): "On the Mask"

The glyph is a yellow-orange mask, shown in profile. The name derives from:

> *xayaca(tl):* mask
> *co:* on, or in

 **XICALHUACAN** (folio 29r): "Place that Has Gourd Bowls"

The glyph is a hand holding a blue gourd bowl. The bowl has two vertical black stripes. The name derives from:

> *xical(li):* gourd bowl
> *hua:* possessive
> *can:* place

 **XICALTEPEC** (folios 33r, 46r): "On the Hill of the Gourd Bowls"

The glyph is a blue gourd bowl with two vertical black bars, perched atop a green hill. The name is formed from:

> *xical(li):* gourd bowl
> *tepe(tl):* hill
> *c:* on, or in

 **XICO** (folio 20v): "In the Navel"

The glyph represents a navel bordered by elements of the traditional glyph for "hill." The name is formed from:

> *xic(tli):* navel
> *co:* on, or in

The "hill" (*tepetl*) element does not form part of the place-name, although it is included in the glyph.

 XICOCHIMALCO (folio 13r): "On the Bee Shield"

The glyph consists of a bee embedded in a round shield. The entire glyph is yellow. The name is formed from:

> *xico(tli):* large honey bee
> *chimal(li):* shield
> *co:* on, or in

Peñafiel (1885:235) translates *xicotli* as honeycomb; Molina (1970: folio 159r) clearly states "large honey bee." Honey bees and their sweet product are discussed by Hernández (1959 2:48–49) and Sahagún (1950–1982 11:93–94); the latter especially emphasizes the effects of the insect's potent sting.

 **XILOÇINCO** (folio 26r): "On the Small Tender Maize Ears"

The glyph shows two young maize ears, one yellow and one red, above the lower half of a man's body. The name is formed from:

> *xilo(tl):* tender ear of maize
> *tzin(tli):* rump
> *tzin:* small
> *co:* on, or in

This glyph in the *Matrícula* (folio 4v) arranges the legs in an unusual running mode.

 **XILOTEPEC** (folios 8r, 31r): "On the Hill of the Young Maize Ears"

The glyph on both folios shows a hill with two young ears of maize (one yellow and one red) on top. The name is formed from:

> *xilo(tl):* young maize ear
> *tepe(tl):* hill
> *c:* on, or in

 **XILOXOCHITLAN** (folio 50r): "Near the *Xiloxochitl*"

The glyph is a tree with red and yellow flowers, and with two rows of teeth in the trunk. The name derives from:

> *xiloxochi(tl):* a tree
> *tlan:* tooth, abundance of

Hernández (1959 1:145–146) describes this hot-land plant as having red (though sometimes white) flowers.

 XIQUIPILCO (folio 10v): "On the Incense Bag"

The glyph is a black and white incense bag. The bag has a handle and three tassels with fringes. The name derives from:

> *xiquipil(li):* incense bag
> *co:* on, or in

Such bags were used by priests; one can be seen in use on folio 63r of *Codex Mendoza*. This bag also stood for the number 8,000 (called *cenxiquipilli*), as on folio 25r of *Codex Mendoza*.

XIUHHUACAN (XIHUACAN) (folios 13r, 38r):
"Place That Has Turquoise"

The glyph consists of a turquoise-and-red-colored ornament. The name is formed from:

xih(uitl): turquoise
hua: possessive
can: place of

XIUHTECÇACATLAN (folio 13r):
"Place of the Yellow-Haired *Xiuhtecuhtli*"

The glyph is a very colorful profile head of the fire god Xiuhtecuhtli. The yellow face has two horizontal red bands painted on it and blue nose and ear ornaments. A red, white, and blue headband with three waving stalks of yellow grass, or *çacate*, tops his head. The name derives from:

xiuhtec(uhtli): Xiuhtecuhtli, the fire god
çaca(tl): grass
tlan: abundance of

Çacate is discussed under Acaçacatla. Clark (1938 2:14) states that the yellow grass symbolizes this god's yellow hair, and that he was also called Tzoncuztli, "Yellow-Haired." This god, complete with horizontal face-stripes and decorative headgear, is illustrated in Sahagún (1950–1982 1: plates 13, 39).

XIUHTEPEC (folios 6r, 7v, 23r):
"On the Hill of Turquoise"

The glyph on all three folios consists of a hill with the glyph for turquoise on top. The round blue stone has four small blue circles on its rim and red inlays in the middle. The name is formed from:

xihui(tl): turquoise
tepe(tl): hill
c: on, or in

XOCHIACAN (folio 10r):
"Place of Aromatic Flowers"

The glyph consists of a man enjoying the aroma of a colorful flower. Tiny black dots range from the flower to the man's nose. The name is formed from:

xochi(tl): flower
a(uiac): soft and aromatic, pleasant
can: place

While the glyph for water (*atl*) is normally used to produce the "a" sound, in this case a glyphically interesting variation is employed.

XOCHICHIVCA (folio 27r):
"Place Where Flowers Are Cultivated"

The glyph is a hand grasping a fluffy white flower with yellow stamens. The name derives from:

xochi(tl): flower
chiua: to make (cultivate)
ca(n): place where

XOCHIMILCAÇINCO (folio 24v):
"On the Small Place of the Xochimilca"

The glyph consists of two flowers on top of a rectangular plot of ground. The lower half of a man's body emerges from the side of the plot. The name is formed from:

xochi(tl): flower
mil(li): cultivated field
Xochimilca: people of the town of Xochimilco
tzin(tli): rump
tzin: small
co: on, or in

XOCHIMILCO (folios 2v, 6r):
"On the Fields of Flowers" or "In the Place of the Xochimilca"

The glyph on both folios consists of a rectangular plot of land on which sit two pert and colorful flowers. The name is formed from:

xochi(tl): flower
mil(li): cultivated field
Xochimil(ca): a group living in the southern Valley of Mexico
co: on, or in

XOCHIQUAUHTITLAN (folio 50r):
"Among Many Liquidambar Trees"

The glyph consists of a tree with yellow flowers and red roots, and two rows of teeth in the trunk. The name is formed from:

xochi(tl): flower
quahu(itl): tree
tlan(tli): tooth, abundance of
titlan: among

Clark (1938 2:53) suggests that the tree represents the *xochiocotzoquahuitl*, or sweet gum tree (*Liquidambar styraciflua L.*).

XOCHITEPEC (folio 23r):
"On the Hill of Flowers"

The glyph is a blue, red, and yellow flower on top of a green hill. The name derives from:

xochi(tl): flower
tepe(tl): hill
c: on, or in

XOCHIYETLA (folio 12r):
"Where There Are Many Tobacco Flowers"

The glyph shows a fluffy white flower with red and yellow stamens above a smoking tube. The name derives from:

xochi(tl): flower
ye(tl): tobacco
tla(n): abundance of

Smoking often accompanied feasts, and as Hernández (1959 2:176) notes, a mixture of tobacco, aromatic herbs, and liquidambar filled the tubes, and powdered charcoal was smeared on the outside of the tubes.

XOCHTLAN (folio 13r):
"Where There Are Many Flowers"

The glyph shows a man's head in profile: the man's hair is short on top and long in back; he has a hole in his septum for a nose plug and wears a prominent red headband. A fluffy white flower with yellow stamens attaches to the front of the headband. The name is formed from:

xoch(itl): flower
tlan: abundance of

The individual and his accoutrements may resemble an inhabitant of the Pacific coast, as Xochtlan was situated there, in the vicinity of Tehuantepec.

XOCONOCHCO (folios 15v, 18r, 47r):
"On the Sour Cactus Fruit"

The glyph in all three representations is a green prickly pear cactus with yellow and red fruits and red roots. The name is formed from:

xoco(c): sour
noch(tli): fruit of the prickly pear cactus
co: on, or in

The *xoconochtli* variety of prickly pear cactus had sour fruits and leaves and grew as tall as a tree (Hernández 1959 1:312). Clark (1938 2:51) identifies it as *Opuntia imbricata*.

XOCOTITLAN (folios 10v, 35r):
"Near the Fruit"

The glyph is a green hill with a profile head on top. On folio 10v the head is very white with two black bands across the eye and cheek. The figure wears a headband; two stalks with fruits rise from the headband. On folio 35r the face is tan in color, and the headband lacks the back-tie. The image is that of the god Xiuhtecuhtli, appropriately adorned for the monthly feast of Xocotl uetzi, "Xocotl Falls." This festival is illustrated in the *Codex Magliabechiano* (folio 26). The name derives from:

xoco(tl): fruit
titlan: near, among

Clark (1938 2:38) suggests that this refers specifically to Xocotepetl, a hill near Toluca.

XOCOTLA (folio 39r):
"Where There Are Many Fruits"

The glyph is a green tree with yellow fruit, red roots, and two rows of teeth on the trunk. The *Matrícula* version of this glyph (folio 10r) shows red fruit. The name derives from:

xoco(tl): fruit
tla(ntli): tooth, abundance of

Xocotl is a general term in Nahuatl referring to fruits with a sour taste (Hernández 1959 1:90).

XOCOYOCAN (folio 54r):
"Place of Fruit Trees"

The glyph consists of a tree with yellow fruits above a single footprint. The name derives from:

xocoyo: tree that has fruit (*xocotl*)
o: ohtli, road; the sound "o"
can: referring to a place

Xocotl is a general term referring to fruits with a sour taste (Hernández 1959 1:90).

XOCOYOLTEPEC (folio 41r): "On the Hill of the *Xocoyolli*"

The glyph is a lower leg and foot with a jaguar leg band (with two bells and a red strap) and a white sandal (with red thongs). Two stems with broad leaves emerge from the leg. The entire assemblage is set against the backdrop of a green hill. The name derives from:

xo(tl): foot
coyol(li): bell
  xocoyol(li): wood sorrel (*Oxalis* sp.)
tepe(tl): hill
c: on, or in

The inclusion of branches provides the clue that the plant, and not the literal "foot-bell," is intended. The *De la Cruz-Badiano Herbal* illustrates two varieties of the wood sorrel, both with slender stems and relatively broad leaves, useful in treating scales and cataracts (Gates 1939:9, 17).

XOLOCHIUHYAN (folios 13r, 38r): "Place Where Attendants or Slaves Are Made"

The glyphs show an old man's head with white hair, wrinkled face, and white bib. The name derives from:

xoloch(tic): wrinkled
  xolo: attendant or slave
chihua: to make
yan: place of

Peñafiel (1885:243) suggests that the first element is derived from *xolocha-hui:* "to grow wrinkled with age." This glyph appears earlier on the corresponding *Matrícula* folio (9v), immediately following Yztapan.

XOLOTLAN (folio 13v): "Place of Xolotl"

The glyph is the head of Xolotl, god of twins, monstrosities, and the ball court. The name derives from:

xolo(tl): Xolotl, god of the ball court, of twins, and of monstrosities
tlan: abundance of, place of

This deity is described and illustrated by Nicholson (1971b:418–419, fig. 3).

XOMEYOCAN (folio 29r): "Place Full of Elder Trees"

The glyph is a hand grasping a fruit or leaf of a leafy green plant. Two footprints march below. The name derives from:

xo(cotl): fruit
ma: to take
  xome(tl): elder tree
o(htli): road
  yo(tl): pertaining to
  xomeyo: pertaining to (full of) elder bushes
can: place

Hernández (1959 1:130) describes the *xometontli,* or small elder tree.

XONOCTLA (XONOTLA) (folio 51r): "Place of Much *Jonote*"

The glyph is the god Xolotl, with three green branches atop. There is no tooth (*tlantli*) glyph. In the *Matrícula de Tributos* (folio 15r), the Xolotl figure is drawn quite differently, the branches are brown, and the tooth glyph is included at the bottom. The name is formed from:

Xolo(tl): god of twins, the ball courts, etc.
xono(tl): a plant
tla(n): abundance of

The region where this town is located abounds in the plant *jonote* (from *xonotl*), from which cordage and baskets are made yet today. Santamaría (1974:643) identifies the plant as *Heliocarpus americanus.* The inclusion of the Xolotl glyph provides the clue that the relevant plant name begins with the "xo" sound. Clark (1938 2:54) interprets this place glyph as "In the Growing Xolotl."

XOXOVTLA (folio 23r): "Where There Is Much Green" or "Place of Many Precious Greenstones"

The glyph consists of two teeth on a blue disk; they rest on top of a hill. The name is formed from:

xoxouh(qui): green/blue
tla(n): tooth, abundance of

Molina (1970: folios 18r, 161v) defines *xoxouhqui* as both green and a blue "color of the sky." Clark (1938 2:28) suggest that *xoxouhqui ytztli*, "a precious emerald-colored stone," is intended.

YACAPICHTLAN (YACAPICHTLA) (folios 8r, 24v): "Where There Are Many Pointed Things"

The glyph on both folios consists of a hill with a brown built-in nose. Below the nose lurks a small black insect. The name is formed from:

yaca(tl): nose
peç(otli): insect
  yacapitz(auac): something pointed
tla(n): abundance of

YANCUITLAN (folios 12r, 43r): "Where There Are New Towns" or "Place of the New Town"

The glyphs in both cases are white rectangles with two teeth below. The rectangle on folio 12r shows two narrow, crosshatched columns; that on folio 43r shows a border. The place glyph in the *Matrícula* (folio 12r) resembles the *Mendoza* glyph on folio 43r. The name derives from:

yancui(c): something new
tlan(tli): tooth, abundance of

The white color seems to convey the idea of newness. The name for this town in Mixtec is *Yodzocahi* (M. E. Smith 1973:176).

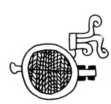

YAONAHUAC (folio 51r): "Near the War"

The glyph consists of battle paraphernalia: a yellow woven shield, an obsidian-bladed club, and a highly stylized glyph for "good sound." The name is formed from:

yao(yotl): war or battle
nahua(tl): good sound
c: on, or in
  nahuac: near

Peñafiel (1885:249) identifies the "sound" glyph as a yellow cloud, the symbol for fire (*tlachinolli*).

YAOTLAN (folio 46r): "Where There Are Many Enemies" or "Place of War"

The glyph is a plain white round shield (with border indicated); a yellow club passes behind the shield. The name is formed from:

yao(tl): enemy
  yao(yotl): war
tlan: abundance of

The shield and weapon (customarily arrows or a war club) serve as glyphic symbols of war in Nahuatl documents (see, for example, part 1 of *Codex Mendoza*). No *tlantli* glyph is included on this place glyph.

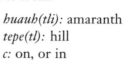

YAUHTEPEC (folios 8r, 24v): "On the Hill of the Amaranth" or "On the Hill of *Yauhtli*"

The glyph on folio 8r shows a hill from which emerge yellow flowers bundled together with a "sacred white knotted cord" (Clark 1938 2:6). The glyph on folio 24v shows the flowers attached to the nock end of an arrow (ibid.:30). The name derives from:

huauh(tli): amaranth
tepe(tl): hill
c: on, or in

Clark (ibid.:6, 30) suggests that the name stands for Yauhtli, a name for the god Tezcatlipoca.

YAYAVQUITLALPA (folio 51r): "On the Brown Land"

The glyph shows a field divided into three segments, two brown and one whitish. The name derives from:

yaya(ctic): brown
qui: thing
tlal(li): land
pa(n): on

The locative *pan* is not expressed glyphically. Clark (1938 2:54) suggests an alternative translation, "On the Disputed Land," with *yayaotla* meaning "dispute." Yet the translation as "brown land" parallels that of Tlatlauhquitepec. Interpretations of this glyph by Peñafiel (1885:247–248) and Macazaga Ordoño (1979:183) as "On New Lands" (Yancuictlalpan) are clearly erroneous.

YCÇOCHINANCO (folio 42r):
"On the Yucca *Chinampa*"

The glyph has a rectangular plot of land at its base; a yucca plant with green (live) and brown (dead) leaves sits on the plot. The name is formed from:

yczo(tli): yucca
chinam(itl): chinampa, or enclosure
co: on, or in

The yucca plant (*Yucca aloifolia* L.) is described by Sahagún (1950–1982 11:110, 205); its rough, scaly trunk can be seen in this glyph.

YCHCA ATOYAC (folio 40r):
"On the River of Cotton"

The glyph combines a stone and a fluffy cotton boll on a river of water. The name is formed from:

ichca(tl): cotton
atoya(tl): river
atoyate(tl): pebble
c: on, or in

Clark (1938 2:44) suggests that the *ichcatl* (cotton) element stands for *iciuhca* (swift).

YCHCATEOPAN (folios 37r, 39r):
"On the Temple of Cotton"

The glyph is a plump cotton boll on a stair-stepped temple pyramid. The name derives from:

ichca(tl): cotton
teopan(tli): temple
pan: on

Clark (1938 2:41) offers the possibility that *ichcatl* serves here as an ideograph for *ixcaua*, "to suffer from neglect." Peñafiel (1885:126) interprets the place glyph literally.

YCHCATLA (folio 40r):
"Where There Is Much Cotton"

The glyph consists of a fluffy boll of cotton. The name is formed from:

ichca(tl): cotton
tla(n): abundance of

As in the folio 40r glyph for Ychcatlan, no *tlantli* locative glyph is drawn here.

YCHCATLAN (folios 40r, 54r):
"Where There Is Much Cotton"

On folio 40r the glyph is a fluffy cotton boll. On folio 54r the glyph is a billowy white cotton boll sitting atop a pair of teeth. The name is formed from:

ichca(tl): cotton
tlan: abundance of

The *tlantli* glyph is absent on the folio 40r glyph, and on its *Matrícula* mate.

YCPATEPEC (folio 15v):
"On Top of the Hill"

The glyph shows a ball of thread on top of a hill. The name is formed from:

icpa(tl): thread
icpa(c): on top of
tepe(tl): hill
c: on, or in

The use of a ball of thread to convey the notion of "on top of" can also be seen on folio 10v (Oztoticpac).

YOALAN (YOALLAN) (folios 6r, 37r, 39r):
"Place of Night"

This is the glyph representing night: a dark, decorated circle with red and white eyes around its perimeter and in its center. The name is formed from:

yoal(li): night
(t)lan: abundance of

Clark (1938 2:42) suggests that the glyph refers to the lord of the night, Yoaltecuhtli.

YOALTEPEC (folios 8r, 40r):
"On the Hill of Night"

The glyph on folio 8r consists of the glyph for "night" (a dark circle with red and white eyes around its rim and in its center). This glyph rests atop a green hill. On folio 40r "night" is represented by only a half-circle. The image in the *Matrícula* (folio 10v) more closely resembles that on *Mendoza* folio 40r. The name is formed from:

yoal(li): night
tepe(tl): hill
c: on, or in

YOLOXONECUILA (folio 16v): "Where There Are Many Heart-Staffs" or "In the Place of *Macuilxochitl*"

The glyph shows a red and yellow heart attached to an elongated red curlicue. The name is formed from:

> *yollo(tli):* heart
> *xonecuil(li):* notched staff offered to the gods
> *(t)la(n):* abundance of

The red curlicue must represent the staff. Clark (1938 2:20) mentions that this was the badge of the god Macuilxochitl ("Five Flower"), a god of pleasure. Clark extends his interpretation of the glyph to translate the town name as "In the Place of Macuilxochitl." Indeed, this god's staff features a prominent heart (Sahagún 1950–1982 1: plate 14; *Codex Magliabechiano* 1983: folio 60r).

YOPICO (folio 20r): "In the Place of the *Yopes*"

The glyph is the peaked cap of the god Xipe Totec. The name derives from:

> *yopi(tzontli):* Xipe Totec's cap
> *Yopi(me):* a group living in the Pacific coastal area of Mexico (modern state of Guerrero)
> *co:* on, or in

This cap was so characteristic of the god Xipe that it served as an ideograph for the group of people most closely associated with this "Flayed God," the Yopes. This glyph also appears on folio 47r of *Codex Mendoza* and 13r of the *Matrícula de Tributos*, representing the month of Tlacaxipehualiztli, during which this deity was especially honored.

YTZUCAN (folio 42r): "Place of Obsidian"

The glyph consists of an obsidian knife containing a row of teeth along the right side. Three footprints complete the glyph. The name derives from:

> *itz(tli):* obsidian
> *o(htli):* road
> *yo(tl):* pertaining to
> *can:* place of

The footprints provide the notion of road and the phonetic value "o." The knife with teeth is an aspect of Tezcatlipoca (Clark 1938 2:45). Peñafiel (1885:129) derives the name "Place Where the Face Is Painted," from *itzoca*, "to dirty the face."

YXCOYAMEC (folio 51r): "On the Face of the Peccary"

The glyph is a wild boar, with an eye glyph on the body. The name is formed from:

> *ix(telolotli):* eye
> *coyame(tl):* peccary
> *c:* on, or in

The eye (*ixtelolotli*) provides the phonetic equivalent for face (*ixtli*). Anderson and Dibble (Sahagún 1950–1982 11:10) identify the animal as a peccary (*Pecari angulatus crassus*), while Clark (1938 2:54) and Peñafiel (1885:131) identify it as *Dicotyles torquatus*. Hernández (1959 2:310–311) describes this beast and its habitat.

YXICAYAN (folio 40r): "Place Where Water Seeps Out"

The glyph is a hill with water dripping from its base. The name derives from:

> *ixica:* to seep or ooze
> *a(tl):* water
> *yan:* place where

YXMATLATLAN (folio 46r): "Place of the Blue Face (Tlaloc)"

The glyph consists of the head of the rain god, Tlaloc. The face and snaking mouth and "nose" are blue; the "fangs" are red and white. The head is ornamented with a yellow maize ear, white paper headgear, red and white tassels, and a turquoise earplug. The name derives from:

> *ix(tli):* face
> *matla(ltic):* dark blue color
> *tlan:* abundance of

The "blue face" serves as a symbolic description of the god Tlaloc, who is clearly depicted in the glyph. In this rendering, the *tlantli* locative is omitted.

YXQUEMECAN (folio 21v):
"Place of Maguey-Fiber Capes"

The glyph consists of a man's face in profile covered by a white cloth. The name is formed from:

> *ix(tli):* face
> *quemi(tl):* cape
> > *ichquemi(tl):* maguey-fiber cape
> *can:* place of

YZAMATITLA (folio 24v):
"Near the Ceiba Trees"

The glyph shows a curved obsidian claw on top of a bound roll of paper. The name is formed from:

> *itz(tli):* obsidian (knife)
> *yz(titl)* or *yztetl:* claw
> *ama(tl):* paper
> > *ytzama(tl):* ceiba tree
> *titla(n):* near or among

Hernández (1959 1:87) describes the *ytzamatl*, indicating that it grew in Huaxtepec, the province where this town is located.

YZCUINCUITLAPILCO (folio 8r):
"On the End of Everyone" or "Place of the Commoners"

The glyph is the bottom half of a black-spotted dog; the dog has an exceptionally long tail. The name derives from:

> *itzcuin(tli):* dog
> > *izquin(tin):* everybody
> *cuitlapil(li):* tail (end)
> *co:* on, or in

Orozco y Berra (1960 1:414) feels that the name refers to *cuitlapilli atlapilli* (commoners, *macehuales*); hence, "In the Place of the *Macehuales*."

YZCUINTEPEC (folio 16r):
"On the Hill of the Dog"

The glyph is a black-spotted dog crouching on a hill. The name derives from:

> *itzcuin(tli):* dog
> *tepe(tl):* hill
> *c:* on, or in

YZHUATLAN (folio 13v):
"Where There Are Many Dried Maize Husks"

The glyph is a stalk of white leaves, probably of maize. The name derives from:

izua(tl): leaf, dried maize husk
tlan: abundance of

Peñafiel (1885:132) identifies *izuatl* as green maize leaves; Anderson and Dibble (in Sahagún 1950–1982 11:279) define the same term as dried maize husks. Clark (1938 2:15) identifies this cluster as "scrubbing brushes of leaves."

YZMIQUILPAN (folio 27r):
"On the *Itzmiquilitl*"

The glyph consists of a plot of ground, a curved green plant, and a red and white knife. The name is formed from:

> *itz(tli):* obsidian (knife)
> *mil(li):* cultivated plot of land
> *quil(itl):* edible plant
> > *itzmiquil(itl):* a creeping plant
> *pan:* on

The colors on the knife signal its use in human sacrifices (Peñafiel 1885:128). Sahagún (1950–1982 11:134, plate 464a) describes and illustrates this leafy plant.

YZTACALCO (folio 17v):
"In the Salt House"

The glyph is a house with smoke and small black dots in a hole in the roof; drops of water fall into a bowl inside the entrance. The name derives from:

> *izta(tl):* salt
> *cal(li):* house
> *co:* on, or in

Salt is being obtained in this front-facing house through evaporation, as Clark (1938 2:22) observes. Yzta-calco was located on a small island in Lake Texcoco (Sanders, Parsons, and Santley 1979: map 19).

YZTAC TLALOCAN (folios 13v, 15v):
"On the White Tlaloc"

The glyph is the blue face of Tlaloc framed by a white headdress and resting on a white hill. On folio 15v only parts of the face and the ear ornament are blue. The name derives from:

> *iztac:* white
> *tlaloc:* Tlaloc, god of rain
> *can:* place

YZTAPAN (folio 38r): "On the Salt"

The glyph is a white bordered circle with small black dots inside. A single footprint rests on top of the circle. The name derives from:

izta(tl): salt
pan(o): to cross a river on foot
pan: on

Clark (1938 2:41) suggests that "salt pan" is intended.

 YZTATLAN (folio 13v): "Where There Is Much Salt"

The glyph is a white bordered disk full of little black dots resting on top of two teeth. The name derives from:

izta(tl): salt
tlan(tli): tooth
tlan: abundance of

Aside from the disk (probably a salt pan), there is nothing special in the glyph to identify the small dots as salt (as opposed to the usual alternatives of chalk, sand, and lime).

 YZTEPEC (YTZTEPEC) (folios 6r, 23r, 51r): "On the Hill of Obsidian"

The glyphs on all three folios show obsidian blades atop a hill. The obsidian in folio 6r is stylistically different from those on the other two folios. The name derives from:

itz(tli): obsidian (knife)
tepe(tl): hill
c: on, or in

Clark (1938 2:4, 29) feels that the obsidian stands for *ichtli*, or maguey. However, if that meaning were intended, such a plant could be easily represented pictographically.

 YZTEYOCAN (YTZTEYOCAN) (folios 17v, 48r): "Place Pertaining to Obsidian"

The glyph consists of a piece of obsidian set atop a stone. Three footprints march along below the stone on the folio 48r glyph. The name derives from:

itz(tli) or *itzte(tl)*: obsidian
te(tl): stone
o(htli): road
yo-: pertaining to
can: referring to a place

Clark (1938 2:52) feels that *yztetl* or *yztitl*, "claw," may be involved, suggested by the shape of the obsidian in the glyph. However, Sahagún (1950–1982 11:227), describing the properties of obsidian, speaks of the *itztetl* (scraper), which comes from the thick obsidian core. This may be the intent of the glyphic pictogram: a curved scraper emerging from the obsidian core. In the folio 48r place glyph, the road (*ohtli*) element has phonetic value.

 YZTITLAN (folio 16v): "Where There Are Many Claws"

The glyph is a formidable-looking claw. The name derives from:

izti(tl): claw
tlan: abundance of

 YZTLA (folio 23r): "Place of Much Obsidian"

The glyph is a piece of hooked obsidian on top of two teeth. The name derives from:

itz(tli): obsidian (knife)
tla(n): tooth, abundance of

Clark (1938 2:29) feels that the obsidian stands for *ixtli*, "agave."

PERSONAL NAMES

 ACAÇITLI (folio 2r): "Reed Hare"

The glyph should be the one attached to the individual glossed "Oçelopan." That glyph shows the brown head of a hare with a reed atop its head. The name derives from:

aca(tl): reed
citli: hare

The hare is described by both Sahagún (1950–1982 11:12–13) and Hernández (1959 2:297).

 ACAMAPICH (folio 2v twice): "Handful of Reeds"

Both glyphs for this name show a hand grasping a bundle of arrow reeds. The name derives from:

aca(tl): reed
mapich(tli): handful

ACUEYOTL (folio 18r): "Wave"

The glyph is a single stream of water with a shell at its tip. This glyph is unglossed, and Clark (1938 1:59) suggests the above interpretation. The name derives from:

> *a(tl):* water
> *cue(chtli);* shell
> *yotl:* full of, pertaining to

 AGUEXOTL (folio 2r): "Water Willow"

The glyph of this name, more properly glossed "Ahuexotl," is a leafy tree with water curling about its roots. The name derives from:

> *a(tl):* water
> *huexotl:* willow

This tree is described by Sahagún (1950–1982 11:110).

 AHUIÇOÇIN (folio 13r): "Revered *Ahuitzotl*"

The glyph is a crouching gray animal with water running along its back and long, curling tail. The name derives from:

> *ahuitzo(tl):* ahuitzotl, a water animal
> *tzin:* revered (or small)

This animal and its mystical qualities are described in great detail by Sahagún (1950–1982 11:68–70) and more cursorily by Hernández (1959 2:393). It is identified as a water-opossum by Clark (1938 1:37). As in other personal names, *-tzin* here means "revered" rather than "small."

 ATONAL (folio 7v): "Water Day" or "Water Summertime"

The glyph is a yellow-bordered canal full of water; four red circles are arranged on the water. The name derives from:

> *a(tl):* water
> *tonal(li):* day, summertime, heat of the sun

 ATOTOTL (folio 2r): "Water Bird"

The glyph is the head of a green bird with a stream of water wrapped about its neck. The name derives from:

> *a(tl):* water
> *tototl:* bird

The *atototl*, or American bittern, was a water bird that was so named because "it is a drowner of people" (Sahagún 1950–1982 11:57). The bird is also discussed by Hernández (1959 2:347).

 AXAYACAÇIN (AXAYACAÇI) (folios 10r, 19r): "Face of Water"

The glyph on both folios shows a stream of water spilling down the front of a man's face. The name is formed from:

> *a(tl):* water
> *xayaca(tl):* face, mask
> *tzin:* revered (also small)

When attached to a person's (or god's) name, the suffix *-tzin* carries the meaning of "revered" rather than "small."

 CHIMALPUPUCA (folio 4v twice): "Smoking Shield"

Both glyphs of this name show a shield with smoke spewing from the top of the shield. The shield is yellow with a blue border; both glyphs also show seven white feather balls in the shield, while one adds three horizontal bands. The name derives from:

> *chimal(li):* shield
> *popoca:* to smoke

 HUEHUE MOTECÇUMA (folio 7v): "Angry Lord, the Elder"

The glyph for this ruler, in this rendering, shows his usual additional name, "Ilhuicamina." The glyph is a stylistic vision of the sky being pierced from below with an arrow. The name is formed from:

> *huehue:* great, or old
> *tec(uhtli):* lord, or judge
> *moçuma:* to frown in anger
>
> +
>
> *ilhuica(tl):* sky
> *mina:* to shoot an arrow

The full name yields "Great Angry Lord, Archer of the Skies." Clark (1938 1:32) suggests that "Courageous lord" may be more seemly, citing an alternate meaning for *çuma.* The glyph for this ruler in the *Codex Telleriano-Remensis* (folio 31v) is a simple turquoise diadem.

HUIÇILYHUITL (folio 3v): "Hummingbird Feather"

The glyph shows the head of a green hummingbird (with long yellow bill); the head is surrounded by five white feather balls. The name derives from:

huitzi(tzilin): hummingbird
ihuitl: feather

Several varieties of hummingbirds are described by Sahagún (1950–1982 11:24–25).

 MIXCOATL (folio 17v): "Cloud Snake"

The glyph, attached directly to a man's head, is a blue snake with curls along its back. The name derives from:

mix(tli): cloud
coa(tl): snake

This glyph is identical to that for the town of Mixcoac, folio 5v.

 MOQUIHUIX (folios 10r, 19r): "Drunk Face"

The glyph on both folios shows a face, partially painted red and with a curvy yellow or brown nose plug; numerous small black dots in a wavy pattern substitute for hair. The name is formed from:

mocuiqui: he who is ill from much drinking
ix(tli): face

This is probably the correct interpretation, since the nose-ornament glyph is the "nose-crescent" (*yaca-metztli*) characteristic of the *pulque* god Ometochtli, and the dots (replacing hair) could easily represent the fermenting *pulque*. The glyph for this ill-fated ruler in the *Codex Telleriano-Remensis* (folio 36v) is simply a bowl of bubbling *pulque*, while Sahagún (1950–1982 8: plate 21) identifies him with an eye (*ixtelolotli*).

 MOTECÇUMA (folio 15v): "Angry Lord"

The glyph shows the characteristic turquoise diadem with red back-tie on a wig; turquoise nose and ear ornaments accompany the noble headgear. The name derives from:

tec(uhtli): lord, or judge
moçuma: to frown from anger
+
xocoyo(tl): younger child
tzin: revered (or small)

The customary latter part of this ruler's name (Xocoyotzin) is not glyphically represented; his full name would be "Angry Lord, the Younger." Clark (1938 1:42) feels that *xocoyotl* is indicated by the nose and ear ornaments, but Molina does not bear out such a translation. As with other personal names, the *-tzin* suffix means "revered," not "small."

 OÇELOPAN (folio 2r): "Jaguar Banner"

The glyph should be the one attached to the figure glossed "Aca-çitli." That glyph consists of a banner formed from (or decorated with) the characteristic spots of a jaguar. The name derives from:

oçelo(tl): jaguar
pan(tli): banner

 OMEQUAUH (folio 18r): "Two Eagle"

The glyph is an eagle's head with two red and white dots below. The name derives from:

ome: two
quauh(tli): eagle

 QUAPAN (folio 2r): "Eagle Banner"

The glyph consists of a banner made of six brown feathers. The name is formed from:

quauh(tli): eagle
pan(tli): banner

 QUAUHTLATOA (folios 6r, 19r): "Speaking Eagle"

The glyph in both cases shows an eagle's head with a blue speech scroll in front of its beak. Clark (1938 1: 30–31) feels that the scribe(s) made an error here, in both glyph and gloss, and that the Tlatelolco ruler Tlacateotl is the correct personage. The name, nonetheless, derives from:

quauh(tli): eagle
tlatoa: to speak

The ruler Quauhtlatoa is shown in Sahagún (1950–1982 8: plate 20), the glyph again an eagle's head, this time with a profusion of speech scrolls. Tlacateotl is also shown in Sahagún (ibid.: plate 19), his glyph being a sun symbol over a rock. This individual appears in association with Itzcoatl's rule in the *Codex Telleriano-Remensis* (folio 31r).

 TEÇINEUH (folio 2r):
"He Who Expels Someone" or
"He Has Rooted Up Maguey"

The glyph is a full maguey plant with the lower half of a man's body attached to its side. The glyph and gloss do not entirely match; perhaps, as Clark (1938 1:21) suggests, "Meçineuh" (Metzineuh) is meant here. The name derives from:

> *te-:* someone
> *me(tl):* maguey
> *tzin(tli):* rump
>> *tzineua:* to root up trees, destroy towns, or the like

 TENUCH (folio 2r):
"Stone Cactus Fruit"

The glyph is the same one used to designate the city of Tenochtitlan, a prickly pear cactus growing on a rock. The name derives from:

> *te(tl):* stone or rock
> *noch(tli):* prickly pear cactus fruit

The prickly pear cactus is discussed under Tenochtitlan.

 TIÇOÇICATZIN (folio 12r):
"Bloodletter"

The glyph is a leg (with foot) covered with numerous small black dots. The name derives from:

> *teço:* bloodletter
> *(tzi)tzica:* to stick with a spine
> *tzin:* revered (or small)

The more usual rendering of this name is reduced to simply Tizoc. Even though this ruler had a questionable career, the "revered" meaning of *-tzin* would apply. In the *Codex Telleriano-Remensis* (folios 38r, 39r), this ruler's glyph is a spine piercing a stone—*tetl* (stone) + *ço* (to draw blood, to pierce).

 XIUHCAQUI (folio 2r):
"Person Shod with Turquoise-Colored Sandals"

The glyph shows a blue sandal. The name is formed from:

> *xiuh(tic):* turquoise color
> *cac(tli):* sandal
>> *caque:* person shod with sandals or shoes

 XOCOYOL (folio 2r):
"Foot Bell" or "Wood Sorrel"

The glyph consists of a foot and lower leg with an anklet; the ornament is a bell dangling from a red cord. The name is formed from:

> *xo(tl):* foot
> *coyol(li):* bell
>> *xocoyol(li):* wood sorrel

Clark (1938 1:21) suggests "wood sorrel."

 XOMIMITL (folio 2r):
"Foot Arrow" or "Pierced Foot"

The glyph consists of a foot and lower leg with an arrow piercing through the ankle. The name is formed from:

> *xo(tl):* foot
> *mimi(na):* to pierce with a spear or arrow
>> *mitl:* arrow

 YZCOAÇI (folios 5v, 19r):
"Revered Obsidian Serpent"

The glyph on both folios consists of a stylized body and head of a red and yellow snake; sharp obsidian blades cover the back of the serpent and continue stylistically over its head. The name derives from:

> *itz(tli):* obsidian (knife)
> *coa(tl):* snake
> *tzi(n):* revered (also small)

Attached to a personal or god's name, *-tzin* carries the meaning of "revered" rather than "small."

TITLES

 ACATL IYACAPANECATL (folio 68r):
"Lord of the Reed on the Nose"

The glyph quite clearly portrays an arrow reed on a man's nose. The name is formed from:

acatl: reed
i: his
yaca(tl): nose
pani: on
ecatl: signifying affiliation

For more information on the stem **(ca)-tl* signifying national, tribal, or civic affiliation, see Andrews (1975:332–333).

 ATENPANECATL (folio 65r): "Keeper on the Edge of the Water"

The glyph shows water spilling down the back side of lips. The name is formed from:

a(tl): water
ten(tli): lips, edge
pani: on
ecatl: signifying affiliation

For additional information on the stem **(ca)-tl,* signifying national, tribal, or civic affiliation, see Andrews (1975:332–333).

  EZGUAGUACATL (folios 65r, 68r): "Raining Blood"

The glyph for this title, which should more properly read *Ezhuahuacatl,* is the sign for rain striped in red and white. The name derives from:

exaxaua(niliztli): blood rain
catl: signifying affiliation

This interpretation is most consistent with the glyph. For additional alternatives and a thorough analysis, see note 35 to the page descriptions for folio 65r.

 HUIZNAHUATL (HUITZNAHUATL) (folios 66r, 67r): "Thorn Speech"

The glyph is a red and blue maguey thorn; a blue speech scroll rolls out from a small opening in the thorn. The name derives from:

uitz(tli): large thorn or spike
nahuatl: good sound

This exalted individual also appears on folio 67r, though without the glyph for his title.

 MYXCOATLAYLOTLAC (folio 68r): "The Returned Master of the Cloud Snake"

The glyph is an eagle-feather tuft with three footprints marching around the sides and top. The name is formed from:

mix(tli): cloud
coa(tl): snake
tlailo(a): to return
tlac(atl): lord, or man

The word *tlailoa* also carries the meaning of "to get dirty," but the presence of footprints in the glyph probably calls for the word's alternate meaning, "to return." It is surprising, however, and somewhat of a mystery to find the feather tuft in place of the "cloud-snake" glyph, as found in the place-name glyph on folio 5v and the personal name on folio 17v.

 PETLACALCATL (folio 70r): "Keeper of the Reed Coffers"

There is no glyph proper for this title on folio 70r; the pictograph shows a man sitting on a reed mat; the mat rests in front of a house whose base is partially made of reeds. On folio 20r a house made of reeds is glossed *petlacalcatl* (see place-name Petlacalco in this appendix). The name derives from:

petla(tl): reed mat
cal(li): house
  petlacal(li): reed coffer or chest; also tribute storehouse
catl: signifying affiliation

More information on the stem **(ca)-tl,* signifying national, tribal, or civic affiliation, is available in Andrews (1975:332–333).

 QUAUHNOCHTLI (folio 65r): "Eagle Cactus Fruit"

The glyph is an eagle feather on top of a human heart. The name derives from:

quauh(tli): eagle
nochtli: prickly pear cactus fruit
  quauhnochtli: the hearts of sacrificial victims

See the page descriptions for folio 65r for an explanation of this etymology.

TEQUIXQUINAHUACATL (folio 68r): "Saltpeter Speech"

The glyph is a set of lips with small black dots within; a speech scroll emerges from the lips. The name derives from:

tequixqui(tl): saltpeter
nahua(tl): good sound
catl: signifying affiliation

The small black dots represent the saltpeter; the presence of lips (*tentli*) is surely a phonetic prompt alerting the glyph-reader that saltpeter (instead of, say, salt or chalk) is meant. See Andrews (1975:332–333) for more about the **(ca)-tl* stem.

TEZCACOACATL (folios 18r, 65r): "Keeper of the Mirrored Snake"

The glyph consists of the upper part of a graceful red snake. The snake's body is covered with a single row of circles, each containing a dot in its center. The name is formed from:

tezca(tl): mirror
coa(tl): snake
catl: signifying affiliation

The circles here represent the mirror, a magnified version of which is found around the neck of a snake in the place-name glyph for Tezcacoac (folio 20v). Andrews (1975:332–333) provides information about the **(ca)-tl* stem.

TICOCYAHUACATL (folio 65r): "Keeper of the Bowl of Fatigue"

The glyph for this title is a bowl of *pulque*; the bowl boasts the curved symbol for *pulque*, and the beverage foams spiritedly above its container. The name derives from:

teco(matl): clay drinking cup
ciau(i): to be fatigued
acatl: signifying affiliation

A thorough analysis of this rather difficult name appears in the page descriptions for folio 65r, note 61. It may also be noted that *oc(tli)* (*pulque*) is buried in the name and prominent in the glyph. This individual appears on folio 67r, but without his name glyph. See Andrews (1975:332–333) for information on the **(ca)-tl* stem.

TLACATECATL (folio 18r): "Keeper of the High Noble's House" or "Keeper of the Court House" or "Keeper of Men"

The glyph for this man's title seems to be embedded in his hairstyle, the classic "pillar of stone" (*temillotl*) style. The same meaning is conveyed by the term *tecaxitli* (Molina 1970: folio 92r). The name derives from:

tlaca(tl): man, or lord
teca(xitli): pillar of stone
teca(lli): lord's house, or judge's house
catl: signifying affiliation

This personage, in fancy warrior costume but without his distinctive "pillar of stone" hairstyle, also appears on folio 67r. Of all the "governors" on folios 17v and 18r, only two wear their hair in this manner. The other is glossed *Tlacochtectli* but carries the glyph for *Tlacochcalcatl*; he is already problematical. More information on this hairstyle is found in the page descriptions for folio 62r. The **(ca)-tl* suffix is discussed by Andrews (1975:332–333).

TLACATECTLI (folios 17v, 18r): "Lord of Men"

The glyph in all four representations (three on folio 17v, one on folio 18r) is simply a nobleman's turquoise diadem (*xiuhuitzolli*). This diadem hovers above a man's head in all but one case. The exception is caused by the interference of a personal name attached to the man's head; the diadem is directly associated with the man by means of a thin black line. The name derives from:

tlaca(tl): man, or lord
tec(uh)tli: high noble, or judge

TLACOCHCALCATL (folios 18r, 65r): "Keeper of the House of Darts"

The glyph is a house with the nock ends of darts or arrows on top, two on folio 18r, three on folio 65r. The gloss on folio 18r, not matching the glyph, says *Tlacochtectli*. The name derives from:

tlacoch(tli): arrow or dart
cal(li): house
catl: signifying affiliation.

This personage, in his prestigious regalia but sans glyph, also appears on folio 67r. The *(ca)-tl* suffix is discussed by Andrews (1975:332–333).

TLACOCHTECTLI (folios 17v, 18r): "Lord of the Dart"

Glyphs for persons carrying this important title appear four times, twice on each folio. The glyph is uniformly the nock end of an arrow embedded into the man's *xiuhuitzolli*, or turquoise diadem. The name derives from:

> *tlacoch(tli):* arrow or dart
> *tec(uh)tli:* high noble, or judge

TLILANCALQUI (folios 18r, 65r): "Keeper of the House of Darkness"

The glyphs on both folios show a house with black lintel and, on folio 65r, black doorjamb. The houses have somewhat different arrangements of circles looking like Maltese crosses (see page descriptions for folio 65r). The name derives from:

> *tlil(li):* black color
> *(t)lan:* abundance of
> > *tlillan:* in the darkness
> *cal(li):* house
> *qui:* personifier

TOCUILTECATL (folio 65r): "Keeper of the Worm on Blade of Maize"

The glyph is a green worm. The name derives from:

> *toc(tli):* the young blade of maize
> *ocuil(in):* worm or caterpillar
> *tecatl:* signifying affiliation

Andrews (1975:332–333) provides a discussion of the *(ca)-tl* suffix.

APPENDIX F: Warrior Costumes: The *Codex Mendoza* and Other Aztec Pictorials

	1 Cuextecatl	2 Cicitlallo Cuextecatl	3 Tzitzimitl	4 Quaxolotl	5 Patzactli	6 Ocelotl
CODEX MENDOZA *Part 2: Tribute*	folio 41r		folio 20r	folio 28r	folio 49r	folio 25r
CODEX MENDOZA *Part 3: Ethnography*	folio 64r	folio 65r	folio 67r	folio 67r		folio 64r
PRIMEROS MEMORIALES			estampa XXIII	estampa XXV	estampa XXV	estampa I
LIENZO DE TLAXCALA	79			62		45
FLORENTINE CODEX	bk. 12: folio 58v	bk. 9: folio 5v		bk. 8: folio 33v	bk. 9: folio 5r	bk. 2: folio 20r
CODICE AZCATITLAN						
DURAN	vol. 2: *lámina* 40				vol. 2: *lámina* 14	vol. 1: *lámina* 15
CODEX MAGLIA-BECHIANO						folio 30r
CODEX TELLERIANO-REMENSIS		folio 37r				

7	8	9	10	11	12	13	14
Momoyactli	Coyotl	Xopilli	Papalotl	Tozcocolli	Quetzaltototl	Pamitl	Quauhtli
folio 24v	folio 25r	folio 23v	folio 23v	folio 43r	folio 46r		
folio 65r	folio 65r	folio 64r	folio 64r			folio 67r	
	estampa XXII		estampa XXIII	estampa XXVI	estampa XXIII	estampa XXIII	estampa I
34	28			48	43	48	48
						bk. 9: folio 5r	bk. 2: folio 126r
	planche IX						planche XXIV
				vol. 1: lámina 45		vol. 2: lámina 40	vol. 2: lámina 60
						folio 37v	

See page 246, across from foldout, for citations.

APPENDIX G: Shields: The *Codex Mendoza* and Other Aztec Pictorials

	1 Cuexyo	2 Cuexyo Variant 1	3 Cuexyo Variant 2	4 Cuexyo Variant 3	5 Cuexyo Variant 4
CODEX MENDOZA *Part 2: Tribute*	folio 25r	folio 19r	folio 20v	folio 20r	
CODEX MENDOZA *Part 3: Ethnography*	folio 67r	folio 64r	folio 64r		folio 65r
PRIMEROS MEMORIALES	estampa XXII				
LIENZO DE TLAXCALA	B		54	25	59
FLORENTINE CODEX	bk. 2: folio 20r		bk. 8: folio 33v		bk. 8: folio 34r
CODEX TELLERIANO-REMENSIS	folio 39v		folio 42r		
DURAN	vol. 1: lámina 17		vol. 2: lámina 35		vol. 1: lámina 12
CODICE XOLOTL					plancha VII
HISTORIA TOLTECA-CHICHIMECA	folio 42v				folio 42v

6	7	8	9	10	11	12
Xicalcoliuhqui	Quauhtete-poyo	Tlahauitectli	Teocuitlaxapo	Ihuiteteyo	---------	---------
folio 20r	folio 20v	folio 46r				
folio 64r	folio 65r	folio 64r	folio 67r	folio 65r	folio 65r	folio 64r
estampa XXII	estampa XXIV	estampa XXVII	estampa XXII	estampa XXVII		
32	47		57		B	66
	bk. 12: folio 50v		bk. 2: folio 126r	bk. 2: folio 19v		bk. 12: folio 58v
folio 33v		folio 31r	folio 43r	folio 29r	folio 29r	
vol. 1: lámina 15			vol. 1: lámina 15	vol. 1: lámina 16	vol. 2: lámina 42	
plancha VII				plancha VIII		
folio 42v						

See page 246, across from foldout, for citations.

APPENDIX H: *Ehuatl* Styles: The *Codex Mendoza* and Other Aztec Pictorials

	1	2	3
CODEX MENDOZA *Part 2: Tribute*	folio 22r		
MATRICULA DE TRIBUTOS	folio 3r	folio 4v	folio 5r
PRIMEROS MEMORIALES	estampa XXV	estampa XXII	estampa XXII
LIENZO DE TLAXCALA	15	21	52
FLORENTINE CODEX	bk. 12: folio 58v		
CODICE XOLOTL	10	8	7
CODEX TELLERIANO-REMENSIS	folio 42v		
CODEX IXTLILXOCHITL	folio 106r		

4	5	6	7	8
folio 32r				
folio 6v				
estampa XXII	*estampa* XXII	*estampa* XXII		
35	22	37	73	61
7	7	9		

See page 246, across from foldout, for citations.

CITATIONS: APPENDICES F—J

APPENDIX F

Clark 1938: volume 3

Clark 1938: volume 3

Primeros Memoriales 1926

Lienzo de Tlaxcala 1892

Sahagún 1979

Códice Azcatítlan 1949

Durán 1967

Codex Magliabechiano 1970

Codex Telleriano-Remensis 1964–1967

APPENDIX H: *Ehuatl* Styles

Clark 1938: volume 3

Matrícula de Tributos 1980

Primeros Memoriales 1926

Lienzo de Tlaxcala 1892

Sahagún 1979

Códice Xolotl 1951

Codex Telleriano-Remensis 1964–1967

Codex Ixtlilxochitl 1976

APPENDIX G

Clark 1938: volume 3

Clark 1938: volume 3

Primeros Memoriales 1926

Lienzo de Tlaxcala 1892

Sahagún 1979

Codex Telleriano-Remensis 1964–1967

Durán 1967

Codex Xolotl 1951

Historia tolteca-chichimeca 1976

APPENDIX I–J

All citations are from Clark 1938, volume 3.

The name in parentheses refers to the province which appears on the given folio in the tribute section.

All Nahuatl terms are found on the corresponding tribute pages of *Matrícula de Tributos* 1980 (Frances F. Berdan translation), unless otherwise noted (see below).

a. Sahagún 1950–1982 8:23–25 (Anderson and Dibble translation).

b. Glossed analogue found on *Matrícula de Tributos* 1980: folio 16r (Frances F. Berdan translation).

c. Glossed analogue found on *Matrícula de Tributos* 1980: folio 4r (Frances F. Berdan translation).

d. Glossed analogue found on *Matrícula de Tributos* 1980: folio 3v (Frances F. Berdan translation).

e. Glossed analogue found on *Matrícula de Tributos* 1980: folio 15v (Frances F. Berdan translation).

f. Glossed analogue found on *Matrícula de Tributos* 1980: folios 7v, 12r (Frances F. Berdan translation).

Descriptions of the Warrior Insignia
in *Primeros Memoriales* (1926)
estampas XXII—XXVII

Based on Thelma D. Sullivan Translations (*Primeros Memoriales* n.d.: chap. 4, par. 8)

ESTAMPA XXII (LEFT COLUMN)
Three Lords with Their Insignia

(1)   Ce tlacatl tlatoani pilli
        yn itlatq' yn itlaviz
ychcavipil, yxiuheuauh,
yteucuitlacuzcapetl,
ychalchiuhtēteuh, yteucuitlanacvch,
yquetzalpatzac, ychimal
quetzalxicalcvliuhqui, ymaquauh,
ytlaçomaxtli, ytecpilcac.

The accoutrements and insignia of
   a personage, a ruler, a nobleman:
His padded cotton shirt. His turquoise blue tunic. His gold mat necklace. His green stone lip plug. His gold ear plugs. His compressed quetzal feather insignia. His quetzal feather shield with the stepped fret design. His war club. His precious breech cloth. His lordly sandals.

(2)   Oc no çe tlacatl tlatoani
        pilli yn itlatq' yn itlaviz
ychcavipil, ypillivieuauh,
yxiuhtēteuh, ymayanacoch ychayauac
cuzqui, yquetzalpapaluh, ychimal
quetzalcuexyo, ymaquauh,
ytlaçomaxtli, ytlaçocac.

The accoutrements and insignia
   of another personage, ruler, nobleman:
His padded cotton shirt. His tunic of princely feathers. His turquoise lip plug. His June beetle ear plugs. His necklace of green stone and gold and radiating pendants. His quetzal feather butterfly insignia. His quetzal feather Huaxtec shield. His war club. His precious breech cloth. His precious sandals.

(3)   Jnic ei tlacatl pilli yn
        itlatq' yn itlaviz
ychcavipil, ytozeuauh,
ychalchiuhtēteuh, yxiuhnanacuch,
yteucuitlapā, ychalchiuhcuzqui,
ychimal tozmiquizyo, ymaquauh,
ytlaçomaxtli, ytecpilcac.

The accoutrements and insignia
   of a third personage, a nobleman:
His padded cotton shirt. His yellow parrot feather tunic. His green stone lip plug. His turquoise ear plugs. His gold banner. His green stone necklace. His yellow parrot feather death's head shield. His war club. His precious breech cloth. His lordly royal sandals.

ESTAMPA XXII (RIGHT COLUMN)
Three Captains with Their Insignia

(4)   Auh ynic ōcuemitl tiyacaoā
        yn intlaviz
yn itlamamaltuzquaxolotl,
ychcavipil, ytlapalivieuauh,
yteucuitlanacoch, yyacametz,
yteucuitlachipolcuzqui, ychimal
teucuitlaxapo, yquāmaxtli,
ytlaçocac.

And from the second group, the
   brave warriors' insignia:
His yellow parrot feather Xolotl head insignia carried on the back. His padded cotton shirt. His tunic of red feathers. His gold ear plugs. His crescent-shaped nose ornament. His necklace of gold snail shells. His gold disc shield. His eagle feather breech cloth. His lordly sandals.

(5)   Jnic ome tlacatl yn
        itlatqui yn itlaviz
ychcavipil, yaztaeuauh, yxiuhnacoch,
yteucuitlatempilol, yaztapatzac,
ychimal texaxacalo, ytlaçomaztli,
ymaquauh, ytlaçocac.

The accoutrements and insignia
   of a second personage:
His padded cotton shirt. His heron feather tunic. His turquoise ear plugs. His gold lip pendant. His compressed heron feather insignia. His shield with the thick lips design. His precious breech cloth. His war club. His precious sandals.

(6)   Jnic ei tlacatl yn
        itlatqui yn itlaviz
ychcavipil, ytuzcoyouh,
ytezacanecuil, ychimal tlilxapo,
yquāmaxtli, yztaccac, ymaquauh.

The accoutrements and insignia
   of a third personage:
His padded cotton shirt. His yellow parrot feather coyote insignia. His curved lip ornament. His black disc shield. His eagle feather breech cloth. His white sandals. His war club.

ESTAMPA XXIII

Insignia of the Lords

(1)   *quetzalpanitl*
The quetzal feather banners
          insignia.

(2)   *çaquãpanitl*
The black and gold troupial
     feather banners insignia.

(3)   *quetzalquaquavitl*
The quetzal feather horns
          insignia.

(4)   *quetzaltzitzimitl*
The quetzal feather demon of
     the dark insignia.

(5) *quetzalquatlamoyaoallj*
The quetzal feather bestrewn
          head insignia.

(6)   *quetzaltototl*
The quetzal bird insignia.

(7)   *xolopapalotl*
The dark yellow parrot feather
     butterfly insignia.

(8)   *çaquãtonatiuh*
The black and yellow troupial
     feather sun insignia.

(9)   *ometochtlaviztli*
The Two-Rabbit insignia.

(10)   *tzatzaztli*
The warping frame insignia.

(11)   *çaquãpapalotl*
The black and yellow troupial
     feather butterfly insignia.

ESTAMPA XXIV
Insignia of the Lords

(17)   *ananacaztli*
The water ears insignia.

(12)   *teucuitlavevetl*
The gold drum insignia.

(18) *quauhtetepoyo chimalli*
The eagle's foot shield.

(13)   *chamolcvyutl*
The red coyote insignia.

(19) *oçelotetepoyo chimalli*
The jaguar foot shield.

(14)   *xiuhcoyotl*
The turquoise blue coyote
insignia.

(20) *chimalli teucuitlateteyo*
The silver stones shield.

(15)   *quetzalcopilli*
The quetzal feather conical
headpiece insignia.

(21)   *quetzalpuztecqui*
chimalli
The cleft quetzal feather
shield.

(16)   *iztac cvyutl*
The white coyote insignia.

(22) *teucuitlacuzcatl temoltic*
The golden beetle necklace.

(23–
24) *teucuitlaçoyanacvchtli*
The gold palm ear plug.

*nicã tlami ỹ pillatquitl ỹ
tlaviztli etc.*
Here end the noblemen's
accoutrements and insignia.

ESTAMPA XXV

Insignia of the Captains

(LEFT COLUMN)

(1) *chamoleuatl*
The red parrot
feather tunic.

(2) *tlapalquaxolotl*
The red Xolotl
head insignia.

(3) *yztac quaxolotl*
The white Xolotl
head insignia.

(4) *tlacvchpatzactli*
The compressed
dart insignia.

(5) *cueçalpatzactli*
The compressed
macaw feather
insignia.

(6) *cacalpatzactli*
The compressed
crow feather
insignia.

(7) *tlecocomoctli*
The crackling fire
insignia.

(8) *tlapallivitelolotli*
The red feather
ball.

(9) *yztac ivitelolotli*
The white feather
ball.

(10) *macuilpanitl*
The five flag
insignia.

(11) *aztatzũtli*
The heron feather
hair insignia.

(12) *aztacopilli*
The heron feather
conical headpiece
insignia.

ESTAMPA XXVI

Insignia of the Captains

(LEFT COLUMN)

(13) *tvzcocolli*
The yellow parrot
feather serpentine
insignia.

(14) *tlapalitzmitl*
The colored
arrowhead insignia.

(15) *tlilpapalotl*
The black butterfly
insignia.

(16) *xacalli*
The straw hut
insignia.

(MIDDLE COLUMN)

17) *caltzaqualli*
The masonry house
insignia.

(18) *çacacalli*
The grass hut
insignia.

(19) *tzipito*
The fretful child
insignia.

(20) *tlaquimiloli*
The bundle
insignia.

(RIGHT COLUMN)

(21) *mexayacatlaviztli*
The thigh-skin
mask insignia.

(22) *ytzpapalotl*
The obsidian
butterfly insignia.

(23) *tlazimaluapalli*
The maquey fiber
pulling board
insignia.

(24) *vexolotl*
The turkey cock
insignia.

ESTAMPA XXVII

Insignia of the Captains

(LEFT COLUMN)

(25) *yxtlapalpanitl*
  The transverse
  banner insignia.

(26) *tlapalcvyutl*
  The red coyote
  insignia.

(27) *tlecvyutl*
  The fire coyote
  insignia

(28) *chimallaviztli*
  The shield insignia.

(MIDDLE COLUMN)

33) *teçacanecuilo
  chimallj*
  The shield with the
  curved lip
  ornament.

(34) *texoxapo
  chimallj*
  The blue disc
  shield.

(35) *macpalo
  chimallj*
  The hand shield.

(36) *yhuiteteyo
  chimallj*
  The shield with the
  feather border.

(37) *yhuiteteyo
  çouhqui chimallj*
  The shield with the
  open feather
  border.

(38) *tlahavitectlj
  chimallj*
  The whitened
  shield.

(RIGHT COLUMN)

(29) *çitlalcvyutl*
  The star-studded
  coyote insignia.

(30) *tliltic cvyutl*
  The black coyote
  insignia.

(31) *ixcoliuhqui
  chimalli*
  The curved eye
  shield.

(32) *çitlallo chimallj*
  The star-studded
  shield.